THE KARL MARX LIBRARY

EDITED AND TRANSLATED BY

SAUL K. PADOVER

Distinguished Service Professor of Political Science,
Graduate Faculty, New School for Social Research

ALREADY PUBLISHED

On Revolution

On America and the Civil War

On the First International

TITLES IN PREPARATION

On Freedom of the Press and Censorship

On Religion: Christianity, Judaism, and Jews

Also by Saul K. Padover

THE REVOLUTIONARY EMPEROR: JOSEPH II

SECRET DIPLOMACY AND ESPIONAGE

(*with James Westfall Thompson*)

THE LIFE AND DEATH OF LOUIS XVI

JEFFERSON (a biography)

EXPERIMENT IN GERMANY

LA VIE POLITIQUE DES ÉTATS-UNIS

FRENCH INSTITUTIONS: VALUES AND POLITICS

THE GENIUS OF AMERICA

UNDERSTANDING FOREIGN POLICY

THE MEANING OF DEMOCRACY

THOMAS JEFFERSON AND THE FOUNDATIONS OF AMERICAN FREEDOM

· ·

Edited by Saul K. Padover

THOMAS JEFFERSON ON DEMOCRACY

THE COMPLETE JEFFERSON

THOMAS JEFFERSON AND THE NATIONAL CAPITAL

A JEFFERSON PROFILE

THE WRITINGS OF THOMAS JEFFERSON

THE COMPLETE MADISON (also titled: THE FORGING OF AMERICAN FEDERALISM)

THE WASHINGTON PAPERS

THE MIND OF ALEXANDER HAMILTON

WILSON'S IDEALS

THE LIVING UNITED STATES CONSTITUTION

CONFESSIONS AND SELF-PORTRAITS

THE WORLD OF THE FOUNDING FATHERS

NEHRU ON WORLD HISTORY

TO SECURE THESE BLESSINGS

On the First International

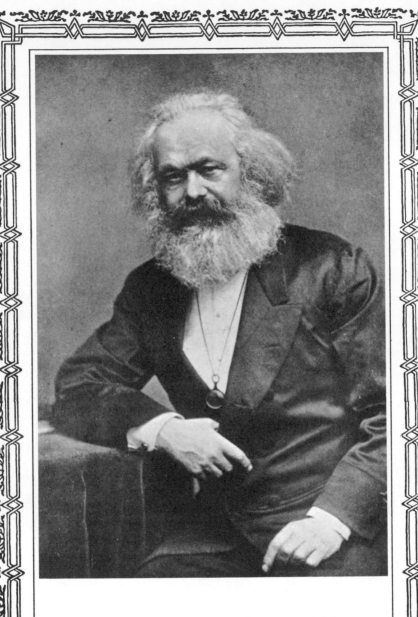

KARL MARX (1818–1883)

THE KARL MARX LIBRARY
VOLUME III

On the First International

KARL MARX

ARRANGED AND EDITED, WITH AN
INTRODUCTION AND NEW TRANSLATIONS
by Saul K. Padover

McGraw-Hill Book Company

NEW YORK   ST. LOUIS   SAN FRANCISCO
DÜSSELDORF   LONDON   MEXICO   PANAMA
SYDNEY   TORONTO

FIRST EDITION

123456789 BPBP 79876543

Library of Congress Cataloging in Publication Data
Marx, Karl, 1818–1883.
  The Karl Marx library.
  Bibliography: v. 1, p. 641–643.
  CONTENTS: v. 1. On revolution. v. 2. On America
and the Civil War. v. 3. On the first international.
  1. Socialism—Collections. I. Title.
HX276.M2773   1972   335.43'08   78-172260
ISBN
        0-07-048076-1
        0-07-048081-8 (pbk.)

Contents

Policies and Programs

Conflicts and Splits

Contents

Letters to the Press

Interviews and Reports

Personal Letters

Contents

Contents

Photographs following pages 176 and 388

Introduction:
Marx's Role in
the First International

IN SEPTEMBER, 1864, when the International Working Men's Association—now known as the First International and referred to in these pages as the International—was founded in St. Martin's Hall, London, Marx was a relatively obscure refugee journalist. Exiled from his native Germany, thrown out of Belgium, and expelled from France, he found refuge in the British capital in 1849. In the fifteen years before the founding of the International, Marx eked out a living from journalism—saved from actual starvation by Frederick Engels, who was in the textile business in Manchester—and spent most of his time writing, reading, and researching (in the British Museum). After the traumatic defeat of the revolutions of 1848–49 in Europe, he became for a time politically inactive.

In London, Marx's main contacts were with other Europeans, particularly German and French radicals and refugees, with many of whom he had intermittent squabbles and disagreements. While showing deep interest in British politics, institutions, and movements—notably the history of Chartism, which was not without influence on his own political thinking—he kept himself, or was kept, aloof from English activists, including trade unionists. With few exceptions, one of them being the Chartist leader and editor Ernest Charles Jones, Marx had no close connection with English radicals or laborites, and vice versa. His was the politically isolated life of an unassimilated continental refugee. The International was to change all this.

It is still not entirely clear why Marx was invited to what turned out to be a historic meeting at St. Martin's Hall. Until about a week before the meeting, on September 28, he apparently knew nothing about any preparations for it. Then he was told about it by Victor

Le Lubez, a thirty-year-old French radical republican living in London, who invited him to come as a representative of German workers. Marx accepted and proposed that he be joined by Johann Georg Eccarius, a tailor living in London, as another German representative. As it turned out, Marx and Eccarius were to become the two mainstays of the International from its inception to its end.

The meeting was jammed with a large number of assorted radicals. There were English Owenites and Chartists, French Proudhonists and Blanquists, Irish nationalists, Polish patriots, Italian Mazzinists, and German socialists. It was an assortment united not by a commonly shared ideology or even by genuine internationalism, but by an accumulated burden of variegated grievances crying for an outlet. The English were against special privilege, the French against Bonapartism, the Irish against Britain, the Poles against Russia, the Italians against Austria, and the Germans against capitalism. There was no necessary or integral interconnection among them—except what Marx later tried to provide in the organization that followed the meeting. Under the chairmanship of Edward Spencer Beesly, an English Positivist historian and professor at London University, radical oratory was given free rein. Marx himself did not speak. He was, as he wrote later, a "silent figure on the platform."

The meeting voted unanimously to appoint a provisional committee to work out a program and membership rules for the proposed international organization. Marx was appointed a member of the committee, which met a week later and, being large and unwieldy, agreed on a small subcommittee to do the actual work. Marx became a member of this crucial subcommittee. The only other German on it was "my old friend, the tailor Eccarius," as Marx wrote to a communist friend in Solingen. The subcommittee met in Marx's house, and so powerful was his intellectual ascendancy and certainty of purpose that the group empowered him to draw up both the program—the Inaugural Address—and the rules—Provisional Statutes—of the new organization. Henceforth Marx was to remain its predominant spirit and the indomitable personality that held the disparate International Association together for eight difficult and often stormy years, until it was shattered by bitter internal dissensions.

In the International Marx saw a great historic opportunity, and seized it. Indeed, it is questionable whether the organization would have survived, or would have had any meaning, without him. His steely will and impassioned commitment to the idea of the revolutionary role of the world proletariat prevented the International from passing into the same oblivion as had other dreams of squabbling radicals, confused in their philosophy and at cross-purposes in their aims.

From the very first, Marx realized that the new organization could be important, primarily because there were among the founders, especially among the English, experienced laborites, and not mere word-spouting intellectuals or semi-intellectuals, as had been the case with the leaders of the continental revolutions of 1848–49. Marx was impressed by the fact that the English founders of the International were mostly trade-union leaders, "the real labor kings of London," as he called them. British labor had shown its power the year before, in March, 1863, at a huge mass meeting in St. James's Hall, which Marx had attended and which he was convinced had prevented Lord Palmerston from openly supporting the confederacy by declaring war on the United States—as, Marx was sure, the British Prime Minister was "on the verge of doing." British labor leadership was, to Marx, obviously an invaluable potential in the proletarian revolution. "Although for years I systematically turned down participation in all 'organizations,' etc.," Marx wrote to a friend in America when he informed him of the founding of the International, "I accepted *this time*, for here was something where it was possible to be effective."

Marx, who was ailing in October, spent a week drafting the Inaugural Address and the Statutes of the International. These were adopted on November 1 and, some three weeks later, published by the provisional committee. The committee then transformed itself into the Central Council—soon to become the General Council—as the governing body of the International. For the next eight years Marx was to try to use the General Council, whose weekly sessions he never failed to attend except when he was ill or absent from London, as a long-range instrument for the furtherance of his revolutionary vision.

To appreciate Marx's role in the International it is necessary to understand the make-up of the General Council. In the first year of its existence, 1864–65, the General Council consisted of eighty-two members, nearly half (forty) of them Englishmen. The others were Germans (twelve), Frenchmen (eleven), Italians (nine), Polish (six), Swiss (two), plus one Hungarian and one Dane. Most of the foreign members, including the Italians and the French, were transients, professional revolutionists rather than workers, and attended the meetings infrequently. Some, like Luigi Wolff, turned out to be spies in the pay of Napoleon III.

The really active and constant members of the General Council consisted of a small group of foreigners and a larger body of Englishmen. The importance of the foreigners was greater than their numbers. They not only attended regularly but also held a balance of power in the Council. Among them were a handful of Germans—notably Eccarius, Jung (German Swiss), Lessner, Lochner, and Pfänder—and one Frenchman, Dupont. The Germans, except for

Marx, were not intellectuals; they were workers, and one of them, Bolleter (who served on the Council only one year), was keeper of a tavern (2 Nassau Street) where workers sometimes held their meetings.

The foreign members came to be known as Marx's "coterie," providing him with a strong and continuing base of support. Some of them occupied key positions throughout most of the life of the International. Thus Jung was the long-time corresponding secretary for Switzerland, then a center of continental radicalism; Dupont was the equally long-time corresponding secretary for France, the most important country on the Continent; and Eccarius was ensconced as the Council's general secretary for four years, as well as the corresponding secretary for America for two. Eccarius was also the International's occasional newspaper correspondent.

This coterie followed Marx's leadership and he, in turn, gave it support, sometimes against his own better judgment, as in the case of Eccarius, a morose communist whose tactlessness and ambition created resentment among latently xenophobic English members. Marx nearly always defended the dour German tailor and thereby made enemies among some of the British. In the end, in 1871, Eccarius broke with his patron, which led the enraged Marx to label him a "scoundrel" and Engels to call him a "traitor to our cause." It is interesting to note that after the Austrian government archives were opened in 1918 they were found to contain materials which led critics to accuse Eccarius of having been a spy who had sold information about the International to the Austrian Government. But although Eccarius was often in desperate need of money, the case against him has not been conclusively proven.

We may note in passing that fear of spies was a regular preoccupation of continental radicals, whether at home or in exile. Marx himself had a touch of paranoia on the subject. The suspiciousness was not without justification, however. In Marx's day, and indeed, for a long time thereafter, radical and revolutionary groups were infiltrated by police spies and secret agents in the pay of Europe's autocratic governments, notably those of Austria, France, Prussia, and Russia. Spies, suspected or real, were frequently exposed and expelled from radical organizations.

The majority of the membership of the General Council throughout its existence in London was, of course, made up of Englishmen. With a few exceptions, they were workers and trade unionists. They represented the traditional skilled trades—bakers, bricklayers, carpenters, furniture makers, house painters, plasterers, printers, and shoemakers. Neither proletarians in the Marxist sense nor *déclassé* in the sense of the European uprooted, they were fairly solid, perhaps even stolid, products of England's stable and orderly society. Although they had the usual class consciousness of workers, these craftsmen were neither at war with Queen and Country nor alienated from their culture. They were essentially reform-minded, as were also the few non-workers on the Council, such as Peter Fox and Cowell Stepney. Fox, like Marx, was a journalist; Stepney, treasurer of the General Council from 1868 to 1870, was a wealthy socialist. In a letter to his German friend Dr. Ludwig Kugelmann, Marx described Stepney as "a very rich and distinguished man, but wholly, if in a somewhat foolish fashion, devoted to the workers' cause."

Marx's *Inaugural Address*, a brochure of approximately ten printed pages, may be considered the basic general charter of the International. A far cry from the *Communist Manifesto*, it reflected both a subtle shift in Marx's political expectations and an awareness of the essentially British—nonrevolutionary—character of the Council.

In the *Address*, as well as in his subsequent activities in, and official writings for, the International, Marx showed more moderation and political realism than he had evinced in his revolutionary days on the Continent. In part, of course, this was due to greater personal maturity and ripening of his thought. He was, after all, a man of forty-six when the International was founded, and had had time to read widely and deeply in nondoctrinaire literature—economics, trade reports, labor statistics, political history, and social analysis in general.

In part, Marx's comparative moderation—he never did renounce the idea of the ultimate triumph of the proletariat—was due to his British experience. For the past fifteen years he had been exposed to British political life, where the parliamentary system, with all its short-comings, did work in practice. Despite existing social and economic inequalities, and widely prevalent class feeling, the British state was not oppressive. Marx, like Voltaire more than a century earlier, found a surprising amount of freedom and public decency in England. Un-like the Continent, Britain suffered neither from police brutality nor from intellectual persecution. There was no official censorship, for example, and elections, though occasionally corrupt, were generally free and open. British orderly rule suggested to Marx, as it did to English Chartists and trade unionists, the possibility—if not the cer-tainty—of achieving social and economic change without a violent overthrow of the whole social order, at least in countries where politi-cal democracy prevailed.[1]

The *Inaugural Address* consisted of two main parts. The first por-

---

1. See Introduction to *Karl Marx on Revolution* (1972), Vol. I of The Karl Marx Library.

tion was devoted to British economic and social conditions, a subject obviously of special interest to the large number of English members of the International. But it was also of intrinsic importance in general political-economic theory, for Britain was then the center of world capitalism, a subject on which Marx had been working, on and off, for some two decades, in preparation of his masterpiece, *Capital.* The example of Britain, in matters such as investments, business enterprise, technological advances, standards of living, and, above all, the role of labor in an increasingly industrialized society, was obviously bound to have an impact on all other countries— including Germany and France—then in various stages of capitalist development. "England," Marx wrote, "heads the Europe of commerce and industry."

The *Address* pointed out that England had undergone an unrivaled expansion of its industry since the defeat of the 1848–49 European revolutions, without comparable benefits for the workers. Marx cited facts and quoted government reports to show the immensity of the wealth on the part of a few—some of them with yearly incomes of £50,000 and upwards—and the shocking pauperism, misery, "broken health, tainted morals, and mental ruin" suffered by working people. "And yet," he wrote, "the period passed since the Revolutions of 1848 has not been without its compensating features," and he cited two victories achieved by English labor in the period between 1848 and 1864. One was the ten-hour day, and the other the cooperative movement.

For a long time, Marx wrote, English economists—Andrew Ure, Nassau William Senior, "and other sages of that stamp"—had predicted that any restriction of the hours of labor "must sound the death knell of British industry, which, vampirelike, could but live by sucking blood, and children's blood, too." The workers' struggle for a shorter working day had raged fiercely not only against avarice but also against the political economy of the middle class, with its "blind rule of the supply and demand laws." Despite this, the Ten Hours' Bill was passed by Parliament. It was, Marx stated, a victory of principle. "It was the first time that in broad daylight the political economy of the middle class succumbed to the political economy of the working class."

A still greater victory "of the political economy of labor over the political economy of property" was the cooperative movement. The value of cooperative experiments, whose seeds were planted by Robert Owen, lay in showing the possibility of modern economic production on a large scale "without the existence of a class of masters employing a class of hands." Cooperative production "cannot be overrated," because, properly organized, it could free workers from domination and exploitation and result in labor toiling, not as reluctant slaves, but "with a willing hand, a ready mind, and a joyous heart."

But, Marx warned, the cooperative movement would be futile if it remained confined to casual efforts of small groups. A few "private workmen" could never be strong enough to stop the growth of big monopolies or free the masses from their misery. To be effective, it was necessary to develop cooperatives on a national scale, supported by national means. Since the "lords of the land and the lords of capital" could be expected to use their political privileges to perpetuate their economic power, labor must use its political power to achieve its economic emancipation.

"To conquer political power," Marx wrote, "has therefore become the great duty of the working classes. They seem to have comprehended this, for in England, Germany, Italy, and France there have taken place simultaneous revivals, and simultaneous efforts are being made at the political organization of the workingmen's party."

Workers in all countries had a common cause, which should unite them. That "bond of brotherhood" was their emancipation from capitalist exploitation. To achieve their aim, workers must organize, under proper leadership, across national frontiers. "One element of success," Marx went on to say, "they possess—numbers; but numbers weigh in the balance only if united by combination and led by knowledge." It was for this purpose that the International Working Men's Association was organized.

In the second part of the *Address* Marx developed briefly a foreign policy for the working class, designed to call labor's attention to the fact that international politics was its vital concern. There was a connection between oppressive and unjust policies pursued by governments at home and abroad. One was an integral part of the other. Labor could not emancipate itself so long as it did not stop governments from following "criminal designs," playing upon "national prejudices," and squandering "in piratical wars the people's blood and treasure" abroad. The policies of Europe's ruling classes had permitted the assassination of Poland and the encroachments and aggressions of Russia —"that barbarous power, whose head is at St. Petersburg, and whose hands are in every cabinet of Europe." Foreign policies aiming at aggressions and oppressions must be counteracted by labor on an international scale. Workers must use "all means in their power," including public denunciations and protests—such as the one in London that had succeeded in preventing the British Government from coming to the support of the slave states in the American Civil War—to vindicate the "laws of morals and justice" that ought to govern nations in their relations with each other. "The fight for such a foreign policy," Marx wrote, "forms part of the general struggle for the emancipation of the working classes."

He concluded with the words: "Proletarians of all countries, unite!"

This was, after all, what the International was all about.

The *Address*, although a document of some importance, did not reach a large audience. It was published only in a few radical papers, the *Bee-Hive* and the *Workman's Advocate* in England and the *Social-Demokrat* in Germany. A thousand copies were printed in a brochure that also included the Statutes of the International and sold for a penny apiece.

Marx was pleased with his production. He sent copies to friends, including Engels in Manchester, Kugelmann in Hanover, and Weyde-meyer in St. Louis, Missouri. One copy went to his uncle, Lion Philips, a Dutch banker for whom Marx had an affectionate admira-tion (and from whom he received financial assistance from time to time). In the covering letter to Philips, Marx, who always wanted to be thought of as a scholarly writer, made an oblique apology for some of his rhetoric. "I had to insert a few useless figures of speech," he wrote with a touch of irony, "out of courtesy to the French and Italians, who always need grandiose phrases."

Philips, who read Marx's composition with sympathy, replied that if his nephew's new organization in London would pursue a policy of nonviolence, it had a chance of success. "I consider the labor question," the Dutch banker wrote in German mixed with English phrases, "as surely the most interesting of our time; nevertheless, I believe that *lasting* improvements can now be achieved in a regular way, without violent convulsions. If your Association remains faithful to *what they declared* on the heads of their *Rules*, then *slowly*, but I believe surely, the good aim will be achieved." World history, Philips reminded his radical nephew, "always marches without haste, but always for-ward."[2]

Marx's leadership of the International, at least in its first years, shows that he and his banker uncle were not far apart in their views of the desirability of moderate politics and the forward march of history. To Marx, history, whatever its pace, moved inexorably in the direction of progress, the latter meaning the achievement of power by the world proletariat as the final consummation of the historic process. But there was no specific timetable. Nor was there any special reason, theoretical or actual, for hurrying the pace through dogmatic policies or rash actions. Indeed, the Marx of the period of the International took the opposite view: that realistic politics and evolutionary policies

---

2. Philips to Marx, December 5, 1864; MS, D 3362, in Institute for International History, Amsterdam.

were more likely to enhance than to retard the march of the proletariat toward its historically predetermined goal.

Hence in the statements and addresses—including the eloquent ones to Presidents Abraham Lincoln and Andrew Johnson—which Marx drafted for and in the name of the International, there was no advocacy of communism or violent revolution or the overthrow of the existing order of society for attainment of the ends of labor. The International's public documents expressed opinions against injustice, against war, against exploitation and oppression; they defended the rights of workers and supported labor strikes not only in England but also in Belgium, France, Germany, Spain, and Switzerland. The International's official position, in short, was reformist rather than revolutionist. In his role as actual, although never titular, head of the International, Marx was careful to avoid extreme formulations, phrasing documents in such a way that they would be, as Engels wrote in 1890, "acceptable to the English trade unions, to the followers of Proudhon in France, Belgium, Italy, and Spain, and to the Lassalleans in Germany." Indeed, Marx often acted as a moderating influence in the sometimes heated weekly sessions of the General Council.[3]

The International was organized as a fairly democratic body, with free elections of members and open discussion. Occasionally it worked through "front" organizations. One of these was the Reform League, which the International helped organize in 1865, putting six of its own Council members on the steering committee of twelve. The Reform League, which Marx called "our work," organized street demonstrations and public meetings in favor of universal suffrage. Marx was highly pleased with these activities. Referring to mass meetings held in Trafalgar Square in June and July, 1866, under the leadership of Benjamin Lucraft, a member of the Council, Marx wrote to Engels (July 7, 1866): "The workers' demonstrations in London, which are marvelous compared with anything we have seen in England since 1849, are purely the work of the International . . . This shows the difference between *working* behind the scenes and not appearing in public, and the democrats' way of making themselves important and *doing nothing.*"

In general, however, the policies and activities of the International

3. From October 5, 1864, to January 2, 1865, the Council met at 18 Greek Street, Soho, in a house owned by a man named Corbet. Then it moved to 18 Bouverie Street, where it remained until June, 1867; this was also the office of the *Commonwealth*, the International's weekly organ until July, 1867. The Council was not always able to pay the rent. "There being nothing in Treasurery [sic]," an 1866 entry in the minutes records, "the Treasurer [William Dell] advanced the quarter's rent by way of a loan." From June, 1868, to February, 1872, the Council met in the hall of the National Sunday League, a Prohibitionist society, 256 High Holborn, W.C. Afterwards the General Council held its meetings at 33 Rathbone Place, Oxford Street.

were public and nonconspiratorial. This, indeed, was one of the reasons for the bitter quarrel, which was to tear the organization apart in the last years of its existence, between the publicity-conscious Marx and the inveterately conspiratorial Bakunin. Marx, as a professional journalist and writer, was always acutely aware of the value of "propaganda," and he strove to have the work of the International publicized as much as possible. In fact, he was so conscious of the power of the printed word—in newspapers, journals, pamphlets, and books—that after the German (first) edition of *Capital* was published in 1867, he worked out (with the enthusiastic assistance of Engels) a careful and systematic campaign for its review and discussion in the German press. Marx, who as a lifelong revolutionist was convinced that "truth" would ultimately prevail, did not believe that it would make its way among men either at random or unaided. It needed guidance and propulsion. In his view, the printing press was the major instrument for the propagation of "truth" and promotion of revolutionary ideas.

The first journal to print the International's official documents and reports was a London weekly which in the course of its existence, between 1861 and 1876, went under somewhat varying titles—*The Bee-Hive, The Bee-Hive Newspaper,* and *The Penny Bee-Hive* (all had a beehive on the masthead). The *Bee-Hive* was not strictly a house organ of the International, but a fairly independent trade-union journal, not above garbling the International's reports. In April, 1870, at the suggestion of an exasperated Marx, the General Council broke with the *Bee-Hive* altogether, and in effect excommunicated it as an enemy of the interests of labor.

But by that time the International had long ceased to rely exclusively on the *Bee-Hive*. By January, 1865, it had at least five publications which it could claim as its own, four of them on the Continent. In London the International took over the *Miner and Workman's Advocate*, renamed it *Workman's Advocate*, and appointed a multinational editorial board, of which Marx was a member, to run it.[4]. The paper championed the usual radical causes, which were also favored by the International: direct taxation, universal manhood suffrage, a shorter work week, cooperatives, and nationalization of land. In 1866 the *Workman's Advocate* was renamed the *Commonwealth*. In the struggle over the editorship, with Marx successfully supporting Eccarius, nationalistic hostilities and personal rivalries surfaced. The French member, Le Lubez, made a ranting speech against "German influence." The Italian, Major Wolff, Mazzini's agent, attacked Jung, Marx's

---

4. Members of the *Advocate*'s board were: Applegarth, Coulson, Cremer, Facey, Odger, and Weston for England; Marx, Eccarius, and Lessner for Germany; Le Lubez for France; Jung for Switzerland.

supporter. The English Cremer and Odger wanted the editorship themselves. In the end, Marx and the continental members, who, except for Le Lubez, followed his leadership, prevailed. The struggle left scars, and the *Commonwealth* itself did not survive long. In July, 1867, it expired from financial inanition and intellectual malnutrition.

Altogether, in the course of its eight-year existence, the International had about one and a half dozen organs, mostly weeklies, in various European cities: Amsterdam, Antwerp, Barcelona, Brussels, Geneva, Madrid, Naples, and Paris. It even had a weekly in Palma de Majorca. Some of these journals, their small circulations limited to the labor unions affiliated with the International, were short-lived; others, among them Bakuninist organs in Switzerland and Proudhonist ones in France, did not follow the line laid down by the General Council in London; but each of them claimed affiliation with the International and, in its own way, reflected some of its aims.

Marx also used friendly papers, labor, leftist, or socialist, as vehicles for the International, to propagate its ideas or to correct misconceptions about its policies. Among publications more or less sympathetic to the International—or at least willing to print its materials and protests—were the *Eastern Post* in London, *Le Réveil* in Paris, the *Social-Demokrat* in Berlin, and the *Volkswille* in Vienna.

The International, under Marx's stimulus, made systematic and determined efforts to have its actions and programs reported also in the "bourgeois" press, of which he was an inveterate reader in many languages. His workroom in London was piled helter-skelter with newspapers, annotated, clipped, and often fumed over. Verbally—and of course theoretically—he was hostile to the bourgeois press as a paid servant of capitalism and enemy of the proletariat, but psychologically he was addicted to newspapers and could not live without them. Passionately believing as he did in the efficacy of the printed word, he could never escape his thrall to newspapers. The bigger the paper's circulation, the greater its influence, and the greater its influence the more it impressed—and often enraged—Marx. It was a proud day for him when the conservative London *Times,* the powerful voice of the British financial and political establishment, took the trouble to publish a document of the International.

"Enclosed," he wrote to Sigfrid Meyer, a German communist in New York, on September 14, 1868, "the issue of the *Times* which contains the Fourth Annual Report of the General Council (written by *me*) and the highly interesting *first leader* of the *Times* on this document. It is the first time that it has put aside the mocking tone against the working class and has taken it 'very' *au sérieux* [seriously]. Spread this news."

Organizationally, the International had somewhat the structure of a federal republic. It had its elected legislative and executive bodies. The constituent base of the International consisted of local sections organized in many cities in England and in Western Europe (except Germany, where foreign affiliations were illegal). The sections were given "charters" and membership cards (costing a penny apiece) by the General Council. In each country the sections were connected with a federal council which, in turn, was in more or less loose contact with London.

The legislative branch of the International was the annual Congress, which met in the month of September for a period of three to five days. Delegates were chosen by the various sections on the basis of their membership. The Congress checked the mandates of the delegates to assure against fraudulent representation. The number of delegates varied with each Congress. There were 60 at the Geneva Congress in 1866, 64 at Lausanne in 1867, 100 at Brussels in 1868, 78 at Basel in 1869, 23 at London in 1871,[5] and 65 at the final one in The Hague in 1872. Marx never attended a Congress on the Continent except that in The Hague, where he went for the purpose of preventing Bakunin and the anarchists from taking over the International.

Congresses followed prepared agendas and, when necessary, worked through *ad hoc* committees. They heard reports, amended the rules, debated issues, voted on policies, and passed resolutions. They also had the power to expel members and to recognize affiliated bodies. The decisions and resolutions of the Congresses were supposed to be binding on the constituent sections and national councils, but in fact they were impossible to enforce. Neither the Congress nor the General Council had the power to make recalcitrant or discontented sections obey decisions, even if they were passed by a majority of the delegates.

The executive of the International was the General Council. It was the guiding and policy-making body—subject, of course, to the approval of the Congress—as well as the communications center. The regular weekly meetings were rarely attended by the full membership. Attendance, except for extraordinary sessions, varied anywhere from around ten to fifteen members, the average being probably about a dozen. During the first three years of its existence the Council had a president—George Odger, a shoemaker—elected annually. In September, 1866, the English members proposed Marx as president, but he declined in favor of Odger's reelection. Marx felt, and probably wisely so, that it was preferable that the nominal head of the Inter-

---

5. Because of the Franco-Prussian War there was no Congress in 1870; the sparsely attended Congress of 1871 was held in London, owing to the still unsettled conditions on the Continent.

national be an Englishman, rather than a European refugee speaking with a heavily Teutonic accent. Soon afterwards, however, Marx, having quarreled with Odger, moved that the presidency be abolished and that meetings of the Council be chaired by a presiding officer chosen weekly. Odger, an ambitious trade unionist, never forgave Marx his loss of the honorific position; in 1871 he was one of the few prominent members of the Council to refuse to sign *The Civil War in France,* which Marx wrote for the International in defense of the Paris Commune.

The work of the Council was carried out by a general secretary (paid ten shillings weekly) and permanent corresponding secretaries for countries in which the International had either direct affiliation or a special interest. Among the former were Austria (and Hungary), Belgium, Denmark, France, Italy, Spain, Switzerland, and the United States; among the latter were Germany, Ireland, and Poland. The secretaries were responsible for maintaining contact with the foreign affiliates or nationality groups, forwarding instructions, writing letters, receiving correspondence, and requesting intelligence, including radical publications.[6] The secretaries, in turn, reported at Council sessions, which they perforce attended regularly.

Some of the Secretaries represented more than one country, and a few had countries reassigned to them. Marx was corresponding secretary for Belgium, and at one time also for Russia (at the request of a group of Russian exiles in Geneva); Engels, after he moved from Manchester to London in 1870, became a member of the Council and corresponding secretary for Italy and Spain, mainly because he was fluent in the languages and literatures of both countries (as he was also in about thirty other tongues, including Persian and Russian).

The Council also served as a final court of appeals. This was particularly true in the last four years of its existence, when it was often called upon to adjudicate among competing jurisdictions, conflicting interpretations, and clashing personalities in and among squabbling sections in Belgium, France, Italy, Switzerland, and the United States. The Council was the lightning rod for, and in some instances the stimulus of, the verbal violence to which radicals, particularly but not exclusively the uprooted and the exiled, tended to be pleasurably addicted. It must be kept in mind that furious squabbles and doctrinal disputes were desperately needed psychological nourishment for the

---

6. Thus, for example, Marx, as secretary for Belgium, wrote to the Dutch and Flemish members of the International in Brussels, ca. December 3, 1870: "We request our Dutch friends to send regularly their organs, *De Workman, Asmodée, De Toekomst, De Werker,* from Antwerp, etc., to the General Council . . . at the following address: Karl Marx, Modena Villas, Maitland Park, Haverstock Hill, London, England."

radicals, particularly the intellectuals and pseudointellectuals who led labor groups. This was, of course, always true of Marx himself. Acrimony provided drama and savor to lives that were otherwise indigent, impotent, and frustrated. Hence as a court of appeals the Council of the International was bound to find itself in a losing position. Satisfying one group usually meant enraging another. As acrimony grew, the Council's decisions tended to be ignored, which in turn led to expulsion of the offending person or section. In the end, expulsion only contributed to the disintegration of the International.

During the first years the International's success was such that it surprised its founders. Progress, Marx wrote to Kugelmann in February, 1865, was "beyond all expectation." Applications for membership kept coming in from Belgium, France, Italy, and Germany. "Cards of Membership," containing a statement of the aims of the International in three languages (English, French, and German), were sold at a penny apiece to members of affiliated groups or unions. Individual membership could be obtained for one shilling annually, but this was rarely paid more than once. The International was, after all, not a "bread-and-butter" organization that provided concrete services, as did trade unions, but an ideological luxury which few workers could afford.

In consequence the International was in financial straits throughout its existence. In 1870, for example, it carried 294 English-speaking individual members on its rolls. At a shilling a head their dues should have added up to about £28; but most of them had not paid in previous years, so that in 1870 they were listed as being £32 in arrears. What income the International had came from affiliated groups. This was always sparse and grudging. The International's income was around £57 for the year 1865; about £30 for 1869; and about £28 for 1870. It managed to eke out its existence only through small contributions from a few dedicated individuals, including the impecunious Marx (who always paid his dues), the well-to-do Engels, and occasional donations from trade unions.

The number of unions affiliated with the International grew steadily, at least during the first four or five years. In England the affiliated unions contained about 18,000 members by the end of 1865. They continued to increase in numbers there as elsewhere. By the end of 1868 a letter to the General Council reported that Belgium already had sixty branches and that there were "1,000 new adherents every week." At the same time, Wilhelm Liebknecht reported from Germany, where membership in foreign organizations was legally *verboten*, that the International could count there on 11,000 indirectly affiliated members. Reports of progress came also from France, Italy,

Spain, and Switzerland. By 1870–71, the period of the Franco-Prussian
War and the tragic Paris Commune, the International was believed to
have a few million members. In the absence of precise data, exact figures are not determinable; moreover, intermittent membership, juris-
dictional conflicts, wavering loyalties, and indirect affiliations make any
definition of "member" or "membership" impossible. What can be
said with certainty is that membership was loose and not disciplined;
that whatever the exact numbers, they were unprecedentedly large
for an international workers' organization; and that they included a
representative cross section of West European labor.

The unions affiliated with the International contained industrial
workers—miners in Belgium, weavers and spinners in Germany,
bronze workers in France—as well as skilled craftsmen and semiskilled
artisans. The English affiliates, for example, represented a varied range
of crafts and occupations which throw an interesting economic light
on Victorian England. Their list included: London Masons' Union;
United Excavators (navvies); Elastic Web Weavers; Block Cutters
and Pattern Drawers; Organ Builders' Society; Coventry Weavers;
Lancashire, Yorkshire, Cheshire Block Printers Union; West End Cabinet Makers; Coach Trimmers; Day-Working Bookbinders; Journeymen Carriers; National Association of Operative Plasterers; Liverpool
and Birmingham House Painters; Liverpool Cigar Makers; New London Society of Basket Makers; and Portmanteau and Trunk Makers.

A number of these were obviously neither industrial nor basic
craft unions, but "service" unions, representing a variety of skills of
an advanced industrial civilization, including occupations for supplying
the needs of a flourishing middle class—cigars, musical organs, port-
manteaus. But to Marx, who was ambiguous about trade unions as
such, any labor organization was important if it could be imbued with
the proper zeal and political purpose.

"If we succeed in reelectrifying the political movement of the
English working class," he wrote to Engels on May 1, 1865, "our Association, without making any fuss, will have done more for the working
class of Europe than has been possible in any other way. And there is
every prospect for success."

Thus he undertook to guide the International, which would in
turn lead the workers, in England and in other industrializing countries. Given his indomitability of purpose and dedication to the
proletarian cause, it was inescapable that he should find himself in the
center of the International's activities. From the very first, other
members, less literate and less sure of themselves or their philosophy
than Marx, were glad to have him take over responsibility and guidance. This was especially true when it came to the all-important func-

tion of elucidating and formulating positions. "I am," he told Engels in 1865, "in fact the head of the thing."

And this was exactly what Marx wanted to be, the head in everything but name. A dedicated revolutionist, eager to change the world, he had long been frustrated by having to be merely a refugee writer and journalist. The International came as a once-in-a-lifetime opportunity for action and expression through an organized channel that had the possibility of reaching the world proletariat. Not even in his younger years in Germany, when he was editor of the radical *Neue Rheinische Zeitung* in the revolutionary era of 1848–1849, had Marx had an opportunity of similar scope for affecting the course of history, as he visualized it.

Marx's health, moreover, was also a consideration. Frequently ill with virtually every known ailment, including chronic carbuncles, furuncles, liver derangements, and weakened lungs, and incapacitated for months at a time, he was not likely to have another chance actively to influence events. His application for restoration of his Prussian citizenship had been rejected by the Berlin Government in 1863, and he knew that he could never again be active in Germany, except, as he said, in a form "acceptable to Herr von Bismarck," whom he hated and sometimes called "Pissmarck." In England, however, he now had a vehicle for action. Here he was not only free to agitate, but to do so, he thought, with every prospect of seriously affecting British and, consequently, European events. "I prefer," he wrote to Kugelmann, "a hundred times more my agitation here through the International Association. Its influence on the English proletariat is direct and of the greatest importance."

Apart from the political, the International also had a personal importance for Marx. It afforded him an opportunity to break out of his relatively isolated existence as a refugee journalist and widen his contacts as well as his social life.

As a member of the Council, he came to know British trade unionists and could not help being affected by their pragmatism and nondoctrinaire attitudes toward labor and social problems. (He did not think the English had the "head" for philosophy, anyhow.) Occasionally he invited some of them to his house, where his charming wife provided food (sometimes a "very frugal dinner," as Marx put it on his invitations) and he supplied very rich conversation. The hardheaded trade unionists had certainly never been exposed to anyone like Dr. Marx, with his vast erudition, philosophic sweep, and positive opinions expressed in fluent English with the heavy Teutonic accent which he never lost. According to all testimony, Marx was an impressive, perhaps overwhelming, conversationalist.

As the guiding spirit of the International, Marx was also a magnet for European visitors. Radicals from all over the Continent would drop in to visit him when in London. Among them were journalists, agitators, politicians, conspirators, and, on occasion, even bona fide labor leaders: Austrians, Belgians, Dutchmen, Frenchmen, Germans, Hungarians, Italians, Poles, Russians, Spaniards, and Swiss. Some of them were later discovered to be spies or double agents, but all of them were welcomed by Marx, who considered them fresh and rich sources of information, especially about outstanding continental political figures and radical personalities. This sort of information was often of dubious veracity, but Marx always believed the worst about bourgeois political leaders and his own opponents.

For Marx, the International involved increasingly heavy burdens and worries. He was constantly "gebothered," as he called it, by the work the organization required. It came to absorb so much of his time that by the end of 1865 he was complaining to Engels that "it weighs on me like an incubus," and that he would throw it off if there were anybody to take his place. But this could have been self-deception.

Was it worth the time? Engels, for one, seems to have been dubious about the whole effort. Another friend, Kugelmann, told Marx bluntly when the latter visited him in Hanover that in giving his energies to the International he was wasting his time on politics, for which he had little aptitude, when he should devote himself entirely to his proper vocation, that of a social and economic critic, for which he had a genius. It was an observation which Marx resented, perhaps because he unconsciously recognized its validity, and it led to a permanent estrangement between the two men.

The fact was that the International did interfere with Marx's own writing. Although undisciplined in his personal habits, he was a hard-working writer and researcher who often stayed up until four o'clock in the morning trying to catch up with his writing and reading. But *Capital*, the major work on which his fame rests, was never actually completed. Marx worked on it intermittently after he published the first installment of his first book on economics, *Critique of Political Economy*, in 1859. Only one volume of *Capital* appeared in Marx's lifetime, and that after many postponements. Volumes II and III of *Capital* were published posthumously by the devoted Engels, from Marx's voluminous notes, in 1885 and 1894.

Marx, however, considered the International worth the sacrifice of his precious time and of the energies that were steadily being depleted by illnesses. For he convinced himself, if not everyone else, that in the International he possessed a great instrument for world revolution, more effective than anything to be found anywhere in Europe.

He was sure that the International, emanating from the most advanced capitalist country in the world, was on the march, and that by being the guiding spirit of its General Council he held the reins of future power. After the Lausanne Congress of 1867 Marx wrote to Engels expressing a sense of triumph, present and to come: "Our Association has made great progress . . . The swine among the English trade unionists, who thought we have gone too 'far,' now come running to us. In addition to the *Courrier Français*, Girardin's *Liberté, Mode, Gazette de France*, etc., have reported on our Congress. *Les choses marchent.* [Things are moving.] And in the next revolution, which is perhaps nearer than it appears, we (that is, you and I), will have this powerful engine in our hands . . . We can be very well content!"

Actually, Marx hoped to shape the International as an instrument that would fit his gradually changing idea of the proletarian revolution. Without surrendering his belief in the ultimate triumph of the proletariat, he had come to view its historic role in more "evolutionary" terms. As early as April, 1856, in a speech delivered at a banquet celebrating the anniversary of the Chartist *People's Paper*, Marx struck a new note. He said that the real revolution which would ultimately emancipate the proletariat lay not in the sort of "noisy" and "confused" actions that had characterized the continental uprisings in 1848–49, but in the development of science and its practical product, technology. Steam, electricity, powered machinery, Marx pointed out, were bringing about basic transformations, first in the economic sphere and then unavoidably in the social superstructure.[7] The obvious implication was that mere proclamations of "revolution," as expressed by Bakuninists, Blanquists, Proudhonists, and other agitators, whose written and oral utterances showed a deplorable ignorance of economics, were little more than excitable phrasemongering and wish fulfillment.

As Marx saw it, particularly after years of assiduous research in economics, science was the true revolutionary force that was transforming society. It was producing a new world of industrialization which was bound to spread and result in an ever larger number of workers to serve the growing industries. At some point in history the working class would become numerous and strong enough to make a successful bid for power. But such action was not automatic, nor could it be pinpointed in time. There would be an interim period during which the working class, apprized (by Marx and Marxists) of its predestined historic role, prepared itself for its fulfillment.

Revolution—that is, actual transformation of the basic forms and

---

7. See Introduction to *Karl Marx on Revolution* (1972), Vol. I of The Karl Marx Library.

institutions of society—thus depended entirely on concrete economic development, and not on the will or wish of some charismatic revolutionist or utopian fantasist. But not all countries were in the same stage of development or moved at the same tempo. Most of the world, including "barbaric" Russia, was still in a preindustrial stage, agricultural or nomadic, and hence not ripe for real revolution. This was something that the wilder radicals of his time, against whom Marx struggled in the International, failed to grasp.

"He," Marx wrote in one of his comments on Bakunin's *State and Anarchy*, "absolutely understands nothing of the social revolution, but only its political phrases; its economic conditions do not exist for him. Since all hitherto existing economic forms, developed or underdeveloped, include the enslavement of workers (be it in the form of wage-workers, peasants, etc.), he believes that in all of them a *radical revolution* is equally possible . . . He wants the European social revolution, founded as it is on the economic basis of capitalist production, to be consummated on the terrain of the Russian or Slavic agricultural and pastoral people . . . The *will*, and not economic conditions, is the basis of his social revolution." Marx thought this was nonsense.

It was within this framework of the economic determinism of revolution that Marx defended London as the locus of the International's General Council. Continental radicals felt that the British capital was insulated from revolutionary activities. They thought a revolutionary headquarters should be where the revolutionists and the revolutionary traditions were: on the Continent, particularly in the French-speaking part.

Marx did not agree. He took the position, which on the face of it seemed paradoxical, that seemingly serene and prosperous London was the ideal place for a headquarters of revolution. What the continentals had was fervor, but zeal was not enough. Revolutionary slogans uttered in Brussels or Geneva or Paris, no matter how exciting, effected no fundamental changes anywhere, in anything. The real revolution, as Marx visualized and explained it, was actually occurring in England, the great and original center of world capitalism, now undergoing its final stages of industrial-economic transformation. In England the revolution—that is, the basic economic one—had gone farther than anywhere else and its example was bound to affect, and ultimately to be followed by, the rest of the world. Hence for those who were charged with the responsibility of charting and guiding the course of future revolution—that is to say, the General Council—the place to be was capitalist London, and, not, say, nonindustrial Geneva or petty-bourgeois Paris. Only in London, the world's center of international finance, commerce, and colonialism, could one properly observe the final development of capitalism and learn the social-political lessons emerging from its maturation. Marx persuaded himself that England had already passed through most of the stages of development which, according to his theory, capitalism had to undergo. In England, he believed, the last stage of capitalism was at hand. Hence for a revolutionist concerned with the real economic processes in their unavoidable historic evolution, no other country was as much worth studying— and organizing politically—as the heart and soul of world capitalism, whose nerve center was London, where the General Council had its headquarters.

Marx elucidated with notable explicitness this theory that Britain was ripening for revolution in the course of his defense of the policies of the General Council against the increasingly disruptive attacks by impatient continental radicals, led by anarchists and other revolutionists, who accused him of having ceased to be a real revolutionary. For a man like Marx, who had devoted his life and sacrificed his personal welfare to the idea and ideal of world revolution, such an accusation stung, the more so as it found credence among radical workers and leaders, notably in the nonindustrialized Latin countries of Europe under the influence of Bakunin and Bakuninists. In a Circular Letter to the Swiss Romansh Council, a center of insurgency and agitation against the General Council in London, Marx defended his position and explained his theory of the imminence of revolution in Britain:

> Although revolutionary *initiative* will probably come from France, England alone can serve as the *lever* for a serious *economic* revolution. It is the only country where there are no longer any peasants and where landed property is concentrated in a few hands. It is the only country where the *capitalist* form—that is, labor combined on a large scale under capitalist entrepreneurs—has taken over practically the whole of production. It is the only country where *the great majority of the population consists of wage laborers.* It is the only country where the class struggle and organization of the working class by the trade unions have attained a certain degree of maturity and universality. It is the only country where, thanks to its domination of the world market, every revolution in economic relationships must directly affect the whole world. While on the one hand landlordism and capitalism have their classic seat in this country, the *material conditions* for their *destruction* are on the other hand the most mature here. The General Council is now in the fortunate position of having its hand directly on this great lever of proletarian revolution.[8]

This being the case, Marx continued, it would be "folly, yea, one might almost say . . . crime," not to take advantage of such a unique

---

8. For the complete text of the Circular Letter, see page 170.

situation. If the International now relinquished London, the revolutionary lever would fall into "purely English hands." This would not do, for without the guidance of the General Council, Englishmen could not carry out their revolution by themselves. British conditions, to be sure, were revolutionary, but Englishmen were not. Their national characteristics being practicality and moderation, they lacked both theory and zeal for revolutionary action. Without the spur of theory, English workers might not even be aware that they were living in a period of imminent revolution or that they were supposed to behave in revolutionary fashion. The General Council alone, Marx argued, was in a position to correct this situation. Marx wrote: "The English have at their disposal all necessary material preconditions for a social revolution. What they lack is the spirit of generalization and revolutionary passion. Only the General Council can provide them with this, and thus accelerate a truly revolutionary movement here and, in consequence, *everywhere*."

Crucial to Marx's maturing theory of revolution, especially as it evolved in the period of the International, was the role of the interim period. The working class, to be sure, was historically predestined to rule, but not necessarily in the immediate future. In the interim the proletariat must bide its time and prepare itself for its role. It must avoid hasty and premature action—such as that of the Paris Commune of 1871, for example—which could be ruinous.

"Where the working class," Marx wrote to Friedrich Bolte, the German socialist leader of the International in New York (November 23, 1871), "is not yet sufficiently far advanced in its organization to undertake a decisive campaign against the collective power, that is, the political power, of the ruling classes, it must in any case be trained for this by constant agitation against (and a hostile attitude to) the policies of the ruling classes. Otherwise it remains a plaything in their hands."

While awaiting the final seizure of power the workers must take advantage of every opportunity to acquire experience and hasten the revolutionary process. They must learn to organize and to use the power of organization, without which nothing could be achieved in the modern world. Above all, they should engage in incessant struggles, even for limited objectives.

In organized action the workers would find invaluable training for their predestined role. They would acquire political experience through the organization of their own parties and mass demonstrations where such activities were legally possible; economic experience through cooperatives and well-led strikes; intellectual experience through the acquisition of skills and technical, as well as cultural, education; fraternal experience through support given to the strivings for independence of oppressed peoples (Irish, Poles); international-affairs experience through consistent opposition to imperialistic and nationalistic wars.

Such organized activities would not only supply the workers with experience but also strengthen their class consciousness and provide them with steady purpose and inspiration. In addition, they would help ripen conditions for real revolution. The final form of the revolution would be forged by these class-oriented struggles. Any other approach Marx wrote, was nothing but "chewed-over general banalities."

To the end of his life, Marx held steadfast to the idea that revolution cannot be merely invented by the imagination, but must be the product of actual conditions that are ripe for the final triumph by the proletariat. On February 22, 1881, about two years before his death, he reiterated this in a blunt letter to Ferdinand Domela Nieuwenhuis, the Netherlands socialist leader who had translated *Capital* into a condensed Dutch version:

> The doctrinal and necessarily fantastic anticipation of the action program of a revolution of the future emerges only from contemporary struggle. The dream of the imminent destruction of the world inspired the early Christians in their struggle with the Roman world empire and gave them certainty of victory. The scientific insight into the unavoidable and continuing disintegration of the dominant order of society, constantly visible before our eyes . . . as well as the gigantically advancing positive development of the means of production—all this serves as a guarantee that at the moment of outbreak of a real proletarian revolution, its very conditions (even if surely not idyllic ones) will directly bring forth the next *modus operandi*.[9]

Such, in essence, was Marx's mature view of revolution, as he developed it in the period when he was striving to use the International as its instrument. These basic ideas were not always clear to his contemporaries, however, particularly those who found him antagonistic. For Marx often lacked precision and had a tendency to state important propositions in generalities. This, together with his tone of dogmatism and anger, was likely to create confusion and opposition.

By the end of 1868 the International began to run into serious trouble on the Continent. It became confronted with a combination of disruptive events beyond its control, without precedent, and, more to the point, not congruent with Marx's theories or expectations. These events, intermeshed in their effects, were a countermovement inside the International, a major European conflict, and a local revolution.

---

9. See *Karl Marx on Revolution*, page 67.

The countermovement was led by Bakunin; the European conflict was the Franco-Prussian War; the local revolution was the Paris Commune of 1871. Marx, although always ready with theories, did not realize that he would not be able to cope effectively with the effects of such an unpredictable combination. In the course of events, he became more and more enraged.

Marx's clash with Bakunin was not only a highlight of the contemporary revolutionary movement, but was also symbolic of European radicalism itself. The two men represented profoundly divergent views of the meaning of revolution and the role of the working class. Theirs was a struggle between the idea of order and that of anarchism, between the concept of collectivism and the passion for individualism. Marx's primary concern was with power achieved through political organization. Bakunin came to reject all authority, proletarian, republican, or monarchical, in favor of individual freedom, total and uncontrolled. "The liberty of man," Bakunin wrote, "consists solely in this, that he obeys the laws of nature, because he has himself recognized them as such, and not because they have been imposed upon him externally by any foreign will whatsoever, human or divine, collective or individual." For Marx, on the other hand, freedom and individualism did not exist outside the scope of organized systems.

The two men, who had first met in Paris in 1844, admired each other's revolutionary passion, but they never understood, liked, or trusted one another. They and their experiences were worlds apart. Marx, the son of a middle-class Rhineland lawyer who admired Rousseau and Voltaire, grew up in an atmosphere of Germanic orderliness, legality, and comparative intellectual freedom. Bakunin, four years older than Marx, was the son of a Russian nobleman and shaped in an environment of czarist despotism, cruel arbitrariness, and feudal backwardness.

Bakunin, a giant of a man, had been an officer in the Imperial Guards. The Czar's harsh repression of the Poles, which he saw and participated in, inspired him to rebellion. First he rebelled against czarism in Russia, then against tyranny everywhere, and finally against all existing institutions. Rejecting national loyalties, he became a fighter for international revolutions. At the time when Marx was pursuing his career as a radical journalist, Bakunin's revolutionary activism began to grow into a legend. But he paid a severe price for it. After fighting in various uprisings in 1848, he was condemned to death by Saxony but handed over to the Austrians, who sentenced him to death anew. He spent several months in jail, in chains. The Austrians delivered him to the Russians, who imprisoned him in the terrible fortresses of Petropavlovsk and Schlüsselburg. He was savagely

xxxvi INTRODUCTION: MARX'S ROLE

maltreated, got scurvy, and lost all his teeth. After five years of solitary confinement he supplicated the Czar for a pardon, and in 1857 was exiled to Siberia for life. Four years later he succeeded in escaping and making his way, via Japan to California, back to Europe. Early in November, 1864, shortly after the International was organized, Marx saw Bakunin for the first time in sixteen years. He thought the Russian had matured and changed for the better.

"I must say," he wrote to Engels on November 4, 1864, "that I liked him very much and more than before . . . In general, he is one of the few people who, after sixteen years, I find has not regressed but developed."

But the sympathy and appreciation were not to last.

On the Continent, Bakunin, increasingly the archetype of the revolutionary activist, first settled in Italy, where he established a journal to preach his own brand of radicalism. He also founded a secret revolutionary society of small groups of conspirators, with branches in France, Poland, and Spain. Then he moved to Switzerland. He was in search of a base from which, as Marx later accused him, to lead the European revolution. In 1867 Bakunin tried to take over the pacifist League of Peace and Freedom and, failing that, joined the International. He became editor of *L'Égalité*, a Geneva weekly, which served as the platform for his ideas.

Jumping from project to project, Bakunin continued to write, scheme, and orate. He rarely completed anything. His fellow exile, the Russian writer Alexander Herzen, said of him that he "took the second month of pregnancy for the ninth." But Bakunin, the giant with the heavy step and Russian peasant blouse, enveloped in perpetual cigarette smoke, had a dramatic impact on audiences. A genuine tribune of the people and a blazing orator, he stirred his hearers, often half-baked radicals, to frenzy with his passionate outpourings against tyranny and hatred of all systems, governments, and organized political activities. Undisciplined and reckless, artless and devious, the demonic Bakunin was, as Marx was to discover belatedly, a very dangerous man.

As can be judged from Bakunin's fragmentary writings, his basic ideas were not only in conflict with the methods and objectives of the International, but also a direct challenge to Marx and the whole German socialist school. Bakunin distrusted Germans as born lackeys, devoid of any sense of freedom, and believed that anything organized by them, or in line with their theories—whether Marxist or Lassallean —would end in despotism in the name of socialism.

It is illuminating to read what amounts to a "dialogue" between Marx and Bakunin, written shortly after the clash between them helped destroy the International. In 1873 Bakunin published a book,

Gossudarstvennost i Anarchiya [*State and Anarchy*], in Geneva. A year or so later Marx read it in the original Russian, made extensive extracts from it, and added his own comments. The Bakunin quotations and the Marx remarks add up to a kind of political drama. They also throw light on some of the more obscure aspects of Marx's thought, particularly his idea of class rule and the dictatorship of the proletariat.

BAKUNIN: . . . We have already expressed our repugnance for the theory of Lassalle and Marx, which recommends to the workers, if not as a final ideal, at least as the next best objective, the founding of a *people's state*, which, to use their expression, would be organized with the *proletariat as the ruling class*. One asks: If the proletariat is to be the ruling class, over whom would it rule? This means that still another proletariat would remain behind as subjects of this new domination, this new state.

MARX: This means that so long as other classes, especially the capitalist, still exist and the proletariat struggles with them (for the capitalist governments are its enemy and the old organization of society has not yet disappeared), the proletariat must use *forcible* means, hence governmental means. So long as it still remains a class, and the economic conditions on which the class rests still exist, and the other classes have not yet disappeared and have to be cleared out of the way by force or transformed, the process of transformation is to be hastened by force.

BAKUNIN: For example, the common peasantry, the peasant mob, which, as is well known, does not enjoy the benevolence of the Marxists, and which finds itself at the lowest level of the culture, will in all probability be ruled by the city and factory proletariat.

MARX: This means that where the peasant exists in the mass as a private property owner, where he even forms a more or less substantial majority, as he does in all the states of the West European continent, where he has not yet disappeared and been replaced by agricultural day laborers, as in England, the following alternatives develop: either he prevents or frustrates every workers' revolution, as he has hitherto done in France; or the proletariat (for the property-owning peasant does not belong to the proletariat, and even where he belongs to it according to his condition, he does not believe that he does) must take governmental measures directly to improve the peasant's condition, so as to win him over to the revolution; measures, however, that in their seed facilitate the transition from private land ownership to collective ownership, so that the peasant arrives at it economically himself; but the government must not offend the peasant by proclaiming, for example, the abolition of the right of inheritance or the abolition of his property; the latter is possible only where the capitalist tenant has displaced the peasant, and the real farm worker is as much a proletarian, a wage laborer, as the city worker, and thus has the same *indirect,* and not direct, interests. Still less must parceled property be strengthened by increasing the size of the parcels through the simple annexation of the large estate by the peasants, as per the Bakuninist revolutionary campaign.

BAKUNIN: Where there is a state, there is unavoidable domination, consequently also (slavery); domination without slavery, hidden or masked, is unthinkable—hence we are enemies of the state.

What does it mean, the proletariat (organized as a ruling class)?

MARX: It means that the proletariat, instead of fighting singly against the economically privileged classes, has attained sufficient strength and organization to be able to apply general means of coercion against them; but it can apply only the economic means that will abolish its own character as *salariat* [wage workers], and hence as a class; with its complete victory, therefore, its rule comes to an end, because its class character has disappeared.

BAKUNIN: Will the whole proletariat perhaps be at the head of the government?

MARX: In a trade union, does the whole union make up its executive committee? In the factory, will all division of labor, as well as the various functions arising therefrom, cease? And in the Bakuninist structure (from the bottom up), will everybody be up? In which case there is no bottom. Will all members of the community administer the common interests of the domain at the same time? In which case there is no difference between community and domain.

BAKUNIN: The Germans amount to approximately 40,000,000. Will, for example, all the 40,000,000 be members of the government?

MARX: Certainly! Since the matter begins with the self-government of the community.

BAKUNIN: Then there will be no govermnent, no state, but if there is a state, there will be also the governed and slaves.

MARX: This merely means: when class rule has disappeared, there will be no state in the present political sense.

BAKUNIN: This dilemma in the theory of the Marxists is explained simply. Under people's government, they understand government of the people through a small number of representatives, selected by the people.

MARX: Jackass! This is democratic twaddle, political drivel. Election —political form, the kind found in the smallest Russian commune and artel. The character of the election does not depend on those labels, but on the economic foundation, the economic interconnection of the voters. The moment these functions have ceased to be political, then (1) there exists no governmental function; (2) the division of the general functions has become merely a technical business, which does not result in domination; (3) election has nothing of the present-day political character.[10]

---

10. From Marx's "Conspectus of Bakunin's *State and Anarchy*," written between 1874 and early 1875, published in *Marx-Engels Werke*, Vol. XVIII (1964), pp. 599–642.

Bakunin did not believe in the Marxist notion of proletarian rule nor in the hope that such a government would, once victorious, fade away. A proletarian dictatorship was still class rule, which meant that a minority would use governmental power to oppress the people. He did not see any difference between one form of domination and another.

"We object," Bakunin wrote in his posthumously published book, *God and the State* (1882), "to all legislation, all authority, and all influence, privileged, patented, official, and legal, even when it has proceeded from universal suffrage, convinced that it must always turn to the profit of a dominating and exploiting minority, against the interests of the immense enslaved majority."

In October, 1868, in Geneva, Bakunin secretly organized an *Alliance Internationale de la Démocratie Socialiste*—International Alliance of Socialist Democracy—which was to function alongside the International Working Men's Association. Bakunin claimed that his Alliance was to restore the "idealism" lacking in the International ("Russian idealism!" Marx snorted contemptuously when he heard about it). The "Alliance" declared itself in favor of the equality of all classes, the abolition of the state, and the rejection of open political struggle on the part of the workers. This program was obviously totally at variance with Marx's philosophy and the aims of the International. When the news of the Alliance first reached Marx in London, his initial reaction was to ignore it as the usual Bakuninist *"fadaise"* [twaddle] and *"Scheisse"* [excrement]. But Marx and his colleagues soon sensed the potential danger and took steps against it.

"But the matter," Marx wrote Engels on December 15, 1868, "has become more serious than I thought . . . This evening the Council has resolved *publicly* to repudiate this interloping society—in Paris, New York, Germany, and Switzerland. I am charged with drafting the repudiation decree."

Accordingly, on December 22, the General Council issued a formal statement, written by Marx, denouncing Bakunin's organization. In effect, it outlawed the Alliance as a branch of the International and declared its statutes "null and void."

Ironically enough, on the same day that Marx drafted the edict repudiating the Alliance, Bakunin wrote him a warm letter full of flattery: "You have asked . . . whether I am still your friend. Yes, more than ever, dear Marx, because I now understand more than ever how very right you are when you follow the grand route of economic revolution and invite us to march along . . . From now on, my fatherland is the International . . . I am your disciple—and I am proud to be."

But Marx was not deceived. The effusive words did not allay his suspicions of either Bakunin's purposes or his nationality. "I do not trust any Russian," he told Engels. Marx was right to be distrustful. While Bakunin formally agreed to dissolve the Alliance and remain faithful to the International, he continued secretly to work against it. His aim was to undermine its leadership with a view to taking over the organization. Bakunin did this with "Russian cunning," as Engels called it, and deliberate deception. In October, 1869, when Herzen asked Bakunin why, in view of his own political convictions, he did not openly break with Marx and the International, the latter replied disingenuously:

> I have honored and praised Marx for tactical reasons and personal politics. Don't you see how all these gentlemen stick together? Our enemies build a phalanx, and one has first to divide them, break them, in order to defeat them more easily. You are more educated than I, and therefore you know better who first said: *Divide et impera* [Divide and conquer]. If I should now start an open war against Marx, three-fourths of the International would turn against me, and I would end on a slippery slope and lose the only ground on which I want to stand.[11]

For about four years, Marx continued to fight Bakunin inside the International. It was a vain effort, first because Bakunin was slippery, and secondly, because he did develop a loyal following in many branches of the International, most effectively so in the important French-speaking and Latin countries. They challenged Marx's leadership of the International and attacked its policies in their publications, especially in *L'Égalité*. Marx became increasingly convinced that behind the anarchists were the diabolical Bakunin's machinations to seize control of the European radical movement. Enraged and baffled, he looked upon the Bakuninists as "Cossacks" and rogues. These Russians in Geneva, he told Engels in August, 1870, "will find that I set *à Corsaire Corsaire et demi*" (one and a half scoundrels against one). It was not an effective response. The rancorous counterattacks and denunciations merely poisoned the atmosphere further and sapped the strength of the International. Its disintegration was hastened by the crises of the Franco-Prussian War and the Paris Commune.

The Franco-Prussian War, which broke out on July 19, 1870, had immediate and long-range consequences for both Europe and the International. It shifted the balance of power in Europe and resulted in significant changes within the belligerent countries. Among other things, it resulted in Germany's becoming a united empire and France a divided republic.

11. Bakunin to Herzen, October 28, 1869; quoted in B. Nicolaevsky and O. Maenchen-Helfen, *Karl Marx. Eine Biographie* (1963), pp. 299–300.

Initially, Marx had mixed feelings about the conflict. The war had been declared by Napoleon III to prevent the unification of Germany, a unification which Marx favored, although not under Prussian militarist hegemony. Hence the Germans were fighting in self-defense. From a personal point of view, moreover, the German in Marx could not avoid a touch of reluctant admiration for the perfectly executed Prussian military campaign, as against the fumbling ineptitude of the French.

Marx also had long detested Napoleon III, the man "with the long nose of a stock-exchange shark," as he called him. He despised the French Emperor as a lackey of the bankers, a destroyer of the French Republic, a political fraud, an unprincipled adventurer, incurably venal and corrupt; and he castigated this "nephew of the uncle" in some of his most brilliant polemical writings, notably *The Class Struggles in France* and *The Eighteenth Brumaire of Louis Bonaparte*. "I have always exposed him, even at his apogee," he told Kugelmann in February, 1871, "as a *mediocre scoundrel*."

Nor was Marx enamored of Wilhelm III, the King of Prussia who became Wilhelm I, Emperor of a united Germany, in 1871. He pictured the Hohenzollern monarch as a pious old ass, flanked by a police spy (Wilhelm Stieber) on one side and a "thief" (Bismarck) on the other, singing the hymn, "*Jesus ist meine Zuversicht*" ["Jesus Is My Shepherd"]. Morally, as between a corrupt French emperor, representing a reactionary and imperialistic bourgeoisie, and a sanctimonious Prussian king, representing a crude and militaristic *Kraut-junkertum* [cabbage squirearchy], there was indeed nothing to choose. "On both sides," Marx remarked as he followed the military campaign, "it is a disgusting spectacle."

Politically, however, Marx thought that a Prussian defeat would solve nothing, while a victory would destroy the power of Napoleon III and disintegrate his empire. This in turn might well lead to the long-awaited revolution in France.

"For my own part," he wrote on July 28, 1870, to his daughter Laura and her French husband, Paul Lafargue, "I should like that both, Prussians and Frenchmen, thrashed each other alternately, and that—as I believe will be the case—the Germans got *ultimately* the better of it. I wish this because the definite defeat of Bonaparte is likely to provoke revolution in France, while the definite defeat of the Germans would only protract the present state of things for twenty years."

A few days before the ignominiously routed Napoleon III surrendered with his army at Sedan, Marx expressed a similar opinion to Engels. "The French," he told him, "need a thrashing."

But matters were obviously not that simple. Marx realized that the war was both a nationalist and an imperialist one, and hence likely to arouse confusing emotions among working people in the belligerent countries. The International owed it to the workers to provide orientation and guidance. On July 23 he completed the *First Address of the International on the Franco-Prussian War*, of which 30,000 copies were printed in German and French and distributed by the General Council. The *Address* appealed to the workers to refrain from supporting the war. It also alerted the German working class to a menace Marx particularly dreaded: that if the war continued, the Prussians might appeal to the Czar for help; the barbaric Russians would then enter Germany and make that country a permanent base for their long-cherished plan to dominate Europe. This was not a new position for Marx. He was always haunted by the fear that Russian hordes, products of total tyranny and backwardness, would some day pour across Europe's frontiers and destroy Western civilization, including the hard-won gains of Europe's relatively free working class. This was a persistent motif in his thinking and writing about foreign policy in general, especially after 1848–49, when the Czar's "Cossacks" helped the Austrian Empire smash the revolutions there.

"In the background of this suicidal strife," Marx warned in the *First Address*, "looms the dark figure of Russia. . . . Whatever sympathy the Germans may justly claim in a war of defense against Bonapartist aggression they would forfeit at once by allowing the Prussian Government to call for, or accept, the help of the Cossacks."

A few days after the French, on September 4, 1870, proclaimed the Third Republic, with a Provisional Government under the leadership of Louis Jules Trochu and Léon Gambetta, Marx issued the *Second Address of the International on the Franco-Prussian War*. In it he appealed to the German workers to protest against the annexation of Alsace-Lorraine, and to work for peace and the recognition of the French Republic. As for the French workers, particularly members of the International, Marx urged them not to be tricked by nationalistic memories, to support the Republic, and to use it for their own ends: "Let them calmly and resolutely improve the opportunities of republican liberty, for the work of their own class organization. It will gift them with fresh Herculean powers for the regeneration of France, and our common task, the emancipation of labor."

It did not work out that way. In Germany, to be sure, there were some workers' demonstrations against the war, and a few socialist leaders, among them August Bebel and Wilhelm Liebknecht, went to jail for opposing it. But the common people in Germany, even outside Prussia, found a new pride in the prowess of German arms. In France, where chauvinism[12] was always endemic, the result of the swift and humiliating defeat at the hands of the Prussians, whom even Marx considered an inferior race because of their presumed Russian origin (*Prussia* comes from the word *Bo-Russia*), also brought out strong nationalistic feelings and, unavoidably, anti-Germanism. The International in London was dominated by Germans in the General Council, and it was obviously not difficult for French Bakuninists and others to stir up suspicion that it was a Prussian tool, as well as to spread rumors that Marx was an agent of Bismarck.

Events in France moved toward their tragic climax. While the Germans were at the walls of a starving and angry Paris, a National Assembly met in Bordeaux and elected Adolphe Thiers, a seventy-four-year-old nationalistic politician-historian who loathed what he called the "vile multitude," as chief executive of the Government of National Defense. The Thiers Government made a peace treaty with Germany (among other things, ceding Alsace-Lorraine), which the Assembly ratified on March 1, 1871. The conservative National Assembly moved to Versailles, symbol of the *ancien régime*, instead of to Paris, hotbed of revolution. On March 18, 1871, Thiers sent regular French troops to disarm the popular National Guard, but they fraternized with the people instead. In the prevailing insurrectionary atmosphere, two Generals, Claude-Martin Lecomte and Clément Thomas—the latter, as Marx pointed out in *The Civil War in France*, a political bullyboy rather than a professional officer—were shot to death. The Versailles army withdrew and Paris was left in the hands of the radicals.

On March 26 Paris elected a municipal council—the *Commune*—under the auspices of the National Guard. *Commune* means township, but in the muddle and bloodshed that soon ensued, the word became confused with *communism*.

In reality, the Commune was neither communistic nor particularly revolutionary. The majority of its members were not even socialists, but republicans and moderates. A minority consisted of the usual hotheads and romantics, among them a handful of foreign radicals, easily intoxicated by their own revolutionary rhetoric, which, as usual, they mistook for reality. This, of course, was in the French tradition, which went back to 1789, 1830, 1848, and 1852, as can be seen from Marx's many writings on the subject.

The Communards were ignorant of basic economic forces and

---

12. The word is, of course, French. It comes from Nicholas Chauvin, a Napoleonic veteran who exaggeratedly glorified everything French.

relationships. This seems to have been true even of those few who were members of the International. When refugee French members of the International left London for France after the proclamation of the French Republic in September, 1870, Marx remarked with acute pessimism that they were going to Paris to commit "stupidities." The Commune seized the public treasury but not individual private property. It did not take over the Bank of France, long the country's most powerful single institution. When its funds started to run low, which they did in a few days, the Commune did occupy the office of the Stamp and Tax Duties, which was public property, and confiscated the coffers of the wine stores in Bercy, which belonged to a public corporation, but this was done out of sheer immediate necessity. A week after the Commune came into existence, on April 2, the London *Times* correspondent reported to his newspaper from Paris: "It is coming to the end of its resources, and must feed, clothe, and pay its army." But the Commune had no prepared or consistent program.

For the Commune was not a planned conspiracy by any revolutionary organization, but a spontaneous effort by Paris radicals and republicans. It quickly fell into the hands of the more muddle-headed Bakuninists, Blanquists, Proudhonists, and other doctrinarians, who had little in common except rancor and a general hatred of established society, particularly the conservative government in Versailles. Insofar as the Communards had a political philosophy, it was neither Marxist nor anarchist, but a vague autonomism. The Communards wanted Paris to be an autonomous and essentially independent commune, united loosely in a federation of other autonomous French communes. Each commune was to enjoy full democratic rights—of conscience, of education, of voting, of labor—and absolute freedom of action within its own borders, without interference by any central government.

"To insure, however, her own independence," to quote the *Journal Officiel de la République Française sous la Commune* (1871), "Paris reserves to herself the liberty of effecting as she may think fit, in her own sphere, those administrative and economic reforms which her population shall demand, of creating such institutions as are proper for developing and extending education, production, commerce, and credit; and of extending the enjoyment of power and property in accordance with the necessities of the moment, the wish of the persons interested, and that data provided by experience."

This sort of murky thinking made little economic or political sense—and it was certainly not in line with Marx's own long-range philosophy of revolution. In fact, most of the rest of France, accustomed to centuries of highly centralized government and administration, refused to follow the example of Paris, although half a dozen cities did set up temporary communes.[13] But the passions—perhaps the correct word would be *fears*—stirred up by Paris drowned out any moderation on all sides.

Early in April, the Thiers Government in Versailles sent against Paris the regular French army, soon reinforced by Marshal MacMahon and his troops, who had surrendered to the Germans at Sedan in 1870 and who were now released from captivity for this purpose. While the victorious Prussians watched with malicious joy from their encampments on the eastern heights overlooking the capital—extending in a semicircle from near St. Denis to Charenton—the French army began to batter its way from the western side into the city.

The National Guard, with its political "generals" and their fancy uniforms, was obviously no match for a professional army, although the common workers fighting in the ranks often displayed unexampled and, indeed, reckless bravery. A contemporary observer described the Guard officers as ridiculous in their vanity. "All these new-made officers," he wrote, "of whom the greater number have never seen fire, imagined that in putting on their uniforms they transformed themselves into very thunderbolts of war." Marx, as he followed the struggle from his vantage point in London, also thought the strategy and tactics of the Commune leaders were "stupid." In the first engagement of the conflict, at the bridge of Neuilly, the National Guard was defeated in an hour, leaving about 200 dead and wounded behind them. The uneven war continued for six weeks, with the Communards bloodily beaten from one barricade to another.

The end came in the week beginning Sunday, May 21, when the Versailles troops took the Bois de Boulogne. By Tuesday they occupied about half of Paris, including Montmartre and most of the Left Bank. By Friday, they had seized virtually the rest of the city, including the Louvre, the Tuileries, the Hôtel de Ville, the Palais Royal, the Place de la Bastille, and the important railroad stations: Gare de l'Est and Gare du Nord. The last holdouts were on the heights of Buttes Chaumont and Le Père Lachaise, in the extreme eastern part of the city, and there, on Sunday, May 28, the remnants of the Communards, some 6,000 men, were simply slaughtered.

Before the struggle had come to an end, as the Versailles troops were relentlessly taking the city and killing captured Communard leaders (among them men like Gustave Flourens, the thirty-three-year-old scientist whom the Marx family knew and loved[14]) without

---

13. Le Creusot, Limoges, Lyon, Marseilles, Narbonne, Toulouse.

14. From London, Mrs. Karl Marx wrote to Wilhelm Liebknecht in Leipzig, April, 1871: "I cannot begin to tell you in what a state of agitation, fear, and despair we all find ourselves in our house . . . Above all, the death of Gustave

trial, the enraged Commune compounded the tragedy by committing excesses of its own. It seized a number of hostages, including Georges Darboy, Archbishop of Paris, and executed them in prison. Communard *pétroleurs* and *pétroleuses* [male and female arsonists] went around the city burning public buildings. They set fire to the Hôtel de Ville, the Tuileries, the Palais de Justice, the Palace of the Legion of Honor, as well as buildings on the Rue de Rivoli.

But the atrocities deliberately committed by the French army against its own people vastly exceeded anything the Communards ever did or even imagined possible. In the week of May 21–28, the so-called "Bloody May Week," the French army, its leaders fueled by the ugliest class hatred, indulged in a vengeful carnage on a scale not to be seen again until the days of Franco and Hitler. No exact figures are available, but the estimates of slain civilians—men and women who looked or were dressed like workers—range from a minimum of 20,000 to a maximum of 36,000. The Twentieth Arrondissement, a working-class district, was laid waste. In a continuing reign of terror, 20,000 were court-martialed and a large number of them condemned to penal colonies. It was, indeed, "class war"[15]—more than confirming anything that Marx had ever written in the *Communist Manifesto* or elsewhere.

Marx followed the course of the Commune with passionate personal involvement. He knew as well as anyone that neither he nor the International had had anything to do with setting up the Commune, and still less with its policies. It is doubtful, indeed, whether most Communards even knew who Marx was. The bits of advice that he sent from London to a few Communard friends, such as the Hungarian revolutionist Leo Frankel, went unheeded. Marx was, in fact, dubious about the wisdom of the Commune, and in subsequent years was to be severely critical of it. "With a minimum quantum of common

Flourens has shocked us most deeply. We were personal friends . . . Flourens, now assassinated . . . was a noble soul through and through. Audacious to the point of rashness, knightly, humane, compassionate, gentle . . . he had a richly developed mind, being himself a scholar and a representative of modern science; young, rich and endowed with fine courteous manners, he had a warm and impulsive nature that made him turn toward the poor, the oppressed, the disinherited. . . ."

15. The "class" nature of the anti-Commune war can be seen from the ongoing courts-martial. Among the 20,000 condemned by them were the following categories: writers (2,901), mechanics (2,664), masons (2,293), carpenters (1,665), sales clerks (1,598), shoemakers (1,491), clerks (1,265), house painters (863), printers (1,819), stone cutters (766), tailors (681), wood polishers (636), gold workers (528), building carpenters (382), leather workers (347), sculptors (283), tinkers (227), foundry workers (224), hat makers (210), seamstresses (206), embroiderers (193), watchmakers (179), gilders (172), carpet makers (159), pattern makers (157), prison wardens (124), bookbinders (106), teachers (106).

sense," he wrote to the Dutch socialist Nieuwenhuis in February, 1881, "it could have achieved a compromise with the Versailles Government, useful for the whole mass of the people—which was then attainable."

But despite private doubts, Marx's heart was with the Commune and its fate. In April, while the Commune was fighting for its life, he referred to it in personal letters as the "most glorious act of our party," praised it as "this exalted revolution," and spoke of the embattled Communards as "heaven-stormers." When the reports of the killings of Communard leaders by the Versailles troops reached London, the whole Marx household was plunged, in the words of his wife, into a bitter "state of agitation, fear, and despair."

The personal involvement became even more intensified when the conservative French press, in search of a scapegoat, found one in Marx. He was depicted on the one hand as an agent of Bismarck, and on the other as the *"grand chef"* [supreme chief] of a diabolical socialist conspiracy. Rumors and pure fabrications about Marx were picked up and reprinted by other newspapers, including German and English, and spread throughout Europe. Two examples:

> From *La Province*, a Bordeaux daily: Paris, April 2. A revelation arriving from Germany has caused a great sensation here. It is now authentically substantiated that Karl Marx, one of the most influential chiefs of the International, was *Private Secretary to Count Bismarck* in the year 1857 and never ceased to remain in contact with his former *patron.*

> From *National Zeitung*, a Berlin daily: " 'Capital,' says Karl Marx, "trades in the strength and life of the workman"; but this new Messiah himself is not a step farther advanced: he takes from the mechanic the money paid him by the capitalist for his labor, and generously gives him in exchange a bill on a state that may possibly exist a thousand years hence. What edifying stories are told about the vile corruption of socialist agitators, what a shameful abuse they make of the money confided to them, and what mutual accusations they throw in each other's faces, are things we have abundantly learned from the Congresses and from the organs of the party. There is here a monstrous volcano of filth, from whose eruptions nothing better could issue than a Parisian Commune.[16]

Marx, of course, reacted as was to be expected, with unrestrained fury. He attacked the lies in angry letters to the press—which only spread them the more—and defended the Commune in a bitterly eloquent pamphlet, *The Civil War in France*, whose immediate effect was further to identify the International with the Commune, by then in

16. This was reprinted in *Public Opinion*, a London weekly, August 19, 1871.

such wide disrepute that some of the English members of the General Council refused to endorse it.

Marx concluded *The Civil War in France* with these impassioned words: "Workingmen's Paris, with its Commune, will be forever celebrated as the glorious harbinger of a new society. Its martyrs are enshrined in the great heart of the working class. Its exterminators history has already nailed to that eternal pillory from which all the prayers of their priests will not avail to redeem them."

But the rhetoric could not hide the immediate reality, which was that the Commune was dead and the International splintered on the Continent, its members either legally persecuted or in hiding. In London too the General Council was disintegrating under various attacks from inside and outside. Refugees from the Commune holocaust indulged in internecine conflict among themselves and with the General Council. Mutual recriminations found their echoes even in the radical press.

Outsiders joined in. Charles Bradlaugh, free-thinker and editor of the *National Reformer,* a London radical weekly, attacked both the International and Marx, whom he accused of being a coward and an agent of Bismarck. "If I were one of his own countrymen," Bradlaugh wrote to the editor of the *Eastern Post* (December 16, 1871), "he might betray me to his government, here he can only calumniate." Marx, hinting that Bradlaugh was a French agent, threatened to sue him for defamation. "For the present," he wrote the *Eastern Post* in reply (December 23), "I shall 'betray him' to the German public by giving the greatest possible circulation to his epistle. If he be kind enough to clothe his libels in a more tangible shape, I shall 'betray him' to an English law court."

Marx was losing touch. The London Conference, which he and Engels prepared and which met from September 17 to 23, 1871, underlined the extent of the International's disintegration. It was attended by only twenty-three delegates, among them French Bakuninists, whom the eternally suspicious Marx treated with harsh arrogance. One of them, Paul Robin, finally washed his hands of the whole affair, sending Marx a note: ". . . in my regret at having to break with you, I believe that I owe you this declaration. I am convinced that in yielding to personal hatreds you have carried or supported unjust accusations against members of the International, the objects of these hatreds, whose sole crime has been in not sharing them."[17]

17. An anonymous penciled note, found among the minutes of the General Council under date of May 29, 1871, stated: "M, a German of acute mind, but like that of Proudhon, of a dissolving tendency, of a domineering temper, jealous of the influence of others, without strong philosophical or religious faith, and I am afraid with more hatred, even if just hatred, than love in his heart."

In 1872, when even Eccarius broke with him, Marx came to the conclusion that the International no longer had any future in Europe. He saw it threatened by twin enemies, bourgeois governments and Bakuninists. He decided, as he wrote to Paul Lafargue in March, 1872, "to prevent hostile elements from seizing" the General Council. In September, 1872, Marx, together with his wife and daughter Eleanor, went to The Hague, where, in a small dance hall on Lombard Straat, the International held its last Congress. It was attended by sixty-five delegates from Western Europe, as well as from Australia and the United States. The Marxists were in a majority and dominated the Congress. In an atmosphere of bitterness they shattered what was left of the International by expelling Bakunin and his followers. Then they accepted Marx's proposal to remove the General Council, with its archives and organizational responsibility, from Europe to America, to keep it out of hostile hands. On the last day of the Congress, September 6, Marx scribbled a note in French, which was signed by his friends and followers:[18] "We are proposing that for the year 1872–1873 the seat of the General Council be transferred to New York. . . ."

This was the end of the International, so far as Europe was concerned. But the General Council, despite Marx's sometimes lengthy epistolary advice to its leaders from London, did not survive long in New York either. There, as can be seen from Marx's correspondence included in this volume, it fell prey to the usual bickerings, splinterings, and countermovements, as well as attempted take-overs by such indigenous American radical groups as those headed by the suffragette Tennessee Claflin. On July 15, 1876, the New York-based General Council, now a splinter group without much legitimacy, held a conference in Philadelphia, attended by fourteen American delegates, and dissolved the International.

The First International left strong memories in the European socialist and labor movements. It served as a precedent for the Second International, founded in Paris in 1889, six years after Marx's death. The Second International, representing Marxist Social Democratic parties, which were making rapid progress on the Continent, particularly in Germany, was torn by clashing interpretations of Marx's thought. Did Marx believe in the possibility of achieving socialism, at least in advanced countries, through democratic means, as he had suggested in his speech in Amsterdam in September, 1872,[19] or did he

18. Maltman Barry, Eugène Dupont, Frederick Engels, Benjamin Le Moussu, Friedrich Lessner, Charles Longuet, J. Patrick McDonnell, Auguste Serraillier, George Sexton, and Walery Wroblewsky.

19. See *Karl Marx on Revolution*, pages 63–65.

exclusively advocate violence and dictatorship? In 1914 the First
World War ended the Second International but not the crucial debate
over what Marx had actually said and meant. A Third International,
built around Lenin's interpretation of revolutionary Marxism, was
founded in March, 1919.[20] Called the Comintern, it became the center
of the world-wide communist movement, at least up to the period of
the Second World War. After 1919 the socialist parties everywhere
split sharply between supporters of the so-called dictatorship of the
proletariat, known as communists, and advocates of social democracy,
the socialists and social democrats. Both sides acted in the name of
Karl Marx.

As for Marx himself, the First International was his last direct
political activity. After its dissolution his virtually uninterrupted ill
health made it increasingly impossible for him to do much serious
work. He did sporadic research for the continuation of *Capital*, engaged in some polemical writings, such as the one exposing Bakunin's
"Plot Against the International," drafted suggestions for socialist
policy, such as the "Critique of the Gotha Program," and kept up a
fairly wide correspondence, particularly letters of criticism, comment,
and advice to foreign socialists, American, French, German, and
Russian. Suffering from laryngitis, bronchitis, a tumor on the lung, and
cruel sleeplessness, he died in London on March 14, 1883, about two
months before his sixty-fifth birthday.

At the graveside service in London's Highgate Cemetery, where
Marx was buried, his lifelong friend and associate, Frederick Engels,
said: "His name and his works will live on through the ages."

This volume—the third in The Karl Marx Library—contains virtually everything Marx wrote in connection with the First International. A number of the materials, including the minutes of the General Council, its addresses, and some speeches and letters to the
press, were originally in English; the rest were written in German or
French. Except when otherwise indicated, the translations are by the
editor. Brief translations and explanations by the editor are given in
brackets in the text. Footnotes are the editor's except for those keyed
"K.M.," etc.

---

20. For the debate between Marxist socialists and communists, see Saul K.
Padover, "Kautsky and the Materialist Interpretation of History," in J. L. Cate
and E. N. Anderson, eds., *Medieval and Historiographical Essays in Honor of
James Westfall Thompson* (University of Chicago Press, 1938), pp. 439–64.

Chronology:
Communist Organizations and
the First International[1]

COMMUNIST ORGANIZATIONS

1834

SUMMER Founding in Paris of the *Bund der Geächteten* (League of Outlaws), a secret organization of about two hundred German handicraftsmen, aiming at the overthrow of princely rule in Germany and the unification of the country.

1836

Proletarian members break with the *Bund der Geächteten* and found in Paris their own secret organization, the *Bund der Gerechten* (League of the Just).

1839

MAY 12 In Paris, the League of the Just joins the *Société des Saisons* (Society of the Seasons), a secret Blanquist organization, in an armed uprising, which is smashed by the Municipal Guard; the German members are expelled from France.

---

1. For a full Chronology of Marx's life, see *Karl Marx on Revolution* (1972), Vol. I of The Karl Marx Library.

1840

FEBRUARY 7   German refugees from France, led by Heinrich
              Bauer and Karl Schapper, found in London the
              Deutsche Arbeiterbildungsverein (German Workers'
              Educational Society), which soon attracts other Eu-
              ropean refugees, thus becoming an international com-
              munist society. (The motto on its membership cards,
              "All Men Are Brothers," was printed in twenty
              languages.)

1841

SEPTEMBER   Wilhelm Weitling, a German communist, begins pub-
             lication in Switzerland of a monthly, *Der Hülferuf
             der deutschen Jugend* (German Youth's Cry for
             Help), written specifically for workers.

1842

JANUARY   Weitling publishes another proletarian monthly, *Die
             Junge Generation* (The Young Generation), which
             has 1,000 subscribers—500 of them in Switzerland,
             400 in Paris, and 100 in London.

1845

SEPTEMBER 22 Founding, in London, of the Fraternal Democrats,
              an international-minded revolutionary organization
              made up of Chartists, French émigrés, members of
              the League of the Just, etc.

1846

EARLY IN   In Brussels, Karl Marx and Frederick Engels found
THE YEAR   the Communist Correspondence Committee, consist-
              ing mostly of German refugee revolutionists.

AUGUST 15   Engels moves the headquarters of the Communist
              Correspondence Committee from Brussels to Paris.

1847

EARLY JUNE   First Congress of the League of Communists, joined
              by members of the League of the Just, adopts new
              statutes. The first article reads: "The aim of the

League is the overthrow of the bourgeoisie, the rule of the proletariat, the breaking-up of the old society based on class laws, and the founding of a new society without classes and without private property."

AUGUST 5 Under the leadership of Marx and Engels, the League of Communists in Brussels organizes a German Labor Association, for the propagation of communism.

NOVEMBER 29–
DECEMBER 8 Second Congress of the League of Communists meets in London, with Karl Schapper as president, Frederick Engels as secretary, and Karl Marx as active participant. This congress commissions Marx and Engels to write the "Manifesto of the Communist Party" (*Communist Manifesto*).

1848

MARCH 3 The Central Committee of the League of Communists, in Brussels, dissolves itself and authorizes Marx to found a new organization in revolutionary Paris.

MARCH 11 The Central Committee of the League of Communists is reconstituted in Paris under Marx's leadership.

MARCH 21–29 Marx and Engels publish, in Paris, the seventeen-point "Demands of the Communist Party in Germany."

APRIL 13 A communist *Arbeiterverein* (Workers' Association), with about three hundred members, is organized in Cologne.

APRIL 25 A *Demokratische Gesellschaft* (Democratic Society) is organized by communists in Cologne.

JUNE 24 Organization of a central committee to combine the communist and revolutionary forces in Cologne.

1849

LATE AUGUST In London, the League of Communists is reorganized, with Marx (who arrived on August 24) as president. Members are Heinrich Bauer, Johann Georg Eccarius, Albert Lehmann, Karl Pfänder, Konrad Schramm, and later Engels, Wilhelm Liebknecht, Karl Schapper, and August Willich.

1850

SEPTEMBER 15 The League of Communists is split between the followers of Marx and those of Schapper and Willich.

SEPTEMBER 29   The League of Communists in Cologne is split the same way.

1851

MAY 10–
JULY 11   In Cologne, active members of the League of Communists, including the Central Committee, are imprisoned.

1852

OCTOBER 4–
NOVEMBER 12   Trial of eleven communists in Cologne, where seven are sentenced to prison; this all but destroys the League.

NOVEMBER 17   In London, at the behest of Marx, the League of Communists is dissolved, on the ground that its activities are no longer appropriate to the new conditions of antirevolutionary reaction on the Continent.

1864

The International Working Men's Association—The First International—founded in London, becomes, in effect, the successor of the communist leagues, although it does not officially call itself communist. Indeed, many of its members, although radical, were not communists, and in the end, fundamental disagreements over policies and tactics were to break up that organization.

FIRST INTERNATIONAL

1864

SEPTEMBER 28   Marx attends founding meeting of the International Working Men's Association (First International),[2] at St. Martin's Hall, London; he becomes a member of the Provisional Committee.

OCTOBER 5   At its first meeting the Provisional Committee selects Marx as a member of the subcommittee to work out a program for the International.

OCTOBER 6–17   Marx is ill and unable to work.

2. Throughout this Chronology the Association is referred to as the International.

OCTOBER 20   The subcommittee meets in Marx's house and empowers him to draft the International's program.

OCTOBER 21–27   Marx drafts the Inaugural Address and Provisional Statutes of the International.

NOVEMBER 1   The Provisional Committee transforms itself into the Central Council (later General Council), the governing organ of the International, and adopts Marx's drafts.

NOVEMBER 8   At Marx's suggestion the Central Council decides to issue reports of its sessions to the press, to avoid distortion.

NOVEMBER 15, 22   The Central Council adopts two resolutions, written by Marx, dealing with conditions for membership (they are published in London, in the *Bee-Hive*, November 26).

NOVEMBER 24   The Inaugural Address and the Provisional Statutes are published in London as brochures.

NOVEMBER 29   The Central Council adopts Marx's "Address of the International Working Men's Association to Abraham Lincoln," congratulating him on his reelection to the American presidency.

DECEMBER 21, 30   "Address and Provisional Rules of the Working Men's Association" is published in *Der Social-Demokrat*, and as a pamphlet by the *Bee-Hive*.

1865

JANUARY 31   Ambassador Charles Francis Adams' January 28 reply to the address to Lincoln, is read at the session of the Central Council.

APRIL 11   Marx is elected the International's corresponding secretary for Belgium. (He held this post until January, 1866.)

MAY 2–9   Marx drafts the International's "Address to Andrew Johnson."

JUNE 20   Marx delivers a lecture, "Wages, Price and Profit," before the General Council of the International.

LATE AUGUST   Marx joins the editorial board of the *Workmen's Advocate*, weekly organ of the International.

SEPTEMBER 25–29   The First Congress of the International, meeting in London, is attended by Belgian, English, French,

Italian, Polish, and Swiss delegates. Marx participates as a German delegate.

1866

JANUARY   Johann Philipp Becker, leader of the Swiss Central Committee of the International, in Geneva, publishes the first issue of *Der Vorbote*, a monthly which becomes the German-language organ of the International, and which continues publication until December, 1871.

SEPTEMBER 2   Marx is elected the International's corresponding secretary for Germany.

SEPTEMBER 3–8   The Second Congress of the International, held in Geneva, is attended by sixty delegates, representing twenty-five sections and eleven cooperating societies in England, France, Germany, and Switzerland. The congress accepts Marx's program, drafted in his "Instructions for the Delegates. . . ."

1867

SEPTEMBER 2–8   The Third Congress of the International is held in Lausanne, attended by sixty-four delegates from England, France, Germany, Italy, and Switzerland. The congress resists Proudhonist attacks on the program adopted in 1866, and reelects the General Council with its headquarters in London.

1868

MARCH–APRIL   Swiss miners win a strike with support not only from the International but from a solidarity movement which it organized in Belgium, England, France, Germany, and the rest of Switzerland. The successful strike enhances the reputation and power of the International.

AUGUST 1   With Marx's encouragement, Wilhelm Eichhoff publishes in Berlin *Die Internationale Arbeiterassociation. Ihre Gründung, Organisation, politischsociale Thätigkeit und Ausbreitung* (The International Working Men's Association. Its Founding, Organization, Political-Social Activities and Spreading). The 102-page brochure contains a history of the Inter-

national, as well as its statutes and Marx's "Inaugural
Address."

SEPTEMBER   The Fourth Congress of the International meets in
6–13   Brussels, with a hundred Belgian, English, French,
German, Italian, Spanish, and Swiss delegates. It
adopts Marx's "Annual Report . . . ," as well as the
General Council's program dealing with strikes, war,
standing armies, and public ownership of lands,
mines, and railroads.

SEPTEMBER 24   Marx is reelected the International's corresponding
secretary for Germany.

DECEMBER 1   Marx is elected archivist of the International.

1869

JULY 3–4   At the initiative of the Nuremberg and Fürth sections of the International, delegates from thirteen
labor unions meet in Nuremberg and resolve to establish a Bavarian Social-Democratic party along the
principles of the International.

LATE AUGUST–
EARLY   Marx writes the "Report . . . of the International . . .
SEPTEMBER   to the Fourth Congress in Basel."

SEPTEMBER   At the Basel congress, attended by seventy-eight
7–11   delegates from Austria, Belgium, England, France,
Germany, Italy, Spain, Switzerland, and the United
States, Marx, who is not present, is unanimously reelected to the General Council. Bakuninists and Proudhonists, attempting to take over the International, are
decisively defeated. The congress, adopting a Marxist program, resolves "that society has the right to
abolish private property in land and to transform it
into common property."

1870

JULY 12   The General Council publishes the agenda for the
Fifth International Congress, scheduled to meet in
Mainz. (The meeting could not be held, owing to the
Franco-Prussian War.)

JULY 19   In London, the General Council authorizes Marx
to draft a statement outlining the International's
position on the Franco-Prussian War.

JULY 23   Marx completes his "First Address of the Interna-
             tional on the Franco-Prussian War," calling on labor
             to take an international, rather than a national, posi-
             tion and advising German workers to be alert against
             the war's becoming one against the French people.
             The "Address" was published in German and French,
             in an edition of 30,000 copies.

SEPTEMBER 9 In his "Second Address of the International on the
             Franco-Prussian War" Marx urges German workers
             to protest the Prussian annexation of Alsace-Lorraine
             and to work for peace, as well as a recognition of
             the French Republic (which had been proclaimed
             on September 4).

OCTOBER 4   Having moved from Manchester to London, Fred-
             erick Engels is unanimously elected a member of the
             General Council and becomes corresponding secre-
             tary for Italy and Spain.

1871

MARCH 18–   Establishment of the Paris Commune, the leadership
   MAY 28   of which consists mostly of Blanquists and Proud-
             honists, with only a handful of Marxist members of
             the International.

APRIL 18–   Marx writes *The Civil War in France*, a pamphlet
   MAY 29   defending the Commune, published in English in
             London and in German in Leipzig. (Engels brought
             out a new edition in 1891.)

JUNE–   Marx organizes financial assistance for refugees from
   DECEMBER the Paris Commune, destroyed in May.

SEPTEMBER   The Congress of the International, held in London
      17–23 and prepared by Marx and Engels, is attended by
             only twenty-three delegates. Germans are absent. In
             the aftermath of the Commune's defeat, the con-
             gress discusses the political role of the proletariat,
             concluding that the working class must constitute
             itself as a political party "for the triumph of the
             social revolution and its final goal—*elimination of
             classes.*"

OCTOBER 3   Marx is elected the International's corresponding
             secretary for Russia.

1872

JANUARY–
EARLY MARCH

Marx, in collaboration with Engels, prepares the anti-Bakunin circular, "Fictitious International." International."

LATE AUGUST

Marx is elected delegate to the Hague Congress of the International.

SEPTEMBER 1

Marx, with his wife and their daughter Eleanor, arrives in The Hague.

SEPTEMBER 2–6

The Congress of the International—destined to be the last one—meets in an atmosphere of strife and bitterness; it is attended by sixty-five delegates from Australia, Austria, Belgium, Denmark, England, France, Germany, Holland, Hungary, Ireland, Poland, Portugal, Spain, Switzerland, and the United States. Delegates are split between followers of Marx and Bakunin. Bakuninists are expelled from the congress. To keep the International from falling into the hands of the European anarchists, the congress resolves to move its headquarters (the General Council) from London to New York. This is the effective end of the International in Europe.

1876

JULY 16

At a conference held in Philadelphia, attended by the New York General Council and fourteen American delegates, it is decided the International is dissolved.

ADDRESSES,
RULES, REPORTS,
AND RESOLUTIONS

DURING the eight years of the First International's existence Marx was not only its leading spirit but also the main draftsman of its important documents. It was a role that fell to him almost naturally, first because of his passionate dedication to the cause for which the International stood—a world-wide organization of workers—and, secondly, because of his intellectual training and literary experience.

Marx was also one of the few members of the governing body of the International—the General Council (first known as the Central Council)—who retained his seat from the beginning, in 1864, to the end, in 1872. Over the years, the Council had a varying membership of about five dozen, many of whom served only for brief periods or intermittently, primarily as signers of important documents (usually drafted by Marx). Thus the Address to Abraham Lincoln was signed by fifty-eight members of the General Council, that to Andrew Johnson by thirty-eight, and the Second Address on the Franco-Prussian War by thirty-three.

The essential—and continuing—work was done by a relatively small group, probably no more than a dozen members in all, and they included the more or less long-time secretaries for the various countries (Marx was secretary for Germany). They met weekly, the number attending averaging anywhere from one and a half dozen to half a dozen. Marx was one of the very few members who attended virtually all the sessions, except when prevented from doing so by absence from London or by illness.

With the exception of Peter Fox, a journalist and member of the General Council from 1864 to 1869, Marx was the only regular and continuous member who was an intellectual by profession. Most of the

[3]

other active members of the General Council were bona fide working people, although not proletarians in the technical sense. They included tailors,[1] carpenters,[2] weavers,[3] shoemakers,[4] furniture makers,[5] as well as at least one watchmaker,[6] one mason,[7] one musical-instrument maker,[8] and one hairdresser.[9]

Hence it was all but inevitable that Marx, the highly educated and articulate scholar, who, moreover, was a writer and journalist by profession, should be the chief draftsman of the International's major addresses and reports.

---

1. Eccarius, Lessner, Maurice, Milner, Stainsby.
2. Applegarth, Cremer, Lochner, Weston.
3. Bradnick, J. Hales, Mottershead.
4. Morgan, Odger, Serraillier.
5. Dell, Lucraft.
6. Jung.
7. Howell.
8. Dupont.
9. Lassassie.

Inaugural Address of the International Working Men's Association*

Workingmen:

It is a great fact that the misery of the working masses has not diminished from 1848 to 1864, and yet this period is unrivaled for the development of its industry and the growth of its commerce. In 1850 a moderate organ of the British middle class, of more than average information, predicted that if the exports and imports of England were to rise 50 percent, English pauperism would sink to zero. Alas! On April 7, 1864, the Chancellor of the Exchequer delighted his parliamentary audience by the statement that the total import and export of England had grown in 1863 "to £443,955,000! That astonishing sum about three times the trade of the comparatively recent epoch of 1843!" With all that, he was eloquent upon "poverty." "Think," he exclaimed, "of those who are on the border of that region," upon "wages . . . not increased"; upon "human life . . . in nine cases out of ten but a struggle of existence!" He did not speak of the people of Ireland, gradually replaced by machinery in the north and by sheepwalks in the south, though even the sheep in that unhappy country are decreasing, it is true, not at so rapid a rate as the men. He did not repeat what then had been just betrayed by the highest representatives of the upper ten thousand in a sudden fit of terror. When garrote panic had reached a certain height the House of Lords caused an inquiry to be made into, and a report to be published upon, transportation and penal servitude. Out came the murder in the bulky Blue Book of 1863 and proved it was, by official facts and figures, that the

---

* Written in English, October 21–27, 1864; printed as a pamphlet, along with the General Rules, under the title *Inaugural Address and Provisional Rules of the International Working Men's Association*, London, 1864.

[5]

worst of the convicted criminals, the penal serfs of England and Scotland, toiled much less and fared far better than the agricultural laborers of England and Scotland. But this was not all. When, consequent upon the Civil War in America, the operatives of Lancashire and Cheshire were thrown upon the streets, the same House of Lords sent to the manufacturing districts a physician commissioned to investigate into the smallest possible amount of carbon and nitrogen, to be administered in the cheapest and plainest form, which on an average might just suffice to "avert starvation diseases." Dr. Smith, the medical deputy, ascertained that 28,000 grains of carbon and 1,330 grains of nitrogen were the weekly allowance that would keep an average adult . . . just over the level of starvation diseases, and he found furthermore that quantity pretty nearly to agree with the scanty nourishment to which the pressure of extreme distress had actually reduced the cotton operatives.[1] But now mark! The same learned doctor was later on again deputed by the medical officer of the Privy Council to enquire into the nourishment of the poorer laboring classes. The results of his research are embodied in the "Sixth Report on Public Health," published by order of Parliament in the course of the present year. What did the doctor discover? That the silk weavers, the needlewomen, the kid glovers, the stocking weavers, and so forth received on an average, not even the distress pittance of the cotton operatives, not even the amount of carbon and nitrogen "just sufficient to avert starvation diseases."

"Moreover"—we quote from the report—"as regards the examined families of the agricultural population, it appeared that more than a fifth were with less than the estimated sufficiency of carbonaceous food, that more than one-third were with less than the estimated sufficiency of nitrogeneous food, and that in three counties (Berkshire, Oxfordshire, and Somersetshire) insufficiency of nitrogeneous food was the average diet." "It must be remembered," adds the official report, "that privation of food is very reluctantly borne, and that, as a rule, great poorness of diet will only come when other privations have preceded it. . . . Even cleanliness will have been found costly or difficult, and if there still be self-respectful endeavors to maintain it, every such endeavor will represent additional pangs of hunger." "These are painful reflections, especially when it is remembered that the poverty to which they advert is not the deserved poverty of idleness; in all cases

1. We need hardly remind the reader that, apart from the elements of water and certain inorganic substances, carbon and nitrogen form the raw materials of human food. However, to nourish the human system, these simple chemical constituents must be supplied in the form of vegetable or animal substances. Potatoes, for instance, contain mainly carbon, while wheaten bread contains carbonaceous and nitrogenous substances in a due proportion.—K. M.

it is the poverty of working populations. Indeed the work which obtains the scanty pittance of food is for the most part excessively prolonged." The report brings out the strange and rather unexpected fact: "That of the divisions of the United Kingdom," England, Wales, Scotland, and Ireland, "the agricultural population of England," the richest division, "is considerably the worst fed"; but that even the agricultural laborers of Berkshire, Oxfordshire, and Somersetshire fare better than great numbers of skilled indoor operatives of the East of London.

Such are the official statements published by order of Parliament in 1864, during the millennium of free trade, at a time when the Chancellor of the Exchequer told the House of Commons that "the average condition of the British laborer has improved in a degree we know to be extraordinary and unexampled in the history of any country or any age." Upon these official congratulations jars the dry remark of the official Public Health Report: "The public health of a country means the health of its masses, and the masses will scarcely be healthy unless, to their very base, they be at least moderately prosperous."

Dazzled by the "Progress of the Nation" statistics dancing before his eyes, the Chancellor of the Exchequer exclaims in wild ecstasy: "From 1842 to 1852 the taxable income of the country increased by 6 percent; in the eight years from 1853 to 1861, it has increased from the basis taken in 1853, 20 percent! The fact is so astonishing to be almost incredible! . . . This intoxicating augmentation of wealth and power," adds Mr. Gladstone, "is entirely confined to classes of property."

If you want to know under what conditions of broken health, tainted morals, and mental ruin that "intoxicating augmentation of wealth and power . . . entirely confined to classes of property" was, and is, being produced by the classes of labor, look to the picture hung up in the last Public Health Report of the workshops of tailors, printers, and dressmakers! Compare the "Report of the Children's Employment Commission" of 1863, where it is stated, for instance, that "the potters as a class, both men and women, represent a much degenerated population, both physically and mentally," that "the unhealthy child is an unhealthy parent in his turn," that "a progressive deterioration of the race must go on," and that "the degenerescence of the population of Staffordshire would be even greater were it not for the constant recruiting from the adjacent country, and the inter-marriages with more healthy races." Glance at Mr. Tremenheere's Blue Book on the "Grievances Complained of by the Journeymen Bakers"! And who has not shuddered at the paradoxical statement made by the inspectors of factories, and illustrated by the Registrar General, that the Lancashire operatives, while put upon the distress pittance of food, were actually improving in health, because of their temporary exclusion by the cotton famine from the cotton factory, and that the mortality of the children was decreasing, because their mothers were now at last allowed to give them, instead of Godfrey's cordial, their own breasts.

Again reverse the medal! The income and property tax returns laid before the House of Commons on July 20, 1864, teach us that the persons with yearly incomes valued by the tax gatherer at £50,000 and upwards had, from April 5, 1862, to April 5, 1863, been joined by a dozen and one, their number having increased in that single year from 67 to 80. The same returns disclose the fact that about 3,000 persons divide among themselves a yearly income of about £25,000,000 sterling, rather more than the total revenue doled out annually to the whole mass of the agricultural laborers of England and Wales. Open the census of 1861 and you will find that the number of the male landed proprietors of England and Wales had decreased from 16,934 in 1851 to 15,066 in 1861, so that the concentration of land had grown in 10 years 11 percent. If the concentration of the soil of the country in a few hands proceeds at the same rate, the land question will become singularly simplified, as it had become in the Roman Empire when Nero grinned at the discovery that half of the province of Africa was owned by six gentlemen.

We have dwelt so long upon these facts "so astonishing to be almost incredible" because England heads the Europe of commerce and industry. It will be remembered that some months ago one of the refugee sons of Louis Philippe publicly congratulated the English agricultural laborer on the superiority of his lot over that of his less florid comrade on the other side of the Channel. Indeed, with local colors changed, and on a scale somewhat contracted, the English facts reproduce themselves in all the industrious and progressive countries of the Continent. In all of them there has taken place, since 1848, an unheard-of-development of industry, and an undreamed-of expansion of imports and exports. In all of them the "augmentation of wealth and power . . . entirely confined to classes of property" was truly "intoxicating." In all of them, as in England, a minority of the working classes got their real wages somewhat advanced; while in most cases the monetary rise of wages denoted no more a real access of comforts than the inmate of the metropolitan poorhouse or orphan asylum, for instance, was in the least benefited by his first necessaries costing £9 15s. 8d. in 1861 against £7 7s. 4d. in 1852. Everywhere the great mass of the working classes were sinking down to a lower depth, at the same rate at least that those above them were rising in the social scale. In all countries of Europe it has now become a truth demonstrable to every unprejudiced mind, and only denied by those whose interest it is to hedge other people in a fool's paradise, that no improvement of machinery, no appliance of science to production, no contrivances of communication, no new colonies, no emigration, no opening of markets, no free trade, nor all these things put together, will do away with the miseries of the industrious masses; but that, on the present false base, every fresh development of the productive powers of labor must tend to deepen social contrasts and point social antagonisms. Death of starvation rose almost to the rank of an institution, during this intoxicating epoch of economical progress, in the metropolis of the British empire. That epoch is marked in the annals of the world by the quickened return, the widening compass, and the deadlier effects of the social pest called a commercial and industrial crisis.

After the failure of the Revolution of 1848 all party organizations and party journals of the working classes were, on the Continent, crushed by the iron hand of force, the most advanced sons of labor fled in despair to the transatlantic republic, and the short-lived dreams of emancipation vanished before an epoch of industrial fever, moral marasm, and political reaction. The defeat of the continental working classes, partly owed to the diplomacy of the English government, acting then as now in fraternal solidarity with the Cabinet of St. Petersburg, soon spread its contagious effects to this side of the Channel. While the rout of their continental brethren unmanned the English working classes, and broke their faith in their own cause, it restored to the landlord and the money lord their somewhat shaken confidence. They insolently withdrew concessions already advertised. The discoveries of new gold lands led to an immense exodus, leaving an irreparable void in the ranks of the British proletariat. Others of its formerly active members were caught by the temporary bribe of greater work and wages, and turned into "political blacks." All the efforts made at keeping up, of remodeling, the Chartist movement failed signally; the press organs of the working class died one by one of the apathy of the masses, and in point of fact never before seemed the English working class so thoroughly reconciled to a state of political nullity. If, then, there had been no solidarity of action between the British and the continental working classes, there was, at all events, a solidarity of defeat.

And yet the period passed since the Revolutions of 1848 has not been without its compensating features. We shall here only point to two great facts.

After a thirty years' struggle, fought with most admirable perseverance, the English working classes, improving a momentaneous split between the landlords and money lords, succeeded in carrying the Ten Hours' Bill. The immense physical, moral, and intellectual benefits hence accruing to the factory operatives, half-yearly chronicled in the reports of the inspectors of factories, are now acknowledged on all sides. Most of the continental governments had to accept the English Factory Act in more or less modified forms, and the English Parliament itself is every year compelled to enlarge its sphere of action. But besides its practical import, there was something else to exalt the marvelous success of this workingmen's measure. Through their most notorious organs of science, such as Dr. Ure, Professor Senior, and other sages of that stamp, the middle class had predicted, and to their heart's content proved, that any legal restriction of the hours of labor must sound the death knell of British industry, which, vampirelike, could but live by sucking blood, and children's blood, too. In olden times, child murder was a mysterious rite of the religion of Moloch, but it was practiced on some very solemn occasions only, once a year perhaps, and then Moloch had no exclusive bias for the children of the poor. This struggle about the legal restriction of the hours of labor raged the more fiercely since, apart from frightened avarice, it told indeed upon the great contest between the blind rule of the supply and demand laws which form the political economy of the middle class, and social production controlled by social foresight, which forms the political economy of the working class. Hence the Ten Hours' Bill was not only a great practical success; it was the victory of a principle; it was the first time that in broad daylight the political economy of the middle class succumbed to the political economy of the working class.

But there was in store a still greater victory of the political economy of labor over the political economy of property. We speak of the cooperative movement, especially the cooperative factories raised by the unassisted efforts of a few bold "hands." The value of these great social experiments cannot be overrated. By deed instead of by argument, they have shown that production on a large scale, and in accord with the behests of modern science, may be carried on without the existence of a class of masters employing a class of hands; that to bear fruit, the means of labor need not be monopolized as a means of dominion over, and of extortion against, the laboring man himself; and that, like slave labor, like serf labor, hired labor is but a transitory and inferior form, destined to disappear before associated labor plying its toil with a willing hand, a ready mind, and a joyous heart. In England, the seeds of the cooperative system were sown by Robert Owen; the workingmen's experiments tried on the Continent were, in fact, the practical upshot of the theories, not invented, but loudly proclaimed, in 1848.

At the same time the experience of the period from 1848 to 1864 has proved beyond doubt that, however excellent in principle and however useful in practice, cooperative labor, if kept within the narrow circle of the casual efforts of private workmen, will never be able to arrest the growth in geometrical progression of monopoly, to free the masses, nor even to perceptibly lighten the burden of their miseries. It is perhaps for this very reason that plausible noblemen, philanthropic middle-class spouters, and even keen political economists have all at once turned nauseously complimentary to the very co-operative labor system they had vainly tried to nip in the bud by deriding it as the utopia of the dreamer, or stigmatizing it as the sacrilege of the socialist. To save the industrious masses, cooperative labor ought to be developed to national dimensions, and, consequently, to be fostered by national means. Yet the lords of land and the lords of capital will always use their political privileges for the defense and perpetuation of their economical monopolies. So far from promoting, they will continue to lay every possible impediment in the way of the emancipation of labor. Remember the sneer with which, last session, Lord Palmerston put down the advocates of the Irish Tenants' Right Bill. The House of Commons, cried he, is a house of landed propri-etors. To conquer political power has therefore become the great duty of the working classes. They seem to have comprehended this, for in England, Germany, Italy, and France there have taken place simul-taneous revivals, and simultaneous efforts are being made at the politi-cal organization of the workingmen's party.

One element of success they possess—numbers; but numbers weigh in the balance only if united by combination and led by knowledge. Past experience has shown how disregard of that bond of brotherhood which ought to exist between the workmen of different countries, and incite them to stand firmly by each other in all their struggles for emancipation, will be chastised by the common discomfiture of their incoherent efforts. This thought prompted the workingmen of differ-ent countries assembled on September 28, 1864, in public meeting at St. Martin's Hall, to found the International Association.

Another conviction swayed that meeting.

If the emancipation of the working classes requires their fraternal concurrence, how are they to fulfill that great mission with a foreign policy in pursuit of criminal designs, playing upon national prejudices, and squandering in piratical wars the people's blood and treasure? It was not the wisdom of the ruling classes, but the heroic resistance to their criminal folly by the working classes of England, that saved the west of Europe from plunging headlong into an infamous crusade for the perpetuation and propagation of slavery on the other side of the Atlantic. The shameless approval, mock sympathy, or idiotic indifference with which the upper classes of Europe have witnessed the mountain fortress of the Caucasus falling a prey to, and heroic Poland being assassinated by, Russia: the immense and unresisted encroachments of that barbarous power, whose head is at St. Petersburg, and whose hands are in every cabinet of Europe, have taught the working classes the duty to master themselves the mysteries of international politics; to watch the diplomatic acts of their respective governments; to counteract them, if necessary, by all means in their power; when unable to prevent, to combine in simultaneous denunciations, and to vindicate the simple laws of morals and justice, which ought to govern the relations of private individuals, as the rules paramount of the intercourse of nations.

The fight for such a foreign policy forms part of the general struggle for the emancipation of the working classes.

Proletarians of all countries, unite!

General Rules of the International Working Men's Association*

Considering,

That the emancipation of the working classes must be conquered by the working classes themselves; that the struggle for the emancipation of the working classes means not a struggle for class privileges and monopolies, but for equal rights and duties, and the abolition of all class rule;

That the economical subjection of the man of labor to the monopolizer of the means of labor—that is, the sources of life—lies at the bottom of servitude in all its forms, of all social misery, mental degradation, and political dependence;

That the economical emancipation of the working classes is therefore the great end to which every political movement ought to be subordinate as a means;

That all efforts aiming at the great end have hitherto failed from the want of solidarity between the manifold divisions of labor in each country, and from the absence of a fraternal bond of union between the working classes of different countries;

That the emancipation of labor is neither a local nor a national, but a social problem, embracing all countries in which modern society exists, and depending for its solution on the concurrence, practical and theoretical, of the most advanced countries;

That the present revival of the working classes in the most industrious countries of Europe, while it raises a new hope, gives solemn

---

* "General Rules and Administrative Regulations of the International Working Men's Association," written in English in October, 1864; approved by the Central Council on November 1 as the "Provisional Rules"; and confirmed by the Geneva Congress in 1866.

warning against a relapse into the old errors, and calls for the immediate combination of the still disconnected movements;

For these reasons—

The International Working Men's Association has been founded. It declares:

That all societies and individuals adhering to it will acknowledge truth, justice, and morality as the basis of their conduct toward each other and toward all men, without regard to color, creed, or nationality;

That it acknowledges *no rights without duties, no duties without rights;*

And in this spirit the following Rules have been drawn up.

1. This Association is established to afford a central medium of communication and cooperation between workingmen's societies existing in different countries and aiming at the same end; viz., the protection, advancement, and complete emancipation of the working classes.

2. The name of the society shall be "The International Working Men's Association."

3. There shall annually meet a General Working Men's Congress, consisting of delegates of the branches of the Association. The Congress will have to proclaim the common aspirations of the working class, take the measures required for the successful working of the International Association, and appoint the General Council of the society.

4. Each Congress appoints the time and place of meeting for the next Congress. The delegates assemble at the appointed time and place without any special invitation. The General Council may, in case of need, change the place, but has no power to postpone the time of meeting. The Congress appoints the seat and elects the members of the General Council annually. The General Council thus elected shall have power to add to the number of its members.

On its annual meetings, the General Congress shall receive a public account of the annual transactions of the General Council. The latter may, in cases of emergency, convoke the General Congress before the regular yearly term.

5. The General Council shall consist of workingmen from the different countries represented in the International Association. It shall from its own members elect the officers necessary for the transaction of business, such as a treasurer, a general secretary, corresponding secretaries for the different countries, etc.

6. The General Council shall form an international agency between the different national and local groups of the Association, so that

the workingmen in one country be constantly informed of the movements of their class in every other country; that an inquiry into the social state of the different countries of Europe be made simultaneously, and under a common direction; that the questions of general interest mooted in one society be ventilated by all; and that when immediate practical steps should be needed—as, for instance, in case of international quarrels—the action of the associated societies be simultaneous and uniform. Whenever it seems opportune, the General Council shall take the initiative of proposals to be laid before the different national or local societies. To facilitate the communications, the General Council shall publish periodical reports.

7. Since the success of the workingmen's movement in each country cannot be secured but by the power of union and combination, while, on the other hand, the usefulness of the International General Council must greatly depend on the circumstance whether it has to deal with a few national centers of workingmen's associations, or with a great number of small and disconnected local societies—the members of the International Association shall use their utmost efforts to combine the disconnected workingmen's societies of their respective countries into national bodies, represented by central national organs. It is self-understood, however, that the appliance of this rule will depend upon the peculiar laws of each country, and that, apart from legal obstacles, no independent local society shall be precluded from corresponding directly with the General Council.

8. Every section has the right to appoint its own secretary corresponding directly with the General Council.

9. Everybody who acknowledges and defends the principles of the International Working Men's Association is eligible to become a member. Every branch is responsible for the integrity of the members it admits.

10. Each member of the International Association, on removing his domicile from one country to another, will receive the fraternal support of the Associated Working Men.

11. While united in a perpetual bond of fraternal cooperation, the workingmen's societies joining the International Association will preserve their existent organizations intact.

12. The present Rules may be revised by each Congress, provided that two-thirds of the delegates present are in favor of such revision.

13. Everything not provided for in the present Rules will be supplied by special Regulations, subject to the revision of every Congress.

Address of the International Working Men's Association to President Lincoln*

Sir:

We congratulate the American people upon your reelection by a large majority. If resistance to the Slave Power was the reserved watchword of your first election, the triumphant war cry of your re-election is Death to Slavery.

From the commencement of the titanic American strife the workingmen of Europe felt instinctively that the star-spangled banner carried the destiny of their class. The contest for the territories which opened the dire epopee, was it not to decide whether the virgin soil of immense tracts should be wedded to the labor of the emigrant or prostituted by the tramp of the slave driver?

When an oligarchy of 300,000 slaveholders dared to inscribe for the first time in the annals of the world "slavery" on the banner of Armed Revolt, when on the very spots where hardly a century ago the idea of one great Democratic Republic had first sprung up, whence the first Declaration of the Rights of Man was issued, and the first impulse given to the European revolution of the eighteenth century; when on those very spots counterrevolution, with systematic thoroughness, gloried in rescinding "the ideas entertained at the time of the formation of the old constitution," and maintained slavery to be "a beneficent institution," indeed, the old solution of the great

---

*From the minutes of the Central (General) Council of the International, November 19, 1864: "Dr. Marx then brought up the report of the subcommittee, also a draft of the address which had been drawn up for presentation to the people of America congratulating them on their having reelected Abraham Lincoln as President. The address is as follows and was unanimously agreed to." The address was presented to Ambassador Charles Francis Adams on January 28, 1865.

problem of "the relation of capital to labor," and cynically proclaimed property in man "the cornerstone of the new edifice"—then the working classes of Europe understood at once, even before the fanatic partisanship of the upper classes for the Confederate gentry had given its dismal warning, that the slaveholders' rebellion was to sound the tocsin for a general holy crusade of property against labor, and that for the men of labor, with their hopes for the future, even their past conquests were at stake in that tremendous conflict on the other side of the Atlantic. Everywhere they bore therefore patiently the hardships imposed upon them by the cotton crisis, opposed enthusiastically the proslavery intervention importunities of their betters—and, from most parts of Europe, contributed their quota of blood to the good cause.

While the workingmen, the true political powers of the North, allowed slavery to defile their own republic, while before the Negro, mastered and sold without his concurrence, they boasted it the highest prerogative of the white-skinned laborer to sell himself and choose his own master, they were unable to attain the true freedom of labor, or to support their European brethren in their struggle for emancipation; but this barrier to progress has been swept off by the red sea of civil war.

The workingmen of Europe feel sure that, as the American War of Independence initiated a new era of ascendancy for the middle class, so the American Antislavery War will do for the working classes. They consider it an earnest of the epoch to come that it fell to the lot of Abraham Lincoln, the single-minded son of the working class, to lead his country through the matchless struggle for the rescue of an enchained race and the reconstruction of a social world.[1]

Signed, on behalf of the International Working Men's Association, the Central Council:
Longmaid, Worley, Whitlock, Fox, Blackmore, Hartwell, Pidgeon, Lucraft, Weston, Dell, Nieass, Shaw, Lake, Buckley, Osborne, Howell, Carter, Wheeler, Stainsby, Morgan, Grossmith, Dick, Denoual, Jourdain, Morrissot, Leroux, Bordage, Bocquet, Talandier, Dupont, L. Wolff, Aldovrandi, Lama, Solustri, Nusperli, Eccarius, Wolff, Lessner, Pfänder, Lochner, Kaub, Bolleter, Rybczinski, Hansen, Schantzenbach, Smales, Cornelius, Petersen, Otto, Bagn-

1. The minutes of the meeting continue: "A long discussion then took place as to the mode of presenting the address and the propriety of having a M. P. with the deputation; this was strongly opposed by many members, who said workingmen should rely on themselves and not seek for extraneous aid. . . . It was then proposed . . . and carried unanimously: That the Secretary correspond with the United States Minister asking to appoint a time for receiving the deputation, such deputation to consist of the members of the Central Council."

agatti, Setacci; George Odger, President of Council; *P. V. Lubez,*
Corresponding Secretary for France; *Karl Marx,* Corresponding
Secretary for Germany; *G. P. Fontana,* Corresponding Secretary
for Italy; *J. E. Holtorp,* Corresponding Secretary for Poland; *H. F.
Jung,* Corresponding Secretary for Switzerland; *William R. Cremer,*
Honorary General Secretary. 18 Greek Street, Soho.

Ambassador Adams' Reply to the Address to President Lincoln

Legation of the United States
London, 28th January, 1865

Sir:

I am directed to inform you that the address of the Central Council of your Association, which was duly transmitted through this Legation to the President of the United [States], has been received by him.

So far as the sentiments expressed by it are personal, they are accepted by him with a sincere and anxious desire that he may be able to prove himself not unworthy of the confidence which has been recently extended to him by his fellow citizens and by so many of the friends of humanity and progress throughout the world.

The Government of the United States has a clear consciousness that its policy neither is nor could be reactionary, but at the same time it adheres to the course which it adopted at the beginning, of abstaining everywhere from propagandism and unlawful intervention. It strives to do equal and exact justice to all states and to all men and it relies upon the beneficial results of that effort for support at home and for respect and good will throughout the world.

Nations do not exist for themselves alone, but to promote the welfare and happiness of mankind by benevolent intercourse and example. It is in this relation that the United States regard their cause in the present conflict with slavery, maintaining insurgence as the cause of human nature, and they derive new encouragement to persevere from the testimony of the workingmen of Europe that the national attitude is favored with their enlightened approval and earnest sympathies.

I have the honor to be, sir, your obedient servant,

Charles Francis Adams

Address of the International Working Men's Association to President Johnson*

Sir:

The demon of the "peculiar institution" for the supremacy of which the South rose in arms, would not allow his worshipers to honorably succumb in the open field. What he had begun in treason, he must needs end in infamy. As Philip II's war for the Inquisition bred a Gérard, thus Jefferson Davis' proslavery war a Booth.

It is not our part to call words of sorrow and horror, while the heart of two worlds heaves with emotion. Even the sycophants who, year after year, and day by day, stick to their Sisyphus work of morally assassinating Abraham Lincoln, and the great Republic he headed, stand now aghast at this universal outburst of popular feeling, and rival with each other to strew rhetorical flowers on his open grave. They have now at last found out that he was a man, neither to be browbeaten by adversity, nor intoxicated by success, inflexibly pressing on to his great goal, never compromising it by blind haste, slowly maturing his steps, never retracing them, carried away by no surge of popular favor, disheartened by no slackening of the popular pulse, tempering stern acts by the gleams of a kind heart, illuminating scenes dark with passion by the smile of humor, doing his titanic work as humbly and homely as Heaven-born rulers do little things with the grandiloquence of pomp and state; in one word, one of the rare men who succeed in becoming great, without ceasing to be good. Such, indeed, was the modesty of this great and good man, that the world only discovered him a hero after he had fallen a martyr.

To be singled out by the side of such a chief, the second victim

* Written in English, May 2–9, 1865; adopted by the General Council on May 9; published in the *Bee-Hive*, May 20, 1865.

to the infernal gods of slavery, was an honor due to Mr. Seward.[1] Had he not, at a time of general hesitation, the sagacity to foresee and the manliness to foretell "the irrepressible conflict"? Did he not, in the darkest hours of that conflict, prove true to the Roman duty to never despair of the Republic and its stars? We earnestly hope that he and his son will be restored to health, public activity, and well-deserved honors within much less than "ninety days."

After a tremendous civil war—but which, if we consider its vast dimension, and its broad scope, and compare it to the Old World's Hundred Years' wars, and Thirty Years' wars, and Twenty-three years' wars, can hardly be said to have lasted ninety days—yours, sir, has become the task to uproot by the law what has been felled by the sword, to preside over the arduous work of political reconstruction and social regeneration. A profound sense of your great mission will save you from any compromise with stern duties. You will never forget that, to initiate the new era of the emancipation of labor, the American people devolved the responsibilities of leadership upon two men of labor—the one Abraham Lincoln, the other Andrew Johnson.

---

1. On April 14, 1865, Secretary of State William H. Seward, ill in bed at his home in Washington, was brutally attacked by Lewis Powell (alias Payne), a fellow conspirator of Booth. Seward's son, Frederick W. Seward, and three other people who came to the rescue were also wounded by the would-be assassin. Seward's wife, an invalid, was so shocked that she died within two months, and his daughter, who witnessed the attack, died within the year. Seward himself gradually recovered.

Marx, Not Mazzini, Wrote the Rules*

CITIZEN Marx made a speech in reference to the proceedings at the previous meeting. He said it was not true, as Major Wolff had stated,[1] that Mazzini had written our Statutes. He, Marx, wrote them after discussion in committee. Several drafts were discussed, Wolff's draft among the rest. On two points they were quite distinguished from each other. Marx spoke of capital oppressing labor. Wolff wanted centralization and understood by workingmen's associations only benefit societies. Mazzini's Statutes were printed at the time of the conference in Naples. It could hardly be true that Mazzini had seen Marx's Address before it was printed, as it was in Marx's pocket, unless Mazzini saw it after it had been put in Le Lubez' hands and before it had been taken to the *Bee-Hive*.

Again Mazzini wrote to Brussels, to Fontaine, a letter which was to be communicated to the Belgian societies, in which he warned them against Marx's socialist views. This was stated by De Paepe at the conference.

Major Wolff was not a member of the Council. Major Wolff ought to have sent a letter informing the Council that he intended to prefer his complaint. He [Marx] protested against the proceedings at the last meeting in the name of himself and the other continental secretaries. He desired a note of this to be taken, as it might be brought before the Congress at Geneva.

---

* From the minutes of the General Council, March 13, 1866.
1. Minutes of March 6, 1866: "Citizen Louis [Luigi] Wolff . . . alleged that there were four falsehoods concerning Mazzini, viz., that the *Reglements* [Rules] were not drawn up by him, that he did not know of Marx's Address, and lastly, that had he known of it he would have opposed its adoption. Fourthly, that Mazzini did not oppose the translation of the Address but only objected to certain passages therein amounting in all to nine or ten words."

Instructions for the Delegates
of the Provisional
General Council*

1. ORGANIZATION OF THE
INTERNATIONAL ASSOCIATION

Upon the whole, the Provisional Central Council recommend the plan of organization as traced in the Provisional Statutes. Its soundness and facilities of adaptation to different countries without prejudice to unity of action have been proved by two years' experience. For the next year we recommend London as the seat of the Central Council, the continental situation looking unfavorable for change.

The members of the Central Council will of course be elected by Congress (5 of the Provisional Statutes) with power to add to their number.

The General Secretary to be chosen by Congress for one year and to be the only paid officer of the Association. We propose £2 for his weekly salary.

The uniform annual contribution of each individual member of the Association to be one half penny (perhaps one penny). The cost price of cards of membership (*carnets*) to be charged extra.

While calling upon the members of the Association to form benefit societies and connect them by an international link, we leave the initiation of this question (*établissement des sociétés de secours mutuels. Appui moral et matériel accordé aux orphelins de l'association*) to the Swiss, who originally proposed it at the conference of September last.

---

* Written in English at the end of August, 1866, and read as the official report at the Geneva Congress of the International, September 3–8, 1866.

2. INTERNATIONAL COMBINATION OF EFFORTS, BY THE AGENCY OF THE ASSOCIATION, IN THE STRUGGLE BETWEEN LABOR AND CAPITAL

a. From a general point of view, this question embraces the whole activity of the International Association which aims at combining and generalizing the till now disconnected efforts for emancipation by the working classes in different countries.

b. To counteract the intrigues of capitalists always ready, in cases of strikes and lockouts, to misuse the foreign workman as a tool against the native workman, is one of the particular functions which our Society has hitherto performed with success. It is one of the great purposes of the Association to make the workmen of different countries not only *feel* but *act* as brethren and comrades in the army of emancipation.

c. One great "international combination of efforts" which we suggest is a *statistical inquiry into the situation of the working classes of all countries to be instituted by the working classes themselves.* To act with any success, the materials to be acted upon must be known. By initiating so great a work, the workmen will prove their ability to take their own fate into their own hands. We propose therefore:

That in each locality where branches of our Association exist the work be immediately commenced, and evidence collected on the different points specified in the subjoined scheme of inquiry.

That the Congress invite all workmen of Europe and the United States of America to collaborate in gathering the elements of the statistics of the working class; that reports and evidence be forwarded to the Central Council. That the Central Council elaborate them into a general report, adding the evidence as an appendix.

That this report together with its appendix be laid before the next annual Congress, and after having received its sanction, be printed at the expense of the Association.

General Scheme of Inquiry, Which May of Course Be Modified by Each Locality

1. Industry, name of.
2. Age and sex of the employed.
3. Number of the employed.
4. Salaries and wages: (a) apprentices; (b) wages by the day or piece work; scale paid by middlemen. Weekly, yearly average.
5. (a) Hours of work in factories. (b) The hours of work with

small employers and in homework, if the business be carried on in those different modes. (c) Night work and day work.

6. Mealtimes and treatment.

7. Sort of workshop and work: overcrowding, defective ventilation, want of sunlight, use of gaslight. Cleanliness, etc.

8. Nature of occupation.

9. Effect of employment upon the physical condition.

10. Moral condition. Education.

11. State of trade: whether season trade or more or less uniformly distributed over year, whether greatly fluctuating, whether exposed to foreign competition, whether destined principally for home or foreign competition, etc.

3. LIMITATION OF THE WORKING DAY

A preliminary condition, without which all further attempts at improvement and emancipation must prove abortive, is the *limitation of the working day*.

It is needed to restore the health and physical energies of the working class—that is, the great body of every nation—as well as to secure them the possibility of intellectual development, sociable intercourse, social and political action.

We propose *eight hours' work* as the *legal limit* of the working day. This limitation being generally claimed by the workmen of the United States of America, the vote of the Congress will raise it to the common platform of the working classes all over the world.

For the information of continental members, whose experience of factory law is comparatively short dated, we add that all legal restrictions will fail and be broken through by capital if the *period of the day* during which the eight working hours must be taken be not fixed. The length of that period ought to be determined by the 8 working hours and the additional pauses for meals. For instance, if the different interruptions for meals amount to one hour, the legal period of the day ought to embrace nine hours, say from 7:00 A.M. to 4:00 P.M., or from 8:00 A.M. to 5:00 P.M., etc. Night work to be but exceptionally permitted in trades or branches of trades specified by law. The tendency must be to suppress all night work.

This paragraph refers only to adult persons, male or female, the latter, however, to be rigorously excluded from *all night work whatever*, and all sort of work hurtful to the delicacy of the sex, or exposing their bodies to poisonous and otherwise deleterious agencies. By adult persons we understand all persons having reached or passed the age of eighteen years.

4. JUVENILE AND CHILDREN'S LABOR (BOTH SEXES)

We consider the tendency of modern industry to make childern and juvenile persons of both sexes cooperate in the great work of social production as a progressive, sound, and legitimate tendency, although under capital it was distorted into an abomination. In a rational state of society *every child whatever,* from the age of nine years, ought to become a productive laborer in the same way that no able-bodied adult person ought to be exempted from the general law of nature, viz.: to work in order to be able to eat, and work not only with the brain but with the hands too.

However, for the present, we have only to deal with the children and young persons of both sexes belonging to the working people. They ought to be divided into three classes, to be treated differently; the first class to range from nine to twelve; the second, from thirteen to fifteen years; and the third, to comprise the ages of sixteen and seventeen years. We propose that the employment of the first class in any workshop or housework be legally restricted to two, that of the second, to four, and that of the third, to six hours. For the third class, there must be a break of at least one hour for meals or relaxation.

It may be desirable to begin elementary school instruction before the age of nine years; but we deal here only with the most indispensable antidotes against the tendencies of a social system which degrades the workingman into a mere instrument for the accumulation of capital, and transforms parents by their necessities into slaveholders, sellers of their own children. The *right* of children and juvenile persons must be vindicated. They are unable to act for themselves. It is, therefore, the duty of society to act on their behalf.

If the middle and higher classes neglect their duties toward their offspring, it is their own fault. Sharing the privileges of these classes, the child is condemned to suffer from their prejudices.

The case of the working class stands quite different. The working man is no free agent. In too many cases, he is even too ignorant to understand the true interest of his child, or the normal conditions of human development. However, the more enlightened part of the working class fully understands that the future of its class, and therefore of mankind, altogether depends upon the formation of the rising working generation. They know that, before everything else, the children and juvenile workers must be saved from the crushing effects of the present system. This can only be effected by converting *social reason* into *social force,* and, under given circumstances, there exists no other method of doing so than through *general laws,* enforced by the power of the state. In enforcing such laws the working class do not fortify governmental power. On the contrary, they transform that power, now used against them, into their own agency. They effect by a general act what they would vainly attempt by a multitude of isolated individual efforts.

Proceeding from this standpoint, we say that no parent and no employer ought to be allowed to use juvenile labor, except when combined with education.

By education we understand three things.

First: Mental education.

Second: Bodily education, such as is given in schools of gymnastics, and by military exercise.

Third: Technological training, which imparts the general principles of all processes of production and simultaneously initiates the child and young person in the practical use and handling of the elementary instruments of all trades.

A gradual and progressive course of mental, gymnastic, and technological training ought to correspond to the classification of the juvenile laborers. The costs of the technological schools ought to be partly met by the sale of their products.

The combination of paid productive labor, mental education, bodily exercise, and polytechnic training will raise the working class far above the level of the higher and middle classes.

It is self-understood that the employment of all persons from nine to seventeen years (inclusively) in night work and all health-injuring trades must be strictly prohibited by law.

5. COOPERATIVE LABOR

It is the business of the International Working Men's Association to combine and generalize the spontaneous movements of the working classes, but not to dictate or impose any doctrinary system whatever. The Congress should therefore proclaim no special system of cooperation, but limit itself to the enunciation of a few general principles.

a. We acknowledge the cooperative movement as one of the transforming forces of the present society based upon class antagonism. Its great merit is to practically show that the present pauperizing and despotic system of the *subordination of labor* to capital can be superseded by the republican and beneficent system of the *association of free and equal producers*.

b. Restricted, however, to the dwarfish forms into which individual wage slaves can elaborate it by their private efforts, the cooperative system will never transform capitalistic society. To convert social production into one large and harmonious system of free and cooperative labor, general social changes are wanted, *changes of the general conditions of society*, never to be realized save by the transfer of the organized forces of society, viz., the state power, from capitalists and landlords to the producers themselves.

c. We recommend to the workingmen to embark in *cooperative production* rather than in cooperative stores. The latter touch but the surface of the present economic system, the former attacks its groundwork.

d. We recommend to all cooperative societies to convert one part of their joint income into a fund for propagating their principles by example as well as by precept, in other words, by promoting the establishment of new cooperative fabrics, as well as by teaching and preaching.

e. In order to prevent cooperative societies from degenerating into ordinary middle-class joint stock companies (*sociétés par actions*), all workmen employed, whether shareholders or not, ought to share alike. As a mere temporary expedient, we are willing to allow shareholders a low rate of interest.

6. TRADE UNIONS. THEIR PAST, PRESENT, AND FUTURE

a. Their past.

Capital is concentrated social force, while the workman has only to dispose of his working force. The contract between capital and labor can therefore never be struck on equitable terms, equitable even in the sense of a society which places the ownership of the material means of life and labor on one side and the vital productive energies on the opposite side. The only social power of the workmen is their number. The force of numbers, however, is broken by disunion. The disunion of the workmen is created and perpetuated by their unavoidable competition among themselves.

Trade unions originally sprang up from the *spontaneous* attempts of workmen at removing or at least checking that competition, in order to conquer such terms of contract as might raise them at least above the condition of mere slaves. The immediate object of trade unions was therefore confined to everyday necessities, to expediencies for the obstruction of the incessant encroachments of capital—in one word, to questions of wages and time of labor. This activity of the trade unions is not only legitimate, it is necessary. It cannot be dispensed with so long as the present system of production lasts. On the contrary, it must be generalized by the formation and the combination of trade unions throughout all countries. On the other hand, unconsciously to themselves, the trade unions were forming centers of organization of the working class, as the medieval municipalities and communes did for the middle class. If the trade unions are required for the guerrilla fights between capital and labor, they are still more important as *organized agencies for superseding the very system of wages labor and capital rule.*

b. Their present.

Too exclusively bent upon the local and immediate struggles with capital, the trade unions have not yet fully understood their power of acting against the system of wage slavery itself. They therefore kept too much aloof from general social and political movements. Of late, however, they seem to awaken to some sense of their great historical mission, as appears, for instance, from their participation, in England, in the recent political movement, from the enlarged views taken of their function in the United States, and from the following resolution passed at the recent great conference of trades delegates at Sheffield: "That this conference, fully appreciating the efforts made by the International Association to unite in one common bond of brotherhood the working men of all countries, most earnestly recommend to the various societies here represented the advisability of becoming affiliated to that body, believing that it is essential to the progress and prosperity of the entire working community."

c. Their future.

Apart from their original purposes, they must now learn to act deliberately as organizing centers of the working class in the broad interest of its *complete emancipation.* They must aid every social and political movement tending in that direction. Considering themselves and acting as the champions and representatives of the whole working class, they cannot fail to enlist the nonsociety men into their ranks. They must look carefully after the interests of the worst paid trades, such as the agricultural laborers, rendered powerless by exceptional circumstances. They must convince the world at large that their efforts, far from being narrow and selfish, aim at the emancipation of the downtrodden millions.

7. DIRECT AND INDIRECT TAXATION

a. No modification of the form of taxation can produce any important change in the relations of labor and capital.

b. Nevertheless, having to choose between two systems of taxation, we recommend the *total abolition of indirect taxes* and the *general substitution of direct taxes*.

Because direct taxes enhance the prices of commodities, the tradesmen adding to those prices not only the amount of the indirect taxes, but the interest and profit upon the capital advanced in their payment;

Because indirect taxes conceal from an individual what he is paying to the state, whereas a direct tax is undisguised, unsophisticated, and not to be misunderstood by the meanest capacity. Direct taxation prompts therefore every individual to control the governing powers while indirect taxation destroys all tendency to self-government.

8. INTERNATIONAL CREDIT

Initiative to be left to the French.

9. POLISH QUESTION

a. Why do the workmen of Europe take up this question? In the first instance, because the middle-class writers and agitators conspire to suppress it, although they patronize all sorts of nationalities, on the Continent, even Ireland. Whence this reticence? Because both aristocrats and bourgeois look upon the dark Asiatic power in the background as a last resource against the advancing tide of working-class ascendency. That power can only be effectually put down by the restoration of Poland upon a democratic basis.

b. In the present changed state of Central Europe, and especially Germany, it is more than ever necessary to have a democratic Poland. Without it, Germany will become the outwork of the Holy Alliance, with it, the cooperator with republican France. The working-class movement will continuoulsy be interrupted, checked, and retarded until this great European question be set at rest.

c. It is especially the duty of the German working class to take the initiative in this matter, because Germany is one of the partitioners of Poland.

10. ARMIES

a. The deleterious influence of large standing armies upon production has been sufficiently exposed at middle-class congresses of all denominations, at peace congresses, economic congresses, statistical congresses, philanthropic congresses, sociological congresses. We think it, therefore, quite superfluous to expatiate upon this point.

b. We propose the general armament of the people and their general instruction in the use of arms.

c. We accept as a transitory necessity small standing armies to form schools for the officers of the militia; every male citizen to serve for a very limited time in those armies.

11. RELIGIOUS QUESTION

To be left to the initiative of the French.

Fourth Annual Report of the General Council of the International*

THE YEAR 1867–68 will mark an epoch in the history of the Association. After a period of peaceable development it has assumed dimensions powerful enough to provoke the bitter denunciations of the ruling classes and the hostile demonstrations of governments. It has entered upon the phases of strife.

The French Government took, of course, the lead in the reactionary proceedings against the working classes. Already last year we had to signalize some of its underhand maneuvers. It meddled with our correspondence, seized our Statutes and the Congress documents. After many fruitless steps to get them back, they were at last given up only under the official pressure of Lord Stanley, the English Minister of Foreign Affairs.

But the Empire has this year thrown off the mask and tried to directly annihilate the International Association by *coups de police* and judiciary prosecution. Begot by the struggle of classes, of which the days of June, 1848, are the grandest expression, it could not but assume alternately the attitudes of the official savior of the bourgeoisie and of the paternal protector of the proletariat. The growing power of the International, having manifested itself in the strikes of Roubaix, Amiens, Paris, Geneva, etc., reduced our would-be patron to the necessity of turning our society to his own account or of destroying it. In the beginning he was ready enough to strike a bargain on very moderate terms. The manifesto of the Parisians read at the Congress of Geneva having been seized at the French frontier, our Paris Executive

* Written September 1, 1868; published in the London *Times* September 9, 1868; in *Der Vorbote*, No. 9, September, 1868; and in the supplement of *Le Peuple Belge*, Brussels, 1868. The text here is from the *Times*.

demanded of the Minister of the Interior the reasons of this seizure. M. Rouher then invited one of the members of the Committee to an interview, in the course of which he declared himself ready to authorize the entry of the manifesto on the condition of some modifications being inserted. On the refusal of the delegate of the Paris Executive, he added, "Still, if you would introduce some words of gratitude to the Emperor, who has done so much for the working classes, one might see what could be done."

M. Rouher's, the sub-Emperor's, insinuation was met by a blank rebuff. From that moment the Imperial Government looked out for a pretext to suppress the Association. Its anger was heightened by the antichauvinist agitation on the part of our French members after the German war. Soon after, when the Fenian panic had reached its climax, the General Council addressed to the English Government a petition demanding the commutation of the sentence of the three victims of Manchester and qualifying their hanging as an act of political revenge. At the same time it held public meetings in London for the defense of the rights of Ireland. The Empire, always anxious to deserve the good graces of the British Government, thought the moment propitious for laying hands upon the International. It caused nocturnal perquisitions to be made, eagerly rummaged the private correspondence, and announced with much noise that it had discovered the center of the Fenian conspiracy, of which the International was denounced as one of the principal organs. All its laborious researches, however, ended in nothing. The public prosecutor himself threw down his brief in disgust. The attempt at converting the International Association into a secret society of conspirators having miserably broken down, the next best thing was to prosecute our Paris branch as a nonauthorized society of more than twenty members. The French judges, trained by the imperialist discipline, hastened, of course, to order the dissolution of the Association and the imprisonment of its Paris Executive. The tribunal had the naïveté to declare in the preamble of its judgment that the existence of the French Empire was incompatible with a workingmen's association that dared to proclaim truth, justice, and morality as its leading principles. The consequences of these prosecutions made themselves felt in the departments, where paltry vexations on the part of the prefects succeeded to the condemnations of Paris. This governmental chicanery, however, so far from annihilating the Association, has given it a fresh impulse by forcing the Empire to drop its patronizing airs to the working classes.

In Belgium the International Association has made immense strides. The coal lords of the basin of Charleroi, having driven their miners to riots by incessant exactions, let loose upon those unarmed men the armed force which massacred many of them. It was in the midst of the panic thus created that our Belgian branch took up the cause of the miners, disclosed their miserable economic condition, rushed to the rescue of the families of the dead and wounded, and procured legal counsel for the prisoners, who were finally all of them acquitted by the jury. After the affair of Charleroi the success of the International in Belgium was assured. The Belgian Minister of Justice, Jules Bara, denounced the International Association in the Chamber of Deputies and made of its existence the principal pretext for the renewal of the law against foreigners. He even dared to threaten he should prevent the Brussels Congress from being held. The Belgian Government ought at last to understand that petty states have no longer any *raison d'être* in Europe except they be the asylums of liberty.

In Italy the progress of the Association has been impeded by the reaction following close upon the ambuscade of Mentana; one of the first consequences was the restriction put upon the right of association and public meeting. But the numerous letters which have come to our hands fully prove that the Italian working class is more and more asserting its individuality quite independently of the old parties.

In Prussia the International cannot exist legally, on account of a law which forbids all relations with foreign societies. Moreover, in regard to the General Union of the German Working Men, the Prussian Government has imitated Bonapartism on a shabby scale. Always ready to fall foul of each other, the military governments are cheek by jowl when entering upon a crusade against their common enemy, the working classes. In spite, however, of all these petty tribulations, small groups spread over the whole surface of Germany had long since rallied round our Geneva center. The General Union of the German Working Men, whose branches are mostly confined to northern Germany, have in their recent Congress held at Hamburg decided to act in concert with the International Working Men's Association, although debarred from joining it officially. In the program of the Nuremberg Congress, representing upwards of a hundred workingmen's societies, which mostly belong to middle and southern Germany, the direct adhesion to the International has been put on the order of the day. At the request of their leading committee we have sent a delegate [Eccarius] to Nuremberg.

In Austria the working-class movement assumes a more and more revolutionary aspect. In the beginning of September a congress was to meet at Vienna, aiming at the fraternization of the workingmen of the different races of the Empire. They had also sent an address to the English and French workingmen in which they declared for the principles of the International. Your General Council had already appointed a delegate [Fox] to Vienna when the Liberal government of Austria, on the very point of succumbing to the blows of the feudal reaction, had the shrewdness to stir the anger of the workingmen by prohibiting their congress.

In the struggle maintained by the building trades of Geneva the very existence of the International in Switzerland was put on its trial. The employers made it a preliminary condition of coming to any terms with their workmen that the latter should forsake the International. The workingmen indignantly refused to comply with this dictate. Thanks to the aid received from France, England, Germany, etc., through the medium of the International, they have finally obtained a diminution of one hour of labor and 10 percent increase of wages. Already deeply rooted in Switzerland, the International has witnessed since that event a rapid increase in the number of its members. In the month of August last the German workingmen residing in Switzerland (about fifty societies) passed at their Congress in Neuenburg [Neuchâtel] a unanimous vote of adhesion to the International.

In England the unsettled state of politics, the dissolution of the old parties, and the preparations for the coming electoral campaign have absorbed many of our most active members, and to some degree retarded our propaganda. Nevertheless, we have entered into correspondence with numerous provincial trade unions, many of which have sent in their adhesion. Among the more recent London affiliations those of the Curriers' Society and the City Men's Shoemakers are the most considerable as regards numbers.

Your General Council is in constant communication with the National Labor Union of the United States. On its last Congress of August, 1867, the American Union had resolved to send a delegate to the Brussels Congress, but, pressed for time, was unable to take the special measures necessary for carrying out the vote.

The latent power of the working classes of the United States has recently manifested itself in the legal establishment of a working day of eight hours in all the workshops of the federal government, and in the passing of laws to the same effect by many state legislatures. However, at this very moment the workingmen of New York, for example, are engaged in a fierce struggle for enforcing the eight hours' law, against the resistance of rebellious capital. This fact proves that even under the most favorable political conditions all serious success of the proletariat depends upon an organization that unites and concentrates its forces; and even its national organization is still exposed to split on the disorganization of the working classes in other countries, which one and all compete in the market of the world, acting and reacting the one upon the other. Nothing but an international bond of the working classes can ever insure their definitive triumph. This want has given birth to the International Working Men's Association. That Association has not been hatched by a sect or a theory. It is the spontaneous growth of the proletarian movement, which itself is the offspring of the natural and irrepressible tendencies of modern society. Profoundly convinced of the greatness of its mission, the International Working Men's Association will allow itself neither to be intimidated nor misled. Its destiny, henceforward, coalesces with the historical progress of the class that bear in their hands the regeneration of mankind.

Report of the General Council to the Fourth Annual Congress*

Citizens:

The delegates of the different sections will give you detailed reports on the progress of our Association in their respective countries. The report of your General Council will mainly relate to the guerrilla fights between capital and labor—we mean the strikes which during the last year have perturbed the continent of Europe, and were said to have sprung neither from the misery of the laborer nor from the despotism of the capitalist, but from the secret intrigues of our Association.

A few weeks after the meeting of our last Congress, a memorable strike on the part of the ribbon weavers and silk dyers occurred in Basel, a place which to our days has conserved much of the features of a medieval town with its local traditions, its narrow prejudices, its purse-proud patricians, and its patriarchal rule of the employer over the employed. Still, a few years ago a Basel manufacturer boasted to an English secretary of embassy that "the position of the master and the man was on a better footing here than in England," that "in Switzerland the operative who leaves a good master for better wages would be despised by his own fellow workmen," and that "our advantage lies principally in the length of the working time and the moderation of the wages." You see, patriarchalism, as modified by modern influences, comes to this—that the master is good and that his wages are bad, that the laborer feels like a medieval vassal and is exploited like a modern wage slave.

That patriarchalism may further be appreciated from an official

---

* Written by Marx at the instruction of the General Council, August 31, 1869. The Fourth Congress was held in Basel September 6–11, 1869.

Swiss inquiry into the factory employment of children and the state of the primary public schools. It was ascertained that "the Basel school atmosphere is the worst in the world, that while in the free air carbonic acid forms only 4 parts of 10,000, and in closed rooms should not exceed 10 parts, it rose in Basel common schools to 20–81 parts in the forenoon, and to 53–94 in the afternoon." Thereupon a member of the Basel Great Council, Mr. Thurneysen, coolly replied, "Don't allow yourselves to be frightened. The parents have passed through schoolrooms as bad as the present ones, and yet they have escaped with their skins safe."

It will now be understood that an economical revolt on the part of the Basel workmen could not but mark an epoch in the social history of Switzerland. Nothing more characteristic than the starting point of the movement. There existed an old custom for the ribbon weavers to have a few hours' holiday on Michaelmas. The weavers claiming this small privilege at the usual time in the factory of Messrs. Dubary and Sons, one of the masters declared, in a harsh voice and with imperious gesticulation, "Whoever leaves the factory will be dismissed at once and forever." Finding their protestations in vain, 104 out of 172 weavers left the workshop without, however, believing in their definite dismissal, since master and men were bound by written contract to give a fourteen days' notice to quit. On their return the next morning they found the factory surrounded by gendarmes keeping off the yesterday's rebels, with whom all their comrades now made common cause. Being thus suddenly thrown out of work, the weavers with their families were simultaneously ejected from the cottages they rented from their employers, who, into the bargain, sent circular letters around to the shopkeepers to debar the houseless ones from all credit for victuals. The struggle thus begun lasted from the ninth of November, 1868, to the spring of 1869. The limits of our report do not allow us to enter upon its details. It suffices to state that it originated in a capricious and spiteful act of capitalist despotism, in a cruel lockout, which led to strikes, from time to time interrupted by compromises, again and again broken on the part of the masters, and that it culminated in the vain attempt of the Basel "High and Honorable State Council" to intimidate the working people by military measures and a quasi state of siege.

During their sedition the workmen were supported by the International Working Men's Association. But that was not all. That society the masters said had first smuggled the modern spirit of rebellion into the good old town of Basel. To again expel that mischievous intruder from Basel became, therefore, their great preoccupation. Hard they tried, though in vain, to enforce the withdrawal from it as a condition of peace, upon their subjects. Getting generally worsted in their war with the International they vented their spleen in strange pranks. Owning some industrial branch establishments at Lörrach, in Baden, these republicans induced the grand-ducal official to suppress the International section at that place, a measure which, however, was soon after rescinded by the Baden Government. The Augsburg *Allgemeine Zeitung*, a paper of world-wide circulation, presuming to report on the Basel events in an impartial spirit, the angry worthies threatened it in foolish letters with the withdrawal of their subscriptions. To London they expressly sent a messenger on the fantastic errand of ascertaining the dimensions of the International general "treasury box." Orthodox Christians as they are, if they had lived at the time of nascent Christianity they would, above all things, have spied into St. Paul's banking accounts at Rome.

Their clumsily savage proceedings brought down upon them some ironical lessons of worldly wisdom on the part of the Geneva capitalist organs. Yet a few months later the uncouth Basel vestrymen might have returned the compliment with usurious interest to the Geneva men of the world.

In the month of March there broke out in Geneva a building trades strike and a compositors' strike, both bodies being affiliated to the International. The builders' strike was provoked by the masters setting aside a convention solemnly entered upon with their workmen a year ago. The compositors' strike was but the winding up of a ten years' quarrel which the men had during all that time in vain tried to settle by five consecutive commissions. As in Basel, the masters transformed at once their private feuds with their men into a state crusade against the International Working Men's Association.

The Geneva State Council dispatched policemen to receive at the railway stations, and sequestrate from all contact with the strikers, such foreign workmen as the masters might contrive to inveigle from abroad. It allowed the *"Jeunesse Dorée,"* the hopeful loafers of *"La Jeune Suisse,"* armed with revolvers, to assault, in the streets and places of public resort, workmen and workwomen. It launched its own police ruffians on the working people on different occasions, and signally on the twenty-fourth of May, when it enacted at Geneva, on a small scale, the Paris scenes which Raspail has branded as *"les orgies infernales des casse-têtes"* ["the infernal orgies of the head-breakers"]. When the Geneva workmen passed in public meeting an address to the State Council calling upon it to inquire into these infernal police orgies, the State Council replied by a sneering rebuke. It evidently wanted, at the behest of its capitalist superiors, to madden the Geneva people into an *émeute* [revolt], to stamp that *émeute* out by armed

force, to sweep the International from Swiss soil, and to subject the
workmen to a Decembrist regime. This scheme was baffled by the
energetic action and moderating influence of our Geneva Federal
Committee. The masters had at last to give way.

And now listen to some of the invectives of the Geneva capitalists
and their press gang against the International. In public meeting they
passed an address to the State Council, where the following phrase
occurs: "The International Committee at Geneva ruins the Canton of
Geneva by decrees sent from London and Paris; it wants here to
suppress all industry and all labor." One of their journals stated that
the leaders of the International were secret agents of the Emperor,
who, at the opportune moment, were likely to turn out public accusers
against this little Switzerland of ours.

And this on the part of the men who had just shown themselves
so eager to transplant at a moment's notice the Decembrist regime to
Swiss soil, on the part of financial magnates, the real rulers of Geneva
and other Swiss towns, whom all Europe knows to have long since
been converted from citizens of the Swiss republic into mere feudato-
ries of the French Crédit Mobilier and other international swindling
associations.

The massacres by which the Belgian Government did answer in
April last to the strikes of the puddlers at Seraing and the coal miners
of Borinage have been fully exposed in the address of the General
Council to the workmen of Europe and the United States. We considered this address the more urgent since, with that constitutional
model government, such workingmen's massacres are not an accident
but an institution. The horrid military drama was succeeded by a
judicial farce. In the proceedings against our Belgian General Committee at Brussels, whose domiciles were brutally broken into by the
police, and many of whose members were placed under secret arrest,
the judge of instruction finds the letter of a workman, asking for 500
"*Internationales*," and he at once jumps to the conclusion that 500
fighting men were to be dispatched to the scene of action. The 500
"*Internationales*" were 500 copies of the *Internationale*, the weekly
organ of our Brussels Committee.

A telegram to Paris by a member of the International, ordering a
certain quantity of powder, is raked up. After a prolonged research,
the dangerous substance is really laid hand on at Brussels. It is powder
for killing vermin. Last, not least, the Belgian police flattered itself, in
one of its domiciliary visits, to have got at that phantom treasure
which haunts the great mind of the continental capitalist, viz., the
International treasure, the main stock of which is safely hoarded at
London, but whose offsets travel continually to all the continental

seats of the Association. The Belgian official inquirer thought it buried in a certain strongbox, hidden in a dark place. He gets at it, opens it forcibly, and there was found—some pieces of coal. Perhaps, if touched by the hand of the police, the pure International gold turns at once into coal.

Of the strikes that in December, 1868, infested several French cotton districts, the most important was that at Sotteville-lès-Rouen. The manufacturers of the Department de la Somme had not long ago met at Amiens, in order to consult how they might undersell the English manufacturers in the English market itself. Having made sure that, besides protective duties, the comparative lowness of French wages had till now mainly enabled them to defend France from English cottons, they naturally inferred that a still further lowering of French wages would allow them to invade England with French cottons. The French cotton workers, they did not doubt, would feel proud at the idea of defraying the expenses of a war of conquest which their masters had so patriotically resolved to wage on the other side of the Channel. Soon after it was bruited about that the cotton manufacturers of Rouen and its environs had, in secret conclave, agreed upon the same line of policy. Then an important reduction of wages was suddenly proclaimed at Sotteville-lès-Rouen, and then for the first time the Norman weavers rose against the encroachments of capital. They acted under the stir of the moment. Neither had they before formed a trade union nor provided for any means of resistance. In their distress they appealed to the International committee at Rouen, which found for them some immediate aid from the workmen of Rouen, the neighboring districts, and Paris. Toward the end of December, 1868, the General Council was applied to by the Rouen Committee, at a moment of utmost distress throughout the English cotton districts, of unparalleled misery in London, and a general depression in all branches of British industry. This state of things has continued in England to this moment. Despite such highly unfavorable circumstances, the General Council thought that the peculiar character of the Rouen conflict would stir the English workmen to action. This was a great opportunity to show the capitalists that their international industrial warfare, carried on by screwing wages down now in this country, now in that, would be checked at last by the international union of the working classes. To our appeal the English workmen replied at once by a first contribution to Rouen, and the London Trades Council resolved to summon, in unison with the General Council, a metropolitan monster meeting on behalf of their Norman brethren. These proceedings were stopped by the news of the sudden cessation of the Sotteville strike. The miscarriage of that economic revolt was largely compensated for by its moral results. It enlisted the Norman cotton workers into the revolutionary army of labor, it gave rise to the birth of trade unions at Rouen, Elboeuf, Darnétal, and the environs; and it sealed anew the bond of fraternity between the English and French working classes.

During the winter and spring of 1869 the propaganda of our Association in France was paralyzed, consequent upon the violent dissolution of our Paris Section in 1868, the police chicaneries in the departments, and the absorbing interest of the French general elections.

The elections once over, numerous strikes exploded in the Loire mining districts, at Lyon, and many other places. The economical facts revealed during these struggles between masters and men struck the public eye like so many dissolving views of the high-colored fancy pictures of working-class prosperity under the auspices of the Second Empire. The claims of redress on the part of the workmen were of so moderate a character and so urgent a nature that, after some show of angry resistance, they had to be conceded, one and all. The only strange feature about those strikes was their sudden explosion after a seeming lull, and the rapid succession in which they followed each other. Still, the reason of all this was simple and palpable. Having during the elections successfully tried their hands against their public despot, the workmen were naturally led to try them after the elections against their private despots. In one word, the elections had stirred their animal spirits. The governmental press, of course, paid as it is to misstate and misinterpret unpleasant facts, traced these events to a secret *mot d'ordre* from the London General Council, which, they said, sent their emissaries from place to place, to teach the otherwise highly satisfied French workmen that it was a bad thing to be overworked, underpaid, and brutally treated. A French police organ published at London, the *"International"*—(see its number of August 3)— has condescended to reveal to the world the secret motives of our deleterious activity. "The strangest feature," it says, "is that the strikes were ordered to break out in such countries where misery is far from making itself felt. These unexpected explosions, occurring so opportunely for certain neighbors of ours, who had first to apprehend war, make many people ask themselves whether these strikes took place on the request of some foreign Machiavelli, who had known how to win the good graces of this all-powerful Association."

At the very moment when this French police print impeached us of embarrassing the French Government by strikes at home, in order to disembarrass Count Bismarck from war abroad, a Prussian paper accused us of embarrassing the Northern German Bund with strikes, in order to crush German industry for the benefit of foreign manufactures.

The relations of the International to the French strikes we shall illustrate by two cases of a typical character. In the one case, the strike of St. Étienne and the following massacre at Ricamaric, the French Government itself will no longer dare to pretend that the International had anything whatever to do with it. In the Lyon case, it was not the International that threw the workmen into strikes, but, on the contrary, it was the strikes that threw the workmen into the International.

The miners of St. Étienne, Rive-de-Giers, and Firminy had calmly, but firmly, requested the managers of the mining companies to reduce the working day, numbering twelve hours' hard underground labor, and revise the wages tariff. Failing in their attempt at a conciliatory settlement, they struck on the eleventh of June. For them it was of course a vital question to secure the cooperation of the miners that had not yet turned out to combine with them. To prevent this, the managers of the mining companies requested and got from the prefect of the Loire a forest of bayonets. On the twelfth of June the strikers found the coal pits under strong military guard. To make sure of the zeal of the soldiers thus lent to them by the government, the mining companies paid each soldier a franc daily. The soldiers paid the companies back by catching, on the sixteenth of June, about sixty miners eager to get at a conversation with their brethren in the coal pits. These prisoners were in the afternoon of the same day escorted to St. Étienne by a detachment (150 men) of the fourth regiment of the line. Before these stout warriors set out, an engineer of the Dorian mines distributed them sixty bottles of brandy, telling them at the same time they ought to have a sharp eye on their prisoners' gang, these miners being savages, barbarians, ticket-of-leave men. What with the brandy, and what with the sermon, a bloody collision was thus prepared for. Followed on their march by a crowd of miners, with their wives and children, surrounded by them on a narrow defile on the heights of the Moncel, Quartier Ricamarie, requested to surrender the prisoners, and, on their refusal, attacked by a volley of stones, the soldiers, without any preliminary warning, fired with their chassepots pell-mell into the crowd, killing fifteen persons, among whom were two women and an infant, and dangerously wounding a considerable number. The tortures of the wounded were horrible. One of the sufferers was a poor girl of twelve years, Jenny Petit, whose name will live immortal in the annals of the working-class martyrology. Struck by two balls from behind, one of which lodged in her leg, while the other passed through her back, broke her arm, and escaped through her right shoulder. "*Les chassepots avaient encore fait merveille.*" ["The rifles have done marvelously again."]

This time, however, the government was not long in finding out that it had committed not only a crime but a blunder. It was not hailed as the savior of society by the middle class. The whole municipal council of St. Étienne tendered its resignation in a document denouncing the scoundrelism of the troops and insisting upon their removal from the town. The French press rang with cries of horror! Even such conservative prints as the *Moniteur Universel* opened subscriptions for the victims. The government *had* to remove the odious regiment from St. Étienne.

Under such difficult circumstances, it was a luminous idea to sacrifice on the altar of public indignation a scapegoat always at hand, the International Working Men's Association. At the judicial trial of the so-called rioters, the act of accusation divided them into ten categories, very ingeniously shading their respective darkness of guilt. The first class, the most deeply tinged, consisted of workmen more particularly suspected to have obeyed some secret *mot d'ordre* from abroad, given out by the International. The evidence was, of course, overwhelming, as the following short extract from a French paper will show: "The interrogatory of the witnesses did not allow 'neatly' to establish the participation of the International Association. The witnesses affirm only the presence, at the head of the bands, of some unknown people, wearing white frocks and caps. None of the unknown ones have been arrested, or appear in the dock. To the question: Do you believe in the intervention of the International Association? a witness replies: I believe it, but without any proof whatever!"

Shortly after the Ricamarie massacres, the dance of economic revolts was opened at Lyon by the silk winders, most of them females. In their distress they appealed to the International, which, mainly by its members in France and Switzerland, helped them to carry the day. Despite all attempts at police intimidation, they publicly proclaimed their adhesion to our society, and entered it formally by paying the statutory contributions to the General Council. At Lyon, as before at Rouen, the female workers played a noble and prominent part in the movement. Other Lyon trades have since followed in the track of the silk winders. Some 10,000 new members were thus gained for us in a few weeks among that heroic population which more than thirty years ago inscribed upon its banner the watchword of the modern proletariat: "*Vivre en travaillant ou mourir en combattant!*" ["Live working or die fighting!"]

Meanwhile the French Government continues its petty tribulations against the International. At Marseilles our members were forbidden meeting for the election of a delegate to Basel. The same paltry trick was played in other towns. But the workmen on the Continent, as elsewhere, begin at last to understand that the surest way to get one's natural rights is to exercise them at one's personal risk.

The Austrian workmen, and especially those of Vienna, although entering their class movement only after the events of 1866, have at once occupied a vantage ground. They marched at once under the banners of socialism and the International, which, by their delegates at the recent Eisenach Congress, they have now joined en masse.

If anywhere, the liberal middle class has exhibited in Austria its selfish instincts, its mental inferiority, and its petty spite against the working class. Their ministry, seeing the Empire distracted and threatened by an internecine struggle of races and nationalities, pounces upon the workmen who alone proclaim the fraternity of all races and nationalities. The middle class itself, which has won its new position not by any heroism of its own, but only by the signal disaster of the Austrian army, hardly able as it is, and knows itself to be, to defend its new conquests from the attacks of the dynasty, the aristocracy, and the clerical party, nevertheless wastes its best energies in the mean attempt to debar the working class from the rights of combination, public meeting, free press, and free thought. In Austria, as in all other states of continental Europe, the International has supplanted the *ci-devant spectre rouge* [former red specter]. When, on the thirteenth of July, a workmen's massacre on a small scale was enacted at Brünn, the cottonopolis of Moravia, the event was traced to the secret instigations of the International, whose agents, however, were unfortunately invested with the rare gift of rendering themselves invisible. When some leaders of the Vienna workpeople figured before the judicial bench, the public accuser stigmatized them as tools of the foreigner. Only, to show how conscientiously he had studied the matter, he committed the little error of confounding the middle-class League of Peace and Liberty with the workingman's International Association.

If the workmen's movement was thus harassed in Cisleithanian Austria, it has been recklessly prosecuted in Hungary. On this point the most reliable reports from Pest and Pressburg have reached the General Council. One example of the treatment of the Hungarian workmen by the public authorities may suffice. Herr von Wenckheim, the Hungarian Home Minister, was just staying at Vienna on public business. Having for months been interdicted from public meetings and even from entertainments destined for the collection of the funds of a sick club, the Pressburg workmen at last sent delegates to Vienna, then and there to lay their grievances before the illustrious Herr von Wenckheim. Puffing and blowing his cigar, the illustrious one received them with the bullying apostrophe, "Are you workmen? Do you work hard? For nothing else you have to care. You do not want public clubs; and if you dabble in politics, we shall know what measures to take against you. I shall do nothing for you. Let the workmen grumble to their hearts' content!" To the question of the workmen whether the good pleasure of the police was still to rule uppermost, the liberal minister replied: "Yes, under my responsibility." After a somewhat prolonged but useless explanation the workmen left the minister, telling him, "Since state matters influence the workmen's condition, the workmen must occupy themselves with politics, and they will certainly do so."

In Prussia and the rest of Germany, the past year was distinguished by the formation of trade unions all over the country. At the recent Eisenach Congress the delegates of 150,000 German workmen, from Germany proper, Austria, and Switzerland, have organized a new democratic social party, with a program literally embodying the leading principles of our Statutes. Debarred by law from forming sections of our Association, they have, nevertheless, formally entered it by resolving to take individual cards of membership from the General Council. At its congress at Barmen, the *Allgemeine Deutsche Arbeiterverein* has also reaffirmed its adhesion to the principles of our Association, but simultaneously declared the Prussian law forbade them joining us.

New branches of our Association have sprung up at Naples, in Spain, and in Holland.

At Barcelona a Spanish, and at Amsterdam a Dutch organ of our Association is now being issued.

The laurels plucked by the Belgian Government on the glorious battlefields of Seraing and Frameries seem really to have roused the angry jealousy of the Great Powers. No wonder, then, that England also had this year to boast a workman's massacre of its own. The Welsh coal miners, at Leeswood Great Pit—near Mold—in Denbighshire, had received sudden notice of a reduction of wages by the manager of those works, whom long since they had reason to consider a most incorrigible petty oppressor. Consequently they collected aid from the neighboring collieries and, besides assaulting him, attacked his house, and carried all his furniture to the railway station, these wretched men fancying in their childish ignorance thus to get rid of him for good and all. Proceedings were of course taken against the rioters; but one of them was rescued by a mob of 1,000 men, and conveyed out of the town. On May 28 two of the ringleaders were to be taken before the magistrates of Mold by policemen under the escort of a detachment of the fourth regiment of the line, "The King's Own." A crowd of miners trying to rescue the prisoners, and, on the resistance of the police and the soldiers, showering stones at them, the soldiers—without any previous warning—returned the shower of stones by a shower of bullets from their breachloaders (Snider fusils). Five persons, two of them females, were killed, and a great many wounded. So far there is much analogy between the Mold and the Ricamarie massacres, but here it ceases. In France the soldiers were only responsible to their commander. In England they had to pass through a coroner's jury inquest; but this coroner was a deaf and daft fool who had to receive the witnesses' evidence through an ear trumpet, and the Welsh jury, who backed him, were a narrowly prejudiced class jury. They declared the massacre "justifiable homicide."

In France the rioters were sentenced to from three to eighteen months' imprisonment, and soon after amnestied. In England they were condemned to ten years' penal servitude! In France the whole press resounded with cries of indignation against the troops. In England the press was all smiles for the soldiers and all frowns for their victims! Still, the English workmen have gained much by losing a great and dangerous illusion. Till now they fancied to have their lives protected by the formality of the Riot Act, and the subordination of the military to the civil authorities. They know now, from the official declaration to Mr. Bruce, the liberal Home Minister, in the House of Commons—first, that without going through the premonitory process of reading the Riot Act, any country magistrate, some fox hunter or parson, has the right to order the troops to fire on what he may please to consider a riotous mob; and second, that the soldier may give fire on his own hook, on the plea of self-defense. The liberal minister forgot to add that under these circumstances every man ought to be armed, at public expense, with a breachloader, in self-defense against the soldier.

The following resolution was passed at the recent General Congress of the English Trades Unions at Birmingham: "That as local organizations of labor have almost disappeared before organizations of a national character, so we believe the extension of the principle of free trade, which induces between nations such a competition that the interest of the workman is liable to be lost sight of and sacrificed in the fierce international race between capitalists, demands that such organizations should be still further extended and made international. And as the International Working Men's Association endeavors to consolidate and extend the interests of the toiling masses, which are everywhere identical, this Congress heartily recommends that Association to the support of the workingmen of the United Kingdom, especially of all organized bodies, and strongly urges them to become affiliated to that body, believing that the realization of its principles would also conclude to lasting peace between the nations of the earth."

During last May a war between the United States and England

seemed imminent. Your General Council, therefore, sent an address to Mr. Sylvis, the president of the American National Labor Union, calling on the United States' working class to command peace where their would-be masters shouted war.

The sudden death of Mr. Sylvis, that valiant champion of our cause, will justify us in concluding this report, as an homage to his memory, by his reply to our letter: "Your favor of the twelfth instant, with address enclosed, reached me yesterday. I am very happy to receive such kindly words from our fellow workingmen across the water: our cause is a common one. It is war between poverty and wealth: labor occupies the same low condition, and capital is the same tyrant in all parts of the world. Therefore I say our cause is a common one. I, in behalf of the working people of the United States, extend to you, and through you to those you represent, and to all the downtrodden and oppressed sons and daughters of toil in Europe, the right hand of fellowship. Go ahead in the good work you have undertaken, until the most glorious success crowns your efforts. That is our determination. Our late war resulted in the building up of the most infamous monied aristocracy on the face of the earth. This monied power is fast eating up the substance of the people. We have made war upon it, and we mean to win. If we can, we will win through the ballot box: if not, then we will resort to sterner means. A little bloodletting is sometimes necessary in desperate cases."

By order of the Council,

R. Applegarth, Chairman
Cowell Stepney, Treasurer
J. Georg Eccarius, General Secretary

First Address of the General Council on the Franco-Prussian War*

To the Members of the International Working Men's
Association in Europe and the United States

IN THE Inaugural Address of the International Working Men's Association of November, 1864, we said: "If the emancipation of the working classes requires their fraternal concurrence, how are they to fulfill that great mission with a foreign policy in pursuit of criminal designs, playing upon national prejudices, and squandering in piratical wars the people's blood and treasure?" We defined the foreign policy aimed at by the International in these words: "To vindicate the simple laws of morals and justice, which ought to govern the relations of private individuals, as the rules paramount of the intercourse of nations."

No wonder that Louis Bonaparte, who usurped his power by exploiting the war of classes in France, and perpetuated it by periodic wars abroad, should from the first have treated the International as a dangerous foe. On the eve of the plebiscite he ordered a raid on the members of the Administrative Committees of the International Working Men's Association throughout France, at Paris, Lyon, Rouen, Marseilles, Brest, etc., on the pretext that the International was a secret society dabbling in a complot for his assassination, a pretext soon after

* Written July 19-23, 1870, this document was translated into German by Wilhelm Liebknecht and published in the Leipzig *Der Volksstaat*, the organ of the Social Democratic Workers' party, on August 7, 1870. Marx reedited and retranslated the German text and published it in *Der Vorbote* of Geneva in August, 1870, and also as a separate leaflet. In 1891 Engels published the First and Second Addresses in the German edition of *The Civil War in France*. In French, the First Address was published in *L'Égalité*, *L'Internationale*, and *Le Mirabeau* on August 7, 1870. The August–September, 1870, issue of *Narodnoye Dyelo* contained a Russian translation.

exposed in its full absurdity by his own judges.[1] What was the real crime of the French branches of the International? They told the French people publicly and emphatically that voting the plebiscite was voting despotism at home and war abroad. It has been, in fact, their work that in all the great towns, in all the industrial centers of France, the working class rose like one man to reject the plebiscite. Unfortunately, the balance was turned by the heavy ignorance of the rural districts. The stock exchanges, the cabinets, the ruling classes, and the press of Europe celebrated the plebiscite as a signal victory of the French Emperor over the French working class; and it was the signal for the assassination, not of an individual, but of nations.

The war plot of July, 1870, is but an amended edition of the *coup d'état* of December, 1851. At first view the thing seemed so absurd that France would not believe its real good earnest. It rather believed the deputy [Jules Favre] who saw the ministerial war talk as a mere stock-jobbing trick. When on July 16 war was at last officially announced to the *Corps Législatif*, the whole opposition refused to vote the preliminary subsidies; even Thiers branded it as "detestable"; all the independent journals of Paris condemned it, and, wonderful to relate, the provincial press joined in almost unanimously.

Meanwhile, the Paris members of the International had again set to work. In the *Réveil* of July 12 they published their manifesto "to the workmen of all nations," from which we extract the following few passages. "Once more," they say, "on the pretext of the European equilibrium, of national honor, the peace of the world is menaced by political ambitions. French, German, Spanish workmen! Let our voices unite in one cry of reprobation against war! . . . War for a question of preponderance or a dynasty can, in the eyes of workmen, be nothing but a criminal absurdity. In answer to the warlike proclamations of those who exempt themselves from the impost of blood, and find in public misfortunes a source of fresh speculation, we protest, we who want peace, labor, and liberty! . . . Brothers of Germany! Our division would only result in the complete triumph of despotism on both sides of the Rhine . . . Workmen of all countries! Whatever may for the present become of our common efforts, we, the members of the International Working Men's Association, who know of no frontiers, we send you as a pledge of indissoluble solidarity the good wishes and the salutations of the workmen of France."

This manifesto of our Paris section was followed by numerous

1. Napoleon III's plebiscite for approval of his policies was held in May, 1870. The trial of the arrested members of the International took place from June 22 to July 5, 1870, and some of them were sentenced for no other reason than their membership.

similar French addresses, of which we can here only quote the declaration of Neuilly-sur-Seine, published in the *Marseillaise* of July 22: "The war, is it just?—No! The war, is it national?—No! It is merely dynastic. In the name of humanity, of democracy, and the true interests of France, we adhere completely and energetically to the protestation of the International against the war."

These protestations expressed the true sentiments of the French working people, as was soon shown by a curious incident. The Society of December 10,[2] first organized under the presidency of Louis Bonaparte, having been disguised in workingmen's smocks and let loose on the streets of Paris to perform the contortions of war fever, the real workmen of the *faubourgs* came forward with public peace demonstrations so overwhelming that Pietri, the prefect of police, thought it prudent to stop all further street politics at once, on the plea that the real Paris people had given sufficient vent to their pent-up patriotism and exuberant war enthusiasm.

Whatever may be the incidents of Louis Bonaparte's war with Prussia, the death knell of the Second Empire has already sounded at Paris. It will end as it began, in a parody. But let us not forget that it is the governments and the ruling classes of Europe who enabled Louis Bonaparte to play for eighteen years the ferocious farce of the Restored Empire.

On the German side, the war is a war of defense, but who put Germany to the necessity of defending herself? Who enabled Louis Bonaparte to wage war upon her? Prussia! It was Bismarck who conspired with that very same Louis Bonaparte for the purpose of crushing popular opposition at home, and annexing Germany to the Hohenzollern dynasty. If the battle of Sadowa[3] had been lost instead of won, French battalions would have overrun Germany as the allies of Prussia. After her victory did Prussia dream one moment of opposing a free Germany to an enslaved France? Just the contrary. While carefully preserving all the native beauties of her old system, she added on all the tricks of the Second Empire, its real despotism and its mock democratism, its political shams and its financial jobs, its high-flown talk and its low legerdemains. The Bonapartist regime, which till then flourished on only one side of the Rhine, had now got its counterfeit on the other. From such a state of things, what else could result but war?

If the German working class allow the present war to lose its strictly defensive character and to degenerate into a war against the

---

2. A secret Bonapartist organization founded in 1849.
3. On July 3, 1866, at Sadowa (Königgrätz) in Bohemia, the Prussians defeated the Austrians.

French people, victory or defeat will alike prove disastrous. All the miseries that befell Germany after her war of independence will revive with accumulated intensity.

The principles of the International are, however, too widely spread and too firmly rooted among the German working class to presage such a sad consummation. The voices of the French workmen have reechoed from Germany. A mass meeting of workmen held at Brunswick on July 16 expressed its full concurrence with the Paris manifesto, spurned the idea of national antagonism to France, and wound up its resolutions with these words: "We are enemies of all wars, but above all of dynastic wars . . . With deep sorrow and grief we are forced to undergo a defensive war as an unavoidable evil; but at the same time we call upon the whole German working class to make the recurrence of such an immense social misfortune impossible by vindicating for the peoples themselves the power to decide on peace and war, and making them masters of their own destinies."

At Chemnitz a meeting of delegates representing 50,000 Saxon workers unanimously adopted a resolution to this effect: "In the name of the German Democracy, and especially of the workmen forming the Social-Democratic party, we declare the present war to be exclusively dynastic . . . We are happy to grasp the fraternal hand stretched out to us by workmen of France . . . Mindful of the watchword of the International Working Men's Association: *Proletarians of all countries, unite*, we shall never forget that the workmen of *all* countries are our friends and the despots of *all* countries our enemies."

The Berlin branch of the International has also replied to the Paris manifesto. "We," they say, "join with heart and hand your protestation . . . Solemnly we promise that neither the sound of the trumpet nor the roar of the cannon, neither victory nor defeat shall divert us from our common work for the union of the children of toil of all countries."

Be it so!

In the background of this suicidal strife looms the dark figure of Russia. It is an ominous sign that the signal for the present war should have been given at the moment when the Muscovite government had just finished its strategic lines of railway and was already massing troops in the direction of the Pruth. Whatever sympathy the Germans may justly claim in a war of defense against Bonapartist aggression they would forfeit at once by allowing the Prussian Government to call for, or accept, the help of the Cossacks. Let them remember that after their war of independence against the first Napoleon, Germany lay for generations prostrate at the feet of the Czar.

The English working class stretch the hand of fellowship to the

French and German working people. They feel deeply convinced that whatever turn the impending horrid war may take, the alliance of the working classes of all countries will ultimately kill war. The very fact that while official France and Germany are rushing into a fratricidal feud, the workmen of France and Germany send each other messages of peace and good will—this great fact, unparalleled in the history of the past—opens the vista of a brighter future. It proves that in contrast to old society, with its economical miseries and its political delirium, a new society is springing up whose international rule will be *Peace,* because its national ruler will be everywhere the same—*labor!* The pioneer of that new society is the International Working Men's Association.

The General Council:

Applegarth, Robert	*Mottershead, Thomas*
Boon, Martin J.	*Murray, Charles*
Bradnick, Fred.	*Odger, George*
Hales, John	*Parnell, James*
Hales, William	*Pfänder*
Harris, George	*Ruehl*
Lessner, Fred.	*Shepherd, Joseph*
Lintern, W.	*Stepney, Cowell*
Legreulier	*Stoll*
Maurice, Zevy	*Schmutz*
Milner, George	*Townshend, W.*

Corresponding Secretaries:

Eugène Dupont, for France
Karl Marx, for Germany
A. Serraillier, for Belgium, Holland, and Spain
Hermann Jung, for Switzerland
Giovanni Bora, for Italy
Anton Zabicki, for Poland
James Cohen, for Denmark
J. G. Eccarius, for the United States

Benjamin Lucraft, Chairman
John Weston, Treasurer
J. Georg Eccarius, General Secretary

Second Address of the General Council on the Franco-Prussian War*

To the Members of the International Working Men's
Association in Europe and the United States

IN our first Manifesto of the twenty-third of July we said: "The death knell of the Second Empire has already sounded at Paris. It will end as it began, in a parody. But let us not forget that it is the governments and the ruling classes of Europe who enabled Louis Napoleon to play for eighteen years the ferocious farce of the Restored Empire."

Thus even before war operations had actually set in, we treated the Bonapartist bubble as a thing of the past.

If we were not mistaken as to the vitality of the Second Empire, we were not wrong in our apprehension lest the German war should "lose its strictly defensive character and . . . degenerate into a war against the French people." The war of defense ended, in point of fact, with the surrender of Louis Bonaparte, the Sedan capitulation, and the proclamation of the Republic of Paris. But long before these events, the very moment that the utter rottenness of the imperialist arms became evident, the Prussian military *camarilla* had resolved upon conquest. There lay an ugly obstacle in their way—King William's own proclamations at the commencement of the war. In his speech from the throne to the North German Diet, he had solemnly declared to make war upon the Emperor of the French, and not upon the French people. On the eleventh of August he had issued

---

* Written September 6–9, 1870; published as a leaflet in English, September 11–13. A German translation by Marx was published in *Der Volksstaat*, September 21, 1870.

a manifesto to the French nation, where he said: "The Emperor Napoleon having made, by land and sea, an attack on the German nation, which desired and still desires to live in peace with the French people, I have assumed the command of the German armies to repel his aggression, and I have been led by military events to cross the frontiers of France."

Not content to assert the defensive character of the war by the statement that he only assumed the command of the German armies "to repel aggression," he added that he was only "led by military events" to cross the frontiers of France. A defensive war does, of course, not exclude offensive operations dictated by "military events."

Thus this pious king stood pledged before France and the world to a strictly defensive war. How to release him from his solemn pledge? The stage managers had to exhibit him as giving, reluctantly, way to the irresistible behest of the German nation. They at once gave the cue to the liberal German middle class, with its professors, its capitalists, its aldermen, and its penmen. That middle class which in its struggle for civil liberty had, from 1846 to 1870, been exhibiting an unexampled spectacle of irresolution, incapacity, and cowardice felt, of course, highly delighted to bestride the European scene as the roaring lion of German patriotism. It revindicated its civic independence by affecting to force upon the Prussian Government the secret designs of that same government. It does penance for its long-continued and almost religious faith in Louis Bonaparte's infallibility by shouting for the dismemberment of the French Republic. Let us for a moment listen to the special pleadings of those stouthearted patriots!

They dare not pretend that the people of Alsace and Lorraine pant for the German embrace; quite the contrary. To punish their French patriotism, Strasbourg, a town with an independent citadel commanding it, has for six days been wantonly and fiendishly bombarded by "German" explosive shells, setting it on fire and killing great numbers of its defenseless inhabitants! Yet the soil of those provinces once upon a time belonged to the whilom German Empire. Hence, it seems, the soil and the human beings grown on it must be confiscated as imprescriptible German property. If the map of Europe is to be remade in the antiquary's vein, let us by no means forget that the Elector of Brandenburg for his Prussian dominions was the vassal of the Polish Republic.

The more knowing patriots, however, require Alsace and the German-speaking part of Lorraine as a "material guarantee" against French aggression. As this contemptible plea has bewildered many weak-minded people, we are bound to enter more fully upon it.

There is no doubt that the general configuration of Alsace, as compared with the opposite bank of the Rhine, and the presence of a large fortified town like Strasbourg, about halfway between Basel and Germersheim, very much favor a French invasion of South Germany, while they offer peculiar difficulties to an invasion of France from South Germany. There is, further, no doubt that the addition of Alsace and German-speaking Lorraine would give South Germany a much stronger frontier, inasmuch as she would then be master of the crest of the Vosges Mountains in its whole length, and of the fortresses which cover its northern passes. If Metz were annexed as well, France would certainly for the moment be deprived of her two principal bases of operation against Germany, but that would not prevent her from constructing a fresh one at Nancy or Verdun. While Germany owns Coblenz, Mainz, Germersheim, Rastatt, and Ulm, all bases of operation against France, and plentifully made use of in this war, with what show of fair play can she begrudge France Strasbourg and Metz, the only two fortresses of any importance she has on that side? Moreover, Strasbourg endangers South Germany only while South Germany is a separate power from North Germany. From 1792 to 1795 South Germany was never invaded from that direction, because Prussia was a party to the war against the French Revolution; but as soon as Prussia made a peace of her own in 1795, and left the South to shift for itself, the invasions of South Germany, with Strasbourg for a base, began, and continued till 1809. The fact is, a *united* Germany can always render Strasbourg and any French army in Alsace innocuous by concentrating all her troops, as was done in the present war, between Saarlouis and Landau, and advancing, or accepting battle, on the line of road between Mainz and Metz. While the mass of the German troops is stationed there, any French army advancing from Strasbourg into South Germany would be outflanked, and have its communications threatened. If the present campaign has proved anything, it is the facility of invading France from Germany.

But in good faith, is it not altogether an absurdity and an anachronism to make military considerations the principle by which the boundaries of nations are to be fixed? If this rule were to prevail, Austria would still be entitled to Venetia and the line of the Mincio, and France to the line of the Rhine, in order to protect Paris, which lies certainly more open to an attack from the northeast than Berlin does from the southwest. If limits are to be fixed by military interests, there will be no end to claims, because every military line is necessarily faulty, and may be improved by annexing some more outlying territory; and moreover they can never be fixed finally and fairly because they always must be imposed by the conqueror upon the conquered, and consequently carry within them the seed of fresh wars.

Such is the lesson of all history. Thus with nations as with individuals. To deprive them of the power of offense, you must deprive them of the means of defense. You must not only garrote but murder. If ever a conqueror took "material guarantees" for breaking the sinews of a nation, the first Napoleon did so by the Tilsit Treaty and the way he executed it against Prussia and the rest of Germany. Yet a few years later his gigantic power split like a rotten reed upon the German people. What are the "material guarantees" Prussia, in her wildest dreams, can or dare impose upon France, compared to the "material guarantees" the first Napoleon had wrenched from herself? The result will not prove the less disastrous. History will measure its retribution, not by the extent of the square miles conquered from France, but by the intensity of the crime of reviving, in the second half of the nineteenth century, *the policy of conquest!*

But, say the mouthpieces of Teutonic patriotism, you must not confound Germans with Frenchmen. What *we* want is not glory, but safety. The Germans are an essentially peaceful people. In their sober guardianship, conquest itself changes from a condition of future war into a pledge of perpetual peace. Of course it is not Germans that invaded France in 1792, for the sublime purpose of bayoneting the revolution of the eighteenth century. It is not Germans that befouled their hands by the subjugation of Italy, the oppression of Hungary, and the dismemberment of Poland. Their present military system, which divides the whole adult male population into two parts—one standing army on service, and another standing army on furlough, both equally bound in passive obedience to rulers by divine right—such a military system is, of course, a "material guarantee" for keeping the peace, and the ultimate goal of civilizing tendencies! In Germany, as everywhere else, the sycophants of the powers that be poison the popular mind by the incense of mendacious self-praise.

Indignant as they pretend to be at the sight of French fortresses in Metz and Strasbourg, those German patriots see no harm in the vast system of Muscovite fortifications at Warsaw, Modlin, and Ivangorod. While gloating at the terrors of imperialist invasion, they blink at the infamy of autocratic tutelage.

As in 1865 promises were exchanged between Louis Bonaparte and Bismarck, so in 1870 promises have been exchanged between Gorchakov and Bismarck. As Louis Bonaparte flattered himself that the War of 1866, resulting in the common exhaustion of Austria and Prussia, would make him the supreme arbiter of Germany, so Alexander flattered himself that the War of 1870, resulting in the common exhaustion of Germany and France, would make him the supreme arbiter of the western Continent. As the Second Empire thought the

North German Confederation incompatible with its existence, so auto-cratic Russia must think herself endangered by a German empire under Prussian leadership. Such is the law of the old political system. Within its pale the gain of one state is the loss of the other. The Czar's paramount influence over Europe roots in his traditional hold on Germany. At a moment when in Russia herself volcanic social agencies threaten to shake the very base of autocracy, could the Czar afford to bear with such a loss of foreign prestige? Already the Muscovite journals repeat the language of the Bonapartist journals after the War of 1866. Do the Teuton patriots really believe that liberty and peace will be guaranteed to Germany by forcing France into the arms of Russia? If the fortune of her arms, the arrogance of success, and dynastic intrigue lead Germany to a dismemberment of France, there will then only remain two courses open to her. She must at all risks become the *avowed* tool of Russian aggrandizement, or, after some short respite, make ready again for another "defensive" war, not one of those newfangled "localized" wars but a *war of races*—a war with the combined Slavonian and Roman races.

The German working class has resolutely supported the war, which it was not in their power to prevent, as a war for German independence and the liberation of France and Europe from that pestilential incubus the Second Empire. It was the German workmen who, together with the rural laborers, furnished the sinews and muscles of heroic hosts, leaving behind their half-starved families. Decimated by the battles abroad, they will be once more decimated by misery at home. In their turn they are now coming forward to ask for "guarantees"—guarantees that their immense sacrifices have not been brought in vain, that they have conquered liberty, that the victory over the imperialist armies will not, as in 1815, be turned into the defeat of the German people; and as the first of these guarantees, they claim an *honorable peace for France*, and the *recognition of the French Republic*.

The Central Committee of the German Social-Democratic Work-ers' party issued, on the fifth of September, a manifesto energetically insisting upon these guarantees: "We protest against the annexation of Alsace and Lorraine. And we are conscious of speaking in the name of the German working class. In the common interest of France and Germany, in the interest of peace and liberty, in the interest of Western civilization against Eastern barbarism, the German workmen will not patiently tolerate the annexation of Alsace and Lorraine. . . . We shall faithfully stand by our fellow workmen in all countries for the common international cause of the Proletariat!"

Unfortunately, we cannot feel sanguine of their immediate success.

If the French workmen amidst peace failed to stop the aggressor, are the German workmen more likely to stop the victor amidst the clangor of arms? The German workmen's manifesto demands the extradition of Louis Bonaparte as a common felon to the French Republic. Their rulers are, on the contrary, already trying hard to restore him to the Tuileries as the best man to ruin France. However that may be, history will prove that the German working class are not made of the same malleable stuff as the German middle class. They will do their duty.

Like them, we hail the advent of the Republic in France, but at the same time we labor under misgivings which we hope will prove groundless. That republic has not subverted the throne, but only taken its place become vacant. It has been proclaimed, not as a social conquest, but as a national measure of defense. It is in the hands of a Provisional Government composed partly of notorious Orléanists, partly of middle-class republicans, upon some of whom the insurrection of June, 1848, has left its indelible stigma. The division of labor among the members of that government looks awkward. The Orléanists have seized the strongholds of the army and the police, while to the professed republicans have fallen the talking departments. Some of their first acts go far to show that they have inherited from the Empire, not only ruins, but also its dread of the working class. If eventual impossibilities are in wild phraseology demanded from the Republic, is it not with a view to prepare the cry for a "possible" government? Is the Republic, by some of its middle-class managers, not intended to serve as a mere stopgap and bridge over an Orléanist restoration?

The French working class moves, therefore, under circumstances of extreme difficulty. Any attempt at upsetting the new government in the present crisis, when the enemy is almost knocking at the doors of Paris, would be a desperate folly. The French workmen must perform their duties as citizens, but at the same time they must not allow themselves to be deluded by the national *souvenirs* [memories] of 1792, as the French peasants allowed themselves to be deluded by the national *souvenirs* of the First Empire. They have not to recapitulate the past, but to build up the future. Let them calmly and resolutely improve the opportunities of republican liberty, for the work of their own class organization. It will gift them with fresh Herculean powers for the regeneration of France, and our common task—the emancipation of labor. Upon their energies and wisdom hinges the fate of the Republic.

The English workmen have already taken measures to overcome, by a wholesome pressure from without, the reluctance of their government to recognize the French Republic.[1] The present dilatoriness of the British Government is probably intended to atone for the anti-Jacobin war and its former indecent haste in sanctioning the *coup d'état*. The English workmen call also upon their government to oppose by all its power the dismemberment of France, which part of the English press is shameless enough to howl for. It is the same press that for twenty years deified Louis Bonaparte as the providence of Europe, that frantically cheered on the slaveholders' rebellion. Now, as then, it drudges for the slaveholder.

Let the sections of the International Working Men's Association in every country stir the working classes to action. If they forsake their duty, if they remain passive, the present tremendous war will be but the harbinger of still deadlier international feuds, and lead in every nation to a renewed triumph over the workman by the lords of the sword, of the soil, and of capital.

Vive la République.

The General Council:

Robert Applegarth; Martin J. Boon; Fred. Bradnick; Cahill; John Hales; William Hales; George Harris; Fred. Lessner; Lopatin; B. Lucraft; George Milner; Thomas Mottershead; Charles Murray; George Odger; James Parnell; Pfaender; Ruehl; Joseph Shepherd; Cowell Stepney; Stoll; Schmutz

Corresponding Secretaries:

Eugène Dupont for France; *Karl Marx* for Germany and Russia; *A. Serraillier* for Belgium, Holland, and Spain; *Hermann Jung* for Switzerland; *Giovanni Bora* for Italy; *Zévy Maurice* for Hungary; *Anton Zabicki* for Poland; *James Cohen* for Denmark; *J. G. Eccarius* for the United States.

William Townshend, Chairman
John Weston, Treasurer
J. Georg Eccarius, General Secretary
256 High Holborn, London, W.C., September 9, 1870

---

1. On September 5, 1870, English trade unions organized mass meetings in London, Birmingham, and other cities urging the government to recognize the Republic.

Resolutions of the London Conference*

I
DESIGNATIONS OF NATIONAL COUNCILS, ETC.

The Conference invites the General Council to limit the number of those members whom it adds to itself, and to take care that such adjunctions be not made too exclusively from citizens belonging to the same nationality.

II
DESIGNATIONS OF NATIONAL COUNCILS

1. In conformity with a Resolution of the Congress of Basel (1869), the Central Councils of the various countries where the International is regularly organized shall designate themselves henceforth as federal councils or federal committees with the names of their respective countries attached, the designation of General Council being reserved for the Central Council of the International Working Men's Association.

2. All local branches, sections, groups, and their committees are henceforth to designate and constitute themselves simply and exclusively as branches, sections, groups, and committees of the International Working Men's Association with the names of their respective localities attached.

3. Consequently no branches, sections, or groups will henceforth

---

* Drafted and prepared by Marx and Engels in September–October, 1871; printed as a pamphlet in English, German, and French, and also in various organs of the International, November–December, 1871. The Conference was held September 17–23, 1871.

be allowed to designate themselves by sectarian names such as positivists, mutualists, collectivists, communists, etc., or to form separatist bodies under the name of sections of propaganda, etc., pretending to accomplish special missions, distinct from the common purposes of the Association.

4. Resolutions 1 and 2 do not, however, apply to affiliated *trade unions*.

III
DELEGATES OF THE GENERAL COUNCIL

All delegates appointed to distinct missions by the General Council shall have the right to attend, and be heard at, all meetings of federal councils, or committees, district and local committees and branches, without, however, being entitled to vote thereat.

IV
CONTRIBUTION OF 1d.[1] PER MEMBER TO THE GENERAL COUNCIL

1. The General Council shall cause to be printed adhesive stamps representing the value of one penny each, which will be annually supplied, in the numbers to be asked for, to the federal councils or committees.

2. The federal council or committees shall provide the local committees, or, in their absence, their respective sections, with the number of stamps corresponding to the number of their members.

3. These stamps are to be affixed to a special sheet of the *livret* or to the Rules which every member is held to possess.

4. On the first of March of each year, the federal councils or committees of the different countries shall forward to the General Council the amount of the stamps disposed of, and return the unsold stamps remaining on hand.

5. These stamps, representing the value of the individual contributions, shall bear the date of the current year.

V
FORMATION OF WORKING WOMEN'S BRANCHES

The Conference recommends the formation of female branches among the working class. It is, however, understood that this resolu-

---

1. The German edition uses "1 Groschen"; in the French edition it is "10 centimes."

tion does not at all interfere with the existence or formation of branches composed of both sexes.

VI
GENERAL STATISTICS OF THE WORKING CLASS

1. The Conference invites the General Council to enforce Article 6 of the original Rules relating to general statistics of the working class, and the resolutions of the Geneva Congress, 1866, on the same subject.

2. Every local branch is bound to appoint a special committee of statistics, so as to be always ready, within the limits of its means, to answer any questions which may be addressed to it by the federal council or committee of its country, or by the General Council. It is recommended to all branches to remunerate the secretaries of the committees of statistics, considering the general benefit the working class will derive from their labor.

3. On the first of August of each year the federal councils or committees will transmit the materials collected in their respective countries to the General Council, which, in its turn, will have to elaborate them into a general report, to be laid before the Congresses or Conferences annually held in the month of September.

4. Trade unions and international branches refusing to give the information required shall be reported to the General Council, which will take action thereupon.

VII
INTERNATIONAL RELATIONS OF TRADE UNIONS

The General Council is invited to assist, as has been done hitherto, the growing tendency of the trade unions of the different countries to enter into relations with the unions of the same trade in all other countries. The efficiency of its action as the international agent of communication between the national trade societies will essentially depend upon the assistance given by these same societies to the general labor statistics pursued by the International.

The boards of trade unions of all countries are invited to keep the General Council informed of the directions of their respective offices.

VIII
AGRICULTURAL PRODUCERS

1. The Conference invites the General Council and the federal councils or committees to prepare, for the next Congress, reports on

the means of securing the adhesion of the agricultural producers to the movement of the industrial proletariat.

2. Meanwhile, the federal councils or committees are invited to send agitators to the rural districts, there to organize public meetings, to propagate the principles of the International, and to found rural branches.

IX
POLITICAL ACTION OF THE WORKING CLASS

Considering the following passage of the preamble to the Rules: "The economical emancipation of the working classes is . . . the great end to which every political movement ought to be subordinate as a means";

That the Inaugural Address of the International Working Men's Association (1864) states: "The lords of land and the lords of capital will always use their political privileges for the defense and perpetuation of their economical monopolies. So far from promoting, they will continue to lay every possible impediment in the way of the emancipation of labor. . . . To conquer political power has therefore become the great duty of the working classes";

That the Congress of Lausanne (1867) has passed this resolution: "The social emancipation of the workmen is inseparable from their political emancipation";

That the declaration of the General Council relative to the pretended plot of the French Internationals on the eve of the plebiscite (1870) says: "Certainly by the tenor of our Statutes, all our branches in England, on the Continent, and in America have the special mission not only to serve as centers for the militant organization of the working class, but also to support, in their respective countries, every political movement tending toward the accomplishment of our ultimate end—the economical emancipation of the working class";

That false translations of the original Statutes have given rise to various interpretations which were mischievous to the development and action of the International Working Men's Association;

In presence of an unbridled reaction which violently crushes every effort at emancipation on the part of the workingmen, and pretends to maintain by brute force the distinction of classes and the political domination of the propertied classes resulting from it;

Considering that against this collective power of the propertied classes the working class cannot act, as a class, except by constituting itself into a political party, distinct from, and opposed to, all old parties formed by the propertied classes;

That this constitution of the working class into a political party is indispensable in order to ensure the triumph of the Social Revolution and its ultimate end—the abolition of classes;

That the combination of forces which the working class has already effected by its economical struggle ought at the same time to serve as a lever for its struggles against the political power of landlords and capitalists—

The Conference recalls to the members of the International:

That in the militant state of the working class, its economical movement and its political action are indissolubly united.

X
GENERAL RESOLUTION AS TO THE COUNTRIES WHERE THE REGULAR ORGANIZATION OF THE INTERNATIONAL IS INTERFERED WITH BY THE GOVERNMENTS

In those countries where the regular organization of the International may for the moment have become impracticable in consequence of government interference, the Association, and its local groups, may be re-formed under various other names, but all secret societies properly so called are and remain formally excluded.

XI
RESOLUTIONS RELATING TO FRANCE

1. The Conference expresses its firm conviction that all persecutions will only double the energy of the adherents of the International, and that the branches will continue to organize themselves, if not by great centers, at least by workshops and federations of workshops corresponding with each other by their delegates.

2. Consequently, the Conference invites all branches vigorously to persist in the propaganda of our principles in France and to import into their country as many copies as possible of the publications and Statutes of the International.

XII
RESOLUTION RELATING TO ENGLAND

The Conference invites the General Council to call upon the English branches in London to form a Federal Committee for London which, after its recognition by the provincial branches and affiliated societies, shall be recognized, by the General Council, as the Federal Council for England.

XIII
SPECIAL VOTES OF THE CONFERENCE

1. The Conference approves of the adjunction of the members of the Paris Commune whom the General Council has added to its number.

2. The Conference declares that the German workingmen have done their duty during the Franco-German War.

3. The Conference fraternally thanks the members of the Spanish Federation for the memorandum presented by them on the organization of the International, by which they have once more proved their devotion to our common work.

4. The General Council shall immediately publish a declaration to the effect that the International Working Men's Association is utterly foreign to the so-called conspiracy of Nechayev, who has fraudulently usurped its name.

XIV
INSTRUCTION TO CITIZEN OUTINE

Citizen Outine is invited to publish in the journal *L'Égalité*[2] a succinct report, from the Russian papers, of the Nechayev trial. Before publication, his report will be submitted to the General Council.

XV
CONVOCATION OF NEXT CONGRESS

The Conference leaves it to the discretion of the General Council to fix, according to events, the day and place of meeting of the next Congress or Conference.

XVI
ALLIANCE DE LA DÉMOCRATIE SOCIALISTE
(ALLIANCE OF SOCIALIST DEMOCRACY)

Considering, that the *"Alliance de la Démocratie socialiste"* has declared itself dissolved (see letter to the General Council, Geneva,

---

2. A Geneva weekly, organ of the Swiss Romansh Federation of the International.

10th August, 1871, signed by Citizen N. Joukowsky, Secretary to the Alliance);

That in its sitting of the 18th September (see No. II of this circular) the Conference has decided that all existing organizations of the International shall, in conformity with the letter and the spirit of the General Rules, henceforth designate and constitute themselves simply and exclusively as branches, sections, federations, etc., of the International Working Men's Association with the names of their respective localities attached;

That the existing branches and societies shall therefore no longer be allowed to designate themselves by sectarian names such as positivists, mutualists, collectivists, communists, etc., or to form separatist bodies under the names of sections of propaganda, *Alliance de la Démocratie socialiste*, etc., pretending to accomplish special missions distinct from the common purposes of the Association;

That henceforth the General Council of the International Working Men's Association will in this sense have to interpret and apply Article 5 of the administrative resolutions of the Basel Congress: "The General Council has the right either to accept or to refuse the affiliation of any new section or group," etc.[3];

The Conference declares the question of the *"Alliance de la Démocratie socialiste"* to be settled.

XVII
SPLIT IN THE FRENCH-SPEAKING PART OF SWITZERLAND

1. The different exceptions taken by the Federal Committee of the Mountain [Jura] sections as to the competency of the Conference are declared inadmissible. (This is but a résumé of Article 1, which will be printed in full in *L'Égalité* of Geneva.)

2. The Conference confirms the decision of the General Council of June 29th, 1870.

At the same time, in view of the persecutions which the International is at present undergoing, the Conference appeals to the feelings of fraternity and union which more than ever ought to animate the working class;

It invites the brave workingmen of the Mountain sections to rejoin the sections of the Romand [Romansh] Federation;

In case such an amalgamation should prove impracticable, it decides that the dissident Mountain sections shall henceforth name themselves the "Jurassian Federation."

---

3. In the German and French editions the word "etc." is replaced by "subject to appeal to the next Congress."

The Conference gives warning that henceforth the General Council will be bound to publicly denounce and disavow all organs of the International which, following the precedents of *Progrès* and *Solidarité*, should discuss in their columns, before the middle-class public, questions exclusively reserved for the local or federal committees and the General Council, or for the private and administrative sittings of the federal or general congresses.

NOTICE

The resolutions not intended for publicity will be communicated to the federal councils or committees of the various countries by the corresponding secretaries of the General Council.

By order and in the name of the Conference,

The General Council:

R. Applegarth, M. J. Boon, Fred. Bradnick, G. H. Buttery, Delahaye, Eugène Dupont (on mission), *W. Hales, G. Harris, Hurliman, Jules Johannard, Fred. Lessner, Lochner, Ch. Longuet, C. Martin, Z. Maurice, Henry Mayo, George Milner, Charles Murray, Pfänder, John Roach, Ruehl, Sadler, Cowell Stepney, Alf. Taylor, W. Townshend, E. Vaillant, John Weston*

Corresponding Secretaries:

A. Serraillier for France; *Karl Marx*, Germany and Russia; *F. Engels*, Italy and Spain; *A. Herman*, Belgium; *J. P. Mac Donnell*, Ireland; *Le Moussu* for the French branches of the United States; *Walery Wroblewski* for Poland; *Hermann Jung* for Switzerland; *T. Mottershead*, Denmark; *Ch. Rochat*, Holland; *J. G. Eccarius*, United States; *Leo Frankel*, Austria and Hungary

Resolutions on the Anniversary of
the Paris Commune*

I

That this meeting assembled to celebrate the anniversary of the 18th March last declares that it looks upon the glorious movement inaugurated upon the 18th March, 1871, as the dawn of the great social revolution which will forever free the human race from class rule.

II

That the incapacity and the crimes of the middle classes, extended all over Europe by their hatred against the working classes, have doomed old society, no matter under what form of government—monarchical or republican.

III

That the crusade of all governments against the International, and the terror of the murderers of Versailles as well as their Prussian

---

* At its session of February 20, 1872, the General Council adopted a resolution "to celebrate the anniversary of the eighteenth of March," that being "the first attempt on the part of the working classes to seize political power." The anniversary meeting, to commemorate the "Social Revolution of Paris" (in the words of the handbill), was held in St. George's Hall on March 18, 1872. Marx wrote these resolutions for the meeting between March 13 and 18, 1872; they were published in La Liberté in French on March 24, and in the International Herald in English on March 30.

conquerors, attest the hollowness of their successes, and the presence of the threatening army of the proletariat of the whole world gathering in the rear of its heroic vanguard crushed by the combined forces of Thiers and William of Prussia.

Report of the General Council to the Fifth Annual Congress*

Citizens:

Since our last Congress at Basel, two great wars have changed the face of Europe: the Franco-German War and the Civil War in France. Both of these wars were preceded, accompanied, and followed by a third war—the war against the International Working Men's Association.

The Paris members of the International had told the French people, publicly and emphatically, that voting the plebiscite was voting despotism at home and war abroad. Under the pretext of having participated in a plot for the assassination of Louis Bonaparte, they were arrested on the eve of the plebiscite, the twenty-third of April, 1870. Simultaneous arrests of Internationalists took place at Lyon, Rouen, Marseilles, Brest, and other towns. In its declaration of May 3, 1870, the General Council stated: "This last plot will worthily range with its two predecessors of grotesque memory. The noisy and violent measures against our French sections are exclusively intended to serve one single purpose—the manipulation of the plebiscite."

In point of fact, after the downfall of the December Empire its governmental successors published documentary evidence to the effect that this last plot had been fabricated by the Bonapartist police itself, and that on the eve of the plebiscite, Ollivier, in a private circular, directly told his subordinates. "The leaders of the International must

* Written at the end of August, 1872; published as a leaflet in Brunswick, 1872; published also in the International organs *Der Volksstaat*, September 18, 1872; *La Liberté*, September 29, 1872; *L'Internationale, International Herald*, October 5, 12, 19, 1872. This text is from *The International Herald*. The Fifth Congress was held in The Hague, September 2–7, 1872.

be arrested or else the voting of the plebiscite could not be satisfactorily proceeded with."

The plebiscitary farce once over, the members of the Paris Federal Council were indeed condemned, on the 8th of July, by Louis Bonaparte's own judges, but for the simple crime of belonging to the International and not for any participation in the sham plot. Thus the Bonapartist government considered it necessary to initiate the most ruinous war that was ever brought down upon France, by a preliminary campaign against the French sections of the International Working Men's Association. Let us not forget that the working class in France rose like one man to reject the plebiscite. Let us no more forget that "the stock exchanges, the cabinets, the ruling classes, and the press of Europe celebrated the plebiscite as a signal victory of the French Emperor over the French working class." (Address of the General Council on the Civil War, July 23, 1870.)

A few weeks after the plebiscite, when the imperialist press commenced to fan the warlike passions among the French people, the Paris Internationalists, nothing daunted by the government persecutions, issued their appeal of the 12th of July, "to the workmen of all nations," denounced the intended war as a "criminal absurdity," telling their "brothers of Germany" that their "division would only result in the complete triumph of despotism on both sides of the Rhine," and declaring that "we, the members òf the International Association, know of no frontiers." Their appeal met with an enthusiastic echo from Germany, so that the General Council was entitled to state,

"The very fact that while official France and Germany are rushing into a fratricidal feud, the workmen of France and Germany send each other messages of peace and good will—this fact, unparalleled in the history of the past—opens the vista of a brighter future. It proves that in contrast to old society, with its economical miseries and its political delirium, a new society is springing up whose international rule will be *Peace*, because its national ruler will be everywhere the same—*Labor*. The pioneer of that new society is the International Working Men's Association." (Address of July 23, 1870.)

Up to the proclamation of the Republic, the members of the Paris Federal Council remained in prison, while the other members of the Association were daily denounced to the mob as traitors acting in the pay of Prussia.

With the capitulation of Sedan, when the Second Empire ended as it began, in a parody, the Franco-German War entered upon its second phase. It became a war against the French people. After her repeated solemn declarations to take up arms for the sole purpose of repelling foreign aggression, Prussia now dropped the mask and proclaimed a war of conquest. From that moment she found herself compelled not only to fight the Republic of France, but simultaneously the International in Germany. We can here but hint at a few incidents of that conflict.

Immediately after the declaration of war, the greater part of the territory of the North German Confederation, Hanover, Oldenburg, Bremen, Hamburg, Brunswick, Schleswig-Holstein, Mecklenburg, Pomerania, and the province of Prussia, were placed in a state of siege, and handed over to the tender mercies of General Vogel von Falkenstein. This state of siege, proclaimed as a safeguard against the threatening foreign invasion, was at once turned into a state of war against the German Internationals.

The day after the proclamation of the Republic of Paris, the Brunswick Central Committee of the German Social Democratic Workers' Party, which forms a section of the International within the limits imposed by the law of the country, issued a manifesto September 5 calling upon the working class to oppose by all means in their power the dismemberment of France, to claim a peace honorable for that country, and to agitate for the recognition of the French Republic. The manifesto denounced the proposed annexation of Alsace and Lorraine as a crime tending to transform all Germany into a Prussian barracks, and to establish war as a permanent European institution. On September 9, Vogel Von Falkenstein had the members of the Brunswick Committee arrested and marched off in chains, a distance of six hundred miles, to Lötzen, a Prussian fortress on the Russian frontier, where their ignominious treatment was to serve as a foil to the ostentatious feasting of the imperial guest at Wilhelmshöhe. As arrests, the hunting of workmen from one German state to another, suppression of proletarian papers, military brutality, and police chicane in all forms, did not prevent the International vanguard of the German working class from acting up to the Brunswick manifesto, Vogel von Falkenstein, by a ukase of September 21 [1870], interdicted all meetings of the Social-Democratic party. That interdict was canceled by another ukase of October 5, wherein he naïvely commands the police spies "to denounce to him personally all individuals who, by public demonstrations, shall encourage France in her resistance against the conditions of peace imposed by Germany, so as to enable him to render such individuals innocuous during the continuance of the war."

Leaving the cares of the war abroad to Moltke, the King of Prussia contrived to give a new turn to the war at home. By his personal order of October 17, Vogel von Falkenstein was to lend his Lötzen captives to the Brunswick District Tribunal, which, on its part, was either to find grounds for their legal durance or else return them to the safe keeping of the dread general.

Vogel von Falkenstein's proceedings were, of course, imitated throughout Germany, while Bismarck, in a diplomatic circular, mocked Europe by standing forth as the indignant champion of the right of free utterance of opinion, free press, and free meetings, on the part of the peace party in France. At the very same time that he demanded a freely elected National Assembly for France, in Germany he had Bebel and Liebknecht imprisoned for having, in opposition to him, represented the International in the German parliament, and in order to get them out of the way during the impending general elections.

His master, William the Conqueror, supported him by a decree from Versailles prolonging the state of siege, that is to say, the suspension of all civil law, for the whole period of the elections. In fact, the King did not allow the state of siege to be raised in Germany until two months after the conclusion of peace with France. The stubbornness with which he was insisting upon the state of war at home, and his repeated personal meddling with his own German captives, prove the awe in which he, amid the din of victorious arms and the frantic cheers of the whole middle class, held the rising party of the proletariat. It was the involuntary homage paid by physical force to moral power.

If the war against the International had been localized, first in France, from the days of the plebiscite to the downfall of the Empire, then in Germany during the whole period of the resistance of the Republic against Prussia, it became general since the rise, and after the fall, of the Paris Commune.

On June 6, 1871, Jules Favre issued his circular to the foreign powers demanding the extradition of the refugees of the Commune as common criminals, and a general crusade against the International as the enemy of family, religion, order, and property, so adequately represented in his own person. Austria and Hungary caught the cue at once. On the thirteenth of June a raid was made on the reputed leaders of the Pest Working Men's Union, their papers were seized, their persons sequestered, and proceedings were instituted against them for high treason. Several delegates of the Vienna International, happening to be on a visit to Pest, were carried off to Vienna, there to undergo a similar treatment. Beust asked and received from his parliament a supplementary vote of £30,000, "on behalf of expenses for political information that had become more than ever indispensable through the dangerous spread of the International all over Europe."

Since that time a true reign of terror against the working class has set in in Austria and Hungary. In its last agonies the Austrian Government seems still anxiously to cling to its old privilege of playing the Don Quixote of European reaction.

A few weeks after Jules Favre's circular, Dufaure proposed to his rurals a law which is now in force, and punishes as a crime the mere fact of belonging to the International Working Men's Association, or of sharing its principles. As a witness before the rural committee of inquiry on Dufaure's bill, Thiers boasted that it was the offspring of his own ingenious brains and that he had been the first to discover the infallible panacea of treating the Internationals as the Spanish Inquisition had treated the heretics. But even on this point he can lay no claim to originality. Long before his appointment as savior of society, the true law which the Internationals deserve at the hands of the ruling classes had been laid down by the Vienna courts.

On July 26, 1870, the most prominent men of the Austrian proletarian party were found guilty of high treason, and sentenced to years of penal servitude, with one fast day in every month. The law laid down was this: "The prisoners, as they themselves confess, have accepted and acted according to the program of the German Working Men's Congress of Eisenach (1869). This program embodies the program of the International. The International is established for the emancipation of the working class from the rule of the propertied class, and from political dependence. That emancipation is incompatible with the existing institutions of the Austrian state. Hence whoever accepts and propagates the principles of the International program commits preparatory acts for the overthrow of the Austrian Government, and is consequently guilty of high treason."

On November 27, 1871, judgment was passed upon the members of the Brunswick Committee. They were sentenced to various periods of imprisonment. The court expressly referred, as to a precedent, to the law laid down at Vienna.

At Pest, the prisoners belonging to the Working Men's Union, after having undergone for nearly a year a treatment as infamous as that inflicted upon the Fenians by the British Government, were brought up for judgment on April 22, 1872. The public prosecutor here also called upon the court to apply to them the law laid down at Vienna. They were, however, acquitted.

At Leipzig, on March 27, 1872, Bebel and Liebknecht were sentenced to two years' imprisonment in a fortress for attempted high treason upon the strength of the law as laid down at Vienna. The only distinctive feature of this case is that the law laid down by a Vienna judge was sanctioned by a Saxon jury.

At Copenhagen the three members of the Central Committee of the International, Brix, Pio, and Geleff, were thrown into prison on the fifth of May [1872] because they had declared their firm resolve to hold an open-air meeting in the teeth of a police order forbidding it. Once in prison they were told that the accusation against them was extended, that socialist ideas in themselves were incompatible with the existence of the Danish state, and that consequently the mere act of propagating them constituted a crime against the Danish constitution. Again the law as laid down in Vienna! The accused are still in prison awaiting their trial.

The Belgian Government, distinguished by its sympathetic reply to Jules Favre's demand of extradition, made haste to propose, through Malou, a hypocritical counterfeit of Dufaure's law.

His Holiness Pope Pius IX gave vent to his feelings in an allocution to a deputation of Swiss Catholics. "Your government," said he, "which is republican, thinks itself bound to make a heavy sacrifice for what is called liberty. It affords an asylum to a goodly number of individuals of the worst character. It tolerates that sect of the International which desires to treat all Europe as it has treated Paris. These gentlemen of the International, who are no gentlemen, are to be feared because they work for the account of the everlasting enemy of God and mankind. What is to be gained by protecting them! One must pray for them."

Hang them first and pray for them afterwards!

Supported by Bismarck, Beust, and Stieber, the Prussian spy-in-chief, the Emperors of Austria and Germany met at Salzburg in the beginning of September, 1871, for the ostensible purpose of founding a holy alliance against the International Working Men's Association. "Such a European alliance," declared the *North German Gazette*, Bismarck's private *Moniteur*, "is the only possible salvation of state, church, property, civilization, in one word, of everything that constitutes European states."

Bismarck's real object, of course, was to prepare alliances for an impending war with Russia, and the International was held up to Austria as a piece of red cloth is held up to a bull.

Lanza suppressed the International in Italy by simple decree. Sagasta declared it an outlaw in Spain, probably with a view to curry favor with the English Stock Exchange. The Russian Government, which since the emancipation of the serfs has been driven to the dangerous expedient of making timid concessions to popular claims today and withdrawing them tomorrow, found in the general hue and cry against the International a pretext for a recrudescence of reaction at home. Abroad, with the intention of prying into the secrets of our Association, it succeeded in inducing a Swiss judge to search, in presence of a Russian spy, the house of Outine, a Russian International, and the editor of the Geneva *Égalité*, the organ of our Romance [Romansh] Federation. The republican government of Switzerland has only been prevented by the agitation of the Swiss Internationals from handing up to Thiers refugees of the Commune.

Finally, the government of Mr. Gladstone, unable to act in Great Britain, at least set forth its good intentions by the police terrorism exercised in Ireland against our sections then in course of formation, and by ordering its representatives abroad to collect information with respect to the International Working Men's Association.

But all the measures of repression which the combined government intellect of Europe was capable of devising vanish into nothing before the war of calumny undertaken by the lying power of the civilized world. Apocryphal histories and mysteries of the International, shameless forgeries of public documents and private letters, sensational telegrams followed each other in rapid succession; all the sluices of slander at the disposal of the venal respectable press were opened at once to set free a deluge of infamy in which to drown the execrated foe. This war of calumny finds no parallel in history for the truly international area over which it has spread, and for the complete accord in which it has been carried on by all shades of ruling class opinion. When the great conflagration took place at Chicago, the telegraph around the world announced it as the infernal deed of the International; and it is really wonderful that to its demoniacal agency has not been attributed the hurricane ravaging the West Indies.

In its former annual reports, the General Council used to give a review of the progress of the Association since the meeting of the preceding Congress. You will appreciate, citizens, the motives which induce us to abstain from that course upon this occasion. Moreover, the reports of the delegates from the various countries, who know best how far their discretion may extend, will in a measure make up for this deficiency. We confine ourselves to the statement that since the Congress at Basel, and chiefly since the London Conference of September, 1871, the International has been extended to the Irish in England and to Ireland itself, to Holland, Denmark, and Portugal, that it has been firmly organized in the United States, and that it has established ramifications in Buenos Aires, Australia, and New Zealand.

The difference between a working class without an International and a working class with an International becomes most evident if we look back to the period of 1848. Years were required for the working class itself to recognize the insurrection of June, 1848, as the work of its own vanguard. The Paris Commune was at once acclaimed by the universal proletariat.

You, the delegates of the working class, meet to strengthen the militant organization of a society aiming at the emancipation of labor and the extinction of national feuds. Almost at the same moment, there meet at Berlin the crowned dignitaries of the old world in order to forge new chains and to hatch new wars.

Long life to the International Working Men's Association!

POLICIES
AND PROGRAMS

EXCEPT for Engels, who became active in the General Council of the International only in the last two years of its life (after he moved to London in 1870), Marx was the only member who was a professional scholar and writer, and who had, moreover, a profound and comprehensive philosophy in regard to the historical role of the working class. He viewed the International as an instrument of that role, and as a clear voice protesting injustice and oppression everywhere. While the International was not essentially a communist organization, Marx, by virtue of his continuing presence in the Council and his undoubted intellectual predominance, was able to imbue it with some of his passion and to make it adopt a number of ideas—in defense of Ireland, Poland, and the Paris Commune, for example—which he formulated in its name.

Poland and the Russian Menace*

MORE than thirty years ago a revolution broke out in France. This was an event not foreseen by St. Petersburg, for shortly before that it had concluded a secret treaty with Charles X for the improvement of Europe's administration and geographic order. Upon the arrival of the news of the revolution, which frustrated all plans, Czar Nicholas assembled the officers of his Guard and delivered to them a brief, warlike speech which ended with the words: To horse, gentlemen! This was no empty threat. Paskevich was sent to Berlin, there to prepare the plan for the invasion of France. Within a few months the plans were ready. The Prussians were to concentrate on the Rhine and the Muscovites were to follow them. But then "the vanguard turned against the main army," as Lafayette said in the Chamber of Deputies. The uprising in Warsaw saved Europe from a second anti-Jacobin war.

Eighteen years later, a new revolutionary eruption, or rather, earthquake, shook the whole Continent. Even Germany began to move, although it had been kept constantly at Russia's apron strings since the so-called War of Independence. Even more astonishing was the fact that, of all German cities, Vienna was the first to set up

* Speech delivered at a meeting on Poland, Cambridge Hall, London, January 22, 1867; published in Polish in *Glos Wolny*, February 10, 1867. The meeting was organized by the General Council of the International, in cooperation with Polish immigrants in London, for the fourth anniversary of the Polish uprising of 1863. *Glos Wolny*, organ of Left-wing Polish immigrants, appeared in London, beginning with January, 1863, three times monthly, under the editorship of Antoni Żabicki. A French translation of the speech, from an English-language manuscript, which Laura Lafargue provided, was published in the Paris socialist paper, *Le Socialisme*, March 15, 1908. This version is translated from the German.

barricades, and to do so with success. This time, for the first time in history, Russia lost its composure. Czar Nicholas no longer turned to the Guard, but published a manifesto to his people in which he complained that the French pestilence had infected even Germany, that it was nearing the borders of the Empire, and that the Revolution in its madness was turning its feverish eyes on Holy Russia. No wonder! he cried out. This Germany, after all, has been for years the refuge of unbelief. The cancer of an infamous philosophy has affected the vital parts of a people that appeared to be so healthy. And he concluded his proclamation with the following appeal to the Germans: "God is with us! Bear it in mind, you heathens, and submit, for God is with us!"

Shortly thereafter he had his faithful servant Nesselrode send a further message to the Germans which dripped with tenderness for this heathenish people.[1] Why this turn? Now the Berliners had not only made a revolution, they had also proclaimed the restoration of Poland, and the Prussian Poles, deceived by the enthusiasm of the people, began to construct military camps in Posen. Hence the flatteries of the Czar. Once again it was the Polish nation, the immortal knight of Europe, that forced the Mongols to retreat! Only after the Germans, especially the Frankfurt National Assembly, betrayed the Poles did Russia begin to breathe again and gather enough strength to deliver the final blow to the Revolution of 1848 in its last refuge, Hungary. And even there, the last knight to oppose Russia was a Pole—General Bem.

Today there are still naïve people who believe that everything would have been different if Poland had ceased to be "a necessary nation," as a French writer put it, yea, even if Poland were only a mere sentimental memory. You know, however, that neither sentiment nor memory is a salable commodity on the exchange. When the last Russian ukase on the insurrection in the Polish kingdom became known in England, the organ of the leading moneybags[2] advised the Poles to become Muscovites. And why should they not, if only to insure the repayment of the six million pounds sterling which the English capitalists had just granted to the Czar? At worst, should Russia seize Constantinople, the *Times* wrote, England would be allowed to seize Egypt in order to secure the route to the great Indian market! In other words: England may leave Constantinople to Russia only if she receives permission from Russia to dispute France's claim to Egypt.

---

1. On July 6, 1848, Nesselrode sent out a circular letter to all the Russian envoys in Germany, attacking the German press for its "calumnies against us." Marx had attacked the circular in an article in the *Neue Rheinische Zeitung* August 3, 1848.
2. The London *Times*, January 7, 1867.

The Muscovite, the *Times* writes, gladly floats loans in England and pays well. He loves English money. He does indeed. How well he likes the English themselves is best described in the *Gazette de Moscou*[3] of December, 1851: "No, the turn of perfidious Albion will finally come, and we will conclude a treaty with that people only in Calcutta."

I ask you, what has changed? Has the danger from the Russian side been lessened? No. Rather, the delusion of the ruling classes of Europe has reached its pinnacle. Above all, nothing has changed in Russia's policy, as her official historian Karamsin admits. Her methods, her tactics, her maneuvers may change, but the pole star—world domination—is immutable. Only a crafty government, ruling over a mass of barbarians, could devise such a plan nowadays. Pozzo di Borgo, the greatest Russian diplomat of modern times, wrote to Alexander I during the Congress of Vienna that Poland was the most important instrument in carrying out Russian intentions for world domination; but it is also an insurmountable obstacle, if the Pole, tired of its unceasing betrayal by Europe, does not become a fearful whip in the hands of the Muscovites. Now, without speaking of the mood of the Polish people, I ask: Has anything taken place that would frustrate Russia's plans or paralyze her actions?

I do not have to tell you that her conquests in Asia are making constant progress. I do not have to tell you that the so-called Anglo-French war against Russia delivered the mountain fortresses in the Caucasus to the latter and gave her domination over the Black Sea and maritime rights—something that Catherine II, Paul, and Alexander II had vainly tried to wrest from England. Railroads unite and concentrate her forces once scattered over a wide area. Her material resources in Congress Poland,[4] which constitute her fortified camp in Europe, have increased colossally. The fortresses of Warsaw, Modlin, Ivangorod, points once selected by Napoleon I, dominate the whole length of the Vistula and comprise a formidable base for attacks on the north, west and south. Pan-Slavic propaganda progresses to the extent that Austria and Turkey become weakened. And what Pan-Slavic propaganda means you can see from 1848–49, when Hungary was invaded, Vienna ravaged, and Italy pulverized by the Slavs who fought under Jellachich, Windischgrätz, and Radetzky. And as if this were not enough, England's crime against Ireland created for Russia a powerful new ally on the other side of the Atlantic.

Peter I once said that to conquer the world, the Muscovites lack

---

3. *Moscovskye Vedomosti*, a Moscow daily, organ of the Russian ruling classes, published from 1756 to 1917.

4. The part of the kingdom of Poland that fell to Russia by the decision of the Congress of Vienna, 1814–15.

nothing except souls.[5] The invigorating spirit that Moscow needs will be acquired only with the engorging of the Poles. What will they then have to throw into the scales? This question is being answered from many points of view. Some say that if she emancipated the peasants, Russia can belong to the family of civilized nations. Others maintain that German power, recently concentrated in the hands of Prussia, can defy all Asiatic attacks. Still others, more radical, place their hope in internal social transformations of Western Europe.[6]

In regard to the first—that is, the emancipation of the serfs—the government has freed itself from the obstacles that the nobility could have put in the way of its centralization. It created a wide field for the recruiting of its army, dissolved the community property of the peasants, isolated them, and strengthened their faith in the Czar as a Little Father. It did not free them from Asiatic barbarism, for it takes centuries to build civilization. Every attempt to elevate the moral level of the peasants is considered a crime and punished as such. I only remind you of the temperance unions, which aimed to save the Muscovite from what Feuerbach calls the substance of his religion, namely, alcohol. Whatever one may expect of the peasant emancipation in the future, it is clear in any case that, for the time being, it has enlarged the powers at the disposal of the Czar.

We now come to Prussia. Once a vassal of Poland, it has become, under the aegis of Russia and because of the partition of Poland, a power of the first rank. If it lost its Polish booty tomorrow, it would merge into Germany, instead of swallowing it. In order to maintain itself as a separate power in Germany, it has to depend on the Muscovite. The most recent extension of its rule has not loosened this tie at all, but rather made it indissoluble and strengthened its antagonism to France and Austria. At the same time Russia is the pillar on which the unrestrained rule of the Hohenzollern dynasty and its feudal vassals rests. Russia is Prussia's shield against the anger of the people.

---

5. In the version in *Le Socialisme* this sentence reads: "The plan of Russian policy remains unchanged; its means of action have grown considerably since 1848, and until now only one thing has remained beyond its reach—and Peter the Great touched on this weak point when he said that for conquering the world, the Muscovites lack nothing except souls."

6. In the version of *Le Socialisme*, the concluding sentences of this paragraph read: "A continental European would perhaps answer me that with the emancipation of the peasants, Russia can belong to the family of civilized nations, that German power, recently concentrated in the hands of Prussia, can defy all Asiatic attacks, and that, finally, the social revolution in Western Europe would put an end to the danger of 'international conflicts.' But an Englishman, who reads only the *Times*, could answer me that, at worst, if Russia conquers Constantinople, England would annex Egypt and thus secure for itself the route to the great Indian market."

Hence Prussia is no wall against Russia, but the latter's tool, destined to invade France and conquer Germany.

And the social revolution—what else is it but a class conflict? It is possible that the conflict between workers and capitalists will be less cruel and bloody than the conflict between feudal lords and capitalists in England and France. Let us hope so. But in any case, such a social crisis, even if it could enhance the energies of the people of the West, would, like any other inner conflict, call forth aggression from outside. Thus Russia would again play the role she did during the anti-Jacobin war and the Holy Alliance—the role of a savior of Order chosen by Providence. It would enlist in its ranks all the privileged classes of Europe. Already, during the February Revolution, it was not only Count Montalembert who had his ear to the ground to hear the hoof beats of the approaching Cossack horses. The Prussian bumpkin-Junkers were not the only ones who, in the representative corporate bodies of Germany, proclaimed the Czar the "Father and Protector." On all the European exchanges shares rose with every Russian victory and fell with every Russian defeat.

Thus Europe faces only one alternative: Either Asian barbarism, under the leadership of the Muscovites, will come down on Europe like an avalanche, or Europe must restore Poland and thereby protect itself against Asia with a wall of twenty million heroes, to win time for the consummation of its social transformation.

On the Fenian Prisoners in Manchester*

Memorial of the General Council of the International
Working Men's Association

To the Right Hon. Gathorne-Hardy, Her Majesty's Secretary of State:
The memorial of the undersigned,[1] representing workingmen's
associations in all parts of Europe, showeth:

That the execution of the Irish prisoners condemned to death
at Manchester will greatly impair the moral influence of England upon
the European continent. The execution of the four prisoners resting
upon the same evidence and the same verdict which, by the free
pardon of Maguire, have been officially declared, the one false, the
other erroneous, will bear the stamp not of a judicial act, but of
political revenge. But even if the verdict of the Manchester jury and
the evidence it rests upon had not been tainted by the British Government itself, the latter would now have to choose between the
bloody-handed practices of old Europe and the magnanimous humanity of the young Transatlantic Republic.

The commutation of the sentence for which we pray will be an
act not only of justice, but of political wisdom.[2]

---

* Written in English, and unanimously adopted at a special meeting of the
General Council, November 20, 1867, this statement was not printed in the
English press. A French translation appeared in *Le Courrier français*, November
24, 1867.
    1. John Weston, chairman; Robert Shaw, secretary for America; Eugène
Dupont, secretary for France; Karl Marx, secretary for Germany; Hermann
Jung, secretary for Switzerland; Paul LaFargue, secretary for Spain; Anton
Zabicki, secretary for Poland; Derkinderen, secretary for Holland; Alexandre
Besson, secretary for Belgium; J. Georg Eccarius, general secretary.
    2. On September 18, 1867, five Fenians were arrested on the charge of killing

By order of the General Council of the International Working Men's Association.

---

a policeman. They were condemned to death. Of the five, one (Maguire) was released, another (Condon) had his sentence commuted to life imprisonment, and the rest (Larkin, Allen, and O'Brien) were executed on November 23, 1867. The executions caused a storm of protest in Ireland and England.

On the Irish Question*

ON December 16 Karl Marx delivered a lecture before the London Workers' Educational Society on the situation in Ireland, from which it appeared that all efforts of the English Government in previous centuries to Anglicize the Irish population had been in vain. The English immigrants, including the aristocrats, who settled there during the Reformation had been turned by Irishwomen into Irishmen, and their progeny has fought against England. The war atrocities committed against the Irish under Queen Elizabeth—the destruction of crops, the removal of the population from one part of the country to another to make room for English colonists—have changed nothing. At that time, gentlemen and merchant adventurers received large tracts of land with the proviso that they colonize them with Englishmen. In Cromwell's time, the descendants of those colonists fought on the side of the Irish against the English. Cromwell sold many of them as slaves to the West Indies. Under the Restoration, Ireland was favored in many ways. Under William III, a new class, interested only in making money, came to power, and in order to compel the Irish to sell their raw materials to England at any price, Irish industry was suppressed. With the help of Protestant penal laws, the new aristocrats were given a free hand under Queen Anne. The Irish parliament became an instrument of oppression. No Catholic could hold an official position, own landed property, make a will, or acquire an inheritance; to be a Catholic bishop was high treason. All these were means of

---

* Summary of a lecture before the German Workers' Educational Society in London, December 16, 1867. The notes, taken down by Johann Georg Eccarius, secretary of the International, were designed for publication in *Der Vorbote* in Geneva. *Der Vorbote* did not publish them.

robbing the Irish of their land; despite that, more than half the English descendants in Ulster remained Catholic. The people were driven into the arms of the Catholic clergy, who thereby acquired their power. All that the English Government succeeded in doing was to plant an aristocracy in Ireland. The cities built by the English became Irish. This is why one finds so many English names among the Fenians.

At the time of the American Revolution, the reins were somewhat loosened. Further concessions became necessary in the period of the French Revolution. Ireland rebelled so quickly that her inhabitants threatened to outflank the English. The English government drove Ireland to rebellion and effected the Anglo-Irish Union [1801] through bribery. The Union gave the reviving Irish industry its death blow. Meagher remarked on one occasion that all Irish industrial branches were destroyed and only the manufacture of coffins was left to us. Possession of land became a matter of life and death; the big landowners leased their lands to speculators, land going through four or five leasing stages before it reached the peasants, who found the price disproportionately high. The country people lived on potatoes and water; wheat and meat were sent to England; rents were consumed in London, Paris, and Florence. In the year 1836, £7,000,000 was sent out to absentee landlords abroad. Together with produce and rents, manure was also exported, and the land became exhausted. Partial famines occurred frequently, but there was a general famine in 1846, the result of a potato blight. 1,000,000 people died of hunger. The potato blight resulted from the exhaustion of the land, produced by English rule.

With the abolition of the Corn Laws, Ireland lost her monopoly in the English market, and the old lease rentals could no longer be paid. The high cost of meat and the bankruptcy of the remaining small landowners contributed to the driving out of small peasants and the transformation of their holdings into sheep meadows. Since 1860, more than half a million acres have been taken out of agricultural use. Production per acre has diminished: oats by 16 percent, flax by 36 percent, potatoes by 50 percent. Now oats are raised only for the English market, and wheat is being imported.

With the exhaustion of the soil, the population has deteriorated physically. The lame, the blind, the deaf mutes, and the mentally ill have increased absolutely in a declining population.

More than 1,100,000 people have been replaced by 9,600,000 sheep. Things of this nature are unheard of in Europe. The Russians replace transported Poles with Russians, not with sheep. Only among the Mongols in China was the question once discussed of razing the cities in order to make room for sheep.

The Irish question is therefore not merely a nationality question, but a land-and-existence question. The slogan is: ruin or revolution; the Irish are all convinced that if anything is to happen, it has to happen quickly. The English should demand separation and leave it to the Irish themselves to solve the question of land ownership. Everything else is useless. If it does not happen soon, the Irish immigration will cause a war of America against England. The domination of Ireland today is nothing but the English aristocracy's collecting money for leases.

Machinery in the Hands of Capitalists*

THE discussion of the proposition, "The influence of machinery in the hands of capitalists," was opened by Citizen Marx.[1] He said what strikes us most is that all the consequences which were expected as the inevitable result of machinery have been reversed. Instead of diminishing the hours of labor, the working day was prolonged to sixteen and eighteen hours. Formerly, the normal working day was ten hours; during the last century the hours of labor were increased by law here as well as on the Continent. The whole of the trade legislation of the last century turns upon compelling the working people by law to work longer hours.

It was not until 1833 that the hours of labor for children were limited to twelve. In consequence of overwork there was no time left whatever for mental culture. They also became physically deteriorated; contagious fevers broke out among them, and this induced a portion of the upper class to take the matter up. The first Sir Robert Peel was one of the foremost in calling attention to the crying evil, and Robert Owen was the first mill owner who limited the hours of labor in his factory. The ten-hours bill was the first law which limited the hours of labor to ten and a half per day for women and children but it applied only to certain factories.

This was a step of progress, insofar as it afforded more leisure time to the workpeople. With regard to production, the limitation has long since been overtaken. By improved machinery and increased intensity of the labor of individuals there is now more work done

---

* From the minutes of the General Council, July 28, 1868.
1. Marx developed this idea in *Capital*, Vol. I, Ch. XV, "Machinery and Modern Industry."

in the short day than formerly in the long day. People are again overworked, and it will soon become necessary to limit the working day to eight hours.

Another consequence of the use of machinery was to force women and children into the factory. The woman has thus become an active agent in our social production. Formerly female and children's labor was carried on within the family circle. I do not say that it is wrong that women and children should participate in our social production. I think every child above the age of nine ought to be employed at productive labor a portion of its time, but the way in which they are made to work under existing circumstances is abominable.

Another consequence of the use of machinery was that it entirely changed the relations of the capital of the country. Formerly there were wealthy employers of labor, and poor laborers who worked with their own tools. They were to a certain extent free agents who had it in their power effectually to resist their employers. For the modern factory operative, for the women and children, such freedom does not exist, they are slaves of capital.

There was a constant cry for some invention that might render the capitalist independent of the workingman; the spinning machine and power loom has rendered him independent, it has transformed the motive power of production into his hands. By this the power of the capitalist has been immensely increased. The factory lord has become a penal legislator within his own establishment, inflicting fines at will, frequently for his own aggrandizement. The feudal baron in his dealings with his serfs was bound by traditions and subject to certain definite rules; the factory lord is subject to no controlling agency of any kind.

One of the great results of machinery is organized labor which must bear fruit sooner or later. The influence of machinery upon those with whose labor it enters into competition is directly hostile. Many hand-loom weavers were positively killed by the introduction of the power loom both here and in India.

We are frequently told that the hardships resulting from machinery are only temporary, but the development of machinery is constant, and if it attracts and gives employment to large numbers at one time it constantly throws large numbers out of employment. There is a continual surplus of displaced population, not as the Malthusian asserts a surplus population in relation to the produce of the country, but a surplus whose labor has been superseded by more productive agencies.

Employed on land, machinery produces a constantly increasing surplus population whose employment is not fluctuating. This surplus flocks to the towns and exercises a constant pressure, a wage-lowering pressure upon the labor market. The state of the East of London is one of the phenomena it produces.

The real consequences are best seen in those branches of labor in which the machine is not employed.

To conclude for the present, machinery leads on one hand to associated organized labor, on the other to the disintegration of all formerly existing social and family relations.

Citizen Weston said the previous speaker had only referred to machinery in the factory districts . . . If a man with a machine could do in ten hours what required ten days if done by hand, this would not diminish the aggregate demand for labor. If it rained hats from heaven for people to wear for nothing that would not diminish the aggregate demand for labor. . . .

Marx told Mr. Weston that he must consider the question of the hats being monopolized as the property of the capitalist.

Hours of Labor*

CITIZEN ECCARIUS then opened the debate on the reduction of the hours of labor question. He said: Forty years ago a man working twelve hours a day would have received sufficient for making a dozen pair of trousers to support a family for two weeks. . . . In 1861 there were 12,000 females employed in the tailoring trade of the metropolis, 3,000 of whom never worked less than fourteen, frequently sixteen or eighteen hours a day, occasionally all night, for seven to ten shillings a week. I know, from good authority, that there are practices quite as bad in other trades where women and children are employed. . . . He then proved, from government statistics, that the development and increase of the powers of production in our staple trades had far outstripped the increased demand for labor or the increased number of persons employed. In proof of this he read a statement from Dr. Marx's work on political economy [*Capital*], according to which the number of adult persons employed diminished by 1,700 between 1856 and 1862; but the number of children under fourteen years of age had increased. . . .

Citizen Milner could not take the same view of the subject. A general reduction of the hours of labor, however desirable, meant a diminution of the production of wealth; the opposition it would encounter from those who had amassed large fortunes out of other people's labor would be too great for the working classes to overcome. He thought a rise of wages could easier be obtained; the reduction of the hours of labor would follow that.

Citizen Marx could not coincide with [Milner], that it would lead to a diminished production, because where the restrictions had been

* From the minutes of the General Council, August 11, 1868.

[95]

introduced, the instruments of production had been vastly more developed than in other trades. It had the effect of introducing more machinery, and made production on a small scale more and more impossible, which, however, was necessary to arrive at social production. The sanitary question was settled. But a reduction of the hours of labor was also indispensable to give the working class more time for mental culture. Legislative restrictions were the first step toward the mental and physical elevation and the ultimate emancipation of the working classes. Nobody denied, nowadays, that the state must interfere on behalf of the women and children; and a restriction of their hours led, in most instances, to a reduction of the working time of the men. England had taken the lead, other countries had been obliged to follow to some extent. The agitation had seriously commenced in Germany, and the London Council was looked to for taking the lead. The principle had been decided at former congresses; the time for action had arrived.

The Belgian Massacres*

To the Workmen of Europe and the United States

THERE passes hardly a week in England without strikes—and strikes upon a grand scale. If on such occasions the government was to let its soldiers loose upon the working class, this land of strikes would become a land of massacres, but not for many a week. After a few such physical force experiments, the powers that be would be nowhere. In the United States, too, the number and scale of strikes have continued to increase during the last few years, and even sometimes assumed a riotous character. But no blood was spilled. In some of the great military states of continental Europe the era of strikes may be dated from the end of the American Civil War. But here again no blood was spilled. There exists but one country in the civilized world where every strike is eagerly and joyously turned into a pretext for the official massacre of the working class. That country of single blessedness is Belgium—the model state of continental constitutionalism, the snug, well-hedged little paradise of the landlord, the capitalist, and the priest. The earth performs not more surely its yearly revolution than the Belgian Government its yearly workingmen's massacre. The massacre of this year does not differ from last year's massacre but by the ghastlier number of its victims, the more hideous ferocity of an otherwise ridiculous army, the noisier jubilation of the clerical and capitalist press, and the intensified frivolity of the pretexts put forward by the governmental butchers.

It is now proved, even by the involuntary evidence of the capitalist

* Approved by the General Council May 4, 1869, and published as a pamphlet in English, French, and German.

press, that the quite legitimate strike of the puddlers in the Cockerill Ironworks, at Seraing, was only converted into a riot by a strong posse of cavalry and gendarmerie suddenly launched upon that place in order to provoke the people. From the ninth to the twelfth of April these stout warriors not only recklessly charged with saber and bayonet the unarmed workmen, they indiscriminately killed and wounded harmless passers-by, forcibly broke into private houses, and even amused themselves with repeated furious onslaughts on the travelers pent up in the Seraing railway station. When these days of horror had passed away it became bruited about that Mr. Kamp, the mayor of Seraing, was an agent of the Cockerill Joint Stock Company, that the Belgian Home Minister, a certain Mr. Pirmez, was the largest shareholder in a neighboring colliery also on strike, and that His Royal Highness the Prince of Flanders had invested 1,500,000 francs in the Cockerill concern. Hence people jump to the truly strange conclusion that the Seraing massacre was a sort of joint stock company *coup d'état*, quietly plotted between the firm Cockerill and the Belgian Home Minister for the simple purpose of striking terror unto their disaffected subjects. This calumny, however, was soon after victoriously refuted by the later events occurring in Le Borinage, a colliery district where the Belgian Home Minister, the said Mr. Pirmez, seems not to be a leading capitalist. An almost general strike having broken out among the miners of that district, numerous troops were concentrated, who opened their campaign at Frameries by a fusillade which killed nine and grievously wounded twenty miners, *after* which little preliminary exploit the Riot Act, singularly enough styled in French "*les sommations préalables*" [preliminary summations], was read, and then the butchery proceeded with.

Some politicians trace these incredible deeds to motives of a sublime patriotism. While just negotiating on some ticklish points with their French neighbor, the Belgian Government, they say, was bound in duty to show off the heroism of its army. Hence that scientific division of arms displaying, first, the irresistible impetuosity of the Belgian cavalry at Seraing, and then the steady vigor of the Belgian infantry at Frameries. To frighten the foreigner, what means more infallible than such homely battles, which one does not know how to lose, and such domestic battlefields, where the hundreds of workmen killed, mutilated, and made prisoners shed so glorious a luster upon those invulnerable warriors who all of them, to a man, get off with their skins safe.

Other politicians, on the contrary, suspect the Belgian ministers to be sold to the Tuileries, and to periodically enact these horrible scenes of a mock civil war with the deliberate aim of affording Louis

Bonaparte a pretext for saving society in Belgium as he has saved it in France. But was Ex-Governor Eyre ever accused of having organized the Negro massacre at Jamaica in order to wrest that island from England and place it into the hands of the United States? No doubt the Belgian ministers are excellent patriots of the Eyre pattern. As he was the unscrupulous tool of the West Indian planter, they are the unscrupulous tools of the Belgian capitalist.

The Belgian capitalist has won fair fame in the world by his eccentric passion for what he calls the liberty of labor (*la liberté du travail*). So fond is he of the liberty of his hands to labor for him all the hours of their life, without exemption of age or sex, that he has always indignantly repulsed any factory law encroaching upon that liberty. He shudders at the very idea that a common workman should be wicked enough to claim any higher destiny than that of enriching his master and natural superior. He wants his workman not only to remain a miserable drudge, overworked and underpaid, but like every other slaveholder he wants him to be a clinging, servile, brokenhearted, morally prostrate, religiously humble drudge. Hence his frantic fury at strikes. With him a strike is a blasphemy, a slave's revolt, the signal of a social cataclysm. Put, now, into the hands of such men—cruel from sheer cowardice—the undivided, uncontrolled absolute sway of the state power, as is actually the case in Belgium, and you will no longer wonder to find the saber, the bayonet, and the musket working in that country as legitimate and normal instruments for keeping wages down and screwing profits up. But in point of fact, what other earthly purpose could a Belgian army serve? When by the dictation of official Europe Belgium was declared a *neutral country*, it ought, as a matter of course, have been forbidden the costly luxury of an army, save, perhaps, a handful of soldiers, just sufficient to mount the royal guard and parade at a royal puppet show. Yet within its 536 square leagues of territory Belgium harbors an army greater than that of the United Kingdom or the United States. The field service of this neutralized army is fatally computed by the number of its *razzias* upon the working class.

It will easily be understood that the International Working Men's Association was no welcome guest in Belgium. Excommunicated by the priest, calumniated by the respectable press, it came soon to loggerheads with the government. The latter tried to get rid of it by making it responsible for the Charleroi colliery strikes of 1867–68, strikes wound up, after the invariable Belgian rule, by official massacres, followed by the judicial prosecution of the victims. Not only was this cabal baffled, but the Association took active steps, resulting in a verdict of not guilty for the Charleroi miners, and, consequently, in a verdict of guilty against the government itself. Fretting at this defeat, the Belgian ministers gave vent to their spleen by fierce denunciations, from the tribune of the Chamber of Deputies, against the International Working Men's Association, and pompously declared they should never allow its General Congress to meet at Brussels. In the teeth of their menaces the Congress met at Brussels. But now at last the International is to succumb before the 536 square leagues of Belgian Omnipotence. Its culpable complicity during the recent events has been proved beyond the possibility of doubt. The emissaries of the Brussels Central Committee for Belgium and some of the local committees stand convicted of several flagrant crimes. In the first instance, they have tried hard to calm the excitement of the workmen on strike and warn them off the government traps. In some localities they have actually prevented the effusion of blood. And last, not least, these ill-boding emissaries observed on the spot, verified by witnesses, noted carefully down and publicly denounced the sanguinary vagaries of the defenders of order. By the simple process of imprisonment they were at once converted from the accusers into the accused. Then the domiciles of the members of the Brussels Committee were brutally invaded, all their papers seized, and some of them arrested on the charge of belonging to an association *"founded for the purpose of attempting the lives and properties of individuals."* In other words, they were impeached of belonging to an Association of Thugs commonly styled the International Working Men's Association. Hunted on by the raving capucinades of the clerical and the savage howls of the capitalist press, this swaggering pygmy government is decidedly anxious to drown itself in a morass of ridicule, after having weltered in a sea of blood.

Already the Belgian Central Committee at Brussels has announced its intention to institute, and afterwards publish the results of, a full inquiry into the massacres of Seraing and Le Borinage. We will circulate their revelations all over the world, in order to open the eyes of the world on the pet fanfaronade of the Belgian capitalist: *La liberté, pour faire le tour du monde, n'a pas besoin de passer par ici (la Belgique).* [Liberty, in traveling around the world, has no need of passing through Belgium.]

Perhaps the Belgian Government flatters itself that having, after the revolutions of 1848–49, gained a respite of life by becoming the police agent of all the reactionary governments of the Continent, it may now again avert imminent danger by conspicuously playing the gendarme of capital against labor. This, however, is a serious mistake. Instead of delaying, they will thus only hasten the catastrophe. By making Belgium a byword and a nickname with the popular masses all over the world, they will remove the last obstacle in the way of the despots bent upon wiping that country's name off the map of Europe.

The General Council of the International Working Men's Association hereby calls upon the workmen of Europe and the United States to open monetary subscriptions for alleviating the sufferings of the widows, wives, and children of the Belgian victims, and also for the expenses incident upon the legal defense of the arrested workmen, and the inquiry proposed by the Brussels Committee.

By order of the General Council of the International Working Men's Association,

R. Applegarth, Chairman
R. Shaw, Secretary for America
Bernard, Secretary for Belgium
Eugène Dupont, Secretary for France
Karl Marx, Secretary for Germany
Jules Johannard, Secretary for Italy
A. Zabicki, Secretary for Poland
H. Jung, Secretary for Switzerland
Cowell Stepney, Treasurer

All contributions for the victims of the Belgian massacre to be sent to the Office of the General Council, 256 High Holborn, London, W.C.

Defense of America Against England*

Fellow Workmen:

In the initiatory program of our Association we stated: "It was not the wisdom of the ruling classes, but the heroic resistance to their criminal folly by the working classes of England, that saved the west of Europe from plunging headlong into an infamous crusade for the perpetuation and propagation of slavery on the other side of the Atlantic." Your turn has now come to stop a war the clearest result of which would be, for an indefinite period, to hurl back the ascendant movement of the working class on both sides of the Atlantic.

We need hardly tell you that there exist European powers anxiously bent upon hurrying the United States into a war with England. A glance at commercial statistics will show that the Russian export of raw produce, and Russia has nothing else to export, was rapidly giving way before American competition when the civil war suddenly turned the scales. To convert the American plowshares into swords would just now rescue from impending bankruptcy that despotic power which your republican statesmen have, in their wisdom, chosen for their confidential adviser. But quite apart from the particular interests

---

* "Address to the National Labor Union of the United States," written in English in the name of the International, May 11, 1869. From the minutes of the General Council, May 11, 1869, recorded by the secretary, J. Georg Eccarius: "Citizen Marx then rose and said that most members would have seen a letter from Professor Goldwin Smith in the *Bee-Hive* [May 8, 1869] respecting the impression made in America by the speech of Senator Sumner, and he, Citizen Marx, had thought it was a proper occasion for the Council to appeal to the workingmen of America to put a stop to these menaces of the Republican party. With this intention he had drawn up an address to the National Labor Union of the United States which, if approved of by the Council, should be adopted and sent to America. He then read as follows . . ."

of this or that government, is it not the general interest of our common oppressors to turn our fast-growing international cooperation into an internecine war?

In a congratulatory address to Mr. Lincoln on his reelection as president, we expressed our conviction that the American Civil War would prove of as great import to the advancement of the working class as the American War of Independence had proved to that of the middle class. And, in point of fact, the victorious termination of the antislavery war has opened a new epoch in the annals of the working class. In the States themselves, an independent working-class movement, looked upon with an evil eye by your old parties and their professional politicians, has since that date sprung into life. To fructify it wants years of peace. To crush it, a war between the United States and England is wanted.

The next palpable effect of the Civil War was, of course, to deteriorate the position of the American workman. In the United States, as in Europe, the monster incubus of a national debt was shifted from hand to hand, to settle down on the shoulders of the working class. The prices of necessaries, says one of your statesmen, have since 1860 risen 78 percent, while the wages of unskilled labor rose 50 percent, those of skilled labor 60 percent only. "Pauperism," he complains, "grows now in America faster than population." Moreover, the sufferings of the working classes set off as a foil the newfangled luxury of financial aristocrats, shoddy aristocrats, and similar vermin bred by wars. Yet for all this the Civil War did compensate by freeing the slave and the consequent moral impetus it gave to your own class movement. A second war, not hallowed by a sublime purpose and a great social necessity, but of the Old World's type, would forge chains for the free laborer instead of tearing asunder those of the slave. The accumulated misery left in its track would afford your capitalists at once the motive and the means to divorce the working class from its bold and just aspirations by the soulless sword of a standing army.

On you, then, depends the glorious task to prove to the world that now at last the working classes are bestriding the scene of history no longer as servile retainers, but as independent actors, conscious of their own responsibility, and able to command peace where their would-be masters shout war.[1]

In the name of the General Council of the International Working Men's Association

---

1. The minutes of the meeting continue: "Citizen Odger took objection to the word *vermin.* Citizen Lucraft rather preferred it and Citizen Marx stated that no other word could be substituted without altering the context . . . It was agreed that all the Council members should sign it and that their occupation should be stated."

British nationality: *R. Applegarth*, carpenter; *M. J. Boon*, engineer; *J. Buckley*, painter, *J. Hales*, elastic web weaver; *Harriet Law; B. Lucraft*, chair maker; *J. Milner*, tailor; *G. Odger*, shoemaker; *J. Ross*, bootcloser; *B. Shaw*, painter; *Cowell Stepney; J. Warren*, trunk maker; *J. Weston*, handrail maker. French nationality: *E. Dupont*, instrument maker; *Jules Johannard*, lithographer; *Paul Lafargue*. German nationality: *G. Eccarius*, tailor; *F. Lessner*, tailor; *W. Limburg*, shoemaker; *Karl Marx*. Swiss nationality: *H. Jung*, watchmaker; *A. Müller*, watchmaker. Belgian nationality: *M. Bernard*, painter. Danish nationality: *J. Cohn*, cigar maker. Polish nationality: *Zabicki*, compositor.

B. Lucraft, Chairman
Cowell Stepney, Treasurer
J. Georg Eccarius, General Secretary

Social Right and Social Necessity*

CITIZEN BOON . . . considered the claim of right preferable to social necessity. . . . He was in favor . . . to claim the soil as natural right.

Citizen Marx was of opinion that . . . there was no opposition to the mines and woods being made common property. The injury caused by the accumulation of land in the hands of the few was granted; it was only with regard to arable land that there was any dispute, the opposition came from the partisans of small farming; small property was the point in dispute.

The plea of social necessity was superior to the claim of abstract right. Everything, every possible form of oppression had been justified by abstract right; it was high time to abandon this mode of agitation. The question was, under what form this right should be realized. There was a social necessity to transform feudal property into peasant property. In England the proprietor had ceased to be a necessity in agriculture.

As for natural right, the animal had a natural right to the soil since it cannot live without it. To push this natural right to its logical consequences would land us at the assertion of every individual to cultivate his own share.

Social right and social necessity determined in what manner the means of subsistence must be procured. Social necessity enforced itself in the course of which factory had arrived where cooperation was compulsory. The fact that no one could produce anything by

---

* From the minutes of the General Council, July 6, 1869, recorded by J. Georg Eccarius.

himself gave the social necessity for cooperation. He was not against giving a more emphatic form to the resolutions.[1]

1. The resolution read: "Confirming the views already expressed by the last Congress that the lands, mines, etc. should be the property of the state for the benefit of the whole people;

"That the individual ownership of large tracts of land, mines, etc., has given a power to the few over the many, incompatible with the freedom of a nation;

"That the only way to realize the natural right of every individual to an interest in the soil of his country is to make land the property of all for all."

The Right of Inheritance*

CITIZEN MARX opened the discussion on the question: The Right of Inheritance. He said the question had been put by the Alliance of Socialist Democrats of Geneva and the Council had accepted it for discussion. The Alliance of Geneva demanded above all the entire abolition of the right of inheritance. There were two forms of inheritance. The testamentary right, or inheritance by will, had come from Rome and had been peculiar to Rome. The father of the Roman family had exercised absolute authority over everything belonging to his household. The Roman family father must not be compared with the father of a family of the present day. The Roman household had included slaves and clients whose affairs and interests the head had been obliged to defend and maintain in public. There had been a superstition that when this man died his ghost remained as a watch in the house to see that things were done right or to torment if things were managed wrong. In the early times of Rome people had sacrificed to this house god; even blood feasts had been celebrated in his honor and to appease his wrath. By and by it had become fashionable to compromise with this spirit by a heir-at-will. It had been the Roman immortality of the soul. The will of the deceased had been perpetuated by a testament, but this testament had not necessarily brought a fortune to the successor who inherited, but the will of the deceased had been looked upon as a religious duty. In course of time these heirs-at-will had laid claim to the fortune too, but even in imperial times had never been allowed more than a fourth by law. That pagan superstition had been transmitted to Christian countries and was the

* From the minutes of the General Council, July 20, 1869, recorded by J. Georg Eccarius.

foundation of the right of will as at present existing in England and the United States.

The German right of inheritance was the intestate right, the family right, which treated an estate as a sort of co-proprietorship of which the father of the family was the manager. When this manager died the property fell to all the children. The Germans had known of no other hereditary rights; the Church of Rome had introduced the Roman right and the feudal system had falsified the German right, because feudal property bearing a military charge could not have been divided. The French Revolution had returned to the German right of inheritance. In England we had all sorts of nonsensical things; the individual had the most absolute right to will away his property, even to disinherit his own offspring, and by this, rule long after he had ceased to exist.[1] This right of will might be left for the middle class to deal with as it was a point which would work against the aristocracy. In Prussia only a little of a man's property could be willed away.

The working class who had nothing to inherit had no interest in the question.

The Democratic Alliance was going to commence the social revolution with the abolition of the right of inheritance. He asked would it be policy to do so?

The proposition was not new. St. Simon had proposed it in 1830.

As an economical measure it would avail nothing. It would cause so much irritation that it would be sure to raise an almost insurmountable opposition which would inevitably lead to reaction. If at the time of a revolution it was proclaimed, he did not believe that the general state of intelligence would warrant its being sustained. Besides, if the working class had sufficient power to abolish the right of inheritance, it would be powerful enough to proceed to expropriation, which would be a much simpler and more efficient process.

To abolish the right to the inheritance of land in England would involve the hereditary functions connected with the land, the House of Lords, etc., and 15,000 lords and 15,000 ladies would have to die before it became available. If, on the contrary, a workingmen's parliament decreed that the rent should be paid into the treasury instead of to the landlord, the government would obtain a fund at once without any social disturbance, while by abolishing the right of inheritance everything would be disturbed and nothing got.

Our efforts must be directed to the end that no instruments of production should be private property. The private property in these things was a fiction, since the proprietors could not use them them-

---

1. The next sentence, "It was what kept the aristocracy in its present position and could be left to the middle class," is crossed out in the minutes.

selves; they only gave them dominion over them, by which they compelled other people to work for them. In a semibarbarous state this might have been necessary, but it was no longer so. All the means of labor must be socialized, so that every man had a right and the means to exercise his labor power. If we had such a state of things the right of inheritance would be of no use. As long as we had not, the family right of inheritance could not be abolished. The chief aim of people in saving for their children was to insure them the means of subsistence. If a man's children were provided for after his death he could not care about leaving them wherewith to get a living, but as long as this was not the case it would only result in hardships, it would irritate and frighten people and do no good. Instead of the beginning it could only be the end of a social revolution. The beginning must be to get the means to socialize the means of labor.

The testamentary right of inheritance was obnoxious to the middle class; with this the state could safely interfere any time. We had legacy duties already, all we had to do was to increase them and make them progressive, as well as the income tax, leaving the smaller amounts, £50 for instance, free. Insofar only it was a working-class question.

All that was connected with the present state of things would have to be transformed, but if testaments were suppressed they would be avoided by gifts during life, therefore it would be better to tolerate them on certain conditions than do worse. First the means for a transformed state of things must be got, then the right would disappear of itself.

Citizen Milner said it was but natural that people should question the right of inheritance seeing that so many were disinherited. Possession was nine points of the law, and in all ages people had striven to get possession of things. If all had the same right, there would be a family right to be divided, but if not, some would be dispossessed and others would keep possession forever. Had one man a right to disinherit another? It led to dualisms in the family. Possession led to dominion and dominion to slavery. . . .

Citizen Marx replied: If the state had the power to appropriate the land, inheritance was gone. To declare the abolition of inheritance would be foolish. If a revolution occurred, expropriation could be carried; if there was no power to do that, the right of inheritance would not be abolished.

Citizen Marx consented to furnish [a resolution] at the next meeting.[2]

---

2. August 3, 1869.

Report of the General Council on the Right of Inheritance*

1. THE RIGHT of inheritance is only of social import insofar as it leaves to the heir the power which the deceased wielded *during his lifetime,* viz., *the power of transferring to himself,* by means of his property, the *produce of other people's labor.* For instance, land gives the living proprietor the power to transfer to himself, under the name of rent, without any equivalent, the produce of other people's labor. Capital gives him the power to do the same under the name of profit and interest. The property in public funds gives him the power to live without labor upon other people's labor, etc.

Inheritance does not *create* that power of transferring the produce of one man's labor into another man's pocket—it only relates to the change in the individuals who yield that power. Like all other civil legislation, the laws of inheritance are not the cause, but the effect, the juridical consequence of the existing economical organization of society, based upon private property in the means of production; that is to say, in land, raw material, machinery, etc. In the same way the right of inheritance in the slave is not the cause of slavery, but on the contrary, slavery is the cause of inheritance in slaves.

2. What we have to grapple with is the cause and not the effect— the economical basis, not its juridical superstructure. Suppose the means of production transformed from private into social prosperity, then the right of inheritance (so far as it is of any social importance) would die of itself, because a man only leaves after his death what he possessed during his lifetime. Our great aim must, therefore, be to supersede those institutions which give to some people, *during their*

---

* Written August 2–3, 1869; endorsed by the General Council, August 3, 1869.

[110]

lifetime, the economical power of transferring to themselves the fruits of the labor of the many. Where the state of society is far enough advanced, and the working class possesses sufficient power to abrogate such institutions, they must do so in a *direct way*. For instance, by doing away with the public debt, they get of course, at the same time, rid of the inheritance in public funds. On the other hand, if they do not possess the power to abolish the public debt, it would be a foolish attempt to abolish the right of inheritance in public funds.

The disappearance of the right of inheritance will be the natural result of a social change superseding private property in the means of production; but the abolition of the right of inheritance can never be the starting point of such a social transformation.

3. It was one of the great errors committed about forty years since by the disciples of St. Simon, to treat the right of inheritance, not as the legal effect, but as the economical cause of the present social organization. This did not at all prevent them from perpetuating in their system of society private property in land and the other means of production. Of course elective and lifelong proprietors, they thought, might exist as elective kings have existed.

To proclaim the abolition of the right of inheritance as the starting point of the social revolution would only tend to lead the working class away from the true point of attack against present society. It would be as absurd a thing as to abolish the laws of contract between buyer and seller, while continuing the present state of exchange of commodities.

It would be a thing false in theory, and reactionary in practice.

4. In treating of the laws of inheritance, we necessarily suppose that private property in the means of production continues to exist. If it did no longer exist among the living, it could not be transferred from them, and by them, after their death. All measures, in regard to the right of inheritance, can therefore only relate to a state of social transition, where, on the one hand, the present economical base of society is not yet transformed, but where, on the other hand, the working masses have gathered strength enough to enforce transitory measures calculated to bring about an ultimate radical change of society.

Considered from this standpoint, changes of the laws of inheritance form only part of a great many other transitory measures tending to the same end.

These transitory measures, as to inheritance, can only be:

a. Extension of the inheritance duties already existing in many states, and the application of the funds hence derived to purposes of social emancipation.

b. Limitation of the testamentary right of inheritance, which—as distinguished from the intestate or family right of inheritance—appears an arbitrary and superstitious exaggeration even of the principles of private property themselves.

Compulsory Education*

THE EDUCATION QUESTION then came on for discussion. Citizen Eccarius read so much of the Geneva Resolutions as referred to training and education of children and adolescents[1] and proposed that it be adhered to. . . .

Citizen Marx said there was a peculiar difficulty connected with this question. On the one hand, a change of social circumstances was required to establish a proper system of education; on the other hand, a proper system of education was required to bring about a change of social circumstances; we must therefore commence where we were.

The question treated at the Congress was whether education was to be national or private.[2] National education had been looked upon as governmental, but that was not necessarily the case. In Massachusetts every township was bound to provide schools for primary education for all the children. In towns of more than 5,000 inhabitants higher schools for technical education had to be provided, in larger towns

---

* From the minutes of the General Council, August 10, 1869.

1. Resolutions of the First Congress Assembled at Geneva, September, 1866: "By education we understand three things. Firstly: mental education. Secondly: Bodily education, such as is given in schools, by gymnastics, and by military exercise. Thirdly: technological training, which imparts the general principles of all processes of production, and simultaneously initiates the child and young person in the practical use and handling of the elementary instruments of all trades. A gradual and progressive course of mental, gymnastic, and technological training ought to correspond with the classification of the juvenile laborers. The costs of the technological schools ought to be partly met by the sale of their products. The combination of paid productive labor, mental education, bodily exercise, and polytechnic training will raise the working class far above the level of the higher and middle classes."

2. General education was also discussed at the Congresses of Geneva (1866), Lausanne (1867), and Brussels (1868).

still higher. The state contributed something but not much. In Massachusetts one-eighth of the local taxes went for education, in New York one-fifth. The school committees which administered the schools were local, they appointed the schoolmasters and selected the books. The fault of the American system was that it was too much localized, the education given depended upon the state of culture prevailing in each district. There was a cry for a central supervision. The taxation for schools was compulsory, but the attendance of children was not. Property had to pay the taxes and the people who paid the taxes wanted that the money was usefully applied. Education might be national without being governmental. Government might appoint inspectors whose duty it was to see that the laws were obeyed, just as the factory inspectors looked after the observance of the factory acts, without any power of interfering with the course of education itself.

The Congress might without hesitation adopt that education was to be compulsory. As to children being prevented from working, one thing was certain: It would not reduce wages and people would get used to it.

The Proudhonists maintained that gratuitous education was nonsense, because the state had to pay for it; of course somebody had to pay, but not those who could least afford it. [Marx] was not in favor of gratuitous college education.

As Prussian education had been talked so much of, he would conclude by observing that the Prussian system was only calculated to make good soldiers.

On the Irish Amnesty Question*

November 16

CITIZEN MARX then opened the debate on the attitude of the British Government on the Irish Question. He said political amnesty proceeds from two sources: (1) When a government is strong enough by force of arms and public opinion, when the enemy accepts the defeat, as was the case in America, then amnesty is given. (2) When misgovernment is the cause of quarrel and the opposition gains its point, as was the case in Austria and Hungary. Such ought to have been the case in Ireland.

Both Disraeli and Gladstone have said that the government ought to do for Ireland what in other countries a revolution would do. Bright asserted repeatedly that Ireland would always be ripe for revolution unless a radical change was made. During the election Gladstone justified the Fenian insurrection and said that every other nation would have revolted under similar circumstances.[1] When taunted in the House he equivocated his fiery declarations against the "policy of conquest" [that] implied that "Ireland ought to be ruled according to Irish ideas." To put an end to the "policy of conquest" he ought to have begun like America and Austria by an amnesty as soon as

---

* From the minutes of the General Council, November 16, 26, 1869, recorded by J. Georg Eccarius. (At the meeting of November 9, Marx proposed "discussion of the following questions: 1. The attitude of the British Government on the Irish Question. 2. The attitude of the English working class toward the Irish. Citizen Marx volunteered to open the debate. The report was adopted and the question ordered to be put on the order of the day.")

1. In December, 1868, Gladstone replaced Disraeli as Prime Minister after promising a solution for the Irish question.

he became minister. He did nothing. Then the amnesty movement in Ireland by the municipalities. When a deputation was about to start with a petition containing 200,000 signatures for the release of the prisoners he anticipated it by releasing some to prevent the appearance of giving way to Irish pressure. The petition came, it was not got up by Fenians, but he gave no answer. Then it was mooted in the House that the prisoners were infamously treated. In this at least the English Government is impartial; it treats Irish and English alike; there is no country in Europe where political prisoners are treated like in England and Russia. Bruce was obliged to admit the fact. Moor wanted an inquiry; it was refused. Then commenced the popular amnesty movement at Limerick. A meeting was held at which 30,000 people were present and a memorial for the unconditional release was adopted. Meetings were held in all the towns in the North. Then the great meeting was announced in Dublin where 200,000 people attended. It was announced weeks beforehand for the tenth of October. The trade societies wanted to go in procession. On the eighth proclamations were issued prohibiting the procession to go through certain streets. Isaac Butt interpreted it as a prohibition of the procession. They went to Fortescue to ask but he was not at home, his secretary Burke did not know. A letter was left to be replied to; he equivocated. The government wanted a collision. The procession was abandoned and it was found afterwards that the soldiers had been supplied with forty rounds of shot for the occasion.

After that Gladstone answered the Limerick memorial of August in a roundabout way. He says the proceedings varied much. There were loyal people and others who used bad language demanding as a right what could only be an act of clemency.

It is an act of presumption on the part of a paid public servant to teach a public meeting how to speak.

The next objection is that the prisoners have not abandoned their designs which were cut short by their imprisonment.

How does Gladstone know what their designs were and that they still entertain them? Has he tortured them into a confession? He wants them to renounce their principles, to degrade them morally. Napoleon did [not] ask people to renounce their republican principles before he gave an amnesty and Prussia attached no such conditions.

Then he says the conspiracy still exists in England and America.

If it did, Scotland Yard would soon be down upon it. It is only "disaffection of seven hundred years' standing." The Irish have declared they would receive unconditional freedom as an act of conciliation. Gladstone cannot quell the Fenian conspiracy in America, his conduct promotes it, one paper calls him the Head Center. He finds fault with the press. He has not the courage to prosecute the press; he wants to make the prisoners responsible. Does he want to keep them as hostages for the good behavior of the people outside? He says "it has been our desire to carry leniency to the utmost point." This then is the utmost point.

When Mountjoy was crowded with untried prisoners, Dr. M'Donnell wrote letter after letter to Joseph Murray about their treatment. Lord Mayo said afterwards that Murray had suppressed them. M'Donnell then wrote to the inspector of prisons, to a higher official. He was afterwards dismissed and Murray was promoted.

He then says: We have advised the minor offenders to be released; the principal leaders and organizers we could not set free.

This is a positive lie. There were two Americans among them who had fifteen years each. It was fear for America that made him set them free. Carey was sentenced in 1865 to five years, he is in the lunatic asylum, his family wanted him home, he could not upset the government.

He further says: To rise in revolt against the public order has ever been a crime in this country. Only in this country. Jefferson Davis' revolt was right because it was not against the English, the government. He continues, the administration can have no interest except the punishment of crimes.

The administration are the servants of the oppressors of Ireland. He wants the Irish to fall on their knees because an enlightened sovereign and parliament have done a great act of justice. They were the criminals before the Irish people. But the Irish was the only question upon which Gladstone and Bright could become ministers and catch the dissenters and give the Irish place hunters an excuse of selling themselves. The church was only the badge of conquest. The badge is removed, but the servitude remains. He states that the government is resolved to continue to remove any grievance, but that they are determined to give security to life and property and maintain the integrity of the empire.

Life and property are endangered by the English aristocracy. Canada makes her own laws without impairing the integrity of the empire, but the Irish know nothing of their own affairs, they must leave them to Parliament, the same power that has landed them where they are. It is the greatest stupidity to think that the prisoners out of prison could be more dangerous than insulting a whole nation. The old English leaven of the conqueror comes out in the statement: We will grant you but you must ask.

In his letter to Isaac Butt he says: "You remind me that I once pleaded for foreigners. Can the two cases correspond? The Fenians

were tried according to lawful custom and found guilty by a jury
of their countrymen. The prisoners of Naples were arrested and not
tried and when they were tried they were tried by exceptional tri-
bunals and sentenced by judges who depended upon the government
for bread."

If a poacher is tried by a jury of country squires he is tried by his
countrymen. It is notorious that the Irish juries are made up of
purveyors to the castle whose bread depends upon their verdict. Oppression is always a lawful custom. In England the judges can be
independent, in Ireland they cannot. Their promotion depends upon
how they serve the government. Sullivan the prosecutor has been made
master of the rolls.

To the Ancient Order of Foresters in Dublin he answered that
he was not aware that he had given a pledge that Ireland was to be
governed according to Irish ideas. And after all this he comes to
Guild Hall and complains that he is inadequate for the task.

The upshot is that all the tenants' rights meetings are broken up;
they want the prisoners [released]. They have broken with the clerical
party. They now demand that Ireland is to govern herself. Moor and
Butt have declared for it. They have resolved to liberate O'Donovan
Rossa by electing him a member of Parliament.

Citizen Marx ended by proposing the following resolution:
Resolved,

That in his reply to the Irish demands for the release of the
imprisoned Irish patriots (in a reply contained in his letter to Mr.
O'Shea, Oct. 18, 1869, and to Mr. Isaac Butt, Oct. 23, 1869) Mr. Gladstone has deliberately insulted the Irish nation;

That he clogs political amnesty with conditions alike degrading
to the victims of misgovernment and the people they belong to;

That having in the teeth of his responsible position publicly and
enthusiastically cheered on the American slaveholders' rebellion, he
now steps in to preach to the Irish people the doctrine of passive
obedience;

That his whole proceedings with reference to the Irish amnesty
question are the true and genuine offspring of that "policy of conquest" by the fiery denunciation of which Mr. Gladstone ousted his
Tory rivals from office;

That the General Council of the International Working Men's
Association express their admiration of the spirited and high-souled
manner in which the Irish people carry on their amnesty movement;

That this resolution be communicated to all the branches of, and
workingmen's bodies connected with, the International Working
Men's Association in Europe and the United States.

Citizen Harris seconded the resolution.

The Chairman thought the discussion had better be postponed till the next week.[2]

November 26

Citizen Mottershead: I regret that Englishmen applauded the statements of Dr. Marx, as some did last week. Ireland cannot be independent. It lies between England and France; if we relinquish our hold, it would only be asking the French to walk in. The Irish movement is not of that high-souled character the Doctor ascribes to it in the resolution. One thing is wrong altogether: if you look to the *Times* and other papers you will find that the Prime Minister commenced the amnesty affair before the Irish moved. Dr. Marx makes it appear that it was a sort of cowardice, fear of America to release the Americans, and then he states that America has not been conciliated. I never found the Irish in the field with the English in any movement, but they have often been against us. I remind you of the Garibaldi riots.[3] I am surprised that Napoleon is held up against Gladstone. Dr. Marx forgot that thousands of the French and Hungarians were amnestied by death in the streets of Paris and at Cayenne. The Austrian Government had fourteen Hungarian generals hung one morning. Robert Blum was shot.

Citizen Marx: Citizen Mottershead has given a history of Gladstone. I could give another, but that has nothing to do with the question before us. The petitions which were adopted at the meetings were quite civil, but he found fault with the speeches by which they were supported. Castlereagh was as good a man as Gladstone and I found today in the *Political Register*[4] that he used the same words against the Irish as Gladstone, and Cobbett made the same reply as I have done.

When the electoral tour commenced all the Irish candidates spouted about amnesty, but Gladstone did nothing till the Irish municipalities moved.

I have not spoken of the people killed abroad, because you cannot

---

2. Marx to Engels, November 18, 1869: ". . . Last Tuesday [November 16] I opened the discussion [at the General Council of the International] on Point No. 1, the *attitude of the British Ministry on the Irish Amnesty Question.* Made a speech of about four-fifths of an hour, much cheered, and then proposed the following resolution on Point No. 1. . . ."

3. Fights between Irishmen and Englishmen at Hyde Park on September 28, 1862, at a workers' meeting honoring Garibaldi and protesting the French occupation of Rome.

4. *Cobbett's Weekly Political Register.*

compare the Hungarian war with the Fenian insurrection. We might compare it with 1798[5] and then the comparison would not be favorable to the English.

I repeat that political prisoners are not treated anywhere so bad as in England.

Citizen Mottershead is not going to tell us his opinion of the Irish; if he wants to know what other people think of the English let him read Ledru-Rollin and other continental writers. I have always defended the English and do so still.

These resolutions are not to be passed to release the prisoners, the Irish themselves have abandoned that.

It is a resolution of sympathy with the Irish and a review of the conduct of the government, it may bring the English and the Irish together. Gladstone has to contend with the opposition of the *Times*, the *Saturday Review*, etc.; if we speak out boldly on the other side, we may support him against an opposition to which he might otherwise have to succumb. He was in office during the Civil War and was responsible for what the government did and if the North was low when he made his declaration, so much the worse for his patriotism.

Citizen Odger is right, if we wanted the prisoners released, this would not be the way to do it, but it is more important to make a concession to the Irish people than to Gladstone.[6]

5. In 1798 an Irish insurrection was severely crushed by the British Government.
6. The resolution was passed. In the minutes as reported in *Reynolds's Newspaper*, November 28, 1869, Marx's concluding sentence reads: "The question was which was most important—to conciliate the Irish, or make this resolution acceptable to Mr. Gladstone."

The Abolition of Landed Property*

THE property in the soil—that original source of all wealth—has become the great problem upon the solution of which depends the future of the working class.

While not intending to discuss here all the arguments put forward by the advocates of private property in land—jurists, philosophers, and political economists—we shall only state firstly that they disguise the original fact of conquest under the cloak of "natural right." If conquest constitutes a natural right on the part of the few, the many have only to gather sufficient strength in order to acquire the natural right of reconquering what has been taken from them. In the progress of history the conquerors attempt to give a sort of social sanction to their original title derived from brute force, through the instrumentality of laws imposed by themselves. At last comes the philosopher who declares those laws to imply the universal consent of society. If indeed private property in land is based upon such a universal consent it evidently becomes extinct from the moment the majority of a society dissent from warranting it. However, leaving aside the so-called "rights" of property, we affirm that the economical development of society, the increase and concentration of people, the necessity to agriculture of collective and organized labor as well as of machinery and similar contrivances, render the nationalization of land a "social necessity," against which no amount of talk about the rights of property will avail.

Changes dictated by social necessity are sure to work their way sooner or later, because the imperative wants of society must be

---

* Memorandum for Robert Applegarth, December 3, 1869. See Marx's letter to Engels, December 4, 1869, page 483.

satisfied, and legislation will always be forced to adapt itself to them.

What we require is a daily increasing production whose exigencies cannot be met by allowing a few individuals to regulate it according to their whims and private interests or to ignorantly exhaust the powers of the soil. All modern methods such as irrigation, drainage, steam plowing, chemical treatment, etc., ought to be applied to agriculture at last. But the scientific knowledge we possess, and the technical means of agriculture we command, such as machinery, etc., never can be successfully applied but by cultivating the land on a large scale. Cultivation on a large scale—even under its present capitalist form that degrades the producer himself to a mere beast of burden —has to show results so much superior to the small and piecemeal cultivation—would it then not, if applied on national dimensions, be sure to give an immense impulse to production? The ever growing wants of the people on the one side, the ever increasing price of agricultural produce on the other, afford the irrefutable proof that the nationalization of land has become a "social necessity." The diminution of agricultural produce springing from individual abuse ceases to be possible as soon as cultivation is carried on under the control, at the cost, and for the benefit of the nation.

France has often been alluded to, but with its peasantry proprietorship it is farther off the nationalization of land than England with its landlordism. In France, it is true, the soil is accessible to all who can buy it, but this very facility has brought about the division of land into small plots cultivated by men with small means and mainly thrown on the resources of the bodily labor of both themselves and their families. This form of landed property and the piecemeal cultivation necessitated by it not only excludes all appliance of modern agricultural improvements, but simultaneously converts the tiller himself into the most decided enemy of all social progress, and above all, of the nationalization of the land. Enchained to the soil upon which he has to spend all his vital energies in order to get a relatively small return, bound to give away the greater part of his produce to the state in the form of taxes, to the law tribe in the form of judiciary costs, and to the usurer in the form of interest; utterly ignorant of the social movement outside his petty field of action; he still clings with frantic fondness to his spot of soil and his merely nominal proprietorship in the same. In this way the French peasant has been thrown into a most fatal antagonism to the industrial working class. Peasantry proprietorship being thus the greatest obstacle to the "nationalization of land," France, in its present state, is certainly not the place where we must look for a solution of this great problem. To nationalize the land and let it out in small plots to individuals or workingmen's societies would, under a middle-class government, only bring about a reckless competition among them, and cause a certain increase of "rent," and thus lend new facilities to the appropriators for feeding upon the producers.

At the International Congress in Brussels, in 1868, one of my friends said: "Small private property is doomed by the verdict of science; great private property by justice. There remains then but one alternative. The soil must become the property of rural associations, or the property of the whole nation. The future will decide the question."

I say on the contrary: "The future will decide that the land cannot be owned but nationally. To give up the soil to the hands of associated rural laborers would be to surrender all society to one exclusive class of producers. The nationalization of land will work a complete change in the relations between labor and capital and finally do away altogether with capitalist production, whether industrial or rural. Only then the class distinctions and privileges will disappear together with the economical basis from which they originate and society will be transformed into an association of "producers." To live upon other people's labor will become a thing of the past. There will no longer exist a government nor a state distinct from society itself." Agriculture, mining, manufacture, in one word all branches of production will gradually be organized in the most effective form. *National centralization of the means of production* will become the natural basis of a society composed of associations of free and equal producers consciously acting upon a common and rational plan. Such is the goal to which the great economic movement of the nineteenth century is tending.

The British Government and the Imprisoned Fenians*

THE silence observed by the European press about the infamies committed by the British oligarchic bourgeois government is due to several reasons. To begin with, the British Government is *rich*, and the press, as you know, is *incorruptible*. Furthermore, the British Government is a model government, recognized as such by the landlords, by the capitalists of the Continent, and even by Garibaldi (see his book): hence one should not speak ill of that ideal government. Finally, the French republicans are so narrow-minded and egoistic in spirit that they reserve all their wrath for the Empire. It would be a crime against freedom of speech to inform their compatriots that in a country of bourgeois freedom people are sentenced to twenty years of hard labor for things punishable with six months' imprisonment in the country of cantonments. Here follow a few details taken from English dailies about the treatment of Fenian prisoners:

Mulcahy, subeditor of the *Irish People*, condemned for having taken part in a Fenian conspiracy, had an iron collar put around his neck at Dartmoor and was hitched to a cart loaded with stones.

O'Donovan Rossa, proprietor of the *Irish People*, was for thirty-five days kept in a dungeon with his arms chained behind his back night and day. He was not even unshackled to take his food—the meager brew that was left for him on the prison floor.

Although Kickham, one of the editors of the *Irish People*, did not have the use of his right hand owing to an abscess, he was made to sit with his companions on a pile of rubbish in the fog and cold of November and to break stones and bricks with his right hand. For

* Written in French, February 21, 1870; published in *L'Internationale*, February 27.

the night he was taken back to his cell, and had nothing more to sustain him than six ounces of bread and a pint of warm water.

O'Leary, an old man of sixty or seventy, was while in prison put on bread and water for three weeks because he did not want to renounce his "paganism" (that, evidently, is what the jailer calls free thinking) and to become either papist, Protestant, Presbyterian, or even Quaker, or embrace one of the numerous religions which the governor of the prison offered for the Irish pagan's choice.

Martin H. Carey is incarcerated in an insane asylum at Millbank; the silence that was imposed on him and other ill treatment made him lose his reason.

Colonel Richard Burke is in no better condition. One of his friends writes that his reason is affected, that he has lost his memory and that his ways, his manners, and his speech indicate insanity.

Political prisoners are transferred from one prison to another as though they were wild beasts. The company of the vilest rogues is imposed on them; they are obliged to scour utensils which were used by these miserables, to wear the shirts and flannels of these criminals, many of whom are afflicted with the most disgusting diseases, and to wash in water which these latter have already used. All these criminals were allowed to speak with visitors until the arrival of the Fenians at Portland. A visiting cage was installed for the Fenian prisoners. It consisted of three compartments separated by thick iron bars; the jailer occupies the central compartment, and the prisoner and his friends cannot see each other but through this double row of bars.

There are prisoners in the docks who eat all the snails, and frogs are considered a delicacy at Chatham. General Thomas Burke declares that he was not surprised to see a dead mouse floating in the soup. The condemned say that it was an unhappy day for them when the Fenians were brought to the prisons. (The routine has become much stricter.)

I shall add a few words to the above:

Last year Mr. Bruce, Minister for the Interior, grand Liberal, grand policeman, grand proprietor of mines in Wales, and a fierce exploiter of labor, was interpellated on the bad treatment of Fenian prisoners and especially O'Donovan Rossa. At first he denied everything; later he was compelled to admit it. Then Mr. Moore, Irish member of the House of Commons, demanded an investigation. It was flatly refused by that radical ministry of which that demisaint (he has been publicly compared to Jesus Christ) Mr. Gladstone is head and the old bourgeois demagogue John Bright is one of the most influential members.

Lately, after the rumors of bad treatment were renewed, a few M.P.s demanded permission from Minister Bruce to visit the prisoners, in order to be able to state the falsity of these rumors. Mr. Bruce refused the permission because, he said, the governors of the prison feared that the prisoners would be excited by visits of that kind.

Last week the Minister for the Interior was again interpellated. He was asked whether it was true that after his nomination as deputy for Tipperary O'Donovan Rossa received corporal punishment (i.e., was whipped); the Minister declared that this did not happen after 1868 (which goes to say that in the course of two to three years the political prisoner was indeed whipped).

I am also sending you extracts concerning Michael Terbert, a Fenian who was sentenced like all the others to hard labor and who served his sentence at Spike Island Convict Prison, Cork County, Ireland. You will see that the coroner himself attributes his death to tortures. The inquest took place last week.

In the course of two years *more than twenty* Fenian workers died or lost their reason by grace of the philanthropy of these good bourgeois, supported by those good landlords.

You probably know that the English press professes a chaste horror of the abominable general emergency laws which embellish beautiful France. But it is general emergency laws that—brief intervals excepted—make up the Irish Charter. Ever since 1793 the English Government has for every possible reason regularly and periodically suspended the operation of the Habeas Corpus Bill (the law which guarantees freedom of person) in Ireland and, in effect, every law save that of brute force. In this manner thousands of people suspected of being Fenian supporters were taken into custody in Ireland without trial or judgment, without even being formally charged. Not content with depriving them of their liberty, the English Government subjected them to most savage tortures. Here is an example:

One of the prisons where suspected Fenians were buried alive is Mountjoy Prison in Dublin. The inspector of that prison, Murray, is a wild beast. He has maltreated prisoners in a manner so savage that a few of them went out of their minds. The prison doctor, M'Donnell, an excellent man (who has played an honorable part in the inquest of Michael Terbert's death), wrote letters of protest for some months, which he at first addressed to Murray himself. Since Murray did not reply to them, he addressed his reports to the superior authorities, but Murray, an expert jailer, intercepted them.

Finally M'Donnell addressed himself directly to Lord Mayo, then Viceroy of Ireland. This was at the time when the Tories (Derby-Disraeli) were in power. What were the results of these actions? The documents related to the affair were published by order of Parliament and . . . Doctor M'Donnell was dismissed from his post! As for Murray, he kept his.

Then came the so-called radical ministry of Gladstone, that delicate, that unctuous, that magnanimous Gladstone, who shed such hot and sincere tears over the lot of Poerio and the other bourgeois maltreated by King Bomba. What did this idol of the progressive bourgeoisie do? While insulting the Irish with his insolent rejection of their amnesty demands, he not only confirmed the Monster Murray in his functions, but in gratitude added a fat sinecure to his post of chief jailer! Such is the apostle of bourgeois philanthropy!

But dust had to be thrown in the eyes of the public; one had to create the impression that something was being done for Ireland, and with grand fanfare he announced a law to regulate the land question (the Land Bill). But all this is nothing but deceit with the ultimate object of creating an impression in Europe, of enticing the Irish judges and barristers with prospects of endless litigations between land-lords and farmers, attracting the landlords with promises of subventions, and luring the richer farmers with some half-concessions.

In the lengthy introduction to his grandiloquent and confused discourse, Gladstone confessed that even the "benevolent" laws which Liberal England had granted Ireland in the past hundred years have unfailingly led to that country's deterioration. And after that naïve confession the selfsame Gladstone persists in torturing the men who want to end this wrongful and imbecile legislation.

The Imprisoned O'Donovan Rossa
and the English Press*

O'DONOVAN ROSSA's letter, which I reported to you in my last article,[1] was the event of last week.

The *Times* printed the letter without comment, the *Daily News* printed a commentary without the letter.

"As was to be expected," the latter newspaper wrote, "Mr. O'Donovan Rossa chose as the theme of his letter the prison regulations to which he has been subjected for a while."

How cruel is this "for a while" when one speaks of a man who has already been incarcerated for five years and has been condemned to hard labor for life!

Mr. O'Donovan Rossa complains, among other things, that he had been "hitched to a cart with a rope around his neck," and this was done in such a way that his life depended on the movements of his English fellow convicts.

"But is it so unjust," cries the *Daily News*, "to put a man in a position where his life depended on the actions of others? Does not the life of a man in a wagon or on a steamer depend upon the actions of others?"

After this energetic piece, the pious casuist reproaches O'Donovan Rossa with not loving the Bible and preferring the *Irish People*.[2] This apposition of Bible and People is designed to delight its readers.

---

* Signed "J. Williams," Jenny Marx's pseudonym, written in French, in collaboration with her father, and published in *La Marseillaise*, March 19, 1870. The text used here is translated from a German version.

1. *La Marseillaise* published a series of eight articles on the Irish Question by "J. Williams" between March 1 and April 24, 1870; see Marx's letter to Engels, March 5, 1870. The article referred to here appeared March 9.

2. The *Irish People*, a Fenian weekly in Dublin, was closed in 1865 and its editors arrested.

"Mr. O'Donovan Rossa," the paper continues, "seems to imagine that prisoners, undergoing punishment for insurrectionary writings, should be supplied with cigars and daily newspapers and, above all, that they must have the right to correspond with their friends unhindered."

Oh, you virtuous Pharisee! You finally admit that O'Donovan Rossa has been condemned to hard labor for life for his "insurrectionary writings," and not, as you had vilely told the French press in your first statement, because of an attempt to murder Queen Victoria.

"Finally," the shameless paper concludes, "O'Donovan Rossa is being treated as what he is, that is, a common convict."

In Mr. Gladstone's special organ, the *Daily Telegraph*, which generally strikes a very crude note, we find a different nuance of the liberalizing press.

"If we deign," this paper declares, "to take notice of O'Donovan Rossa's letter, we do not do it on behalf of the incorrigible Fenians but exclusively for the welfare of France."

"Know ye then," it says, "that a few days ago, in the House of Commons, Mr. Gladstone formerly denied all these shameless allegations, and surely no sensible Frenchman, regardless of what party or class he may belong to, would dare doubt the word of an English gentleman."

But even if, against all expectations, there should be in France parties or men who are so corrupt as to give no credence to the word of an English gentleman like Mr. Gladstone, France should at least be able to resist the well-meaning advice of Mr. Levy,[3] who is in no way a gentleman, and who appeals to her in the following words: "We advise our neighbors, the Parisians, to consider all tales of cruelties, which are allegedly being committed against political prisoners in England, as shameless inventions."

Mr. Levy will permit me to give you an example of the value of the *word* of the gentlemen who make up Gladstone's Cabinet.

You will recall that in my first article I mentioned Colonel Richard Burke, an imprisoned Fenian who, thanks to the benevolent methods of the English Government, went insane. The *Irishman*[4] was the first to report this. Thereupon Mr. Underwood wrote to Mr. Bruce, Home Secretary, and demanded an investigation of the treatment of political prisoners.

Mr. Bruce replied in a letter, published in the English newspapers, that contained the following sentence: "In regard to Richard Burke in the prison in Woking, Mr. Bruce must decline an investigation based

---

3. The publisher of *The Daily Telegraph*.
4. A weekly published first in Belfast and then in Dublin.

on such completely unfounded and extravagant insinuations contained in the excerpts from the *Irishman* that were sent to him."

This statement by Mr. Bruce is dated January 11, 1870. Now, in its most recent issue, the *Irishman* published the reply of the same Secretary to a letter from Madame Barry, Richard Burke's sister, requesting information about the "disquieting" condition of her brother. To the Secretary's reply of February 24, there is added an official report of January 11, wherein the prison doctor and Burke's special guard stated that Burke had become insane.[5] Thus on the same day that Mr. Bruce publicly characterized the reports in the *Irishman* as untrue and completely groundless, he had the overwhelming official proof of its veracity in his pocket! Be it remarked in passing that Mr. Moore, Irish member of the House of Commons, will interpellate the Secretary on the treatment of Colonel Burke.

The *Echo*, a recently established newspaper,[6] pretends to an even stronger liberalism than its governmental brothers. It has its own principles; the principle: to cost one sou, while the other papers cost two, four, or six sous. This price of one sou forces it, on the one hand, to a pseudodemocratic confession of faith, so as not to lose its proletarian subscribers, and on the other hand, to constant caution, so as to win over the respectable subscribers from its competitors.

In a lengthy rigmarole on O'Donovan Rossa's letter, that paper rises to the remarkable conclusion that "perhaps the amnestied Fenians themselves would hesitate to believe the exaggerations of their countrymen." As if Mr. Kickham, Mr. Costello, etc., had not already published reports on the Fenians' sufferings in prison that coincide fully with Rossa's letter! But after all its subterfuges and confused evasions, the *Echo* touches the sore point.

"The publications in the *Marseillaise*," it states, "will cause a scandal that will go around the world. The continental mind is perhaps too narrow to differentiate correctly between the misdeeds of a Bomba and the stern measures of a Gladstone! Hence it would be better to institute an investigation, etc."

The *Spectator*, a liberalizing weekly in Gladstone's camp, is edited on the principle that every genre is bad except the tedious one. Hence it is called in London the paper of the Seven Wise Men. After giving a synopsis of O'Donovan Rossa's letter and chiding him for his aversion to the Bible, this paper of the Seven Wise Men comes to the

5. The report on Colonel Burke appeared in the *Irishman* January 1, 1870; Underwood's letter to Bruce, January 8; Bruce's reply, January 22; the reply to Burke's sister, March 12.

6. The *Echo*, a London newspaper, was founded in 1868 and continued publication until 1907.

following judgment: "The Fenian, O'Donovan Rossa, clearly did not have to endure more than any other convict, but we must admit that we would gladly see a change in this system. It is completely just and also very reasonable to shoot rebels. It may also be just to imprison them as the most dangerous sort of criminals. But it is neither just nor wise to degrade them."

Well spoken, wise Solomon!

Finally, we come to the *Standard*, the leading organ of the Tories, the Conservatives. You know that the English oligarchy consists of two fractions: the landed aristocracy and the plutocracy. If in their family quarrels one takes the side of the plutocrats against the aristocrats, one is called a liberal, yea, even a radical. If, on the other hand, one takes sides with the aristocrats against the plutocrats, one is a Tory.

The *Standard* treated O'Donovan Rossa's letter as an apocryphal romance that perhaps originated with A. Dumas.

"Why did the *Marseillaise*," that paper asks, "not add that Mr. Gladstone, the Archbishop of Canterbury, and the Lord Mayor witnessed the torturing of O'Donovan Rossa every morning?"

In the House of Commons, a member characterized the Tories as a "stupid party." Truly, the *Standard* has earned the title of leading organ of the stupid party!

Before I finish this letter, I must warn the French not to confuse the uproar in the newspapers with the voice of the English proletariat; it is a misfortune for both countries, Ireland and England, that this voice does not find expression in the English press.

It suffices to say that in Hyde Park more than 200,000 men, women, and children of the English working class demanded the liberation of their Irish brothers and that the General Council of the International Working Men's Association, which has its headquarters in London and which counts the acknowledged leaders of the English working class among its members, has branded the treatment of the imprisoned Fenians in the sharpest terms and has come out for the rights of the Irish nation against the English Government.[7]

P. S. As a result of the publication of O'Donovan Rossa's letter in the *Marseillaise*, Gladstone fears that he could be forced by public opinion to order an official parliamentary inquiry into the treatment of political prisoners. To avoid this once again (we know how often his depraved conscience has already opposed it), this diplomat has just published an official, but anonymous, denial of the facts brought out by Rossa.[8]

---

7. See "On the Irish Amnesty Question," September 16, 1869, page 115.
8. An article by Home Secretary Bruce, published anonymously in the *Times*, March 16, 1870.

The French should know that this denial is nothing more than a repetition of the statements of the jailers and the policemen, Knox, Pollock, etc., etc. These gentlemen know very well that Rossa cannot answer them. He will now be watched over more rigorously than ever, but in the next article I will answer them with *facts* whose substantiation does not depend on the good will of the jailers.

Denial of Conspiratorial Methods*

CITIZEN Marx then called the attention of the Council to the circumstances that many members of the Association had been arrested in France and that the government papers had endeavored to spread it abroad that the Association was implicated in a pretended plot against the Emperor [Napoleon III]. To refute those insinuations he proposed the following:

On the occasion of the last pretended complot, the French Government has not only arrested many members of our Paris and Lyon sections, but insinuated by its organs that the International Working Men's Association is an accomplice of that pretended complot. According to the tenor of our Statutes, it is certainly the special mission of all our branches in England, on the Continent, and in the United States to act not only as centers for the organization of the working class, but also to aid, in their different countries, all political movements tending to the accomplishment of our ultimate end, viz., the *economical emancipation of the working class*. At the same time these Statutes bind all the sections of our Association to act in open daylight. If our Statutes were not formal on that point, the very nature of an Association which identifies itself with the working classes would exclude from it every form of secret society. If the working classes, who form the great bulk of all nations, who produce all their wealth, and in the name of whom even the usurping powers always pretend to rule, conspire, they conspire publicly, as the sun conspires against darkness, in the full consciousness that without their pale there exists no legitimate power.

---

* From the minutes of the General Council, May 3, 1870. (This proposal was adopted unanimously.)

If the other incidents of the complot denounced by the French Government are as false and unfounded as its insinuations against the International Working Men's Association, this last complot will worthily range with its two predecessors of grotesque memory. The noisy and violent measures against our French sections are exclusively intended to serve one single purpose—*the manipulation of the plebiscite.*

The Lockout of the Building Trades in Geneva*

The General Council of the International Working Men's Association to the Working Men and Women of Europe and the United States

Fellow Workers:

The master builders of Geneva have, after mature consideration, arrived at the conclusion that "the entire freedom of labor" is best calculated to promote the happiness of the laboring poor. In order to secure this blessing to their workpeople, they resolved to carry into practice, on June 11, a trick of English invention, viz., the lockout of upwards of 3,000 mechanics till then in their employ.

Trade unionism being of recent growth in Switzerland, the same master builders of Geneva used to indignantly denounce it as an English importation. Two years ago they taunted their men with a lack of patriotism for trying to transplant on Swiss soil such an exotic plant as the limitation of the working day with fixed rates of wages per hour. They never doubted but there must be some keen mischief mongers behind the scene, since their own native workmen, if left to themselves, would naturally like nothing better than drudging from twelve to fourteen hours a day for whatever pay the master might find it in his heart to allow. The deluded men, they publicly asserted, were acting under dictation from London and Paris, much the same as Swiss diplomats are wont to obey the behests from St. Petersburg, Berlin, and Paris. However, the men were not to be cajoled, taunted, or intimidated into the persuasion that limiting the daily hours of toil

* Written (in English) at the instruction of the General Council meeting of June 21, 1870, and approved by it on July 5; published as a leaflet in English, German, and French.

to ten, and fixing the rate of wages per hour, was something derogatory to a free citizen, nor could they by any provocation be inveigled into acts of violence affording the masters a plausible pretext for enforcing public repressive measures against the unions.

At last, in May, 1868, M. Camperio, the then Minister of Justice and Police, brought about an agreement that the hours of labor should be nine a day in winter and eleven a day in summer, wages varying from forty-five to fifty centimes an hour. That agreement was signed in the presence of the minister by both masters and men. In the spring of 1869 some masters refused to pay more wages for a day's labor of eleven hours than they had paid during winter for nine hours. The matter was again compromised by making 45 centimes an hour the uniform rate of wages for artisans in the building trade. Although clearly comprised in this settlement, the plasterers and painters had to toil away on the old conditions because they were not yet sufficiently organized to enforce the new ones. On the fifteenth of May last, they claimed to be put on a level with the other trades, and on the flat refusal of the masters, struck work the following week. On the fourth of June the master builders resolved that if the plasterers and painters did not return to work on the ninth, the whole of the building operatives should be locked out on the eleventh. This menace was carried into effect. Not satisfied with having locked out the men, the masters publicly called upon the federal government to forcibly dissolve the union and expel the foreigners from Switzerland. Their benevolent and truly liberal attempts at restoring the freedom of labor were, however, baffled by a monster meeting and a protest on the part of the Swiss nonbuilding operatives.

The other Geneva trades have formed a committee to manage the affairs for the men locked out. Some house owners who had contracted for new buildings with the master builders considered the contracts broken, and invited the men employed on them to continue the work as if nothing had happened. This proposal was at once accepted. Many single men are leaving Geneva as fast as they can. Still there remain some 2,000 families deprived of their usual means of subsistence. The General Council of the International Working Men's Association therefore calls upon all honest workingmen and -women, throughout the civilized world, to assist both by moral and material means the Geneva building trades in their just struggle against capitalist despotism.

By order of the Council,

B. Lucraft, Chairman
John Weston, Treasurer
Georg Eccarius, General Secretary

Program for the Fifth Congress*

1. On the need to abolish the public debt. Discussion of the right to compensation.

2. Relationship between political action and the social movement of the working class.

3. Practical means of converting land property into social property (see footnote).

4. Conversion of banks of issue into national banks.

5. Conditions of cooperative production on a national scale.

6. Need for the working class to draw up general statistics of labor, in conformity with the Geneva Congress resolutions in 1866.

7. Reconsideration by the Congress of the question of ways to stop wars.

Footnote to Point 3: The Belgian General Council has proposed this question: "Concerning the practical means of forming agricultural branches within the International and of establishing solidarity between agricultural proletarians and proletarians of other industries."

The General Council of the International Association believes this question is contained in Point 3.

CONFIDENTIAL COMMUNICATION TO ALL SECTIONS

1. The General Council requests all sections to give their delegates formal instructions concerning the advisability of changing the venue of the General Council for 1870–71.

2. In the event of agreement on the change, the General Council will propose Brussels as the venue for the General Council that year.

---

* Written July 14, 1870; printed in *La Liberté*, July 31, 1870, and in *Der Volksstaat*, August 13, 1870. The text here is from the French.

On the Paris Commune*

. . . or papers. This would be rectified in future as the commercial communications between the Commune and London would be kept up by a traveling agent who would also take charge of our communications.

Serraillier and Dupont had been elected to fill up vacancies in the Seventeenth Arrondissement. Serraillier had written that Dupont was sure to be elected but he had not written since the election; he might have written to Manchester. It appeared that more letters had been written than had arrived.

Félix Pyat and Vésinier were slandering Serraillier and Dupont in Paris and when Serraillier had threatened to prosecute they had denied it. It was urgent to write at once to Paris to state the reasons why Pyat calumniated Serraillier and Dupont, and upon the motion of Citizen Mottershead Citizen Marx was instructed to write.[1]

[Marx continued] The letters had been posted outside the line by Lafargue; they had, therefore, been delayed by rail: both the French and the Prussian governments sifted the letters. Most of the information they contained was old but there were a few facts which the papers had not given. It was stated that the provinces knew as little what was going on in Paris as during the siege. Except where the fighting was going on it had never been so quiet. A great part of the middle class had joined the National Guards at Belleville. The great capitalists had run away and the small tradespeople went with the working class. No one could have an idea of the enthusiasm of the

---

* From the minutes of the General Council, April 25, 1871. (The beginning of Marx's speech is missing from the minutes.)
1. See Marx's letter to Leo Frankel, April 26, 1871, page 526.

people and the National Guards, and the people at Versailles must be fools if they believed that they could ever enter Paris. Paris did not believe in a rising in the provinces and knew that superior forces were brought against it but there was no fear on that account but there was fear of Prussian intervention and want of provisions. The decrees about rent and commercial bills were two master strokes: without them three-fourths of the tradespeople would have become bankrupt. The murder of Duval and Flourens had excited a sentiment of vengeance. The family of Flourens and the Commune had sent a legal officer to have the cause of their death certain but in vain. Flourens had been killed in a house.

About the fabrication of telegrams there was some information. When Brutto had gone through the accounts of the Government of National Defense he had discovered that money had been paid for the construction of an improved portable guillotine. The guillotine had been found and publicly burned by order of the Commune. The gas company had owed the municipality more than a million but had not shown any willingness to refund till their goods had been seized; then a bill to the amount had been given on the Bank of France. The telegrams and correspondents gave altogether different versions of these things. The greatest eyesore was that the Commune governed so cheap. The highest officials only received at the rate of 6,000 francs [per] year, the others only workman's wages.

The Purpose of the London Conference*

THE GENERAL COUNCIL has convened a conference:

In order to come to an agreement with the delegates of the different countries on the measures to be taken to meet the danger faced by the Association in many countries, and to decide on a new organization that would correspond to the needs of the situation;

Secondly, to prepare a response to the different governments which work steadily with all the means at their disposal to destroy the Association;

And finally, to settle the Swiss conflict once and for all.

Other, secondary questions will undoubtedly come up in the course of the Conference and will have to find their solution.

Citizen Marx added that it was necessary to issue a declaration to the Russian Government, which is trying to draw the Association into the affair of the secret society,[1] whose ringleaders are hostile or entirely alien to us.

The Conference is private, but after all the delegates have returned to their homes the General Council will publish those decisions which the Conference considers necessary.

---

* Notes taken in French of a speech at the opening of the London Conference; Protocol of the Session of September 17, 1871.

1. The trial of Sergei Nechayev, which began in July, 1871, in St. Petersburg.

The English Trade Unions*

I

MARX BELIEVES that this decision[1] was not adopted at the Basel Congress; but upon reexamination he recognizes that a decision in this sense was made. That was a pious wish, he thought the thing possible then; now he is convinced that the trade unions would not agree to such a federation. The trade unions, he said, are an aristocratic minority. Poor working people could not belong to them: the great mass of workers who, because of economic development, are daily driven from the villages into the cities, long remain outside the trade unions, and the poorest among them would never belong. The same is true of the workers born in London's East End, where only one out of ten belongs to the trade unions. The farmers, the day laborers, never belong to these trade unions.

The trade unions by themselves are impotent—they will remain a minority. They do not have the mass of proletarians behind them, whereas the International influences these people directly; the International does not need the organization of the trade unions in order to win over the workers—the ideas of the International inspire them immediately. It is the only association in which the workers have complete confidence.

The differences in language, too, militate against an International federation with the trade unions.

---

* Notes taken in French of a speech at the London Conference; Protocol of the Session of September 20, 1871.

1. On September 20 Pierre Louis Delahaye had proposed the establishment of an international federation of labor associations based on administrative decentralization, thus forming a "true commune of the future."

II

Marx did not share Steens's fears regarding the trade unions.[2] The latter could never bring anything about without turning to us—not even those that are best organized and have branches in the United States; the trade unions have remained outside the most important revolutionary movement in England.[3]

Since the existence of the International, the situation has changed. If the trade unions want to make use of their power, they can achieve anything with our help. They have in their statutes one paragraph that forbids them to meddle in politics; they undertook political action only under the influence of the International. For years the General Council has been in contact with the trade unions; there was a Committee;[4] at present it maintains contacts with the trade unions in three big cities—Manchester, Birmingham, and Sheffield.

---

2. The Belgian delegate Eugène Steens expressed the fear that an international trade union would absorb the local unions.

3. The Chartist movement, which began in the 1830s.

4. The Executive Committee of the Reform League, which was founded in 1865.

Political Action of the Working Class*

September 20

CITIZEN LORENZO reminded us to stick to the Rules, and Citizen Bastelica followed his example. In both the original Statutes and the Inaugural Address I read that the General Council is obligated to prepare an agenda for the Congresses for discussion. The program which the General Council prepared for the Conference deals with the organization of the Association, and Vaillant's proposal[1] relates directly to this point. Hence the objection of Lorenzo and Bastelica is unfounded.

In virtually all countries, certain members of the International, invoking the mutilated conception of the Statutes adopted at the Geneva Congress, have made propaganda in favor of abstention from politics; and the governments have been quite careful not to impede this restraint. In Germany, Schweitzer and others in the pay of Bismarck even attempted to harness the cart to government policy. In France this criminal abstention allowed Favre, Picard, and others to seize power on September 4; this abstention made it possible, on March 18, to set up a dictatorial committee composed largely of Bonapartists and intrigants, who, in the first days, lost the Revolution by inactivity, days which they should have devoted to strengthening the Revolution.

---

* Notes taken in French of two speeches at the London Conference; Protocols of the Sessions of September 20, 21, 1871.

1. On September 20 the French delegate Édouard Vaillant proposed a resolution stressing the inseparable connection between political and economic questions, urging that the workers unite their political forces. This idea was unpalatable to the Proudhonists.

In America a recently held workers' congress[2] resolved to occupy itself with political questions and to replace professional politicians with workers like themselves, who were authorized to defend the interests of their class.

In England it is not so easy for a worker to get to Parliament. Since members of Parliament do not receive any compensation, and the worker has to work to support himself, Parliament becomes unattainable for him, and the bourgeoisie knows very well that its stubborn refusal to allow salaries for members of Parliament is a means of preventing the working class from being represented in it.

One should never believe that it is of small significance to have workers in Parliament. If one stifles their voices, as in the case of De Potter and Castiau, or if one ejects them, as in the case of Manuel— the reprisals and oppressions exercise a deep effect on the people. If, on the other hand, they can speak from the parliamentary tribune, as do Bebel and Liebknecht, the whole world listens to them. In the one case or the other, great publicity is provided for our principles. To give but one example: when during the [Franco-Prussian] war, which was fought in France, Bebel and Liebknecht undertook to point out the responsibility of the working class in the face of those events, all of Germany was shaken; and even in Munich, the city where revolutions take place only over the price of beer, great demonstrations took place demanding an end to the war.

The governments are hostile to us, one must respond to them with all the means at our disposal. To get workers into Parliament is synonymous with a victory over the governments, but one must choose the right men, not Tolains.

Marx supports the proposal of Citizen Vaillant, as well as Frankel's amendment, to state it as a premise, and thus strengthen it, that the Association has always demanded, and not merely from today, that the workers must occupy themselves with politics.

September 21

Marx said he had already spoken yesterday in favor of Vaillant's motion, and therefore he would not oppose him today. He replied to Bastelica that at the beginning of the Conference it was already decided that it would take up exclusively the question of organization, and not the question of principles. In regard to the reference to the Rules, he calls attention to the fact that the Statutes and the Inaugural Address, which he has reread, are to be read as a whole.

---

2. The congress of the National Labor Union, held in Baltimore, August 7–10, 1871.

He explained the history of abstention from politics and said that one ought not to let himself be irritated by this question. The men who propagated this doctrine were well-meaning utopians, but those who want to take such a road today are not. They reject politics until after a violent struggle, and thereby drive the people into a formal, bourgeois opposition, which we must battle against at the same time we fight against the governments. We must unmask Gambetta, so that the people are no longer hoodwinked. Marx shares Vaillant's opinion. We must reply with a challenge to all the governments that are subjecting the International to persecutions.

Reaction exists on the whole Continent; it is general and permanent —even in the United States and England—in one form or another.

We must announce to the governments: We know you are the armed power which is directed against the proletarians; we will move against you in a peaceful way where that is possible, and with arms if it should become necessary.

Marx is of the opinion that Vaillant's proposal requires some changes, and he therefore supports Outine's motion.[3]

---

3. Outine had proposed that the General Council be empowered to take up the subject, "The Political Efficacy of the Working Class," and that Vaillant's motion and the amendments by Serraillier and Frankel be taken into consideration; Outine's motion carried.

On Secret Societies*

MARX read the following resolution:

"In those countries where the regular organization of the International may for the moment have become impracticable in consequence of government interference, the Association, and its local groups, may be re-formed under various other names, but all secret societies properly so called are and remain formally excluded."

By secret societies one must not understand actual secret societies, which, on the contrary, must be fought.

In France and Italy, where the political situation is such that the right of assembly is a punishable action, people will be very strongly inclined to let themselves be drawn into secret societies, the result of which is always negative. For the rest, this type of organization is in contradiction to the development of the proletarian movement, because, instead of educating the workers, it subjects them to authoritarian and mystical rules which injure their independence and deflect their consciousness in a false direction.

Marx asks for adoption of his resolution.[1]

---

* Notes taken in French of a speech at the London Conference; Protocol of the Session of September 22, 1871.

1. The resolution was adopted by the Conference.

The Situation of the International in Germany and England*

You know that the organization of the International in Germany cannot exist under its own name, since the law does not allow any local
association to be connected with any international one. But the International exists there despite this, and has undergone an extraordinary
development under the name of the Social-Democratic party, which
has long been associated with the International. At the Dresden Congress[1] the connection has been renewed and solemnly confirmed. It is
therefore superfluous to suggest for Germany measures or declarations
of the sort required for countries where the International is being
persecuted.

Marx remarked further that if he had spoken unfavorably of the
German students, the same could not be said of the German workers.
During the brief [Franco-Prussian] war, which led to a sharpening of
the class struggle, the behavior of the German workers was noble
beyond praise; moreover, the Social-Democratic party understood well
that this war was undertaken by Bonaparte and William more to
stifle modern ideas than for conquest. The whole Brunswick Committee was arrested and taken to a fortress near the Russian frontier,
and most of the members were still in prison under the accusation of
high treason. Bebel and Liebknecht, the representatives of the German
working class, did not hesitate to declare in the Reichstag that they
were members of the International Working Men's Association, that
they protested against the war, and that they refused to vote for any

---

* Notes taken in French of a speech at the London Conference; Protocol of
the Session of September 22, 1871.
    1. The Social-Democratic Workers' Party (Eisenachers) Congress, August
12–15, 1871.

war credits. The government did not dare to have them arrested during the session; only after they went outside did the police seize them and drag them to prison.

During the Commune the German workers, in meetings and through their newspapers, constantly strengthened their solidarity with the revolutionists in Paris. And after the Commune was defeated they held a meeting in Breslau, which the Prussian police vainly tried to prevent; at that meeting, as well as at others in various German cities, they enthusiastically concurred with the Paris Commune. Finally, at the triumphal entry of Kaiser William and his army into Berlin, these victors over the people were received with the cry, "Long live the Commune!"

Citizen Marx added that, in speaking of England, he had forgotten to say the following: It is not unknown to you that there has always been a very strong antagonism between the English and the Irish workers, the causes of which are very simply explained. This antagonism has its source in the differences of language and religion, as well as in the fact that the Irish workers compete for wages with the English workers. In England this antagonism is the obstacle to revolution, and is being cleverly exploited by the government and the ruling classes, which are convinced that the English and Irish workers cannot be united by any bond. It is true: on the political terrain a union would be impossible; on the economic one, the thing is different. On both sides, one could build international sections that would march in common for the same goals. The Irish sections will soon be very numerous.

Resolution of the General Council to Celebrate the Anniversary of the Paris Commune*

I

THAT this meeting assembled to celebrate the anniversary of the eighteenth of March last declares that it looks upon the glorious movement inaugurated upon the eighteenth March, 1871, as the dawn of the great social revolution which will forever free the human race from class rule.

II

That the incapacity and the crimes of the middle classes, extended all over Europe by their hatred against the working classes, have doomed old society no matter under what form of government—monarchical or republican.

III

That the crusade of all governments against the International, and the terror of the murderers of Versailles as well as of their Prussian conquerors, attest the hollowness of their successes, and the presence of the threatening army of the proletariat of the whole world gathering in the rear of its heroic vanguard crushed by the combined forces of Thiers and William of Prussia.

---

* Written March 13–18, 1872; published in *La Liberté*, March 24, 1872, and in the *International Herald*, March 30, 1872.

Resolution on the Establishment of
Working-Class Parties*

AGAINST the collective power of the propertied classes the working class cannot act, as a class, except by *constituting itself into a political party, distinct from, and opposed to, all old parties formed by the propertied classes.*

This constitution of the working class into a political party is indispensable in order to insure the triumph of the social revolution and its ultimate end—*the abolition of classes.*

The combination of forces which the working class has already effected by its economical struggles ought at the same time to serve as a lever for its struggles against the political power of landlords and capitalists.

The lords of the land and the lords of capital will always use their political privileges for the defense and perpetuation of their economical monopolies and for enslaving labor. To conquer political power has therefore become the great duty of the working classes.

---

* Drafted in July, 1872, and adopted by the Hague Congress of the International as Article 7 of the General Statutes, in September, 1872. Printed in French and English.

Vive la Commune!*

Citizens!

With great regret we have to inform you that we are not able to attend your meeting.

When the Commune of Paris succumbed to the atrocious massacre organized by the defenders of "Order," the victors little thought that ten years would not elapse before an event would happen in distant Petersburg[1] which, maybe after long and violent struggles, must ultimately and certainly lead to the establishment of a Russian Commune.

That the King of Prussia who had prepared the Commune by besieging Paris and thus compelling the ruling bourgeoisie to arm the people—that that same King of Prussia, ten years after, besieged in his own capital by socialists, would be able to maintain his throne only by declaring the state of siege in his capital Berlin.[2]

On the other hand, the continental governments who after the fall of the Commune by their persecutions compelled the International Working Men's Association to give up its formal, external organization—these governments who believed they could crush the great International Labor Movement by decrees and special laws—little did they think that ten years later that same International Labor Move-

---

* Written in English by Marx and Engels to the Chairman of the Slavonic Meeting in Celebration of the Anniversary of the Paris Commune, March 21, 1881. The meeting was held in London under the chairmanship of the Russian revolutionist Leo Hartmann.

1. On March 1, 1881, Czar Alexander II was assassinated by members of the secret revolutionary society Narodnaya Volya (People's Will).

2. In the spring of 1880 the German antisocialist law of 1878 was extended for another five years.

ment, more powerful than ever, would embrace the working classes
not only of Europe but of America also; that the common struggle
for common interests against a common enemy would bind them together into a new and greater spontaneous International, outgrowing
more and more all external forms of association.

Thus the Commune which the powers of the old world believed to
be exterminated, lives stronger than ever, and thus we may join you in
the cry: *Vive la Commune!*

CONFLICTS
AND SPLITS

Throughout its existence the First International—specifically, the General Council—had to face a number of conflicts, the major ones centering on national prejudices, personal rivalries, and ideological discords. Many continental members resented the idea that the center of an international workers' movement should be in insular London, rather than on the mainland of Europe, where labor was both radical and embattled. Others were jealous of the predominance of Englishmen and of Germans, most notably Marx. The English were considered too unrevolutionary and the Germans too disciplined. Finally, there was ideological conflict, which, in the end, tore the International apart.

Michael Bakunin personified all the areas of conflict within the International. A Russian professional revolutionist, with explosive energies and primitive passions, of gigantic stature and unquenchable appetites—Marx described him as a "monster, a huge mass of flesh and fat that can hardly walk"—Bakunin was a racist, an anti-Semite, an anti-German, and an antibourgeois; and to him, all orderly thought and behavior was bourgeois. His torrential eloquence swept audiences, particularly ignorant and embattled workers with a grievance. He appealed to anarchy.

A Russian, Baron Wrangel, who heard Bakunin speak, recalled him thus:

"The speech was without logical consistency . . . Mighty words, exclamations, thunderclaps, lion's roar, raging storm, flashing lightnings, something elemental, inflammatory. This man was the born Tribune, created for revolution. Revolution was his natural being . . . Bakunin's speech made a thrilling impression. If he had asked his listeners to cut each other's throats, they would undoubtedly have done it."

Trouble began the moment Bakunin joined the International. In

1868 he founded in Geneva his own group, the Alliance of Socialist Democracy, aiming ultimately to take over the International and turn it into what he considered a genuinely revolutionary organization—that is, one that would destroy the whole existing social and economic system of Europe. He did not believe, as Marx and the International did, in organized political action by labor. He was sure Marx was an agent of Bismarck and hence an enemy of revolution. Marx, in turn, believed that Bakunin and his "Cossacks," being Russians, were almost by definition enemies of European civilization.

The conflict between the International, led by Marx, and Bakunin, who had passionate and devoted followers in Belgium, Switzerland, Italy, and Spain, raged for about four years, leading to bitter disunion and poisonous intrigues. It ended with the expulsion of the Bakuninists by the Hague Congress in September, 1872. To prevent the Bakuninists from seizing control of what was left of the International's organization, including the archives, Marx proposed on September 6, 1872, that the seat of the General Council be transferred from London to New York. This was done, but the International did not survive in the New World. It dissolved in Philadelphia four years later.

Marginal Remarks on the Program and Rules of Bakunin's International Alliance of Socialist Democracy*

Program and Rules of the Alliance	Marx's Remarks
The socialist minority of the League of Peace and Freedom having separated itself from the League as a result of the majority vote at the Bern Congress, the majority being formally opposed to the fundamental principle of all workers' associations—that of economic and social equalization of classes and individuals—has thereby adhered to the principles proclaimed by the workers' congresses held in Geneva, Lausanne, and Brussels. Several members of this minority, belonging to various nations, have suggested to us to form a new International Alliance of Socialist Democracy, established entirely within the big International Working Men's Association, but having a special mission to study political and philosophical questions on the basis of the grand principle of universal and genuine equality of all human beings on earth.	equality of classes!
	established within and established against!
Convinced, on our part, of the usefulness of such an enterprise that would provide sin-	

---

* Notations made in the margins of a leaflet containing the program and rules of the International Alliance of Socialist Democracy, founded by Bakunin in Geneva in October, 1868. Marx's marginal notes were probably written December 15, 1868. The text here is a translation from the French made by the Institute of Marxism-Leninism, Moscow.

cere socialist democrats of Europe and America with the means of being understood and of affirming their ideas, without any pressure from the false socialism which bourgeois democracy finds necessary to apply these days, we consider it our duty, together with our friends, to take the initiative in forming this new organization.

So socialist democrats are not understood through the International

Therefore we have established ourselves as the central section of the International Alliance of Socialist Democracy, and we publish today its Program and Rules.

What modesty! They establish themselves as the central authority, clever lads!

Program of the International Alliance of Socialist Democracy

1. The Alliance declares itself atheist; it wants abolition of cults, substitution of science for faith and human justice for divine justice.

As if one could declare—by royal decree—abolition of faith!

2. It wants above all political, economic, and social equalization of classes and individuals of both sexes, commencing with abolition of the right of inheritance, so that in future enjoyment be equal to each person's production, and so that, in conformity with the decision taken at the last workers' congress in Brussels, the land, instruments of labor, like all other capital, on becoming collective property of the entire society, shall be used only by the workers, that is, by agricultural and industrial associations.

Hermaphrodite man! Just like the Russian Commune! The old Saint-Simon panacea!

3. It wants for all children of both sexes, from birth, equal conditions of development, that is, maintenance, education, and training at all degrees of science, industry, and the arts, being convinced that this equality, at first only economic and social, will increasingly lead to a great natural equality of individuals, eliminating all kinds of artificial inequalities, historical products of a social organization as false as it is iniquitous.

Empty phrase!

4. Being the foe of all despotism, not

recognizing any political form other than republican, and rejecting completely any reactionary alliance, it also rejects any political
action which does not have as its immediate
and direct aim the triumph of the workers'
cause against capital.

5. It recognizes that all the existing political and authoritarian states, more and more
reducing their activities to simple administrative functions of public service in their respective countries, will have to dissolve into a universal union of free associations, like the agricultural and industrial ones.

> If they are reducing
> themselves they will
> not have to dissolve,
> but disappear sponta-
> neously.

6. Since the social question can only have
a final and real solution on the basis of international or universal solidarity of the workers
of all countries, the Alliance rejects any policy
based on self-styled patriotism and on rivalry
between nations.

> There is rivalry and
> rivalry, my dear Rus-
> sian!

7. It wants the universal association of all
local associations on the basis of Liberty.

Rules

1. The International Alliance of Socialist
Democracy constitutes a branch of the International Working Men's Association and accepts all its general rules.

> The International As-
> sociation does not
> admit any "Interna-
> tional branches."

2. The Founder Members of the Alliance
are organizing provisionally a Central Bureau
at Geneva.

> New Central Council!

3. Founder Members belonging to the
same country constitute the national bureau
of their country.

4. National bureaus are to establish in all
regions local groups of the Alliance of Socialist Democracy, which, through their respective national bureaus, will ask the Central
Bureau of the Alliance to admit them into the
International Working Men's Association.

> The Rules of the
> International do not
> recognize this "media-
> tory power."

5. All local groups will form their bureau
according to the customary procedure ac-

cepted by the local sections of the International Working Men's Association.

6. All members of the Alliance must pay a monthly contribution of ten centimes, half of which will be retained for their own needs by each national group, and the other half will go to the Central Bureau for its general requirements.

In countries where this sum will be judged to be too high, the national bureaus, in accord with the Central Bureau, will have the power to reduce it.

7. At the annual Working Men's Congress the delegation of the Alliance of Socialist Democracy, as a branch of the International Working Men's Association, will hold public meetings in a separate building.

New taxes absorbing our own contributions!

They want to compromise us under our own patronage!

Members of the Geneva Initiating Group

J. Philipp Becker.—M. Bakunin.—Th. Rémy.—Antoine Lindegger.—Louis Nidegger.—Valérien Mroczkowsky.—Jean Zagorsky.—Phil. Zöller.—A. Ardin.—Ch. Perron.—J. Gay.—J. Friess.—Fr. Rochat.—Nikolai Zhukovsky.—M. Elpidin.—Zampérini.—E. Becker.—Louis Weiss.—Perret.—Marauda.—Edouard Crosset.—A. Blanchard.—A. Matis.—C. Raymond.—Mme. Alexeyeva [Barteneva].—Mme. Bakunin.—Mme. Suzette Croset.—Mme. Rosalie Sanguinède.—Mme. Désirée Gay.—Mme. Jenny Guinet.—Antoine Dunaud.—J. Maulet.—Guerry.—Jacques Courtois.—John Potot.—André Bel.—Fr. Bofféty.—Ch. Guyot.—Ch. Postleb.—Ch. Détraz.—J. Croset.—J. Sanguinède.—C. Jaclard.—L. Coulin.—Fr. Gay.—Blaise Rossety.—Jos. Marilly.—C. Brechtel.—L. Monachon.—Fr. Mermillod.—Donat-father.—L. J. Cheneval.—J. Bédeau.—L. H. Fornachon.—Pinière.—Ch. Grange.—Jacques Laplace.—S. Pellaton.—W. Rau.—Gottlob Walter.—Adolphe Hae-

Asinus Asinorum! And Madame Bakunin!

berling.—Perrié.—Adolphe Catalan.—Marc Héridier.—Louis Allement.—A. Pellergin-Druart.—Louis de Coppet.—Louis Dupraz.—Guillmeaux.—Joseph Baquet.—Fr. Pisteur.—Ch. Ruchet.—Placide Margarittaz.—Paul Garbani.—Etienne Borret.—J. J. Scopini.—F. Crochet.—Jean Jost.—Léopold Wucher.—G. Filliétaz.—L. Fulliquet.—Ami Gandillon.—V. Alexeyev [Bartenev].—François Chevallier.

Jules Johannard
Eugène Dupont

The Founder Members of the International Alliance of Socialist Democracy having decided to start a paper under the name *La Révolution*, to be the press organ of this new Association, the provisional Central Bureau will begin publication as soon as it has 300 shares, of 10 francs each and payable in four installments, one every three months, from January 1, 1869. Accordingly, the provisional Central Bureau is appealing to all national bureaus of the Alliance and inviting them to begin subscriptions in their own countries. As these subscriptions are considered voluntary gifts which give no right to receipt of the paper, the national bureaus must simultaneously compile a list of subscribers.

and they have the cheek to announce in Switzerland that I shall contribute articles to *La Révolution*, without informing me!

The paper will appear once a week.

Subscription cost:

one year   6 fr.
six months   3 fr. 50

On behalf of the provisional Central Bureau:

Secretary, JEAN ZAGORSKY
8 Rue Montbrillant

N. B. The national bureaus are requested to send the Central Bureau the money received for the shares and subscriptions before January 1.

The International Working Men's Association and Bakunin's International Alliance of Socialist Democracy*

JUST ABOUT a month ago a certain number of citizens formed in Geneva the Central Initiating Committee of a new international society named the International Alliance of Socialist Democracy, stating it was their "special mission to study political and philosophical questions on the basis of the grand principle of . . . equality, etc." The program and rules printed by this Initiating Committee were only communicated to the General Council of the International Working Men's Association at its meeting on December 15. According to these documents, the said International Alliance is "established entirely within the . . . International Working Men's Association," at the same time as it is established entirely outside of the Association.

Besides the General Council of the International Association, elected at the Geneva, Lausanne, and Brussels workingmen's congresses, there is to be, in line with the initiating rules, another Central Council in Geneva, which is self-appointed. Besides the local groups of the International Association, there are to be local groups of the International Alliance, which "through their . . . national bureaus," operating outside the national bureaus of the International Association, "will ask the Central Bureau of the Alliance to admit them into the International Working Men's Association"; the Alliance Central Committee thereby takes upon itself the right of admittance to the International Association. Lastly, the General Congress of the International Association will have its parallel in the General Congress of the International Alliance, for, as the initiating rules say, "At the annual Working Men's Congress the

* Written in French and approved by the General Council on December 22, 1868. This text is a translation from the French made by the Institute of Marxism-Leninism, Moscow.

delegation of the Alliance of Socialist Democracy, as a branch of the International Working Men's Association, will hold public meetings in a separate building."

Considering,

That the presence of a second international body operating within and outside the International Working Men's Association will be the most infallible means of its disorganization;

That every other group of individuals, anywhere at all, will have the right to imitate the Geneva initiating group and, under more or less plausible excuses, to bring into the International Working Men's Association other international associations with other "special missions";

That the International Working Men's Association will thereby soon become a plaything for intriguers of every race and nationality;

That the Rules of the International Working Men's Association anyway admit only local and national branches into the Association (see Article 1 and Article 6 of the Rules);

That sections of the International Association are forbidden to give themselves rules or administrative regulations contrary to the General Rules and Administrative Regulations of the International Association (see Article 12 of the Administrative Regulations);

That the Rules and Administrative Regulations of the International Association can only be revised by the General Congress in the event of two-thirds of the delegates present voting in favor of such a revision (see Article 13 of the Administrative Regulations).

The General Council of the International Working Men's Association unanimously agreed at its meeting on December 22, 1868, that:

1. All articles of the Rules of the International Alliance of Socialist Democracy, defining its relations with the International Working Men's Association, are declared null and void;

2. The International Alliance of Socialist Democracy may not be admitted as a branch of the International Working Men's Association;

3. These resolutions be published in all countries where the International Working Men's Association exists.

By order of the General Council
of the International Working Men's Association

Letter of the General Council to the Alliance of Socialist Democracy*

Citizens:

According to Article I of its Statutes, the International Working Men's Association admits "all working men's societies . . . aiming at the same end, viz., the protection, advancement, and complete emancipation of the working classes."

Since the various sections of workingmen in the same country, and the working classes in different countries, are placed under different circumstances and have attained to different degrees of development, it seems almost necessary that the theoretical notions which reflect the real movement should also diverge.

The community of action, however, called into life by the International Working Men's Association, the exchange of ideas facilitated by the public organs of the different national sections, and the direct debates at the General Congresses are sure by and by to engender a common theoretical program.

Consequently, it belongs not to the functions of the General Council to subject the program of the Alliance to a critical examination. We have not to inquire whether, yes or no, it be a true scientific expression of the working-class movement. All we have to ask is whether its general tendency does not run against the general tendency of the International Working Men's Association, viz., the complete emancipation of the working class?

One phrase in your program lies open to this objection. It occurs [in] Article 2: "*Elle (l'Alliance) veut avant tout l'égalisation politique,*

---

* Written in English and French, March 9, 1869; copies sent to all sections of the International.

économique, et sociale des classes." ["The Alliance wants above all political, economic, and social equalization . . . of classes."]

The *"égalisation des classes,"* literally interpreted, comes to the "harmony of capital and labor" (*"l'harmonie du capital et du travail"*) so persistently preached by the bourgeois socialists. It is not the logically impossible "equalization of classes," but the historically necessary, superseding "abolition of classes" (*abolition des classes*), this true secret of the proletarian movement, which forms the great aim of the International Working Men's Association.

Considering, however, the context in which that phrase *"égalisation des classes"* occurs, it seems to be a mere slip of the pen, and the General Council feels confident that you will be anxious to remove from your program an expression which offers such a dangerous misunderstanding.

It suits the principles of the International Working Men's Association to let every section freely shape its own theoretical program, except the single case of an infringement upon its general tendency. There exists, therefore, no obstacle to the transformation of the sections of the Alliance into sections of the International Working Men's Association.

The dissolution of the Alliance and the entrance of its sections into the International Working Men's Association once settled, it would, according to our Regulations, become necessary to inform the General Council of the residence and the numerical strength of each new section.

Confidential Communication*

INCLUDING CIRCULAR OF JANUARY 1, 1870,
TO THE SWISS ROMANSH COUNCIL

THE RUSSIAN BAKUNIN (although I have known him since 1843, I pass over everything that is not absolutely necessary for an understanding of the following) had a meeting with Marx in London shortly after the founding of the International. Marx received him in the International, for which Bakunin promised to work to the best of his ability. Bakunin went to Italy, received there the Provisional Statutes and the Address to the Working Classes, which Marx sent him, replied "very enthusiastically," and did nothing. After years during which one heard nothing from him, he emerged again in Switzerland. There he joined, not the International, but the *Ligue de la Paix et de la Liberté.*[1] After the congress of this Peace League (Geneva, 1867), Bakunin gets himself elected to its *executive committee,* but in it he finds opponents who not only do not allow him any "dictatorial" influence but also watch him as a "Russian suspect." Shortly after the Brussels Congress of the International (September, 1868), the Peace League held its congress in Bern. This time, B. appeared as a firebrand and—it is to be remarked in passing—denounced the Occidental bourgeoisie in the same tone that the Muscovite optimists use to attack Western civilization in order to minimize their own barbarism. He proposed a series

---

* Written March 28, 1870, and sent by Marx, in his capacity as the International's corresponding secretary for Germany, as a Confidential Communication to Dr. Ludwig Kugelmann, with the request that he submit it to Wilhelm Bracke and other members of the German Social-Democratic Workers' party commitee.
1. The League of Peace and Liberty, founded in 1867; among its prominent members were Victor Hugo and Giuseppe Garibaldi.

of resolutions which, absurd in themselves, were designed to instill fear
in the bourgeois cretins and to allow Herr Bakunin to leave the Peace
League and to enter the International with éclat. It suffices to say
that the program he proposed at the Bern Congress contained such
absurdities as "equality" of "classes," "abolition of the right of inheritance as the beginning of the social revolution," etc.—senseless
prattle, a garland of hollow notions which pretended to be chilling; in
short, an insipid improvisation designed to achieve a certain momentary
effect. Bakunin's friends in Paris (where a Russian[2] is co-publisher of
the *Revue Positiviste*) and in London publicly announced his withdrawal from the Peace League as an *événement* [event] and proclaimed his grotesque program—this *olla podrida* [spiced-up stew] of
polished commonplaces—as something strangely fearsome and original.

In the meantime, B. joined the Branche Romande [Romansh
Branch] of the International (in Geneva). It took him years before
he decided on this step. But it was only a few days before Herr
Bakunin decided to overthrow the International and transform it into
his instrument.

Behind the back of the London General Council—which was informed only after everything was seemingly ready—he established
the so-called *Alliance des Démocrates Socialistes*. The program of this
Alliance was none other than the one B. had proposed at the Bern
Peace [League] Congress. Thus from the outset the Alliance showed
itself to be a propaganda organization of specifically Bakuninist private
mysticism, and B. himself, one of the most ignorant of men in the field
of social theory, suddenly figures here as a sect founder. However, the
theoretical program of this Alliance was pure farce. Its serious side lay
in its practical organization. For this Alliance was to be an *international* one, with its central committee in Geneva, that is, under
Bakunin's personal direction. At the same time it was to be an "integral" part of the International Working Men's Association. Its branches
were to be represented at the "next Congress" of the International
(in Basel) on the one hand, and to have its own separate sessions
alongside the former on the other hand, etc. etc.

The human material chiefly at Bakunin's disposal consisted of the
then-majority of the Federal Romansh Committee of the International
in Geneva. J. Ph. Becker, whose propaganda zeal occasionally runs
away with his head, was pushed forward. In Italy and Spain, Bakunin
had some allies.

The General Council in London had been thoroughly informed.

2. Grigory N. Vyrubov, a Russian crystallographer, co-founder of *La Philo-
sophie Positive. Revue*, a journal published between 1867 and 1883 to propagate
the ideas of Auguste Comte.

But it quietly let Bakunin go on until the moment when he was forced by J. Ph. Becker to submit the statutes (and program) of the Alliance of Socialist Democracy to the General Council for approval. Thereupon followed a far-reaching decision—entirely "judicial" and "objective," yet in its "basic considerations" full of irony—which concluded as follows:

1. The General Council does *not* admit the Alliance as a branch of the International.

2. All paragraphs of the statutes of the Alliance which deal with the relationship of the International are declared *null and void*.

In the basic considerations it was demonstrated clearly and strikingly that the Alliance is nothing but a machine for the disorganization of the International.

This came as an unexpected blow. Bakunin had already transformed *L'Égalité*, the central organ of the French-speaking members of the International in Switzerland, into *his* organ; in addition, he founded in Locle a little private journal—*Progrès*. *Progrès* still plays that role under the editorship of a fanatical Bakunin follower, Guillaume.

After several weeks of reflection, the Central Committee of the Alliance—under the signature of Perron, a Genevan—finally sent a reply to the General Council. In it the Alliance, out of zeal for the cause, offered to sacrifice its independent organization, but only on one condition, namely, a declaration by the General Council that it recognizes the Alliance's "radical" principles.

The General Council replied: It is not its function to sit in theoretical judgment on the programs of the various sections. Its only task is to see to it that the latter are *not in direct contradiction with its Statutes and their spirit*. Hence the General Council must insist that the absurd phrase "equality of classes" be stricken out and replaced by the phrase "abolition of classes" (which was done). For the rest, the members of the Alliance can join the International, *after the dissolution of its own independent international organization* and after a list of the various branches has been supplied to the General Council (which, let it be noted, was never done).

With this, the incident was closed. The Alliance dissolved itself *nominally*, but *factually* continued under the leadership of Bakunin, who at the same time dominated the Geneva *Comité Romand Fédéral* of the International. Added to its list of organs there was the *Federación* in Barcelona (and after the Basel Congress, also the *Eguaglianza* in Naples).

Bakunin then sought to achieve his aim—to transform the International into his private instrument—by other means. Through the Geneva Romansh Committee of the General Council he proposed that the "question of inheritance" be put on the agenda of the Basel Congress. The General Council agreed, in order to be able to hit Bakunin on the head directly. Bakunin's plan was this: When the Basel Congress accepts the "principles" (?) he proposed in Bern, he will show the world that he has not gone over to the International, but the International has gone over to him. The simple consequence: The London General Council (whose opposition to the rehashing of the St.-Simonist *vieillerie* [rubbish] was known to Bakunin) must resign and the Basel Congress would *move the General Council to Geneva;* that is, the International would fall under the dictatorship of Bakunin.

Bakunin put his full conspiracy into motion, in order to assure himself of a majority in the Basel Congress. Even fake mandates were not lacking, such as those of Herr Guillaume for Locle, etc. Bakunin himself importuned mandates from Naples and Lyon. All sorts of calumnies against the General Council were spread. Some were told that it was dominated by the *élément bourgeois* and others that it was the seat of *communisme autoritaire.*

The result of the Basel Congress is known. Bakunin's proposals did not go through, and the General Council remained in London.

The anger of this defeat—Bakunin had perhaps tied up a hoped-for success with private speculations in "his heart's spirit and feeling"—was aired in irritated utterances in *L'Égalité* and *Progrès.* These papers in the meantime assumed more and more the form of official oracles. Now one and now the other of the Swiss sections [of the International] was put under excommunication because, despite Bakunin's express instructions, it participated in political movements, etc. Finally the long restrained fury against the General Council broke into the open. *Progrès* and *L'Égalité* sneered, attacked, declared that the General Council did not fulfill its duties, for example, in connection with the quarterly bulletins; the General Council must rid itself of direct control over England and establish a separate central committee to occupy itself with English affairs; the resolutions of the General Council in regard to the Fenian prisoners were an infringement of its functions, since it is not supposed to concern itself with local political questions. Furthermore, *Progrès* and *L'Égalité* took the side of Schweitzer, and the General Council was categorically challenged to declare itself officially and publicly on the Liebknecht-Schweitzer question. The journal *Le Travail* (in Paris), into which Schweitzer's Paris friends smuggled articles favorable to him, was praised for this by *Progrès* and *L'Égalité,* the latter demanding that *Le Travail* make common cause against the General Council.

Hence the time has come for taking decisive steps. The enclosed is an exact copy of the General Council's circular to the Romansh

Central Committee in Geneva. The document [written in French] is too long to translate into German.

CIRCULAR TO THE SWISS ROMANSH FEDERAL COUNCIL*

IN ITS extraordinary session of January 1, 1870, the General Council resolved:

1. We read in *L'Égalité* of December 11, 1869:

"It is certain that the General Council is neglecting extremely important matters. We remind the General Council of its obligations under Article I of the Regulations: The General Council is obliged to carry out the decisions of the Congress . . . We could put enough questions to the General Council for its replies to make up quite a lengthy document. They will come later. . . . Meanwhile . . . etc."

The General Council does not know of any article, either in the Statutes or in the Rules, which *obliges* it to enter into correspondence or into polemic with *L'Égalité* or to provide "answers" to "questions" from any newspapers.

Only the Swiss Romansh Federal Council represents the branch societies in the General Council. When the Federal Council directs questions or reprimands to us, and does it by the only legitimate means —that is, through its secretary—the General Council will always be ready to reply. But the Romansh Federal Council has the right neither to abdicate its functions to *L'Égalité* and *Progrès* nor to permit them to be usurped by these newspapers.

Generally speaking, the General Council's correspondence with national and local committees cannot be published without doing great harm to the general interests of the International.

Hence if other organs of the International were to follow the example of *Progrès* and *L'Égalité* the General Council would be faced with the alternative of either discrediting itself publicly by its silence or violating its obligations by replying publicly.

L'Égalité joined *Progrès* (a paper which is not sent to the General Council) in inviting *Le Travail* (a Paris paper which has not hitherto declared itself an organ of the *International,* and which is also not sent to the General Council) to demand explanations from the General Council. That is almost a League of Public Welfare![3]

2. Assuming that the questions put by *L'Égalité* come from the Romansh Federal Council, we are going to answer them, but only on

---

* Marx wrote this circular about January 1, 1870.

3. A feudal association founded in France in 1464, to oppose the policies of Louis XI.

condition that such questions are never put to us again in such a manner.

3. *The Question of a Bulletin.* In the Resolutions of the Geneva Congress, which are inserted in the Rules, it is laid down that the national committees shall send the General Council *documents* dealing with the proletarian movement and that the General Council shall thereupon publish them as bulletins in the *different languages* as often *as its means permit.* ("As often as its means permit, the General Council shall publish a report," etc.)

The General Council's obligation was thus made dependent on conditions which have never been fulfilled. Even the statistical inquiry provided for in the Rules, decided on by consecutive general congresses, and requested by the General Council year after year, has never been made. As for means, the General Council would long ago have ceased to exist without the regional contributions from England and the personal sacrifices of its members.

Thus the Rule adopted by the Geneva Congress has remained a dead letter.

In regard to the Basel Congress, it did not discuss fulfillment of these existing Rules, but only the opportunity of issuing a bulletin in good time, and *it did not make any resolution* on this. (See the German account, published in Basel under the eyes of the congress.)

For the rest, the General Council believes that the basic purpose of the bulletin is at the moment perfectly fulfilled by the various organs of the International published in various languages and exchanged among them. It would be absurd to do by expensive reports what is being done already without cost. Moreover, a bulletin which published what is not printed in the organs of the International would only help our enemies to see behind the scenes.

4. *The Question of the Separation of the General Council from the Federal Council for England.* Long before the founding of *L'Égalité,* this proposal used to be made repeatedly in the General Council by one or two of its English members. It was always rejected almost unanimously.

Although revolutionary *initiative* will probably come from France, England alone can serve as the *lever* for a serious *economic* revolution. It is the only country where there are no longer any peasants and where landed property is concentrated in a few hands. It is the only country where the *capitalist* form—that is, labor combined on a large scale under capitalist entrepreneurs—has taken over practically the whole of production. It is the only country where *the great majority of the population consists of wage laborers.* It is the only country where the class struggle and organization of the working class by the trade unions have attained a certain degree of maturity and universality. It is the only country where, thanks to its domination of the world market, every revolution in economic relationships must directly affect the whole world. While on the one hand landlordism and capitalism have their classic seat in this country, the *material conditions* for their *destruction* are on the other hand the most mature here. The General Council is now in the fortunate position of having its hand directly on this great lever of proletarian revolution; what folly, yea, one might almost say what crime it would be to let this lever fall into purely English hands!

The English have at their disposal all necessary material preconditions for a social revolution. What they lack is the spirit of generalization and revolutionary passion. Only the General Council can provide them with this, and thus accelerate a truly revolutionary movement here and, in consequence, *everywhere*. The great successes we have already achieved in this respect are attested by the most intelligent and most eminent newspapers of the ruling classes, such as, for example, the *Pall Mall Gazette*, the *Saturday Review*, the *Spectator*, and the *Fortnightly Review*, not to mention the so-called radicals in the House of Commons and the House of Lords who until recently still exerted a great influence on the leaders of the English workers. They accuse us publicly of having poisoned and practically stifled the "English spirit" of the working class and of having driven it to revolutionary socialism.

The only way of bringing about this change is to do what the General Council of the International Association is doing. As the General Council, we are able to initiate measures (for example, the founding of the Land and Labour League) which later, after their execution, appear to the public as spontaneous movements of the English working class.

If a Federal Council were to be established outside the General Council, what would be the immediate effects? The Federal Council would find itself placed between the General Council of the International and the General Council of the Trade Unions, and would have no authority. Furthermore, the General Council of the International would have its great lever taken out of its hands. If we preferred noisy quackery to serious action behind the scenes, we would perhaps commit the mistake of replying publicly to *L'Égalité*'s question why "the General Council permits such a burdensome accumulation of functions."

England should not simply be compared to other countries. It must be considered as the *metropolis of capital*.

5. *The Question of the General Council's Resolution on the Irish*

Amnesty. While England is the bulwark of landlordism and capitalism, Ireland is the only point where the great blow against official England can really be struck.

First, Ireland is the bulwark of English landlordism. If it fell in Ireland, it would also fall in England. In Ireland this is a hundred times easier, because *the economic struggle there is concentrated exclusively in landed property*, because the struggle there is at the same time a *national* one, and because the people there are more revolutionary and more embittered than in England. In Ireland landlordism is maintained solely by the English army. The moment the forced union between the two countries ends, a social revolution will break out in Ireland, even if in outmoded form. English landlordism would not only lose a substantial source of its wealth, but also its greatest moral force—that of *representing the domination of England over Ireland*. On the other hand, by maintaining the power of their landlords in Ireland, the English proletariat makes them invulnerable in England itself.

Second, the English bourgeoisie has not only exploited the Irish misery to keep down the working class in England by forced immigration of poor Irishmen, it has also divided the proletariat into two hostile camps. The revolutionary ardor of the Celtic worker does not go well with the solid but slow nature of the Anglo-Saxon worker. On the contrary, in all the big industrial centers in England there is a profound antagonism between the Irish and English proletarians. The average English worker hates the Irish worker as a competitor who lowers wages and the standard of life. He feels national and religious antipathies for him. He regards him practically in the same way that the poor whites in the southern states of North America regard the black slaves. This antagonism between the proletarians in England is artificially nourished and kept alive by the bourgeoisie. It knows that this split is the true secret of maintaining its power.

This antagonism is reproduced also on the other side of the Atlantic. The Irish, driven from their native soil by the oxen and the sheep, reassemble in North America, where they constitute a conspicuous and ever growing section of the population. Their only thought, their only passion, is hatred for England. The English and American governments (that is, the classes they represent) nourish these passions in order to perpetuate the covert struggle between the United States and England, and thereby prevent a sincere and serious alliance between the working classes on both sides of the Atlantic and, consequently, their emancipation.

Furthermore, Ireland is the only pretext the English Government has for maintaining a large standing army, which in case of necessity, as has happened before, can be loosed against the English workers after getting its military training in Ireland.

Finally, England today is seeing a repetition of what happened on a gigantic scale in ancient Rome. A nation that enslaves another forges its own chains.

The position of the International on the Irish Question is thus clear. Its first task is to hasten the social revolution in England. To this end, the decisive blow must be struck in Ireland.

The General Council's resolution on the Irish amnesty serves only as an introduction to other resolutions which will affirm that, apart from ordinary international justice, it is a precondition for the emancipation of the English working class to transform the present forced union (that is, the enslavement of Ireland) into an equal and free confederation, if possible, or complete separation, if need be.

For the rest, the naïve doctrines of *L'Égalité* and *Progrès* about the connection, or rather the nonexistence of any connection, between the social and political movements have never, to the best of our knowledge, been recognized by any of our International congresses. They run counter to our Statutes, which state: "That the economical emancipation of the working classes is therefore the great end to which every political movement ought to be subordinate as a means."

The words "as a means" were left out in the French translation made in 1864 by the Paris Committee. When questioned by the General Council, the Paris Committee excused itself by the difficulties of its political position.

There are other mutilations of the original text of the Statutes. The first clause of the Statutes reads as follows: ". . . The struggle for the emancipation of the working classes means . . . a struggle . . . for equal rights and duties, and the abolition of all class rule."

The Paris translation speaks of "equal rights and duties"; that is, it reproduces a general phrase found virtually in all democratic manifestoes of the past hundred years and differently interpreted by different classes, but it omits the concrete demand: *The abolition of all class rule.*

Further, in the second clause of the Statutes one reads: "That the economical subjection of the man of labor to the monopolizer of the means of labor—that is, the sources of life," etc.

The Paris translation substitutes the word "capital" for "the means of labor—that is, the sources of life," although the latter expression includes the land as well as the other means of labor.

The original and authentic text was restored in the French translation published as a pamphlet in Brussels by *La Rive Gauche* in 1866.

6. *The Question of Liebknecht-Schweitzer. L'Égalité* writes: "Both of these groups belong to the International." This is false. The

Eisenach group (which *Progrès* and *L'Égalité* would like to transform into Citizen Liebknecht's group) belongs to the International. The Schweitzer group does not belong to it.

Schweitzer even explained at length in his newspaper, *Social-Demokrat*, why the Lassallean organization could not join the International without destroying itself. He spoke the truth without realizing it. His artificial, sectarian organization stands in opposition to the historical and spontaneous organization of the working class.

Progrès and *L'Égalité* have summoned the General Council to declare publicly its "opinion" on the personal differences between Liebknecht and Schweitzer. Since Citizen Johann Philipp Becker (who is slandered as much as Liebknecht in Schweitzer's paper) is a member of *L'Égalité*'s editorial board, it seems truly strange that its editors are not better informed about the facts. They should have known that Liebknecht, in the *Demokratisches Wochenblatt*, publicly invited Schweitzer to accept the General Council as arbiter over their differences, and that Schweitzer has no less publicly refused to recognize the authority of the General Council.

For its part, the General Council has left no stone unturned to put an end to this scandal. It instructed its secretary for Germany to enter into correspondence with Schweitzer; this has been done for two years, but all efforts by the Council have broken down in the face of Schweitzer's firm resolve to preserve his autocratic power, together with his sectarian organization, at all costs.

It is up to the General Council to determine the favorable moment when its public intervention in this conflict will do more good than harm.

7. Since *L'Égalité*'s accusations are public and could be considered as emanating from the Romansh Federal Council in Geneva, the General Council is to communicate this reply to all committees corresponding with it.

By Order of the General Council

Marx's letter continues:

The French Committee (despite the fact that Bakunin has intrigued mightily in Lyon and Marseilles and has won over a few young hotheads), as well as the *Conseil Général Belge* (Brussels), have declared themselves *in entire agreement* with this General Council rescript.

The copy for Geneva (because the secretary for Switzerland, Jung, was very busy) had been somewhat delayed. Hence it crossed an official statement which Perret, the secretary of the Geneva Romansh Central Committee, sent to the General Council.

For the crisis broke out in Geneva before the arrival of our letter there. Some of the editors of *L'Égalité* rebelled against the Bakuninist-dictated direction. Bakunin and his followers (among them six *Égalité* editors) wanted to force the Geneva Committee to dismiss the recalcitrants. But the Geneva Committee had long been tired of Bakunin's despotism and was reluctant to be dragged in against the General Council, in opposition to the German Swiss Committee. Hence it endorsed the *Égalité* editors who had displeased Bakunin. Whereupon the six other editors submitted their resignation from the editorial board, hoping thereby to bring the paper to a standstill.

In reply to our communication the Geneva Central Committee stated that *Égalité*'s attack took place against its wishes, that it had never approved the policy it preached, that the paper would henceforth be edited under strict supervision, etc.

Thereupon Bakunin withdrew from Geneva to Tessin. Now he has control—at least as far as Switzerland is concerned—only over *Progrès* (Locle).

Soon thereafter Herzen died. Bakunin, who from the time when he began to pose as the leader of the European labor movement slandered his old friend and patron Herzen, upon the latter's death immediately began to trumpet his eulogies. Why? Because Herzen, despite his personal wealth, received from the pseudosocialist Pan-Slavic party, which was friendly to him, 25,000 francs annually for propaganda. Through his loud eulogies Bakunin managed to have this money directed to him and thereby entered into "Herzen's inheritance"—*malgré sa haine de l'héritage* [despite his hatred of the right in inheritance]—pecuniarily and morally *sine beneficio inventarii* [without legal permission of the estate].

At the same time a young Russian refugee colony settled in Geneva, consisting of students, who were really honest and who showed their honesty by adopting opposition to Pan-Slavism as the main point of their program.

They are publishing a journal, *La Voix du Peuple*, in Geneva.

About two weeks ago they applied to London, sending in their program and asking approval for the establishment of a Russian branch. The approval was granted.

In a separate letter to Marx they requested him to represent them provisionally in the General Council. This too was accepted. At the same time they indicated—and seemed thereby to want to apologize to Marx—that their next step must be to tear off Bakunin's mask publicly, because that man speaks two entirely different languages, one in Russia and another one in Europe.

Thus the game of this highly dangerous intrigant—at least on the terrain of the International—will soon be played out.

Karl Marx in the 1870s, aged about fifty-five. This photograph, by Mayall, hung in Stalin's office.

(Top) The destruction of the Vendôme Column at the order of the Commune, May 16, 1871. (Bottom) Attack by the insurgents on the Paris Hôtel de Ville, January 22, 1871.

(Top) Demonstration of solidarity with the Paris Commune, held in London, April, 1871. (Bottom) Proclamation of the Paris Commune before the Hôtel de Ville, the city hall, in Paris.

Leading members of the Paris Commune, most of them Marx's friends or associates: (Top) Gustave-Paul Cluzeret (1823-1900), escaped to Belgium. (Left to right) Raoul Rigault (1846-1871), shot by the Versailles Government. Louis-Charles Delescluze (1809-1871), fell on the barricades; Felix Pyat (1810-1889), immigrated to England. (Left to right, bottom) Pascal Grousset (1844-1909), deported to New Caledonia, fled in 1874; Charles-Théophile Ferré (1845-1871), shot by the Versailles Government; Adolphe-Alphonse Assi (1841-1886), deported to New Caledonia.

Proclamation of the Commune inside the Paris Hôtel de Ville, March 28, 1871.

Marx was under continuous police surveillance. This Dutch police telegram of April 14, 1872, reads: "Chief of Police Amsterdam—I have learned that today the Congress of the International will end and that tomorrow a number of delegates, including Marx, will meet with the Amsterdam section. Vanschermbeek."

Michael Bakunin(1814-1886), Russian anarchist who was in conflict with Marx in the International Working Men's Association, the First International.

Henri Louis Tolain (1828-1897), leader of the Paris Section of the First International.

James Guillaume (1844-1916), a French follower of Bakunin.

Pierre Joseph Proudhon (1809-1865), French social theorist and utopian whom Marx criticized in The Poverty of Philosophy.

August Bebel (1840-1913), a Marxist and a leading founder of the German Social Democratic party.

French socialist Charles Longuet (1839-1903) and his wife, Marx's daughter Jenny (1844-1883).

French socialist Paul Lafargue (1842-1911), a member of the Paris Commune and husband of Marx's daughter Laura.

Ferdinand Lassalle (1825-1864), founder of the German Labor Association in 1863, and a friend and enemy of Marx. Lassalle was killed in a duel.

Wilhelm Liebknecht (1826-1900), a friend of Marx and a founder, with August Bebel, of the German Social Democratic party.

A page of the *Minute Book of the General Council of the First International* (meeting of July 28, 1868), with a motion by Marx that a delegate be sent to the Congress of the German Workers' Unions to be held at Nuremberg.

The Bee-Hive*

CITIZEN MARX proposed that the Council should cut off all connections with the *Bee-Hive*. He said it had suppressed our resolutions and mutilated our reports and delayed them so that the dates had been falsified, even the mention that certain questions respecting the Irish prisoners were being discussed had been suppressed.

Next to that, the tone of the *Bee-Hive* was contrary to the Rules and platform of the Association. It preached harmony with the capitalists, and the Association had declared war against the capitalists' rule.

Besides this, our branches abroad complained that by sending our reports to the *Bee-Hive* we gave it a moral support and led people to believe that we endorsed its policy. We would be better without its publicity than with it.

On the Irish Coercion Bill it had not said a word against the government.

---

* From the minutes of the General Council, April 26, 1870. On November 22, 1864, the General Council had declared the *Bee-Hive*, a British trade-union weekly, to be the organ of the International. Marx's motion to sever the connection was carried.

Jules Favre and the Paris Government
of National Defense*

CITIZEN MARX said as there were several English members present he had a very important statement to make. At the last meeting at St. James's Hall Odger spoke of the French Government contrary to truth.[1] In our Second Address we said the brand of infamy attaches to some of the members of the provisional government from the Revolution of 1848. Odger said there was not a blame attached to them. Favre can only be received as the representative of the Republic, not as the spotless patriot Jules Favre. The way that is now talked about him put Favre in the foreground and the Republic almost out of sight. One example of Favre's doings. After the Revolution of 1848 Favre became Secretary of the Interior; on account of Flocon being ill, Ledru-Rollin chose Favre. One of the first things he did was to bring back the army to Paris, which afterwards enabled the bourgeoisie to shoot the workpeople down. Later, when the people became convinced that the Assembly consisted of middle-class men, the people made a demonstration in favor of Poland, on which occasion the people ran into the Assembly.[2] The president entreated Louis Blanc to speak to them and pacify them, which he did. A war with Russia would have saved the Republic. The first thing Jules Favre did

---

* From the minutes of the General Council, January 17, 1871. The minutes were written by the secretary, J. Georg Eccarius.

1. At meetings of the British Positivists on January 6 and 10, 1871, urging the recognition of the French Republic, George Odger, a British trade-union member of the International's General Council, spoke in praise of the Paris government.

2. On May 15, 1848, a mass demonstration in Paris, led by Auguste Blanqui, demanded the dissolution of the Constituent Assembly. It was dispersed by the National Guard.

a few days after was to ask for authority to prosecute Louis Blanc as an accomplice of the invaders. The Assembly thought he was instructed by the government to do [so] but all the other members of the government denounced [this measure] as the private affair of Favre. The Provincial Government conspired to provoke the insurrection of June. After the people were shot down Favre proposed that the Executive Committee should be abolished.[3] On the twenty-seventh he drew up the decree to transport the prisoners without trial; 15,000 were transported. In November the Assembly was compelled to examine some not yet transported. In Brest alone 1,000 had to be liberated. Of the most dangerous, who were tried by a military commission, many had to be liberated, others were only sentenced to short terms of imprisonment. Afterwards motions were made for an amnesty, Favre always opposed. He was one of the men who insisted for a commission of inquiry of the whole revolution except February. He was instrumental in the passing of the most infamous press laws[4] that ever existed and of which Napoleon made good use. Favre had certain relations with the Bonapartists under the July Monarchy and he used all his influence to get Napoleon into the National Assembly. He interested himself to bring about the expedition to Rome,[5] which was the first step for the establishment of the Empire.

---

3. The Executive Committee, set up by the Constituent Assembly on May 10, 1848, was in power until June 24, 1848, when General Cavaignac took over as dictator.

4. The press laws of August 9 and 11, 1848, provided that periodicals make heavy financial deposits before publication, and also called for punishment of those who criticized the government, the social system, and private property.

5. In April, 1849, France, in alliance with Austria and Naples, invaded Italy and put an end to the Roman Republic.

Activities of the Alliance of
Socialist Democracy*

THE CONFLICT began with the creation of the Alliance of Socialist Democracy, founded by Bakunin and others in Geneva. Marx read the two reports, of [December 22], 1868, and of March [9], 1869, against the Alliance; in the second report, the dissolution of the Alliance and the publication of the number of its members and sections were made a condition of the latter's admission to the International. These conditions have never been fulfilled; the Alliance has never really dissolved, but always maintained a kind of organization. The organ of the Geneva sections, *L'Égalité*, in its issue of December 11, 1869, rebuked Marx for not having done his duty by replying to its articles; to which the General Council replied that it was not his duty to enter into a newspaper polemic, but that he was, nevertheless, prepared to answer the questions and complaints of the Romansh Federal Council. This Circular Letter was sent to all the sections; they all approved the attitude of the General Council. The Swiss Council disavowed *L'Égalité* and broke with its management. The management was changed, and ever since then the organs of the followers of the Alliance have been *Le Progrès* and, later, *La Solidarité*. Then at the Congress in Locle[1] it came to an open split between the two parties, the Romansh Federation and the Jura Federation (Alliance). The General Council let the matter rest; it absolutely forbade the new Council to act as the Romansh Federal Council alongside the existing one. Guillaume, who, contrary to our Statutes, preached abstention

* Notes of a speech before a committee of the London Conference, September 18, 1871. These notes were made in German by Frederick Engels.
  1. The Congress of the Romansh Federation of the International, held at La-Chaux-de-Fonds, Canton of Le Locle, April 4 to 6, 1870.

from all political activities, at the outbreak of the [Franco-Prussian] war published an appeal,[2] calling for the creation of an army in support of France, in the name of the International, which is even more contrary to our Statutes.

---

2. James Guillaume and Gaspard Blanc, "To the Sections of the International," published at Neuchâtel, September 5, 1870.

Resolutions on the Rules of the French Section of 1871*

October 17

To Citizen Members of the French Section of 1871

Citizens:

Considering the following articles of the administrative resolutions voted on by the Basel Congress: Article 4. "Every new section or society which comes into existence and wishes to join the International must immediately notify the General Council of its adherence."

Article 5. "The General Council is entitled to accept or to refuse the affiliation of every new society or group," etc.

The General Council confirms the Rules of the French Section of 1871 with the following modifications:

1. That in Article 2 the words "justify his means of sustenance" be erased and that it should simply be said: to be admitted as a member of the section a person must present guarantees of morality, etc.

Article 9 of the General Rules states:

"Everybody who acknowledges and defends the principles of the International Working Men's Association is eligible to become a member. Every branch is responsible for the integrity of the members it admits."

In dubious cases a section may well take information about means of sustenance as a "guarantee of morality," while in other cases, like those of refugees, workers on strike, etc., absence of means of suste-

---

* Adopted by the General Council on October 17 and November 7, 1871. This text is a translation from the French by the Institute of Marxism-Leninism, Moscow.

nance may well be a guarantee of morality. But to ask candidates to justify their means of sustenance as a general condition to be admitted to the International would be a bourgeois innovation contrary to the spirit and letter of the General Rules.

2.(a) Considering that Article 4 of the General Rules states:

"The Congress . . . elects the members of the General Council . . . with power to add to their number"; that consequently the General Rules recognize only two ways of election for General Council members: either their election by the Congress, or their cooption by the General Council; that the following passage of Article 11 of the Rules of the French Section of 1871: "One or several delegates shall be sent to the General Council" . . . is therefore contrary to the General Rules which give no branch, section, group, or federation the right to send delegates to the General Council.

That Article 12 of the Regulations prescribes: "Every section is at liberty to make rules and bylaws for its local administration, suitable to the peculiar circumstances of the different countries. But these bylaws must not contain anything contrary to the General Rules and Regulations."

For these reasons:

The General Council cannot admit the above-mentioned paragraph of the Rules of the French Section of 1871.

(b) It is quite true that the different sections existing in London have been invited to send delegates to the General Council, which, so as not to violate the General Rules, has always proceeded in the following manner:

It has first determined the number of delegates to be sent to the General Council by each section, reserving itself the right to accept or refuse them depending on whether it considered them able to fulfill the general functions allotted them. These delegates became members of the General Council not by virtue of the fact that they were delegated by their sections but by virtue of the right of coopting new members accorded to the Council by the General Rules.

Having acted upon the decision taken by the last Conference both as the General Council of the International Working Men's Association and as the Central Council for England, the Council in London thought it useful to admit, besides the members that it coopted directly, members originally delegated by their respective sections.

It would have been a big mistake to identify the electoral procedure of the General Council of the International Working Men's Association with that of the Paris Federal Council, which was not even a national council nominated by a national congress like, for example, the Brussels Federal Council or that of Madrid.

The Paris Federal Council being only a delegation of the Paris sections, the delegates of these sections could well be invested with an imperative mandate with a council where they had to defend the interests of their section. The General Council's electoral procedure is, on the contrary, defined by the General Rules and its members would not accept any other imperative mandate than that of the General Rules and General Regulations.

(c) The General Council is ready to admit two delegates from the French Section of 1871 on the terms prescribed by the General Rules and never contested by the other sections existing in London.

3. In Article 11 of the Rules of the French Section of 1871, this paragraph appears:

"Every member of the section should refuse any delegation to the General Council other than that of his section."

Interpreted literally, this paragraph could be accepted, since it says only that a member of the French Section of 1871 should not present himself to the General Council as a delegate from another section.

But if we take into consideration the paragraph that precedes it, Article 11 means nothing else but completely changing the General Council's composition and making out of it, contrary to Article 3 of the General Rules, a delegation of London sections where the influence of local groups would be substituted for that of the whole International Working Men's Association.

The meaning of the paragraph in Article 11 from the rules of the French Section of 1871 is clearly confirmed by the obligation which it imposes for opting between the title of member of the section and the function of member of the General Council.

For these reasons the General Council cannot admit the above-mentioned paragraph, since it is contrary to the General Rules and deprives it of its right to recruit forces everywhere in the general interest of the International Working Men's Association.

4. The General Council is sure that the French Section of 1871 will understand the necessity for the proposed modifications and will not hesitate to bring its rules into conformity with the letter and spirit of the General Rules and Regulations and that it will thereby forestall any discord which, in the present circumstances, could only hinder the progress of the International Working Men's Association.

Greetings and equality.

In the name and by order of the General Council, the Corresponding Secretary for France,

Auguste Serraillier

November 7

I. PRELIMINARY REMARKS

The General Council considers that the ideas expressed by the French Section of 1871 about a radical change to be made in the articles of the General Rules concerning the constitution of the General Council have no bearing on the question which it ought to discuss.

With regard to the insulting references to the General Council made by that section, these will be judged for what they are worth by the councils and federal committees of the various countries.

The Council merely wishes to note:

That *three years* have not yet elapsed since the Basel Congress (which met on September 6–11, *1869*), as the above-mentioned section deliberately asserts;

That in 1870, on the eve of the Franco-Prussian War, the Council addressed a general circular to all the federations, including the Paris Federal Council, proposing that the seat of the General Council be transferred from London;

That the replies received were unanimously in favor of retaining the present seat of the Council and of prolonging its term of office;

That in 1871, as soon as the situation permitted, the General Council summoned a Conference of Delegates, this being the only action possible in the given circumstances;

That at this Conference delegates from the Continent gave voice to the misgivings in their respective countries that the cooption of too large a number of French refugees would destroy the international character of the General Council;

That the Conference (see its "Resolutions, etc.," XV) "leaves it to the discretion of the General Council to fix, according to events, the day and place of meeting of the next Congress or Conference which might replace it."

With regard to the said section's claim to exclusive representation of "the French revolutionary element," because its members include ex-presidents of Paris workers' societies, the Council remarks:

The fact that this or that person has in the past been president of a workers' society may well be taken into account by the General Council, but does not in itself constitute the "right" to a seat on the Council or to represent the "revolutionary element" on that body. If this were so, the Council would be obliged to grant membership to M. Gustave Durand, former president of the Paris Jewelers' Society and secretary of the French Section in London. Moreover, members of the General Council are bound to represent the principles of the International Working Men's Association, rather than the opinions and interests of this or that corporation.

II. OBJECTIONS PRESENTED BY THE FRENCH SECTION OF 1871 AT THE GENERAL COUNCIL MEETING OF OCTOBER 31 TO THE RESOLUTIONS OF OCTOBER 17

1. With respect to the following passage from Article 2 of the section's rules: "In order to be admitted as a member of the section, a person must provide information as to his means of sustenance, present guarantees of morality," etc., the section remarks: "The General Rules make the sections responsible for the morality of their members, and, as a consequence, recognize the right of sections to demand guarantees at their own discretion."

On this argument, a section of the International founded by teetotalers could include in its rules this type of article: "To be admitted as a member of the section, a person must swear to abstain from all alcoholic drinks." In short, it would always be possible for individual sections to impose in their local rules the most absurd and incongruous conditions of admittance into the International, under the pretext that they "think it necessary in this way" to discharge their responsibility for the integrity of their members.

In its Resolution I of October 17, the General Council stated that there may be "cases in which the absence of any means of sustenance may well be a guarantee of morality." It is of the opinion that the section repeated this point unnecessarily when it said that "refugees" are "above suspicion by virtue of the eloquent proof of their poverty."

As to the phrase that strikers' "means of sustenance" consist of "the strike fund" this might be answered by saying, first, that this "fund" is often fictitious.

Moreover, official English inquiries have shown that the majority of English workers, who, generally speaking, enjoy better conditions than their brothers on the Continent, are forced as a result of strikes and unemployment, or because of insufficient wages or terms of payment and many other causes, to resort incessantly to pawnshops or to borrowing money, that is, to "means of sustenance" about which one cannot demand information without interfering in an unqualified manner in a person's private life.

There are two alternatives.

Either the section sees "means of sustenance" purely as "guarantees of morality," in which case the General Council's proposal that "to be admitted as a member of the section a person must provide guarantees of morality" serves the purpose since it assumes (see the resolution of October 17) that "in dubious cases the section may well take information about means of sustenance as a guarantee of morality."

Or in Article 2 of its rules the section deliberately refers to the furnishing of information about "means of sustenance" as a condition for admission, over and above the "guarantees of morality" which it is empowered to require, in which case the General Council affirms that "it is a bourgeois innovation contrary to the letter and spirit of the General Rules."

2. With respect to the General Council's rejection of the following clause of Article 11 of the section's rules: "One or several delegates shall be sent to the General Council," the section states: "We are not unaware . . . that the wording of the General Rules confers on it" (the General Council) "the right to accept or reject delegates."

This is a patent demonstration of the fact that the section is not familiar with the essence of the General Rules.

In actual fact, the General Rules, which recognize only *two* ways of election to the General Council, namely, election by the Congress or cooption by the Council itself, *nowhere* state that the Council has the right to accept or reject delegates from the sections or groups.

The admission of delegates proposed by the London sections has always been a purely administrative measure on the part of the General Council, which in this case only made use of its power of cooption (see clause 2 of the resolution of the General Council of October 17).

The exceptional circumstances which led the General Council to have recourse to cooption of this kind were explained at sufficient length in its resolution of October 17.

In the same resolution (2c) the Council declared that it would admit delegates from the French Section of 1871 on the same conditions as those from the London sections. It cannot, however, be expected to give serious consideration to a demand that would grant this section a privileged position contrary to the General Rules.

By the inclusion of the following paragraph in Article 11 of its rules: "One or several delegates shall be sent to the General Council," the French Section of 1871 is claiming the right to send delegates to the General Council allegedly basing itself on the General Rules. It acted as though fully convinced that it possessed this imaginary right, and even before the section had been recognized by the General Council (see Article VI of the Administrative Resolutions of the Basel

Congress), it did not hesitate to send "by right" to the General Council meeting of October 17 two delegates, armed with "imperative mandates" in the name of the twenty full members of the section. Finally, in its latest communication it again insists on "the duty and right to send delegates to the General Council."

The section attempts to justify its claims by seeking a precedent in the position of Citizen Herman on the General Council. It pretends to be unaware of the fact that Citizen Herman was coopted into the General Council at the recommendation of the Belgian Congress, and in no way represents the Liège section.

3. With respect to the General Council's refusal to recognize the following passage in the section's rules: "Each member of the section should refuse any delegation to the General Council other than that of his section," the section states: "In response to this, we shall limit ourselves to the observation that our rules pertain to our section alone; our agreements are of no concern or relevance to anyone but ourselves, and this claim in no way contradicts the General Rules, which include no provision on this subject."

It is difficult to comprehend how the Rules which include no provision on the right of delegation to the General Council should suddenly specify the conditions of this delegation. On the other hand, it is not so difficult to see that the section's own rules do not apply outside its field of competence. Nevertheless, it cannot be admitted that the specific rules of any section "are of no concern or relevance to anyone" but that section alone. For were the General Council to approve Article 11 of the rules of the French Section of 1871, for example, it would be obliged to insert it into the rules of all the other sections, and this article, once it began to apply generally, would completely nullify the right of cooption conferred on the Council by the General Rules.

For these reasons:

1. The General Council reaffirms in their entirety its resolutions of October 17, 1871;

2. In the event of these resolutions not being accepted by the section before the Council's meeting on November 21, the corresponding secretaries should bring the following documents to the notice of the Federal Councils or Committees of the respective countries or, where these do not exist, to the notice of the local groups: the rules of the French Section of 1871, the mandate of that section's delegates presented to the General Council at its meeting on October 17, the General Council's resolutions of October 17, the reply of the French Section of 1871 presented to the General Council at its meeting on October 31, and the Council's final resolutions of November 7.

Nechayev's Misuse of the Name of the International*

THE Conference of the Delegates of the International Working Men's Association, assembled at London September 17–23, 1871, has charged the General Council to declare publicly:

That Nechayev[1] has never been a member or an agent of the International Working Men's Association;

That his assertions to have founded a branch at Brussels and to have been sent by a Brussels branch on a mission to Geneva are false;

That the above-said Nechayev has fraudulently used the name of the International Working Men's Association in order to make dupes and victims in Russia.

By order of the General Council, etc.

---

* Written October 14, 1871.

1. Sergei Nechayev was closely connected with Bakunin while in exile in Switzerland, whence he was extradited to Russia in 1872. He died in the Peter-Paul's Fortress prison after seven years' confinement. On November 25, 1872, Marx wrote to Nicolai F. Danielson in St. Petersburg: "As a result of Nechayev's extradition and the intrigues of his master, Bakunin, I am very worried about the safety of yourself and that of some other friends. Those fellows are capable of any vileness." See Marx's letter to Frau Liebknecht, January 13, 1871, page 519.

Fictitious Splits in the International*

UNTIL NOW the General Council has completely refrained from any interference in the International's internal squabbles and has never replied publicly to the overt attacks launched against it during more than two years by some members of the Association.

But if the persistent efforts of certain meddlers to deliberately maintain confusion between the International and a society[1] which has been hostile to it since its inception allowed the General Council to maintain this reserve, the support which European reaction finds in the scandals provoked by that society at a time when the International is undergoing the most serious trial since its foundation obliges it to present a historical review of all these intrigues.

I

After the fall of the Paris Commune, the General Council's first act was to publish its Address on the Civil War in France, in which it came out in support of all the Commune's acts which, at the moment, served the bourgeoisie, the press, and all the governments of Europe as an excuse to heap the most vile slander on the vanquished Parisians. Within the working class itself some still failed to realize that their cause was lost. The Council came to understand the fact, among other things, by the resignation of two of its members, Citizens

---

* Written by Marx and Engels between the middle of January and March 5, 1872, and adopted by the General Council as a private circular; published in French as a pamphlet, *Les Prétendues Scissions dans l'Internationale*, in Geneva in 1872. The text used here is based on a translation by Progress Publishers, Moscow.

1. The International Alliance of Socialist Democracy.

Odger and Lucraft, who repudiated all support of the Address. It may be said that the unity of views among the working class regarding the Paris events dates from the publication of the Address in all the civilized countries.

On the other hand, the International found a very powerful means of propaganda in the bourgeois press and particularly in the leading English newspapers, which the Address forced to engage in a polemic kept going by the General Council's replies.

The arrival in London of numerous refugees from the Commune made it necessary for the General Council to constitute itself as a relief committee and function as such for more than eight months, besides carrying on its regular duties. It goes without saying that the vanquished and exiles from the Commune had nothing to hope for from the bourgeoisie. As for the working class, the appeals for aid came at a difficult moment. Switzerland and Belgium had already received their contingent of refugees whom they had either to support or send on to London. The funds collected in Germany, Austria, and Spain were sent to Switzerland. In England, the big fight for the nine-hour working day, the decisive battle of which was fought at Newcastle, had exhausted both the workers' individual contributions and the funds set up by the trade unions, which could be used, incidentally, according to the rules, only for labor conflicts. Meanwhile, by working diligently and sending out letters, the Council managed to accumulate, bit by bit, the money which it distributed weekly. The American workers responded more generously to its appeal. It is unfortunate that the Council could not avail itself of the millions which the terrified bourgeoisie believed the International to have amassed in its safes!

After May, 1871, some of the Commune's refugees were asked to join the Council, in which, as a result of the war, the French side was no longer represented. Among the new members were some old Internationalists and a minority composed of men known for their revolutionary energy whose election was an act of homage to the Paris Commune.

Along with all these preoccupations, the Council had to prepare for the Conference of Delegates that it had just called.

The violent measures taken by the Bonapartist government against the International had prevented the holding of the Congress at Paris, which had been provided for by a resolution of the Basel Congress. Using the right conferred upon it by Article 4 of the Rules, the General Council, in its circular of July 12, 1870, convened the Congress at Mainz. In letters addressed at the same time to the various federations, it proposed that the General Council should transfer its seat from England to another country and asked that delegates be provided with definite mandates to that effect. The federations unanimously insisted that it should remain in London. The Franco-Prussian War, which began a few days later, made it necessary to abandon any plans for convening the Congress. It was then that the federations which we consulted authorized us to fix the date of the next Congress as may be dictated by the political situation.

As soon as the political situation permitted, the General Council called a private Conference, acting on the precedents of the 1865 Conference and the private administrative meetings of each Congress. A public Congress was impossible and could only have resulted in the continental delegates being denounced at a moment when European reaction was celebrating its orgies; when Jules Favre was demanding from all governments, even the British, the extradition of refugees as common criminals; when Dufaure was proposing to the Rural Assembly a law banning the International, a hypocritical counterfeit of which was later presented by Malou to the Belgians; when in Switzerland a Commune refugee was put under preventive arrest while awaiting the federal government's decision on the extradition order; when hunting down members of the International was the ostensible basis for an alliance between Beust and Bismarck, whose anti-International clause Victor Emmanuel was quick to adopt; when the Spanish Government, putting itself entirely at the disposal of the butchers of Versailles, was forcing the Madrid Federal Council to seek refuge in Portugal; at a time, lastly, when the International's prime duty was to strengthen its organization and to accept the gauntlet thrown down by the governments.

All sections in regular contact with the General Council were invited in good time to the Conference, which, even though it was not to be a public meeting, nevertheless faced serious difficulties. In view of the internal situation France was, of course, unable to elect any delegates. In Italy, the only organized section at the time was that of Naples; but just as it was about to nominate a delegate it was broken up by the army. In Austria and Hungary, the most active members were imprisoned. In Germany, some of the more well-known members were prosecuted for the crime of high treason, others landed in jail, and the party's funds were spent on aid to their families. The Americans, though they sent the Conference a detailed memorandum on the situation of the International there, employed the delegation's money for maintaining the refugees. All federations, in fact, recognized the necessity of substituting the private Conference for a public Congress.

After meeting in London from September 17 to 23, 1871, the Conference authorized the General Council to publish its resolutions;

to codify the Administrative Regulations and publish them with the General Rules, as reviewed and corrected, in three languages; to carry out the resolution to replace membership cards with stamps; to reorganize the International in England; and, lastly, to provide the necessary money for these various purposes.

Following the publication of the Conference proceedings, the reactionary press of Paris and Moscow, of London and New York denounced the resolution on working-class policy as containing such dangerous designs—the *Times* accused it "of coolly calculated audacity"—that it would outlaw the International with all possible speed. On the other hand, the resolution that dealt a blow at the fraudulent sectarian sections gave the international police a long-awaited excuse to start a noisy campaign ostensibly for the unrestricted autonomy of the workers whom it professed to protect against the despicable despotism of the General Council and the Conference. The working class felt itself so "heavily oppressed," indeed, that the General Council received from Europe, America, Australia, and even the East Indies reports about the admission of new members and the formation of new sections.

II

The denunciations in the bourgeois press, like the lamentations of the international police, found a sympathetic echo even in our Association. Some intrigues, directed ostensibly against the General Council but in reality against the Association, were hatched in its midst. At the bottom of these intrigues was the inevitable International Alliance of Socialist Democracy, fathered by the Russian Michael Bakunin. On his return from Siberia, the latter began to write in Herzen's *Kolokol* preaching the idea of Pan-Slavism and racial war, conceived out of his long experience. Later, during his stay in Switzerland, he was nominated to head the steering committee of the League of Peace and Freedom, founded in opposition to the International. When this bourgeois society's affairs went from bad to worse, its president, Mr. G. Vogt, acting on Bakunin's advice, proposed to the International's Congress which met at Brussels in September, 1868, that it make an alliance with the League. The Congress unanimously proposed two alternatives: either the League should follow the same goal as the International, in which case it would have no reason for existing; or else its goal should be different, in which case an alliance would be impossible. At the League's congress, held in Bern a few days later, Bakunin made an about-face. He proposed a makeshift program whose scientific value may be judged by this single phrase: "economic and social equalization of classes." Backed by an insignificant minority, he broke with the League in order to join the International, determined to replace the International's General Rules by the makeshift program, which had been rejected by the League, and to replace the General Council by his personal dictatorship. To this end, he created a special instrument, the International Alliance of Socialist Democracy, intended to become an International within the International.

Bakunin found the necessary elements for the formation of this society in the relationships he had formed during his stay in Italy, and in a small group of Russian emigrants, serving him as emissaries and recruiting officers among members of the International in Switzerland, France, and Spain. Yet it was only after repeated refusals of the Belgian and Paris federal councils to recognize the Alliance that he decided to submit for the General Council's approval his new society's rules, which were nothing but a faithful reproduction of the "misunderstood" Bern program. The Council replied with the following circular dated December 22, 1868. . . .[2]

A few months later, the Alliance again appealed to the General Council and asked whether, *yes or no*, it accepted its *principles*. If yes, the Alliance was ready to dissolve itself into the International's sections. It received a reply in the following circular of March 9, 1869 . . .[3]

Having accepted these conditions, the Alliance was admitted to the International by the General Council, misled by certain signatures affixed to Bakunin's program and supposing it recognized by the Romansh Federal Committee in Geneva, which on the contrary had always refused to have any dealings with it. Thus it had achieved its immediate goal: to be represented at the Basel Congress. Despite the dishonest means employed by his supporters, means used solely on this occasion in an International Congress, Bakunin was deceived in his expectation of seeing the Congress transfer the seat of the General Council to Geneva and give an official sanction to the old St. Simon rubbish, the immediate abolition of hereditary rights which he had made the practical point of departure of socialism. This was the signal for the open and incessant war which the Alliance waged not only against the General Council but also against all International sections that refused to adopt this sectarian clique's program and particularly the doctrine of total abstention from politics.

2. See "The International Working Men's Association and Bakunin's International Alliance of Socialist Democracy," page 162.
3. See "Letter of the General Council to the Alliance of Socialist Democracy," page 164.

Even before the Basel Congress, when Nechayev came to Geneva, Bakunin got together with him and founded, in Russia, a secret society among students. Always hiding his true identity under the name of various "revolutionary committees," he sought autocratic powers based on all the tricks and mystifications of the time of Cagliostro. The main means of propaganda used by this society consisted in compromising innocent people in the eyes of the Russian police by sending them communications from Geneva in yellow envelopes stamped in Russian on the outside "secret revolutionary committee." The published accounts of the Nechayev trial bear witness to the infamous abuse of the International's name.

The Alliance commenced at this time a public polemic directed against the General Council, first in the Locle *Progrès*, then in the Geneva *Égalité*, the official newspaper of the Romansh Federation, where several members of the Alliance had followed Bakunin. The General Council, which had scorned the attacks published in *Progrès*, Bakunin's personal organ, could not ignore those from *L'Égalité*, which it was bound to believe were approved by the Romansh Federal Committee. It therefore published the circular of January 1, 1870.[4]

Meanwhile, before having read this circular, the Romansh Federal Committee had already expelled supporters of the Alliance from the editorial board of *L'Égalité*.

The January 1, 1870, circular, like those of December 22, 1868, and March 9, 1869, was approved by all International sections.

It goes without saying that none of the conditions accepted by the Alliance have ever been fulfilled. Its sham sections have remained a mystery to the General Council. Bakunin sought to retain under his personal direction the few groups scattered in Spain and Italy and the Naples section which he had detached from the International. In the other Italian towns he corresponded with small cliques composed not of workers but of lawyers, journalists, and other bourgeois doctrinaires. At Barcelona some of his friends maintained his influence. In some towns in the South of France the Alliance made an effort to found separatist sections under the direction of Albert Richard and Gaspard Blanc, of Lyon, about whom we shall have more to say later. In a word, the International within the International continued to operate.

The big blow—the attempt to take over the leadership of French Switzerland—was to have been executed by the Alliance at the Chaux-de-Fonds Congress, opened on April 4, 1870.

The battle began over the right to admit the Alliance delegates,

4. For full text of the circular, see page 170.

which was contested by the delegates of the Geneva Federation and the Chaux-de-Fonds sections.

Although on their own calculation the Alliance supporters represented no more than a fifth of the Federation members, they succeeded, thanks to repetition of the Basel maneuvers, in procuring a fictitious majority of one or two votes, a majority which, in the words of their own organ (see *Solidarité* of May 7, 1870), represented no more than *fifteen* sections, while in Geneva alone there were thirty! On this vote, the French-Switzerland Congress split into two groups which continued their meetings independently. The Alliance supporters, considering themselves the legal representatives of the whole of the Federation, transferred the Federal Committee's seat to Chaux-de-Fonds and founded at Neuchâtel their official organ, *Solidarité*, edited by Citizen Guillaume. This young writer had the special job of decrying the Geneva "factory workers," those odious "bourgeois," of waging war on *L'Égalité*, the Federation newspaper, and of preaching total abstention from politics. The authors of the most important articles on this theme were Bastelica in Marseilles and Albert Richard and Gaspard Blanc in Lyon, the two big pillars of the Alliance.

On their return, the Geneva delegates convened their sections in a general assembly which, despite opposition from Bakunin and his friends, approved their actions at the Chaux-de-Fonds Congress. A little later, Bakunin and the more active of his accomplices were expelled from the old Romansh Federation.

Hardly had the Congress closed when the new Chaux-de-Fonds Committee called for the intervention of the General Council in a letter signed by F. Robert, secretary, and by Henri Chevalley, president, who was denounced two months later as a thief by the Committee's organ, *Solidarité*, on July 9. After examining the case of both sides, the General Council decided on June 28, 1870, to keep the Geneva Federal Committee in its old functions and invite the new Chaux-de-Fonds Federal Committee to take a local name. In the face of this decision which foiled its plans, the Chaux-de-Fonds Committee denounced the General Council's *authoritarianism*, forgetting that it had been the first to ask for its intervention. The trouble that the persistent attempts of the Chaux-de-Fonds Committee to usurp the name of the Romansh Federal Committee caused the Swiss Federation obliged the General Council to suspend all official relations with the former.

Louis Bonaparte had just surrendered his army at Sedan. From all sides arose protests from International members against the war's continuation. In its address of September 9, the General Council, denouncing Prussia's plans of conquest, indicated the danger of her triumph for the proletarian cause and warned the German workers that they would themselves be the first victims. In England the General Council organized meetings which condemned the pro-Prussian tendencies of the court. In Germany the International workers organized demonstrations demanding recognition of the Republic and "an honorable peace for France". . . .

Meanwhile, his bellicose nature gave the hotheaded Guillaume (of Neuchâtel) the brilliant idea of publishing an *anonymous* manifesto as a supplement and under cover of the official newspaper *Solidarité*, calling for the formation of a Swiss volunteer corps to fight the Prussians, something which he had doubtless always been prevented from doing by his abstentionist convictions.

Then came the Lyon uprising. Bakunin rushed there and, supported by Albert Richard, Gaspard Blanc, and Bastelica, installed himself on September 28 in the town hall—where he *refrained* from posting a guard, however, lest it be viewed as a political act. He was driven out in shame by some of the National Guard at the moment when, after a difficult accouchement, his decree on the abolition of the state had just seen the light of day.

In October, 1870, the General Council, in the absence of its French members, coopted Citizen Paul Robin, a refugee from Brest, one of the best-known supporters of the Alliance, and, what is more, the instigator of several attacks on the General Council in *L'Égalité*, where, since that moment, he has acted constantly as official correspondent of the Chaux-de-Fonds Committee. On March 14, 1871, he suggested the calling of a private Conference of the International to sift out the Swiss trouble. Foreseeing that important events were in the making in Paris, the Council flatly refused. Robin returned to the question on several occasions and even suggested that the Council take a definite decision on the conflict. In July 25 the General Council decided that this affair would be one of the questions for the Conference due to be convened in September, 1871.

On August 10 the Alliance, hardly eager to see its activities looked into by a Conference, declared itself dissolved as from the sixth of August. But on September 15 it reappeared and requested admission to the Council under the name of the Atheist Socialist Section. According to Administrative Resolution No. V of the Basel Congress, the Council could not admit it without consulting the Geneva Federal Committee, which was exhausted after its two years of struggle against the sectarian sections. Moreover, the Council had already told the Young Men's Christian Association that the International did not recognize theological sections.

On August 6, the date of the dissolution of the Alliance, the

Chaux-de-Fonds Federal Committee renewed its request to enter into official relations with the Council and said that it would continue to ignore the June 28 resolution and to regard itself, in relation to Geneva, as the Romansh Federal Committee, and that it was "up to the General Congress to judge this affair." On September 4 the same Committee challenged the Conference's competence, even though it had been the first to call for its convocation. The Conference could have replied by questioning the competence of the Paris Federal Committee, which the Chaux-de-Fonds Committee had, before the siege of Paris, asked to deliberate on the Swiss conflict. But it confined itself to the General Council decision of June 28, 1870 (see the reasons given in *L'Égalité* of Geneva, October 21, 1871).

III

The presence in Switzerland of some of the outlawed French who had found refuge there put some life back into the Alliance.

The Geneva members of the International did all they could for the emigrants. They came to their aid right from the beginning, initiated a wide campaign, and prevented the Swiss authorities from serving an extradition order on the refugees as demanded by the Versailles government. Several risked grave danger by going to France to help the refugees reach the frontier. Imagine the surprise of the Geneva workers when they saw several of the ringleaders, such as B. Malon,[5] immediately come to an understanding with the Alliance people and with the help of N. Zhukovsky, ex-secretary of the Alliance, try to found at Geneva, outside of the Romansh Federation, the new "Socialist Revolutionary Propaganda and Action Section." In the first article of its rules it "pledges allegiance to the General Rules of the International Working Men's Association, while reserving for itself

---

5. Do the friends of B. Malon, who have been advertising him in a stereotyped way for the last three months as the founder of the International, who have called his book the only independent work on the Commune, know the attitude taken by this assistant to the Mayor of Batignolles on the eve of the February elections? At that time, B. Malon, who did not yet foresee the Commune and saw nothing more than the success of his election to the Assembly, plotted to get himself put on the list of the four committees as a member of the International. To these ends he insolently denied the existence of the Paris Federal Council and submitted to the committees the list of a section founded by himself at Batignolles as coming from the entire Association. Later, on March 19, he insulted in a public document the leaders of the great Revolution on the eve of their consummating it. Today this anarchist from top to toe prints or has printed what he was saying a year ago to the four committees: I am the International! B. Malon has hit on a way of parodying Louis XIV and Perron the chocolate manufacturer at one and the same time. It was Perron who declared that his chocolate was the *only* edible chocolate!—K.M., F.E.

the complete freedom of action and initiative to which it is entitled as a logical consequence of the principle of autonomy and federation recognized by the Rules and Congresses of the Association."

In other words, it reserves for itself full freedom to continue the work of the Alliance.

In a letter from Malon of October 20, 1871, this new section for the third time asked the General Council for admission to the International. Conforming to Resolution V of the Basel Congress, the Council consulted the Geneva Federal Committee, which vigorously protested against the Council's recognizing this new "seedbed of intrigues and dissentions." The Council acted, in fact, in a rather "authoritarian" manner, so as not to bind the whole Federation to the will of B. Malon and N. Zhukovsky, the Alliance's ex-secretary.

Solidarité having gone out of business, the new Alliance supporters founded the *Révolution Sociale* under the supreme management of Madame André Léo, who had just said at the Lausanne Peace Congress that Raoul Rigault and Ferré were the two sinister figures of the Commune who, up till then (up till the execution of the hostages), had not stopped calling for bloody measures, albeit in vain.

From its very first issue the newspaper hastened to put itself on the same level as *Figaro, Gaulois, Paris-Journal,* and other disreputable sheets which have been throwing mud at the General Council. It thought the moment opportune to fan the flames of national hatred, even within the International. It called the General Council a German Committee led by a Bismarckian brain.[6]

After having definitely established that certain General Council members could not boast of being "Gauls first and foremost," the *Révolution Sociale* could find nothing better than to take up the second slogan put in circulation by the European police and to denounce the Council's "authoritarianism."

What, then, were the facts on which this childish rubbish rested? The General Council had let the Alliance die a natural death and, in agreement with the Geneva Federal Committee, had prevented it from being resurrected. Moreover, it had suggested to the Chaux-de-Fonds Committee that it take a name which would permit it to live in peace with the great majority of International members in French Switzerland.

Apart from these "authoritarian" acts, what use did the General Council make, between October, 1869, and October, 1871, of the

---

6. Here is the national composition of the Council: twenty Englishmen, fifteen French, seven Germans (of whom five are founding members of the International), two Swiss, two Hungarians, one Pole, one Belgian, one Irishman, one Dane, and one Italian.—K.M., F.E.

fairly extensive powers that the Basel Congress had conferred upon it?

1. On February 8, 1870, the Paris "Society of Positivist Proletarians" applied to the General Council for admission. The Council replied that the principles of the Positivists, the part of the society's special rules concerning capital, were in flagrant contradiction with the preamble of the General Rules; that the society had therefore to drop them and join the International not as "Positivists" but as "proletarians," while remaining free to reconcile their theoretical ideas with the Association's general principles. Realizing the justness of this decision, the section joined the International.

2. At Lyon there was a split between the 1865 Section and a recently-formed section in which, amid honest workers, the Alliance was represented by Albert Richard and Gaspard Blanc. As had been done in similar cases, the judgment of a court of arbitration, formed in Switzerland, was turned down. On February 15, 1870, the recently formed section besides asking the General Council to resolve the conflict by virtue of Resolution VII of the Basel Congress, sent it a ready-made resolution excluding and branding the members of the 1865 Section, which was to be signed and sent back by *return mail*. The Council condemned this unprecedented procedure and demanded that the necessary documents be produced. In reply to the same request, the 1865 Section said that the accusatory documents against Albert Richard, which had been submitted to the court of arbitration, were in Bakunin's possession and that he refused to give them up. Consequently it could not completely satisfy the desires of the General Council. The Council's decision on the affair, dated March 8, met with no objection from either side.

3. The French section in London, which had admitted people of a more than dubious character, had been gradually transformed into a concern virtually controlled by Mr. Félix Pyat. He used it to organize damaging demonstrations calling for the assassination of Louis Bonaparte, etc., and to spread his absurd manifestoes in France under cover of the International. The General Council confined itself to declaring in the Association's organs that Mr. Pyat was not a member of the International and it could not be responsible for his actions. The French branch then declared that it no longer recognized either the General Council or the Congresses; it plastered the walls of London with handbills proclaiming that with the exception of itself the International was an antirevolutionary society. The arrest of French members of the International on the eve of the plebiscite, on the pretext of a conspiracy, plotted in reality by the police and to which Pyat's manifestoes gave an air of credibility, forced the General Council to publish in *La Marseillaise* and *Réveil* its resolution of May 10, 1870, de-

claring that the so-called French branch had not belonged to the International for over two years, and that its agitation was the work of police agents. The need for this *démarche* was proved by the declaration of the Paris Federal Committee, published in the same newspapers, and by that of the Paris members of the International during their trial, both declarations referring to the Council's resolution. The French branch disappeared at the outbreak of the war, but, like the Alliance in Switzerland, it was to reappear in London with new allies and under other names.

During the last days of the Conference, a French Section of 1871, about thirty-five members strong, was formed in London among the Commune refugees. The first "authoritarian" act of the General Council was to publicly denounce the secretary of this section, Gustave Durand, as a French police spy. The documents in our possession prove the intention of the police first to assist Durand to attend the Conference and then to secure for him membership in the General Council. Since the rules of the new section directed its members not to accept any delegation to the General Council other than from its section, Citizens Theisz and Bastelica withdrew from the Council.

On October 17 the section delegated to the Council two of its members, holding imperative mandates; one was none other than Mr. Chautard, ex-member of the artillery committee. The Council refused to admit them prior to an examination of the rules of the 1871 Section.[7] Suffice it to recall here the principal points of the debate to which these rules gave rise. Article 2 states: "To be admitted as member of the section, a person must provide information as to his means of sustenance, present guarantees of morality, etc."

In its resolution of October 17, 1871, the Council proposed deleting the words "provide information as to his means of sustenance." "In dubious cases," said the Council, "a section may well take information about means of sustenance as a 'guarantee of morality,' while in other cases, like those of refugees, workers on strike, etc., absence of means of sustenance may well be a guarantee of morality. But to ask candidates to provide information as to their means of sustenance as a general condition to be admitted to the International would be a bourgeois innovation contrary to the spirit and letter of the General Rules." The section replied: "The General Rules make the sections responsible for the morality of their members and, as a consequence, recognize their right to demand such guarantees as they deem necessary."

---

7. A little later, this Chautard whom they had wanted to put on the General Council was expelled from the section as an agent of Thiers' police. He was accused by the same people who had judged him worthy among all others of representing them on the General Council.—K.M., F.E.

To this the General Council replied November 7: "On this argument, a section of the International founded by *teetotalers* could include in its own rules this type of article: To be admitted as a member of the section, a person must swear to abstain from all alcoholic drinks. In other words, the most absurd and most incongruous conditions of admittance into the International could be imposed by sections' rules, always on the pretext that they intend, in this way, to be assured of the morality of their members. . . . 'The means of sustenance of strikers,' adds the French Section of 1871, 'consist of the strike fund.' This might be answered by saying, first, that this 'fund' is often fictitious. . . . Moreover, official English questionnaires have proved that the majority of English workers . . . are forced—by strikes or unemployment, by insufficient wages or terms of payment, as well as many other causes—to resort incessantly to pawnshops or to borrowing money. These are means of sustenance about which one cannot demand information without interfering in an unqualified manner in a person's private life. There are thus two alternatives: either the section is only to seek guarantees of morality through means of sustenance, in which case the General Council's proposal serves the purpose. . . . Or the section, in Article 2 of its rules, intentionally says that the members have to provide information as to their means of sustenance as a condition of admission, over and above the guarantees of morality, in which case the Council affirms that it is a bourgeois innovation, contrary to the letter and spirit of the General Rules."

Article 11 of their rules states: "One or several delegates shall be sent to the General Council."

The Council asked for this article to be deleted "because the International's General Rules do not recognize any right of the sections to send delegates to the General Council." "The General Rules," it added, "recognize only two ways of election for General Council members: either their election by the Congress, or their cooption by the General Council. . . ."

It is quite true that the different sections in London had been invited to send delegates to the General Council, which, so as not to violate the General Rules, has always proceeded in the following manner: It has first determined the number of delegates to be sent by each section, reserving itself the right to accept or refuse them depending on whether it considered them able to fulfill the general functions assigned to them. These delegates became members of the General Council not by virtue of their nomination by their sections, but by virtue of the right that the Rules accord the Council to coopt new members. Having operated up to the decision taken by the last Conference both as the International Association's General Council and as the Central Council for England, the London Council thought it expedient to admit, besides the members that it coopted directly, also members nominated initially by their respective sections. It would be a serious mistake to identify the General Council's electoral procedure with that of the Paris Federal Council, which was not even a national Council nominated by a national Congress like, for example, the Brussels Federal Council or that of Madrid. The Paris Federal Council was only a delegation of the Paris sections. . . . The General Council's electoral procedure is defined in the General Rules . . . and its members would not know how to accept any other imperative mandate than that of the Rules and General Regulations. . . . If we take into consideration the article that precedes it, Article 11 means nothing else but a complete change of the General Council's composition, turning it, contrary to Article 3 of the General Rules, into a delegation of the London sections, in which the influence of local groups would be substituted for that of the whole International Working Men's Association. Lastly, the General Council, whose first duty is to carry out the Congress resolutions (see Article 1 of the Geneva Congress' Administrative Regulations), said that it "considers that the ideas expressed by the French Section of 1871 about a radical change to be made in the articles of the General Rules concerning the constitution of the General Council have no bearing on the question. . . ."

Moreover, the Council declared that it would admit two delegates from the section on the same conditions as those of the other London sections.

The 1871 Section, far from being satisfied with this reply, published on December 14 a "declaration" signed by all its members, including the new secretary, who was shortly expelled as a scoundrel from the refugee society. According to this declaration, the General Council, by refusing to usurp the legislative functions, was accused of "a gross distortion of the social idea."

Here are some samples of the good faith displayed in the drawing up of this document:

The London Conference approved the conduct of the German workers during the [Franco-Prussian] war. It was apparent that this resolution, proposed by a Swiss delegate [Outine], seconded by a Belgian delegate, and approved unanimously, referred only to the German members of the International, who paid and are still paying for their antichauvinist behavior during the war by imprisonment. Furthermore, in order to avoid any possible misinterpretation, the Secretary of the General Council for France [Serraillier] had just explained the true sense of the resolution in a letter published by the journals *Qui Vive!, Constitution, Radical, Émancipation, Europe,* etc.

Nonetheless, eight days later, on November 20, 1871, fifteen members of the "French Section of 1871" inserted in *Qui Vive!* a "protest" full of abuse against the German workers and denouncing the Conference resolution as irrefutable proof of the General Council's "pan-Germanic idea." On the other hand, the entire feudal, liberal, and police press of Germany seized avidly upon this incident to demonstrate to the German workers how their international dreams had come to naught. In the end the November 20 protest was endorsed by the entire 1871 Section in its December 14 declaration.

To show "the dangerous slope of authoritarianism down which the General Council [was] slipping," the declaration cited "the publication by the very same General Council of an official edition of the General Rules as revised by it."

One glance at the new edition of the Rules is enough to see that each new article has, in the appendix, reference to the original sources establishing its authenticity! As for the words "official edition," the first Congress of the International decided that "the official and obligatory text of the Rules and Regulations" would be published by the General Council (see "Working Congress of the International Working Men's Association held at Geneva from September 3 to 8, 1866," page 27, note).

Naturally enough, the 1871 Section was in continuous contact with the dissidents of Geneva and Neuchâtel. One Chalain, a member who had shown more energy in attacking the General Council than he had ever shown in defending the Commune, was unexpectedly rehabilitated by B. Malon, who had earlier leveled very grave charges against him in a letter to a Council member. The French Section of 1871, however, had scarcely launched its declaration when civil war exploded in its ranks. First Theisz, Avrial, and Camélinat withdrew. Thereafter the section broke up into several small groups, one of which was led by Mr. Pierre Vésinier, expelled by the General Council for his slander against Varlin and others, and then expelled from the International by the Belgian Commission appointed by the Brussels Congress of 1868. Another of these groups was founded by B. Landeck, who had been relieved by the sudden flight of police prefect Pietri, on September 4, of his obligation, "scrupulously fulfilled, not to engage any more in political affairs, nor in the International in France" (see "Third Trial of the International Working Men's Association in Paris, 1870," p. 4).

On the other hand, the mass of French refugees in London have formed a section which is in complete harmony with the General Council.

IV

The men of the Alliance, hidden behind the Neuchâtel Federal Committee and determined to make another effort on a vaster scale to disorganize the International, convened a Congress of their sections at Sonvillier on November 12, 1871. Back in July two letters from *maître* Guillaume to his friend Robin had threatened the General Council with an identical campaign if it did not agree to recognize them to be in the right "vis-à-vis the Geneva bandits."

The Sonvillier Congress was composed of sixteen delegates claiming to represent nine sections in all, including the new "Socialist Revolutionary Propaganda and Action Section" of Geneva.

The Sixteen made their debut by publishing the anarchist decree declaring the Romansh Federation dissolved, and the latter retaliated by restoring to the Alliance members their "autonomy" by driving them out of all sections. However, the Council had to recognize that a stroke of good sense brought them to accept the name Jura Federation, which the London Conference had given them.

The Congress of Sixteen then proceeded to "reorganize" the International by attacking the Conference and the General Council in a "Circular to All Federations of the International Working Men's Association."

Those responsible for the circular accused the General Council primarily of having called a Conference instead of a Congress in 1871. The preceding explanations show that these attacks were made directly against the International as a whole, which had unanimously agreed to convene a Conference, at which, incidentally, the Alliance was conveniently represented by Citizens Robin and Bastelica.

The General Council has had its delegates at every Congress; at the Basel Congress, for example, it had six. The Sixteen claim that "the majority of the Conference was fraudulently assured in advance by the admission of six General Council delegates with a deciding vote."

In actual fact, among the General Council delegates at the Conference, the French refugees were none other than the representatives of the Paris Commune, while its English and Swiss members could take part in the sessions only on rare occasions, as is attested to by the minutes, which will be submitted before the next Congress. One Council delegate had a mandate from a national federation. According to a letter addressed to the Conference, the mandate of another [Marx] was withheld because of the news of his death in the papers. That left one delegate. Thus the Belgians alone outnumbered the Council by six to one.

The international police, who in the person of Gustave Durand were kept out, complained bitterly about the violation of the General Rules by the convening of a "secret" conference. They were not conversant enough with our General Regulations to know that the administrative sittings of the Congress *have to be in private.*

Their complaints, nonetheless, found a sympathetic echo with the Sonvillier Sixteen, who cried out: "And on top of it all, a decision of this Conference declares that the General Council will itself fix the time and place of the next Congress or of the Conference to replace it; thus we are threatened with the suppression of the General Congresses, these great public sessions of the International."

The Sixteen refused to see that this decision was affirmed before the various governments only to show that, despite all the repressive measures, the International was firmly resolved to hold its general meetings one way or another.

At the general assembly of the Geneva sections, held on December 2, 1871, which gave a bad reception to Citizens Malon and Lefrançais, the latter put forward a proposal confirming the decrees passed by the Sonvillier Sixteen and censuring the General Council, as well as disavowing the Conference. The Conference had resolved that "the Conference resolutions which are not due to be published shall be communicated to the federal councils of the various countries by the corresponding secretaries of the General Council."

This resolution, which was in complete conformity with the General Rules and Regulations, was fraudulently revised by B. Malon and his friends to read as follows: "Some Conference resolutions shall be communicated only to the federal councils and to the corresponding secretaries."

They further accused the General Council of having "violated the principle of sincerity" in refusing to hand over to the police, by means of "publicity," the resolutions which were aimed exclusively at reorganizing the International in the countries where it is proscribed.

Citizens Malon and Lefrançais complain further that "the Conference aimed a blow at freedom of thought and its expression . . . in conferring upon the General Council the right to denounce and disavow any publicity organ of the sections or federations that discussed either the principles on which the Association rests, or the respective interests of the sections and federations, or finally the general interests of the Association as a whole (see *L'Égalité* of October 21)."

What, then, had *L'Égalité* of October 21 published? It had published a resolution in which the Conference "gives warning that henceforth the General Council will be bound to publicly denounce and disavow all newspapers calling themselves organs of the International which, following the precedents of *Progrès* and *Solidarité*, discuss in their columns, before the middle-class public, questions exclusively reserved for the local or federal committees and the General Council, or for the private and administrative sittings of the Federal or General Congresses."

To appreciate properly the spiteful lamentation of B. Malon we must bear in mind that this resolution puts an end once and for all to the attempts of some journalists who wished to substitute themselves for the main committees of the International and to play therein the role that the journalists' bohemia is playing in the bourgeois world. As a result of one such attempt the Geneva Federal Committee had seen some members of the Alliance edit *L'Égalité*, the official organ of the Romansh Federation, in a manner completely hostile to the latter.

Incidentally, the General Council had no need of the London Conference to "publicly denounce and disavow" the improper use of the press, for the Basel Congress had decided (Resolution II) that: "All newspapers countenancing attacks on the Association must be immediately sent by the sections to the General Council."

"It is evident," says the Romansh Federal Committee in its December 20, 1871, declaration (*L'Égalité*, December 24), "that this article was adopted not in order that the General Council might keep in its files newspapers which attack the Association, but to enable it to reply, and to nullify in case of need, the pernicious effect of slander and malevolent denigrations. It is also evident that this article refers in general to all newspapers, and that if we do not want to leave the attacks of the bourgeois papers without retaliation, it is all the more necessary to disavow, through our main representative body, i.e., the General Council, those newspapers whose attacks against us are made under cover of the name of our Association."

Let us note in passing that the *Times*, that Leviathan of the capitalist press, *Progrès* (of Lyon), a publication of the liberal bourgeoisie, and the *Journal de Genève*, an ultrareactionary paper, have brought the same charges against the Conference and used virtually the same terms as Citizens Malon and Lefrançais.

After having challenged the convocation of the Conference and, later, its composition and its allegedly secret character, the Sixteen's circular challenged the Conference resolutions.

Stating first that the Basel Congress had surrendered its rights "having authorized the General Council to grant or refuse admission to, or to suspend, the sections of the International," it accuses the Conference, farther on, of the following sin: "This Conference has . . . taken resolutions . . . which tend to turn the International, which is a free federation of autonomous sections, into a hierarchical and authoritarian organization of disciplined sections placed entirely under the control of a General Council which may, at will, refuse their admission or suspend their activity"!

Still farther on, the circular once more takes up the question of the Basel Congress having allegedly "distorted the nature of the General Council's functions."

The contradictions contained in the circular of the Sixteen may be summed up as follows: the 1871 Conference is responsible for the resolutions of the 1869 Basel Congress, and the General Council is guilty of having observed the Rules which require it to carry out Congress resolutions.

Actually, however, the real reason for all these attacks against the Conference is of a more profound nature. In the first place, it thwarted, by its resolutions, the intrigues of the Alliance men in Switzerland. In the second place, the promoters of the Alliance had, in Italy, Spain, and part of Switzerland and Belgium, created and upheld with amazing persistence a calculated confusion between the program of the International Working Men's Association and Bakunin's makeshift program.

The Conference drew attention to this deliberate misunderstanding in its two resolutions on proletarian policy and sectarian sections. The motivation of the first resolution, which makes short work of the political abstention preached by Bakunin's program, is given fully in its recitals, which are based on the General Rules, the Lausanne Congress resolution, and other precedents.[8]

---

8. The Conference resolution on political action of the working class reads as follows:

"Considering the following passage of the Preamble to the Rules: 'The economical emancipation of the working classes is the great end to which every political movement ought to be subordinate as a means';

"That the Inaugural Address of the International Working Men's Association (1864) states: 'The lords of land and the lords of capital will always use their political privileges for the defense and perpetuation of their economical monopolies. So far from promoting, they will continue to lay every possible impediment in the way of the emancipation of labor. . . . To conquer political power has therefore become the great duty of the working classes';

"That the Congress of Lausanne (1867) has passed this resolution: 'The social emancipation of the workmen is inseparable from their political emancipation';

"That the declaration of the General Council relative to the pretended plot of the French Internationals on the eve of the plebiscite (1870) says: 'Certainly by the tenor of our Statutes, all our branches in England, on the Continent, and in America have the special mission not only to serve as centers for the militant organization of the working class, but also to support, in their respective countries, every political movement tending toward the accomplishment of our ultimate end—the economical emancipation of the working class';

"That false translations of the original Statutes have given rise to various interpretations which were mischievous to the development and action of the International Working Men's Association;

We now pass on to the sectarian sections:

The first phase of the proletariat's struggle against the bourgeoisie is marked by a sectarian movement. That is logical at a time when the proletariat has not yet developed sufficiently to act as a class. Certain thinkers criticize social antagonisms and suggest fantastic solutions thereof, which the mass of workers is left to accept, preach, and put into practice. The sects formed by these initiators are abstentionist by their very nature, i.e., alien to all real action, politics, strikes, coalitions, or, in a word, to any united movement. The mass of the proletariat always remains indifferent or even hostile to their propaganda. The Paris and Lyon workers did not want the St.-Simonists, the Fourrierists, the Icarians, any more than the Chartists and the English trade unionists wanted the Owenists. These sects act as levers of the movement in the beginning, but become an obstruction as soon as the movement outgrows them; after which they became reactionary. Witness the sects in France and England, and lately the Lassalleans in Germany, who after having hindered the proletariat's organization for several years ended by becoming simple instruments of the police. To sum up, we have here the infancy of the proletarian movement, just as astrology and alchemy are the infancy of science. If the International were to be founded it was necessary that the proletariat go through this phase.

Contrary to the sectarian organizations with their vagaries and rivalries, the International is a genuine and militant organization of the proletarian class of all countries united in their common struggle against the capitalists and the landowners, against their class power organized in the state. The International's Rules, therefore, speak of only simple "workers' societies," all aiming for the same goal and accepting the same program, which presents a general outline of the

---

"In presence of an unbridled reaction which violently crushes every effort at emancipation on the part of the working men, and pretends to maintain by brute force the distinction of classes and the political domination of the propertied classes resulting from it;

"Considering that against this collective power of the propertied classes the working class cannot act, as a class, except by constituting itself into a political party, distinct from, and opposed to, all old parties formed by the propertied classes;

"That this constitution of the working class into a political party is indispensable in order to ensure the triumph of the Social Revolution and its ultimate end—the abolition of classes;

"That the combination of forces which the working class has already effected by its economical struggles ought at the same time to serve as a lever for its struggles against the political power of landlords and capitalists—

"The Conference recalls to the members of the International:

"That in the militant state of the working class, its economical movement and its political action are indissolubly united."—K.M., F.E.

proletarian movement, while leaving its theoretical elaboration to be guided by the needs of the practical struggle and the exchange of ideas in the sections, unrestrictedly admitting all shades of socialist convictions in their organs and Congresses.

Just as in every new historical phase old mistakes reappear momentarily only to disappear forthwith, so within the International there followed a resurrection of sectarian sections, though in a less obvious form.

The Alliance, which considers the resurrection of the sects a great step forward, is in itself conclusive proof that their time is over: for if initially they contained elements of progress, the program of the Alliance, in the tow of a "Mohammed without the Koran," is nothing but a heap of pompously worded ideas long since dead and capable only of frightening bourgeois idiots or serving as evidence to be used by the Bonapartist or other prosecutors against members of the International.[9]

The Conference, at which all shades of socialism were represented, unanimously acclaimed the resolution against sectarian sections, fully convinced that this resolution, stressing once again the International's true character, would mark a new stage of its development. The Alliance supporters, whom this resolution dealt a fatal blow, construed it only as the General Council's victory over the International, through which, as their circular pointed out, the General Council assured "the domination of the special program" of some of its members, "their personal doctrine," the orthodox doctrine," "the official theory, and the only one permissible within the Association." Incidentally, this was not the fault of those few members, but the necessary consequence, "the corrupting effect," of the fact that they were members of the General Council, for "it is absolutely impossible for a person who has power" (!) "over his fellows to remain a moral person. The General Council is becoming a hotbed of intrigue."

According to the opinion of the Sixteen, the General Rules of the International should be censured for the grave mistake of authorizing the General Council to coopt new members. Thus authorized, they claim, "the Council could, whenever it saw fit, coopt a group numerous enough to completely change the nature of its majority and its tendencies."

They seem to think that the mere fact of belonging to the General

---

9. Recent police publications on the International, including the Jules Favre circular to foreign powers and the report of Sacaze, a deputy in the rural assembly, on the Dufaure project, are full of quotations from the Alliance's pompous manifestos. The phraseology of these sectarians, whose radicalism is wholly restricted to verbiage, is extremely useful for promoting the aims of the reactionaries.—K.M., F.E.

Council is sufficient to destroy not only a person's *morality*, but also his common sense. How else can we suppose that a majority will transform itself into a minority by voluntary cooptions?

At any rate, the Sixteen themselves do not appear to be very sure of all this, for they complain farther on that the General Council has been "composed for five years running of the same persons, continually reelected," and immediately afterwards they repeat: "Most of them are not regular mandatories, not having been elected by a Congress."

The fact is that the body of the General Council is constantly changing, though some of the founding members remain, as in the federal councils in Belgium, French Switzerland, etc.

The General Council must fulfill three essential conditions if it is to carry out its mandate. In the first place, it must have a numerically adequate membership to carry on its diverse functions; second, a membership of "workingmen belonging to the different nations represented in the International Association"; and, lastly, laborers must be the predominant element therein. Since the exigencies of the worker's job incessantly cause changes in the membership of the General Council, how can it fulfill all these indispensable conditions without the right of cooption? The Council nonetheless considers a more precise definition of this right necessary, as it indicated at the recent Conference.

The reelection of the General Council's original membership, at successive Congresses at which England was definitely underrepresented, would seem to prove that it has done its duty within the limits of the means at its disposal. The Sixteen, on the contrary, view this only as a proof of the "blind confidence of the Congresses," carried at Basel to the point of "a sort of voluntary abdication in favor of the General Council."

In their opinion, the Council's "normal role" should be "that of a simple correspondence and statistical bureau." They justify this definition by adducing several articles extracted from an incorrect translation of the Rules.

Contrary to the rules of all bourgeois societies, the International's General Rules touch only lightly on its administrative organization. They leave its development to practice, and its regularization to future Congresses. Nevertheless, inasmuch as only the unity and joint action of the sections of the various countries could give them a genuinely international character, the Rules pay more attention to the Council than to the other bodies of the organization.

Article 6 of the original Rules states: "The General Council shall form an international agency between the different national and local groups," and proceeds to give some examples of the manner in which it is to function. Among these examples is a request to the Council to see that "when immediate practical steps should be needed—as, for instance, in case of international quarrels—the action of the associated societies be simultaneous and uniform."

The article continues: "Whenever it seems opportune, the General Council shall take the initiative of proposals to be laid before the different national or local societies."

In addition, the Rules define the Council's role in convening and arranging Congresses, and charge it with the preparation of certain reports to be submitted thereto. In the original Rules so little distinction is made between the independent action of various groups and unity of action of the Association as a whole, that Article 6 states: "Since the success of the workingmen's movement in each country cannot be secured but by the power of union and combination, while, on the other hand, the activity of the General Council will be more effective . . . the members of the International Association shall use their utmost efforts to combine the disconnected workingmen's societies of their respective countries into national bodies, represented by central national organs."

The first administrative resolution of the Geneva Congress (Article I) says: "The General Council is commissioned to carry the resolutions of the Congress into effect."

This resolution legalized the position that the General Council has held ever since its origin: that of the Association's *executive delegation*. It would be difficult to carry out orders without enjoying moral "authority" in the absence of any other "freely recognized authority." The Geneva Congress at the same time charged the General Council with publishing "the official and obligatory text of the Rules."

The same Congress resolved (Administrative Resolution of Geneva, Article 14): "Every section has the right to draw up its own rules and regulations adapted to local conditions and to the laws of its own country, but they must not contain anything contrary to the General Rules and Regulations."

Let us note, first of all, that there is not the least allusion either to any special declarations of principles or to any special tasks which this or that section should set itself apart from the common goal pursued by all the groups of the International. The issue simply concerns the right of sections to adapt the General Rules and Regulations to local conditions and to the laws of their country.

In the second place, who is to establish whether or not the particular rules conform to the General Rules? Evidently, if there were no "authority" charged with this function, the resolution would be null and void. Not only could police or hostile sections be formed, but also the intrusion of declassed sectarians and bourgeois philanthropists into the Association could warp its character and, by force of numbers at Congresses, crush the workers.

Since their origin, the national and local federations have exercised in their respective countries the right to admit or reject new sections, according to whether or not their rules conformed to the General Rules. The exercise of the same function by the General Council is provided for in Article 6 of the General Rules, which allows local independent societies, i.e., societies formed outside the federal body in the country concerned, the right to establish direct contacts with the General Council. The Alliance did not hesitate to exercise this right in order to fulfill the conditions set for the admission of delegates to the Basel Congress.

Article 6 of the Rules deals further with legal obstacles to the formation of national federations in certain countries where, consequently, the General Council is asked to function as a Federal Council (see Minutes of the Lausanne Congress, etc., 1867, p. 13).

Since the fall of the Commune these legal obstacles have been multiplying in the various countries, making action by the General Council therein, designed to keep doubtful elements out of the Association, more necessary than ever. That is why the French committees recently demanded the General Council's intervention to rid themselves of informers, and why in another great country [Austria] members of the International requested it not to recognize any section which has not been formed by its direct mandates or by themselves. Their request was motivated by the necessity to rid themselves of *agents-provocateurs*, whose burning zeal manifested itself in the rapid formation of sections of unparalleled radicalism. On the other hand, the so-called antiauthoritarian sections do not hesitate to appeal to the Council the moment a conflict arises in their midst, or even to ask it to deal severely with their adversaries, as in the case of the Lyon conflict. More recently, since the Conference, the Turin "Workers' Federation" decided to declare itself a section of the International. As the result of the split that followed, the minority formed the Emancipation of the Proletariat Society. It joined the International and began by passing a resolution in favor of the Jura people. Its newspaper, *Il Proletario*, is filled with outbursts against all authoritarianism. When sending in the society's subscriptions, the secretary [Carlo Terzaghi] warned the General Council that the old federation would probably also send its subscriptions. Then he continues: "As you will have read in *Il Proletario*, the Emancipation of the Proletariat Society . . . has declared . . . its rejection of all solidarity with the bourgeoisie, who, under the mask of workers, are organizing the Workers' Federation," and begs the Council to "communicate this resolution to all sections and to refuse the ten centimes in subscriptions in the event of their being sent."[10]

Like all the International's groups, the General Council is required to carry on propaganda. This it has accomplished through its manifestoes and its agents, who laid the basis for the first organizations of the International in North America, in Germany, and in many French towns.

Another function of the General Council is to aid strikers and organize their support by the entire International (see General Council reports to the various Congresses). The following fact, *inter alia*, indicates the importance of its intervention in the strike movement. The Resistance Society of the English Foundrymen is in itself an international trade union with branches in other countries, notably in the United States. Nonetheless, during a strike of American foundrymen the latter found it necessary to invoke the intercession of the General Council to prevent English foundrymen being brought into America.

The growth of the International obliged the General Council and all federal councils to assume the role of arbiter.

The Brussels Congress resolved that: "The federal councils are obliged to send a report every quarter to the General Council on their administration and financial state" (Administrative Resolution No. 3).

Lastly, the Basel Congress, which provokes the bilious wrath of the Sixteen, occupied itself solely with regulating the administrative relations engendered by the Association's continuing development. If it extended unduly the limits of the General Council's powers, whose fault was it if not that of Bakunin, Schwitzguebel, F. Robert, Guillaume, and other delegates of the Alliance, who were so anxious to achieve just that? Or will they accuse themselves of "blind confidence" in the London General Council?

Here are two resolutions of the Basel Congress: "No. IV. Each new section or society which is formed and wishes to be part of the International must immediately announce its adhesion to the General Council," and "No. V. The General Council has the right to admit or reject the affiliation of any new society or group, subject to appeal at the next Congress."

As for local independent societies formed outside the federal body, these articles only confirm the practice observed since the Internation-

---

10. At this time these were the *apparent* ideas of the Emancipation of the Proletariat Society, as represented by its corresponding secretary, a friend of Bakunin. Actually, however, this section's tendencies were quite different. After expelling this double-dealing traitor for embezzlement and for his friendly relations with the Turin police chief, the society set forth its explantions, which cleared up all misunderstanding between it and the General Council—K.M., F.E.

al's origin, maintenance of which is a matter of life or death for the Association. But extending this practice and applying it indiscriminately to every section or society in the process of formation is going too far. These articles do authorize the General Council to intervene in the internal affairs of the federations; but they have never been applied in this sense by the General Council. It defies the Sixteen to cite a single case where it has intervened in the affairs of new sections desirous of affiliating themselves with existing groups or federations.

The resolutions cited above refer to sections in the process of formation, while the resolutions given below refer to sections already recognized:

"VI. The General Council has equally the right to suspend until the next Congress any section of the International. VII. When conflicts arise between the societies or branches of a national group, or between groups of different nationalities, the General Council shall have the right to decide the conflict, subject to appeal at the next Congress, which will decide definitely."

These two articles are necessary for extreme cases, although up to the present the General Council has never had recourse to them. The review presented above shows that the Council has never suspended any section, and in cases of conflict has only acted as arbiter at the request of the two parties.

We arrive, at last, at a function imposed on the General Council by the needs of the struggle. However shocking this may be for supporters of the Alliance, it is the very persistence of the attacks to which the General Council is subjected by all the enemies of the proletarian movement that has placed it in the vanguard of the defenders of the International Working Men's Association.

V

Having dealt with the International, such as it is, the Sixteen proceed to tell us what it should be.

First, the General Council should be nominally a simple correspondence and statistical bureau. Once it has been relieved of its administrative functions, its correspondence would be concerned only with reproducing the information already published in the Association's newspapers. The correspondence bureau would thus become needless. As for statistics, that function is possible only if a strong organization, and especially, as the original Rules expressly say, a common direction are provided. Since all that smacks very much of "authoritarianism," however, there might perhaps be a bureau, but certainly no statistics. In a word, the General Council would disappear. The federal councils, the local committees, and other "authoritarian" centers would go by the same token. Only the autonomous sections would remain.

What, one may ask, will be the purpose of these "autonomous sections," freely federated and happily rid of all superior bodies, "even of the superior body elected and constituted by the workers"?

Here it becomes necessary to supplement the circular by the report of the Jura Federal Committee submitted to the Congress of the Sixteen: "In order to make the working class the real representative of humanity's new interests," its organization must be "guided by the idea that will triumph. To evolve this idea from the needs of our epoch, from mankind's vital aspirations, by a consistent study of the phenomena of social life, to then carry this idea to our workers' organizations—such should be our aim," etc. Lastly, there must be created "amid our working population a real revolutionary socialist school."

Thus the autonomous workers' sections are in a trice converted into *schools*, of which these gentlemen of the Alliance will be the masters. They "evolve" the idea by "consistent" studies which leave no trace behind. They then "carry this idea to our workers' organizations." To them the working class is so much raw material, a chaos into which they must breathe their Holy Spirit before it acquires a shape.

All of which is but a paraphrase of the old Alliance program, which begins with these words: "The socialist minority of the League of Peace and Freedom, having separated itself from the league," proposes to found "a new Alliance of Socialist Democracy . . . having a special mission to study political and philosophical questions . . ."

This is the "idea" that is being "evolved" therefrom: "Such an enterprise . . . would provide sincere socialist democrats of Europe and America with the means of being understood and of affirming their ideas."[11]

That is how, on its own admission, the minority of a bourgeois society slipped into the International shortly before the Basel Congress

11. The gentlemen of the Alliance, who continue to reproach the General Council for calling a private Conference at a time when the convocation of a Congress would have been the height of treachery or folly—these absolute proponents of clamor and publicity—organized within the International, in contempt of our Rules, a real secret society directed against the International itself with the aim of bringing its sections, unbeknown to them, under the sacerdotal direction of Bakunin.

The General Council intends to demand at the next Congress an investigation of this secret organization and its promoters in certain countries, such as Spain, for example.—K.M., F.E.

with the exclusive aim of utilizing it as a means for posing before the working masses as a hierarchy of a secret science that may be expounded in four phrases and whose culminating point is "the economic and social equalization of the classes."

Apart from this "theoretical mission," the new organization proposed for the International also has its practical aspect. "The future society," says the circular of the Sixteen, "should be nothing but a universalization of the organization which the International will establish for itself. We must therefore take care to bring this organization as near as possible to our ideal. . . . How could one expect an egalitarian and free society to grow out of an authoritarian organization? That is impossible. The International, embryo of the future human society, must be, from now on, the faithful image of our principles of liberty and federation."

In other words, just as the medieval convents presented an image of celestial life, so the International must be the image of the New Jerusalem, whose embryo the Alliance bears in its womb. The Paris Communards would not have failed if they had understood that the Commune was "the embryo of the future human society" and had cast away all discipline and all arms, that is, the things which must disappear when there are no more wars!

Bakunin, however, the better to establish that despite their "consistent study" the Sixteen did not hatch this pretty project of disorganization and disarmament in the International when it was fighting for its existence, has just published the original text of that project in his report on the International's organization (see *Almanach du Peuple pour 1872, Genève*).

VI

Now turn to the report presented by the Jura Committee at the Congress of the Sixteen. "A perusal of the report," says their official organ, *Révolution Sociale* (November 16), "will give the exact measure of the devotion and practical intelligence that we can expect from the Jura Federation members."

It begins by attributing to "these terrible events"—the Franco-Prussian War and the Civil War in France—a "somewhat demoralizing influence . . . on the situation within the International's sections."

If, in fact, the Franco-Prussian War could not but lead to the disorganization of the sections because it drew great numbers of workers into the two armies, it is no less true that the fall of the Empire and Bismarck's open proclamation of a war of conquest provoked in Germany and England a violent struggle between the bourgeoisie, which sided with the Prussians, and the proletariat, which more than ever demonstrated its international sentiments. This alone should have been sufficient for the International to have gained ground in both countries. In America, the same fact produced a split in the vast German proletarian émigré group, the internationalist party definitely dissociating itself from the chauvinist party.

On the other hand, the advent of the Paris Commune gave an unprecedented boost to the expansion of the International and to a vigorous support of its principles by sections of all nationalities, except the Jura sections, whose report continues thus: "The beginning of the gigantic battle . . . has caused people to think . . . some go away to hide their weakness. . . . For many this situation" (within their ranks) "is a sign of decrepitude," but "on the contrary . . . this situation is capable of transforming the International completely," according to their own pattern. This modest wish will be understood after a deeper examination of so propitious a situation.

Leaving aside the dissolved Alliance, since replaced by the Malon section, the Committee had to report on the situation in twenty sections. Among them, seven simply turned their backs on the Alliance. This is what the report has to say about it: "The section of box makers and that of engravers and designers of Bienne have never replied to any of the communications that we sent them. The sections of Neuchâtel craftsmen, i.e., joiners, box makers, engravers, and designers, have made no reply to letters from the Federal Committee. We have not been able to obtain any news of the Val-de-Ruz section. The section of engravers and designers of Locle have given no reply to letters from the Federal Committee."

That is what is described as *free* intercourse between the autonomous sections and their Federal Committee.

Another section, that "of engravers and designers of the Courtelary district, after three years of stubborn perseverance . . . at the present time . . . is forming a resistance society"—independent of the International, which does not in the least deter them from sending two delegates to the Congress of the Sixteen.

Next come four completely defunct sections: "The central section of Bienne has currently been dissolved; one of its devoted members wrote to us recently, however, saying that all hope of seeing the rebirth of the International at Bienne is not lost. The Saint-Blaise section has been dissolved. The Catébat section, after a brilliant existence, has had to yield to the intrigues woven by the masters" (!) "of this district in order to dissolve this valiant" (!) "section. Lastly, the Corgémont section also has fallen victim of intrigues on the part of the employers."

The central section of the Courtelary district follows, which "took the wise step of suspending its activity"; which did not deter it from sending two delegates to the Congress of the Sixteen.

Now we come to four sections whose existence is more than problematical. "The Grange section has been reduced to a small nucleus of socialist workers. . . . Their local action is paralyzed by their numerically modest membership. The central section of Neuchâtel has suffered considerably from the events, and would inevitably have disbanded except for the dedication and activity of some of its members. The central section of Locle, hovering between life and death for some months, ended up by being dissolved. It has been reconstituted quite recently, however," evidently for the sole purpose of sending two delegates to the Congress of the Sixteen. "The Chaux-de-Fonds section of socialist propaganda is in a critical situation. . . . Its position, far from getting better, tends rather to deteriorate."

Next come two sections, the study circles of Saint-Imier and of Sonvillier, which are mentioned only in passing, without so much as a word about their circumstances.

There remains the model section, which, to judge by its name of central section, is nothing but the residue of other defunct sections. "The central section of Moutier is certainly the one that has suffered least. . . . Its Committee has been in constant contact with the Federal Committee . . . no sections have yet been founded . . ."

That is easily explained: "The action of the Moutier section was particularly favored by the excellent attitude of a working population . . . given to their traditional ways; we would like to see the working class of this district make itself still more independent of political elements."

One can see, in fact, that this report "gives the exact measure of the devotion and practical intelligence that we can expect from the Jura Federation members."

They might have rounded it off by adding that the workers of Chaux-de-Fonds, the original seat of their committee, have always refused to have anything to do with them. Just recently, at the general assembly of January 18, 1872, they replied to the circular of the Sixteen by a unanimous vote confirming the London Conference resolutions and also the French Switzerland Congress resolution of May 1871: "To exclude forever from the International Bakunin, Guillaume, and their supporters."

Is it necessary to say anything more about the courage of this sham Sonvillier Congress, which, in its own words, "caused war, open war within the International"?

Certainly these men, who make more noise than their stature

warrants, have had an incontestable success. The whole of the liberal and police press have openly taken their side; they have been backed in their personal slander of the General Council and the insipid attacks aimed against the International by ostensible reformers in many lands: by the bourgeois republicans in England, whose intrigues were exposed by the General Council; by the dogmatic free-thinkers in Italy who, under the banner of Stefanoni, have just formed a "Universal Rationalist Society" with permanent headquarters in Rome, an "authoritarian" and "hierarchical" organization of monasteries for atheist monks and nuns, whose rules provide for a marble bust in the Congress hall for every bourgeois who donates ten thousand francs; and lastly by the Bismarck socialists in Germany who, apart from their police mouthpiece, the *Neuer Social-Demokrat*, played the role of "white shirts" for the Prusso-German Empire.

The Sonvillier conclave, in a pathetic appeal, requests all sections of the International to insist on the urgency of an immediate Congress "to curb the consistent encroachments of the London Council," according to Citizens Malon and Lefrançais, but actually to replace the International with the Alliance. This appeal received such an encouraging response that they immediately set about falsifying a resolution voted at the last Belgian Congress. Their official organ (*Révolution Sociale*, January 4, 1872) writes as follows: "Lastly, which is even more important, the Belgian sections met at the Congress of Brussels on December 24 and 25 and voted unanimously for a resolution identical with that of the Sonvillier Congress, on the urgency of convening a General Congress."

It is important to note that the Belgian congress voted the very opposite. It charged the Belgian congress, which was not due to meet until the following June, to draft new General Rules for submission to the *next Congress* of the International.

In accordance with the will of the vast majority of members of the International, the General Council is to convene the annual Congress only in September, 1872.

VII

Some weeks after the Conference, Albert Richard and Gaspard Blanc, the most influential and most ardent members of the Alliance, arrived in London. They came to recruit, among the French refugees, aides willing to work for the restoration of the Empire, which, according to them, was the only way to rid themselves of Thiers and to avoid being left destitute. The General Council warned all concerned, including the Brussels Federal Council, of their Bonapartist plots.

In January, 1872, they dropped their mask by publishing a pamphlet entitled *The Empire and the New France. Call of the People and the Youth to the French Conscience*, by Albert Richard and Gaspard Blanc, Brussels, 1872.

With the modesty characteristic of the charlatans of the Alliance, they declaim the following humbug: "We who have built up the great army of the French proletariat . . . we, the most influential leaders of the International in France,[12] . . . happily, we have not been shot, and we are here to flaunt in their faces (to wit: ambitious parliamentarians, smug republicans, sham democrats of all sorts) the banner under which we are fighting, and despite the slander, threats, and all manner of attacks that await us, to hurl at an amazed Europe the cry that comes from the very heart of our conscience and that will soon resound in the hearts of all Frenchmen: 'Long Live the Emperor!' Napoleon III, disgraced and scorned, must be splendidly reinstated"; and Messrs. Albert Richard and Gaspard Blanc, paid out of the secret funds of Invasion III, are specially charged with this restoration.

Incidentally, they confess: "It is the normal evolution of our ideas that has made us imperialists."

Here is a confession that should give pleasure to their coreligionists of the Alliance. As in the heyday of *Solidarité*, A. Richard and G. Blanc mouth again the clichés about "abstention from politics" which, on the principle of their "normal evolution," can become a reality only under the most absolute despotism, with the workers abstaining from any meddling in politics, much like the prisoner abstaining from a walk in the sun.

"The time of the revolutionaries," they say, "is over . . . communism is restricted to Germany and England, especially Germany. That,

---

12. Under the heading "To the Pillory!" *L'Égalité* (of Geneva), February 15, 1872, had this to say:

"The day has not yet come to describe the story of the defeat of the movement for the Commune in the South of France; but what we, most of whom witnessed the deplorable defeat of the Lyon insurrection on April 30, can announce today is that one of the reasons for the insurrection's failure was the cowardice, the treachery, and the thievery of G. Blanc, who intruded everywhere carrying out the orders of A. Richard, who kept in the shade.

"By their carefully prepared maneuvers these rascals intentionally compromised many of those who took part in the preparatory work of the insurrectionary Committees.

"Further, these traitors managed to discredit the International at Lyon to such an extent that by the time of the Paris revolution the International was regarded by the Lyon workers with the greatest distrust. Hence the total absence of organization, hence the failure of the insurrection, a failure which was bound to result in the fall of the Commune, which was left to rely on its own isolated forces! It is only since this bloody lesson that our propaganda has been able to rally the Lyon workers around the flag of the International.

"Albert Richard was the pet and prophet of Bakunin and company."—K.M., F.E.

moreover, is where it had been developed in earnest for a long time, to be subsequently spread throughout the International, and this disturbing expansion of German influence in the Association has in no small degree contributed to retarding its development, or rather, to giving it a new course in the sections of central and southern France, whom no German has ever supplied with a slogan."

Perhaps this is the voice of the great hierophant, who ever since the Alliance's foundation has taken upon himself, in his capacity as a Russian, the special task of representing the Latin races? Or do we have here "the true missionaries" of the *Révolution Sociale* (November 2, 1871) denouncing "the backward march which endeavors to foist German and Bismarckian mentality on the International"?

Fortunately, however, the true tradition has survived, and Messrs. Albert Richard and Gaspard Blanc have not been shot! Thus, their own "contribution" consists in "setting a new course" for the International in central and southern France to follow, by an effort to found Bonapartist sections, *ipso facto* basically "autonomous."

As for the constitution of the proletariat as a political party, as recommended by the London Conference, "After the restoration of the Empire, we"—Richard and Blanc—"shall quickly deal not only with the socialist theories but also with any attempts to implement them through revolutionary organization of the masses." Briefly, exploiting the great "autonomy principle of the sections" which "constitutes the real strength of the International . . . especially in the Latin countries" (*Révolution Sociale*, January 4), these gentlemen base their hopes on anarchy within the International.

Anarchy, then, is the great war horse of their master Bakunin, who has taken nothing from the socialist systems except a set of slogans. All socialists see anarchy as the following program: Once the aim of the proletarian movement, i.e., abolition of classes, is attained, the power of the state, which serves to keep the great majority of producers in bondage to a very small exploiter minority, disappears, and the functions of government become simple administrative functions. The Alliance draws an entirely different picture. It proclaims anarchy in proletarian ranks as the most infallible means of breaking the powerful concentration of social and political forces in the hands of the exploiters. Under this pretext it asks the International, at a time when the Old World is seeking a way of crushing it, to replace its organization with anarchy. The international police want nothing better for perpetuating the Thiers republic, while cloaking it in a royal mantle.

Resolutions on the Split in the United States Federation*

I. THE TWO FEDERAL COUNCILS

Article 1. Considering that central councils are but instituted in order to secure, in every country, to the workingmen's movement the power of union and combination" (Article 7 of the General Rules); that, consequently, the existence of two rival central councils for the same federation is an open infraction of the General Rules;

The General Council calls upon the two professional federal councils at New York to reunite and to act as one and the same provisional Federal Council for the United States until the meeting of an American General Congress.

Article 2. Considering that the efficiency of the Provisional Federal Council would be impaired if it contained too many members who have only recently joined the International Working Men's Association;

The General Council recommends that such new-formed sections as are numerically weak should combine among each other for the appointment of a few common delegates.

II. GENERAL CONGRESS OF THE UNITED STATES FEDERATION

Article 1. The General Council recommends the convocation, for July 1, 1872, of a General Congress of the delegates of sections and affiliated societies of the United States.

---

* Written in English about March 5, 1872, and passed by the General Council March 5, 12, 1872. Published in *La Emancipación*, April 6, in *Woodhull and Claflin's Weekly*, May 4, in *Der Volksstaat*, May 8, 1872.

Article 2. To this Congress will belong the appointment of the members of the Federal Council for the United States. It may, if convenient, empower the Federal Council thus appointed to add to itself a certain limited number of members.

Article 3. This Congress will have the sole power of determining the bylaws and regulations for the organization of the I.W.A. in the United States, "but such bylaws and regulations must not contain anything contrary to the General Rules and Regulations of the Association" (Administrative Regulation V, Article 1).

III. SECTIONS

Article 1. Considering that Section No. 12 at New York has not only passed a formal resolution by virtue of which "each section" possesses "the independent right" to construe, according to its fancy, "the proceedings of the several congresses" and the "General Rules and Regulations," but moreover has fully acted up to this doctrine, which, if generally adopted, would leave nothing of the I.W.A. but its name;

That the same section has never ceased to make the I.W.A. the vehicle of issues some of which are foreign to, while others are directly opposed to, the aims and purposes of the I.W.A.;

For these reasons the General Council considers it its duty to put in force Administrative Resolution VI of the Basel Congress and to declare Section No. 12 *suspended* till the meeting of the next General Congress of the I.W.A., which is to take place in September, 1872.

Article 2. Considering that the I.W.A., according to the General Rules, is to consist exclusively of "workingmen's societies" (see Article 1, Article 7, and Article 11 of the General Rules);

That, consequently, Article 9 of the General Rules to this effect: "Everybody who acknowledges and defends the principles of the I.W.A. is eligible to become a member," although it confers upon the active adherents of the International who are not workingmen the right either of individual membership or of admission to workingmen's sections, does in no way legitimate the foundation of sections exclusively or principally composed of members not belonging to the working class;

That for this very reason the General Council was some months ago precluded from recognizing a Slavonian section exclusively composed of students;

That according to the General Regulations V, 1, the General Rules and Regulations are to be adapted "to local circumstances of each country";

That the social conditions of the United States, though in many other respects most favorable to the success of the working-class movement, peculiarly facilitate the intrusion into the International of bogus reformers, middle-class quacks, and trading politicians;

For these reasons the General Council recommends that in future there be admitted no new American section of which two-thirds at least do not consist of wage laborers.

Article 3. The General Council calls the attention of the American Federation to Resolution II, 3, of the London Conference relating to "sectarian sections" or "separatist bodies pretending to accomplish special missions" distinct from the common aim of the Association, viz., to emancipate the man of labor from his "economical subjection to the monopolizer of the means of labor," which "lies at the bottom of servitude in all its forms, of all social misery, mental degradation, and political dependence" (see Preamble to the General Rules).

The So-Called Split in the International*

CITIZEN Marx said two declarations had been drawn up to be issued to the public if the Council approved of them; the first had reference to the debate in the House of Commons upon the Baillie-Cochrane motion, the second to the so-called split in the International. He then proceeded to read the first, which was as follows:

The performances of the Versailles Rural Assembly, and of the Spanish Cortes, with intent to extinguish the International, very properly aroused a noble spirit of emulation in the breasts of the representatives of the Upper Ten Thousand in the British House of Commons. Accordingly, on April 12, 1872, Mr. B. Cochrane, one of the most representative men, as far as upper-class intellect is concerned, called the attention of the House to the sayings and doings of that formidable society. Being a man not much given to reading, he had qualified himself for his task by a journey of inspection to a few of the continental headquarters of the International, undertaken last autumn, and had, on his return, hastened to secure, by a letter to the *Times*, a kind of provisional protection for his right of priority to this subject. His speech in Parliament betrays what in any other man would be considered a willful and premeditated ignorance of what he is talking about. With one exception the many official publications of the International are unknown to him; in their stead he quotes a jumble of passages from petty publications by private individuals in Switzerland, for which the International, as a body, is as much responsible as the British Cabinet is for the speech of Mr. Cochrane. According to that speech, "the great majority of those who joined the society

* From the minutes of the General Council, April 16, 1872.

in England, and their number was 180,000, was totally ignorant of the principles it was intended to carry out, which were carefully concealed from them while they were giving their subscriptions."

Now the principles intended to be carried out by the International are laid down in the Preamble to the General Rules, and Mr. Cochrane is in happy ignorance of the fact that no one can enter the Association without giving his express adhesion to them. Again, "the society, as originally constituted, was founded upon the principles of the trade unions, and no political element was then introduced into it."

Not only does the preamble to the original General Rules contain a strong political element, but the political tendencies of the Association are very fully developed in the Inaugural Address, published in 1864, contemporaneously with these Rules. Another wonderful discovery is this, that Bakunin was "charged" to reply, in the name of the International, to the attacks of Mazzini, which is simply an untruth. After giving a quotation from Bakunin's pamphlet, he continues: "We might smile at such bombastic nonsense, but when these papers emanated from London" (from which they did *not* emanate) "was it surprising that foreign governments should take alarm?"

And is it surprising that Mr. Cochrane should become their spokesman in England? Another charge is that the International had just started "a newspaper" in London, which is another untruth. However, let Mr. Cochrane console himself, the International has plenty of organs of its own in Europe and America, and in almost all civilized languages.

But the gist of the whole speech is contained in the following: "He should be able to show that the Commune and the International Association were, in reality, one, and that the International Society located" (?) "in London had given orders to the Commune to burn Paris, and to murder the archbishop of that city."

And now for the proofs. Eugène Dupont, as chairman of the Brussels Congress of September, 1868, truly stated that the International aimed at a social revolution. And what is the secret link between this statement of Eugène Dupont in 1868 and the deeds of the Commune in 1871? That "only last week Eugène Dupont was arrested in Paris, to which he had gone secretly from the country. Now this M. Eugène Dupont was a member of the Commune and also a member of the International Society."

Unfortunately for this very conclusive mode of reasoning, A. Dupont, the member of the Commune, who has been arrested in Paris, was not a member of the International, and E. Dupont, the member of the International, was not a member of the Commune. The second proof is: "Bakunin said, at Geneva, July, 1869, when the Congress met under his presidency: 'The International proclaims itself atheist.' "

Now there never took place an International Congress at Geneva in July, 1869; Bakunin never presided at any International Congress and was never charged to make declarations in its name. Third proof: The *Volksstimme*, the International organ at Vienna, wrote: "For as the red flag is the symbol of universal love, let our enemies beware, lest they turn it into the symbol of universal terror."

The same paper, moreover, stated in so many words that the General Council in London was, in fact, the General Council of the International, that is to say, its central administrative delegation. Fourth proof: In one of the French trials of the International, Tolain ridiculed the assertion of the public prosecutor that "it was sufficient for the president of the International" (who does not exist) "to raise his finger to command obedience over the whole surface of the globe."

The muddling brain of Mr. Cochrane turns Tolain's denial into a confirmation. Fifth proof: The manifesto of the General Council on the Civil War in France, from which Mr. Cochrane quotes the defense of the reprisals against the hostages, and of the use of fire, as measures of warfare, necessary under the circumstances. Now as Mr. Cochrane approves of the massacres committed by the Versaillais, are we to infer that he had *ordered* them, although he is surely innocent of the murder of anything but game? Sixth proof: "There was a meeting held between the leaders of the International and the Commune before the burning of Paris."

This is exactly as true as the report which a short time ago went the rounds of the Italian press to the effect that the General Council of the International had sent, on a tour of inspection to the Continent, its truly and well-beloved Alexander Baillie-Cochrane, who reported most satisfactorily on the flourishing state of the organization, and stated that it counted seventeen million members. Final proof: "In the decree of the Commune which commanded the destruction of the column of the Place Vendôme, the approval of the International is signified."

Nothing of the kind is stated in that decree, although the Commune was no doubt fully aware that the whole International all over the world would applaud this resolution.

Such then is the, according to the *Times* newspaper, irrefutable evidence for Cochrane's statement that the Archbishop of Paris was killed and Paris burned by the direct order of the General Council of the International in London. Compare his incoherent rant to the report of M. Sacaze on the law against the International in Versailles, and you will be able to realize the distance still existing between a French Rural and a British Dogberry.

Of Mr. Cochrane's *fidus Achates* [devoted follower], Mr. Eastwick, we should say with Dante: "Look at him and pass on," were it not for his absurd assertion that the International is responsible for the *Père Duchêne* of Vermersch, whom the learned Mr. Cochrane calls Vermuth.

If it is an unmixed pleasure to have an opponent like Mr. Cochrane, it is a grievous calamity to have to undergo the patronage, as far as it goes, of Mr. Fawcett. If he is bold enough to defend the International against forcible measures, which the British Government neither dares nor cares to take, he has at the same time that sense of duty and high moral courage which compel him to pass upon it his supreme professorial condemnation. Unfortunately, the pretended doctrines of the International which he attacks are but concoctions of his own poor brain. "The state," he says, "was to do this and that, and find money to carry out all their projects. The first article of the program was that the state should buy up all the land, and all the instruments of production, and let them out at a fair and reasonable price to the people."

As to the buying up of the land by the state under certain circumstances and the letting of it out to the people at a fair and reasonable price, let Mr. Fawcett settle that with his theoretical teacher Mr. John Stuart Mill, and with his political Chief Mr. John Bright. The second article "proposes that the state should regulate the hours of labor."

The historical learning of our Professor shines out brilliantly when he makes the International the author of the British Factory and Workshops' Acts, and his economical proficiency comes out to equal advantage in his appreciation of those acts. Third article—"That the state should provide gratuitous education."

Such broad facts as the existence of gratuitous education in the United States and Switzerland, and their beneficial results, what are they compared to the gloomy vaticinations of Professor Fawcett? Fourth article—"That the state should lend capital to cooperative societies."

There is here a slight mistake; Mr. Fawcett mixes up the demands put forth by Lassalle, who died before the foundation of the International, with the principles of the International. By the by, Lassalle invoked the precedent of the state loans which, under the pretext of agricultural improvements, and by the instrumentality of Parliament, the British landed proprietors had so generously granted to themselves. Fifth article—"As the coping stone, it was proposed that the whole revenue of the country should be raised by a graduated tax upon property."

This is really too bad; to make the demands of Mr. Robert Gladstone and his Liverpool middle-class financial reformers the "coping stone" of the International!

This great political economist, Mr. Fawcett, whose claim to scientific fame rests entirely upon a vulgarization, for the use of schoolboys, of Mr. John Stuart Mill's compendium of political economy, confesses that "the confident predictions" (for the free-traders) "of five and twenty years ago had been falsified by facts." At the same time he is confident of his ability to allay the giant proletarian movement of our days by repeating over and over again, in a still more diluted form, the very same stale phrases by which those false predictions of twenty-five years ago were propped up. His sham defense of the International, which is in reality a humble apology for his former pretended sympathies with the working classes, will, it is to be hoped, open the eyes of such English workingmen as are still taken in by the sentimentalism under which Mr. Fawcett hitherto tried to hide his scientific nullity.

Now if Mr. B. Cochrane represents the political intellect and Mr. Fawcett the economical science of the British House of Commons, how does this "pleasantest of all London clubs" compare with the American House of Representatives, which on December 13, 1871, passed an act for the establishment of a Labor Statistics Office and declared that this act was passed at the express desire of the International Working Men's Association, which the House recognized as one of the most important facts of the present age?

The "American Split"*

OCTOBER *15, 1871, was published in the journal of Woodhull (a banker's woman, free-lover, and general humbug) and Claflin (her sister in the same line) an "Appeal of Section No. 12" (founded by Woodhull, and almost exclusively consisting of middle-class humbugs and worn-out Yankee swindlers in the reform business; Section 9 is founded by Miss Claflin).*

"An Appeal of Section No. 12" (to the English-speaking citizens of the United States) (dated August 30, 1871, signed by W. West, secretary of Section 12).

The following excerpts are from this Appeal:

"The object of the International is simply to emancipate the laborer, male and female, by the conquest of political power." "It involves first, the Political Equality and Social Freedom of men and women alike."

"Political Equality means the personal participation of each in the preparation, administration, and execution of the laws by which all are governed." "Social Freedom means absolute immunity from impertinent intrusion in all affairs of exclusively personal concernment, such as religious belief, the sexual relation, habits of dress, etc."

"The proposition involves, secondly, the establishment of a Universal Government ... Of course, the abolition of ... even differences of language are embraced in the program."

"Section No. 12" invites the formation of "English-speaking sections" in the United States upon this program.

---

* Notes made in English, German, and French, May, 1872. Throughout this selection italics are used to indicate material written in English.

That the whole organization for place hunting and electoral purposes:

"If practicable, for the convenience of political action, there should be a section formed in every primary election district."

"There must ultimately be instituted in every town a municipal committee or council corresponding with the common councils; in every state a state committee or council corresponding with the state legislature, and in the nation a national committee or council corresponding with the United States National Congress."

"The work of the International includes nothing less than the institution, within existing forms, of another form of government, which shall supersede them all."

This Appeal—and the formation from it *of all sorts of middle-class humbug sections, free-lovers, spiritists, spiritist Shakers, etc.*—caused the split, and the demand by Section 1 (German) of the old Council that Section 12 be expelled and that no section be admitted to membership unless it consisted of at least two-thirds workers.

First, five dissidents formed a separate Council on November 19, 1871, which consisted of Yankees, Frenchmen, and Germans.

In Woodhull's, etc., journal, November 18, 1871, Section 12 protested (West as secretary) against Section 1 and declared, among other things:

"The simple truth is that Political Equality and Social Freedom for all alike, of all races, both sexes, and every condition, are necessary precursors of the more radical reforms demanded by the International."

"The extension of equal citizenship to women, the world over, must precede any general change in the subsisting relations of capital and labor." "Section 12 would also remonstrate against the vain assumption, running all through the Protest" (of Section 1) *"under review, that the International Working Men's Association is an organization of the working classes. . . ."*

Prior to that, in Woodhull's Journal, October 21, 1871, Section 12 *asserts:*

"The independent right of each section to have, hold, and give expression to its own constructions of said proceedings of the several Congresses, and the Rules and Regulations" (!) *"of said General Council, each section being alone responsible for its own action."*

Woodhull's, etc., journal, November 25, 1871. Protest of Section 12 against "Address of Section 1" (the same address that you had printed in Italian, etc., papers).

"It is not true that the 'common understanding or agreement' of the workingmen of all countries, of itself, standing alone, constitutes the Association. . . . The statement that the emancipation of the

working classes can only be conquered by themselves cannot be denied, yet it is true so far as it describes the fact that the working classes cannot be emancipated against their will."

December 3, 1871. The new Federal Council for North America formally founded (Yankees, Germans, Frenchmen).

December 4. The old Council (10 Ward Hotel) denounces the swindlers in a circular to all sections of the International in the United States. It states, among other things:

"In the Committee" (of the old Central Committee) "which was to be a defense against all reform swindles, the majority finally consisted of practically forgotten reformers and panacea-mongers. . . . Thus it came about that the people who preached the evangel of free love sat fraternally beside those who wanted to bring to the whole world the blessing of a single common language—land cooperativists, spiritualists, atheists, and deists—each striving to ride his own hobbyhorse. Particularly Section 12, Woodhull . . . The first step that has to be taken here to further the movement is to organize and at the same time arouse the revolutionary element to be found in the opposing interests of capitalists and workers. . . .

"The delegates of Sections 1, 4, 5, 7, 8, 11, 16, 21, 23, 24, 25, and others, having seen that all efforts to control this mischief were in vain, decided, after the adjournment of the old Central Council sine die (December 3, 1871), to establish a new one, which would consist of real workers and which would exclude all those who would only confuse the question" (*New Yorker Democrat,* December 9, 1871).

West *elected as delegate* of the new Council.

It is to be noted that the new Council quickly filled up with new delegates, mostly from the new sections founded by Section 9 (Claflin) and Section 12 (Woodhull), *riffraff,* mostly; moreover, insufficiently strong or numerous to elect the necessary officers.

Meanwhile, the Woodhull journal (West, etc.) lied unashamedly when it asserted that it was sure of the support of the General Council.

Both councils appealed to the General Council. Various sections, for example, the French Section No. 10 (New York), and several Irish sections, withdrew their delegates from both councils until the General Council made its decision. Lies of the Woodhull journal, in an article of December 2 entitled: *"Section 12 Sustained. The Decision of the General Council."* (This was the decision of the General Council, November 5, 1871, which, on the contrary, sustained the Central Committee against the claims of Section 12, which tried to replace it as Yankees.)

Resolutions of the General Council, March 5 and 12, 1872.

The fate of the International in the United States depended on it.

(In passing, the humbug cult which the Woodhull journal has pursued to date should be noted.)

As soon as the resolutions reached New York, the fellows of the Counter Committee began to follow their old tactics. They had first discussed the original split in the most notorious New York bourgeois papers. Now they did the same against the General Council (presenting the matter as a conflict between Frenchmen and Germans, between socialism and communism), to the joyous cry of all labor-hating organs.

Very characteristic were the marginal comments in *Woodhull's journal, May 4, 1872*, on the resolutions of the General Council.

Before that also: *Woodhull's journal, December 15, 1871.*

"No new test of membership, as that two-thirds or any part of a section shall be wage slaves, as if it were a crime to be free, was required."

(Particularly in the composition of the Counter Council.)

Woodhull's journal, May 4, 1872:

". . . In this decree of the General Council its authors presume to recommend that in future no American section be admitted of which two-thirds at least are not wage slaves. Must they be politically slaves also? As well one thing as the other. . . ." "The intrusion into the International Working Men's Association of bogus reformers, middle-class quacks, and trading politicians is mostly to be feared from that class of citizens who have nothing better to depend upon than the proceeds of wage slavery."

Meanwhile, as the Presidential elections approached, the cloven hoof showed itself—namely, that the International should serve in the election of—Madame Woodhull!

Apropos. *In article signed W. West, in Woodhull's, etc., journal, March 2, 1872*, one reads:

"The issue of the 'Appeal' of Section 12 to the English-speaking citizens of the United States in August last was a new departure in the history of the International, and has resulted in the recognition by the General Council of Political Equality and Social Freedom of both sexes alike, and of the essential political character of the work before us."

Woodhull's, etc., journal, March 2, 1872. Under the title, *"The Coming Combination Convention,"* the statement:

"There is a proposition under consideration by the representatives of the various reformatory elements of the country looking to a grand consolidated convention to be held in this city in May next, during Anniversary week. . . . Indeed, if this convention in May acts wisely, who can say that the fragments of the defunct Democratic

party will come out from them and take part in the proposed convention . . . Every body of radicals everywhere in the United States should, as soon as the call is made public, take immediate steps to be represented in it."

(Apropos. The Woodhull journal, I can't find the date, comforts the *spiritist sections* with the thought of telling the General Council to go to the devil.)

Woodhull, etc. journal, April 6, 1872:

"Every day the evidence that the convention called for the 9 and 10 May by representatives of the various reforms . . . is to be a spontaneous uprising of the people increases in volume."

National Women Suffrage Association supplements this:

"This Convention will . . . consider the nominations for President and Vice-President of the United States."

Ditto under the title:

"The Party of the People to secure and maintain human rights, to be inaugurated in the United States in May, 1872."

The Appeal was headed by the signature: *Victoria C. Woodhull,* followed by *Theodore H. Banks, R. W. Hume* (Banks one of the founders of the *Counter Council*). In this Appeal: the convention will consider *"nominations for President and Vice-President of the United States."* Specially invited are:

"Labor, land, peace, and temperance reformers, and Internationals and Women Suffragists—including all the various suffrage associations —as well as all others who believe the time has come when the principles of eternal justice and human equality should be carried into our halls of legislation."

Woodhull, etc., Weekly, April 13, 1872. The Presidency dodge is presented ever more clearly. This time, for a change:

". . . Internationals, and other labor reformers—the friends of peace, temperance and education, and by all those who believe that the time has come to carry the principles of true morality and religion into the State House, the Court and the Market Place."

Under the title: *"The Party of the People, etc.,"* a new Appeal, always with Victoria C. Woodhull at the head, followed by the chief scamps of the Counter Council, Th. H. Banks, R. W. Hume, G. R. Allen, William West, G. W. Maddox (the subsequent president of the Apollo meeting), J. T. Elliott (the English secretary of the Counter Council), T. Millot (delegate of French Section 2).

Woodhull, etc., Weekly (it isn't called Journal), *April 20, 1872. Continuation of the same dodge.*

The lists grow, always headed by V. C. Woodhull (There are also "Honorables" among them.)

Woodhull, etc., Weekly, April 27, 1827 [1872]. Continuation of the same ballyhoo. (Begins to print the list of delegates.)

Woodhull, etc., Weekly, May 4, 1872. Continuation of the dodge. (Constant reprinting of same and of enlarged lists.)

Woodhull, etc., Weekly, May 25, 1872. At last (Apollo Hall scandal, May 9, 10, 11), *Woodhull for President of United States, F. Douglass for Vice-President. (Maddox of Counter Council, president of the convention, first day.) Laughingstock of New York and United States.*

The rest, officials of the *Counter Council:* John T. Elliott, vice-president, G. R. Allen, secretary (and member of *Committee on Resolutions and Platform*). In the latter *committee, Th. H. Banks* (one of the five founders of the *Counter Council,* November 19, 1871). Also Mrs. Maria Huleck on one of the *committees.* In the *Central National Committee of New York* there figure: G. R. Allen, Th. H. Banks (next to Colonel Blood, member of Section 12 and lover of Victoria), J. B. Davis.

Breakup of the Counter Council.

Section 2 (French) removes Laugrand (until then the *French secretary of the Counter Council*) as delegate. They accuse the fellow *"of using the organization for political purposes, and as a sort of adjunct to the free-love branch of the women's rights' party. . . . Citizen Millot"* (he proposed the withdrawal of Section 2 from the Counter Council, which was accepted) *"stated upon the introduction of the Resolution that only three sections—9 (Claflin), 12 (Woodhull), and 35—were represented in the Apollo Hall 'odds and ends' convention, by scheming men for political purposes, and that the delegation in the said convention pretending to act for the Federal Council was a spurious one and self appointed"* (But the *Federal Counter Council* did not repudiate them.) (*The World,* May 13, 1872.)

Section 6 (German) removes its delegate, E. Grosse (ex-private secretary of Herr von Schweitzer) and threatens to withdraw if the Counter Council does not accept all the resolutions of the General Council.

Le Socialiste (New York), May 18, 1872:

"Section 2 of New York at its Sunday meeting, May 12, adopted the following resolutions:

"Considering, etc., etc.,

"That Section 2 has reason to believe that the union of Jewelers refuses to affiliate with the International, and that meanwhile a delegate continues to represent it in the Federal Council;

"That Section 2 has reasons to think that other delegates represent fictitious sections or those that are composed of only six to eight members;

"Section 2 declares: That an investigation is necessary," etc. . . .

"Considering that, rightly or wrongly, Section 12 has been suspended by the General Council, acting by virtue of the authority given to it by the Congress of Basel, Section 2 protests against the Federal Council having a delegate from Section 12 with a deliberative voice.

"Finally, considering that the International is an Association of workers, having for its objective the emancipation of workers by workers themselves:

"Section 2 protests against the admission of sections in which the majority is made up of nonworkers."

Other resolutions of Section 2:

"Section 2,

"Recognizing the principle of women's right to vote, in view of the insinuations of Citizeness Woodhull, at the meeting in Apollo Hall, leading the public to believe that the International supports her candidacy,

"Declares:

"That for the present the International cannot and should not be taken in tow by any American political party; for none of them represents the workers' aspirations; none of them has for its objective the economic emancipation of the workers.

"Section 2 had thought:

"That our sole objective ought to be, for the present, the organization and the solidarity of the working class in America."

Under the title "Internationals, watch out!," the same issue of *Socialiste* states, among other things:

"The International is not, and cannot be, persecuted in America; the politicians, far from aiming at its destruction, think only of using it as a lever and supporting point for the triumph of their personal views. Should the International let itself be dragged into this path, it would cease to be the Association of Workers and become a ring of politicians.

"For a long time now there have been cries of alarm; but the convention in Apollo Hall, nominating, in the name of the International, Madame Woodhull as candidate for the Presidency, should henceforth open the eyes of the less perceptive. Internationals of America, watch out!"

The World, May 20, 1872:

Sitting of Counter Council, May 19, 1872. Maddox (of Apollo

Hall) in the chair. Withdrawal of eight delegates (for eight sections) (French and German).

Herald, May 20, 1872, reports the same sitting under the heading: "The French" (are) "insulted and leave in disgust. . . . Terrible slang used. But 1,500 members in the United States. A split among the Internationals of London. The Woodhull crowd victorious."

Resolution of General Council of May 28, 1872, by which—in reply to the questions put by the German Section of St. Louis and the French Section of Nouvelle Orléans—the Old Council (Provisional Federal Council for the United States) is alone recognized.

Criticism of Eccarius*

CITIZEN MARX then entered into the charge against Eccarius;[1] he said that the split in the American sections took place on the nineteenth of November last, and the first letters came to hand about it in December and the beginning of January, but at that time the quarrels among the English members of the Council precluded the Council from dealing with the subject. Then came the Swiss dispute, which was of more importance as it affected the very existence of the International. It was in reality caused by a secret society within the Association. Then there was the manifesto [*Fictitious Splits in the International*], a longer document than the Address on the Civil War, to be written, calling the French members together to consult upon it, and the debate upon it by the Council to be dealt with before the Council could turn its attention to the American affairs—but as soon as the matters referred to had been disposed of, the subject was brought on and the matters referred to the subcommittee. Now the object of referring matters to the subcommittee was to save time, and he found that it would expedite business by bringing the subject before the Council, for while engaged with the other affairs he had written to Eccarius and Hales for the correspondence which he received as well as that which Le Moussu had received. He found that Eccarius had received a letter from Gregory, a letter from Hubert, and a private letter . . .[2] Le Moussu had received a letter from Laugrand and one from Section 10. One had also come addressed to Dupont. Hales had received one from Hubert, one from Elliott, and one from Grosse belonging to the new

---

* From the minutes of the General Council, May 11, 1872.
1. See Marx's letter to Eccarius, May 3, 1872, page 562.
2. The sentence is incomplete in the minutes.

Counter-Council, and one from Nicholson of the old Council. That those letters were sent to Hales was the fault of the Americans and not the fault of the Council, but none of them contained any new facts; beyond what had appeared in the American press there was nothing except a demand for rules made by Grosse. On his own part he had received nothing whatever from the Counter-Council and nothing official from the old. He had received private correspondence which had continued from the time when he corresponded with the[3] German sections as German corresponding secretary. But he had long ago written informing them that his official functions had ceased and he had a reply acknowledging the receipt of it. The resolutions were drawn up and the Council accepted [them], even Eccarius himself voting most of them, and yet after their adoption he refused to send them. Now he contended that the decisions of the Council ought not to be subject to the caprice of an individual, and could not recognize the right of any officer to set aside the action of the Council, whatever it might be. But knowing that Eccarius had refused, he had sent the resolutions to the old Council and Le Moussu had sent them to the new one, so that they reached both parties, but that did not exculpate Eccarius. He did more than simply refuse to carry out his duty, he wrote a letter stating that he refused to send the resolutions and said things that were said to have influenced one of the Councils into refusing the acceptance of the resolutions and had thereby lowered the influence of the Council. He thought it necessary to press the charge, but before formulating any resolution he would ask Eccarius what he had written.

Citizen Eccarius said he was in the same position as Hales; he kept no copies, and should decline to answer; he should stand on the principle of English law, which was that those who prosecute should prove. The split was caused by Sorge asking twenty-two delegates to show their credentials, and demanding that two-thirds of the sections should be composed of wage slaves. Since then an Irish section had tried to bring about a reconciliation but failed. The Council had no right to pass resolutions three months after that the sections had refused in December. If the subcommittee had met and consulted the matter might have been so arranged that the Council would not be implicated.

Citizen Barry said he thought a member had the right to entertain an opinion even though the Council had passed resolutions with which he disagreed, but he had no right to hold office to give effect to his own, when they were opposed to the majority. When he could not conscientiously carry out the will of the Council, he ought to resign. On the other hand he would be quite right in refusing to tolerate any interference with his duties.

---

3. Half the line is blank in the minutes.

Citizen Jung didn't think a member of the Council had a right to advocate opinions that had been condemned by the Council or that were contrary to its declarations; he had a right to hold them but not to advocate them, when he wished to do so he should first resign.

Citizen Eccarius said that a letter had been printed which said "that the report sent threw a new light upon the subject and the writer regretted that it had not come to hand when the resolutions were before the Council." That purported to have been written by the secretary for America. He didn't write it.

Citizen Hales said he wrote that letter but he sent it unofficially and did not sign himself as American secretary. It was printed without the context, which would give an altogether different aspect to it. He would stand by the letter as a whole.

Citizen Marx considered Hales had been guilty of grave indiscretion, as he had compromised the Council.

Citizen Engels agreed with the remarks of Citizen Marx. With respect to the defense of Citizen Eccarius, the Council had nothing to do with British law. It had a right to know: Had Eccarius written the letter he was charged with writing? Yes or No?

Citizen Jung read an extract from a letter written by Cristenet, a member of the new Council, which said that Eccarius' letter in which he announced his resignation had done much to reawake ill feeling; many of the sections would have accepted the resolutions only for it.

Citizen Eccarius thought when the charge was made the proofs would be forthcoming, but instead of the proofs being produced he was asked to acknowledge his guilt. He should refuse to give any answer until the letter was in his hand. It had all along been assumed that he had been guilty of criminal correspondence, and he should let those who made the charge prove it.

Citizen Marx said he said nothing about criminal correspondence, but he did say it was a crime if Eccarius wrote the letter which had the damaging character— of destroying the influence of the Council.

With regard to the demand that the charge should be proved, he would point out that this was not an ordinary tribunal where there was a defendant and a prosecutor. It was a question of the conservation of the influence of the Council. Under the circumstances, he saw nothing but that the matter should be adjourned, and the letter written for.

Citizen Eccarius said that had already been done.

Citizen Engels said that the sentimentality of the previous sitting, when it was said it was cruel to let charges hang over a man's head, etc., only made the cry for delay more comical. Of course the matter must be delayed, but he was quite convinced . . .

Refutation of a Second General Council*

Citizen Marx submitted the following declaration which upon the motion of Citizen Hales, seconded by Citizen Mayo, was adopted.

Some weeks ago a pamphlet was published under the title *Universal Federalist Council of the International Working Men's Association and of the Republican Socialist Societies Adhering*. This pamphlet pretends nothing less than to inaugurate a *coup d'état* within the International. It announces the formation of a second General Council, and it denounces both the organization of the International and the administration of its General Council. Now who are the members of this new self-constituted Council, and the authors of these denunciations? Among the names affixed to the document we find, first, that of Citizen John Weston, a member of the General Council and its former treasurer, who in a letter to the Council declares his name to have been made use of without his authority. Second, six delegates from the Universal Republican League, a society entirely foreign to the International. Third, two delegates from an "International Republican Federalist Section," which section is totally unknown to the International. Fourth, two delegates from the Land and Labour League, which society does not form any part of the International. Fifth, two self-styled delegates of the German Arbeiterbildungsverein [Workers' Educational Society] but in fact delegates of a few Germans who were excluded from that society on account of their openly avowed hostility to the International. Last, four delegates of two French societies counting together less than a score of members, and which the General Council had declined to admit as branches; among these we find M. Vésinier, excluded from the International by a committee appointed

* From the minutes of the General Council, May 21, 1872.

[242]

by the Brussels Congress in 1868, and M. Landeck, whom the hasty flight of Louis Bonaparte's prefect of police, on the fourth of September, 1870, liberated from the engagement he had voluntarily taken toward that officer, and "scrupulously kept, not to occupy himself any more, in France, either with politics or with the International" (see the published report of the third trial of the International at Paris), and who only lately was expelled from the Society of the Communard Refugees in London.

It must be evident, even to the signatories of this document, that a conclave of such entire strangers to the International has exactly as much right to meddle with its organization and to constitute itself its General Council, as the General Council of the International has to interfere with the organization and to declare itself the Board of Directors of the Great Northern Railway.

No wonder that these men are utterly ignorant of the history and organization of the International. How should they be expected to know that according to our Rules the General Council has to render its accounts to the General Congresses, and not to them? Or that when in 1870 the breaking out of the war prevented the Congress meeting, a unanimous vote of all federations empowered the General Council to continue in office until political circumstances should permit the convocation of a public Congress? As to the fund collected by the General Council in favor of the refugees, the sum total received has, from time to time, been acknowledged in the published reports of the Council meetings, and our treasurer, Citizen Jung, 4 Charles Street, Northampton Square, Clerkenwell, holds the receipts for every farthing expended, which receipts, as well as the accounts, can be inspected any day by any of the donors. Such an inspection will show not only that the Council has devoted a great portion of its time to this object, quite foreign to its regular functions, but also that itself, as a body, and its individual members, have contributed to the refugee fund within the limits of their means.

Since the growth and power of the International have become what they are, the only way in which rival and hostile societies can attempt to attack it with any chance of success is to usurp its name in order to undermine its strength. This has been so well understood by the whole press gang of the governments, and of the ruling classes, that the same papers, from police press to so-called democratic and republican, which carefully suppress every official declaration of the General Council always hasten to keep all Europe well informed of insignificant and ridiculous manifestations like that of the "Universal Federalist Council."

Citizen Marx then reverted to the American question; he said he did not think any motion was necessary as the American Congress was near at hand, but he thought a review of the action taken by the Council would prove that it had done right. He didn't concern himself with the quarrels of the two sections, for he believed there were faults on both sides, but the position he took was that the resolutions were necessary to keep the Association in its proper limits. (1) They recommended the two sections to unite: that was only carrying on the Rules. (2) In recommending sections numerically weak to amalgamate, the Council was mainly following a suggestion which emanated from Section 6, which belonged to the new Council. In advising the calling of a Congress in July, the Council took a course which had been accepted; to have called it later would have prevented the sections from sending delegates to the General Congress in September. The resolution which suspended Section 12 was the only executive resolution, and the only one for which the Council was responsible to the Congress. The suspension was rendered necessary by the appeal which it issued, an appeal which had created confusion and misunderstanding and upon which new sections had been founded. They had demanded to be put in the place of the New York Federal Council. Not only that but their protest showed that they did not understand the principles of the Association. They objected to the term "wage slaves," saying that they must necessarily be political slaves, the proper persons to be entrusted with the management being the small self-employers; besides, their other peculiar theories caused a great deal of misconception as to the real objects of the Association.

The new Council itself did not seem to care much either way about the matter, for Hubert's letter seemed to intimate that it would not have mattered if the Council had only censured the other party. The resolution requiring all new sections to be composed of two-thirds wage slaves was necessary to prevent the Association being used for trading purposes.

The period was a most critical one, and it was necessary that there should not be any mistake as to the principles of the Association. The work of the Association did not concern the real Yankees so much as [it] did some of the other elements. The Yankees were instinctively speculators. The greatest labor interest in the States was Irish, next German, third the Negroes, and fourth the Yankees themselves. The document sent to the London Conference from America called attention to the danger which would result from middle-class intrusion and said that reform societies did not understand the labor question, and yet those societies were continually growing and workingmen were being led away by them. Seven of the signatories to that document belonged to the new Council.

Citizen Eccarius said: Whether it was right or not an impression prevailed that the section had been the victim of an intrigue. For a long time the Council could not get anyone to act in America. Jessup simply corresponded, Sylvis might have done more had he lived, Hume was furnished with credentials, and Cluseret announced himself as general organizer, but it was not until November, 1870, when steps were taken to form a Central Council. It was recognized as a Provisional Council for New York, and since then the work of organization had gone on. Section 9 dated from 1848. It was in reality the New Democracy, which had always advocated the nationalization of the land. Three of its officers were Allen, a painter, Ira Davis, whose doors had always been open to the poor and distressed, [and] Maddox. The New Democracy dissolved itself to get rid of West but he got in again by starting a section. There soon got to be two elements on the Council; the Germans in Chicago and other places appointed members of Section 1, Sorge's section, as their delegates on the Federal Council until out of eleven members six were on the Council. Last October Sorge announced he was going to resign; and only five voted against when Sorge proposed dissolution to get rid of West. It was arranged that they should reorganize and a meeting was fixed, but seven remained behind and constituted themselves a new committee, and on the day when the new committee was to have met, the seven met beforehand and appointed president, treasurer, secretary, and demanded credentials from twenty-two of the delegates when they arrived, telling them to wait a fortnight. The result was that they met and constituted themselves a committee and declined to recognize what Sorge had done. They all say that they object to the interference of the middle-class reformers—all statements to the contrary being invented by their opponents. They intended to work with the bona fide working-class elements and meant to bring in the New York trade unions. Whether true or not, they considered themselves the victims of an intrigue.

Citizen Marx said he was quite ready to admit that the resolutions might be misrepresented, as in the Swiss dispute. Eccarius had gone into details. He would bring details too—a French section and an Irish one joined the old Council immediately the decision of the General Council was known; from San Francisco and New Orleans complaints had come of the new Council; Nicholson wrote that great danger would result from unauthorized versions of the principles being promulgated. Section 10 sent word that the old Council represented the interest of the worker while the new was composed of politicians who wanted to make capital out of the Association. The workingmen refused to join so long as the Association was identified with particular doctrines.

Citizen Eccarius said that the antagonism of the Pennsylvania miners arose from the defense of the Commune, the reason being that there were many Irish among them and they forgot everything in the shooting of the priests—being Catholics.

The English section of San Francisco withdrew its delegate from the old Council.

Citizen Marx said that the Irish only took action after the decision of the General Council.

Citizen Hales said he wished to say one word in justification of the letter he had written; he stood to the statement he made, he felt that the Council had acted in the dark. Information had been withheld and he charged Citizen Eccarius with having withheld it. What he had just stated he ought to have stated before the adoption of the resolutions: he knew the circumstances, and let the Council vote in ignorance.

Citizen Engels said it was all very well for Hales to try and justify himself, but he thought it looked very awkward for Hales after what had just been said; he should move that Hales's letter be written for, as well as that of Eccarius—it was necessary to deal with one as well as the other.

Citizen Hales said he would admit that the letter as printed was correct, but if it was necessary to send for it he would second the proposition; he wanted the matter to be gone into.

It was then decided that Citizen Le Moussu should act as secretary for America provisionally—and as such that he should write for the letter of Hales.

Strengthening the General Council*

CITIZEN MARX then brought on the question of the General Congress. He proposed that it be held in Holland, leaving it to the Dutch to fix upon the town, and that Citizen Cournet be instructed to write and ask them [to] decide immediately. The Belgians themselves proposed Holland in 1870.

Citizen Vaillant asked if it could be held in Holland.

Citizen Marx said he had already received information from Holland in the affirmative.

Citizen Serraillier seconded the proposition and it was carried unanimously.

It was then proposed by Citizen Marx, seconded by Citizen Johannard, and carried unanimously that it should be held on the first Monday in September.

Citizen Marx then said that there was no doubt but that the question of organization would be the principal subject that would be brought before the Congress. The struggles that had taken place had sufficiently shown that. In dealing with it, it would be well to divide the subject in sections relating to the General Council and Federal Councils. The proposition of Bakunin would simply reduce the General Council into a bureau of statistics, which would not be worth having a Council for. The papers could give all the information that could be collected, and it must be remembered that as yet no statistics had been gathered, although the General Council had urged upon the sections time after time the necessity of something being done with respect to them.

The proposition of the Belgian Federal Council was logical, for it

---

* From the minutes of the General Council, June 11, 1872.

[247]

went in for the suppression of the General Council as being no longer necessary. It was contended that the federal councils could do all that was necessary. Federal councils, it was contended, were established or were being established in all countries and they could take the management into their own hands. The *Emancipación* of Spain in criticizing that proposition said it would be the death of the Association. It was not even consistent, as, to be logical, federal councils ought to be abolished at the same time. Nevertheless he should not be opposed to accepting the proposition as an alternative, as an experiment, though he was certain it would only demonstrate the absolute necessity of the reestablishment of the General Council; if the policy of strengthening the hands of the General Council was rejected he was prepared to go in for it, but under no circumstances would he accept the proposition of Bakunin to retain the General Council and make it a nullity.

Citizen Serraillier proposed and Citizen Johannard seconded that the question of reorganization be the first subject for discussion at the Congress; carried unanimously.

Citizen Eccarius said he had considered the subject a great deal lately and he had arrived at the same conclusion as Marx, namely, that the hands of the Council should be strengthened; he proposed that the proposition for abolishing the General Council be rejected.

To Spanish Sections of the International*

Citizens,

We hold proof that within the International, and particularly in Spain, there exists a secret society called the Alliance of Socialist Democracy. This society, whose center is in Switzerland, considers it its special mission to guide our great Association in the direction of its own particular inclinations and lead it toward goals unknown to the vast majority of International members. Moreover, we know from the Seville *Razon* that at least three members of your Council belong to the Alliance.

When this society was formed in 1868 as an open society, the General Council was obliged to refuse it admission to the International so long as it preserved its international character, for it pretended to form a second international body functioning within and without the International Working Men's Association. The Alliance was admitted to the International only after promising to limit itself to being purely a local section in Geneva (see the private circular of the General Council on "Fictitious Splits," etc., page 7 onwards).

If the character and organization of this society were already contrary to the spirit and the letter of our Rules when it was still public, its secret existence within the International, in spite of its promise, represents no less than treason against our Association. The International knows but one type of members, all with equal rights and duties; the Alliance divides them into two classes, the initiated and the uninitiated, the latter doomed to be led by the former by means of an organization of whose very existence they are unaware. The

---

* Written by Marx and Engels, August 8, 1872, to the Spanish Federal Council; published in *La Emancipación*, August 17, 1872.

[249]

International demands that its members should acknowledge Truth, Justice, and Morality as the basis of their conduct; the Alliance obliges its supporters to hide from the uninitiated members of the International the existence of the secret organization, the motives and even the aim of their words and deeds. The General Council had already announced in its private circular that at the coming Congress it would demand an inquiry into this Alliance, which is a veritable conspiracy against the International. The General Council is also aware of the measures taken by the Spanish Federal Council on the insistence of the gentlemen of the Alliance in the interests of their society, and is determined to put an end to this underhand dealing. With this end in view, it requests from you for the report it will be presenting at the Hague Congress:

1. A list of all the members of the Alliance in Spain, with indication of the functions they fulfill in the International;

2. An inquiry into the nature and activities of the Alliance, and also into its organization and ramifications outside Spain;

3. A copy of your private circular of July 7 [1872];

4. An explanation of how you reconcile your duties toward the International with the presence in your Council of at least three notorious members of the Alliance.

Unless it receives *a categoric and exhaustive answer by return*, the General Council will be obliged to denounce you publicly in Spain and abroad for having violated the spirit and the letter of the General Rules, and having betrayed the International in the interests of a secret society that is not only alien but hostile to it.

Greetings and fraternity.

On behalf of the General Council,
Secretary for Spain,
Frederick Engels

A Plot Against the International*

I

SINCE the International Working Men's Association undertook to unite the scattered forces of the proletariat in a single union, in order to become the living representative of the common interests which unite the workers, it necessarily had to keep an open door for socialists of every shading. Its founders and the representatives of workers' organizations of both continents who sanctioned the General Statutes of the Association at the International Congresses forgot that the very breadth of its program would allow the *déclassés* to creep in and to build in the bosom of the Association secret organizations whose activities would be aimed, not against the bourgeoisie and the existing governments but against the International itself. Such was the case of the Alliance of Socialist Democracy.

At the Hague Congress, the General Council ordered an investigation of this secret organization. The Congress set up a committee of five members, Citizens Cuno, Lucain, Splingard, Vichard, and Walter

---

* Chapters I, II, and IX from *A Plot Against the International Working Men's Association:* Report Ordered by the Hague Congress on the Doings of Bakunin and the Alliance of Socialist Democracy; written by Marx and Engels, with the assistance of Paul Lafargue, in French, between April and July, 1873, and published as a brochure, *L'Alliance de la Démocratie Socialiste et l'Association Internationale des Travailleurs* [*The Alliance of Socialist Democracy and the International Working Men's Association*] (London and Hamburg, 1873). It was translated into German by S. Kokosky and published under the title, *Ein Complot gegen die Internationale Arbeiter-Association* (Brunswick, 1874). The text and the title used here are from the German translation, as edited by Engels and as compared with the French original. The German text was also published in the New York *Arbeiter-Zeitung*.

(who withdrew), which gave its report at the September 7 session. The Congress resolved that:

1. Michael Bakunin, as founder of the Alliance, be expelled from the International for a personal action.[1]

2. James Guillaume, as a member of the Alliance, be expelled.

3. The documents relating to the Alliance be published.

Because the members were scattered in various countries, the above-mentioned Investigating Committee found itself completely unable to publish the documents basic to the report; therefore Citizen Vichard, the only committee member living in London, submitted documents to the Protocol Committee,[2] which now publishes them in the following report on its own responsibility.

The documents relating to the Alliance were so extensive that during the sessions of the Congress the committee had time to take cognizance of only the most important ones for a practical decision; thus, for example, most of the Russian documents were not submitted. Hence the report submitted to the Congress by the committee no longer suffices today, since it included only a part of the business in question. In order to make the meaning and significance of those documents comprehensible to the reader, we are forced to appear as historians of the Alliance.

The documents we are publishing belong to several categories. Some of them have already been published as individual pieces, mostly in French; nevertheless, they must be brought together with the others, for only in interconnection with each other do they appear in a new light. The published part contains the program of the official Alliance. Other documents belong to the International, still others to the Spanish branch of the secret Alliance, whose existence was divulged by members of the Alliance in the spring of 1871. Those who had carefully followed the Spanish movement in that period will only find more precise details of facts which belong more or less to the public. The significance of these documents does not lie in their being published for the first time, but in their being put together for the first time in such a way that it reveals the common secret activity which produced them; above all, however, they are important when compared with the two following categories. The first consists of documents in the Russian language, which show the true program and

---

1. At the order of Bakunin, Sergei Nechayev wrote to Lyubavin in February, 1870, threatening the latter with reprisals if he did not release Bakunin from the obligations he had undertaken in connection with the Russian translation of Marx's *Capital*.

2. The Hague Congress appointed a Protocol Committee—Marx, Engels, Dupont, Frankel, Serraillier, and Le Moussu—to work on the documents of the Congress.

activity of the Alliance. These documents had hitherto remained hidden by the language, unknown in the West, in which they were written, and this circumstance has enabled its authors to give free vent to their fantasies and rhetoric. The faithful translation we are submitting here will give the reader the opportunity to ascertain the intellectual, moral, political, and economic worth of the heads of the Alliance.

The last category consists of only one document: the secret statutes of the Alliance; it is the only document of any size that is being published for the first time in this report. It will perhaps be asked whether it is permitted revolutionists to publish statutes of a secret society, of an alleged conspiracy. Well, these secret statutes are among the documents whose publication was expressly demanded by the Alliance Committee at the Hague Congress, and no delegate, not even the minority member of the committee, voted against it. Thus this publication has been expressly ordered by the Congress, whose instructions we must carry out; but in regard to the matter itself, we have to say the following:

We are dealing here with a society which, under the mask of the most extreme anarchism, does not aim its attacks against the existing governments but against the revolutionists who do not submit to its orthodoxy and its leadership. Founded by a minority at a bourgeois congress, it crept into the ranks of the International Working Men's Association, the leadership of which it first tried to seize, and then worked to destroy it when its plan was frustrated. In the most shameless way, it sought to substitute its sectarian program and its limited ideas for the all-embracing program and noble aspirations of our Association; it organized its secret sections within the public sections of the International, in many instances succeeding in taking over the latter by prior common conspiratorial action; it publicly attacked in its papers all the elements that refused to submit to its domination; it provoked open war—these are its own words—in our ranks. To attain its objective, no means and no dishonesty were too low; lies, slanders, intimidation, violence, cowardly deception, all were equally right for it. Finally, in Russia, it entirely replaced the International, in whose name it committed common crimes, chicaneries, and one murder, for which the government and the bourgeois press have made our Association responsible. And the International is expected to keep silent because the society which is guilty of all these actions is a secret one! The International has in its hands the statutes of this society, its deadly enemy—statutes in which it openly declares itself to be a new Society of Jesus and claims that it is its right and its duty to use all Jesuitical means. Those statutes make immediately clear all the hostilities to

which the International had been exposed from that side; and it is
expected that it should not publish these statutes because it would
mean denouncing a secret organization!

Against all these intrigues there is only one means, but one of
shattering effectiveness: complete exposure. To expose this devious-
ness in its context is to make it ineffectual. To accord it the protection
of our silence would be not only naïveté, which the heads of the Alliance would rightly ridicule, but also a cowardice. More than that, it
would be an act of treason against those Spanish Internationals who, as
members of the secret Alliance, in their proceedings did not support
the latter when they became aware that it was openly hostile to the
International. Moreover, everything in the secret statutes can be found
in the Russian-language documents, but in even more sharply defined
form, published by Bakunin and Nechayev themselves. The statutes
only strengthen their content.

Let the leaders of the Alliance inveigh against denunciations. We
denounce them for their contempt for workers and their benevolence
toward governments, for which they have performed such good
services that they disorganized the proletarian movement. The Zurich
Tagwacht was quite right when it stated in a reply to Bakunin:

"If you are not a paid agent, it is nevertheless clear that no paid
agent could have done more harm than you did."[3]

                                   II

The Alliance of Socialist Democracy was entirely of bourgeois
origin. It did not emanate from the International; it is an offspring of
the Peace and Freedom League, a stillborn society of bourgeois republicans. The International was already well established when
Michael Bakunin took it into his head to play the role of emancipator
of the proletariat. The International could offer him only a field of
activity common to all members. To amount to anything in it, he
would first have had to earn his spurs by constant and self-sacrificing
work; but he believed he would find better prospects and an easier way
on the side of the bourgeois in the League.

Hence in September, 1867, he had himself elected a member of the
permanent committee of the Peace League and took his role seriously;
one can even say that he and Barni, today a deputy in Versailles, were

---

3. *Die Tagwacht* was a German-language Zurich weekly, organ of the Social-
Democratic party in Switzerland, and of the Swiss sections of the International
from 1869 to 1873. The quotation is from an anonymous article, "*Noch Einiges
über Bakunin*," published October 5, 1872.

the souls of that committee. Posing as the theoretician of the League, Bakunin was to publish a work, *Federalism, Socialism, and Anti-theologism,*[4] under its auspices. He soon became convinced, however, that the League was an insignificant organization and that the liberals, of which it consisted, saw in the congresses only a means of combining a pleasure trip with high-sounding speeches, whereas the International, on the contrary, grew from day to day. It then occurred to him to engraft the League upon the International. To carry out this plan, Bakunin had Elpidin propose him, in July, 1868, as a member of the Central Section [of the International] in Geneva. On the other hand, he had the committee of the League adopt a proposal to suggest at the Brussels Congress of the International that the two societies form an offensive and defensive alliance; and to get the approval of the Congress for this lively proceeding, he composed a confidential circular, which he had the committee send out to the "gentlemen" of the League. In the circular he avowed that the League, hitherto an impotent farce, could acquire importance only if it confronted the alliance of oppressors, "the alliance of nations with the alliance of workers. . . . We can be something only if we become the sincere and earnest representatives of millions of workers."

He was to be the providential apostle of the League, and was to bless the working class with a self-chosen bourgeois parliament, which would leave the political leadership in his care.

"To become a salutary and real power," the circular concludes, "our League must become the *pure political expression* of the great economic and social interests and principles which today are being triumphantly developed and spread by the great International Working Men's Association in Europe and America."

The Brussels Congress had the temerity to reject that proposal of the League. Great was Bakunin's disappointment and fury. On the one hand, the International eluded his patronage. On the other, Professor Gustave Vogt, president of the League, reprimanded him sharply.

"Either," he wrote to Bakunin, "you were not sure of the success of our invitation, in which case you compromised the League; or you knew what a surprise your friends in the International had in store for us, in which case you deceived us in an unworthy way. I ask you, what can we tell our congress?"

Bakunin replied to him in a letter that was read to everybody who would listen:

"I could not foresee," he wrote, "that the Congress of the Interna-

---

4. This incomplete brochure was published in Bern, 1867–1868.

tional would answer us in such a rude and arrogant way; we owe this to the intrigues of a certain coterie of Germans who abhor Russians (to his hearers he explained specifically that this was a Marxist coterie). You ask me what we should do. I claim the honor of making a reply to this gross insult from the tribune of our congress in the name of our committee."

Instead of keeping his word, Bakunin turned coat. He presented to the congress of the League in Bern a program of a fantasy-socialism wherein he demanded equalization of classes and individuals, in an effort to trump the ladies of the League who demand equalization of the sexes. Defeated once more, he and his tiny minority withdrew from the congress and went to Geneva.

The alliance between bourgeois and workers which Bakunin dreamed of was not to be confined to a public alliance. The secret statutes of the Alliance of Socialist Democracy (see Document No. 1[5]) show indications that Bakunin laid the foundations of a secret society in the bosom of the League itself, which was to take over the leadership of the latter. Not only are the names of the leading groups identical with those of the League (permanent central committee, central bureau, national committees), but it is also stated in the secret statutes that the "founding members of the Alliance are to a large extent the former members of the congress at Bern." In order to proclaim himself chief of the International, he had first to become the head of another army, whose loyalty to his person would be assured by a secret organization. Once he publicly planted his society in the International, he planned to have it branch out in all the sections and thereby achieve absolute control. For this purpose he founded in Geneva the (public) Alliance of Socialist Democracy. On the surface it was merely a public society, which, of course, although entirely merged in the International, was to have a separate international organization, a central committee, a national bureau, and sections independent of our own Association; it was to have its own public congress alongside our own annual one. But this public Alliance harbored within itself another, the more secret alliance of the international brothers, the Hundred Guardists of Dictator Bakunin.

The secret statutes of the "Organization of the Alliance of the International Brothers" show that in that Alliance there are "three grades": "(1) the international brothers; (2) the national brothers; (3) the semisecret and semipublic organization of the International Alliance of Socialist Democracy."

---

5. The document is entitled "Secret Organization of the International Alliance of Socialist Democracy," and describes its organizational structure.

1. The international brothers, whose number is restricted to "one hundred," constitute the sacred College. They are under a central committee and a national committee, which are organized as an executive bureau and a supervisory committee. These committees themselves are responsible to the "Constituent," or General Assembly, consisting of at least two-thirds of the International brothers. The Alliance-brothers "have no other fatherland than the general revolution, no other foreign country and no other enemy than reactionaries. They reject all politics of conciliation and compromise and consider reactionary all political movements that do not have the triumph of their principles as their immediate and direct aim."

Since, however, this article postpones the political activity of the "Hundred" indefinitely, and since these irreconcilable ones do not intend to forgo the advantages of public office, Article 8 provides: "No brother is to accept any public service except with the approval of the committee to which he belongs."

When we come to discuss Spain and Italy,[6] we will see how eager the heads of the Alliance were to put this Article into practice. The international brothers "are brothers . . . each must be sacred to all the others, more than a brother by birth; every brother is to count on the help and support of all others up to the extinction of possibilities."

The Nechayev affair will reveal to us the meaning of this mysterious extinction of possibilities.

"All the international brothers know each other. No political secret must ever exist among them. No one is to belong to any secret society without the positive approval of his committee or, in case of necessity, if he demands it, without that of the central committee, and even then he can belong to it only on condition that he reveals to them [his brothers] the secrets which may interest them directly or indirectly."

The Piétris and the Stiebers use only subordinate and lost people as spies, but the Alliance, in sending the false brothers into secret societies to betray the latter's secrets, assigns the role of spies to those very same men who, according to its plan, are to take over the leadership of the "general revolution." In addition, this revolutionary buffoon of the vulgar also dons the crown of the comic:

"An international brother can only be he who has accepted the whole program with all its theoretical and practical consequences, who combines intelligence, energy, honor," (!) "and reliability with revolutionary passion—who has the devil in his body."

2. The national brothers are to be organized by the international

---

6. Parts IV and V of this brochure, omitted here, deal with the activities of the Alliance in Spain and Italy.

brothers along the same plan as national associations in every country; but under no circumstances must they even suspect the existence of an international organization.

3. The secret International Alliance of Socialist Democracy, whose membership is being substantially recruited everywhere, has in its permanent central committee a legislative organ, which, whenever it meets, transforms itself into the "secret General Assembly of the Alliance." This assembly takes place annually at the Congress of the International, or, in extraordinary cases, by convocation by the Central Bureau, or rather, by the Geneva Central Section.

The Geneva Central Section is "the permanent delegation of the permanent Central Committee" and the "executive council of the Alliance." It consists of two subdivisions: the Central Bureau and the Supervisory Committee. The Central Bureau, consisting of from three to seven members, is the actual executive authority of the Alliance:

"It receives its cues from the Geneva Central Section and, for its part, sends its instructions, not to say its orders, to all the national committees, from which it is to receive secret reports at least once a month."

This Central Committee has discovered the means of being fish and meat, secret and public, at the same time, for as part "of the secret Central Section, the Central Bureau is a secret organization; . . . but as a public directory of the public Alliance it is a public organization."

One sees thus that Bakunin had already organized the whole secret and public direction of his "dear Alliance" before it actually existed in fact, and that in any election the participating members were merely the marionettes of a puppet show managed by him. Moreover, he did not mind admitting it, as we shall soon see. The Geneva Central Section, whose task it is to provide cues to the Central Bureau, is itself only a comedy, for its majority decisions are binding on the Bureau only after the latter, "by a majority of its members, decides to appeal to the General Assembly, which then has to be convened within three weeks. An Assembly thus convened can make decisions only if two-thirds of its members are present."

One sees that the Central Bureau has surrounded itself with all constitutional guarantees to secure its independence.

One could be naïve enough to believe that this autonomous Central Bureau might at least have been freely chosen by the Geneva Central Section. By no means; the provisional Central Bureau has been "presented to the Geneva founding group as having been elected provisionally by all the founding members of the Alliance, who to a large extent were members of the Bern Congress and who returned home" (with the exception of Bakunin) "after they had handed over their power of attorney to Bakunin."

The founding members of the Alliance are therefore nothing more than a couple of secessionist bourgeois of the Peace League.

Thus: the permanent Central Committee, which has arrogated to itself all constituent and legislative power over the whole Alliance, has elected itself. The permanent executive delegation of this permanent Central Committee—the Geneva Central Section—has elected itself, instead of being chosen by that committee. The executive Central Bureau of this Geneva Central Section, instead of being elected by it, was forced upon it by a group of individuals, who jointly "handed over their power of attorney to Bakunin."

Thus "Citizen B" is the pivot of the Alliance. And in order to assert his function as such, the secret statutes of the Alliance state literally:

"Its visible form of government is to be a presidency of a federated republic."

A presidency in which the president already existed beforehand, the permanent "Citizen B."

Since the Alliance is an international society, the national committee in every country is to be made up "of all those nationals who are members of the Central Committee."

To constitute a National Committee, only three members are required. In order to assure the bureaucratic order of successive appeal, "the National Committee is to serve as the *sole* mediating organ between the Central Bureau and all the local groups in their country."

The national committees must "undertake the organization of the Alliance in their countries, but in such a way that it is always dominated by the members of the permanent Central Committee and represented at the congresses."

This is what is called the Alliance language: organize from the bottom up. These local groups have only the right to bring their programs and regulations to the national committees, in order "that they be submitted to the Central Bureau for approval; without such approval, the local groups can be no part of the Alliance."

Once this despotic and hierarchical secret organization had been engrafted on the International, the next necessary step for its completion was merely to disorganize the latter. For this purpose, it sufficed to anarchize and autonomize its sections and to transform its central organs into mere mailboxes, "correspondence and statistical bureaus," as was actually attempted later.

The revolutionary past of the permanent "Citizen B" was not glorious enough to permit him the hope of permanently maintaining his dictatorship over the secret Alliance, let alone the public Alliance, which he had sequestrated in his favor. He had to conceal it under democratized shadowboxing. Hence the secret statutes provide that the provisional Central Bureau (read: the permanent Citizen) was to function until the Alliance's first General Assembly, which was then to choose the new permanent members of the Central Bureau. But "since it was of urgent necessity that the Central Bureau should always consist only of members of the permanent Central Committee, the latter, by means of the Central Committee, must see to it that all local groups be so organized and led that they send to the Assembly only members of the permanent Central Committee as delegates, or, in default, only such persons who are completely loyal and devoted to the leadership of their respective national committees, so that the permanent Central Committee always has the upper hand in the whole organization of the Alliance."

These instructions were not handed out by some Bonapartist minister or prefect on the day of election, but from the quintessential antiauthoritarian man, the archanarchist, the apostle of organization from the bottom up, the Bayard of the autonomy of the sections and of the federation of autonomous groups, Saint Michael Bakunin, for the protection of his Permanence.

We have examined the organization created for the perpetuation of "Citizen B's" dictatorship. Let us now look into its program.

"The Association of international brothers wants a general, at the same time social, philosophical, economical, and political revolution, so that in the present order of things, founded as it is on property, exploitation, domination, and the authority principle—be that religious or metaphysical or bourgeois-doctrinaire, yea, even Jacobin-revolutionary—no stone would be left unturned, first in all of Europe and then in the rest of the world. With the slogan: peace to the workers, freedom to the oppressed, and death to the rulers, exploiters, and trustees of every sort! we want to destroy all the states and all the churches, together with all their religious, political, juridical, financial, police, educational, economic, and social arrangements and laws, so that all these millions of poor human beings who have been deceived, enslaved, martyred, exploited until now should be freed from their official and officious managers and benefactors, and cooperative societies as well as individuals would at last breathe in complete freedom."

This is what one may call *revolutionary revolutionism!* To attain this abracadabra goal, the first condition is not to fight the existing states and governments with the usual revolutionary means, but, on the contrary, with the means of ringing, doctored phrases—to seize "the political system altogether and its natural consequence, as a basis, individual property."

Thus what is involved here is not the overthrow of the Bonapartist, Prussian, or Russian state, but the abstract state, the state as such, a state that exists nowhere. But even if the international brothers, in their embittered struggle against this state which lies in the clouds, knew how to get out of the way of the killers, the jails, and the bullets which the actual states save for ordinary revolutionists, we have also seen how they have reserved for themselves at the same time a necessary right, which they obtained only by papal dispensation, of making use of all the advantages the actual bourgeois states offer them. Fanelli, the Italian deputy, Soriano, official in the government of Amadeus of Savoy, and perhaps also Albert Richard and Gaspard Blanc, Bonapartist police agents, have shown us how obliging the Pope is in this respect. . . . And the police are hardly worried about the "Alliance, or, to speak openly, the conspiracy," of Citizen B against this abstract notion of the state.

The first act of the revolution must thus be the abolition of the state by decree, as Bakunin did in Lyon on September 28 [1870], although such abolition of the state is necessarily an authoritarian act. For him, the state means all political, revolutionary, or reactionary authority, "for we care little whether it calls itself church, monarchy, constitutional state, bourgeois republic, or even revolutionary dictatorship. We detest and reject them all on the same ground, as the unfailing source of exploitation and despotism."

Yea, he declares that all revolutionists who desire the "construction of revolutionary states" on the day after the revolution are even more dangerous than all the existing governments, and that "we, the international brothers, are the natural enemies of these revolutionists," for it is the first duty of the international brothers to disorganize the revolution.

The reply to these gasconades on the immediate abolition of the state and on the establishment of anarchy can already be found in the Confidential Circular of the last General Council: *Fictitious Splits in the International*.[7] . . .

Nevertheless, let us follow the anarchistic evangel to its consequences; let us assume that the state is abolished by decree. According to Article 6, the consequences of this act would be: bankruptcy of the state, suspension of private debts incurred with the authority of the state, suspension of all tax payments and dues, dissolution of the

---

7. See page 190. The paragraph omitted here, beginning, "Anarchy, then, is the great war horse of their master Bakunin . . ." is on page 222.

army, the judiciary, the bureaucracy, the police, and the priests, abolition of the official administration of justice, accompanied by an auto-
da-fé of all titles to property, of all the juridical and civil papers and
documents, the confiscation of all productive capital and work tools
in favor of cooperative labor societies which, all together, would
"constitute the commune." This commune will give those who have
been robbed the minimum necessities, leaving them free to earn more
through their own labor.

The event in Lyon has shown that the abolition of the state by
mere decree does not suffice by a long way to fulfill all these fine
promises. Two companies of the bourgeois National Guard, on the
other hand, sufficed to destroy this brilliant dream and to drive Bakunin in all haste to Geneva, with the wonder-working decree in his
pocket. Nor could he assume sufficient stupidity among his followers
not to see the necessity of giving them some sort of plan that would
assure the carrying out of his decree. This plan was as follows:

"For the organization of the commune: a federation of barricades
in permanence and the installation of a council of the revolutionary
commune by the delegation of one or two deputies from each barricade, one for the street or district; the deputies are equipped with
imperative mandates and are always held responsible and revocable"
(they are funny things, these Alliance barricades, on which one edits
mandates, instead of fighting). "The communal council thus organized
can select from its midst special executive committees for every branch
of the revolutionary commune's administration."

The insurgent capital of a commune so constituted then declares to all the other communes of the country that it forgoes all
claims to rule them; it requests that they organize themselves in a
revolutionary way and send their responsible and revocable delegates,
armed with imperative mandates, to some previously arranged place of
assembly, there to constitute a federation of insurgent associations,
communes, and provinces, and to organize a revolutionary authority
strong enough to triumph over reaction. This organization would not
confine itself to the commune of the insurgent country; other provinces and countries could participate, while "the provinces, communes,
cooperative societies, and individuals that take the side of reaction
remain excluded."

The abolition of frontiers is here of a piece with the most in-
dulgent toleration of the reactionary provinces, which are not prevented from igniting a civil war again.

Thus in this anarchist organization of the tribune-barricades we
have, first, the communal council, then the executive committees,
which, in order to be able to execute anything, must nevertheless be

provided with some power and be supported by the public authority; there is in addition a federal parliament, whose main task it would be to organize the public authority. This parliament, like the communal council, must assign the executive authority to one or more committees, which, by this very fact, are equipped with an authoritarian character that would emerge ever more sharply out of the necessities of the struggle. Hence we have all the elements for a restoration of the "authoritarian state" at its most complete, and it does not matter whether we call this machine "a revolutionary commune organized from the bottom up." The name does not change the thing; organizations from the bottom up exist in every bourgeois republic and the imperative mandates even date back to the Middle Ages. Moreover, Bakunin himself recognizes this when (in Article 8) he attaches to his organization the name of "new revolutionary state."

As to the practical value of this new revolutionary plan, in which one is debating instead of fighting, let us not waste any words on it.

But now we come to the secret of all these magic boxes with their double and triple bottoms. In order that the orthodox program be followed and anarchism take pains to appear on its good behavior, "it is necessary that, amidst the popular anarchy which will constitute the life and the entire strength of the revolution, the unity of thought and of revolutionary action find an organ. This organ is to be the secret and universal Association of the international brothers.

This Association starts with the conviction that revolutions will never be made either by individuals or by secret societies: They are made by themselves, by the force of things, by the movement of events and facts. They lie for a long time in the depth of the instinctive consciousness of the masses of the people, and then they come to an eruption . . . All that a well-organized secret society can do, above all, is to further the revolution at birth, in that it spreads ideas corresponding to the mass instincts among the people, and to organize —not the revolutionary army; the army must always be the people (the cannon fodder)—a revolutionary general staff, composed of dedicated, energetic, intelligent individuals and, above all, of sincere and not ambitious or vain friends of the people, who possess the ability to serve as mediators between the revolutionary idea (monopolized by it) and the people's instincts.

"The number of these individuals, therefore, does not have to be large. *One hundred firmly and earnestly united revolutionists suffice* for the international organization of all of Europe. Two or three hundred revolutionists suffice for the organization of the biggest country."

Thus, for once, we see a different picture. Anarchy, the "unchained life of the people," the "evil passions," etc., no longer suffice.

To insure the success of the revolution, *unity of thought and action* is necessary. The members of the International seek to create unity through propaganda, discussion, and the public organization of the proletariat; Bakunin, on the other hand, needs only a secret organization of a hundred men, the privileged representatives of the revolutionary idea, and a revolutionary general staff, commanded by an available, self-elected and permanent "Citizen B." Unity of thought and action means nothing but orthodoxy and blind obedience. *Perinde ac cadaver.*[8] We find ourselves in the middle of the Society of Jesus.

The declaration that the one hundred international brothers must serve "as mediators between the revolutionary idea and the people's instincts" creates an unbridgeable chasm between the revolutionary idea of the Alliance and the proletarian masses. It proclaims the impossibility of recruiting the Hundred Guards from anywhere but the privileged classes.

IX

While the International left the working class in the various countries the fullest freedom in its movements and efforts, it managed at the same time to unite the whole working class and, for the first time, make the ruling classes and their governments feel the cosmopolitan power of the proletariat. The ruling classes and the governments have recognized this fact by concentrating their attacks on the executive organ of our overall organization, the General Council. These attacks sharpened increasingly after the fall of the Commune. And it was precisely that moment that the Alliancers chose to declare open war on the General Council! In consequence, their influence, that mighty weapon in the hands of the Internationals, became a weapon aimed at the International. This influence was the fruit of a struggle, not against the enemies of the proletariat, but against the International itself. They maintained that the General Council's mania for domination won a victory over the autonomy of the sections and the national federations. Hence, they claimed, there was nothing left for them to do but to decapitate the International in order to save autonomy.

In fact, the men of the Alliance knew that if they did not seize this decisive moment, their dreams of the hundred international brothers secretly leading the workers' movement was done for. Their attacks found an approving echo in the police press of all countries.

Their high-sounding phrases about autonomy and free federation,

---

8. Like a cadaver: a reference to Ignatius Loyola's demand that young Jesuits obey their elders blindly and absolutely.

and their war cries against the Council in general, were nothing but a trick to mask their real aim: to disorganize the International and thereby subject it to the secret, hierarchical, and autocratic rule of the Alliance.

Autonomy of the sections, free federation of autonomous groups, antiauthoritarianism, anarchy—these are phrases quite appropriate to a "society of the *déclassés*, without profession and without outlet," a society that conspired within the bosom of the International in order to subject it to a secret dictatorship and force on it the program of Mr. Bakunin!

If one strips this program of its melodramatic tinsel, the following emerges:

1. All the abominations through which, as by a decision of fate, the life of the declassed from the higher social strata move, are praised as so many ultrarevolutionary virtues.

2. Necessity is made a basic principle, in order to lure a small, carefully sought out minority of workers. These are flattered by separating them from the workers with a secret initiation, by letting them participate in a treacherous game of intrigue with secret government, and by preaching to them that they would completely overthrow the old society if they gave their "evil passions" free rein.

3. The chief means of propaganda consist of misleading the youth with invented tales—lies about the growth of the secret organizations' power, prophecies of an imminent outbreak of revolution prepared by them, etc.—and of compromising the most progressive men of the propertied classes in the eyes of government, in order to exploit them pecuniarily.

4. The economic and political struggle of the workers and their emancipation are replaced with the all-destroying actions of this gang of convicts as the highest personification of the revolution. In a word, the scoundrelism kept down by the workers themselves, for the purpose of "revolutions according to the classic Western model," must now be let loose, in order voluntarily to put at the disposal of the reactionaries a well-disciplined band of *agents provocateurs*.

It is difficult to decide which of the two, the grotesque or the infamous, predominates in the theoretical fantasies and the practical attacks of the Alliance. Nonetheless, it did succeed in creating within the International a concealed struggle that hindered our Association's activities for two years and finally led to the defection of some of the sections and federations. Hence the decisions against the Alliance taken by the Hague Congress were acts of pure duty; it could not permit the International, this great creation of the proletariat, to be caught in the traps of the scum of the exploiting classes. As for those who wanted to deprive the General Council of the powers without which the International would have been only a scattered, disconnected, and, to use the language of the Alliance, "amorphous" mass, we can see them only as traitors or simpletons.

The Committee:
E. Dupont, F. Engels, Leo
Frankel, A. Le Moussu,
Karl Marx, Aug. Serraillier

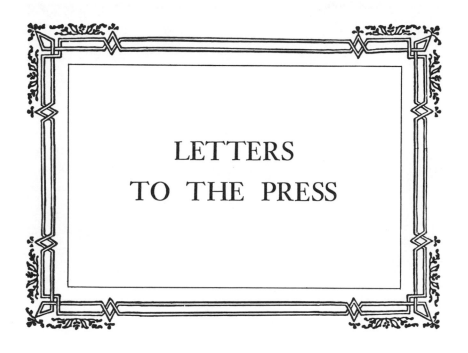

LETTERS
TO THE PRESS

Among Marx's activities as the leading spirit of the First International was writing letters to the press. The letters, not all of which were published, were mainly protests—reactions, sometimes vehement ones, to attacks, errors, omissions, distortions, and occasionally outright fabrications about the International in the "bourgeois" newspapers, as well as in hostile radical papers. Most of the letters in this section deal with the Paris Commune and its consequences for the International.

Letters were often sent to the radical press to clarify the position of the International or to attack its opponents, such as the Bakuninists and Proudhonists. The radical papers were an essential medium for the propagation of Marx's views and those of the International. Among them the following were the most important:

The Bee-Hive, a London trade-union weekly, for a time the organ of the International.

La Cigale, a weekly of the International in Brussels.

The Commonwealth, a weekly of the International in London.

Le Courrier Français, a Proudhonist weekly in Paris (a daily from June, 1867, to 1868).

Le Courrier International, a bilingual (French and English) weekly in London, in 1867 an organ of the International.

Demokratisches Wochenblatt, a labor weekly in Leipzig, published by Liebknecht.

The Eastern Post, a labor weekly in London.

L'Égalité, a French-language weekly in Geneva, organ of the Romansh Federation of the International.

L'Eguaglianza, a weekly of the International in Naples.

La Emancipación, a weekly of the International in Madrid.

La Federación, a weekly of the International in Barcelona.

The International Herald, a labor weekly in London.

Journal de l'Association Internationale des Travailleurs, a monthly (1865–1866) of the International in Geneva.

La Liberté, a Brussels daily, organ of the International.

La Marseillaise, a left-wing republican daily in Paris.

Narodnoye Dyelo, after April, 1870, a Russian-language daily of the International in Geneva.

El Obrero, a weekly of the International in Palma (Majorca).

Le Progrès, a French-language Bakuninist (anti-General Council) newspaper in Le Locle, Switzerland.

Le Rappel, a left-wing republican daily in Paris.

Le Réveil, from May, 1869, to January, 1871, a left-wing republican daily in Paris.

La Révolution Sociale, a Bakuninist weekly in Geneva.

La Rive Gauche, a left-wing republican weekly in Paris, edited by Charles Longuet.

Der Social-Demokrat, a daily organ of the General German Workers Association in Berlin.

La Solidaridad, a weekly of the International in Madrid.

La Solidarité, a Bakuninist weekly in Neuchâtel in 1870, and in Geneva in 1871.

La Tribune du Peuple, a labor weekly in Brussels.

La Vérité, a republican-radical daily in Paris, supporting the Commune.

Der Volksstaat, organ of the Social-Democratic Workers Party (Eisenacher) in Leipzig, twice weekly from October, 1869, to July, 1873, and three times weekly until September, 1876.

Volkswille, a labor weekly in Vienna.

Der Vorbote, a German-language organ of the International in Geneva.

De Werker, a Flemish-language organ of the International in Antwerp.

De Werkman, a weekly of the International in Amsterdam.

Woodhull and Claflin's Weekly, published in New York from 1870 to 1876.

The Workman's Advocate, a labor weekly in London, organ of the International from 1865 to February, 1866, when it was reorganized as The Commonwealth.

The International's Motion on Poland*

AFTER the two motions mentioned in issue No. 30 of your newspaper, made by Messrs. Beales and Leverson at the meeting on Poland in London on March 1, had been adopted, Mr. Peter Fox (Englishman), in the name of the International Working Men's Association, moved: "that an integral and independent Poland is an indispensable necessity for a democratic Europe and that, so long as this condition remains unfulfilled, revolutionary triumphs on the Continent can only be short-lived preludes to prolonged periods of rule by the counterrevolution."

After a brief historical sketch of the evils that befell Europe as a result of Poland's loss of freedom and Russia's policy of conquest, Mr. P. Fox pointed out that the position of the liberal parties on this question does not coincide with that of the democratic society in whose name he speaks. The motto of conservative Europe is: An enslaved Europe with an enslaved Poland as its foundation. The motto of the International Association is, on the other hand: A free Europe, based on a free and independent Poland.

Mr. Eccarius (German worker, vice-president of the International Working Men's Association) supported the motion and explained at length Prussia's participation in the various partitions of Poland. He concluded with the words: "The destruction of the Prussian monarchy is the condition *sine qua non* for the establishment of Germany and the restoration of Poland."

M. Le Lubez, French member of the International Working Men's Association, also spoke for the motion, which was *adopted unanimously amidst prolonged applause by the membership.*

* Written April 13, 1865; published in *Der Weisse Adler* (Zurich), April 22, over the signature of Hermann Jung, corresponding secretary for Switzerland.

The *Daily News* and a couple of other "liberal" London dailies *suppressed* this part of the report out of chagrin at the triumph of the International Working Men's Association, without whose collaboration, be it remarked in passing, the meeting on Poland at St. Martin's Hall could not have taken place at all. In the name of the International Working Men's Association, I request you to make this correction.

The International and English Workingmen's Association*

THE unusual seriousness of the English and particularly the London newspapers in respect of the International Working Men's Association and its Brussels Congress (the *Times* alone devoted four leading articles to it) has stirred up a real witches' Sabbath in the German bourgeois papers. They, the German papers, take the English papers to task for their error in believing that the International Working Men's Association in England is important! They have discovered that the English trade unions, which through the International Working Men's Association have given considerable support in cash to the Paris, Geneva, and Belgian workers in their fight against capital, have absolutely *no* connection with that very same International Working Men's Association!

"Apparently all this is based," we have in writing from London, "on the assertion of a certain M. Hirsch, whom Schulze-Delitzsch sent especially to London to kick up such a fuss. M. Hirsch says so, and M. Hirsch is an honorable man! The honorable Hirsch aroused the suspicions of London trades unionists because he bore no letters of recommendation from the International Working Men's Association. They simply made a fool of him. No wonder then that Hirsch kicked up a fuss. If he had been taken seriously, it would have been quite easy to have let him know, without any particular show of frankness, what the whole of London knows—that the General Trades Council in London consists of six or seven people, of which three, Odger (secretary of the General Trades Council and shoemakers'

---

* Written October 4, 1868; published in *Demokratisches Wochenblatt*, October 17. The text used here is based on a translation from the German by Progress Publishers, Moscow.

delegate), R. Applegarth (delegate of the Amalgamated Carpenters and Joiners), and Howell (delegate of the bricklayers and secretary of the Reform League), are simultaneously members of the General Council of the International Working Men's Association. He would have discovered further that the rest of the affiliated trades unions (there are about fifty in London alone, not counting the provincial trades unions) are represented on the General Council of the International Working Men's Association by another five members, namely, R. Shaw, Buckley, Cohn, Hales, and Maurice; furthermore, every union has the right and habit of sending delegates to the General Council for special purposes. Further, the following English organizations are represented on the General Council of the International Working Men's Association:

"Cooperative societies, which sent three delegates to the Brussels Congress, by Wlm. Weston[1] and Williams;

"The Reform League, by Dell, Cowell Stepney, and Lucraft; all three are also on the Executive Committee of the Reform League;

"The National Reform Association, set up by the late agitator Bronterre O'Brien, by its President, A. A. Walton, and Milner;

"Lastly, the atheist popular movement by its well-known orator Mrs. Harriet Law and Mr. Copeland.

"It is clear that not one significant organization of the British proletariat exists which is not directly, by its own leaders, represented on the General Council of the International Working Men's Association. Finally, there is the *Bee-Hive*, under George Potters' editorship, the official organ of the English trade unions, which is at the same time the official organ of the International's General Council, on whose meetings it reports weekly.

"The discoveries of the honorable Hirsch and the subsequent jubilation in the German bourgeois press have provided just the right fodder for the London correspondent of *Weser-Zeitung* and the London correspondent of *Augsburgerin*,[2] who signs himself △. This person—for one and the same person writes for the two papers—lives, for reasons best known to himself, in a remote corner a few hours out of London. Here he takes his shameful extracts from the *Times*, *Morning Star*, and *Saturday Review*, and serves them up with an aesthetic fish sauce to suit the taste of his public. From time to time, as is the case here, he also digs up the gossip of German papers and has it reprinted under a false date in *Weser-Zeitung* and *Augsburgerin*. The said correspondent of *Weser-Zeitung* and *Augsburgerin* is none

---

1. Probably John Weston.
2. The Augsburg *Allgemeine Zeitung*.

other than the notorious literary lumpen proletarian Élard Biscamp. Long rejected by any decent society, this unfortunate seeks consolation in the bottle for the broken heart caused him by Prussia annexing his native Kur-Hesse and his friend Edgar Bauer."

The General Council Accepts the
Russian Section in Geneva*

Citizens,

At its meeting of March 22 the General Council declared by unanimous vote that your program and rules accord with the general rules of the International Working Men's Association. It immediately admitted your section into the International. I am pleased to accept your proposal to take on the honorable duty of being your representative on the General Council.

You say in your program ". . . that the imperial yoke oppressing Poland is a brake equally hampering the political and social emancipation of both nations—the Russian just as much as the Polish."

You might add that Russia's rape of Poland provides a pernicious support and real reason for the existence of a military regime in Germany, and, as a consequence, on the whole Continent. Therefore, in working on breaking Poland's chains, Russian socialists take on themselves the lofty task of destroying the military regime; that is essential as a precondition for the overall emancipation of the European proletariat.

A few months ago I received from St. Petersburg Flerovsky's work *The Condition of the Working Class in Russia.* This is a real eye opener for Europe. Russian optimism, which is spread over the Continent even by the so-called revolutionaries, is mercilessly exposed in this work. It will not detract from its worth if I say that in one or two places it does not fully satisfy criticism from the purely theoretical point of view. It is the book of a serious observer, a tireless worker,

* Written March 24, 1870; printed in *Narodnoye Dyelo*, April 15. This text is from the Russian translation.

an unbiased critic, a great artist, and, above all, of a person intolerant of oppression in all its forms and of all national anthems, and ardently sharing all the sufferings and all the aspirations of the producing class.

Such works as Flerovsky's and those of your teacher Chernyshevsky do real honor to Russia and prove that your country is also beginning to take part in the movement of our age.

Fraternal greetings,

Karl Marx

French Press Forgeries

To the Editor of the London Times*

Sir:

   In your issue of March 16 your Paris correspondent asserts: "Karl Marx . . . wrote to one of his chief followers in Paris a letter in which he declares that he is not in agreement with the position taken by the members of the Association (the International) in that city," etc.

   Your correspondent has obviously taken this assertion from *Paris-Journal* of March 14, which promises to publish the alleged letter in full. *Paris-Journal* of March 19 actually publishes a letter from London of February 28, 1871, which allegedly is supposed to have been signed by me and whose contents correspond with your correspondent's assertion. I permit myself to declare that the letter is a shameless forgery from beginning to end.

To the Editor of Der Volksstaat†

   Paris-Journal, one of the most successful organs of the Paris police press, published in its March 14 issue an article under the sensational heading, "*Le Grand Chef de l'Internationale*" ("*Grand Chef*" is probably the French translation of Stieber's "*Hauptchef*" [Main Chief]). "He is, as is known," the article begins, "a German and, what is

---

* Written by Marx and Engels; published March 22, 1871. This text is a translation from a German version.
   † Published March 29, 1871. This letter also appeared in *Der Vorbote* on April 23 and in *Zukunft* March 26, 1871. An abridged version was printed in *L'Égalité* March 31, 1871.

[278]

even worse, a Prussian. His name is Karl Marx, he lives in Berlin, etc. Well now! This Karl Marx is dissatisfied with the behavior of the French members of the International. This alone is typical of him. He finds that they are always dabbling too much in politics and not enough in social questions. That is his conviction, and he has just formulated it very precisely in a letter to his brother and friend, Citizen Serraillier, one of the Paris high priests of the International. Karl Marx requests the French members of the International, particularly the Parisians, not to lose sight of the fact that their society has one single aim: organization of labor and the future of the workers' societies. But they are disorganizing labor instead of organizing it, and he believes that the delinquents must again be called to respect the Association's Statutes. We declare that we shall use the chance to publish this remarkable letter of Mr. Karl Marx as soon as it has been communicated to members of the International."

In its March 19 issue *Paris-Journal* actually did print a letter, allegedly signed by me, which was immediately reprinted by the whole reactionary Paris press, and then found its way into the London papers. Meanwhile, *Paris-Journal* had found out that I live in *London*, not in Berlin. So this time it dated the letter from London, contrary to its first announcement. This subsequent correction suffers, however, from the fault that it makes me correspond with my friend Serraillier, who lives in London, by a roundabout route via Paris. The letter, as I have already explained in the *Times*, is a shameless *forgery* from beginning to end.

The same *Paris-Journal* and other Paris organs of the "good press" spread the rumor that the Paris Federal Council of the International had taken a decision, which lay outside its competency, to expel the Germans from the International Working Men's Association. The London dailies hastily seized on this welcome piece of news and maliciously began to write in their leading articles about the finally accomplished suicide of the International. Unfortunately, the *Times* today carries the following announcement from the General Council of the International Working Men's Association:

"A statement has gone the rounds of the English press that the Paris members of the International Working Men's Association had so far joined the so-called Anti-German League as to declare all Germans to be henceforth excluded from the International. This statement is the reverse of fact. Neither the Federal Council of our Association in Paris nor any of the Paris sections represented by that Council have ever passed any such resolution. The so-called Anti-German League, as far as it exists at all, is the exclusive work of the upper and middle classes; it was started by the Jockey Club, and kept up by the adhesions of the Academy, of the Stock Exchange, of some bankers and manufacturers, etc. The working class had nothing whatever to do with it.

"The object of these calumnies is evident. A short time before the outbreak of the late war, the International was made the general scapegoat for all untoward events. This is now repeated over again. While the Swiss and the Russian press accuse it of having created the late outrages upon Germans at Zurich, French papers, such as the *Courrier de Lyon, Courrier de la Gironde*, the Paris *Liberté*, etc., tell of certain secret meetings of "Internationals" having taken place at Geneva and Bern, the "Prussian Ambassador in the chair," in which meetings a plan was concocted to hand over Lyon to the United Prussians and Internationals for the sake of plunder."[1]

This was the General Council's explanation. It is in the nature of things that dignitaries and the ruling classes of the old society, which can hold onto their power and the exploitation of the producing masses of the people only by national battles and conflicts, recognize their common enemy in the International Working Men's Association. To destroy it, *all* means are fair.

Karl Marx,
Secretary of the General Council of
the International Working Men's
Association for Germany

To the Editor of the London Times*

Sir:

Will you allow me to again intrude upon your columns in order to contradict widely spread falsehoods?

A Lombard telegram, dated Paris, March 30, contains an extract from the *Gaulois* which, under the sensational heading, "Alleged Organization of the Paris Revolution in London," has adorned the London papers of Saturday last. Having during the late war successfully rivaled the *Figaro* and the *Paris-Journal* in the concoction of Münchhausiades[1] that made the Paris *petite presse* a byword all over the world, the *Gaulois* seems more than ever convinced that the newsreading public will always cling to the tenet, *"Credo quia absurdum*

---

1. The letter, published in the London *Times*, March 23, 1871, was signed by J. Georg Eccarius, general secretary of the International.

---

* Written in English, April 3, 1871; published April 4.
1. The fabulous lies connected with the legendary German Baron von Münchhausen.

est" ["I believe because it is absurd"]. Baron Münchhausen himself, would he have undertaken to organize at London "in the early part of February," when M. Thiers did not yet hold any official post, "the insurrection of the eighteenth of March," called into life by the attempt of the same M. Thiers to disarm the Paris National Guard? Not content to send MM. Assi and Blanqui on an imaginary voyage to London, there to conspire with myself in secret conclave, the *Gaulois* adds to that conclave two imaginary persons—one "Bentini, general agent for Italy," and one "Dermott, general agent for England." It also graciously confirms the dignity of "supreme chief of the *Internationale*," first bestowed upon me by the *Paris-Journal.* These two worthies notwithstanding, the General Council of the International Working Men's Association will, I am afraid, continue to transact its business without the incumbrance of either "chief" or "president."

I have the honor to be, sir, yours obediently,

Karl Marx

To the Editor of De Werker*

Citizen!

My alleged letter to the members of the International in Paris is, as I have already written to the *Times* of March 22, purely a fabrication of the *Paris-Journal,* one of those boulevard papers hatched in the imperial sewer. For the rest, it seems that all the organs of Europe's "good press" have received directives to use forgery as their strongest weapon against the International.

In the eyes of the honorable champions of religion, order, family, and property, the crime of forgery is not the slightest sin.

Greetings and fraternity,

Karl Marx

To the Editor of La Liberté*

Monsieur:

In Citizen G. Lefrançais' book, *Study of the Communalist Movement in Paris in 1871,*[1] which I examined only a few days ago, there is the following sentence on page 92:

"The letter later written by Karl Marx, the chief inspirer of the

---

* Written in French; published April 8, 1871.

---

* Written in French; published March 17, 1872.

1. *Étude sur le Mouvement Communaliste à Paris, en 1871* (Neuchâtel, 1871).

German Section of the International, on the elections of February 8, in which he criticized the participation of the French Section with a certain bitterness, shows sufficiently that—whether correctly or incorrectly—the International was then little inclined to meddle actively in politics."

Immediately upon publication of my so-called letter to Serraillier, I declared in the *Times*, the *Courrier de l'Europe*, the Berlin *Zukunft*, etc., that the letter was an invention of the *Paris-Journal*. Serraillier, for his part, publicly exposed a police journalist as the author of that letter. Since practically all the organs of the International and even a few Paris newspapers published our statements, I am truly astonished to see that Citizen Lefrançais accepted the newspaper lie manufactured by Henri de Pène.

I remain, sir, faithfully yours,
Karl Marx

Apropos Jules Favre's Circular
Against the International*

Sir:

On June 6, 1871, M. Jules Favre issued a circular to all the European powers calling upon them to hunt down the International Working Men's Association. A few remarks will suffice to characterize that document.

In the very preamble of our Statutes it is stated that the International was founded "September 28, 1864, at a public meeting held at St. Martin's Hall, Long Acre, London." For purposes of his own Jules Favre puts back the date of its origin behind 1862.

In order to explain our principles, he professes to quote "their" (the International's) "sheet of the twenty-fifth of March, 1869." And then what does he quote? The sheet of a society which is not the International. This sort of maneuver he already recurred to when, still a comparatively young lawyer, he had to defend the *National* newspaper, prosecuted for libel by Cabet. Then he pretended to read extracts from Cabet's pamphlets while reading interpolations of his own—a trick exposed while the court was sitting, and which, but for the indulgence of Cabet, would have been punished by Jules Favre's expulsion from the Paris bar. Of all the documents quoted by him as documents of the International, not one belongs to the International. He says, for instance, "The Alliance declares itself atheist, says the General Council, constituted in London in July, 1869."

---

* Written by Marx and Engels in English, June 12, 1871; printed in the London *Times*, June 13, and in the *Eastern Post*, June 17, 1871. The letter was also printed in French—in *L'Internationale* June 18, *La Liberté* June 17, and *L'Égalité* June 27, 1871; in German—in *Der Volksstaat* June 21; and in Spanish—in *Emancipación* June 26, 1871.

The General Council never issued such a document. On the contrary, it issued a document which quashed the original statutes of the "Alliance"—*L'Alliance de la Démocratie Socialiste*, at Geneva— quoted by Jules Favre.

Throughout his circular, which pretends in part also to be directed against the Empire, Jules Favre repeats against the International but the police inventions of the public prosecutors of the Empire, which broke down miserably even before the law courts of that Empire.

It is known that in its two addresses (of July and September last) on the late war, the General Council of the International denounced the Prussian plans of conquest against France. Later on, Mr. Reitlinger, Jules Favre's private secretary, applied, though of course in vain, to some members of the General Council for getting up by the Council a demonstration against Bismarck, in favor of the Government of National Defense; they were particularly requested not to mention the Republic. The preparations for a demonstration with regard to the expected arrival of Jules Favre in London were made—certainly with the best of intentions—in spite of the General Council, which, in its address of the ninth of September, had distinctly forewarned the Paris workmen against Jules Favre and his colleagues.

What would Jules Favre say if, in its turn, the International were to send a circular on Jules Favre to all the cabinets of Europe, drawing their particular attention to the documents published at Paris by the late M. Millière?

I am, sir, your obedient servant,

John Hales,
Secretary to the General Council
of the International Working Men's Association

Lies About the International*

THE GENERAL COUNCIL of this Association has instructed me to state in reply to your leader of June 19, 1871, on the "International," the following facts:

The pretended Paris manifestoes, published by the *Paris-Journal* and similar journals—manifestoes which are mere fabrications of the Versailles police—you place on the same line as our "Address on the Civil War in France."

You say: "The 'political notes' published by Professor Beesly, and quoted the other day in these columns, are quoted also, with entire approval, in the Address of the Council, and we can now understand how justly the Ex-Emperor was entitled to be called the savior of society."

Now the Council, in its Address, quotes nothing from the "political notes" except the testimony of the writer, who is a known and honorable French savant, as to the personal character of the "Internationals" implicated in the last Paris revolution. What has this to do with the "Ex-Emperor" and the society saved by him? The "program" of the Association was not, as you say, "prepared" by Messrs. Tolain and Odger "seven years ago." It was issued by the Provisional Council, chosen at the public meeting held at St. Martin's Hall, Long Acre, on September 28, 1864. M. Tolain has never been a member of that Council, nor was he present at London when the program was drawn up.

You say that Millière was "one of the most ferocious members of

---

* Written to the London *Times* on or after June 19, 1871; not printed by the *Times*.

the Commune." Millière has never been a member of the Commune. "We," you proceed, "should also point out that Assi, lately president of the Association," etc.

Assi has never been a member of the International, and as to the dignity of "president of the Association," it has been abolished long ago—1867.

Authorship of *The Civil War in France**

Sir:

A Council consisting of more than thirty members cannot, of course, draw up its own documents. It must entrust that task to some one or other of its members, reserving to itself the right of rejecting or amending. The address on the *Civil War in France*, drawn up by myself, was unanimously adopted by the General Council of the International, and is therefore the official embodiment of its own views. With regard, however, to the personal charges brought forward against Jules Favre & Co., the case stands otherwise. On this point the great majority of the Council had to rely upon my trustworthiness. This was the very reason why I supported the motion of another member of the Council [Engels] that Mr. John Hales, in his answer to Mr. Holyoake, should name me as the author of the Address.[1] I hold myself alone responsible for those charges, and hereby challenge Jules Favre & Co. to prosecute me for libel. In his letter Mr. Llewellyn Davies says: "It is melancholy to read the charges of personal business so freely flung by Frenchmen at one another."

---

* This letter, published in the *Eastern Post*, July 1, 1871, was in reply to one by George Jacob Holyoake in the *Daily News* of June 20, 1871, charging that *The Civil War in France* was not the work of the General Council, "though manifestly revised by some Saxon or Celtic pen." The minutes of the General Council, June 27, 1871, record that "Citizen Marx then called attention to the fact that he had sent a letter to the *Daily News* which had been mutilated by the editor. It showed that the English press was as vile as that on the Continent. He then handed it to the Secretary to be sent to the *Eastern Post*."

1. Engels to the editor of the *Daily News*, June 23, 1871: "Sir, I am instructed by the General Council . . . to state, in reply to Mr. George Jacob Holyoake's letter in Tuesday's *Daily News* . . . The Address, like many previous publications of the Council, was drawn up by . . . Dr. Karl Marx, was adopted unanimously and 'revised' by nobody."

Does this sentence not somewhat smack of that pharisaical self-righteousness with which William Cobbett so often taunted the British mind? Let me ask Mr. Llewellyn Davies which was worse, the French *petite presse* fabricating in the service of the police the most infamous slanders against the Communards, dead, captive, or hidden, or the English press reproducing them to this day, despite its professed contempt for the *petite presse*. I do not consider it a French inferiority that such serious charges, for instance, as those brought forward against the late Lord Palmerston,[2] during a quarter of a century, by a man like Mr. David Urquhart, could have been burked in England but not in France.

Karl Marx

---

2. Urquhart's criticism of Palmerston's foreign policy was published in the 1830s and 1840s in *The Portfolio*, a collection of diplomatic documents.

Defense of the Commune Against Charges by Ambassador Washburne*

To the New York Central Committee for the United States Sections
of the International Working Men's Association

Citizens,

The General Council of the Association consider it their duty to
communicate publicly to you evidence on the conduct, during the
French Civil War, of Mr. Washburne, the American Ambassador.

I

The following statement is made by Mr. Robert Reid, a Scotch-
man who has lived for seventeen years in Paris, and acted during the
Civil War as a correspondent for the London *Daily Telegraph* and
the *New York Herald*. Let us remark, in passing, that the *Daily Telegraph*, in the interests of the Versailles Government, falsified even
the short telegraphic despatches transmitted to it by Mr. Reid.

Mr. Reid, now in England, is ready to confirm his statement by
affidavit.

"The sounding of the general alarm, mingled with the roar of the
cannon, continued all night. To sleep was impossible. Where, I
thought, are the representatives of Europe and America? Can it be
possible that in the midst of this effusion of innocent blood they should
make no effort at conciliation? I could bear the thought no longer;

---

* Written July 11, 1871. Published in the *New York Sun*, August 1, 1871, as
well as in a number of the organs of the International, this letter was first printed
as a leaflet in London.

and knowing that Mr. Washburne was in town, I resolved at once to go and see him. This was, I think, on the seventeenth of April; the exact date may, however, be ascertained from my letter to Lord Lyons, to whom I wrote on the same day. Crossing the Champs Elysées, on my way to Mr. Washburne's residence, I met numerous ambulance wagons filled with the wounded and dying. Shells were bursting around the Arc de Triomphe, and many innocent people were added to the long list of M. Thiers' victims.

"Arriving at No. 95 Rue de Chaillot, I inquired at the concierge's for the United States Ambassador, and was directed to the second floor. The particular flight or flat you dwell in is, in Paris, an almost unerring indication of your wealth and position—a sort of social barometer. We find here a marquis on the first front floor, and a humble mechanic on the fifth back floor—the stairs that divide them represent the social gulf between them. As I climbed up the stairs, meeting no stout flunkies in red breeches and silk stockings, I thought, 'Ah! The Americans lay their money out to the best advantage—we throw ours away.'

"Entering the secretary's room, I inquired for Mr. Washburne.—Do you wish to see him personally?—I do.—My name having been sent in, I was ushered into his presence. He was lounging in an easy chair, reading a newspaper. I expected he would rise; but he remained sitting with the paper still before him, an act of gross rudeness in a country where the people are generally so polite.

"I told Mr. Washburne that we were betraying the cause of humanity if we did not endeavor to bring about a conciliation. Whether we succeeded or not, it was at all events our duty to try; and the moment seemed the more favorable, as the Prussians were just then pressing Versailles for a definite settlement. The united influence of America and England would turn the balance in favor of peace.

"Mr. Washburne said, '*The men in Paris are rebels. Let them lay down their arms.*' I replied that the National Guards had a legal right to their arms; but that was not the question. When humanity is outraged, the civilized world has a right to interfere, and I ask you to cooperate with Lord Lyons to that effect.—Mr. Washburne: 'These men at Versailles will listen to nothing.'—'If they refuse, the moral responsibility will rest with them.'—Mr. Washburne: 'I don't see that. I can't do anything in the matter. You had better see Lord Lyons.'

"So ended our interview. I left Mr. Washburne sadly disappointed. I found a man rude and haughty, with none of those feelings of fraternity you might expect to find in the representative of a democratic republic. On two occasions I had had the honor of an interview with Lord Cowley, when he was our representative in France. His frank, courteous manner formed a striking contrast to the cold, pretentious, and would-be-aristocratic style of the American Ambassador.

"I also urged upon Lord Lyons that, in the defense of humanity, England was bound to make an earnest effort at reconciliation, feeling convinced that the British Government could not look coldly on such atrocities as the massacres of the Clamart Station and Moulin Saquet, not to speak of the horrors of Neuilly, without incurring the malediction of every lover of humanity. Lord Lyons answered me verbally through Mr. Edward Malet, his secretary, that he had forwarded my letter to the government, and would willingly forward any other communication I might have to make on that subject. At one moment matters were most favorable for reconciliation, and had our government thrown their weight in the balance, the world would have been spared the carnage of Paris. At all events, it is not the fault of Lord Lyons if the British Government failed in their duty.

"But to return to Mr. Washburne. On Wednesday forenoon, the twenty-fourth of May, I was passing along the Boulevard des Capucines when I heard my name called and, turning around, saw Dr. Hossart standing beside Mr. Washburne, who was in an open carriage amidst a great number of Americans. After the usual salutations, I entered into a conversation with Dr. Hossart. Presently the conversation became general on the horrid scenes around; when Mr. Washburne, addressing me with the air of a man who knows the truth of what he is saying,—'*All who belong to the Commune, and those that sympathize with them, will be shot.*' Alas! I knew that they were killing old and young for the crime of *sympathy*, but I did not expect to hear it semiofficially from Mr. Washburne; yet, while he was *repeating* this sanguinary phrase, there was still time for him to save the Archbishop."

II

"On the twenty-fourth of May, Mr. Washburne's secretary came to offer to the Commune, then assembled at the Mairie of the Eleventh Arrondissement, on the part of the Prussians, an intervention between the Versaillais and the Federals on the following terms:

" 'Suspension of hostilities.

" 'Reelection of the Commune on the one side, and of the National Assembly on the other.

" 'The Versailles troops to leave Paris, and to take up their quarters in and around the fortifications.

" 'The National Guard to continue to guard Paris.

" 'No punishment to be inflicted upon the men serving or having served in the Federal Army.'

"The Commune, in an extraordinary sitting, accepted the propositions, with the proviso that two months should be given to France in order to prepare for the general elections of a Constituent Assembly.

"A second interview with the secretary of the American Embassy took place. At its morning sitting of the twenty-fifth of May, the Commune resolved to send five citizens—among them Vermorel, Delescluze, and Arnold—as plenipotentiaries to Vincennes, where, according to the information given by Mr. Washburne's secretary, a Prussian delegate would then be found. That deputation was, however, prevented from passing by the National Guards on duty at the gate of Vincennes. Consequent upon another and final interview with the same American secretary, Citizen Arnold, to whom he had delivered a safe-conduct, on the twenty-sixth of May went to St. Denis, where he was—*not* admitted by the Prussians.

"The result of this American intervention (which produced a belief in the renewed neutrality of, and the intended intercession between the belligerents by, the Prussians) was, at the most critical juncture, to paralyze the defense for two days. Despite the precautions taken to keep the negotiations secret, they became soon known to the National Guards, who then, full of confidence in Prussian neutrality, fled to the Prussian lines, there to surrender as prisoners. It is known how this confidence was abused by the Prussians, shooting by their sentries part of the fugitives, and handing over to the Versailles Government those who had surrendered.

"During the whole course of the Civil War, Mr. Washburne, through his secretary, never tired of informing the Commune of his ardent sympathies, which only his diplomatic position prevented him from publicly manifesting, and of his decided reprobation of the Versailles Government."

This statement, No. II, is made by a member of the Paris Commune [Serraillier], who, like Mr. Reid, will in case of need confirm it by affidavit.

To fully appreciate Mr. Washburne's conduct, the statements of Mr. Robert Reid and that of the member of the Paris Commune must be read as a whole, as part and counterpart of the same scheme. While Mr. Washburne declares to Mr. Reid that the Communals are "rebels" who deserve their fate, he declares to the Commune his sympathies with its cause and his contempt of the Versailles Government. *On the same twenty-fourth of May*, while, in presence of Dr. Hossart and many Americans, informing Mr. Reid that not only the Communards but even their mere sympathizers were irrevocably doomed to death, he informed, through his secretary, the Commune that not only its members were to be saved, but every man in the Federal army.

We now request you, dear citizens, to lay these facts before the working class of the United States, and to call upon them to decide whether Mr. Washburne is a proper representative of the American Republic.

Accusations of Corruption*

To the Editor of Public Opinion*

Sir:

In your publication of today you translate from the Berlin *National Zeitung*, a notorious organ of Bismarck's, a most atrocious libel against the International Working Men's Association, in which the following passage occurs:

" 'Capital,' says Karl Marx, 'trades in the strength and life of the workman'; but this new Messiah himself is not a step farther advanced; he takes from the mechanic the money paid him by the capitalist for his labor, and generously gives him in exchange a bill on a state that may possibly exist a thousand years hence. What edifying stories are told about the vile corruption of socialist agitators, what a shameful abuse they make of the money confided to them, and what mutual accusations they throw in each other's faces, are things we have abundantly learned by the Congresses and from the organs of the party. There is here a monstrous volcano of filth, from whose eruptions nothing better could issue than a Parisian Commune."

In reply to the venal writers of the *National Zeitung*, I consider it quite sufficient to declare that I have *never* asked or received one single farthing from the working class of this or any other country.

Save the General Secretary, who receives a weekly salary of ten shillings, all the members of the General Council of the International do their work *gratuitously*. The financial accounts of the General Council, annually laid before the General Congresses of the Associa-

---

* Written in English, August 19, 1871; published August 26.

tion, have always been sanctioned unanimously without provoking any discussion whatever.

I am, sir, your obedient servant,

Karl Marx

(*Comment by Editor:* In our last number we published, under the title, "A German View of the *Internationale*," an article from the Berlin *National Zeitung* criticizing the proceedings of the International Society. M. Karl Marx complains of a paragraph in that article as conveying an imputation of personal corruption or impropriety against himself and his colleagues in the Society. We gladly publish his letter. We at once disclaim the intention of making any such imputation as that which he has understood to be conveyed by the paragraph in question; and we are sorry that anything has appeared in our columns capable of such a meaning.)

To the Editor of the Evening Standard*

Sir:

In your number of the 2d September, your Berlin correspondent publishes "the translation of an interesting article on the International which has appeared in the *Cologne Gazette*," which article charges me with living at the expense of the working classes. Up to the 30th August, the date of your correspondent's letter, no such article appeared in the *Cologne Gazette*, from which paper, therefore, your correspondent could not translate it. On the contrary, the article in question appeared, more than a fortnight ago, in the Berlin *National Zeitung;* and an English translation of it, literally identical with the one given by your correspondent, figured in the London weekly paper, *Public Opinion,* as far back as the 19th August. The next number of *Public Opinion* contains my reply to those slanders, and I hereby summon you to insert that reply, of which I enclose a copy, in the next number of your paper. The Prussian Government have reasons of their own why they push, by every means in their power, the spreading of such infamous calumnies through the English press. These articles are but the harbingers of impending government prosecutions against the "International."

I am, sir, your obedient servant,

Karl Marx

---

* Written in English, September 4, 1871; published September 6.

Forged Manifestoes*

Sir:

After the General Secretary of the General Council of the International Working Men's Association, Mr. John Hales, read in the *Daily News* that Mr. Renaut ascribed to the International a manifesto which calls on the peasants to burn all castles, etc., he immediately sent to Mr. L. Bigot, the defender of Assi, the following telegram:

"The appeal to incendiarism, which is ascribed to the International, is a forgery. Be prepared to make a declaration under oath before an English judge."

I hasten to join him in calling the attention of the French public, through the medium of your worthy journal, to the fact that *all manifestoes that have been printed in Paris under the name of the International since the French Government troops entered Paris—all these manifestoes, without exception, are forgeries.*

I not only vouch for this declaration with my word of honor, but am also prepared to make a declaration under oath ("the affidavit") before an English judge.

I have reason to believe that these infamous productions do not come directly from the police, but from a certain Mr. B . . . , a person allied with one of those Paris papers which the *Standard* (a Tory newspaper) in one of its recent issues characterized as *"organes du demimonde."*

Accept the assurance of my high esteem,

Karl Marx

---

* Written in French to the editor of *Vérité;* published August 30, 1871.

A Short Relation of My Daughter Jenny on the Persecutions . . . at the Hands of the French Government*

MARX *sent his daughter's letter, reproduced below, to the editors of* Woodhull & Claflin's Weekly, *in New York, with the following covering letter, in English, dated September 23, 1871:*

Mesdames:

I have the honor to send you, for insertion in your *Weekly*—if you judge the contribution sufficiently interesting for your readers— a short relation of my daughter Jenny on the persecutions she and her sisters, during their stay at Bagnères de Luchon (Pyrenees), had to undergo at the hands of the French Government. This tragico-comical episode seems to me characteristic of the République-Thiers. . . .

I have the honor, Mesdames, to remain,

Yours most sincerely,

Karl Marx

Madame:

The following private letter (originally written to a friend) may serve the public interest, if by means of it some light is thrown upon the arbitrary proceedings of the present French Government, who, with supreme contempt for personal security and liberty, do not scruple to arrest foreigners, as well as natives, on altogether false pretenses:

Monsieur Lafargue, my brother-in-law, his wife and children, my youngest sister, and myself, had spent the months of June and July

---

* Written in English and dated September, 1871; published October 21, 1871.

at Bagnères de Luchon, where we intended remaining until the end of September. I hoped, by a prolonged stay in the Pyrenees, and by a daily use of the mineral waters for which Luchon is famous, to recover from the effects of a severe attack of pleurisy. *Mais dans la République-Thiers l'homme propose et la police dispose.* [But in Thiers' Republic, man proposes and the policeman disposes.] On the first or second day in August, M. Lafargue was informed by a friend that he might daily expect a domiciliary visit of the police, when, if found, he would surely be arrested, on the pretext that he had paid a short visit to Paris during the time of the Commune, had acted as emissary of the International in the Pyrenees, and last, but not least, because he is the husband of his wife, consequently the son-in-law of Karl Marx. Knowing that under the present government of lawyers the law is a dead letter, that persons are continually locked up, no reason whatever being assigned for their arrest, M. Lafargue follows the advice given him, crosses the frontier, and settles down at Bosost, a small Spanish town. Several days after his departure, on the sixth of August, Madame Lafargue, her sister Eleanor, and I visit M. Lafargue at Bosost. Madame Lafargue, finding that her little boy is not well enough to leave Bosost on the same day (she was very anxious on the child's account, having lost his brother a few days before), resolved to remain with her husband for a day or two. My sister Eleanor and I therefore returned alone to Luchon.

Without accident we succeeded in getting along the rugged Spanish roads, and safely reached Fos. There the French customhouse officials ask us the usual questions and look into our carriage to see whether there are any contraband goods. As we have nothing but our cloaks with us, I tell the coachman to drive on, when an individual—no other than the Procureur de la République, M. le Baron Desgarre—steps forward, saying: "In the name of the Republic, follow me." We leave our carriage and enter a small room, where we find a forbidding-looking creature—a most unwomanly woman—waiting to search us. Not wishing to let this coarse-looking person touch us, we offer to take off our dresses ourselves. Of this the woman will not hear. She rushes out of the room, whither she soon returns, followed by the Procureur de la République, who in the most ungentlemanly manner thus apostrophizes my sister: "If you still will not allow this woman to search you, I shall do so." My sister replies: "You have no right to come near a British subject. I have an English passport." Seeing, however, that an English passport does not inspire M. le Baron Desgarre with much respect, for he looks as though he were in good earnest, ready to suit his actions to his words, we allow the woman to have her way. She unpicks the very seams of our dresses, makes us take off even our stockings. I fancy I can still feel her spiderlike fingers running through my hair. Having only found a newspaper on me and a torn letter on my sister, she runs with these to her friend and ally, M. le Baron Desgarre. We are reconducted to our carriage—our own coachman, who had acted as our "guide" during our whole stay in the Pyrenees, and had grown much attached to us, is forced away, replaced by another coachman, two officers are installed in the carriage opposite us, and thus we are driven off, a cartful of customhouse officers and police agents following us. After a time, finding, no doubt, that after all we are not such very dangerous characters, that we do not make any attempts to murder our sentinels, our escort is left behind and we remain in the charge of the two officers in the carriage. Thus guarded, we are driven through village after village, through St. Béat, the inhabitants of which comparatively large town collect in crowds, evidently taking us to be thieves, or at least smugglers. At eight o'clock, thoroughly tired out, we arrive at Luchon, cross the *Quinconces*, where hundreds of people are assembled to listen to the band, it being Sunday and the height of the season. Our carriage stops before the *hôtel* of the Prefect, M. le Comte de Kératry. That personage not being at home, still guarded, we are kept waiting before his door for at least half an hour. At length orders are given for us to be taken back to our house, which we find surrounded by gendarmes. We at once go upstairs, wishing to refresh ourselves by washing our faces (we had been out since five o'clock in the morning), but as a gendarme and an agent in plain clothes follow us even into our bedroom, we return to the drawing room, unrefreshed, to await the arrival of the Prefect. The clock strikes nine, ten; M. de Kératry has not come—he is listening to the band on the *Quinconces*, and, we hear, is determined to stay until the last chord of the music has died away. Meanwhile, quantities of *mouchards* [police spies] drop in, they walk into the room as if it were their own and make themselves quite at home, settling down on our chairs and sofa. Soon we are surrounded by a motley crowd of police agents, which devoted servants of the Republic, it is easy to see, have served their term of apprenticeship under the Empire—they are masters of their honorable calling. They have recourse to impossible tricks and dodges to inveigle us into a conversation, but, finding all their efforts to do so are vain, they stare at us as only "professionals" can stare, until, at half-past ten, the Prefect puts in an appearance, flanked by the Procureur General, M. Delpech, the Juge d'Instruction, Juge de Paix, the Commissaires of Toulouse and Luchon, etc. My sister is told to step into an adjoining room: the Commissaire of Toulouse and a gendarme accompany her. My interrogatory commences. I refuse to give any information concerning my brother-in-law and other relatives and friends. With regard to myself I declare I am under medical treatment, and have come to Luchon to take the waters. For more than two hours M. de Kératry by turns exhorts, persuades, and at length threatens me, that if I choose to persist in my refusal to act as a witness, I shall be looked upon as an accomplice. "Tomorrow," he says, "the law will *compel* you to give your deposition on oath; for, let me tell you, M. Lafargue and his wife have been arrested." At this I felt alarmed, because of my sister's sick child.

At length my sister Eleanor's turn comes. I am ordered to turn my back while she speaks. An officer is placed in front of me lest I should attempt to make some sign. To my annoyance I hear my sister is being led by degrees to say yes or no to the numberless questions put to her. Afterward I found out by what means she had been made to speak. Pointing to my written declaration, M. de Kératry (I could not see his gestures, my back being turned) affirmed the contrary of what I had really said. Therefore, anxious not to contradict me, my sister had not refuted the statements said to have been made by me. It was half-past two before her examination was ended. A young girl of sixteen, who had been up since five A.M., had traveled nine hours on an intensely hot day in August, and only taken food quite early at Bosost, cross-examined until half-past two in the morning!

For the rest of the night the Commissaire of Toulouse and several gendarmes remained in our house. We went to bed, but not to sleep, for we puzzled our heads how to get a messenger to go to Bosost to warn M. Lafargue, in case he had not yet been arrested. We looked out of the window. Gendarmes were walking about in the garden. It was impossible to get out of the house. We were close prisoners— not even allowed to see our maid and landlady. On the following day, landlady and servant were examined on oath. I was again questioned for more than an hour by the Procureur General, M. Delpech, and the Procureur de la République. That tongue-valiant hero, M. le Baron Desgarre, read long extracts to me, pointing out the penalties I am liable to incur by persisting in my refusal to act as witness. The eloquence of these gentlemen was, however, lost on me. I quietly but firmly declared my resolution not to take the oath, and remained unshaken.

My sister's examination only lasted a few minutes this time. She also resolutely refused to take the oath.

Before the Procureur General left us, we asked for permission to write a few lines to our mother, fearing the news of our arrest might get into the papers and alarm our parents. We offered to write the letter in French, under the very eyes of M. Delpech. It was only to consist of a few sentences, such as we are well, etc. The Procureur refused our request, on the pretext that we might have a language of our own; that the words—we are well—might convey some hidden meaning.

These magistrates outdid Dogberry and Verges. The following is another instance of their utter imbecility. Having found, as our maid told us, a quantity of commercial letters belonging to M. Lefargue, in which reference was made to the exportation of sheep and oxen, they exclaimed, "Oxen, sheep, intrigues, intrigues; sheep—Communists, oxen—Internationals."

For the remainder of that day and night we were again committed to the care of several gendarmes, one of whom even sat opposite us while we were dining.

On the following day, the eighth, we had a visit from the Prefect and a person whom we supposed to be his secretary. Of this interview a most inaccurate and fantastical account appeared in the *France*, and was from thence transferred into a great number of other papers. But to return to the Prefect.

M. de Kératry, after making a very lengthy preface, informed us most blandly that the authorities had been mistaken; that it had been found that there was no foundation for the charge made against M. Lafargue, who was innocent, and therefore at liberty to return to France. "As for your sister and yourself," said M. de Kératry, thinking, I suppose, that a bird in the hand is worth two in the bush, "there is much more against you than against M. Lafargue" (thus we were being suddenly transformed from witnesses into accused), "and in all likelihood you will be expelled from France. However, an order from the government for your liberation will come in the course of the day." Then, assuming a paternal tone, he said, "Anyhow, let me advise you to moderate your zeal in the future—'*pas trop de zèle*' "! Upon which the supposed secretary said abruptly, "And the International—is the association powerful in England?" "Yes," I answered, "most powerful, and so it is in all other countries." "Ah," exclaimed M. de Kératry, "the International is a religion!" Before he made his exit, M. de Kératry once more assured us, on his word of honor, that Paul Lafargue was free, and asked us at once to write to Bosost to tell him so, and to invite him to return to France. Now I fancied I could see the red ribbon of the Legion d'Honneur adorning the buttonhole of de Kératry, and as I have a notion that the honor of the Knights of the Legion d'Honneur must be something very different to the honor of common mortals, I thought it best to be prudent, and so instead of advising M. Lafargue to return to Luchon, I intended to do the contrary, and begged of a friend to send him the means wherewith to travel further into Spain.

Followed about by our shadows, the gendarmes, we waited in vain for the promised order for our release. At eleven o'clock at night, the Procureur de la République walked into our room; but instead of bringing us the order for our liberation, M. Desgarre asked us to get ready a trunk and to follow him to *"une maison particulière"* [a private house]. I knew this proceeding was illegal—but what could we do? There were only a few women in the house with us, whereas the Procureur was accompanied by several gendarmes. Therefore, not wishing to afford the cowardly bully M. Desgarre the satisfaction of using brute force, we give orders to our weeping maid to get ready our dresses, etc., and having attempted to console the daughter of our landlady by telling her we should soon return, we got into a carriage occupied by two gendarmes, in the dead of night, in a strange country, to be taken whither we knew not.

The *gendarmerie* barracks proved to be our destination; a bedroom having been shown us, our door having been duly barricaded outside, we were left alone. In this place we remained the following day until past five o'clock, when, determined to know what all this meant, I desired to have an interview with the Prefect. M. de Kératry came. I asked him how it was we had been taken to the *gendarmerie* after he had promised us our liberty.

"Thanks to my intercession," answered he, "you have been allowed to spend the night at the *gendarmerie*. The government" (M. Thiers) "would have sent you to the prison of St. Godins, near Toulouse." Then M. de Kératry handed me a letter containing 3,000 francs, which had been sent to M. Lafargue by his banker at Bordeaux, and which he, M. de Kératry, had hitherto detained; declared we were free, were not to be expelled from France, but, like M. Lafargue, at liberty to remain in the country.

This time we were imprudent enough to inform Madame Lafargue of what M. de Kératry had said with regard to her husband.

On the tenth we received a *laissez-passer* to go over to Spain, but our English passport was not returned us. During ten days we applied for it in vain. M. de Kératry wrote he had sent it to Paris, and could not get it back, though he had repeatedly written for it.

We now saw we had only been turned out of the small *gendarmerie* of Luchon to be locked up in the great *gendarmerie*, the Republic-Thiers. We were still prisoners. Without a passport there was no getting out of France, in which country we were evidently to be kept, until some event or other should afford a pretext for again arresting us.

The police organs of Toulouse were daily accusing us of acting as emissaries of the International on the French and Spanish frontiers. "But," added they, "the Prefect is taking energetic measures in order to reassure the inhabitants of the Haute Garonne." Now, it is true, a *laissez-passer* to go over into Spain had been given us, but the experience of Madame Lafargue in that country was not of a nature to encourage us to seek a refuge in the land of El Cid.

The facts we learned from Madame Lafargue carry us back to the sixth of August.

I mentioned above that our coachman had been compelled to leave us at Fos. Whereupon M. Desgarre, the Procureur de la République, and several "gentlemen" of the police, attempted to persuade him, in the most plausible manner, to return to Bosost, and on false pretenses to get M. Lafargue to go to Fos. Fortunately an honest man is more than a match for half a dozen police agents. The shrewd young fellow guessed there was some trick at the bottom of all this glib talk, and flatly refused to fetch M. Lafargue; consequently gendarmes and *douaniers* [customs men], with the Procureur at their head, set out on an expedition to Bosost. M. le Baron Desgarre, whose discretion is the better part of his valor, had previously declared he would not go to Fos to capture M. Lafargue without a sufficient escort; that he could do nothing with one or two gendarmes against a man like M. Lafargue, most likely given to the use of firearms. M. Desgarre was mistaken— not a bullet, but kicks and cuffs were reserved for him. On his return from Bosost he attempted to interfere with peasants celebrating their village feast. The brave mountaineers, who love their freedom as much as their own mountain air, gave the noble baron a sound thrashing, and sent him about his business, a sadder if not a wiser man! But I am anticipating.

I was saying that M. Desgarre and his followers started for Bosost. They soon reached that town, and soon found the hotel at which the Lafargues were staying, for the inhabitants of Bosost only possess two hotels, or rather inns. They are not yet sufficiently civilized to have the orthodox number of public houses. Now, while M. Desgarre is standing before the front door of the Hotel Masse, M. Lafargue, aided by his good friends, the peasants, gets out of the house by the back gate, climbs the mountains, and escapes along paths known only to guides, goats, and English tourists—all the regular roads being guarded by Spanish carabiniers. The Spanish police had enthusiastically taken up the cause of their French brethren. Madame Lafargue is made to feel all the blessings arising from the International Association of the police. At three o'clock in the morning her bedroom is suddenly broken into, and in rush four Spanish officers, with their carbines pointed to the bed in which she and her child are sleeping. The poor sick baby, suddenly awakened, frightened, begins to scream; but that doesn't prevent the Spanish officers from looking in every hole and cranny of the room for M. Lafargue. Finally, convinced that their prey has escaped them, they declare they will carry off Madame Lafargue. At this the master of the hotel—a most worthy man—interferes, saying he is sure the Spanish Government will not accord the extradition of a lady. He was right. Madame Lafargue was allowed to remain at Bosost, but was ever after subjected to the annoyance of being followed about by police agents. At the hotel a troop of spies established their headquarters. One Sunday even the Prefect and the Procureur de la République took the trouble to travel all the way from Luchon to Bosost for the purpose of seeing Madame Lafargue. As, however, they did not succeed in satisfying their curiosity, they consoled themselves by playing at *rouge et noir*, which, together with baccarat, forms the only serious occupation of the *petits gras* [little fat men] from Versailles, now staying at the Pyrenees.

But I must not forget to explain how it was that M. de Kératry had not succeeded in seeing Madame Lafargue. The fact is that a French peasant from Luchon had informed some Spanish friends of his at Bosost of M. de Kératry's intended visit, and they, of course, at once warned Madame Lafargue.

The French and Spanish population of the Pyrenees form a league, offensive and defensive, against their respective governments. In our case they acted as spies upon the official spies of the Prefect—though repeatedly stopped at the French frontiers, they were untiring in their attempts to bring us news. Although M. de Kératry gave orders to the effect that no one, *not even guides,* should be allowed to cross over to Bosost, unless provided with a proper pass. This measure, of course, did not prevent our having messages brought us as heretofore; it only served to embitter still more the peasants of the Pyrenees, already so hostile to the Rurals of Versailles.

In other parts of France I have since heard that the peasants are quite as much opposed to their *so-called* representatives, the governing Rurals. M. Thiers fulfills a great revolutionary mission! By means of his prefects, priests, *gardes champêtres*, and gendarmes he will before long provoke a general rising of the peasantry!

Of M. Lafargue's escape Madame Lafargue had informed us a few days after our release from the *gendarmerie*. Later on, we heard from a native of Bosost that M. Lafargue had been arrested at Huesca, and that the Spaniards had made the offer of his extradition to the French Government. On the very day we received this news our English passport was returned us by the Juge de Paix. So in order to put an end to the state of anxiety in which we knew Madame Lafargue must be placed, tied down as she was to Bosost by her sick child, not knowing what had become of her husband, we at once made up our minds to travel to Huesca, in order to beg the governor of that district to let us know the real intentions of the Spanish government with respect to M. Lafargue. On reaching San Sebastián we heard to our joy that M. Lafargue had been set at liberty. So we immediately returned to England.

I cannot conclude this letter without giving a short sketch of the treatment to which Madame C——, our landlady, and the servant were subjected on the sixth of August, during our absence; for, compared with them, we had always been treated with great courtesy. At eleven o'clock in the morning, the Prefect, Procureur General, Procureur de la République, etc., made a raid upon our house. Enraged at not being able to lay hands on M. Lafargue, they vented their wrath on Madame C——, an invalid, suffering from heart disease in an advanced stage, and upon our maid. That poor girl was treated most roughly, because she would not tell where her master had gone.

This the Prefect, however, succeeded in learning from a boy, employed by Madame C——as gardener, and whom he straightway sent up to Fos, there to lie in wait for us behind a hedge, in order to give warning of our arrival to the Procureur de la République & Co.

If, during the campaign against the Prussians, M. de Kératry had employed the same art of protecting his flanks and rear from surprise, of surprising detachments of the enemy by establishing videttes and sending out scouts, things would have gone better in Brittany—that is to say, if one may judge from the success of De Kératry's tactics at Fos!

Our landlady was not allowed to light a fire in her own kitchen; was ordered, instead of sleeping in her bed, to lie down on the floor. With the latter order she, however, refused to comply. Catching hold of her son, a child not three years of age, the Prefect said he must be the son of M. Lafargue. Madame C—— repeatedly declared he was mistaken—but in vain; at length, really anxious to prove her child's identity (she feared he might be carried off), she exclaimed: "Why, the boy only speaks the patois of the district." For a moment or two the Prefect looked as if even that argument had failed to convince him. Perhaps M. de Kératry, believing as he does that the "International is a religion," was pondering on the miracle of the cloven tongues descending on the apostles.

One of the reasons why Madame C—— was so much ill used was because she had never in her life heard of the International, and therefore could not give an account of the doings of that mysterious society at Luchon, which, by the way, would have been an impossible task for the best initiated member—at least previous to the period at which M. de Kératry commenced at Luchon his active propaganda for the

International Association. Then Madame C—— had been guilty of speaking of her tenant, M. Lafargue, in very high terms. But the head and front of her offending was in her inability to point out hidden bombs and petroleum.

Yes! It is a fact, bombs and petroleum were searched for in our house.

Taking up a small night lamp, used for warming the baby's milk, the assembled magistrates examined it; handling it with great caution, as if it were some diabolical machine by means of which petroleum might have been discharged into the streets of Paris. From Luchon to Paris. Even Münchhausen never indulged in such a stretch of imagination. The French government are *capable de tout* [capable of anything]. They really believe in the truth of the wild petroleum fables—the coinage of their own distempered brains. They do think the women of Paris are "neither brute nor human, neither man nor woman"—but "petroleum"—a species of salamander, delighting in their native element—fire.

They almost come up to Henri de Pène, of the *Paris-Journal*, their prophet and teacher, who, as I am told, now actually fancies that the famous letters manufactured by himself in my father's name have not been written by Henri de Pène but by Karl Marx.

One could afford to treat with silent contempt a government run mad, and to laugh at the farces in which the pottering pantaloons employed by that government play their muddling and meddling parts, did not these farces turn out to be tragedies for thousands of men, women, and children. Think only of the *"petroleuses"* before the court-martial of Versailles, and of the women who, for the last three months, are being slowly done to death on the pontoons [prison ships].

Jenny Marx

No Honorary Membership*

ON PAGE 2 of the *Frankfurter Zeitung*, No. 326, is a report, dated London, November 18, which runs as follows:

"At its last meeting the London Section of the International passed the following resolution: 'The outstanding services of Sir Charles Dilke to the people's cause give him the right to recognition by the people; therefore he is invited to accept the title of honorary member of the International Working Men's union.' At an earlier meeting Kossuth was elected member."

The International does not recognize any honorary membership. In all probability the above-mentioned decision relates to a small London society which first called itself "The International Democratic Association" and later changed its name to "The Universal Republican League." It has no connection whatsoever with the International.

In the name of the General Council of the International Working Men's Association,

Corresponding Secretary for Germany,

Karl Marx

---

* Published in the *Frankfurter Zeitung und Handelsblatt*, November 28, 1871.

Controversy with Charles Bradlaugh*

To the Editor of the Eastern Post*

Sir:

In his last epistle to you,[1] Mr. Charles Bradlaugh makes the report of the sitting of the General Council of December 12th—a sitting from which I was absent in consequence of illness—the pretext for discharging upon me his ruffianism. He says, "I feel indebted to Karl Marx for his enmity." My enmity to Mr. Charles Bradlaugh! Ever since the publication of the "Address on the Civil War in France," Mr. Bradlaugh's voice has chimed in with the world-wide chorus of slander against the "International" and myself. I treated him, like the other revilers, with contemptuous silence. This was more than the grotesque vanity of that huge self-idolater could stand. I "calumniated" him because I took no notice of his calumnies. My silence drove him mad; in a public meeting he denounced me as a *Bonapartist* because, in the "Address on the Civil War," I had, forsooth, laid bare the historic circumstances that gave birth to the Second Empire. He now goes a step further and transforms me into a *police agent of Bismarck*. Poor man! He must needs show that the lessons he has recently received at

---

* Written in English, December 20, 1871; published December 23.
1. Bradlaugh to the editor of the *Eastern Post*, December 16, 1871: "Sir: So much of the report of the International Society as relates to me is absolutely untrue. The £7 was not 'sent' at all, it was taken at the conclusion of the lecture away in a kindly and thankful spirit by the proper authorities for their fellow refugees. Up to this moment the money has not been returned, nor has any proposal even been made to return it. I feel indebted to Karl Marx for his enmity. If I were one of his own countrymen he might betray me to his government, here he can only calumniate. Yours, C. Bradlaugh."

Paris from the infamous Emile de Girardin and his *clique* are not lost upon him.[2] For the present I shall "betray him" to the German public by giving the greatest possible circulation to his epistle. If he be kind enough to clothe his libels in a more tangible shape, I shall "betray him" to an English law court.

I am, sir, yours obediently,

Karl Marx

To the Editor of the Eastern Post*

Sir:

In the *National Reformer* of January 7, Mr. Charles Bradlaugh says: "We only meant to allege that Dr. Marx had, in former times, given information to his own government."

I simply declare that this is a calumny, as ridiculous as it is infamous. I call upon Mr. Bradlaugh to publish any fact that could afford him even the slightest pretext for his statement. For his personal tranquillity I add that he shall not be "challenged."

I am, sir, yours obediently,

Karl Marx

---

2. John Hales, Secretary of the General Council, to the editor of the *Eastern Post*, December 23, 1871: ". . . With reference to Mr. Bradlaugh's insinuation against Dr. Marx, I say that it is as lying as it is malicious, and with that I leave the matter, knowing that Dr. Marx needs no vindicator. But I would make one remark about Mr. Bradlaugh—"Those who live in glass houses should not throw stones. Mr. Bradlaugh has been on one or two missions to Paris lately. I know of no workmen's organization which employs secret emissaries, and as Mr. Bradlaugh has not a reputation for working for nothing, I would ask whether there was any connection between his visits and the recent Bonapartist intrigues. Dirty tools are usually employed to do dirty work, and it is well known that the Bonapartists are not particular as to what instruments they use."

---

* Written in English, January 16, 1872; published January 20.

Lies About a Conversation*

Monsieur:

In *Figaro* of September 11 there is a report of a conversation which I was supposed to have had with the correspondent of *Soir*.[1] The *Figaro* press can allow itself all sorts of calumnies without anyone's making the effort to pillory it properly; but when the venal imagination of a correspondent goes so far as to put into my mouth grave accusations against my friends in the erstwhile General Council, I cannot avoid declaring that he has violated the decent rules of truth when he dares to maintain that he has ever exchanged a single word with me.

I take this opportunity to let our friends and foes know that I never thought of withdrawing from the International, and that the removal of the General Council to New York was proposed by me and many other members of the old General Council.

The report that Bakunin and his henchman Guillaume have been expelled as leaders of a so-called Federal Party is a lie. The expulsion of Bakunin and Guillaume was connected with their founding a secret society, the Alliance of Socialist Democracy, inside the International, a secret society which claimed to carry out the aims of the International, whose principles were entirely opposed to it.

The resolution of the London Conference on the political effectiveness of the working class had been approved by the great majority of Congresses and was included in the General Statutes.

---

* Written in French at The Hague, September 12, 1872; published in *Le Corsaire*, a Paris republican daily, September 15.

1. A Paris republican daily supporting Thiers.

[310]

The working-class public in the Hague and in Amsterdam was highly in favor of the Congress.

So much for the worth of the reports in the reactionary press.

I have the honor to greet you,

Karl Marx

The Expulsion of Bakuninists*

THE LEADING ARTICLE in No. 84 of the *Volksstaat*—"On the Hague Congress. III"—contains a factual error relating to me, the correction of which I consider necessary, even if only, be it noted, because it appears in the *Volksstaat*. If I considered it worth the effort to correct all the lies, slanders, infamies, and even the involuntary "errors" of the press that is inimical to me, there would not be left a moment for real work!

The article mentioned says: "Lafargue was so little Marx's 'adjutant' that when it came to the expulsion of Schwitzguébel, Guillaume's comrade, he refrained from voting, even though the proposal for exclusion was made by Marx himself."

That proposal was made by a Congress Investigating Committee, not by me. What I proposed in the Congress was the exclusion of the Alliance and the appointment of an Investigating Committee for this purpose. Others besides me appeared before that Committee as witnesses for the prosecution. Only toward the end of the inquiry, at the last moment, and for that matter during a session of the Congress, was I summoned. Prior to that, a member of the Committee sought a private meeting with me to clarify purely factual questions. I declined the invitation, to avoid even the semblance of a personal influence on the Committee.

During my examination before the Committee, I did not say a word either about Schwitzguébel or his ringleader Guillaume. I mentioned only one [G. T. Marago] presumably Alliance man in the Congress, in order to express my conviction that he was not a member of the "secret" Alliance, or at least had left it long ago.

* Published in *Der Volksstaat*, October 26, 1872.

In the last session of the Congress I voted *for* the expulsion of Schwitzguébel, because the proofs of his membership in the "secret" Alliance were the same as those of Guillaume's. Under these circumstances, Schwitzguébel's touching poor-sinner speech could not change my vote. It may be remarked in passing that Mr. Guillaume deliberately *lies*—something, by the way, that every member of a "secret" society is obliged to do—when he states in the *Bulletin Jurassien* that Schwitzguébel had declared himself in solidarity with him. On the contrary. Guillaume declared with great emphasis that Schwitzguébel stands or falls with him, but the latter remained deaf to this cry *in extremis!* In his poor-sinner speech, he did not mention Guillaume once, and this was the speech that prejudiced the majority in his favor. As member of the committee for the publication of the proceedings of the Congress, I naturally could look closely into its record.

In regard to Lafargue, it is to be noted that the *Biedermann* [philistine] Biedermann lies when he designates him as delegate for Barcelona. Lafargue was delegate of the Portuguese Federal Council, of the New Madrid Federation, and another Spanish section.

Karl Marx

INTERVIEWS
AND REPORTS

FOR most of his life Marx lived and worked in London in relative obscurity. He was known primarily to radicals, both English and continental, a number of whom were members of the General Council of the First International, of which Marx was the dominant intellectual figure.

Marx, as well as the International, achieved sudden notoriety during and after the Paris Commune of 1871. The Commune, a brief proletarian dictatorship, was destroyed in May, 1871, in an orgy of political murder unprecedented in the annals of Europe up to that time. In one week about 20,000 civilians, virtually all of them working people, were butchered by the troops of Adolphe Thiers' conservative Versailles government. In a continuing reign of terror scores of thousands of other workers, artisans, and craftsmen were court-martialed, imprisoned, and condemned to penal colonies.

Both conservative France and conservative Europe needed a scapegoat for the horrors connected with the Commune, and they found it in the First International and its "chief," Karl Marx. Press and politicians spread the canard that the Commune was hatched in a secret conspiracy by the Marx-dominated International in London.

To Marx, the bitter irony was that he was opposed in principle to conspiracies of any kind—which was why he fought Bakunin and the Bakuninists so strongly—and had little, if anything, to do with either the founding or the policies of the Commune. He was acquainted and had contact with a few of the Communards, to be sure, but the Commune as such had no connection with Marx or the General Council in London. He did, however, defend the Commune, despite reservations about its policies.

As a result of the Commune, Marx became famous—or infamous—throughout the Western world, including the United States. He was written up in the continental press, and, for the first time, big newspapers interviewed him.

This section contains, among other things, interviews published by some leading American publications. They give Marx's views frankly and directly.

Interview with Karl Marx, the Head of *L'Internationale**

REVOLT OF LABOR AGAINST CAPITAL—THE TWO FACES OF *L'INTERNATIONALE*—TRANSFORMATION OF SOCIETY—ITS PROGRESS IN THE UNITED STATES

London, July 3

YOU HAVE ASKED ME to find out something about the International Association, and I have tried to do so. The enterprise is a difficult one just now. London is indisputably the headquarters of the Association, but the English people have got a scare, and smell International in everything as King James smelled gunpowder after the famous plot. The consciousness of the Society has naturally increased with the suspiciousness of the public; and if those who guide it have a secret to keep, they are of the stamp of men who keep a secret well. I have called on two of their leading members, have talked with one freely, and I here give you the substance of my conversation. I have satisfied myself of one thing, that it is a society of genuine workingmen, but that these workmen are directed by social and political theories of another class. One man whom I saw, a leading member of the Council, was sitting at his workman's bench during our interview, and left off talking to me from time to time to receive a complaint, delivered in no courteous tone, from one of the many little masters in the neighborhood who employed him. I have heard this same man make eloquent speeches in public inspired in every passage with the energy of hate

---

* Written by R. Landor; published in the *New York World*, July 18, 1871, and reprinted in *Woodhull & Claflin's Weekly*, August 12, 1871.

toward the classes that call themselves his rulers. I understood the speeches after this glimpse at the domestic life of the orator. He must have felt that he had brains enough to have organized a working government, and yet here he was obliged to devote his life to the most revolting taskwork of a mechanical profession. He was proud and sensitive, and yet at every turn he had to return a bow for a grunt and a smile for a command that stood on about the same level in the scale of civility with a huntsman's call to his dog. This man helped me to a glimpse of one side of the nature of the International, the result of

Labor Against Capital

of the workman who produces against the middleman who enjoys. Here was the hand that would smite hard when the time came, and as to the head that plans, I think I saw that too, in my interview with Dr. Karl Marx.

Dr. Karl Marx is a German doctor of philosophy, with a German breadth of knowledge derived both from observation of the living world and from books. I should conclude that he has never been a worker in the ordinary sense of the term. His surroundings and appearance are those of a well-to-do man of the middle class. The drawing room into which I was ushered on the night of the interview would have formed very comfortable quarters for a thriving stockbroker who had made his competence and was now beginning to make his fortune. It was comfort personified, the apartment of a man of taste of easy means, but with nothing in it peculiarly characteristic of its owner. A fine album of Rhine views on the table, however, gave a clue to his nationality. I peered cautiously into the vase on the side-table for a bomb. I sniffed for petroleum, but the smell was the smell of roses. I crept back stealthily to my seat, and moodily awaited the worst.

He has entered and greeted me cordially, and we are sitting face to face. Yes, I am tête-à-tête with the revolution incarnate, with the real founder and guiding spirit of the International Society, with the author of the address in which capital was told that if it warred on labor it must expect to have its house burned down about its ears—in a word, with the

Apologist for the Commune

of Paris. Do you remember the bust of Socrates? The man who died rather than profess his belief in the Gods of the time—the man with the fine sweep of profile for the forehead running meanly at the end into a little snub, curled-up feature, like a bisected pothook, that formed the nose. Take this bust in your mind's eye, color the beard black, dashing it here and there with puffs of gray; clap the head thus made on a portly body of the middle height, and the Doctor is before you. Throw a veil over the upper part of the face, and you might be in the company of a born vestryman. Reveal the essential feature, the immense brow, and you know at once that you have to deal with that most formidable of all composite individual forces—a dreamer who thinks, a thinker who dreams.

I went straight to my business. The world, I said, seemed to be in the dark about the International, hating it very much, but not able to say clearly what thing it hated. Some, who professed to have peered further into the gloom than their neighbors, declared that they had made out a sort of Janus figure with a fair, honest workman's smile on one of its faces, and on the other a murderous conspirator's scowl. Would he light up the case of mystery in which the theory dwelt?

The professor laughed, chuckled a little I fancied, at the thought that we were so frightened of him. "There is no mystery to clear up, dear sir," he began, in a very polished form of the Hans Breitmann dialect, "except perhaps the mystery of human stupidity in those who perpetually ignore the fact that our Association is a public one, and that the fullest reports of its proceedings are published for all who care to read them. You may buy our rules for a penny, and a shilling laid out in pamphlets will teach you almost as much about us as we know ourselves.

R. [Landor]: Almost—yes, perhaps so; but will not the something I shall not know constitute the all-important reservation? To be quite frank with you, and to put the case as it strikes an outside observer, this general claim of depreciation of you must mean something more than the ignorant ill will of the multitude. And it is still pertinent to ask, even after what you have told me, what is the International Society?

Dr. M.: You have only to look at the individuals of which it is composed—workmen.

R.: Yes, but the soldier need be no exponent of the statecraft that sets him in motion. I know some of your members, and I can believe that they are not of the stuff of which conspirators are made. Besides, a secret shared by a million men would be no secret at all. But what if these were only the instruments in the hands of a bold, and, I hope you will forgive me for adding, not overscrupulous conclave?

Dr. M.: There is nothing to prove it.

R.: The last Paris insurrection?

Dr. M.: I demand firstly the proof that there was any plot at all—that anything happened that was not the legitimate effect of the circumstances of the moment; or the plot granted, I demand the proofs of the participation in it of the International Association.

R.: The presence of the communal body of so many members of the Association.

Dr. M.: Then it was a plot of the Freemasons, too, for their share in the work as individuals was by no means a slight one. I should not be surprised, indeed, to find the Pope setting down the whole insurrection to their account. But try another explanation. The insurrection in Paris was made by the workmen of Paris. The ablest of the workmen must necessarily have been its leaders and administrators; but the ablest of the workmen happen also to be members of the International Association. Yet the Association, as such, may be in no way responsible for their action.

R.: It will seem otherwise to the world. People talk of secret instructions from London, and even grants of money. Can it be affirmed that the alleged openness of the Association's proceedings precludes all secrecy of communication?

Dr. M.: What association ever formed carried on its work without private as well as public agencies? But to talk of secret instruction from London, as of decrees in the matter of faith and morals from some center of papal domination and intrigue, is wholly to misconceive the nature of the International. This would imply a centralized form of government for the International, whereas the real form is designedly that which gives the greatest play to local energy and independence. In fact the International is not properly a government for the working class at all. It is a bond of union rather than a controlling force.

R.: And of union to what end?

Dr. M.: The economical emancipation of the working class by the conquest of political power. The use of that political power to the attainment of social ends. It is necessary that our aims should be thus comprehensive to include every form of working-class activity. To have made them of a special character would have been to adapt them to the needs of one section—one nation of workmen alone. But how could all men be asked to unite to further the objects of a few? To have done that the Association must have forfeited its title to International. The Association does not dictate the form of political movements; it only requires a pledge as to their end. It is a network of affiliated societies spreading all over the world of labor. In each part of the world some special aspect of the problem presents itself, and the workmen there address themselves to its consideration in their own way. Combinations among workmen cannot be absolutely identical in detail in Newcastle and in Barcelona, in London and in Berlin.

In England, for instance, the way to show political power lies open to the working class. Insurrection would be madness where peaceful agitation would more swiftly and surely do the work. In France a hundred laws of repression and a mortal antagonism between classes seem to necessitate the violent solution of social war. The choice of that solution is the affair of the working classes of that country. The International does not presume to dictate in the matter and hardly to advise. But to every movement it accords its sympathy and its aid within the limits assigned by its own laws.

R.: And what is the nature of that aid?

Dr. M.: To give an example, one of the commonest forms of the movement for emancipation is that of strikes. Formerly, when a strike took place in one country it was defeated by the importation of workmen from another. The International has nearly stopped all that. It receives information of the intended strike, it spreads that information among its members, who at once see that for them the seat of the struggle must be forbidden ground. The masters are thus left alone to reckon with their men. In most cases the men require no other aid than that. Their own subscriptions or those of the societies to which they are more immediately affiliated supply them with funds, but should the pressure upon them become too heavy and the strike be one of which the Association approves, their necessities are supplied out of the common purse. By these means a strike of the cigar makers of Barcelona was brought to a victorious issue the other day. But the Society has no interest in strikes, though it supports them under certain conditions. It cannot possibly gain by them in a pecuniary point of view, but it may easily lose. Let us sum it all up in a word. The working classes remain poor amid the increase of wealth, wretched amid the increase of luxury. Their material privation dwarfs their moral as well as their physical stature. They cannot rely on others for a remedy. It has become then with them an imperative necessity to take their own case in hand. They must revise the relations between themselves and the capitalists and landlords, and that means they must transform society. This is the general end of every known workmen's organization; land and labor leagues, trade and friendly societies, cooperative stores and cooperative production are but means toward it. To establish a perfect solidarity between these organizations is the business of the International Association. Its influence is beginning to be felt everywhere. Two papers spread its views in Spain, three in Germany, the same number in Austria and in Holland, six in Belgium, and six in Switzerland. And now that I have told you what the International is you may, perhaps, be in a position to form your own opinion as to its pretended plots.

R.: And Mazzini, is he a member of your body?

Dr. M. (laughing): Ah, no. We should have made but little progress if we had not got beyond the range of his ideas.

R.: You surprise me. I should certainly have thought that he represented most advanced views.

Dr. M.: He represents nothing better than the old idea of a middle-class republic. We want no part of the middle class. He has fallen as far to the rear of the modern movement as the German professors, who, nevertheless, are still considered in Europe as the apostles of the cultured democratism of the future. They were so at one time—before '48, perhaps, when the German middle class, in the English sense, had scarcely attained its proper development. But now they have gone over bodily to the reaction, and the proletariat knows them no more.

R.: Some people have thought they saw signs of a positivist element in your organization.

Dr. M.: No such thing. We have positivists among us, and others not of our body who work as well. But this is not by virtue of their philosophy, which will have nothing to do with popular government, as we understand it, and which seeks only to put a new hierarchy in place of the old one.

R.: It seems to me, then, that the leaders of the new international movement have had to form a philosophy as well as an association themselves.

Dr. M.: Precisely. It is hardly likely, for instance, that we could hope to prosper in our war against capital if we derive our tactics, say, from the political economy of Mill. He has traced one kind of relationship between labor and capital. We hope to show that it is possible to establish another.

R.: And the United States?

Dr. M.: The chief centers of our activity are for the present among the old societies of Europe. Many circumstances have hitherto tended to prevent the labor problem from assuming an all-absorbing importance in the United States. But they are rapidly disappearing, and it is rapidly coming to the front there with the growth, as in Europe, of a laboring class distinct from the rest of the community and divorced from capital.

R.: It would seem that in this country the hoped-for solution, whatever it may be, will be attained without the violent means of revolution. The English system of agitating by platform and press until minorities become converted into majorities is a hopeful sign.

Dr. M.: I am not so sanguine on that point as you. The English middle class has always shown itself willing enough to accept the verdict of the majority, so long as it enjoyed the monopoly of the voting power. But mark me, as soon as it finds itself outvoted on what it considers vital questions we shall see here a new slaveowner's war.

I have here given you as well as I can remember them the heads of my conversation with this remarkable man. I shall leave you to form your own conclusions. Whatever may be said for or against the probability of its complicity with the movement of the Commune, we may be assured that in the International Association the civilized world has a new power in its midst with which it must soon come to a reckoning for good or ill.

The International—Dr. Marx and the *New York Herald* Correspondent in Consultation*

London, July 20

I HAVE PAID a visit today to Dr. Karl Marx, the Corresponding Secretary of the International Society for Germany and Holland. I found him at his house, a neat little villa in Maitland Park, where he is just now very busily engaged in receiving and assisting escaped Communists who find their way to London, and who are for the most part destitute of the means of existence. He seemed disposed to talk very freely about the Commune and the International and willing to have his views given to the world through the columns of the *New York Herald*, although he blames that paper severely for the principles sustained by it during the course of the Communal struggle. Having seen some of the letters in the *Herald* concerning Dombrowsky, he remarked that I was very much in the wrong to suppose that Dombrowsky was the only man the Commune had produced; that he could point to many equally honest and brave, although they had not prob-

* This interiview was published in the *New York Herald*, August 3, 1871. Selections from it were also published in *Le Gaulois*, a conservative Paris daily. Marx protested to both newspapers that the interview was published in distorted form. He wrote to Friedrich Bolte, in New York, on August 25, 1871: "I sent a statement to the *New York Herald*, repudiating all responsibility for the tasteless and entirely false report of its correspondent about his conversation with me." His letter to the editor of the *Herald*, dated August 17, 1871, read: "Sir: In the *Herald* of August 3, I find a report about a conversation between me and your correspondent. I take the liberty of stating that I must repudiate all responsibility for the statement ascribed to me in the report, in regard both to persons connected with the recent events in France and to any political or economic views. Of what I am supposed to have said, partly I said it differently and partly I did not say it at all." Marx sent a copy of this letter to the editor of *Le Gaulois* on August 24, 1871, asking that it be published.

ably distinguished themselves as he had done; that Wroblewsky, for instance, was as good a man, although not so well educated in military matters, and that he equally with Dombrowsky had the confidence of the Commune. I observed, however, that when, in the course of the conversation, I asked his

Opinions Respecting the Prominent Leaders of the Commune

they coincided most strangely with my own, as already expressed at various times in the columns of the *Herald*—a fact which was noticeable in the course of the conversation that followed. He informed me that Dombrowsky's brother, who was in command at Asnières when the Versailles troops entered at the Auteuil Gate, had escaped and was now in London, safe and well, as was Rosveicsky, Wroblewsky's chief of staff, and many others whom I had seen during those dark and bloody days.

No Information About Escaped Chiefs

To my question as to which of the insurgent chiefs had escaped and which were still in Paris he declined answering, as many of them, although escaped from Paris, were not yet out of danger, and he did not wish to give the Versailles . . .[1] any clue as to their whereabouts.

The International and the Commune

Correspondent: Did the International have as much to do with the outbreak of the Commune as people imagine?
Dr. Marx: No. A great deal of nonsense has been talked and written about the detailed and widespread schemes for revolt planned by the International, not a word of which is true. The truth is that the International and the Commune

Worked Together

for a certain period, because they both found themselves fighting the same enemy; but that the leaders of the insurrection were acting under orders received from the International Central Committee of London is absurd. Here

We Knew Nothing of the Attack Upon Montmartre

on the eighteenth of March until the whole city was in the possession of the National Guard, and most assuredly we had no means of giving

---

1. Word faded in the newspaper.

orders had we been so disposed. We always leave the people to act as circumstances and the events of the moment may dictate, only aiding them with our counsel and advice. That is what was done at Paris, with the difference that we had no chance to counsel or advise until the insurrection became an accomplished fact. The government attempted to disband the National Guard, and the latter drove out the government almost before the International knew of it even.

The London Instructions

Correspondent: Did you give them any advice afterwards?
Dr. Marx: I did.
Correspondent: What was the nature of it?
Dr. Marx: Immediately after the affair of the twenty-second of March I advised them to march upon Versailles, and to not delay it later than the twenty-fifth. Had they done this success would have been certain. The government had just taken flight, everything was in disorder, everybody was frightened, the soldiers would not fight and victory was easy and sure. They lost the golden opportunity through the want of capacity on the part of their leaders, and from that I knew what would be the result, and predicted it when communicating with our branch committees. Had the National Guard been well commanded even as late as the morning of the third of April, when they attempted the sortie under

Bergeret and Flourens

they might even then have succeeded. In the first place there was no necessity for going out right under the guns of Mont Valérien and exposing raw troops to a formidable artillery fire; they might have taken another road. This is not all. The commander of Valérien had promised to remain neutral, but he had been replaced by another officer two days before this sortie, and although Flourens had received due notice of it he, it seems, had in the flurry of the moment forgotten this important fact until it was recalled to his mind in thunder tones by the cannon of the fortress.

Fiery Philanthropist Flourens[2]

Correspondent: It was certainly a remarkable thing for a general to forget.

---

2. Gustave Flourens was executed for his activities as a Commune leader. Marx to Engels, February 10, 1870: "The crackbrained youngster Flourens is the little son of the late Flourens [Pierre Jean–Marie], Perpetual Secretary of the Academy [of Sciences], who throughout his almost 100 years' lifetime

Dr. Marx: General! He was no general. He was a republican—a great philanthropist—the kindest-hearted man in the world; a great scholar, but he appeared absolutely crazy when talking on politics, and he was no more capable of commanding an army than a child ten years old.

Belligerent Bergeret

Correspondent: What is your opinion of Bergeret?

Dr. Marx: Utterly incapable. An ambitious man, who had nothing to recommend him but his violence. I am not even sure that he is honest.

Correspondent: Was he not a member of the International?

Dr. Marx: I never saw his name upon our books, nor heard of him before the affair of the eighteenth of March. He may have been a member of the International, but I do not believe that he ever was.

Cloudy Cluseret[3]

Correpsondent: And Cluseret?

Dr. Marx: I will have something to tell you of Cluseret which I would not like to have disclosed yet, as he may be still in danger. He is not nor never was a member of the International. (Here he gave me some very interesting facts about Cluseret and in connection with the Commune, which I am not at liberty to give to the public.)

Rossel[4]

Correspondent: And your opinion of Rossel, the fiery and impetuous Minister of War?

---

went along with whatever government was in existence, being in turn Bonapartist, Legitimist, Orléanist, and Bonapartist again. In the later years of his life he made himself noted by his fanatical opposition to Darwin." Marx to Engels, April 28, 1870: "Flourens has visited me several times. He is a very fine fellow. His dominant characteristic is audacity. Yet he has great scientific knowledge. For a year he lectured on ethnology at the University of Paris, has been everywhere, in Southern Europe, Turkey, Asia Minor, etc. Is full of illusions and revolutionary impatience, but a very jolly fellow with all that, and not of the "stern" heman school. He has been proposed for membership in our Council, which he attended twice as a guest. It would be very good if he remained here longer. It is worth while to influence him."

3. Marx to Engels, September 10, 1870: ". . . the lousy, pushy, vain and very ambitious gossip Cluseret . . ." Marx to Engels, October 19, 1870: "But the jackasses Bakunin and Cluseret came to Lyon and spoiled everything. As both belong to the International, they unfortunately had enough influence to mislead our friends. They seized City Hall—for a short period—and issued the craziest laws about abolition of the state and similar idiocies . . . As for Cluseret himself, he behaved like a fool and a coward."

4. Marx's writings and correspondence contain no reference to Rossel at all.

Dr. Marx: I hardly know. He was evidently a very ambitious man, and, I think, honest, as he was an officer of acknowledged merit and could have got a much better position in the Versailles army than that assigned to him by the Commune at the outset. Nevertheless he did some very strange things. It was he more than Bergeret, probably, who conspired against Cluseret and caused the arrest of the latter. He denounced him secretly to a great many members of the Commune, and then astonished them all by bestowing upon him the highest praise, and he had him securely locked up in the Mazas [prison].

Correspondent: That is a story I had never heard before.

Dr. Marx: It is true nevertheless. And it was this double-dealing that led him in his turn to be suspected by the Commune. They thought he must be a consummate hypocrite.

Correspondent: But they suspected everybody?

Dr. Marx: Yes, probably, with two or three exceptions. But you cannot blame them, they have been betrayed so often. The republic has been overthrown in every case by the treason of its most trusted generals. Later, France herself has been lost by the treason of such men as Bazaine and Bourbaki and the stupidity of others, as Mac-Mahon. Can we blame them for being suspicious?

Alphabetical Assy[5]

Correspondent: Was Assy a member of the International?

Dr. Marx: No, he never was. But his name was on the list of clubs that used to meet in Paris during the siege; and he was only elected because his name begins with an A. In making up the list of candidates for Paris there was one wanting, and upon looking over the names of those inscribed alphabetically that of Assy occurred among the first, and he was fixed upon because they had no time to look further. He is an idiot, and I doubt his honesty. Many think him to be a *mouchard* in the employ of the Versailles government.

Silly Cecilia[6]

Correspondent: And La Cecilia?

Dr. Marx: I believe him to be not only an ass but a traitor.

5. Marx to Léon Bigot, July 11, 1871 (draft of a letter): "I declare that the letter ascribed to me, in which I am supposed to speak about M. Assi, is *a forgery* . . . With one exception, I have never had anything to do with M. Assi, privately or publicly. . . ."

6. Marx to Jenny Longuet, August 14, 1874: "Mr. General Cecilia bored me the day before yesterday for three to four hours. Among other things, he informed me that . . . he is establishing a school for French refugee children. The

Poor Pyat[7]

Correspondent: And Félix Pyat?

Dr. Marx: A great blower, and a still greater coward.

Humanitarian Hugo[8]

Correspondent: And Victor Hugo?

Dr. Marx: Undoubtedly a great poet, but one of those men who are always ready to espouse any cause which may happen to please their fancy. Not to be depended upon.

Rebellious Rochefort

Correspondent: And what do you think of Rochefort?

Dr. Marx: Rochefort has some good points. He made a bold fight against the Empire, and during the time of the Commune he criticized both sides severely, gave them about equal portions of hard blows, and, I believe, had both equally incensed against him. It must be admitted that his criticisms were correct as well as savage. Still, he was only a sort of literary bohemian without any education except what he picked up in the streets—a full-grown *gamin* and that was all— although he displayed in many cases a great deal of good sound sense, a fact which nobody understands better than his opponents, whatever they say to the contrary.

Members of the Commune Who Were Internationals

Correspondent: What members of the Commune were members of the International?

Dr. Marx: Of the most prominent members of the Commune only five were of the International—Flourens, Dombrowsky, Duval, Rigault (now dead), and Wroblewsky (supposed to have escaped).

Correspondent: What are the fundamental principles of the International?

Dr. Marx: The answer to that question would be a very complicated one, and would probably take more time than we have at our disposal. I can give you a few of our publications, however, which will answer the question more satisfactorily and more concisely than could be done in any conversation.

---

curriculum would include also instruction in hygiene, as well as *social economy*, for the latter of which I should be so kind as to write a primer on the English model. . . ."

7. Marx to Leo Frankel, April 26, 1871 (draft of a letter): "The vileness of this man [Pyat] is nourished by one source: *hatred of the International.*"

8. Victor Hugo was not a member of the International or the Paris Commune.

He here gave me several small tracts and showed me the first volume of a large work by himself, entitled, *Der Produktions Prozess des Kapitals*, wherein he said I would "find the question of labor and capital discussed at length," warning me, however, that I would find the first chapter something abstruse and difficult to understand, especially for a foreigner.

Correspondent: What is the principal object of your attack now, monarchy or capital—that is, as you understand it, monopoly.

Dr. Marx: Both. One is the natural result of the other, or, rather, both belong to an age and a civilization that are fast passing away. The feudal system, slavery, monarchy, capital, monopoly—all are bound to follow each other in rapid succession and pass from the earth. The feudal system went first, then slavery; monarchy is going fast, so fast that we scarcely considered it worthy of our steel, and monopoly, or capital, must and will follow. The struggle will be a bitter one, it will bring to the surface all the scum of humanity; it will bring in its train all the miseries that the evil passions of men let loose invariably bring, but it is necessary and inevitable. Capital will never be warned in time, and it will have to take the consequences. What better is the condition of the man who works for a dollar a day—that is, sells himself for a day at a time for just enough to support life—than that of the Negro slave who is clothed and fed by his master?

Capital Is, After All, Only Another Form of Slavery

and the condition of the laborer is about the same in either case. Take the arguments used by the former slaveholders in the southern states of America in defense of slavery and you will find them identical with those used by capitalists and monopolies today. "What right have you to compel these Negroes to work for your profit alone when you only give them the bare necessities of life?" The answer is ready—"I bought them."

The Land Question

"What right have you to 1,000,000 acres of the land that God gave for the support of 1,000,000 men while those men are starving?" The answer is the same—"I bought it," or "It was given me by the king." Had anyone a right to sell; had the king a right to give? That is a question about which they do not trouble themselves in the least. But you have this stuff about the sacredness of private property while men are starving and dying of want and cold and nakedness all around them, or living lives of misery and wretchedness and enduring hardships that even brutes are not subjected to.

Children Compelled to Labor

The recent exposé of children as young as four years working in the backfields is a case in point. Here are children—girls and boys of from eight to ten years old—carrying forty pounds of earth upon their heads a distance of fourteen miles a day, living in the mud like beasts until they have almost lost the semblance of the human form divine; and yet the men who have grown rich from the blood and sweat and toil and suffering of these poor, miserable little creatures— these men who call themselves respectable, who go to church on Sundays in their carriages—come to me and talk about the sacredness of private property forsooth! So talked the cotton planter of the South. So talks every heavy-handed infamy that has ever disgraced humanity.

No Civil War in England

Correspondent: Do you look for a civil war soon in England?
Dr. Marx: We do not intend to make war. We hope to be able to gain our rights in a legal and lawful way by act of Parliament, and

It Is the Aristocracy and the Moneyed Men Who Will Rebel

It is they who will attempt a revolution. But we have the force of numbers. We shall have the strength of intelligence and discipline. Let them put us down if they can.

Success in England Soon

Correspondent: Do you expect to succeed soon in England?
Dr. Marx: Sooner than in any other country, for the reason that labor and capital are already organized upon

The Cooperative System

where the work is done by many skilled hands, each doing a part, and where all sorts of labor-saving machines are used on the farm and in the factory. Labor is already cooperative. It is only necessary to make the profits mutual by dividing them equally among those engaged in it, indeed of giving them all to our own. In this respect the labor system in England is much better adopted to our needs, and to the changes which must inevitably take place, than that existing in France, where land as well as manufactures are parceled out in small quantities, and where the laborer works, as it were, . . .[9]

The Attainment of Capital

Correspondent: You look then upon great conglomerations of capital, of labor, of machinery, where many hands work together for the cultivation of a single product or class of products, or the manufacture of a single article or class of articles, as more conducive to your laws of progress than the system of absolute division and possession of property into small lots.

Dr. Marx: I do; because the transformation will be more . . .[10] But I see where you wish to drive me. You would say that if capital is thus assisting progress, it must be a good thing—a proposition which I do not altogether deny. I look upon

The Present State of Capital

as a stage of development, and a necessary stage in human progress, which must naturally develop itself into a higher form of perfection, just as the flower must fall to give way to the fruit, or the blade of green must spring before the corn can ripen. The present system has led to the beginning of railroads, the extension of commerce, the covering of the ocean with steamers, the opening of great forests, of cutting canals and piercing mountains with tunnels and bringing the poles and the antipodes, the remotest parts of the earth, to communication with each other.

All This Is Progress

but at what a cost of human toil and suffering has it been brought about! And now that we are fairly launched upon our course, now that we no longer need this system, an unjust and cruel one, we will cast it aside and adopt something better and nobler.

The First Step in England

Correspondent: What would be your first step if you should come into power in Parliament?

Dr. Marx: Evidently to set aside the Queen, the House of Lords, and declare the republic.

---

9. Five words faded.
10. Two words faded.

Correspondent: And then?

Dr. Marx: And then we would proceed to the transformation of all great properties, such as manufactures and—all the land, in favor of the state, which should work them for the benefit of every person engaged in producing. The drones, or those who would not work, should have nothing.

Correspondent: That is, you would turn the whole country into a series of joint stock companies, to be run by a government or governments elected for that purpose?

Dr. Marx: That is my meaning.

Correspondent: Do you think it would succeed?

Dr. Marx: I do. Just as joint stock companies do succeed now.

Objections

Correspondent: We have some experience of that sort in America, where a plan of that sort could succeed if it ever did. But we have found that whenever the government undertook to run a railroad, or a canal, or a mine, or anything of that sort, it invariably ran it into the ground

Dr. Marx: That may be, but the system has never yet had a fair trial.

Correspondent: Besides, have you not observed that as soon as the laborer gets a little money he becomes an aristocrat, goes over to the enemy's camp and commences looking down with scorn upon his companions of yesterday?

Dr. Marx: Yes: I have observed that. But it does not change the general aspect of the question. It is only changing the units of the problem from one side to the other without changing the sum total.

Correspondent: But how will you find men who will not do this? How will you, in a word, find men who will not look upon their own personal interests before that of their constituents?

Dr. Marx: It would of course be difficult, but it would have to be done.

Correspondent: What kind of property do you think ought to be worked upon

The Cooperative and Mutual Principle

Dr. Marx: All kinds that require cooperation to work them to the best advantage. Lands, forests, railroads, canals, telegraphs, quarries, collieries, mines, and manufactories.

Correspondent: That is, you would take them from their present possessors, work them for the benefit of those actually engaged in the manufacture and production, giving the present owners just as much as they could earn by the sweat of their brow?

Dr. Marx: That is our doctrine.

Strength of the International

Correspondent: How many members do you count all over the world?

Dr. Marx: I would give about two million as the minimum figure.

Correspondent: Has the society a very full treasury?

Without a Treasury

Dr. Marx: No. We have very little money on hand; but whenever we need it we always get enough by volunteer contributions to answer our purposes. It is a mistake to suppose that we have a large amount of money always ready to assist strikes and to foment troubles between employers and employees. We, on the contrary, discourage

Strikes

as often doing more harm than good, except in cases of absolute necessity. When the workmen are positively obliged to strike we assist them with small amounts of money, but we never give them enough to encourage them in striking when not absolutely driven to it. Besides this we discountenance violence, and except in cases where a government uses force to put us down, we hope to succeed by legal and lawful means.

Annual Dues

Correspondent: What is the yearly amount that each member is expected to pay?

Dr. Marx: One penny, the greater part of which is used in keeping up local organizations. Our organization is very economical, however, and a small amount from each member when required for any special purpose produces a good round sum. No officer of the International receives enough to live upon from his salary alone. He must work besides in order to support himself.

Assisted the Belgian Workmen

Correspondent: Did you assist the Belgians in the late strikes?

Dr. Marx: Yes; we sent them in all about five hundred pounds.

The International in Russia

Correspondent: Have you a strong organization in Russia?

Dr. Marx: No; it is impossible as yet. The government permits nothing of the sort. There is a revolution coming in Russia, however, slowly, but surely. There are two classes there that are greatly discontented with the recent abolition of serfdom—the laborer, whose position has not been in the least improved by it, and the smaller nobility, who have been ruined by it—and these two elements, once they can be induced to work together, will overthrow that tyrannical form of government easily when the first weak czar succeeds to the throne.

The Society in the United States

Correspondent: Have you a strong organization in the United States?

Dr. Marx: Yes, but we apprehend no violence or trouble there, unless, indeed, some of your great iron or other monopolists should take it into their hands to employ force to put down strikes, as they had done in one or two instances, in which case they will be swept away like chaff before the wind.

The Aims of the Society in America

Correspondent: What are the principal aims of the society in the United States?

Dr. Marx: To emancipate the workingman from the rule of politicians, and to combat monopoly in all the many forms it is assuming there, especially that of the public lands. We want no more monstrous land grabs, no more grants to swindling railroad concerns, no more schemes for robbing the people of their birthright for the benefit of a few purse-proud monopolists. More than that, let these men be warned in time; their ill-gotten goods shall be taken from them, and their wealth shall vanish like the baseless fabric of a vision. We oppose also all protectionist measures, which make all the necessaries of life dear to the poor man merely to put money into the pockets of a few aristocrats, who know how to buy over your corrupt politicians.[11]

---

11. From the minutes of the General Council, July 23, 1867: "Citizen Marx had received letters; one from New York [from Friedrich Sorge, July 10, 1867] announcing the affiliation of the Communist Club, which rejects all revealed religion and every [doctrine] not founded upon the perception of concrete objects. It advocates the destruction of individual property, the equality of all persons, and its members bind each other to carry these maxims into practice. The other letter was from a kindred association at Hoboken, N.J., also announcing its adhesion. It called upon the Council to send documents, and spoke of the

The Destruction of the Public Property No Part of the Program

Correspondent: Is the destruction of public property, such as the burning of the Hôtel de Ville of Paris and the Tuileries, any part of your program?

Dr. Marx: I do not see how you can ask such a question. The wanton destruction of property can in no case further the interests of the workingman. The burning of the Tuileries and the Hôtel de Ville were ordered as simple war measures, such as any general might be compelled to take in order to defend himself, just as the burning of Moscow or the bombardment of Strasbourg or the destruction of property everywhere is considered one of the necessary evils of war. Besides, I do not see why public property should be held more sacred than private property, which Mr. Thiers did not spare when he was shelling without the slightest possible reason the Avenue de la Grande Armée and the Champs Elysées.

The French Refugees

Correspondent: You have of course seen a great many refugees from Paris. Have you seen any yet who believed in

The *Pétroleuses*

Dr. Marx: That story is one of the greatest outrages perpetrated in any civilized country. I am sure that not a single woman or child can be convicted upon evidence that would hang a dog of pouring petroleum in houses or of attempting to burn the city; and yet hundreds have been shot for it, and thousands transported and sent to Cayenne. Whatever burning took place was done by men.

Correspondent: I must say that I have the same conviction. I have never yet seen a single person who ever actually saw a woman or child with petroleum. Were those proclamations that appeared in Paris just before the elections, purporting to be from the International, and those reports of sittings of International Committees that were given in the *Paris-Journal* genuine?

A Story Gotten Up by the Monarchists

Dr. Marx: Not one of them was genuine. They were simply gotten up by the monarchists, to frighten the people into voting for their candidates. It is the usual style of their tactics.

---

great danger there was of the workingmen of America being traduced by the professional politicians—the greatest rascals under the sun, who were advocating workingmen's measures to retain their places. Senator Wade had made an almost communistic speech the other day, but had explained it away to a bourgeois audience."

Not in Connection with the Italian *Carbonari*

Correspondent: Are you in connection with the *Carbonari* of Italy?

Dr. Marx: Not now. We were formerly, but they wished to form one grand consolidated society which should be moved by a single will, a despotism of the worst kind, and a very good thing for political conspiracies, but not for an association of free men working openly and neither trying to conceal their intentions nor their principles.

A Sketch of Dr. Marx

Dr. Marx is, I should judge, between fifty and fifty-five years of age,[12] with white hair and beard, black mustache, a deeply lined, thoughtful forehead, the German cast of countenance in all its force and peculiarities, and is evidently an educated and intelligent man, although he allows himself to be borne away by his extravagant utopian ideas with regard to property.

The International Misrepresented

My opinion of the International is that it has been greatly misrepresented and overrated. It will never accomplish what it hopes for, because there is something in the human heart antagonistic to its principles. But it may accomplish something for workingmen by uniting them, inducing them to act together, to help each other and prevent their being pitted against each other in order to cut down their wages by their employers. They will be able within a certain measure to dictate terms to their employers and to up the price of their labor, but this is all they ever can or ever ought to accomplish.

As to Dr. Marx's theory of the abolition of property, even the poorest mechanic in the United States will scout at it, hoping, as they all do, to one day have property of their own.

---

12. Born in 1818, Marx was then fifty-three years old.

The Reds in Session—Authentic Account of the Seventh Anniversary of the International in London*

London, September 26

THE SEVENTH ANNIVERSARY of the International was celebrated last night by the members of the General Council and a select committee of friends, most of them members and officers of the Paris Commune. The festival commenced with a substantial repast of roast beef, veal, mutton, boiled ham, and a boiled leg of mutton. The boiled leg of mutton occupied the place of honor in front of the chair. The juice of the grape was provided in its native purity by a winegrower of St. Macaire, a member of the Commune, occupied during the reign of the Commune in the Ministry of Public Works, and, now, like many of his colleagues, a refugee in London. There was a plentiful supply and ample justice was done to it. When all was ready the question as to who was to preside was raised. "Karl Marx," was the reply. He asked the reason why? He could see but one reason, that he was the oldest man in the company (he is fifty-three). He was answered that in consideration of the position he occupied as member of the Council he was the man for the chair. His objection was that he could not carve. He can cut up a hostile cabinet or government, but was afraid to lay hands on a boiled leg of mutton. The difficulty, however, was removed and he was voted in the chair by acclamation.

The Seats of Honor

were occupied, the right of the chair by General Wroblewski and the left by Colonel Dombrowski, brother of the fallen General Dombrow-

* Published in the *New York World*, October 15, 1871.

ski, of the Commune. Next to them sat the two Misses Marx. Colonel Dombrowski did the carving with a dexterity as if handling the carving knife in a ham and beef shop was the occupation of his life. Both the revolutionary general and the Colonel are young enough to live till all the existing governments shall have been finally overthrown, and they look and are the most unpresuming and pleasant young great men I have ever had the good fortune to be in company with, yet there is a determination in their expressions that convinces you at once that they are not to be trifled with. Among all the refugees present there is not a man as old as forty years, and many are under thirty years of age; it is, in reality, a young generation of revolutionists.

The Speech of the Chairman

was short but to the purpose. He modestly apologized for having consented to occupy the chair, which he had only done because someone must occupy the chair, and being the oldest man present was the only reason why he had consented. Concerning the International, he said that the great success which had hitherto crowned its efforts was due to circumstances over which the members themselves had no control. The foundation of the International itself was the result of these circumstances, and by no means due to the efforts of the men engaged in it. It was not the work of any set of clever politicians: all the politicians in the world could not have created the situation and circumstances requisite for the success of the International. The International had not put forth any particular creed. Its task was to organize the forces of labor and link the various workingmen's movements and combine them. The circumstances which had given such a great development to the association were the conditions under which the workpeople were more and more oppressed throughout the world, and this was the secret of the success. The events of the last few weeks had unmistakably shown that the working class must fight for its emancipation. The persecutions of the government against the International were like the persecutions of ancient Rome against the primitive Christians. They, too, had been few in numbers at first, but the patricians of Rome had instinctively felt that if the Christians succeeded the Roman Empire would be lost. The persecutions of Rome had not saved the Empire, and the persecutions of the present day against the International would not save the existing state of things.

What was new in the International was that it was established by the workingmen themselves and for themselves. Before the foundation of the International all the different organizations had been societies founded by some radicals among the ruling classes for the working classes, but the International was established by the working-men for themselves. The Chartist movement in this country had been started with the consent and assistance of middle-class radicals, though if it had been successful it could only have been for the advantage of the working class. England was the only country where the working class was sufficiently developed and organized to turn universal suffrage to its own proper account. He then alluded to the revolution of February as a movement that had been favored by a portion of the bourgeoisie against the ruling party. The revolution of February had only given promises to the working classes and had replaced one set of men of the ruling class by another. The insurrections of June had been a revolt against the whole ruling class, including the most radical portion. The workingmen who had lifted the new men into power in 1848 had instinctively felt that they had only exchanged one set of oppressors for another and that they were betrayed.

The Last Movement

was the Commune, the greatest that had yet been made, and there could not be two opinions about it—the Commune was the conquest of political power by the working classes. There was much misunderstanding about the Commune. The Commune could not found a new form of class government. In destroying the existing conditions of oppression by transferring all the means of labor to the productive laborer, and thereby compelling every able-bodied individual to work for a living, the only base for class rule and oppression would be removed. But before such a change could be effected a proletarian *dictature* would become necessary, and the first condition of that was a proletarian army. The working classes would have to conquer the right to emancipate themselves on the battlefield. The task of the International was to organize and combine the forces of labor for the common struggle.

Theodor Cuno's Reminiscences of the Hague Congress*

[IN DÜSSELDORF] I organized a section of the International, which sent me as its delegate to the International Congress at the Hague. . . .[1]

One of the highest periods of my life as a social outcast was my participation in the proceedings of the International Congress. . . .

I arrived at the Hague when the Congress had just been called to order. The meeting took place in a common dancing hall in Lombard-straat, about fifty by twenty feet, with a balcony on one side, where a few spectators were sitting, among them reporters of several local and foreign papers. . . .

When I entered the hall I saw a number of tables arranged like a horseshoe, around which the most interesting assembly had gathered I have ever seen in my life. Many of them I knew personally, of others I had seen pictures, others again had been described to me and others I recognized from their typical national exterior as the representatives of Spain, Italy, France, England, and America . . . I saw Johann Philipp Becker, as he had been described to me: a giant with a long black beard, high forehead, broad shoulders. . . .

Then I saw Engels: He was sitting to the left of the presiding officer, smoking, writing, and eagerly listening to the speakers. When I introduced myself to him he looked up from his paper, and seizing my hands he joyfully said: "Everything goes well, we have a big majority."

It was the deciding battle, you know, between Marx and Bakunin —the question had to be decided, whether the International was to be

---

* From Theodor Cuno, *Reminiscences*, written in English for the Moscow Institute of Marxism-Leninism, 1932.

1. September 2–7, 1872.

a well-disciplined army, able to fight an organized enemy, or whether it was to be split up into a hundred thousand particles every one of the members imagining himself to be a general, and Bakunin the great, infallible dictator leading them all by the nose by flattering their vanity and thereby making them his blindly obeying tools.

Engels' face I knew from a photograph, but he was thinner than the picture showed him to be. He is a tall, bony man with sharp-cut features, long, sandy whiskers, ruddy complexion and little blue eyes. His manner of moving and speaking is quick, determined, and convinces the observer that the man knows exactly what he wants and what will be the consequences of his words and actions. In conversation with him one learns something new with every sentence he utters. His brain contains a mighty treasury of scientific knowledge; Engels speaks more than a dozen languages, acquired for the sole purpose of carrying the movement into as many countries of the Old World.

Opposite Engels sat Paul Lafargue, Marx's son-in-law, who had been conducting the fight against Bakunin's secret society in Spain. Introducing me to Lafargue, Engels exclaimed: "Here we have them both, our fighters from Spain and Italy!"

Marx was sitting behind Engels. I recognized him immediately with his big, woolly head. His complexion was dark, his hair and beard were gray. He wore a black broadcloth suit, and when he wanted to look at anybody or anything intently he pressed a monocle into his right eye. Engels took me to him; and he received me affably, requesting me to give him an account of different occurrences in Spain and Italy when the session was adjourned. . . .

And now the Congress could proceed with its regular business . . . Then the report of the General Council was read, Marx, Engels, and other members of the Council alternating in the reading. The report was written in English, French, and German . . . When speaking, Marx was not very fluent; in fact he was not a practiced orator, while Engels spoke in a conversational tone, often sarcastic and humorous, "burschicosically," as we Germans are in the habit of describing the conversation among college students. When Marx was speaking he from time to time dropped his monocle and then slowly reinserted it in its place at his right eye. Being fifty-five years old at that time, Marx was still in a vigorous physical condition, his bushy hair and beard being only in part streaked with gray and white. His complexion was a pale yellow . . . His fellow students had conferred upon him the nickname, "*Der Mohr*," American boys would probably call him "Nigger." His wife and children always called him "*Der Mohr*," considering him to be more of a jolly comrade than a stern and bossy parent. . . .

From The Hague most of us went to Amsterdam, where the local members hired a hall to hold a public propaganda meeting. The hall was small and there were no chairs nor benches so that the small attendance had to listen to the speakers *stante pede* . . . Marx was the first and principal speaker. What he said, I don't remember. Anyhow I did not stay long but with some of the French comrades went out to take in the sights of the old canal-cut Amsterdam. . . .

When the Congress had adjourned the delegates were invited by Marx and Engels to a shore dinner at Scheveningen, the watering resort near The Hague. We all went there and before dining had a swim in the sea. Never having bathed in sea water, I went out nearly a quarter of a mile, and could not return as the tide was going out and the rushing waves were too strong for me. But there was Frederick Engels, who had seen that I was in danger. Being a stronger man and a better swimmer than I was, he swam out to me, grabbed me by one arm and thus enabled me to return safely to the shore.

At Scheveningen Marx also introduced me to his daughters, the one married to Paul Lafargue and the other to one of the French delegates (I don't remember his name,[2] old age playing tricks on me). Eleanor Marx, whom we used to call "Tussy," being the third daughter. When Marx introduced me to Lafargue, he said: "Cuno, I am told that you are going to America, so you may do there what one of my daughters has done towards solving the color question, by marrying a nigger, for Lafargue is of colored descent." I promised to do my best, but circumstances prevented me from carrying out my promise, as there were no Negro ladies at New York, where I lived for over fifty years, for me to marry. . . .

---

2. Charles Longuet.

A Reply on the First International—Mr. George Howell's History of the International Working Men's Association*

I BELIEVE IT worth while to illustrate by a few notes the most recent contribution—see the *Nineteenth Century* of July last—to the extensive spurious literature on the International's history, because its last expounder, Mr. George Howell, an ex-workman and ex-member of the General Council of that Association, may erroneously be supposed to have drawn his wisdom from sources not generally accessible.

Mr. Howell sets about his "History" by passing by the facts that, on September 28, 1864, I was present at the foundation meeting of the International, was there chosen a member of the provisional General Council, and soon after drew up the Inaugural Address and the General Statements of the Association, first issued at London in 1864, then confirmed by the Geneva Congress of 1866. So much Mr. Howell knew, but, for purposes of his own, prefers to make "a German Doctor named Karl Marx" first appear at the London "Congress opened on September 25, 1865." There and then, he avers, the said "Doctor" had "sown the seeds of discord and decay by the introduction of the Religious Idea."

In the first instance, no "congress" of the International took place in September, 1865. A few delegates from the main continental branches of the Association met at London for the sole purpose of conferring with the General Council on the Program of the "First Congress," which was to assemble at Geneva in September, 1866. The real business of the Conference was transacted in private sittings, not

---

* Marx wrote this article in July, 1878, and sent it to the editor of *Nineteenth Century*, who refused to print it. It was published by Harriet Law in the *Secular Chronicle*, August 4, 1878. The text used here is from the British magazine *Labour Monthly*, which reprinted the piece in September, 1954.

at the semipublic meetings in Adelphi Terrace, exclusively made mention of by the exact historian Mr. George Howell.

Like the other representatives of the General Council, I had to secure the acceptance by the Conference of our own program, on its publication thus characterized in a letter to the *Siècle* by the French historian Henri Martin: "The breadth of view and the high moral, political, and economic conceptions which have decided the choice of questions composing the program of the International Congress of Workingmen, which is to assemble next year, will strike with a common sympathy all friends of progress, justice, and liberty in Europe."

The program of the General Council contained not one syllable on "Religion," but at the instance of the Paris delegates the forbidden dish got into the bill of fare in store for the prospective Congress, in this dressing: "Religious Ideas" (not "The Religious Idea," as Howell's spurious version has it), "their influence on the social, political, and intellectual movement." The topic of discussion thus introduced by the Paris delegates was left in their keeping. In point of fact, they dropped it at the Geneva Conference of 1866, and no one else picked it up. The London "Congress" of 1865, the "introduction" there by "a German Doctor named Karl Marx" of the "Religious Idea," and the fierce feud thence arising within the International—this, his triple myth, Mr. George Howell caps by a legend. He says: In the Draft-Address to the American people with regard to the abolition of slavery, the sentence, "God made of one blood all nations of men," was struck out, etc.

Now the General Council issued an address, not to the American people, but to its President, Abraham Lincoln, which he gracefully acknowledged. The address, written by me, underwent no alteration whatever. As the words "God made of one blood all nations of men" had never figured in it, they could not be "struck out." The attitude of the General Council in regard to the "Religious Idea" is clearly shown by the following incident: One of the Swiss branches of the Alliance founded by Michael Bakunin, and calling itself *Section des athées Socialistes*, requested its admission to the International from the Geneva Council, but got the reply: "Already in the case of the Young Men's Christian Association the Council has declared that it recognizes *no theological sections.* (See page 3 of *Les Prétendues scissions dans l'Internationale Circular du Conseil Général*, printed at Geneva.)"

Even Mr. George Howell, at that time not yet become a convert by close study of the *Christian Reader*, consummated his divorce from the International, not at the call of the "Religious Idea," but on grounds altogether secular. At the foundation of the *Commonwealth* as the "special organ" of the General Council, he canvassed keenly the "proud position" of editor. Having failed in his "ambitious" attempt, he waxed sulky, his zeal grew less and less, and soon after he was no more heard of. During the most eventful period of the International he was therefore an outsider.

Conscious of his utter incompetence to trace the history of the Association, but at the same time eager to spice his article with strange revelations, he catches at the appearance, during the Fenian troubles, of General Cluseret in London, where, we are told, at the Black Horse, Rathbone Place, Oxford Street, the General met "a few men—fortunately Englishmen," in order to initiate them into his "plan of a general insurrection." I have some reason to doubt the genuineness of the anecdote, but suppose it to be true, what else would it prove but that Cluseret was not such a fool as to intrude his person and his "plan" upon the General Council, but kept both of them wisely in reserve for "a few Englishmen" of Mr. Howell's acquaintance, unless the latter himself be one of these stout fellows in buckram who, by their "fortunate" interference, contrived to save the British Empire and Europe from universal convulsion.

Mr. George Howell has another dark secret to disclose.

At the beginning of June, 1871, the General Council put forth an Address on the Civil War in France, welcomed on the part of the London press by a chorus of execration. One weekly fell foul of the "infamous author," cowardly concealing his name behind the screen of the General Council. Thereupon I declared in the *Daily News* that I was the author. This stale secret Mr. George Howell reveals, in July, 1878, with all the consequentiality of the man behind the curtain. "The writer of that Address was Dr. Karl Marx . . . Mr. George Odger and Mr. Lucraft, both of whom were members of the Council when it" (sic!) "was adopted, repudiated it on its publication." He forgets to add that the other nineteen British members present acclaimed the Address. Since then, the statements of this Address have been fully borne out by the *enquêtes* [inquiries] of the French Rural Assembly, the evidence taken before the Versailles courts-martial, the trial of Jules Favre, and the memoirs of persons far from hostile to the victors. It is in the natural order of things that an English historian of Mr. George Howell's sound erudition should haughtily ignore French prints, whether official or not. But I confess to a feeling of disgust when, on such occasions for instance as the Hoedel and Nobiling attempts,[1] I behold great London papers ruminating the base calumnies which their own correspondents, eyewitnesses, had been the first to refute.

---

1. Hoedel and Nobiling attempted in June, 1878, to assassinate Emperor Wilhelm I, and Bismarck tried to use this as a pretext to attack the German Social Democrats.

Mr. Howell reaches the climax of snobbism in his account of the exchequer of the General Council. The Council in its published Report to the Congress of Basel (1869) ridicules the huge treasure with which the busy tongue of the European police and the wild imagination of the capitalist had endowed it. It says, "If these people, though good Christians, had happened to live at the time of nascent Christianity, they would have hurried to a Roman bank there to pry into St. Paul's balance." Mr. Ernest Renan, who, it is true, falls somewhat short of Mr. George Howell's standard of orthodoxy, even fancies the state of the primitive Christian communes sapping the Roman Empire might be best illustrated by that of the International sections.

Mr. George Howell, as a writer, is what the crystallographer would call a "pseudomorph," his outer form of penmanship being but imitative of the manner of thought and style "natural" to the English moneyed man of sated virtue and solvent morals. Although he borrows his array of "figures" as to the resources of the General Council from the accounts yearly laid by that same Council before a public "International Congress," Mr. George Howell must not derogate from his "imitative" dignity by stooping to touch the obvious question: how came it to pass that, instead of taking comfort from the lean budgets of the General Council, all the governments of Continental Europe took fright at "the powerful and formidable organization of the International Working Men's Association, and the rapid development it had attained in a few years." (See *Circular of the Spanish Foreign Minister to the Representatives of Spain in Foreign Countries*.) Instead of laying the Red Ghost by the simple process of shaking at its face the sorry returns of the General Council, why, in the name of common sense, did the Pope and his bishop exorcise the International, the French Rural Assembly outlaw it, Bismarck—at the Salzburg meeting of the emperors of Austria and Germany—threaten it with a Holy Alliance Crusade, and the White Czar commend it to his terrible "Third Division," then presided over by the emotional Schouvaloff?

Mr. George Howell condescends to admit: "Poverty is no crime, but it is fearfully inconvenient." I admit, he speaks by book. The prouder he ought to have felt of his former fellowship with a Working Men's Association, which won world-wide fame and a place in the history of mankind, not by length of purse, but by strength of mind and unselfish energy.

However, from the lofty standpoint of an insular "philistine," Mr. George Howell reveals to the "cultured people" of the *Nineteenth Century*, that the International was a "failure," and has faded away. In reality, the social democratic workingmen's parties organized on more or less national dimensions, in Germany, Switzerland, Denmark, Portugal, Italy, Belgium, Holland, and the United States of America, form as many international groups, no longer single sections thinly scattered through different countries, and held together by an eccentric General Council, but the working masses themselves in continuous, active, direct intercourse, cemented by exchange of thought, mutual services, and common aspiration.

After the fall of the Paris Commune, all working-class organization in France was of course temporarily broken, but is now in an incipient state of re-forming. On the other hand, despite all political and social obstacles, the Slavs, chiefly in Poland, Bohemia, and Russia, participate at present in this international movement to an extent not to be foreseen by the most sanguine in 1872. Thus instead of dying out, the International did only pass from its first period of incubation to a higher one where its already original tendencies have in part become realities. In the course of its progressive development, it will yet have to undergo many a change, before the last chapter of its history can be written.

Interview with Karl Marx*

London, December 18 [1878]

IN A LITTLE VILLA at Haverstock Hill, the northwest portion of
London, lives Karl Marx, the cornerstone of modern socialism. He was
exiled from his native country—Germany—in 1844, for propagating
revolutionary theories. In 1848 he returned, but in a few months was
again exiled. He then took up his abode in Paris, but his political
theories procured his expulsion from that city in 1849, and since that
year his headquarters have been in London. His convictions have
caused him trouble from the beginning. Judging from the appearance
of his home, they certainly have not brought him affluence. Persistently during all these years he has advocated his views with an
earnestness which undoubtedly springs from a firm belief in them,
and, however much we may deprecate their propagation, we cannot
but respect to a certain extent the self-denial of the now venerable
exile.

Your correspondent has called upon him twice or thrice, and each
time the Doctor was found in his library, with a book in one hand and
a cigarette in the other. He must be over seventy years of age.[1] His
physique is well knit, massive, and erect. He has the head of a man
of intellect, and the features of a cultivated Jew. His hair and beard
are long, and iron-gray in color. His eyes are glittering black, shaded
by a pair of bushy eyebrows. To a stranger he shows extreme caution.
A foreigner can generally gain admission; but the ancient-looking

---

* Published in the *Chicago Tribune*, January 5, 1879, signed "H."
1. Marx was sixty.

German woman [Helene Demuth] who waits upon visitors has instructions to admit none who hail from the Fatherland, unless they
bring letters of introduction. Once into his library, however, and
having fixed his one eyeglass in the corner of his eye, in order to take
your intellectual breadth and depth, so to speak, he loses that self-
restraint, and unfolds to you a knowledge of men and things throughout the world apt to interest one. And his conversation does not run
in one groove, but is as varied as are the volumes upon his library
shelves. A man can generally be judged by the books he reads, and you
can form your own conclusions when I tell you a casual glance revealed Shakespeare, Dickens, Thackeray, Molière, Racine, Montaigne,
Bacon, Goethe, Voltaire, Paine; English, American, French blue
books; works political and philosophical in Russian, German, Spanish,
Italian, etc., etc. During my conversations I was struck with

His Intimacy with American Questions

which have been uppermost during the past twenty years. His knowledge of them, and the surprising accuracy with which he criticized
our national and state legislation, impressed upon my mind the fact that
he must have derived his information from inside sources. But, indeed,
this knoweldge is not confined to America, but is spread over the
face of Europe. When speaking of his hobby—socialism—he does not
indulge in those melodramatic flights generally attributed to him, but
dwells upon his utopian plans for "the emancipation of the human
race" with a gravity and an earnestness indicating a firm conviction
in the realization of his theories, if not in this century, at least in the
next.

Perhaps Dr. Karl Marx is better known in America as the author
of *Capital*, and the founder of the International Society, or at least its
most prominent pillar. In the interview which follows, you will see
what he says of this Society as it at present exists. However, in the
meantime I will give you a few extracts from the printed general rules
of

The International Society

published in 1871, by order of the General Council, from which you
can form an impartial judgment of its aims and ends. The Preamble
sets forth "that the emancipation of the working classes must be
conquered by the working classes themselves; that the struggle for the
emancipation of the working classes means not a struggle for class
privileges and monopolies, but for equal rights and duties, and the
abolition of all class rule; that the economical subjection of the man

of labor to the monopolizer of the means of labor—that is, the sources of life—lies at the bottom of servitude in all its forms, of all social misery, mental degradation, and political dependence; that all efforts aiming at" the universal emancipation of the working classes "have hitherto failed from want of solidarity between the manifold divisions of labor in each country," and the Preamble calls for "the immediate combination of the still-disconnected movements." It goes on to say that the International Association acknowledges "no rights without duties, no duties without rights"—thus making every member a worker. The Association was formed at London "to afford a central medium of communication and cooperation between the workingmen's societies in the different countries," aiming at the same end, namely: "the protection, advancement, and complete emancipation of the working classes." "Each member," the document further says, "of the International Association, on removing his domicile from one country to another, will receive the fraternal support of the associated working-men."

The Society Consists

of a General Congress, which meets annually; a general Council, which forms "an international agency between the different national and local groups of the Association, so that the workingmen in one country can be constantly informed of the movements of their class in every other country." This Council receives and acts upon applications of new branches or sections to join the International, decides differences arising between the sections, and, in fact, to use an American phrase, "runs the machine." The expenses of the General Council are defrayed by an annual contribution of an English penny per member. Then come the federal councils or committees, and local sections, in the various countries. The federal councils are bound to send one report at least every month to the General Council, and every three months a report on the administration and financial state of their respective branches. Whenever attacks against the International are published, the nearest branch or committee is bound to send at once a copy of such publication to the General Council. The formation of female branches among the working classes is recommended.

The General Council

comprises the following: R. Applegarth, M. T. Boon, Frederick Bradnick, G. H. Buttery, E. Delahaye, Eugène Dupont (on mission), William Hales, G. Harris, Hurliman, Jules Johannard, Harriet Law, Frederick Lessner, Lochner, Charles Longuet, C. Martin, Zevy Maurice,

Henry Mayo, George Milner, Charles Murray, Pfänder, John Roach, Ruhl Sadler, Cowell Stepney, Alfred Taylor, W. Townshend, E. Vaillant, John Weston. The corresponding secretaries for the various countries are: Leo Frankel, for Austria and Hungary; A. Herman, Belgium; T. Mottershead, Denmark; A. Serraillier, France; Karl Marx, Germany and Russia; Charles Rochat, Holland; J. P. McDonnell, Ireland; Frederick Engels, Italy and Spain; Walery Wroblewski, Poland; Hermann Jung, Switzerland; J. G. Eccarius, United States; Le Moussu, for French branches of United States.

During my visit to Dr. Marx I alluded to the platform given by J. C. Bancroft Davis in his official report of 1877 as the clearest and most concise exposition of socialism that I had seen. He said it was taken from the report of the socialist reunion at Gotha, Germany, in May, 1875. The translation was incorrect, he said, and he

Volunteered Correction

which I append as he dictated:

First: Universal, direct, and secret suffrage for all males over twenty years, for all elections, municipal and state.

Second: Direct legislation by the people. War and peace to be made by direct popular vote.

Third: Universal obligation to militia duty. No standing army.

Fourth: Abolition of all special legislation regarding press laws and public meetings.

Fifth: Legal remedies free of expense. Legal proceedings to be conducted by the people.

Sixth: Education to be by the state—general, obligatory, and free. Freedom of science and religion.

Seventh: All indirect taxes to be abolished. Money to be raised for state and municipal purposes by a direct progressive income tax.

Eighth: Freedom of combination among the working classes.

Ninth: The legal day of labor for men to be defined. The work of women to be limited, and that of children to be abolished.

Tenth: Sanitary laws for the protection of life and health of laborers, and regulation of their dwelling and places of labor, to be enforced by persons selected by them.

Eleventh: Suitable provision respecting prison labor.

In Mr. Bancroft Davis' report there is

A Twelfth Clause

the most important of all, which reads: "State aid and credit for industrial societies, under democratic direction." I asked the Doctor why he omitted this, and he replied:

"When the reunion took place at Gotha, in 1875, there existed a division among the Social Democrats. The one wing were partisans of Lassalle, the others those who had accepted in general the program of the International organization, and were called the Eisenach party. That twelfth point was not placed on the platform, but placed in the general introduction by way of concession to the Lassallians. Afterwards it was never spoken of. Mr. Davis does not say that it was placed in the program as a compromise having no particular significance, but gravely puts it in as one of the cardinal principles of the program."

"But," I said, "socialists generally look upon the transformation of the means of labor into the common property of society as the grand climax of the movement."

"Yes; we say that this will be the outcome of the movement, but it will be a question of time, of education, and the institution of higher social status."

"This platform," I remarked, "applies only to Germany and one or two other countries."

"Ah!" he returned, "if you draw your conclusions from nothing but this, you know nothing of the activity of the party. Many of its points have no significance outside of Germany. Spain, Russia, England, and America have platforms suited to their peculiar difficulties. The only similarity in them is the end to be attained."

"And that is the supremacy of labor?"

"That is the

Emancipation of Labor"

"Do European socialists look upon the movement in America as a serious one?"

"Yes: it is the natural outcome of the country's development. It has been said that the movement has been improved by foreigners. When labor movements became disagreeable in England, fifty years ago, the same thing was said; and that was long before socialism was spoken of. In America, since 1857 only has the labor movement become conspicuous. Then trade unions began to flourish; then trades assemblies were formed, in which the workers in different industries united; and after that came national labor unions. If you consider this chronological progress, you will see that socialism has sprung up in that country without the aid of foreigners, and was merely caused by the concentration of capital and the changed relations between the workmen and their employers."

"Now," asked your correspondent, "what has socialism done so far?"

"Two things," he returned. "Socialists have shown the general universal struggle between capital and labor—

The Cosmopolitan Chapter

in one word—and consequently tried to bring about an understanding between the workmen in the different countries, which became more necessary as the capitalists became more cosmopolitan in hiring labor, pitting foreign against native labor not only in America, but in England, France, and Germany. International relations sprang up at once between the workingmen in the different countries, showing that socialism was not merely a local, but an international problem, to be solved by the international action of workmen. The working classes move spontaneously, without knowing what the ends of the movement will be. The socialists invent no movement, but merely tell the workmen what its character and its ends will be."

"Which means the overthrowing of the present social system," I interrupted.

"This system of land and capital in the hands of employers, on the one hand," he continued, "and the mere working power in the hands of the laborers to sell as a commodity, we claim is merely a historical phase, which will pass away and give place to

A Higher Social Condition

We see everywhere a division of society. The antagonism of the two classes goes hand in hand with the development of the industrial resources of modern countries. From a socialistic standpoint the means already exist to revolutionize the present historical phase. Upon trade unions, in many countries, have been built political organizations. In America the need of an independent workingmen's party has been made manifest. They can no longer trust politicians. Rings and cliques have seized upon the legislatures, and politics has been made a trade. But America is not alone in this, only its people are more decisive than Europeans. Things come to the surface quicker. There is less cant and hypocrisy than there is on this side of the ocean."

I asked him to give me a reason for the rapid growth of the socialistic party in Germany, when he replied: "The present socialistic party came last. Theirs was not the utopian scheme which made headway in France and England. The German mind is given to theorizing, more than that of other peoples. From previous experience the Germans evolved something practical. This modern capitalistic system, you must recollect, is quite new in Germany in comparison to other states. Questions were raised which had become almost antiquated in

France and England, and political influences to which these states had yielded sprang into life when the working classes of Germany had become imbued with socialistic theories. Therefore, from the beginning almost of modern industrial development, they have formed an

Independent Political Party

They had their own representatives in the German parliament. There was no party to oppose the policy of the government, and this devolved upon them. To trace the course of the party would take a long time; but I may say this: that, if the middle classes of Germany were not the greatest cowards, distinct from the middle classes of America and England, all the political work against the government should have been done by them."

I asked him a question regarding the numerical strength of the Lassallians in the ranks of the Internationalists.

"The party of Lassalle," he replied, "does not exist. Of course there are some believers in our ranks, but the number is small. Lassalle anticipated our general principles. When he commenced to move after the reaction of 1848, he fancied that he could more successfully revive the movement by advocating cooperation of the workingmen in industrial enterprises. It was to stir them into activity. He looked upon this merely as a means to the real end of the movement. I have letters from him to this effect."

"You would call it his nostrum?"

"Exactly. He called upon Bismarck, told him what he designed, and Bismarck encouraged Lassalle's course at that time in every possible way."

"What was his object?"

"He wished to use the working classes as a set-off against the middle classes who instigated the troubles of 1848."

"It is said that you are the head and front of socialism, Doctor, and from your villa here pull the wires of all the associations, revolutions, etc., now going on. What do you say about it?"

The old gentleman smiled: "I know it.

It Is Very Absurd

yet it has a comic side. For two months previous to the attempt of Hoedel, Bismarck complained in his *North German Gazette* that I was in league with Father Beck, the leader of the Jesuit movement, and that we were keeping the socialist movement in such a condition that he could do nothing with it."

"But your International Society in London directs the movement?"

"The International Society has outlived its usefulness and exists no longer. It did exist and direct the movement; but the growth of socialism of late years has been so great that its existence has become unnecessary. Newspapers have been started in the various countries. These are interchanged. That is about the only connection the parties in the different countries have with one another. The International Society, in the first instance, was created to bring the workmen together, and show the advisability of effecting organization among their various nationalities. The interests of each party in the different countries have no similarity. This specter of the Internationalist leaders sitting at London is a mere invention. It is true that we dictated to foreign societies when the Internationalist organization was first accomplished. We were forced to exclude some sections in New York, among them one in which Madam Woodhull was conspicuous. That was in 1871. There are several American politicians—I will not name them—who wish to trade in the movement. They are well known to American socialists.

"You and your followers, Dr. Marx, have been credited with all sorts of incendiary speeches against religion. Of course you would like to see the whole system destroyed, root and branch."

"We know," he replied after a moment's hesitation, "that violent measures against religion are nonsense; but this is an opinion: as socialism grows,

Religion Will Disappear

Its disappearance must be done by social development, in which education must play a great part."

"The Reverend Joseph Cook, of Boston,—you know him—"

"We have heard of him; a very badly informed man upon the subject of socialism."

"In a lecture lately upon the subject, he said, 'Karl Marx is credited now with saying that, in the United States, and in Great Britain, and perhaps in France, a reform of labor will occur without bloody revolution, but that blood must be shed in Germany, and in Russia, and in Italy, and in Austria.'"

"No socialist," remarked the Doctor, smiling, "need predict that there will be a bloody revolution in Russia, Germany, Austria, and possibly in Italy if the Italians keep on in the policy they are now pursuing. The deeds of the French Revolution may be enacted again in those countries. That is apparent to any political student. But those revolutions will be made by the majority. No revolution can be made by a party,

But by a Nation"

"The reverend gentleman alluded to," I remarked, "gave an extract from a letter which he said you addressed to the Communists of Paris in 1871. Here it is: 'We are as yet but 3,000,000 at most. In twenty years we shall be 50,000,000—100,000,000 perhaps. Then the world will belong to us, for it will be not only Paris, Lyon, Marseilles, which will rise against odious capital, but Berlin, Munich, Dresden, London, Liverpool, Manchester, Brussels, St. Petersburg, New York— in short, the whole world. And before this new insurrection, such as history has not yet known, the past will disappear like a hideous nightmare; for the popular conflagration, kindled at a hundred points at once, will destroy even its memory!' Now, Doctor, I suppose you admit the authorship of that extract?"

"I never wrote a word of it. I never write

Such Melodramatic Nonsense

I am very careful what I do write. That was put in *Le Figaro*, over my signature, about that time. There were hundreds of the same kind of letters flying about then. I wrote to the London *Times* and declared they were forgeries; but if I denied everything that has been said and written of me, I would require a score of secretaries."

"But you have written in sympathy with the Paris Communists?"

"Certainly I have, in consideration of what was written of them in leading articles; but the correspondence from Paris in English papers is quite sufficient to refute the blunders propagated in editorials. The Commune killed only about sixty people; Marshal MacMahon and his slaughtering army killed over 60,000. There has never been a movement so slandered as that of the Commune."

"Well, then, to carry out the principles of socialism do its believers advocate assassination and bloodshed?"

"No great movement," Karl answered, "has ever been inaugurated

Without Bloodshed

The independence of America was won by bloodshed, Napoleon captured France through a bloody process, and he was overthrown by the same means. Italy, England, Germany, and every other country gives proof of this, and as for assassination," he went on to say, "it is not a new thing, I need scarcely say. Orsini tried to kill Napoleon; kings have killed more than anybody else; the Jesuits have killed; the Puritans killed at the time of Cromwell. These deeds were all done or attempted before socialism was born. Every attempt, however, now made upon a royal or state individual is attributed to socialism. The socialists would regret very much the death of the German Emperor at the present time. He is very useful where he is; and Bismarck has done more for the cause than any other statesman, by driving things to extremes."

I asked Dr. Marx

What He Thought of Bismarck

He replied that "Napoleon was considered a genius until he fell; then he was called a fool. Bismarck will follow in his wake. He began by building up a despotism under the plea of unification. His course has been plain to all. The last move is but an attempted imitation of a *coup d'état;* but it will fail. The socialists of Germany, as of France, protested against the war of 1870 as merely dynastic. They issued manifestoes foretelling the German people that, if they allowed the pretended war of defense to be turned into a war of conquest, they would be punished by the establishment of military despotism and the ruthless oppression of the productive masses. The Social-Democratic party in Germany, thereupon holding meetings and publishing manifestoes for an honorable peace with France, were at once prosecuted by the Prussian Government, and many of the leaders imprisoned. Still their deputies alone dared to protest, and very vigorously too, in the German Reichstag, against the forcible annexation of French provinces. However, Bismarck carried his policy by force, and people spoke of the genius of a Bismarck. The war was fought, and when he could make no more conquests, he was called upon for original ideas, and he has signally failed. The people began to lose faith in him. His popularity was on the wane. He needs money, and the state needs it. Under a sham constitution he has taxed the people for his military and unification plans until he can tax them no longer, and now he seeks to do it with no constitution at all. For the purpose of levying as he chooses, he has raised the ghost of socialism, and has done everything in his power

To Create an *Émeute*"

"You have continual advice from Berlin?"

"Yes," he said; "my friends keep me well advised. It is in a perfectly quiet state, and Bismarck is disappointed. He has expelled forty-eight prominent men—among them Deputies Hasselman and Fritsche and Rackow, Bauman, and Auer, of the *Freie Presse.* These men kept the workmen of Berlin quiet. Bismarck knew this. He also knew that there were 75,000 workmen in that city upon the verge of starvation.

Once those leaders were gone, he was confident that the mob would rise, and that would be the cue for a carnival of slaughter. The screws would then be put upon the whole German Empire; his petty theory of blood and iron would then have full sway, and taxation could be levied to any extent. So far no *émeute* has occurred, and he stands today confounded at the situation and the ridicule of all statesmen."

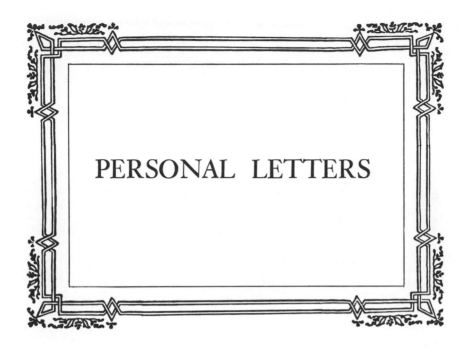

PERSONAL LETTERS

Marx's personal letters about the First International, most of which are given here in English translation for the first time, cover the period from the founding of the I.W.A. in 1864 to its dissolution in Europe in 1873. Up to August, 1870, the majority of these letters were written to Engels, Marx's most intimate friend and confidant. After Engels moved to London, on September 22, 1870, this correspondence ceased, since he and Marx saw each other almost daily. The other letters were written mostly to members of the International abroad, including those who lived in the United States, where the headquarters of the International was transferred in 1872.

This group of letters is in effect a running account of the work of the International, the problems it faced, the clashes of rival personalities and nationalistic biases, and the unceasing factional struggles, of which the most dramatic—and fateful—was the one with Michael Bakunin and his anarchists in Switzerland, France, Italy, and Spain. The correspondence also throws light on the rise and development of Europe's labor and socialist parties, notably the German Social Democratic party, in which Marx took a special interest. Marx's letters, often angry and indiscreet, blunt and bitterly partisan, but also not infrequently brilliant, are a rich and indispensable source for understanding, not only Marx himself, but also European—and, to a lesser extent, American[1]—radicalism in the latter half of the nineteenth century.

---

1. See Marx's letters to Sorge, and especially the long one to Bolte of November 23, 1871.

Dear Friend:

I was pleased to get, through your letter of September 28, a sign of life from the Rhenish workers.

B. Becker or M. Hess? I know them both; they are old members of the movement. Both are honest. Neither of them is capable of leading an important movement. Becker is essentially a weak man; Hess a confused head. So it is difficult to decide between the two. I also think it is quite a matter of indifference as to which of the two you choose, for in a decisive moment the necessary men will be found.

I have had an inquiry from Berlin, for example, whether I would accept the presidency.[1] I replied that it was impossible, because for the time being I am forbidden to settle in Prussia.[2] But I would consider it a *good party demonstration*, both against the Prussian Government and against the bourgeoisie, if the labor congress elected me, for I could then make a public reply why I could not accept the position. Specifically, such a step would be important for the following reasons: On September 28 there took place in London a big public labor meeting of English, German, French, and Italian workers. In addition, the Parisian workers had sent a special deputation, headed by Tolain, a workman who had been selected by the working class in Paris as a candidate for the *Corps législatif* at the last election.

At this meeting a committee was elected—an *international* committee for representing workingmen's interests—which is in direct

---

1. In September and October, 1864, Wilhelm Liebknecht wrote to Marx about becoming president of the General German Labor Association.

2. Marx wrote and then crossed out the following words: "In addition, if I were at the head, the government would immediately suppress the whole thing."

contact with the Paris workers and also contains leaders of the London workers. I was elected representative of the German workers (together with my old friend, the tailor Eccarius). Therefore, if I were to be appointed by the German Congress—even though I would have to decline the election now—the committee, and with it the London and Paris workers, would consider it a demonstration by the German workers. Next year the committee will call an international workers' congress in Brussels. Unfortunately I cannot participate personally, because I am still exiled from the model state of Belgium, as well as from France and Germany.

I will send you copies of the [*Communist*] *Manifesto* as soon as a *reliable* opportunity occurs.

You are getting this letter through one of my friends from Barmen [C. Siebel].

During all of the past year I have been sick (afflicted with carbuncles and furuncles). If not for that, my work on political economy —*Capital*—would have appeared already. I hope to finish it finally in a few months and deliver the bourgeoisie a theoretical blow from which it will never recover.

Farewell, and depend on it that the working class will always have a faithful champion in me.

Your

K. M.

---

*From letter to Frederick Engels (in Manchester)**
LONDON, NOVEMBER 4, 1864

Dear Frederick:

. . . Some time ago London workers sent an address about Poland to Paris workers and summoned them to common action in this matter.

The Parisians on their part sent over a deputation headed by a worker called Tolain, *the real workers' candidate at the last election in Paris,* a very nice fellow. (His companions too were quite nice lads.) A public meeting in St. Martin's Hall was summoned for September 28, 1864, by Odger (shoemaker, president of the Council here of all London trade unions and also especially of the Trade Unions Suffrage Agitation Society, which is connected with Bright), and Cremer, mason and secretary of the Masons' Union. (These two organized the big meeting of the trade unions in St. James's Hall for

* Based on a translation by I. Lasker for Progress Publishers, Moscow, 1955.

North America, under Bright, ditto the Garibaldi demonstrations.) A certain Le Lubez was sent to ask me if I would take part on behalf of the German workers, and especially if I would supply a German worker to speak at the meeting, etc. I provided them with Eccarius, who came off splendidly, and ditto was present myself as a mute figure on the platform. I knew that this time real "powers" were involved on both the London and Paris sides and therefore decided to waive my usual standing rule to decline any such invitations.

(Le Lubez is a young Frenchman, i.e., in his thirties, who has however grown up in Jersey and London, speaks English excellently, and is a very good intermediary between the French and English workers.) (Music teacher and French lessons.)

At the meeting, which was packed to *suffocation* (for there is now evidently a revival of the working classes taking place),[1] Major Wolff (Thurn-Taxis, Garibaldi's adjutant) represented the London Italian Working Men's Society. It was decided to found a "Working Men's International Association, the General Council of which should be in London and should act as an "intermediary" between the workers' societies in Germany, Italy, France, and England. Ditto that a General Working Men's Congress should be summoned in Belgium in 1865. A provisional committee was appointed at the meeting: Odger, Cremer, and many others, some of them old Chartists, old Owenites, etc., for England; Major Wolff, Fontana, and other Italians for Italy; Le Lubez, etc., for France; Eccarius and I for Germany. The committee was empowered to coopt as many members as it chose.

So far so good. I attended the first meeting of the committee. A subcommittee (including myself) was appointed to draft a declaration of principles and provisional statutes. Being unwell I was prevented from attending the meeting of the subcommittee and the meeting of the whole committee which followed.

In these two meetings which I had missed—that of the subcommittee and the subsequent one of the whole committee—the following had taken place:

Major Wolff had handed in the réglement [statutes] of the Italian Workers' Societies (which possess a central organization but, as later transpired, are really associated benefit societies) to be used for the new association. I saw the stuff later. It was evidently a compilation of Mazzini's, so you already know the spirit and phraseology in which the real question, the workers' question, was dealt with. Also how nationalities were shoved in.

In addition an old Owenite, Weston—now a manufacturer himself, a very amiable and worthy man—had drawn up a program of indescribable breadth and full of the most extreme confusion.

---

1. This parenthetical phrase was written in English.

The subsequent general committee meeting instructed the sub-committee to remodel Weston's program, ditto Wolff's regulations. Wolff himself left in order to attend the Congress of Italian Working Men's Associations in Naples and get them to decide on joining the London Central Association.

Another meeting of the subcommittee—which I again failed to attend, because I was informed of the rendezvous too late. At this a "declaration of principles" and a new version of Wolff's statutes were put forward by Le Lubez and accepted by the committee for submission to the general committee. The general committee met on October 18. As Eccarius had written me that delay would be dangerous I appeared, and was really frightened when I heard the worthy Le Lubez read out an appallingly wordy, badly written, and utterly undigested preamble, pretending to be a declaration of principles, in which Mazzini could be detected everywhere, the whole being crusted over with the vaguest tags of French socialism. Added to this the Italian statutes were taken over in the main, and these, apart from all their other faults, aim at something which is in fact utterly impossible, a sort of central government of the *European* working classes (with Mazzini in the background, of course). I put up a mild opposition and after a lot of talking backwards and forwards Eccarius proposed that the subcommittee should submit the thing to further "editing." On the other hand the "sentiments" contained in Lubez' declaration were voted for.

Two days later, on October 20, Cremer (for the English), Fontana (Italy), and Le Lubez assembled in my house. (Weston was prevented.) Hitherto I had never had the documents (those of Wolff and Le Lubez) in my hand so could not prepare anything, but was firmly determined that if possible not one single line of the stuff should be allowed to stand. In order to gain time I proposed that before we "edited" the preamble we should "discuss" the rules. This took place. It was an hour after midnight by the time the first of forty rules was agreed to. Cremer said (and this was what I had aimed at): We have nothing to put before the committee, which meets on October 25. We must postpone the meeting till November 1. But the subcommittee can get together on October 27 and attempt to reach a definite conclusion. This was agreed to and the "papers" "left behind" for my opinion.

I saw that it was impossible to make anything out of the stuff. In order to justify the extremely strange way in which I intended to present the "sentiment" already "voted for," I wrote an Address to the Working Classes (which was not in the original plan: a sort of review of the adventures of the working classes since 1845); on the pretext that everything material was included in this address and that we ought not to repeat the same things three times over, I altered the whole preamble, threw out the declaration of principles, and finally replaced the forty rules with ten. Insofar as international politics come into the address, I speak of countries, not of nationalities, and denounce Russia, not the lesser nations. My proposals were all accepted by the subcommittee. Only I was obliged to insert two phrases about "duty" and "right" into the preamble to the statutes, ditto "truth, morality, and justice," but these are placed in such a way that they can do no harm.

At the meeting of the general committee my address, etc., was agreed to with great enthusiasm (unanimously). The discussion on the method of printing, etc., takes place next Tuesday. Le Lubez has a copy of the address to translate into French and Fontana one to translate into Italian. (For a start there is a weekly paper called the *Bee-Hive*, edited by Potter the trade unionist, a sort of *Moniteur*.) I myself am to translate the stuff into German.

It was very difficult to frame the thing so that our view should appear in a form acceptable from the present standpoint of the workers' movement. In a few weeks the same people will be holding meetings for the franchise with Bright and Cobden. It will take time before the reawakened movement allows the old boldness of speech. It will be necessary to be *fortiter in re, suaviter in modo* [bold in matter, mild in manner]. As soon as the stuff is printed you will get it. . . .

Yours,

K. M.

From letter to Engels (in Manchester)
LONDON, NOVEMBER 14, 1864

Dear Engels:

. . . In a few days you will receive the [Inaugural] "Address" and the "Provisional Rules," etc. The thing was not quite as difficult as you think, because one always had to deal with "workers." The only literary man in the Association is the Englishman Peter Fox, author and agitator, one of the people from the *National Reformer* (atheism, but at the same time anti-Holyoake). I am sending you the very friendly note which he sent me about the "Address." Mazzini is rather disgusted that his people cosigned, *mais il faut faire bonne mine à mauvais jeu* [but it is necessary to put a good face on a bad play]. . . .

Yours,

K. M.

From letter to Ludwig Kugelmann (in Hanover)
LONDON, NOVEMBER 29, 1864

Honored Friend:
You will receive by post today six copies of the "Address of the International Working Men's Association," which was written by me. Would you be so kind as to transmit one to Madame Markheim (in Fulda) with my best regards? Also one to Herr Miquel.

The Association, or rather its committee, is important, because the chiefs of the London trade unions are in it, the same people who prepared the enormous reception for Garibaldi and through the mass meeting in St. James's Hall [March 26, 1863] prevented Palmerston's plan for a war with the United States. The chiefs of the Paris workers are also in contact. . . .

Faithfully yours,
K. M.

From letter to Lion Philips (in Zaltbommel)
LONDON, NOVEMBER 29, 1864

Dear Uncle:
I hope you are completely well, despite the abominable weather. Here everything is all right, except that, to the great alarm of the whole family, a very malevolent carbuncle under my left breast, which broke out earlier this month, tormented me for two or three weeks. Otherwise, everything has been all right. . . .

The enclosed "Address" was written by me. This is how it came about: In September, the workers of Paris sent a deputation to the workers of London for a demonstration in favor of Poland. On that occasion an international workers' committee was established. The matter is not without importance, because (1) in London, at the head of it are the same people who prepared the gigantic reception for Garibaldi and who, by the mass meeting, headed by Bright, in St. James's Hall, *prevented war with the United States.* In a word, they are real labor leaders of London, being, with one or two exceptions, workingmen themselves. (2) The Paris contingent is headed by M. Tolain (himself also a workingman) & Co.; that is, the same people who, in the last elections in Paris, were prevented only by an intrigue of Garnier-Pagès, Carnot, etc., from entering the *Corps Législatif* as the representatives of the workers there. And (3) on the Italian side, they are the representatives of four or five hundred workers' clubs, which held their general congress in Naples a few weeks ago and which the *Times* itself considered important enough to devote a couple of dozen columns to.[1]

Not in the "Address" itself, but in the introduction to the "Statutes," I had to insert a few useless figures of speech out of courtesy to the French and Italians, who always need grandiose phrases. . . .

Your devoted nephew,

K. M.

From letter to Joseph Weydemeyer (in St. Louis)
LONDON, NOVEMBER 29, 1864

Dear Weiwi:

. . . I am sending you by post four copies of the printed "Address," which was written by me. The newly established International Working Men's Committee, in whose name it was published, is not without significance. For its English members consist mostly of heads of the local trade unions, that is, the real labor kings of London, the same people who prepared the gigantic reception for Garibaldi and who, by the huge meeting in St. James's Hall (under Bright's chairmanship), prevented Palmerston from declaring war against the United States, which he was on the verge of doing. From the French side, the members are insignificant, but they are the direct organs of the leading "workers" in Paris. There is likewise contact with the Italian unions, which will soon hold their congress in Naples. Although for years I systematically turned down participation in all "organizations," etc., I accepted this time, because this was something in which it was possible to be effective. . . .

Yours,

K. M.

---

1. The London *Times*, November 4, 1864.

From letter to Engels (in Manchester)
LONDON, DECEMBER 2, 1864

Dear Fred:

... The worst thing about such agitation is that one is harassed as soon as one participates. For example, there was again the question of the Address to Lincoln, and again I had to draft the thing (which is much more difficult than a substantial work), so that the phraseology appropriate to this sort of writing should at least distinguish itself from the usual democratic vulgar-phraseology. Fortunately, Mr. Fox will draft the Polish address, occasioned by November 29, the anniversary of the Polish revolution of 1830.

In the committee, since the Address to Lincoln was to be handed to Adams, some of the Englishmen—because it was customary—wanted the deputation to be introduced by a member of Parliament. This lust was defeated by a majority of the English and the unanimous vote of the continental members, who declared that such old English customs ought to be abolished. On the other side, M. Le Lubez, as a real *crapaud* [toad], wanted the Address directed not to Lincoln but to the American people. I made him properly ridiculous and explained to the English that French democratic etiquette is not worth a farthing more than monarchical etiquette. . . .

Yours,

K. M.

From letter to Engels (in Manchester)
LONDON, DECEMBER 10, 1864

Dear Fred:

... Today's *Miner and Workman's Advocate*—the gazette of the mine workers in England and Wales—carries my Address. The Bricklayers of London (over 3,000 men) declared their accession to the International—fellows who had *never* hitherto joined any movement.

Last Tuesday we had a subcommittee session, where Mr. Peter Fox (his real name is P. Fox André) submitted to us an address on Poland. (Things of this kind are always treated in a subcommittee prior to consideration by the General Council). The thing is not badly written, and Fox had made the effort of applying at least a tincture of "classes," a concept otherwise alien to him. His actual profession is foreign policy, and he has had dealings with the working class as such only as a propagandist for atheism.

Easy though it is to put through anything rational among the English workers, one must nevertheless be on guard the moment literati, bourgeois, or half-literati participate in the movement. Fox, like his friend Beesly (professor of Political Economy at the University of London, he presided at the founding meeting in St. Martin's Hall) and other "democrats," have—in contrast to what they, not without reason, call the English aristocratic tradition and, as its continuation, the English democratic tradition of 1791–92—a fanatical "love" for France, which, so far as foreign policy is concerned, they extend not only to Napoleon I but also even to Boustrapa [Napoleon III]. Well! Mr. Fox, not content to tell the Poles in his address (which, for the rest, is to appear, not as an address of the International as a whole, but only as an address of the English portion on the Polish question, under the sanction of the International as a whole) what is true—namely, that in regard to the Poles the French nation has a better tradition than the English one—winds up his address mainly consoling the Poles that the English working classes have developed a passion of friendship for the French democrats. I opposed this, unfolding an irrefutable tableau of the constant betrayal of the Poles by the French, from Louis XV to Bonaparte III. At the same time I called attention to what was thoroughly *improper*—namely, that the Anglo-French alliance should be shown as the "core" of the International Association only in a democratic edition. In short, Fox's address was adopted by the sub-committee on condition that he alter the ending in accord with my proposals. Jung, the Swiss secretary (from French Switzerland), stated that, as a minority member, he would propose to the General Council that it reject the address as altogether "bourgeois."

Our Major Wolff has been imprisoned by the Piedmontese in the fortress Alexandria for the time being.

Louis Blanc wrote to the General Secretary, Cremer, that he approves the "Address," and regrets not having been able to attend the meeting in St. Martin's Hall, etc. Altogether, his letter is aimed at nothing else than to be invited as an honorary member. Suspecting that attempts of this sort would be made, I had fortunately already put through the bylaw providing that nobody (except workers' societies) ought to be *invited*, and that no person could be an honorary member.

Greetings.

Yours,

K. M.

Letter written in English to Hermann Jung (in London) *
MANCHESTER, ca. JANUARY 8, 1865

My Dear Jung:

I was quite indignant when I read in *Bee-Hive* and *Miner* this week what had happened at our last committee meeting:

"It was unanimously decided to invite Messrs. Beesly, Grossmith, Beales, and Harrison for the soirée that was to take place on the sixteenth."[1]

I do not mention the complete anachronism, namely, that no such decision had been made at the session of last Tuesday.

What I am objecting to is the absolute untruth that Mr. Grossmith has been invited.

This Grossmith, although he rarely if ever attends our sessions, figures in all our addresses as a member of our committee.

How can our committee invite a *member of our committee* to a soirée *arranged by our committee?* Is this perhaps a sort of premium won for regular absences from our weekly meetings?

Since I shall not be able to return to London before the end of next week, I would be obliged to you if at next Tuesday's meeting [January 10] you would ask who is the author of the report in *Bee-Hive* and *Miner*.

Who empowered this author to make our committee, *without its knowledge,* a mouthpiece for the glorification of Mr. Grossmith?

You will understand without further ado how important it is to nip in the bud any attempt to transform our committee into a tool of local ambitions or any other kind of intrigues.

I would be grateful to you if you would let me know at the above address[2]—assuming that you have raised the objection—what answer you received.[3]

Greetings and fraternity.

K. MARX

---

* From a German translation.
1. A celebration of the founding of the International, held in London's Cambridge Hall on January 16, 1865.
2. Marx was staying with Engels at 58 Dover Street, Manchester.
3. On January 11, 1865, Jung informed Marx that his protest was read at the January 10 meeting and that the author of the report, William R. Cremer, saw his mistake and Grossmith's name was withdrawn from the protocol.

Draft of letter to Johann Baptist von Schweitzer (*in Berlin*)
LONDON, JANUARY 16, 1865

Sir:

Your *Social-Demokrat*, despite its short existence, has already printed its second attack on the International Association. I am only awaiting the third, publicly to dissolve, together with my friends, all contact with your paper. In such a declaration I will be forced to discuss "critically" certain things hitherto not brought to the fore out of party considerations, which will not please certain gentlemen. The first attack on the International Association was contained in a silly passage from B. Becker's *Botschaft*.[1] I am not holding you responsible for that, precisely because it is a *Botschaft* [message] and you unfortunately have an official relationship to the General German Workers *Association* (which is very much to be distinguished from working class).

It is different with Moses Hoses' insolently mendacious chatter,[2] which, out of consideration for me and my friends, you should *under no circumstances* have accepted, and which you could have accepted only with the *intention of provoking me.*

In regard to Moses' bungling piece itself, I shall, after receiving certain information from Paris, make a public statement about it. In regard to your own acceptance of the disgraceful article, I beg you to let me know whether I am to consider it as a declaration of war by the *Social-Demokrat*.

Your obedient servant,

K. MARX

Letter to Engels (*in Manchester*)
LONDON, JANUARY 25, 1865

Dear Frederick:

Enclosed letters: (1) from Weydemeyer, (2) from Schily, (3) from Liebknecht. I must have all three back. (4) from Schweitzer, and (5) a scrap about Vogt, which I also want back.

1. *"Botschaft des Präsidenten"* ["Message of the President"], *Social-Demokrat*, December 30, 1864.
2. Moses Hess, "Workingmen's Associations," *Social-Demokrat*, January 13, 1865.

For an understanding of letters (2) and (3) and (4), the following: I don't know whether you get the *Social-Demokrat* (or whether you subscribe to it). (If neither is the case, then Bender, who ordered six issues for resale, can always send you one from here.)

In the *Social-Demokrat* [January 13, 1865] there was a report by the jackass Moses Hess that *we* approached *L'Association* (journal of the Paris Associations) to have our [Inaugural] Address translated (whereas, on the contrary, it was Massel who *proposed* this to Schily) and to join the Association; but that they rejected it, because *we* had originally turned to Tolain, etc., who are Plon-Plonists.[1] Tolain himself has admitted this, etc.

I found this scrap of paper the day after my return from Manchester. So I wrote a furious letter to Paris and Berlin.[2] From Schily's and Schweitzer's letters, it develops that the whole thing is due to the asininity (perhaps conjugated with malice) of Hess and the asininity *toute pure* [pure and simple] of Liebknecht.

The matter caused a great scandal in the local Committee here. Le Lubez, entirely on Tolain's side, declared the whole thing to be a slander, since fellows like Horn (Einhorn, a rabbi) and that bag of platitudes, Jules Simon (of *La Liberté*[3]), are in the committee of *L'Association.* Nevertheless, at my suggestion, it was resolved not to send the 500 membership cards to Paris until Schily has given a further report from there.

The Association is progressing splendidly here. At its soirée, which I did not attend, there were about 1,200 persons (there would have been three times more if the hall had been large enough), which brought to our very depleted exchequer approximately £15.

We received application for admission from Geneva, as well as from different parts of England.

In the course of February there will be a meeting for the Poles (particularly to collect money for the *new* emigration, with Lord Townshend as chairman), organized by the (English) Polish League, the local Polish association, and our own Association.[4]

What do you say to Lassalle's "testament," as described by Liebknecht? Was it not his own Sickingen[5] who wanted to force Charles V "to place himself at the head of the movement?"

At the stormy demand of Schweitzer (and also to make up for having scolded him, instead of Liebknecht, for the blunder in *Social-*

---

1. Marx's nickname for Napoleon III was Plon-Plon.
2. See Marx's letter to Johann Baptist von Schweitzer, January 16, 1865.
3. *La Liberté de Penser*, a Paris journal published 1848–51.
4. The meeting for Poland took place on March 1, 1865.
5. Ferdinand Lassalle was the author of a "historical tragedy," *Franz von Sickingen* (Berlin, 1859), in which Emperor Charles V played a role.

Demokrat), I sent him yesterday an article on Proudhon.[6] You will find that in it a few very bitter blows, presumably applying to Proudhon, fall on the hump of and are meant for our "Achilles." [Lassalle].

Apropos. Each secretary of our Association will receive next week a packet of cards of membership (in the Association, of course, and not in the "committees"), which he is to dispose of (one shilling for annual subscription, a penny for the card). You must dispose of some of them in Manchester. There will not be many. But write me how many I ought to send for this purpose. It is in fact one of the ways and means of the Association.

My compliments to Mrs. Burns. Will she perhaps become a member? Ladies are admitted.

Yours truly,

K. M.

From letter to Engels (*in Manchester*)
LONDON, FEBRUARY 1, 1865

Dear Frederick:

... You must excuse the English scraps in my letter on the ground that yesterday's sitting of the General Council lasted until one o'clock ("quaff" and "smoke" are *excluded* from these "sittings"). First came the reply from Lincoln,[1] which you will perhaps see tomorrow in the *Times,* and in any case in the *Daily News* and the *Star.*[2] While the old man's reply, published in yesterday's *Evening Star,* to the London Emancipation Society (of which such luminaries as Sir Charles Lyell and the "world historical" person, alias "K. Blind," are members) dismissed those fellows quite dryly with a couple of formal phrases, as he had done in his previous answer to the Manchester branch of the Emancipation Society—his letter to us is, in truth, all one could expect, particularly the naïve assurance that the United States cannot enter directly into "propaganda." At any rate, it is so far the only reply on the part of the old man that is more than a strictly formal one.

6. Marx's article, sent to Schweitzer in the form of a letter on January 24, 1865, was published in *Der Social-Demokrat* February 1, 3, and 5, 1865.

1. The Address to Abraham Lincoln was presented to Ambassador Charles Francis Adams on January 28, 1865, and the Ambassador replied on that day.
2. The London *Times* and the *Express* published Adams' reply February 6, 1865.

Second, a deputy who is connected with the Poles (*aristocrats*) in the "Literary Society," was present, carrying from the latter the assurance that they are *democrats,* and that every Pole is now a democrat, since, on account of the aristocracy being too thoroughly melted together, it would be crazy not to see that a restoration of Poland without a peasant insurrection is impossible. Whether or not these fellows believe what they say, it seems that the last lesson did not strike them in vain.[3]

Third, there were statements from different trade unions about their joining. The same from a society in Brussels, which promises to establish branches throughout Belgium.

Furthermore, I had to hand in an issue of the *Daily St. Louis Press*[4] which arrived yesterday, wherein there is a leading article about our "Address to the Workingmen" and an excerpt from it obviously arranged by Weydemeyer.

But now the strangest thing.

Cremer, our honorary general secretary, received a written invitation, in addition to a private visit, from a provisional committee which is meeting privately in a London tavern next Monday. Aim: a mass meeting for manhood suffrage. President: Richard Cobden!

The joke is this: The fellows, as Ernest Jones has already informed us, have failed entirely in Manchester. Hence they adopted a broader platform, wherein, in place of manhood suffrage, registration "for paying poor rate" now figures. So it says in the printed Circular we received. But since, after various indications made it clear to them that nothing less than manhood suffrage could bring about any co-operation whatever on the part of the working-class, they have declared themselves in favor of the latter. A large demonstration in London would, "on the other hand," bring about similar ones in the provinces, so write the provincials, who have "already" perceived that they are incapable of setting the ball agoing.

The next order of business was this: Should our Association, that is, the Council, accede to the wish of the fellows (among them the old sham city agitators like Sam Morley, etc.) and send a few deputies to their provisional committee to observe the transactions as "observers?" Second, should we give these fellows our *direct* support after they have obligated themselves to accept the slogan of manhood suffrage and called a public meeting for this purpose? For the latter is as decisive for these fellows as it was in the American affair. Without the trade unions no mass meeting is possible, and without us the trade

---

3. The "lesson" was the Polish insurrection of 1863–64.
4. The *St.-Louis Daily Press,* a labor paper which appeared from 1864.

unions are not to be had. This is also the reason why the gentlemen are turning to us.

The opinions were *very* divided, to which Bright's latest imbecility in Birmingham contributed greatly.[5]

At my motion, it was resolved: (1) to send deputies (in my proposal I excluded foreigners; but Eccarius and Le Lubez were elected as "Englishmen" and *silent* witnesses), but only as mere "observers"; (2) so far as the meeting is concerned, to act with them, if, *first,* manhood suffrage is directly and publicly proclaimed in the program, and *second,* if the men *chosen by us* enter into the definitive committee, so they can keep an eye on the fellows and, as I have made it clear to all, compromise them in the event of any deliberate new treason. I am writing to E. Jones about the matter today.

Yours,

K. M.

From letter to Engels (in Manchester)
LONDON, FEBRUARY 3, 1865

Dear Frederick:

. . . "Once again," in No. 16 of the *Social-Demokrat,* which carries my letter on Proudhon, interlarded with typos, Moses Hess denounces the International Association[1] "already" for the second time. Yesterday I wrote a furious letter to Liebknecht about it and told him that this is *absolutely the last* warning; that I do not give a farthing for a "good will" that does the work of ill will; that I cannot properly explain to the local members of the "International Committee" that such things are done with *bonne foi* [good will] out of pure stupidity; that the lousy sheet continues its fulsome praise of Lassalle, even though it is now known what treason he contemplated;[2] and that it cravenly flirts with Bismarck while it has the impudence to have the Plon-Plonist Hess accuse us here of Plon-Plonism, etc. . . .

Yours,

K. M.

---

5. Marx to Engels January 30, 1865: "Mr. Bright has again spoiled everything for himself here in London among the workers with his speech against the application of the ten-hour bill to the Birmingham trades. Such a bourgeois is really incorrigible. And the fellow did that at a moment when he wants to defeat the oligarchs through the workers!"

1. "The International Working Men's Association," February 1, 1865.
2. On January 20, 1865, Liebknecht wrote to Marx informing him that Ferdinand Lassalle had been secretly negotiating with Bismarck.

From letter to Engels (*in Manchester*)
LONDON, FEBRUARY 10, 1865

Dear Frederick:

. . . To Moses' great pain, the International Association has attracted great attention among the workers in Paris. As a result of Moses' stupidity, Tolain withdrew (we did *not* accept his resignation officially). H. Lefort (editor of *Avenir*,[1] etc.), who is also a member of the editorial committee of *L'Association*, has, at his request, received an appointment as literary defender (attorney general) of *our* Association in Paris. The latter has already been attacked (one paragraph in the Statutes) by Horn. This Jew Horn will soon notice that there are other Germans besides Moses Hess. Fribourg has opened a *bureau de renseignement* [information office] for us; cards of membership were sent to him yesterday. . . .

Greetings.

Yours,
K. M.

Letter to Victor Le Lubez (*in London*)
LONDON, FEBRUARY 15, 1865

My Dear Le Lubez:

The success of our Association warns us to be careful. In my opinion, the admission of Mr. Beales to our Council would spoil the whole thing.[1] I consider him an honest and well-meaning man; nevertheless, he is a bourgeois politician, and cannot be anything else. He is weak, mediocre, and ambitious. He wants to run for Parliament from Marylebone in the next election. This fact alone should exclude him from admission to our Council. We ought not to be the springboard for petty parliamentary ambitions.

You may be sure that with the admission of Beales, *le ton cordial, sincère, et franc* [the cordial, sincere, and frank tone] which characterizes our present discussions would disappear and be replaced by *word mongering*. Beales would be followed by Taylor, that unbearable clown and lickspittle.

---

1. *L'Avenir National,* a democratic daily in Paris.

1. See Marx's letter to Engels, February 25, 1865.

In the eyes of the public, the admission of Beales would give our Association an entirely different character: We would become one of the numerous societies he honors with his patronage. Wherever he sets his foot, others of his class would follow, and our hitherto successful efforts to free the English workers' movement from any middle-class or aristocratic tutelage would be in vain.

I know beforehand that the questions, primarily of a social nature, which would come up after Beales's admission would force him to withdraw. We will have to prepare manifestoes on the land question, etc., which he cannot sign. Is it not much better not to admit him at all, rather than give him a chance later to break away from us?

I know that after the foolish step by Mr. Dell there will be some difficulties with this candidacy.

I assume that the whole matter could be settled quietly by discussions with the leading English members of the Council before it is laid before the committee.

Fraternally yours,

K. MARX

Apropos. For all his enthusiasm for Poland, Mr. Beales has hitherto not done anything more than, under the leadership of [Lord Townshend], confuse all announcements about Poland. Yesterday he again did the same thing out of the same motives.

From letter to Ludwig Kugelmann (in Hanover)
LONDON, FEBRUARY 23, 1865

Honored Friend:

. . . I prefer a hundred times my agitation here through the International Association. Its influence on the English proletariat is direct and of the greatest importance. We are now making a stir over the General Suffrage Question, which of course has an *entirely different significance* from what it has in Prussia.

On the whole, the progress of the Association is beyond all expectations, here, in Paris, in Belgium, Switzerland, and Italy. Only in Germany, of course, Lassalle's successors oppose me, (1) because they are madly afraid of losing their importance, and (2) because they know of my avowed opposition to what the Germans call "*Realpolitik*" (it is this sort of "reality" that puts Germany so far behind all civilized countries).

Since every person who redeems a card for one shilling can become a member of the Association; since the French have chosen this form of individual membership (ditto the Belgians), because the law prohibits them from joining us as an "Association"; since the same is true in Germany—I have decided to ask my friends here and those in Germany to establish small societies, regardless of the number of members in each locality, each member to redeem an English card of membership. Since the English Association is *public*, nothing stands in the way of this procedure, not even in France. I would be pleased if you too in your immediate circle would establish contact with London in this way . . .

Yours,

K. M.

From letter to Engels (in Manchester)
LONDON, FEBRUARY 25, 1865

Dear Fred:

. . . The International Association succeeded in having the committee for the establishment of the new Reform League so constituted as to have the *whole leadership* in our hands.[1] I have written the details to E. Jones.

In Paris such a split broke out among our own plenipotentiaries that we sent Le Lubez there for explanation and arbitration. In his credentials, Schily was added as his adjunct, and I sent Schily private instructions. We could have issued 20,000 [membership] cards in Paris, but since each group accused the other of being in the service of Plon-Plon, the issuance of cards had to be suspended. Under this military despotism there is, naturally, a great deal of mutual suspicion (it seems to me that this time both sides do themselves an injustice), and the fellows are incapable of coming to agreement and understanding either through meetings or through the press. There is an additional circumstance: The workers seem to take pride in *excluding* every literary man, etc., which is folly, since they need the latter in the press, but excusable, owing to the continual treason of the literary men. On the other hand, the latter suspect every workers' movement which is in opposition to them.

(Speaking of these "literary men" reminds me that local workers, in the transformation of the *Bee-Hive*, which is to take place in three

---

1. The Reform League was founded, under the auspices of the International, at a meeting in London's St. Martin's Hall on February 23, 1865.

PERSONAL LETTERS

months, will want to make me the editor and have already so informed me. However, I will think it over on all twenty-four sides before I undertake one step or the other.)

So you have in Paris, on the one side, Lefort (a literary man, who is also rich, hence a "bourgeois," but of the purest reputation and, so far as *la belle France* is concerned, the actual founder of our Association); and on the other, Tolain, Fribourg, Limousin, etc., who are workers. Well, I shall report the outcome to you. At any rate, I am informed by an acquaintance, Wolff, who has just returned from Paris, that the participation in the International there is intense. The *Débats*,[2] too, has mixed into the affair.

In regard to the London unions, etc., we get new affiliations daily, so that gradually we are becoming a power.

But here also the difficulties begin. Already, Mr. Beales (the registered barrister from Middlesex, one of the most popular men in London now, president of the Polish League, co-founder of the Reform League, in fact the go-between of Workingman and Middle Class, in addition honest and well meaning) has had himself proposed as a member of our Council. The occasion came about when we worked with him on a subcommittee preparing the Polish meeting for next Wednesday (under Marquis Townshend). It was most awkward for me. Of course I could have *violently* prevented the thing, since several continentals would have voted with me. But I did not like any such division. Hence through private letters to the principal English members I arranged that Beales's proposer would not bring forth his motion again. The "official" reasons were given: (1) that in the next parliamentary elections Beales will stand for Marylebone and that our Association must by all means avoid any semblance of serving the interests of any parliamentary ambition; (2) that Beales and ourselves would mutually work better if we sailed on different vessels. For the rest, other parliamentarians, such as Taylor, etc. (fellows who hang around Mazzini), let us know in passing that the time for a Polish meeting "is not opportune." I replied through our Council that the Working Class has its own Foreign Policy, which cares not at all about what the middle class considers opportune. They always consider it opportune to goad on the Poles at the beginning of a new outbreak, betray them during its progress by their diplomacy, and desert them when Russia has thrown them down. In fact, the meeting is above all for the purpose of financial support. Should the poor émigrés (this time mostly workingmen and peasants and hence in no way protected by Prince Zamoyski & Co.) starve to death because the English middle

---

2. *Journal des Débats Politiques et Littéraires*, a Paris daily.

class does not consider it opportune just now even to mention the name of Poland?

Enclosed an excerpt from Herr Blind in the *Morning Star*. Mazzini, who had declared to Fontana that Blind was a liar, was nevertheless furious that *his* local Italian workers' association[3] had sent my "Address" in Italian into the world without omitting passages—for example, those on the middle class—whose omission Mr. Mazzini had expressly demanded.

Yours,

K. M.

From letter to Engels (*in Manchester*)
LONDON, MARCH 13, 1865

Dear Engels:

. . . Apart from the incessant furuncles, I have been hellishly harassed in recent days—last night, for example, I did not get to bed until four in the morning. Next to the work on my book [*Capital*], the International Association takes an enormous amount of my time, since I am in fact the head of the thing. And what a loss of time! (Particularly now, with all the French affairs, the elections, etc.). Take, for example, the French shit:

February 28. Tolain and Fribourg arrive from Paris. Meeting of the Central Council, to which they report and fight with Le Lubez until midnight. Then a night session in Bolleter's pub, where I had to sign some 200 membership cards. (I have now changed this idiocy by having our handwriting engraved in the plate, and only the General Secretary signs by hand. Still, the 1,000 existing cards, from the old edition, must be signed in the old style).

March 1. Polish meeting.[1]

March 4. Meeting of the subcommittee on the French question, lasting until one o'clock in the morning.

March 6. Meeting of the subcommitee on ditto, lasting until one o'clock in the morning.

March 7. Meeting of the Central Council, until midnight . . .

---

3. The *Associazione di Mutuo Progresso* was founded by Italian workers in London in June, 1864. Under Mazzini's influence the Association's honorary president was Giuseppe Garibaldi. In January, 1865, the Association joined the International.

---

1. At St. Martin's Hall, on the anniversary of the Polish uprising of 1863–64.

(This session of March 7, where Le Lubez was thrown into a complete fit, was most distressing and stormy, and created the impression, especially on the English, that the Frenchmen really stand in need of a Bonaparte.) . . .

Well, *mon cher, que faire?* One has to say B the moment one says A.

From letter to Engels (in Manchester)
LONDON, APRIL 11, 1865

Dear Fred:

. . . This evening I again attended a meeting of the International, for the first time in three weeks. While I was absent, a revolution took place. Le Lubez and Denoual resigned from the Association; Dupont was appointed French secretary. As a result of Le Lubez's intrigues and particularly those of Major Wolff, who is a tool in Mazzini's hands, the Italian delegates Lama and Fontana also resigned. Pretext: Lefort (who in the meantime had announced his resignation in the journal *L'Association*) must retain his post as defender general [of the International] in the Paris press. The Italian Working Men's Club did not resign from the Association, but no longer has any representative in the Council. In the meantime I will lay counter mines against Mazzini in Florence through Bakunin. The English Shoemakers' Union—5,000 men strong—joined the Association during my absence.

How is the cotton crisis? I want information on that point.

In all haste.

Yours,

K. M.

Draft in French of letter to Léon Fontaine (in Brussels)
LONDON, APRIL 15, 1865

Dear Citizen:

In its last session (see enclosure), the Central Council appointed an interim secretary for Belgium in place of Citizen Le Lubez, whose resignation as a member of the Council was accepted unanimously. Citizen Dupont replaces him as secretary for France.

If you wish, I will give you later a short report on the unpleasant incidents that had taken place in the Central Council. In my view, the driving force is a person foreign to our Council, known as an Italian patriot [Mazzini], but an archenemy of the rights of the proletariat, without which republicanism would be merely a new form of bourgeois despotism. Nevertheless, he has gone so far as to demand that all passages aimed against the bourgeoisie be stricken from the Italian translation of the "Address," as one person—one of his blindest tools [Fontana]—has admitted to me.

Despite such regrettable incidents and the more or less voluntary withdrawal of a few people, our Association marches on victoriously. Founded only a few months ago, today it has practically 12,000 members in England alone.

The Central Council would be much obliged to you if you would send me *an official report on the present state of our Association in Belgium.*

In your correspondence, please separate the official letters, which go to the archives of the Central Council, from the private communications which you may be so kind as to send me.

My address is:

A. Williams, Esq.,[1] 1 Modena Villa, Maitland Park, Haverstock Hill, N. W. London.

Greetings and fraternity,

KARL MARX

Letter to Hermann Jung (in London)
LONDON, APRIL 25, 1865

Dear Jung:

Monday evening [May 1] (about eight o'clock, or later, if that hour is too early for you), I am inviting you to a small supper in my house, to meet Ernest Jones. In addition to you, only Odger, Cremer, and P. Fox. If I had invited more guests, there would have been too many for the purpose of that evening. This, *entre nous* [between us].

I have just written to Cremer that he immediately fill out the authorization for P. Vinçard, which Dupont must transmit to Vinçard right away. It would be best if Dupont would expedite the matter *direct*, without the roundabout way via Fribourg.

---

1. Marx often used the cover name A. Williams when there was danger of police interception of correspondence.

Vinçard has already written to Le Lubez that he would not accept if he did not receive the mandate direct from London.[1] Le Lubez had promised, in a letter to Fribourg, to report this to the Central Council, but had not done so. Later, I have reason to believe, Fribourg "forgot" the thing deliberately.

More of what happened in Paris (and was, in general, good) I will report to you orally; in the meantime, keep Dupont informed. *Salute and fraternity.*

K. MARX

From letter to Engels (in Manchester)
LONDON, MAY 1, 1865

Dear Fred!

You must excuse me that I am writing you only today and that I broke my last promise to you. This did not happen because "it is far too pleasant to break one's word," but because I am actually overworked, as the work on my book [*Capital*], on the one hand, and the International Association, on the other, take up an extraordinary amount of time. . . .

The great success of the International Association is this:

The Reform League is our work. The workingmen on the inner Committee of Twelve (six middle-class men and six workingmen) are all members of our Council (including Eccarius). We have baffled all attempts of the middle class to mislead the working class. The movement in the provinces is this time wholly dependent on that of London. Ernest Jones, for example, had despaired till we set the ball agoing. If we succeed in reelectrifying the political movement of the English working class, our Association, without making any fuss, will have done more for the working class of Europe than has been possible in any other way. And there is every prospect for success. . . .

Greetings.

Yours,
K. M.

---

1. At its session of March 7, 1865, the Central Council voted in favor of Pierre Vinçard, a labor journalist, as leader of the Paris Section. Vinçard, however, declined on April 30.

Founders of the First International. (Top, left) Benjamin Lucraft (1809-1897), a furniture maker. (Top, right) Eugène Dupont (c. 1831-1888), a leading French member of the International in London. (Center) Johann Georg Eccarius (1818-1889), a tailor. (Bottom, left) Hermann Jung (1830-1901), a watchmaker. (Bottom, right) Friedrich Lessner (1825-1910), a tailor.

The founding of the International Working Men's Association, the First International, St. Martin's Hall, London, September 28, 1864. Marx is near the speaker's chair.

INTERNATIONAL
WORKING MEN'S
ASSOCIATION.

CENTRAL COUNCIL, 18 GREEK STREET, LONDON, W.

FOUNDED ON 28th SEPTEMBER, 1864, AT A

PUBLIC MEETING held at St. MARTIN'S HALL, London.

The Address and Statutes issued by the Provisional Central Council fully explain the Association's objects and aspirations, which, however, may be summed up in a few words. It aims at the protection, advancement, and complete emancipation, economical and political, of the Working Classes. As a means to this great end it will promote the establishment of solidarity between the manifold divisions of labour in EACH COUNTRY, and the co-operation of the Working Classes of DIFFERENT COUNTRIES.

Its Organization, with a Central Medium at London, and numerous affiliated Branches in Europe and America, will assist in uniting the Working Classes of all Countries in a perpetual bond of fraternal co-operation. Annual Congresses of Delegates, elected by the affiliated Working Men themselves, will create for the Working Classes a public and powerful European representation.

The *Executive Council on behalf of the Operative Bricklayers Society* assembled at the *25 Hatfield Street Blackfriars London* having subscribed to the principles, and applied to enter the fraternal bond, are hereby admitted as an affiliated Branch of the Association.

Dated the *21th* of *February* 1865

G. ODGER, *President of Council*
G. W. WHEELER, *Honorary Treasurer.*

E. DUPONT, *Corresponding Sec. for France.*
K. MARX, do. Germany.
E. HOLTORP, do. Poland.

H. IUNG *Corresponding Sec. for Switzerland.*
L. LEWIS. do. America.

W. R. CREMER, *Honorary General Secretary.*

Application from the Operative Bricklayers Society, February 21, 1865, for affiliation with the First International.

INTERNATIONAL
Working Men's Association

Assoc^n Intern^le des Ouvriers . Assoc^le Intern^le Operai
Intern^l Arbeiter Assoc^n

CARD OF MEMBERSHIP.

This is to Certify that Cit. H. Jung .... was admitted

a Member of the above Association *in September* *1864*

and paid as his Annual Subscription *for the year 1869 0. 2. 0*

R. Shaw   Corresponding Secretary for America.

Jesmond's Cor. Sec. for Belgium. | *Jules Johannard* .... Italy.
Eugene Dupont .. France. | *Anthony Zabicki* ...... Poland.
Karl Marx .. Germany. | *H. Jung* .. Switzerland.
Abell Steffeg .. Treasurer. | *J. George Eccarius* Sec^e Genl Council.

Rückseite.

The emancipation of the working classes must be accomplished by the working classes themselves, the struggle for their emancipation means a struggle for equal rights & duties and the abolition of all class rule. The economical subjection of the man of labour to the monopoliser of the means of labour lies at the bottom of servitude in all its forms of social misery, mental degradation, and political dependence. The economical emancipation of the working classes is therefore the great end to which every political movement ought to be subordinate as a means. All efforts aiming at that great end have hitherto failed from the want of solidarity between the manifold divisions of labour in each country and from the absence of a fraternal bond of union between the working classes of different countries. The emancipation of labour is neither a local nor a national, but a social problem embracing all countries in which modern society exists, depending for its solution on the concurrence practical and theoretical of the most advanced countries.

L'émancipation des travailleurs doit être l'œuvre des travailleurs eux mêmes, les efforts des travailleurs pour conquérir leur émancipation ne tendent qu'à établir pour tous des droits et des devoirs égaux et à anéantir la domination de toute classe. L'assujettissement économique du travailleur aux détenteurs des moyens de travail, c'est-à-dire des sources de la vie, est la cause première de sa servitude politique, morale, matérielle. L'émancipation économique des travailleurs est conséquemment le grand but auquel tout mouvement politique doit être subordonné comme moyen. Tout les efforts faits jusqu'ici ont échoué faute de solidarité entre les ouvriers des diverses professions dans chaque pays, et d'une union fraternelle entre les travailleurs des diverses contrées. L'émancipation du travail n'étant un problème ni local ni national, mais social, embrasse tous les pays dans lesquels la vie moderne existe et nécessite pour sa solution leur concours théorique et pratique.

Die Emancipation der Arbeiterklasse muss durch die Arbeiterklasse selbst erobert werden, der Kampf für die Emancipation der Arbeiterklasse ist kein Kampf für neue Klassenvorrechte, sondern für die vernichtung aller Klassenherrschaft. Die oekonomische unterwerfung des Arbeiters unter den Aneigner der Arbeitsmittel, d. h. der Quellen des Lebens liegt der Knechtschaft in aller ihren Formen zu Grunde, dem socialen Elend der geistigen erniedrigung und der politischen Abhängigkeit. Die oekonomische Emancipation der Arbeiterklasse ist daher das grosse Ziel dem jede politische Bewegung als Mittel dienen muss. Alle nach diesem Ziel strebenden versuche sind bisher gescheitert aus Mangelan Einigung unter den verschiedenen Arbeitszweigen jeden Landes und unter der Arbeiterklassen der verschiedenen Laender. Die Emancipation der Arbeiter ist weder eine lokale, noch eine nationale sondern eine gesellschaftliche Aufgabe. Sie umfasst alle Laender worin die moderne Gesellschaft besteht. Sie kann nur gelöst werden durch das planmaessige Zusammenwirken dieser Laender.

First International membership card for Hermann Jung, a German watchmaker in London (signed also by Marx as secretary for Germany), for the year 1869. The text is in English, French, and German.

Karl Marx in 1867, at the time he published Capital *and was most active in the First International.*

Victoria Claflin Woodhull (1838-1927), American feminist and editor of Woodhull & Claflin's Weekly.

Tennessee Celeste Claflin (1846-1923), American feminist and editor, sister of Victoria Claflin Woodhull.

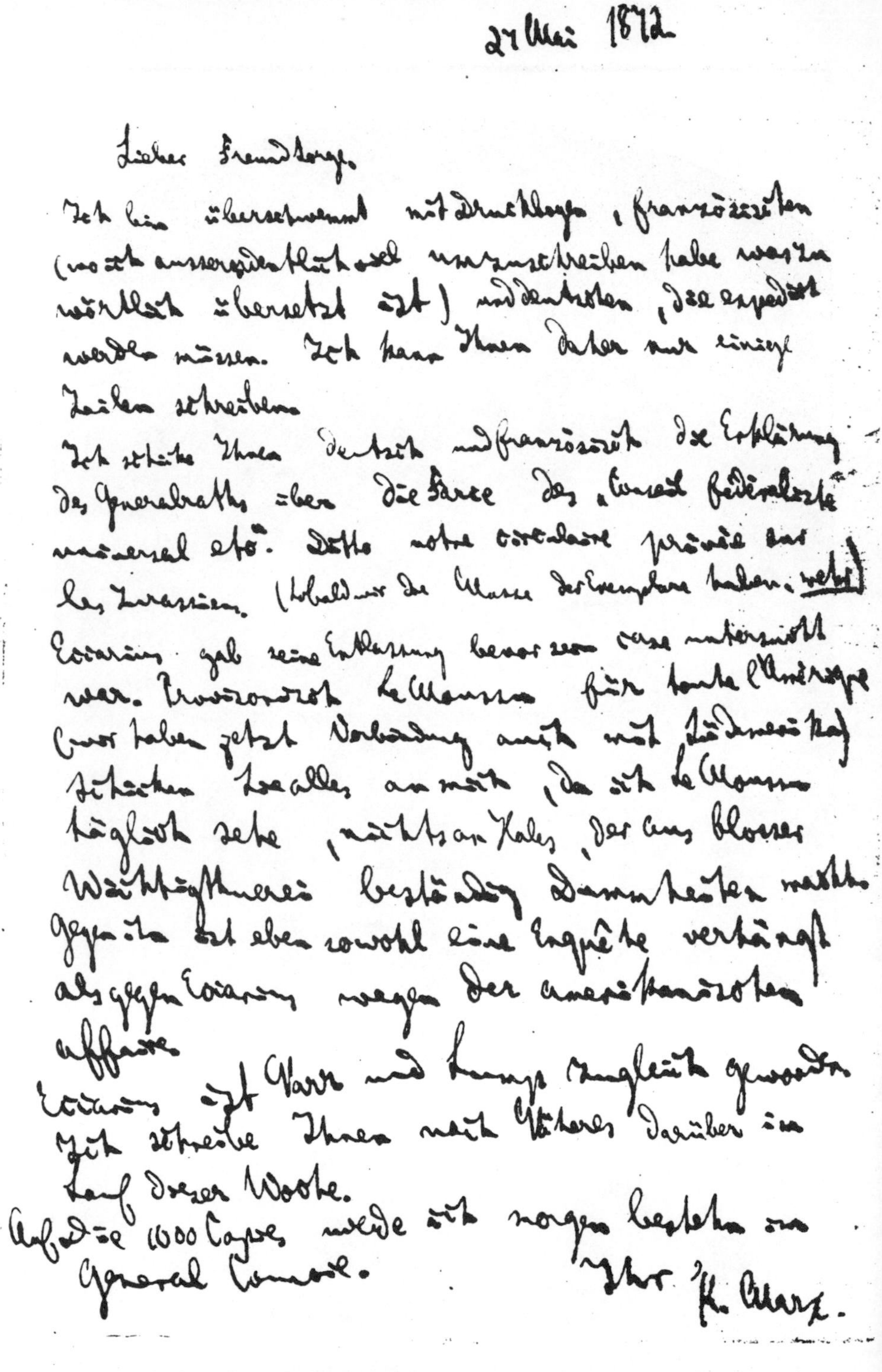

27 Mai 1872

[handwritten letter in German cursive]

Letter from Marx to Friedrich Adolph Sorge, a leading American member of the First International, May 27, 1872.

Friedrich Adolph Sorge (1828-1906), the German-born communist with whom Marx corresponded.

Joseph Weydemeyer (1818-1866), German communist who immigrated to the United States and served as Union colonel in the Civil War; a long-time friend of Marx.

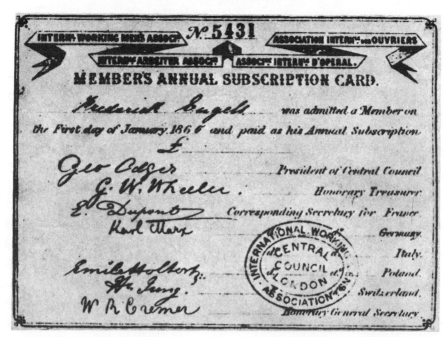

(Top) Frederick Engels' "annual subscription card" for dues to the First International. (Bottom) Notice of a First International public meeting in London.

	September				October				November				December			Present	Absent
	6	13	20	27	4	11	18	25	1	8	15	22	29	6	13	20	Present	Absent
Applegarth		+		+											2		2	14
Boon	+	+		+	+									+			5	11
Bradnick		+			+	+	Out of town								3		3	13
Caihil				+											1		1	15
Cohn		+				+									2		2	14
Eccarius	+	+	+	+	+	+	+	+	+	+	+	+	+	+	+	+	16	
Engels			+	+	+	+	+	+		+	+	+	+		11		11	1
Hales J.		+	+		+	+	+							+	6		6	10
Hales W.		+			+	Out of Town									2		2	14
Harris	+	+	+	+		+	+	+		+	+	+	+		12		12	4
Jung	+	+	Ill												2		2	4
Lapatine			+	+	+	+	+	+	+	+	+	Out of Town			10		10	4
Lessner		+	+	+	+	+	+	+			+		+	+	12		12	4
Lucraft		+	+	+										+	4		4	12
Marx	+	+	+	+	+	+	+	+	+		+	+	+	+	15		15	1
Milner	+	+	+	+		+	+	+		+	+		+	+	+	12	12	4
Motteshead		+													1		1	15
Murray			+	Gone to America											1		1	15
Maurice	Ill														—	No	No	16
Odger															No		No	16
Parnell	Out of Town														No		No	16
Pfänder		+			+	+	+	+		+	+	+		8	8	8	8
Rühl				+											1		1	15
Stepney	Out of Town									+	+	+	+	+			
Townshend	+	+		+	+	+	+	+	+	+		+		+	12		12	4
Weston	+	+	+												3		3	15
Jalicki															No		No	16
Robin											+	+	+	+	+	+		
Kolb	+										+	+	+		3	1	3	1

Weekly attendance record of the members of the General Council of the First International, September through December, 1870.

Frederick Engels (1820-1895), Marx's lifelong friend and collaborator. (Portrait taken in London in the 1870s.)

Jeremiah O'Donovan Rossa (1831-1915), Irish rebel and Fenian leader whom Marx and the First International supported.

INTERNATIONAL INSTITUTE OF SOCIAL HISTORY, AMSTERDAM.

Ferdinand Domela Nieuwenhuis (1846-1919). A Dutch social-democratic leader who brought out an abridged edition of Capital *in Dutch in 1881.*

Marx and Engels

Dear Fred:

. . . As everywhere else, so naturally also among the London workers there exists a knot of asses, fools, and rogues rallying around a scoundrel. The scoundrel in this case is George Potter, a rat of a man, supported by a venal but witty and, as a stump orator, dangerous Irishman named Connolly. Although the bourgeois hate Potter as chief strike manager, they nevertheless support him against our people because they smell venality in him, whereas they know that our people are true men. This Potter derives his power from the fact that he is currently the manager of the *Bee-Hive*, the official organ of the trade unions, although he uses it against the *official councils* of these unions, which are in our hands. Since this paper is a stock company, it is necessary to divide as many shares as possible (five shillings per share) among our workers. I personally have obligated myself to raise the money for thirty shares. I count on £5 from you (single-handed or with friends), £1 from Dronke, to whom I will write, and the rest I will pay myself (even though, for a person in my situation, my function in the Central Council costs me *much* money). The money must be at hand this week, since next week the general assembly of the shareholders will take place. If we are strong enough (and Odger, for example, has guaranteed fifty shares) to select the directors, we will have the scoundrel Potter (who is only the manager) under our thumbs. The matter is of decisive importance for the whole movement.

E. Jones was here, very amiable, socially speaking. But between ourselves, he courts our Association only to use it for his election propaganda. Of the twelve [membership] cards I sent him, he brought back eleven, not having sold a single one, while poor Schily, for example, accounted for twenty-four by himself. I told Jones he should take them back, that I would dispose of them later but that I could not appear before the English workers with such news. By and by he will find out that, if only for speculative reasons, he should not have treated the matter so lightly and almost contemptuously. I will write him that he should hand over the [copies of the Inaugural Address] to you. You can give them to anybody. With him they are dead ballast. Moreover, I do not like it that he came here to wangle a position as Recorder [Judge] from Sir G. Grey.

Today I am to present the "Address to President Johnson." M. Le Lubez wants to get into the Council again—as delegate for Deptford—

the same chap who resigned as *delegate for France*—but his admittance (we have to confirm the delegates) will not run quite so smoothly as he seems to fancy. I would be pleased if you would establish in Manchester a branch, even if only of six men, and have yourself elected correspondent for London. For the correspondents are *eo ipso* [also] members of the Central Council and have a seat and voice in it when in London.

In Lyon, Neufchâteau (département des Vosges), and St. Denis new branches have been established. The French branches (except Paris) for legal reasons are not in touch with Paris but directly with London. . . .

Yours,

K. M.

Letter to Wilhelm Liebknecht (in Berlin)
LONDON, MAY 9–29, 1865

Dear Library:[1]

I would prefer it if the translation of the "Address" [to President Johnson] were to appear in *Reform* and *Rheinische Zeitung*. It must, of course, be pointed out that the original was in English, and it would do no harm if I were mentioned as the author. The bourgeois papers are still resentful that of all the A. Lincoln replies to the various congratulatory addresses upon his reelection, only the one to us was more than a formal acknowledgment of receipt.

Salute.

Yours,

K. M.

From letter to Engels (in Manchester)
LONDON, MAY 13, 1865

Dear Fred:

. . . *Quoad* [in regard to] E. Jones, it is necessary to march with him for the time being. At the next Manchester conference[1] (next

---

1. Marx's nickname for Liebknecht.

---

1. A conference of electoral reform organizations organized by the liberal-radical National Reform Union in Manchester, May 15–16, 1865.

Tuesday) he and his will figure together with our own delegates (Odger and Cremer on the part of the International Association), Howell (bricklayer, one of the members of our Council) as secretary of the Reform League, and Beales and Jones, a stonemason, as the bourgeois representatives of the same league.

Without us, the Reform League would never have come into existence, or would have fallen into middle-class hands. The splendid defeat of Baines's Bill[2] (which will bring in its wake a change of ministry and the coming in of the Tories), originally supported by the government, which wanted some such small measure for the hustings, took place in the lower house with direct reference to the newly posed "extravagant" demands of the working class (that is, our men). . . .

Salute.

Yours,

K. M.

Apropos. Monsieur Le Lubez, who has miscalculated his own importance and dangerousness, wants now to return to the Central Council in the capacity of representative "for Greenwich"! We replied that we must *d'abord* [first] await the arrival of certain letters which he had written to France at the moment of conflict.[3] . . .

From letter to Engels (in Manchester)
LONDON, MAY 20, 1865

Dear Fred:

Enclosed, a clipping containing my Address to Johnson.[1] . . .

This evening, a special session of the International. A good old type, an old Owenist, Weston (carpenter), has put forward the propositions which he always defends in the *Bee-Hive*:

1. That a general rise in the rate of wages would be of no use to workers;

2. That therefore, etc., the trade unions have a *harmful* effect.

If these two propositions, in which he alone in our society believes, were accepted, we should be turned into a laughingstock, both on

2. In early May, 1865, the House of Commons defeated a bill, introduced by Sir Edward Baines, to restrict suffrage in the towns. The working class, including the International, fought for universal suffrage.

3. As the International's corresponding secretary for France, Le Lubez carried on a correspondence with Émile Lefebvre, attempting to influence him against the General Council and the leadership of the Paris Section.

1. See "Address . . . to President Johnson," page 20.

account of the trade unions here, and because of the epidemic of strikes
that now prevails on the Continent.

On this occasion—as nonmembers are also admitted to this meeting
—he will be supported by a native-born Englishman who has written
a pamphlet to this effect. I am, of course, expected to supply the refu-
tation. I should really have worked out my reply for this evening, but
considered it more important to keep working on my book [*Capital*],
and so I shall have to depend on improvisation.[2]

I know beforehand, of course, what the two main points are:

1. That the *wages of labor* determine the value of commodities;

2. That when the capitalists pay five instead of four shillings today,
they will sell their commodities for five shillings instead of four shillings tomorrow (being enabled to do so by the increased demand).

Insipid though this is, and connected only with the most extreme
superficiality of the phenomenon, it is, nevertheless, not easy to explain
to ignorant people all the economic questions that compete here. You
can't compress a course of political economy into one hour. But we
shall do our best.[3] . . .

Greetings.

Yours,

K. M.

From letter to Engels (in Manchester)
LONDON, JUNE 24, 1865

Dear Fred:

. . . In regard to the International Association, only the following
should be mentioned:

The Italian gentlemen *came back*, and last Tuesday [June 20]
they announced that they again chose Major Wolff as their delegate.
Mr. Mazzini seems to have become convinced that he may perhaps
find us useful, whereas we do not care a farthing for him.

A Yankee named Leon Lewis (momentarily in Paris) became
American secretary. He is worth nothing in my opinion, although he
has a great deal of money and much ambition. The fellow imagined
that through the paper, the *Commoner*, which he established, he
would be able to revolutionize England in twenty-four hours, or at

---

2. Marx gave his report on "Wages, Price and Profit," at the General Council
meetings of June 20 and 27, 1865; see his letter to Engels, June 24, 1865.
3. The last two sentences were written in English.

least in six months. He offered us the paper, which has yet to appear, as our organ, but found that we made very businesslike and by no means enthusiastic conditions, and therefore he and his wife, who is also a great statesman, have gone "temporarily" to Frankfurt, in order, according to my surmise, to see whether he would be more successful in finding a "lever" there.

I would like your opinion on the following point:

In the General Council I read a paper (which would make up perhaps two printed sheets) on the question, brought in by Mr. Weston, of the effects of a general rise in wages. The first part of it is a reply to Weston's nonsense, the second part a theoretical explanation, insofar as the occasion called for one.[1]

Now they want to print it. On the one hand, this would perhaps be useful to me, as they are in contact with John Stuart Mill, Professor Beesly, Harrison, etc. On the other hand, I have doubts:

1. Since to have "Mr. Weston" as an opponent is not very flattering;

2. Since the second part contains, in extraordinarily concise but relatively popular form, much that is new, taken from my book,[2] while at the same time a number of points must necessarily be passed over. Question, whether it is wise to excerpt this in such a way. I believe you can decide the matter much better than I, since you can judge more objectively from a distance.

I also had great trouble, because of pressure from Schily, J. Ph. Becker, and a part of the Paris Committee, in putting off the Congress announced for this year. I nevertheless succeeded decisively in winning over the local Council to the idea that, in view of the election agitation, etc., this year only a temporary (private) conference should take place *in London*, to which the foreign central committees would send one delegate each (not the affiliated societies, but their administrative committees). I am sure the Brussels Congress would have been sunk. The situation was not yet ripe for it.

Our Eccarius has become a chief London campaign agitator, and if this were not now the proper tailor season he would have accepted the offer (with £2 weekly) to agitate in the country. He has his own dryly humorous way of speaking, which particularly appeals to the English. . . .

Yours,

K. M.

---

1. The paper was published by Marx's daughter Eleanor in 1898, under the title *Value, Price and Profit*.

2. Engels to Marx, July 15, 1865: "I do not believe that you would gain many laurels in a pen struggle with Mr. Weston, and as a debut into English economic literature this would certainly not be good. Otherwise I do not see much harm done in excerpting a few things from your book."

Draft in French of letter to Léon Fontaine (in Brussels)
LONDON, JULY 25, 1865

Dear Citizen:

Some time ago I sent you a letter through an Englishman who wanted to visit Germany via Brussels. Up to now I have received no news either from you or from the Englishman. I will not ask now for an answer to my letter, but will speak only of actual happenings.

M. Le Lubez has returned to the Central Council as delegate of an English branch, and the Italian Society in London has made in Mr. Wolff its representative in the Council.[1]

M. Charles Limousin, one of our correspondents in Paris, no longer able to find a printer in Paris after the seizure of *La Tribune Ouvrière*,[2] moved to Brussels in the hope of bringing out a newspaper there. There he informed himself on the state of our affairs. He was told that the *Société Fédérative*—after it had unanimously resolved to join our Association at its own request—withdrew:

1. Because it insisted on the right to select its own correspondent and not to be pressured by the General Council;

2. Because it refused to pay for the membership cards, although it had itself hitherto charged one franc fifty.

According to M. Limousin's letter, the *Société* then applied to the book printers union, but with the same result and the same difficulties.

In regard to the selection of a correspondent, the Central Council conceded the federated associations the right to choose their own. It only reserved for itself the right of confirmation. In Brussels, matters went differently, because no Association has as yet been constituted there. Would it not be possible to make enough of a compromise to have you accepted by the societies as correspondent, while at the same time they select an administrative committee, as happened in Paris and Geneva?

As to the financial contributions, the societies will readily see that the General Council would be prevented from taking any overall action if the constituent societies refused to pay their dues. It seems that the objection is aimed only against *double* dues. Should it not be

---

1. See Marx's letters to Engels, June 24, 1865, and March 24, 1866.
2. *La Tribune Ouvrière,* a labor weekly which came out in Paris in June, 1865, and was closed by the Government after its fourth issue in July; it was edited by Tolain, Fribourg, and Varlin, and other members of the Paris Section of the International.

possible to settle these matters amicably? The General Council will accept any concession compatible with its responsibility.

I for my part am convinced that your measures have been dictated exclusively by your zeal for the common cause; I appeal to this zeal, and beg you to undertake ways and means for mutual understanding and further collaboration. I would be very grateful for an immediate reply, primarily because I must report to the General Council about this, and also because there is to take place a *preliminary* conference of the different administrative committees in London, on September 25.

The General Council has come to the conclusion that there can be no congress this year, and that a preliminary conference would first have to prepare for one.

Greetings and fraternity,

Ch. Marx

From letter to Engels (in Manchester)
LONDON, JULY 31, 1865

Dear Engels:

. . . In regard to the International, the situation is this:

I handed over to Cremer the £5 for the purchase of shares in *Bee-Hive*. But since Cremer, Odger, etc., then went to Manchester, the whole thing fell through, and Potter had the better of it. They resolved to postpone the matter until the next meeting of the shareholders (yearly). But I do not believe that anything good will come of it. First, because in the meantime the quarrel between Odger and Potter has become a public scandal. Second, because the *Miner and Workman's Advocate* has offered itself to us. (Apropos. In a brief meeting with the *Miner* we obligated ourselves to provide correspondence for it free of charge. If, therefore, you have time now and then to write an article on foreign politics [*Prussian*, etc.], send it to me for the paper).

In accordance with our Statutes, a public congress was to be held in Brussels this year. The Parisians, the Swiss, and also a number of people here are urging it furiously. Under present conditions—specifically, lack of time for the General Council to prepare the necessary papers—I see only disgrace in such a congress. Despite great resistance from the other side, I succeeded in transforming the public congress in Brussels into a private, *préalable* [preliminary] conference in London (September 25), where only delegates of the administrative committees will attend and where the future congress will be prepared. The *official* reasons for the postponement of the congress were given:

1. The necessity of a *préalable* understanding among the executive committees.

2. The obstacles to the Association's propaganda, because of the strikes in France and the elections, the reform movement, and the workingmen's exhibitions[1] in England.

3. The Alien Bill,[2] recently urged in Belgium, which made it impossible to make Brussels a rendezvous of the International Working Men's Association. . . .

Yours,

K. M.

Letter written in English to Wilhelm Liebknecht (in Leipzig)
LONDON, SEPTEMBER 20, 1865

Dear Miller:[1]

I received yours yesterday afternoon, too late to post a letter here. *Illness* had much to do with my protracted silence. There were other reasons which I think useless now to dwell upon.[2] Much business pressing upon my time just now, I can only return these few lines.

A report (English, of course) on your part is very important. It must be here on Monday next (25 September). It cannot arrive in time unless you send me the letter *directly* by the Leipzig post.

The Swiss have chosen two delegates, M. Dupleix, a Frenchman, and Mr. Philipp Becker, a German.[3]

Old Hatzfeldt dwells at Paris, where the old hag is intriguing with

1. The workingmen's exhibitions were a part of the Anglo-French Industrial Exhibition which opened in London on August 8, 1865.

2. At the end of June, 1865, despite protests, the Belgian Government renewed for the tenth time the triennial Alien Bill (for the expulsion of undesirable foreigners), first passed in 1835.

1. Liebknecht's alias.

2. Marx to Engels, August 5, 1865: "I have not answered Liebknecht . . . for a long time . . . My silence was due to the fact that I have been very busy and, moreover, had enough to do with my own troubles. On the other hand, I was actually furious with him over the imbecility with which he introduced me in the Berlin Lassalle Society. . . ."

3. Delegates to the conference held in London, September 25-29, 1865.

the "horn-bearing" father of "socialism," Moses [Hess], her most cringing slave.[4] It was at her instigation that he inserted his "warning" in the *Nordstern* and his slander in the *Social-Demokrat*.[5] She is now concocting with him the "Apotheosis" of her own belated "Oedipus."[6] The London correspondent of the *Social-Demokrat* seems to be the cracked Weber. All these things have been reported to me from Paris. As to myself, I carefully abstain from taking any notice whatever of what is going on in the Berlin and Hamburg "organs" of the movement. This so-called movement is so disgusting a thing that the less you hear of it the better.

We have founded here a weekly paper of our own, the *Workman's Advocate*. You will oblige by sending correspondence (English) for it to my address.

Yours truly,

A. WILLIAMS

Letter to Hermann Jung (in London)
LONDON, SEPTEMBER 30, 1865

Dear Jung:

I am expecting you tomorrow (Sunday) for dinner (a very frugal one); I have also invited De Paepe and Becker. Please be so kind as also to invite Kaub in my name. This morning I am so pressed by business of all kinds that I cannot afford to write two letters.[1]

Yours fraternally,

K. MARX

---

4. Marx to Engels, November 30, 1867: "Since Moses is a cousin of Hirsch's, it does not surprise me that he himself wears antlers. He bears it proudly." This is both a pun—since *Hirsch* means *deer* in German—and a reference to Hess's wife Sibylle, who was known to cuckold him.
5. As the Paris correspondent of the *Social-Demokrat*, Hess wrote, in the August 30, 1865, issue, that the Congress of the International contained among its leaders "a number of demagogues sitting far from where there is shooting." This infuriated Marx.
6. Ferdinand Lassalle.

---

1. Most of the last sentence was written in English.

From letter to Engels (in Manchester)
LONDON, NOVEMBER 20, 1865

Dear Engels:

. . . The *Workman's Advocate* is still as weak as it was. Nevertheless, it must attract, since it appeared in enlarged form last week. I do
not know any more details, as I will attend the meeting of the International tomorrow for the first time. The Parisians have published a
report on the Conference and at the same time on the program prepared by us for the next Congress. This has been published in all the
liberal, quasi-liberal and republican Paris papers.[1] How well it has
been received you can see from the following report by Fox on the
last session of our Council, which I clipped from the *Workman's
Advocate*. Our Parisians are somewhat disconcerted that the paragraph
on Russia and Poland, which they did *not* want to be included, is
precisely the one that caused the greatest sensation. I hope that in your
spare hours you will devote some time to writing something for the
Advocate from time to time. . . .

Greetings.

Yours,

K. M.

Letter to Hermann Jung (in London)
LONDON, NOVEMBER 20, 1865

My Dear Jung:
The QUESTIONS ARE AS FOLLOWS:[1]

I. Questions affecting the International Association

1. Questions of its organization.
2. Arrangements for mutual help for members of the Association.
Moral and material support for orphans of members of the Association.

---

1. Reports on the London Conference of the International, September 25-29,
were published in *L'Opinion Nationale*, October 8; *L'Avenir National*, October
12; and *Le Siècle*, October 14, 1865.

1. This letter was written to serve as an agenda for the planned International
Congress in Geneva, September 3-8, 1866. On November 25, 1865, Marx outlined
a more or less similar program in a letter to César De Paepe, a member of the
International in Brussels.

II. Social questions

1. Cooperative work.
2. Reduction of working hours.
3. Woman and child labor.
4. Trade unions. Their past, their present, their future.
5. Combined efforts in the struggle between capital and labor with the help of the International Association.
6. International credit: Establishment of international credit institutions, their form and their mode of operations.
7. Direct and indirect taxes.
8. Standing armies and their relations to production.

III. International Policy

The necessity for the elimination of the Muscovite influence in Europe through the realization of the rights of nations to self-determination and the restoration of Poland on a democratic and social foundation.

IV. Philosophical question

The religious idea and its relation to social, political, and intellectual development.

The other resolutions relative to the congress, etc., you will find in the *Workman's Advocate* issue that contains the report on the three days' session of the conference.[2]

Don't forget to demand an *official* report through Vésinier.

Send me Kaub's address, which I have mislaid.

Fraternally yours,

K. MARX

Letter written in English to Wilhelm Liebknecht (in Leipzig)
LONDON, NOVEMBER 21, 1865

My Dear Miller:

Since the conference held at this place I fell again very sick. Afterwards I had to leave London[1] for family affairs. Hence my protracted

2. "Great International Conference of Working Men," in the *Workman's Advocate*, September 30, 1865.

1. Marx visited Engels in Manchester October 20–November 3, 1865.

silence. As to your report, I could *not* lay it before the conference, because I was too personally introduced in it. As to your Berlin speech, there were some very disagreeable blunders in it which could only emanate from yourselves, because they alluded to facts only known to you, but half forgotten and wrongly reproduced by you. But this is a thing of the past.

I have received your Berlin letter, and I shall answer your questions. I have at present neither the *time* nor the means to go to Berlin. Even if I could, you know very well that all and every sort of agitation would be out of the question. The Prussian Government has not in vain declared that the amnesty, as far as I was concerned, still excluded me from Prussia, and only gave me leave to travel as a Foreigner through the Bismarckian world.[2]

The *Workman's Advocate* I shall send you one of these days some numbers of. You can write to it on *every* subject you please, social or political. Till now it is a paper of good will, very mediocre, to be sure. Of course I myself do not have and have not had yet any time to contribute to it, although I am one of its directors. (By my continual relapse into damned ill health I was forced to interrupt the finishing of my book and must now apply to it all my time, part of which is, with all that, absorbed by the International Association.) Engels has promised to contribute, but not yet done so. And the same is the case with other people.

The Conference has resolved that a Public Congress is to take place on the end of May, at Geneva. A program of questions to be there debated has been resolved upon. But nobody can assist who does not belong to a society connected with us, and being sent as a delegate of such society. I now call upon you *very seriously* (I shall do the same at Mayence [Mainz] through Stumpf, and shall write to the Berliners on it) to enter the Association with some men, few or many, we do not care. I shall send you cards which I have prepaid, so that you can *give them away* gratis. But now go to work! Every society (whatever its number) can become a member by paying five shillings per block of cards. The cards, on the other hand, which cost one shilling each, give the right to individual membership, which is important for all workingmen going to foreign countries. But treat this money matter as quite secondary. The principal thing is to win members, individual or through societies, in Germany. At the Conference, Solingen was the only place represented. (They had given

---

2. On January 12, 1861, King Wilhelm I of Prussia granted an amnesty to political refugees. In the spring of that year Marx visited Berlin and applied for renaturalization; the Prussian Government rejected his application.

a delegate's mandate to our old friend Becker, whom you are very mistaken in if you consider him a tool of Megara Hatzfeldt.)

In my next letter I shall send you the program (of questions to be laid before the Congress). All the Paris liberal and republican papers have made a great ado over our Association. Henri Martin, the well-known historian, had a most enthusiastic leader about it in the *Siècle*.[3] I have heard nothing from Quenstedt.[4]

A thing which will rather surprise you is this: Shortly before the arrival of the workingmen's letter from Berlin, I received from that same place—*"centre et foyer des lumières"* [center and focus of enlightenment], of course—a letter from Lothar Bucher, inviting me to become the London financial-article writer for the *Preussische Staats-Anzeiger*,[5] and giving me to understand that anybody *der noch bei Lebzeiten im Staat wirken will*, *"sich an die Regierung ralliiren" muss* [who still wants to be active in the country during his lifetime "must rally to the government"]. I answered him in a few lines he is not likely to exhibit. Of course, you must not publish all this in the papers, but you can communicate it, under the seal of discretion, to your friends. Freiligrath's London shop—viz., the London branch of the Bank of Switzerland—will be closed, never to reopen again, before 1866.

Give my best compliments to Madame and Alice.

Yours truly,

A. WILLIAMS

Some curious letters, written long time since, during his stay at London, by Bernhard Becker to Dr. Rode, have fallen into my hands.

I have opened this letter again, and by that operation somewhat torn it, in order to add that during the past spring I had sent a letter to Dr. Kugelmann, together with cards of membership for our Association. I have received *no answer* from him. The letter of which you speak has never arrived here. Please, write him about this. If he writes to me, let him do so under the address of "A. Williams, Esq.," and not the other one.

---

3. October 14, 1865.
4. Liebknecht's Berlin acquaintance, Quenstedt, offered to help with reviews of *Capital* when the book came out.
5. Berlin daily, organ of the Prussian Government.

From letter to Engels (in Manchester)
LONDON, DECEMBER 26, 1865

Dear Fred:

You must excuse me for thanking you only today, in the name of the family, for your Christmas present, and for not having written you at all for such a long time. I have been very bothered all that time and have been losing so much time in running around, transactions right and left, in order to satisfy A, only thereby to fall into the clutches of B, so that my work has to be confined largely to the night, and good intentions to tend to my correspondence fall by the wayside every day.

As for the International Association and all that goes with it, it weighs on me like an incubus and I would be glad to shake it off. But it cannot be done just now. For one thing, various bourgeois—headed by Mr. Hughes, M.P.—have had the idea of transforming the *Workman's Advocate* into a regular funded paper, and as one of the directors I must watch the transactions so that no foul play takes place. On the other hand, the Reform League, one of our creations has had an enormous triumph in its St. Martin's Hall meeting, the biggest purely labor meeting that has occurred here since I have lived in London. The men of *our* committee were in charge and spoke in our sense. If I were to withdraw tomorrow, the bourgeois element, which is displeased to see us (foreign infidels) behind the scenes, would get the upper hand. Owing to the complete fiasco of the labor movement in Germany, the labor elements in Switzerland have grouped themselves the more around the sections of the International Association there. The first number of the *Journal de l'Association International des Travailleurs, Section de la Suisse Romande,* appeared in Geneva in the middle of this month, and soon a similar organ will come out there in German, under Becker's editorship, which will have a chance because of the death of the *Nordstern* and the discrediting of the *Social-Demokrat.* (Old Becker asks for articles and has commissioned me to write you urgently for same, as *pro nunc* [at present] he has no collaborators.) Finally, in France, owing to the lack of all other centers of movement, the Association is making great progress. Thus if I should withdraw under these circumstances I would do it great harm; and yet on the other hand it is no small matter for me, given my present lack of time, to attend about three meetings in the West End or the City every week, a session of the International Council here, a standing committee there, a *Workman's Advocate* directors' or share-holders' meeting elsewhere. In addition, all kinds of writing. . . .

Happy New Year! Also to Mrs. Lizzy.

Yours,

K. M.

From letter to Engels (in Manchester)
LONDON, JANUARY 5, 1866

Dear Fred:

. . . Some intrigues against the International have developed, and I need your cooperation. More details later. For now only this: M. Le Lubez and Vésinier (the latter aware that an inquiry into his past is now in progress; he is again in Brussels) have here a French Branch (in fact, an opposition branch), to which Longuet, the editor of *Rive Gauche,* belongs, and with which the whole Proudhonist gang in Brussels is connected. First Vésinier published lengthy smears against us in *L'Echo de Verviers,* of course anonymously. Then the London Branch published, in the *same* paper that carries the slanders against our Association (and, among other things, also lies about Tolain and Fribourg being Bonapartists), a program, a draft of future Statutes which *they,* the true ones, are to present to the Congress.

The essential nerve of the polemic is the Polish question. The fellows have all tied up with the Proudhon-Herzen Muscovitism. I will send you the oracles' previous articles against Poland in the *Tribune du Peuple,*[1] and you must write a reply,[2] be it for our Geneva paper (the "German"[3]) or for *The Workman's Advocate.* The Russian gentlemen have found their newest allies in the Proudhonized portion of *Jeune France.*

---

1. Hector Denis, "*La question polonaise et la démocratie*" ["The Polish Question and Democracy"], May–June, 1864.

2. Engels wrote a series of articles, "What Does the Working Class Have to Do With Poland," in *The Commonwealth,* March 24 and 31, and May 5, 1866.

3. *Der Vorbote.*

From letter to Johann Philipp Becker (in Geneva)
LONDON, ca. JANUARY 13, 1866

Dear, best Becker:

You will be angry with me "justly" and at the same time "un-justly" (you know from Heinzen that I am a "Sophist"). Apart from the fact that I have to copy 1,200 pages of manuscript [of *Capital*] and my publisher is already long vexed with me, and apart from the terrible loss of time which, in this Babylon, the Central Committee, the Standing Committee, and the Directors' Committee take from me, I had to suffer most troublesome and difficult "private business," which forced me to leave London for a time[1] and which is not settled yet, etc., etc.

From the enclosed note which I (or rather, my wife) received today, you will see that a packet which I sent you *about fourteen days* ago was confiscated by the worthy French police. It contained mainly copies of the *Manifesto of the Communist Party.* Also a note in which I answered your questions briefly, informing you that Bender agrees that I publish your Appeal,[2] in *English*, in the *Workman's Advocate*, ditto a report on the activities of the Swiss, etc.

The reason why we decided not to publish an official report on the [London] conference was essentially that—apart from lack of money and because the Statutes oblige us to lay before the Congress a general report, and thus to avoid double *emploi* [work]—to let the public know the facts of the case, especially the very "fragmentary" nature of the conference, would do us more harm than good, and would offer our opponents a useful handle. We knew that two members of the Central Committee, Le Lubez and Vésinier, waited only to seize the opportunity by the forelock. Events have confirmed this. First came Vésinier's denunciation of the Central Committee and the conference in *L'Écho de Verviers.*[3] Immediately thereafter, in the same paper, Le Lubez's declaration of principle and a draft of statutes which he, in the name of the French Branch in London which he founded as counterweight to us, thought to impose on the Association. In the meantime this intrigue has been thwarted. The branch has deserted its founder. Its two best men, Longuet (editor of *Rive Gauche*) and

---

1. Marx stayed with Engels in Manchester October 20–November 2, 1865.
2. In November, 1865, Becker issued a circular letter to Swiss workers urging them to join the German Section of the International in Switzerland.
3. Anonymous articles, December 16, 18, 1865.

Crespelle, joined the Central Committee. The latter has resolved that Vésinier must prove his calumnies or be expelled. . . .

Here the movement has gone well in one way and badly in another. The Reform League, which was founded by us, held a mass meeting for universal suffrage, and it was bigger than anything seen in London. Only workingmen spoke. The *Times* itself was frightened and published two leading articles on the "odious" *casus* [case].[4] On the other hand, this movement takes up too much of the time of our best workers.

The *Workman's Advocate* is weak. Now under Eccarius' editorship, it will improve.[5] The difficulties in raising enough money for it are enormous. . . .

The German sections would do best to join Geneva for the time being and to enter into continuous contact with you. As soon as something like this happens, let me know, so that I can at last report here some progress in Germany. . . .

Yours,

K. Marx

From letter to Engels (*in Manchester*)
LONDON, JANUARY 15, 1866

Dear Fred:

Laura has entirely forgotten to send you the copies of the *Tribune*,[1] which I had put aside a week ago. She is doing it today, sending also the *Workman's Advocate* . . .

In the meantime, we have printed to death the wretched intrigues of Vésinier in Belgium and Le Lubez in London. The editor of *Rive Gauche* and friend of Rogeard's—Longuet—also Mr. Crespelle—the two most intelligent members of the branch founded by Le Lubez—have also become members of our Central Committee. The [French] Branch has declared itself against him, and for us. The Central Committee has summoned Vésinier "to substantiate his accusations, or be expelled." . . .

You will be amused by the wiseacre Denis' last prayer to Proud-

4. December 13, 14, 1865.
5. See Marx's letter to Engels, February 10, 1866.

1. *La Tribune du Peuple.*

hon.[2] This "sensational writer," with his half-baked learning, his Lassalle-like parading of science about which he knows nothing, with his seemingly critical superiority to the socialist sectarians, has done much damage.

Le Lubez is a cipher. Fox rightly calls him "*Le Père enfantin*,"[3] but Vésinier is entirely the fellow for the Russians. Not worth much as a writer, as his *La Vie du Nouveau César*[4] and other pamphlets against Bonaparte show. But he has talent, great rhetorical power, much energy, and, above all, is unscrupulous through and through.

Yours,

K. M.

Letter to Wilhelm Liebknecht (in Leipzig)
LONDON, JANUARY 15, 1866

Dear Library:

Happy New Year!

You must excuse my silence, ditto the brevity of this letter. You would not believe how my time is eaten up. Illness,[1] always recurring periodically, bad luck through all kinds of accidents, being in demand by the International Association, etc., all these have confiscated all the free movements needed to make a fair copy of my manuscript. I hope to take Volume I personally to the publisher in March. (The whole, in two volumes, will appear *simultaneously*, however. The thing *is good*.)

Now in summary.

I am sending you by post today the last two issues of the *Workman's Advocate*, of which Eccarius is now editor. Should you contribute articles (political, social, or whatever you wish), as I hope you will, send them to me.

I am enclosing cards of membership. I paid for them. Hence you can give them to whomever you want; all you have to do is inscribe the name, put a o behind £, and one shilling behind o.

---

2. *L'Anti-Proudhon* (Rennes, 1860), a discussion of Proudhon's *De la Justice dans la Révolution et dans l'Église* (3 vols., Paris, 1858).

3. The French Saint-Simonian writer Barthélemy Prosper Enfantin used to be called "Père Enfantin"; spelling the latter word with a small "e" makes it a pun, meaning "childish father."

4. *The Life of the New Caesar* (Geneva, 1865).

---

1. Marx to Engels, February 10, 1866: "This time, my life was in danger. My family did not know how serious the case was. If the thing [liver illness and carbuncles] recurs three or four more times in the same form, I am a dead man."

The conditions are generally these: *An association as such*, if it wants to join, has to pay five shillings annually for an *association card*. If, however, all the members join as *individuals*, they must use the cards which I am sending you. This is useful for the workers. The cards serve as a passport abroad, and the confrères in London, Paris, Brussels, Lyon, Geneva, etc., find them work.

The Association has made great progress. It already possesses an official English journal, the *Workman's Advocate;* a Brussels one, *La Tribune du Peuple;* a French one in Geneva, *Journal de l'Association International des Travailleurs, Section de la Suisse Romande;* and a German one in Geneva, *Der Vorbote*, that will appear in a few days. The latter's address is: 6 rue du Môle, Geneva, J. P. Becker, in case you wish to write to the old man from time to time (which I hope you do).

I hope that you will soon make it possible for me to announce the establishment of a Leipzig association and to propose correspondence from it. (In *English*. It could also be of service to the *Workman's Advocate*.) The numbers do not matter, although the more the better.

Should your people enter en masse, as an association, you can see that the total cost of five shillings, paid yearly, is nothing.

J. P. Becker writes me:

"Sections will be established in Leipzig, Gotha, Stuttgart, and Nuremberg; should we admit them here in the meantime until there is a large enough number to form a Central Committee in Germany?"

I have replied in the affirmative. As various branches may exist in any one city, you and yours can connect with us directly.

I have received a second letter from Berlin. I am finally writing them today. Ditto a letter from Dr. Kugelmann.

Greetings.

Yours,

K. M.

Next time I will report to you the questions that will be taken up at the Geneva Congress.

From letter to Ludwig Kugelmann (in Hanover)
LONDON, JANUARY 15, 1866

Dear Friend:

Happy New Year and best thanks for your friendly letter.

You must excuse the brevity of this letter on the ground of my over-busyness. Next time I will write at greater length.

I am enclosing two membership cards [to the International], and in my next letter I will report to you the questions to be discussed at the public congress in Geneva, next May.[1]

Our Association has made great progress. It already possesses three official organs: the *Workman's Advocate* in London; *La Tribune du Peuple* in Brussels; a French one in Switzerland, *Journal de l'Association International des Travailleurs, Section de la Suisse Romande* (Geneva). A German-Swiss journal, *Der Vorbote*, under the editorship of J. P. Becker, will appear in a few days. (Address: 6 rue du Môle, Geneva, J. P. Becker, in case you want to send him some occasional correspondence, political or social.)

We have succeeded in bringing into the movement the only really big workers' organization, the English trade unions, which had hitherto occupied itself exclusively with wage problems. With its help, the English organization [Reform League] which we founded for effecting universal suffrage (half of the central committee consists of members—workers—of our own Central Committee) held a mass meeting, at which only workers spoke. The effect of it you see from the fact that the *Times* devoted two succeeding leaders [editorials] to this meeting.[2] . . .

Your devoted

K. MARX

From letter to Engels (in Manchester)
LONDON, FEBRUARY 10, 1866

Dear Fritz:

. . . There was a great crisis in the *Workman's Advocate*, which is coming out tomorrow as the *Commonwealth*, a change brought about by the bourgeois element and by *my* absence from the Council. Nevertheless, from my sickbed, through epistolary threats, I was able to frustrate the intrigue to the point that Eccarius, instead of some gentleman from the *Nonconformist*,[1] became editor, and an editorial supervision committee, meeting weekly, was appointed. It consists of me, Howell, Weston, and Miall (the publisher-editor of the *Nonconformist* and our publisher now), four atheists against one "Protestant." *Your*

1. It was postponed until September 3–8, 1866.
2. December 13, 14, 1865.

1. A radical weekly which appeared in London between 1841 and 1879.

article[2] is now *urgently* necessary for poor Eccarius (since the intrigues are massive and I cannot support him; my writing time is entirely taken up by my book). . . .
Salute.

Yours,
K. M.

From letter to Engels (in Manchester)
LONDON, MARCH 10, 1866

Dear Fred:
. . . In the International Council and the [*Commonwealth*] editorial board everything is in a mess, and one has a great urge to revolt against the absent "tyrants" and let the whole business get stuck in the mire. My wounds (from the last carbuncles) are sufficiently healed (no new ones have followed yet) so that I could go out next Monday and Tuesday, but on the other hand, I can hardly bear the late sessions in a corner of Fleet Street,[1] and what is even worse, I am still so nervously irritated that I can hardly keep the storms "inside the bounds of pure reason," but rather, am prone to violent outbursts, which is purposeless.
When will Polish article No. 1 finally arrive?[2]

Yours,
K. M.

From letter to Engels (in Manchester)
MARGATE, MARCH 24, 1866

Dear Fred:
. . . Before I left London (which I did on Wednesday, March 14), although I was still in a miserable condition, I had to attend successive evening sessions on March 12 and 13, first that of the shareholders of the *Commonwealth*, and on the thirteenth that of the Central Council.

---

2. On Poland; see Marx's letter to Engels, January 5, 1866.

---

1. From January, 1866, to June 25, 1867, the meetings of the General Council were held at No. 18 Bouverie Street, near Fleet Street.
2. See Marx's letter to Engels, January 5, 1866.

In the *Commonwealth* meeting Mr. Cremer had arranged everything for getting rid of Eccarius, which would well have happened if
I had not been present. The only result of the session, therefore, was
that Mr. Cremer "voluntarily" resigned from the editorial board. What
happened subsequently I do not know, since everything was settled
"provisionally," for only one week, and the general shareholders'
meeting was adjourned until March 19. Nevertheless, here too it will
be: *Beati possidentes* [Happy are the possessors]—and Eccarius, as a
result of that session, was the *possidens*.

The intrigue in the General Council was closely tied to the
rivalries and jealousies connected with the journal (Mr. Howell wanted
to be editor in chief and Mr. Cremer ditto). M. Le Lubez used this
occasion to rant against German influence, and in the session of March
6 there was a fine and quietly prepared scene. For suddenly Major
Wolff appeared and gave a solemn speech in his name, that of Mazzini,
and that of the Italian society against the reply to Vésinier's attack
which Jung had sent to the *Echo de Verviers* in the name of the General Council. He very vehemently attacked Jung and (by implication)
me. The old Mazzinism of Odger, Howell, Cremer, etc., was aired. Le
Lubez stoked the fire, and at all events, a resolution was passed which
more or less included an *amende honorable* [apology] to Mazzini,
Wolff, etc. You see, the matter was serious. (Of the foreigners, only
a few were present, and none voted.) It would have been a very artful
stroke on the part of Mazzini to let me develop the Association and
then appropriate it for himself. He demanded that the English recognize him as the chief of the continental democracy, as if the English
had to appoint *us* chiefs!

On Saturday (March 10), the foreign secretaries of the Association
met in my house to hold a council of war (Dupont, Jung, Longuet,
Lafargue, Bobczynski). It was decided that I must under all circumstances appear at the Council on Tuesday (the thirteenth) and protest
against the proceedings in the name of *all* the foreign secretaries. For
the proceedings had been irregular, since Wolff had ceased to be a
member of the Council; hence no resolution regarding a matter in
which he was personally implicated should have been passed in his
presence. Furthermore, I was to explain Mazzini's relationship partly
to our Association and partly to the Continental Workingmen's
parties, etc. Finally, the Frenchmen were to bring with them Cesare
Orsini (by the by, a personal friend of Mazzini's), who was to give
evidence on Mazzini, Wolff, and the state of "socialism" in Italy.

The whole thing went well, beyond expectations; but unfortunately, because of the Reform League shit,[1] the English element was

---

1. See Marx's letter to Engels, February 25, 1865.

not strongly represented. In any case, it became clear to the English (in reality, only a minority is meant here) that the whole continental element sticks with me to a man, and that despite Le Lubez's insinuations, *German* influence is not the question. Le Lubez attempted to persuade them that I, as leader of the *English* element in the Council, held down the rest of the *continental* elements; but the English gentlemen, on the contrary, have now become convinced that through the continental element I would completely hold them in check if they made any asinine leaps. More about this next time. . . .

Yours,

K. M.

From letter to Engels (in Manchester)
MARGATE, APRIL 2, 1866

Dear Fred:

D'abord [first], received the £10 with my best thanks.

During my absence, a *changement de décoration* [change of decoration] has taken place in the *Commonwealth*, or rather *de direction* [of direction], which comes into being next week. Odger, editor; Fox, subeditor; the "son of toil" [Eccarius] is engaged to write a weekly article for 10 shillings; Cremer out of a job; he has also handed in his resignation as general secretary of the International Association. On the whole, I have nothing against the change. Eccarius could hardly (or at least should not) fancy that he would be entrusted with nominal direction of the paper after it had established itself. I have warned him in vain. It was a "political" mistake on my part to yield to his pressure and to recommend him, as I did in a letter, for the position now vacated. If I had not been sick, he would have knocked in vain. I knew beforehand that the thing would fall on my back. The avoidance of all appearance of personal aims or misuse of personal influence for secret objectives, as well as a good understanding with the English, must naturally be more important for us than satisfying Eccarius' more or less justified ambitions.

Dry natures like Eccarius also possess a certain dry egoism, which easily misleads them. When the Reform League decided on its big meeting in St. Martin's Hall, the Council of the League chose him as one of the public speakers. The fellows from Potter's clique protested against him as a foreigner. I expressly warned him not to accept his "brief." He, however, thought himself to be above it all, and titillated

himself with the important role in the metropolitan movement. And
he was a dead failure. The poor fellow had, of course, experienced a
life of disappointments, and the honorary post of vice-president of the
International, etc., which the English gave him spontaneously, deceived
him to the point that he thought he could once and for all take
vengeance for his whole past. If he had followed my advice, operated
slowly, maintained a modest posture, everything would have gone for
the best with him. When, despite his lack of discipline and obstinacy,
I went into the muck in his defense, I was motivated to do it out of
the consideration that he had always worked for us and had never
reaped any fruits. But one always makes blunders when one permits
oneself to be influenced by such considerations.

As for the paper itself, its danger—due to lack of funds—lies in
the growing attacks from the preponderance of the *Nonconformist*
clique. . . .

Yours,

K. M.

From letter to Engels (in Manchester)
MARGATE, APRIL 6, 1866

Dear Fred:

. . . I must tell you frankly that things go very badly with the
International, the more so as, owing to the impatience of the French,
the date of the Congress has been set for the *end of May*.[1]

The fact is this, that the English leaders in London, after we
created a position for them (why is every Englishman incapable of
doing two things at the same time?), are very *cool* in our narrow
movement. My absence of almost three months[2] has done *extraordinary*
harm. WHAT TO DO? In France, Belgium, Switzerland (and even here
and there in Germany, and even sporadically in America), the International has made great and steady progress. In England, the reform
movement, which we brought into being, has practically killed us.
The matter would be unimportant if the Congress had not been announced for the end of May and if the Parisians, for whom this movement is the *only possible one*, had not made it practically impossible,

---

1. The date of the First Congress of the International, to meet in Geneva,
was later changed from May to September 3, 1866.

2. From January to April Marx was ill with carbuncles; he was on a cure in
Margate from March 15 to April 10, 1866.

through their own journal, *Le Congrès*,[3] to prorogue the Congress. The English will soon realize the lousiness of the reform movements as they now exist. After my return, a threat of flirtation with the Potter clique, etc., would have put everything back on the proper track. But there is no time. For the English, the failure of the Congress itself is a blunder. But for us? *A European disgrace!* I see, in fact, no way out. The English have neglected everything too much for the Congress to be possible in any decent form. *Que faire?* [What to do?] Do you think I should go to Paris to explain to the people there how impossible the Congress is now? Reply soon.[4] Only in an understanding with the Parisians do I see a way out. Otherwise, I know, their position is endangered if no Congress takes place. *Que faire?* M. Vésinier has *challenged* our Parisians. They are to come to Belgium and shoot it out with him. The imbecile. As to Orsini, I knew that you could do nothing. But I could not refuse the recommendation to you.[5]

Yours,

K. M.

Letter written in English to Wilhelm Liebknecht (in Leipzig)
MARGATE, APRIL 6, 1866

My Dear Miller:

You see from the address that I have been banished to the seaside by my medical adviser.

After having received your last letter, and some letters on the part of our Berlin friends, my sickness assumed a really dangerous character. For some time it was very doubtful whether or not that decomposition of the blood, under which I labor, should get the better of me. It was only toward the middle of March that I was bodily enabled

---

3. Early in 1866 the Paris Section of the International published a brochure, *Congrès Ouvrier*, containing a garbled translation of the International's Statutes, as well as plans for the proposed Congress.

4. Engels to Marx, April 10, 1866: ". . . I would under no circumstances go to Paris. You are protected there by nobody, and the police will lay hold without constraint."

5. Marx to Engels, March 15, 1866: "My dear Frederick, The bearer of these lines is citizen Orsini [Cesare], the brother of the immortal martyr [Felice], and a member of our Association. He leaves England for the United States, whence he will return in some months. Your advice on commercial matters may, perhaps, prove useful to him. At all events, you will be delighted to make his personal acquaintance."

to remove myself to this place. I am now restored, and shall very soon return to London. But again a quarter of year has been lost!

Write me immediately under my London address.

After my return, I shall send you regularly the *Commonwealth* (under which altered title the *Workman's Advocate* is now published). It is only since a few weeks that it has been registered for transmission abroad. Eccarius is no longer the editor, but only a contributor. It was to be foreseen, that as soon as the paper should get some sort of standing, a Foreigner would not be allowed to retain the nominal leadership.

Write me

   1. about the state of "our" movement in Germany,
   2. about the state of German politics.

Yours truly,

K. M.

My best compliments to Madame.

From letter to Engels (*in Manchester*)
LONDON, APRIL 23, 1866

Dear Fred:

  . . . In the International, the situation is this: Since my return, discipline has been completely restored. Also, the International's successful intervention in the tailors' strike (through letters of the secretaries for France, Belgium, etc.) has caused a sensation among the local trade unions. In regard to the Geneva Congress, I decided to contribute to its success so far as I can here, but not to attend personally. I thereby shake off all personal responsibility for its leadership.

As for the *Commonwealth*, the encroachments of Miall & Co. would be more bearable if they at least rested on the pretext of really valuable financial contributions. But the fellows are very prodigal with good advice and naggings, and very thrifty with cash, so that the paper's entire existence is reprieved only from week to week. Its readership widens weekly, but a penny paper, to be successful, has to be funded for at least a year in advance. To make it self-supporting in less time than that is quite out of the question. If the paper is not worse than it is just now, it is only thanks to Fox, who has to carry on a constant struggle. . . .

Tout à vous,

K. M.

Letter written in English to Wilhelm Liebknecht (in Leipzig)
LONDON, MAY 4, 1866

My Dear Friend:

As I am at this moment, after so long an interruption of work, very busily engaged in making up for lost time, you will excuse me for writing this time only a few lines.

I shall send you today the last number of the *Commonwealth*. The financial position of the paper is such that it struggles from week to week and is altogether disabled from paying one farthing for Foreign Correspondence. Its circulation is increasing, but you know that a penny paper wants at least 20,000 subscribers, and cannot even then make the two ends meet without a goodly number of advertisements. The *Commonwealth* is of too recent an origin to come up to those requisites.

The Congress at Geneva has been postponed for the second of September next.[1] The Society is rapidly spreading, particularly in France. Italian societies have also recently joined. The propaganda in London has taken a new start, principally due to the circumstances that the successful strikes of the London tailors and wire workers were due to our intervention, which prevented the import of working-men from France, Switzerland, Belgium, which had been contemplated by the masters. This proof of its immediate practical importance has struck the practical English mind.[2]

For the same purpose you find, on the last page of this letter, an *"avis"* [warning] to the German tailors which I call upon you to have inserted in such German papers as you have access to. At the same time you will oblige me by sending me a copy or two of some papers in which the *"avis"* will have been inserted, telling me at the same time the names of all other papers that should have reprinted it. Kugelmann might also be useful for this purpose.

My best compliments to Mrs. Liebknecht. I feel exceedingly thankful for her friendly interest in my welfare.

Yours fraternally,

A. WILLIAMS

1. The Congress met in Geneva, September 3–8, 1866.
2. At the end of March, 1866, the apprentice tailors went out on strike and the masters imported German tailors to put it down. The International took steps to warn the immigrant tailors, in England as well as in Europe; this led to a settlement of the strike in favor of the apprentices, and an increase in the membership of the International. The strike of the wire workers, in April, 1866, was also helped by the International and led the former to join it.

Warning

Some time ago, London apprentice tailors formed a general union to assert their claims against the London master tailors, who are mostly big capitalists. It is not only a question of raising wages to meet the cost of living, but also to put an end to the exceptional brutality with which workers are treated in this trade. The masters sought to break the union by recruiting apprentices in Belgium, France, and Switzerland. The secretaries of the Central Council of the International Working Men's Association thereupon published a warning in Belgian, French, and Swiss newspapers, the success of which was complete. The maneuver of the London masters was thwarted, they had to surrender and satisfy the just demands of the workers. Defeated in England, the masters tried to bring about a reaction in Scotland. In consequence of the events in London, they were forced to agree to a 15 percent rise in wages in Edinburgh too. Secretly, however, they sent agents to Germany, to recruit apprentice tailors in Hanover and Mecklenburg for importation to Edinburgh. The first shipment of them has already taken place.[3] The aim of this importation is the same as that of the importation of Indian coolies to Jamaica—*perpetuation of slavery*. Should the Edinburgh masters succeed in breaking their agreement because of the importation of Germans, a repercussion in England would be unavoidable. Nobody would expiate for this more than the German workers themselves, who are more numerous in Great Britain than workers of any other country. The newly imported ones, entirely helpless in a foreign land, would soon sink to a position of pariah.

It is, furthermore, a point of honor for the German workers to show foreign countries that, like their brothers in France, Belgium, and Switzerland, they know how to represent the common interest of their class and not hand themselves over as weak-minded bondsmen of capital in the struggle against labor.

By order of the Central Council of the International Working Men's Association,

KARL MARX

German apprentice tailors who desire more information about British conditions are requested to write to the German branch committee of the London tailors union, under the address: Albert F. Haufe, Crown Public House, Hedden Court, Regent Street, London.

---

3. On May 1, 1866, Engels wrote to Marx from Manchester: ". . . a cargo of 57 *German tailors* arrived in Edinburgh, to put down a strike, and two other cargoes are expected. Probably from Hamburg. Can you not find out the details in Edinburgh and put a stop to this?"

From letter to Engels (in Manchester)
LONDON, MAY 17, 1866

Dear Fred:

... Mr. Mazzini did not rest until he founded an "International Republican Committee" against us. In it, jackass Holtorp, Langiewicz, Ledru, Kinkel, Blind, I believe also—Bolleter! Our Association is having an effect daily. Only in Germany, because of jackass Liebknecht (good fellow as he is!), there is nothing doing. ...

Greetings.

Yours,
K. M.

From letter to Engels (in Manchester)
LONDON, JUNE 9, 1866

Dear Fred:

... This evening I am compelled to go to a session of the "directors and friends" of the *Commonwealth.* The thing is on its last legs. Apart from its extreme financial difficulties, it has internal political ones. Since that jackass of a Bradford manufacturer, Mr. Kell (who donated £50, his brother ditto, and promised more), totally dominates Miall, Dr. Bridges, Professor Beesly, [and] Harrison (the Comteists) threatened him not only with their resignation but also with making a public declaration.

I am tired of the stuff, and this evening I will tell the fellows to *sell* their bankrupt institution to Kell & Co., to put an end to this ridiculous situation where a Bradford manufacturer edits a London "workers' organ." If they refuse, I will hand in my resignation in any case. For some time yet the paper will not be able to survive on its own funds, and is therefore dependent on bourgeois advances, losing its character thereby. I had developed much patience in this connection, because I had always hoped that the workers themselves would strive sufficiently to carry on the thing independently, and since I did not want to be a spoilsport. ...

Greetings.

Yours,
K. M.

Letter to Engels (*in Manchester*)
LONDON, JUNE 20, 1866

Dear Fred:

The damn weather has a particularly disagreeable effect on my physique; and this is the reason why I have not hitherto acknowledged the "wine" or written otherwise. It is not possible for me to go to Manchester, for I cannot leave the house in my present state; moreover, I must be here on account of the International, where my French friends have once already taken advantage of my absence to act stupidly under these trying circumstances.

In regard to the local newspapers, it is my view that in case the matter does not work out in Manchester, you should send a strong military article to the *Times*, where you can present yourself as the English correspondent of the Darmstadt *Militär-Zeitung*. Political considerations are not to be taken into account, since one London paper is as bad as another, and since the widest publicity is involved.

You must now keep me "critically" *au courant* with the affairs in Italy and Germany.

Yesterday there was a discussion in the International Council on the present [Austro-Prussian] war. It had been announced beforehand and our room was very full. The Italian gentry also sent us representatives again. The discussion wound up, as was to be expected, with the "question of nationality" in general and the attitude we should take toward it. This subject was adjourned until next Tuesday.

The French, who were numerously represented, gave vent to their cordial dislike for the Italians.

Moreover, the representatives of "Young France" (*nonworkers*) came out with the announcement that all nationalities and even nations were "antiquated prejudices." Proudhonized Stirnerism. Everything is to be dissolved into small "groups" or "communes," which in turn are to form an "association," but no state. And this "individualization" of humanity and the corresponding "mutualism" are to go on while history comes to a stop in all other countries and the whole world waits until the French are ripe for a social revolution. Then they will demonstrate the experiment to us, and the rest of the world, overwhelmed by the force of their example, will follow suit. Exactly what Fourier expected of his model phalanstery. Moreover, whoever encumbers the "social" question with the "superstitions" of the old world is a "reactionary."

The English laughed a lot when I began my speech by saying that my friend Lafargue, etc., who had abolished nationalities, had spoken *French* to us, i.e., a language which nine-tenths of the audience did not understand. I also suggested that by the negation of nationalities he appeared, quite unconsciously, to assume their absorption into the model French nation.

For the rest, the situation is difficult now, because on the one hand, the silly English Italianism, and on the other the fake French polemics against it, must be equally combated. In particular, every demonstration that would involve our Association in a one-sided direction must be prevented.

Greetings.

Yours,

K. M.

From letter to Engels (in Manchester)
LONDON, JULY 7, 1866

Dear Fred:

. . . The workers' demonstrations[1] in London, fabulous compared with anything we have seen in England since 1849, are purely the work of the International. Mr. Lucraft, for instance, the leader in Trafalgar Square, is one of our Council. This shows the difference between *working* behind the scenes and not appearing in public, and the democrats' way of making oneself important in public and *doing nothing.*

The *Commonwealth* will soon give up the ghost. Fox is leaving it next week. Apropos. Stumpf writes me from Mainz that the demand for your book, *The Condition,* etc.,[2] among the workers is growing daily and that you simply must bring out another edition, if only for party reasons. At the same time, he believes, from his personal experience, that after the war the "labor question" will come prominently to the fore in Germany. . . .

Greetings.

Yours,

K. M.

---

1. Mass meetings on June 27 and July 2 in Trafalgar Square, demanding manhood suffrage.
2. *The Condition of the Working Class in England* (1845).

From letter to Ludwig Kugelmann (in Hanover)
LONDON, AUGUST 23, 1866

My Dear Friend:
    . . . Although I am devoting much time to the Geneva Congress,[1]
I cannot, and do not want to, go there, because no prolonged interruption of my work[2] is possible. I consider that this work which I
am doing is much more important for the working class than anything
that I, personally, could do at a congress *quelconque* [of any
kind]. . . .

Yours very sincerely,

K. MARX

Letter to Johann Philipp Becker (in Geneva)
LONDON, AUGUST 31, 1866

Dear Becker:
    It is absolutely necessary that *Jung* be president of the Congress.
    1. Because he speaks the three languages, English, French, and
German.
    2. Jung *really represents* the Central Council, while Odger (who,
furthermore, knows only his mother tongue) has *not* been chosen by
the Central Council. We elected four delegates, with Jung at the
head; Odger was to attend only if he could borrow money himself
(of course, with our guarantee). He has done *nothing* for the Association.
    3. Cremer and Odger have woven a very cheap intrigue to prevent,
even on the last day, the departure of Jung and Eccarius.
    4. Odger wants to be elected president of the Congress in order
to impress the English and, next year, to foist himself as president of
the Central Council against the wishes of the great majority of the
Council.
    5. Cremer and Odger have both betrayed us in the Reform League,
where they made compromises with the bourgeoisie against our wishes.
    6. Herr Cremer has become entirely demoralized. He speculates for

1. September 3–8, 1866.
2. On *Capital*.

a "paid" position only not to have to work. Hence he must under no circumstances be elected general secretary (the only paid position) of the Congress. One should elect Fox, if only for the good reason that the General Secretary must know more than one language.

9.[1] The president of the Central Council must NOT be elected by the Congress, but here in London by *local leaders only*.

10. At the election of the president of the Congress, you must say at the outset, so as to save time, etc., that an international congress can be presided over only by a single person.

11. Convey this matter to Dupleix.

12. I would appreciate it if, before the Congress begins, Eccarius would translate into German for you the Instructions[2] I wrote for the London delegates in the name of the Central Committee.

Greetings and a handshake.

Yours,

K. M.

From letter to Engels (in Manchester)
LONDON, SEPTEMBER 26, 1866

Dear Fred:

. . . In a demonstration against the French gentlemen—who want to exclude all *travailleurs manuels* [manual workers], first from the International Association and then from the possibility of being chosen delegates to the Congress—the English yesterday proposed *me* as *president of the Central Council.* I stated that I could under no circumstances accept and that, for my part, I proposed Odger, who was reelected, although a few, despite my statement, voted for me. For the rest, Dupont gave me the key to an understanding of Tolain and Fribourg. They plan to come out as *workers'* candidates for the *Corps legislatif* [in Paris], on the "principle" that *only workers* can represent workers. It was, therefore, extremely important for those gentlemen to proclaim this principle at the Congress.[1]

In yesterday's session of the Central Council there were all kinds of scenes. Mr. Cremer, for example, fell from the clouds, and in his

---

1. Marx omitted points 7 and 8.
2. See "Instructions for the Delegates of the Provisional General Council," page 23.

---

1. A proposal to this effect was made by the delegate, Henri Tolain, at the Geneva Congress.

place, Fox was named general secretary. Cremer restrained his fury only with very great effort. Another scene took place when Mr. Le Lubez was officially informed of his exclusion from the Central Council *par décret* [by decree]. In an hour-long speech, he played the oppressed soul, spewing poison and gall on the Parisian members, treating himself with astonishing respect, and murmuring all kinds of suspicions about the intrigues which kept the nationalities friendly to him (Belgium and Italy) out of the Congress. In the end he demanded—and this comes up for discussion next Tuesday—a vote of confidence from the Central Council.[2]

Salute.

Yours,

K. M.

From letter to Ludwig Kugelmann (in Hanover)
LONDON, OCTOBER 9, 1866

Dear Friend:

. . . And now to some general comments.

I had great fears about the first Congress at Geneva. But in general it has come out well, beyond my expectations. Its effect in France, England, and America was unhoped-for. I could not and would not attend myself, but did write the program for the London delegation. I deliberately confined myself to those points that would allow an immediate understanding and cooperation among workers and would give direct nourishment and impetus to the needs of the class struggle and the organization of workers as a class. The Parisian gentlemen had their heads full of the emptiest Proudhonist phrases. They prattle about science and they know nothing. They scorn all *revolutionists*, that is, action deriving from the class struggle itself, all concentrated social movement, and also objectives (such as, for example, a shorter work day) attainable by political means. Under the pretext of freedom and antigovernmentalism or antiauthoritarian individualism, these gentlemen—who had so passively endured the most miserable despotism for the past sixteen years, and still do!—in fact advocate the ordinary bourgeois system, but Proudhonistically

---

2. At the Central Council's meeting, which took place, not on Tuesday, October 2, but on October 16, 1866, it was decided to submit the matter to a subcommittee; the latter, on October 23, confirmed the unanimous decision to exclude Le Lubez from the Central Council.

idealized! Proudhon has caused enormous harm. First, his sham criticism of and his sham opposition to the utopians (he himself is merely a petty-bourgeois utopian, whereas in the utopia of a Fourier, Owen, etc., one finds the glimmerings and the visionary expression of a new world) attacked and corrupted the *"jeunesse brillante"* [glittering youth] and the students, then the workers, especially the Parisians, who as workers in the luxury trades belonged very much to the old muck, without knowing it. Ignorantly vain, pretentious, gossipy, emphatically arrogant, they were on the verge of spoiling everything, since they rushed to the Congress in large numbers which had no relation to the number of their members. In my report, I shall rap their knuckles.

The simultaneous American labor congress at Baltimore[1] has given me great joy. The slogan there was organization for the struggle against capital, and remarkably enough, out of a correct workers' instinct, most of the demands I had formulated for the Geneva Congress were made there too.

The reform movement here, which our Central Council has called into life (*quorum magna pars fui*) [in which I played a large role], has now assumed immense and irresistible dimensions. I have always remained behind the scenes, and will not bother with the thing further, once it starts moving.

Yours,

K. MARX

From letter to Ludwig Kugelmann (in Hanover)
LONDON, OCTOBER 13, 1866

Dear Friend:

. . . The London Council of the English Trade Unions (its secretary is our president, Odger) is consulting at this moment as to whether it should declare itself as the British Section of the International Association. If it does that, then the government of the working class here goes over to us in a certain sense, and we can "push on" the movement very much.

Greetings.

Yours,

K. M.

---

1. The trade-union congress at Baltimore, Md., August 20–25, 1866, which decided to found a National Labor Union.

From letter to Engels (in Manchester)
LONDON, DECEMBER 31, 1866

Dear Fred:
   . . . Apropos. The French Government confiscated and placed in
the police archives papers and documents which were taken across
the frontier by French members after the Geneva Congress. Through
Lord Stanley, the Foreign Minister, we claimed the papers as "British
property." And in fact poor Bonaparte had to deliver them all back
to us.[1] Isn't this fine! . . .
   Greetings.

Yours,
K. M.

From letter to Engels (in Manchester)
LONDON, APRIL 2, 1867

Dear Engels:
   . . . Our International has celebrated a great victory. We had
arranged for financial support from the London trade unions for the
Paris bronze workers who were on strike. As soon as the masters saw
this, they gave in. The thing has stirred up a great fuss in the French
papers, and we are now an established power in France. . . .
   Greetings.

Yours,
K. M.

1. From the minutes of the General Council, January 1, 1867: "The General
Council then, on the motion of Fox, passed the following resolution: That the
General Council . . . tenders its thanks to Lord Stanley for his just and efficacious
intervention with the French Government with a view to obtain for the said
General Council the papers and letters belonging to it, which were seized upon
the person of Jules Gottraux, a British subject, on September 30, 1866. Fox was
directed and undertook to communicate this resolution to Lord Stanley."

From letter to Sigfrid Meyer (in New York)
HANOVER,[1] APRIL 30, 1867

Dear Friend:

So far as the International Working Men's Association is concerned, it has become a power in England, France, Switzerland, and Belgium. Do organize in America as many branches as possible. Contribution per member is one penny (about one silver groschen) yearly. Still, every community donates what it can. The Congress this year will be in Lausanne, on September 3. Each community may send one representative. Write me about this matter, about what has happened to you in America, and about the general situation. If you remain silent, I will consider it proof that you have not yet forgiven me.

With warmest regards.

Yours,
KARL MARX

From letter to Ludwig Büchner (in Darmstadt)
HANOVER, MAY 1, 1867

Dear Sir:

. . . I consider it of the highest importance to free the French from the false views in which Proudhon, with his idealized petty-bourgeoisness, has buried them. At the Geneva Congress, as well as in the connections that I, as a member of the General Council of the International Working Men's Association, have had with the French Branch, I have repeatedly encountered the most repulsive consequences of Proudhonism. . . .

Faithfully yours,
KARL MARX

---

1. From April 17 to May 15, 1867, Marx was visiting his friend Dr. Ludwig Kugelmann in Hanover.

From letter to Engels (in Manchester)
LONDON, AUGUST 31, 1867

Dear Fred:
 . . . For the Congress of the International in Lausanne,[1] delegates from here: Eccarius, Lessner, Dupont. In addition, the president of the Coventry Ribbon Weavers, and A. Walton, Esq. (from Wales). Eccarius has been given the correspondenceship of the *Times*—at the latter's request.
 From all reports from Paris, it looks very shaky for Bonaparte there. Salute.

Yours,
K. M.

From letter to Engels (in Manchester)
LONDON, SEPTEMBER 4, 1867

Dear Fred:
 . . . The following will explain to you the article *"Les Conditions de la Paix,"* in *Le Courrier Français*[1] (which you must *return* to me after reading):
 You know that in the General Council I spoke against joining the peace windbags.[2] My speech lasted about half an hour. Eccarius, as recording secretary, gave a report to the *Bee-Hive*[3] in which he mentioned only a few words of my remarks. Its reprint in the *Courrier* also left out the sentences about the necessity of armies vis-à-vis Russia and the cowardice of the fellows. Nevertheless, there has been a great uproar over all this. The donkeys of the Peace Congress, whose London agent is M. de Colleville, *changed* their original program and smuggled into the new one, which is much more democratic, the words: "the harmonizing of economic interests with

1. September 2–8, 1867.

1. September 2, 1867; the article was by Lucien Dubois.
2. At the General Council session of August 13, 1867, Marx spoke against the International's joining the Peace Congress on the ground that disarmament would leave Europe open to Russian conquest.
3. Published August 17, 1867.

liberty," a loose phrase that can also mean mere free trade. They bombarded me with letters and even had the insolence to send me the enclosed trash with their new program. The insolence consists of the fact that in their address they refer to me as "member of the Geneva, etc., Congress." The *Courrier*, their liveliest spokesman in Paris, deserted them, as you will see. Because of a private letter I wrote to Vermorel (whom I don't know) about a fortnight ago, the same *Courrier* changed its policy in regard to Russia.

The main thing is that these great gentlemen of the Peace Congress —Victor Hugo, Garibaldi, L. Blanc, etc.—had ignored our International Association with the most extreme superiority. I have now forced them to recognize us as a power.

I received the first two issues of a Naples paper: *Libertà e Giustizia*. In issue No. 1 they declare themselves for our organ. I gave it to Eccarius for submission to the Congress. No. 2, which I will send you, contains a very good attack on Mazzini.[4] I presume that Bakunin is behind it. . . .

Yours,

K. M.

From letter to Engels (in Manchester)
LONDON, SEPTEMBER 11, 1867

Dear Fred:

. . . At the next Congress, in Brussels, I shall personally deal with these jackasses of Proudhonists. I have managed the whole thing diplomatically and did not want to come out *personally* until my book was published and our Association had struck root. For the rest, I will give them a hiding in the Official Report of the General Council (despite all their efforts, the Parisian babblers could not prevent our reelection).

Meanwhile our Association has made great progress. The wretched *Star*, which tried to ignore us entirely, declared yesterday in its leading article that we are more important than the Peace Congress. Schulze-Delitzsch could not prevent his "Workers' Association" in Berlin from joining us. The swine among the English trade unionists, who thought we had gone too "far," now come running to us. In addition to the *Courrier Français*, Girardin's *Liberté*, *Siècle*, *Mode*, *Gazette de France*, etc. have reported on our Congress. *Les choses*

---

4. "*La Questione Romana*," in *Libertà e Giustizia*, August 24, 1867.

marchent. [Things are moving.] And in the next revolution, which is perhaps nearer than it appears, we (that is, you and I) will have this powerful engine in our hands. Compare with this the results of Mazzini's, etc., operation since thirty years![1] And without financial means! With the intrigues of the Proudhonists in Paris, of Mazzini in Italy, of the jealous Odger, Cremer, and Potter in London, with the Schulze-Delitzschites and Lassalleans in Germany! We can be very well content! . . .

Yours,

K. M.

From letter to Engels (in Manchester)
LONDON, SEPTEMBER 12, 1867

Dear Fred:

. . . I am entirely in agreement with you *quoad* Eccarius. A worker, specifically one of Eccarius' critical dryness, lacks diplomatic finesse. He writes for the *Times*[1] as if he were writing for the *Neue Rheinische Zeitung*. Nevertheless, the thing does no harm. Here in London, they say: The International Association, etc., must be very strong to have the *Times* report on it specially. Eccarius' sneers are considered the *Times*'s sneers.

The lousy French Swiss, very strongly represented [at the Lausanne Congress], gave the Paris French chatterboxes free play. Old Becker committed the main blunder. He broke down our agenda in order to burst forth with *his freedom proposal.* This gave the Parisians the opportunity to completely eliminate the whole thing.

But it did not matter. The main thing is having the Congress, not what happens in it. In our General Report *on se moquera bien* [we will make good fun of] the Paris wiseacres. To the latter's great sorrow, it was resolved that those *who do not pay* (and the Parisians have not paid a sou) cannot be delegates in the future. At the next Congress, in Brussels, twenty Englishmen and thirty Germans will be needed. As to the Belgians themselves, they can send only one delegate per five hundred members, and therefore they will not be very

---

1. This sentence was written in English.

1. On September 6, 7, 9, 10, and 11, 1867, the *Times* published a series of articles, "International Working Men's Congress," written anonymously by Eccarius, criticizing the confusion and talkativeness of the French Proudhonist delegates at the Lausanne Congress.

numerous. In addition, they are rather rebellious against the Parisians.

Notabene: The worst is that we do not have a single person in Paris who could make contact with *anti*-Proudhonist sections among the workers (and they are in the majority). If Dupont were in Paris for a few weeks, everything would be in order, but the police keep a sharp eye on him.

By and by, in private letters, I will chastise Vermorel for his asininities in regard to German politics. I must proceed *gradatim* [gradually], and therefore I deliberately start with the United States, Russia, and Turkey, because this is "neutral" territory as between Germans and French.

Laura and Lafargue are now translating part of the Preface for *Le Courrier Français*.[2]

Salute.

Yours,

K. M.

From letter to Engels (in Manchester)

LONDON, OCTOBER 4, 1867

Dear Fred:

. . . *Ad vocem* [regarding] the International Association. At my proposal, the office of president was abolished, after Odger's reelection had already been proposed. Fox, who at every opportunity shows great hostility to Eccarius behind his back, gave notice that at the next session (Tuesday) he would bring up Eccarius' articles in the *Times* for censure by the Council. To Fox's great surprise, I also gave notice that next Tuesday I would bring up the "secret letter" he wrote to Becker urging him "to do all in his power to remove the seat of the Central Council from London."[1] Fox, who is made up of caprices and crotchets, imagines that he must build an "opposition party" inside the Council against what he calls the "German dictatorship" there. He will get a surprise at his successes in this line! . . .

Salute.

Yours,

K. M.

---

2. The French translation of the Preface to *Capital* was published in *Le Courrier Français*, October 1, 1867.

---

1. On August 29, 1867, on the eve of the Lausanne Congress, Fox wrote Johann Philipp Becker a "personal and confidential" letter suggesting that the seat of the General Council be moved from London to Geneva.

From letter to Engels (in Manchester)
LONDON, OCTOBER 9, 1867

Dear Fred:

. . . Yesterday Eccarius was to be beheaded by Fox. The arraignment by the latter lasted more than an hour. He had put together the worst passages with great malice and used all the arts of an Old Bailey lawyer, including constant attacks on me. In my rebuttal I socked him so that in his final reply he lost all his composure and self-control. Everybody participated in the discussion. Result: My motion (rather, amendment) to "pass to the agenda" was adopted by an enormous majority. Nevertheless, during the debate Eccarius was properly dressed down. . . .

Yours,
K. M.

From letter to Engels (in Manchester)
LONDON, NOVEMBER 30, 1867

Dear Fred:

. . . If you have read the papers, you will have seen that (1) the Memorial of the International Council for the Fenians[1] was sent to Hardie, and that (2) the debate on Fenianism (last Tuesday week[2]) was reported in the *Times*.[3] Reporters from the Dublin papers *Irishman* and *Nation* were also present. I came very late (I have had a fever for about two weeks and it passed only two days ago) and really had no intention of speaking first, because of my uncomfortable physical condition, and second, because of the ticklish situation. However, Weston, the chairman, wanted to force me to, and so I moved for an adjournment, which obligated me to speak last Tuesday [November 26]. As a matter of fact, what I prepared for Tuesday last was not a speech but points for a speech. But the Irish reporters failed to come; we waited for them until nine o'clock, although the place is open only until nine-thirty. At my instigation, Fox (because of a quarrel

1. See "On the Fenian Prisoners in Manchester," page 87.
2. November 19.
3. The *Times*, November 21, 1867.

in the Council, he had not shown up for two weeks, and, moreover, he had sent in his resignation as a member of the Council, with rude attacks on Jung) had prepared a long speech. After the opening of the meeting, I therefore stated that I would yield the floor to Fox on account of the belated hour. Actually—because of the executions in Manchester that had taken place in the meantime—our subject, Fenianism, was likely to inflame the passions to such heat that I (but not the abstract Fox) would have been forced to hurl revolutionary thunderbolts instead of a factual analysis of the situation and the movement, as I had intended to do. The Irish reporters, therefore, by staying away and delaying the opening of the meeting, did me a great service. I do not like to mix with people like Roberts, Stephens, etc.

Fox's speech was good, for one thing, because it was delivered by an *Englishman*, and for another, because it dealt only with the political and international aspects. For that very reason, however, he moved only on the surface. The resolution he brought forth was absurd and inane. I opposed it and had it referred to the Standing Committee.

What the English do not yet know is that since 1846 the economic content and therefore the political aim of English domination in Ireland has entered an entirely new phase, and that, precisely because of this, Fenianism is characterized by a socialistic tendency (in the negative sense, directed against the appropriation of the land) and by being a lower-orders movement. What can be more ridiculous than to confuse the barbarities of Elizabeth or Cromwell, who wanted to supplant the Irish with English colonists (in the Roman sense), with the present system, which wants to supplant them with sheep, pigs, and oxen! The system of 1801–46 (evictions in that period were exceptional, occurring mainly in Leinster, where the soil is particularly favorable to cattle raising), with its usurious rents and middlemen, collapsed in 1846. The repeal of the Corn Laws, partly the result of, or at any rate hastened by, the Irish famine, deprived Ireland of its *monopoly* of England's corn supply in normal times. Wool and meat became the slogan, hence conversion of tillage into pasture. Hence systematic consolidation of farms from then on. The Encumbered Estates Act, which turned a mass of previously enriched middlemen into landlords, hastened the process. *Clearing of the Estate of Ireland!* is now the only purpose of English rule in Ireland. The stupid English Government in London, of course, knows nothing itself of this immense change since 1846. But the Irish know it. From Meagher's Proclamation (1848) down to the election manifesto of Hennessy (Tory and Urquhartite) (1866), the Irish have expressed their consciousness of it in the clearest and most forceful manner.

The question now is, what shall we advise the *English* workers?

In my opinion, they must make *repeal of the Union* (in short, the joke of 1783, only democratized and adapted to the conditions of the time) an article of their pronunciamento. This is the only *legal* and, therefore, the only possible form of Irish emancipation which can be admitted in the program of an English party. Experience must show later whether a mere personal union can continue to subsist between the two countries. I half think it can, if it takes place in time.

What the Irish need is:

1. Self-government and independence from England.

2. An agrarian revolution. With the best intentions in the world, the English cannot accomplish this for them, but they can give them the legal means of accomplishing it themselves.

3. Protective tariffs against England. Between 1783 and 1801 every branch of Irish industry flourished. The Union, which overthrew the protective tariffs established by the Irish parliament, destroyed all industrial life in Ireland. The bit of linen industry offers no substitute whatever. The Union of 1801 had the same effect on Irish industry as the measures for the suppression of the Irish woolen industry, etc., taken by the English Parliament under Anne, George II, etc. As soon as the Irish are independent, necessity will turn them into protectionists, as it did Canada, Australia, etc. Before I present my views in the Central Council (next Tuesday [December 3], this time fortunately *without* the presence of reporters), I would like you to give me your opinion in a few lines.

Greetings.

Yours,

K. M.

From letter to Engels (in Manchester)
LONDON, JANUARY 11, 1868

Dear Fred:

The "Geck"[1] has been bustling about here in London for some time. He also visited Borkheim, to whom he made speeches as to you, but with better success, since he knew how to flatter our B's vanity. After he squeezed money for ten shares from the latter, and after he had consumed his wines, he did not let himself be seen again. For an understanding of his further activities in London, the following, pro-

---

1. "Geck," coxcomb or fop, is Marx's pun on the name of Amand Goegg.

visionally: Cremer, who as you know has been removed as secretary of the International Council for some time now and who, out of anger, resigned from the Council, was not reelected by the last Congress. Mr. Odger was reelected. At my suggestion, the office of president (annual) was abolished, and replaced by a chairman to be chosen at every session. Odger, angry at this, has held himself aloof from our principles. Well! Mr. "Geck," via Le Lubez, trickily attached himself to Odger (who had inducted him into the London Trades Council) and to Cremer. They set up a London Committee, with Beales as president, etc. In short, it is a story against the International Working Men's Association. (At the initial meeting, Geck also brought in the noble Blind.) The fellows had the effrontery to invite me to their second meeting. Eccarius, in a badly written article in the *Bee-Hive* of last Saturday,[2] denounced Geck and Consorts. . . .

Yours,

MOHR[3]

Letter to Engels (in Manchester)
LONDON, MARCH 16, 1868

Dear Fred:

Enclosed from Kugelmann a letter from a young Bielefeld manufacturer.[1] I am especially amused by the latter's idea that I must once have been a sewing machine "employing manufacturer."[2] If the fellows only knew how little I know about all this stuff!

Also unavoidable is the question: What now? People want all prescriptions to be miracle cures, not seeing the fire-and-iron cures which have already been quite effective.

Strange how this Dollfus (Alsace) has achieved his false renown! This humbug, who is way below such Englishmen as Briggs, etc., has so arranged his contracts with his workers—contracts which only degenerate rabble would make—that in reality they produce his own serf colonies, which in fact are well treated "as serfs" and thereby exploited as neatly as any others. This brute has therefore introduced in the *Corps législatif* the paragraph of the Press Law about the *"vie*

---

2. "The Geneva Peace Congress," January 4, 1868.
3. "Moor," Marx's nickname.

1. A letter from the linen manufacturer Gustav Meyer to Marx, enclosed in Kugelmann's letter of March 13, 1868.
2. The two words are written in English.

privée qui doit être murée" ["private life, which should be behind walls"].[3] In this, his philanthropic tricks are illuminated here and there.

The way the English in Ireland now treat political prisoners, or suspects, or even those merely imprisoned in ordinary jails (such as Pigott of the *Irishman* and Sullivan of the *News*), exceeds anything perpetrated on the Continent—Russia excepted. They are dogs!

Salute.

Yours,

K. M.

From letter to Ludwig Kugelmann (in Hanover)
LONDON, APRIL 6, 1868

Dear Kugelmann:

. . . The Irish Question predominates here now. It has been exploited by Gladstone & Co., of course, only in order to get back into office, and above all, to have an electoral cry at the next elections, which will be based on household suffrage.[1] For the moment, this turn of affairs is harmful to the workers' party. The intriguers among the workers, such as Odger, Potter, etc., who want to get into the next Parliament, now have a new excuse for attaching themselves to the bourgeois Liberals.

However, this is only a penalty which England—and hence also the English working class—is paying for the great crime it has been committing against Ireland for many centuries. And in the long run it will benefit the English working class itself. Specifically, the English Established Church in Ireland—or what they used to call here the Irish church—is the religious bulwark of English *landlordism* in Ireland, and at the same time the outpost of the Established Church in England itself (I am speaking here of the Established Church as a *landowner*). The overthrow of the Established Church in Ireland will mean its downfall in England, and both will be followed by the destruction of landlordism, first in Ireland, and then in England. But I

---

3. In the French Press Law, passed on March 6, 1868, Article 11 states: "Publications in journals in regard to private life are violations of law and will be punished with a fine of 500 francs."

---

1. The parliamentary elections of November, 1868, were conducted under the 1867 Reform Bill, which provided for household suffrage for all those who paid a minimum of £10 rent annually. The number of voters was thus nearly doubled. The Reform Bill did not apply in Scotland and Ireland, or to women.

have long been convinced that the social revolution must begin *seriously* from the bottom, that is, from land ownership.

Moreover, the whole thing will have the very useful consequence that, once the Irish church is dead, the Protestant Irish tenants in the province of Ulster will make common cause with the Catholic tenants in the three other provinces of Ireland, whereas up till now landlordism has been able to exploit this religious antagonism. . . .

Yours,

K. Marx

From letter to Engels (in Manchester)
LONDON, JUNE 20, 1868

Dear Fred:

. . . Last Tuesday's [June 16] session of the International. Prior to that I received papers which made a rescinding of the resolutions about the Congress unavoidable. *D'abord* [to begin with], the statement of the Minister of Justice, Bara, that the Congress should not take place in Brussels. Second, a printed manifesto of the Brussels and Verviers committees, wherein they throw the gauntlet at the Minister. Third, letters from De Paepe and Vandenhouten that we would ruin the Association if we held the Congress in Belgium. It would be rumored as a concession to the government, etc.

I do not even mention the lousy intrigues of Vésinier, Pyat, etc., who are here now. They, of course, are spreading the rumor that we are working at Bonaparte's dictate.

They expected a great scandal in that last session and therefore they sent us auditors. They were very disappointed when I, after reading the relevant documents, withdrew my resolutions. I turned the thing so: The [Belgian] law against foreigners was in no way a special threat to the International. It was *general*. The International, however, would have made a concession to the government if it had chosen Brussels as its meeting place under such a law. Now the matter is reversed. After the Belgian Government had directly threatened and provoked us, we would make it a concession if we removed the Congress from Brussels. At the same time, I made a few very disdainful jokes over the heroic tone assumed by the attackers of my resolutions (Odger, etc.) before they knew the changed circumstances. The only danger that could have been incurred was that of cheap martyrdom and ridicule. Mrs. Law cried out "Hear, hear" several times and expressed her approval by pounding on the table. At any rate, I brought it to the point that the laughter was turned against Odger, etc., and that the rescinding of the resolutions did not appear to be a victory for them. . . .

Greetings.

Yours,

K. M.

From letter to Engels (in Manchester)
LONDON, JUNE 23, 1868

Dear Fred:

. . . Vésinier is making a stink here in the French Branch against Dupont and Jung, both of whom he decries as "Bonapartists." During my absence he attended a session of the Central Council (to which he had no right) and wrote an incredible report in *Cigale* (Brussels paper).[1] The discussion was over the location of the next Congress.

Letter to Engels (in Manchester)
LONDON, JULY 7, 1868

Dear Fred:

The children are doing well. Yesterday, for the first time, they were outdoors for half an hour. They are still peeling strongly. As soon as this is over, they will be movable.

In the last few days I have been extraordinarily hard-pressed by the baker, cheesemonger, assessed taxes, God and the devil.

You will recall that for the last eighteen years the local German Workers' Educational Society has been celebrating the June [1848] insurrection. Only in the past few years have the French (their local society now exists as a branch of the International[1]) participated in this. And the old *meneurs* [leaders] have always stayed away, I mean the *petits grands hommes* [little great men].

1. Pierre Vésinier attacked Dupont and Jung in *Cigale* June 21, 1868. The Belgian Section of the International protested Vésinier's attack a week later, June 28, 1868, in the same paper.

1. The French Section of the International was founded in London in the fall of 1865.

This year, in public meeting, M. Pyat came and read an alleged address of the Paris Commune (this euphemism of the same Pyat, who yields nothing to Blind in this line), wherein the assassination of Bonaparte was advocated,[2] as he did also in his *"Lettre aux étudiants"* exactly a year ago. The French Branch, supported by other screamers, acclaimed this. Vésinier had it printed in *Cigale* and *Espiègle*, Belgian papers, and left it to Pyat to explain to the International.

Thereupon we received a letter from the Brussels Committee, which presently carries on much propaganda under increasingly difficult circumstances (Charleroi Affair[3]). Content of the letter: This demonstration threatens to tumble the whole International on the Continent. Will the French Branch never give up the old demagogical rhetoric, etc., etc.? To think that our people are sitting in jail in Paris at the same time.[4] Yesterday *we* issued a statement (to be printed in Brussels) disavowing any connection between Pyat and the International.[5]

In reality, I regard the whole affair (naturally supported by the French Branch's background of enormous stupidities) as an intrigue of the old parties, the republican jackasses of 1848, especially the *petits grands hommes* who represent them in London. Our Association is a thorn in their flesh. Having vainly tried to work against it, the next best thing is naturally to compromise it. Pyat is just the fellow to do this *de bonne foi* [in good faith]. Hence the more clever ones are pushing him forward.

What could be more comical than this squinting melodrama writer and charivari man of 1848, this toastmaster of 1848, who now plays Brutus, but at a safe distance!

The local French Branch, if it does not cease its jackasseries, will have to be thrown out of the Association. Fifty such clowns, who on public occasions can gather around them shriekers of all nationalities, must not be permitted to endanger the International Association at a moment when, because of the conditions on the Continent, it is beginning to be a serious power.

Salute.

Greetings.

Yours,

K. M.

---

2. See Marx's letter to Kugelmann, December 5, 1868.

3. In March, 1868, there was a bloody clash between striking miners and gendarmes in Charleroi.

4. In May, 1868, nine members of the Paris Section of the International were sentenced to three months' imprisonment and 100-franc fines.

5. On July 7, 1868, the General Council passed a resolution that "Félix Pyat . . . has no connection with the Association"; it was published in the Belgian papers *Liberté, Cigale,* and *Tribune du Peuple.*

From letter to Engels (in Manchester)
LONDON, JULY 29, 1868

Dear Fred:

. . . There are all kinds of scandals here relating to Pyat, the French Branch, and the General Council. More about it tomorrow.[1] Now only this. In his second program for the congress of the General German Labor Association in Hamburg,[2] Schweitzer has one point about the International Working Men's Association and another one about my book [*Capital*]. The program also appeared in the *Zukunft*. On the other hand, A. Bebel, president of the Labor Association, meeting in Nuremberg,[3] sent an invitation to the General Council. We are asked to send delegates (Eccarius will go). Its joining the International and acceptance of our program are practically *assured*. Finally, we received an invitation from Vienna, where the Austrian fraternal labor festival will be celebrated at the beginning of September. We sent a mandate to Fox, who is in Vienna, to represent us. Of the private negotiations between Wilhelmchen [Liebknecht] and Schweitzer I know only what the former writes me. Against this, I know from other sources that in the same degree that Wilhelmchen has discredited himself among workers, with his overeager alliance with the South German pettifoggers, the influence of Schweitzer, who is a crafty dog, has grown. Hence Wilhelm saw himself in need of concluding a cartel, now in existence, with Schweitzer, who was, in addition, clever enough to have his title of nobility taken away by a Prussian court "because of *lèse majesté*." It is now up to me—I mean as a member of the General Council—to remain nonpartisan as between the various *organized* labor groups. It is their business, and not mine, whom they want for a leader. As secretary for Germany, I must reply to everybody who writes me in his official position as president, etc. In this sense I also wrote to Schweitzer (always with an eye to the possibility of the whole correspondence being published). Still, it is high time to be able to show influence among German workers in Germany, after the intrigues of the 1848 democracy against us. . . .

Salute.

Yours,

MOHR

1. See Marx's next letter to Engels, August 4, 1868.
2. August 22–26, 1868.
3. On July 23, 1868, Bebel sent his invitation to the congress, which met in Nuremberg September 5–7, 1868.

From letter to Engels (*in Manchester*)
LONDON, AUGUST 4, 1868

Dear Fred:

. . . The swinish French Branch has made us a fine scandal. The Pyatists have published a *blâme* [censure] against the General Council in *Cigale*. Their channel—the notorious Vésinier. We simply passed over this vote of censure and moved to *l'ordre du jour* [order of the day]. Thereupon a meeting of the French Branch, which developed into a free-for-all. Dupont, Jung, Lafargue, Johannard, Lassassie, and divers others withdrew from this rabble of scamps. The rabble now numbers perhaps fifteen members, although they claim to us to represent the "*souveraineté du peuple*" [sovereignty of the people]. We are "*des endormeurs*" [wheedlers], "*des ambitieux*" [ambitious ones], etc. Apart from this little scandal which these philistines made in the obscure little Belgian paper, they are naturally nowhere. . . .

Salute.

Yours,
K. M.

From letter to Engels (*in Manchester*)
LONDON, AUGUST 29, 1868

Dear Fred:

. . . Dupont has received a mandate from Naples, to represent the branch there.[1] Since the Mentana affair,[2] as we read in the Italian reports, a general reaction has taken place, in particular the right of meeting and association has been practically destroyed there.

In Paris, fortunately, our old members still *sit*. The Paris Committee will send one *délégué* [delegate] to Brussels; but on the other hand, the various *corps de métier* [craft unions], eight to nine.[3] Our people have written us from prison in order to "compromise politically" these *corps de métier* men, so that they can no longer return. The length

---

1. At the Brussels Congress, held September 6–13, 1868.
2. French and papal troops defeated Garibaldi's volunteers at Mentana, in the Rome province, on November 3, 1867.
3. About ten delegates of the French craft unions—mechanics, tinsmiths, wagon makers, bookbinders, cabinetmakers, goldsmiths, cotton printers, etc.— attended the Brussels Congress.

to which the Paris police will go you can see from the fact that they put a certain "Monsieur Dupont" from London among the wives of prisoners to spy on them. He was a police agent, but the comedy miscarried everywhere for him. Eccarius went as our delegate to Nuremberg[4] today. From there he goes to Brussels. He is the correspondent from the *Times* for both meetings.

The so-called French Branch, under the direction of Messrs. Pyat and Vésinier, is sending a delegate to Brussels in order—*horribile dictu* [horrible to say]—to impeach us!

If Moore is still there, tell him it would be well if he could pay me his contribution to the International Working Men's Association *before Tuesday*. We are weakly represented in Brussels, and every shilling we can raise now will be used to send another member there. Tuesday next[5] is our last sitting this year before the Congress.

Greetings.

Yours,

K. M.

Letter to Johann Georg Eccarius and Friedrich Lessner
(in Brussels)
LONDON, SEPTEMBER 10, 1868

Dear Eccarius and Lessner!

First my thanks to Lessner for his long and interesting letter.[1]

You two must not permit the Congress to last longer than this week. Up to now—as far as England is concerned—there has been as yet no ridicule.

Should the Belgians and French again bring forth masses of new stuff for the agenda, you should let them know that it won't do, since

1. The Germans are represented quite poorly because their own congresses are taking place in Germany at the same time.

2. England is practically not represented at all, because of the suffrage campaign there.

3. The German Swiss are not represented at all, because they joined only recently, and their long-existing branches exhausted their means in the Geneva strike.[2]

---

4. The conference of German Workers' Associations, September 5–7, 1868.
5. September 1.

1. In a letter to Marx, September 8, 1868, Lessner gave a detailed report on the Brussels congress.
2. A strike of 3,000 Geneva building-trade workers in March and April, 1866.

4. The debates are conducted one-sidedly in the French language.

5. That, therefore, one must avoid making *decisions on general theoretical questions,* as this would later only provoke protests from the non-Belgian and non-French side.

The [Franco-Prussian] war naturally interests the public most. Ponderous declamations and inflated phrases do no harm here. The decision to be taken in this matter is simply that the working class is not yet sufficiently organized to throw any decisive weight into the scales; but that the Congress, in the name of the working class, protests and denounces the originators of the war; that a war between France and Germany is a civil war, ruinous for both countries and ruinous for Europe altogether. The observation that the war can only serve the interests of the Russian Government can hardly be expected to get support from the French and Belgian gentlemen.

Regards to friend Becker.

K. MARX

Should the *crédit mutuel* be mentioned, Eccarius must simply explain that the workers in England, Germany, and the United States have nothing to do with Proudhonistic dogmas and consider the question of credit as secondary.

The resolutions of the Congress are to be reported to the London papers by telegraph. Hence nothing that is blameworthy!

K. M.

From letter to Engels (in Manchester)
LONDON, SEPTEMBER 12, 1868

Dear Fred:

Fortunately, the Congress is ending today, and up to Thursday [September 10]—our reports go that far—it has compromised itself only minimally. But one must always anxiously expect some failure, as the Belgians have an enormous majority there. M. Tolain and other Parisians wanted to move the General Council to Brussels. They are very jealous of London. It is great progress that the Proudhonist "brave Belgians" and French who, at the congresses of Geneva (1866) and Lausanne (1867), declaimed against the trade unions, etc., are now fanatically for them. The "brave Belgians," with all their boasting, had not prepared for anything. The correspondent of the *Daily News,* for example, had for three days tried in vain to find out the place of the meeting, until he accidentally encountered Jung and Stepney. The meeting place was, in fact, not rented in advance, and the "brave

Belgians" wanted to charge the cost to the General Council, which they owe (as they do the French) 3,000 francs (for their 250 attendants, etc.). The money is now being raised through private collections among the delegates. . . .

Greetings.

Yours,

K. M.

Letter to Hermann Jung (in London)
LONDON, SEPTEMBER 14, 1868

Dear Jung:

Today's *Times* publishes Eccarius' reports of September 9 and 10.

In the discussion on machinery, he worsens Lessner's speech, which was much better in the *Daily News*. Lessner quoted my book [*Capital*], as you can see in the *Daily News*. Eccarius suppresses the citation.

But even better. In the *Daily News*, the resolution on machinery, etc., was designated as being the *proposal of the General Council*. In the *Times*, Eccarius transformed this into his *personal proposal*. Here is a point whereon you must lay hold of him. His egoism is in need of a thump to set him right again.

Yours,

K. M.

Letter to Sigfrid Meyer (in New York)
LONDON, SEPTEMBER 14, 1868

Dear Meyer:

Enclosed the issue of the *Times* which contains the Fourth Annual Report of the General Council (written by *me*) and the highly interesting *first leader* of the *Times* on this document. It is the first time it has put aside the mocking tone against the working class and has taken it "very" *au sérieux* [seriously]. Spread this news. Inform Jessup about it.

I have to reply to both your letters,[1] the first to me and the second

---

1. See Marx's letter to Meyer and Vogt, October 28, 1868.

to Eccarius, which has been handed me in his absence (he is not yet back from Brussels).

In regard to the first letter, it is your fault if Sorge (who is altogether unknown to me) received the mandate. If you wanted simply to give him a recommendation for a specific purpose, you should have definitely written so. From the tenor of your letter I thought Sorge was *your and A. Vogt's man.* So be more careful in the future! But you also made a second mistake when you handed the mandate over to Sorge instead of writing to me about the misunderstanding.

The mistake has been made, but can be rectified.

The Brussels Congress has renewed the General Council's seat in London. But this has to be considered a *new* Council, which is to *review* all the *old* mandates. Write me, therefore, whether you and A. Vogt want mandates. Write me also in what way we should revoke Sorge's mandate, or whether we should inform him that the General Council has changed the mandates.

Drury was here for some time. Recently, shortly before the Brussels Congress, he was proposed as the International Working Men's Association's plenipotentiary to the American labor union and its congress. We did not agree then, because the person who made the proposal was suspect to us. Do first observe the man more closely yourself or have friends do so.

There are no more issues of the *Commonwealth.* Agitational writings, in our sense, do not exist in England since last year. *My book has not yet been translated into English.* Eccarius, generally very efficient and at the same time very ambitious, has *deliberately avoided* speaking of it in the *Commonwealth* and on other occasions. He loves to appropriate my ideas to *himself.* At the Brussels Congress Lessner used my book in his speech on machinery. The correspondent of the *Daily News* reported this. Eccarius, who reported the sessions of the Congress to the *Times, suppressed* it. His behavior is the more stupid in that he not only owes his knowledge to me, but also his post as general secretary of the General Council. I alone supported him (also in the *Commonwealth*) against the attacks from the English and French sides. He relies on his previous experience with me, that I keep my eye only on business and overlook personal stupidities! I will *not* give him your letter.

The more clippings from the American press about my book you can send me, the better. Do send them to me!

I am enclosing a card. It was sent to us with a letter, in order to enter into contact with us. Address: G. W. Randall, secretary, Workingmen's Institute, 3 Tremont Row, Room 52, Boston, N.E.

My acquaintances in America have been lost to me for years. I am in contact only with [Hermann] Meyer in St. Louis, the friend of our J. Weydemeyer (who died last year).

Write everything you can find out about the relationship between the railroads and public lands. You have perhaps forgotten that the General German Labor Association, at its Hamburg congress, gave my book recognition by a Resolution of its own.

Write to Randall at my suggestion as the German secretary of the General Council.

Best regards to A. Vogt and yourself.

Yours,

K. M.

From letter to Engels (in Manchester)
LONDON, SEPTEMBER 16, 1868

Dear Engels:

. . . The policy of sending the Report[1] to the *Times* only has justified itself. It forced all the London papers, with the exception of the deeply indignant Levy,[2] to speak out. The *Times* did not take Eccarius' reports from Nuremberg. It bit only when it received the Report from me. Yesterday's *Morning Advertiser* (to Blind's sorrow) had a first leader in favor of the International and against the *Times*. The *Star* declared the [Brussels] Congress to be a *"success."* The *Standard*, which attacked us at first, sneaks in yesterday a leading article in favor of the working class. It smites the capitalists and will itself now make fun of the land question. The *Journal des Débats* regrets that the English, Germans, and Belgians, as the resolution on the land question shows, belong to the *"secte communiste"* and that the French, for their part, again produce *"les déclamations ridicules de Proudhon."*

There is much dissatisfaction with Eccarius, and next Tuesday he will be subjected to a salutary storm. The points of accusation against him are these:

He took practically no part in the Congress and afterwards posed in the *Times* as the leading mind there. He appropriated, again in the *Times*, the proposals of the General Council as his private property

---

1. Marx's "Fourth Annual Report of the General Council of the International" was published in the London *Times*, September 9, 1868.
2. Publisher of the *Daily Telegraph*.

and similarly the consequent applause as coming to him. He suppressed the speeches of the others as much as possible, and, in order to flatter the *Times, falsified* Dupont's final speech. In addition, Lessner has a grievance that Eccarius suppressed the fact that he (Lessner) had read passages from my book and that only under high pressure did he include in his correspondence the resolution on my book, and finally that he had falsified the German resolution on the war. He wrote that a European war would be a civil war, instead of using the words of the German resolution, which said: "A war between France and Germany is a civil war to the *profit of Russia*." He left out the latter entirely. Instead he ascribed to the Germans and English the Belgian nonsense, "to *strike* against war."

On the other hand, he profited from his reports. The long and the short of it is that he will be told that in future he will figure only as *reporter,* with the Council paying his travel expenses and the *Times* paying for his articles. But he will *no longer* be appointed *delegate.* So beware of the conflict of fractions.

Lessner says that if we achieved so much at the Congress, even though it was almost entirely Belgian (with an admixture of French) and we were so meagerly represented, it was due to the fact that on all decisive points the Belgian workers, despite their Brussels *leaders,* voted with London. Moses [Hess] is said to have made the best speech against the Proudhonists.[3] Tolain was so furious that he did not appear at the banquet. Not only was the Central Council reappointed, but the list of members, purged by us, was accepted. Vésinier is to send the proof of his suspicions of Tolain to a committee in Brussels within four weeks.[4] If they are nothing (and they are nothing), the Congress has already conditionally expelled him from the Association as a slanderer. The delegate of the French Branch brought in an act of accusation against the General Council, which also contained a modest demand that the French member of the General Council be appointed by the French Branch. This was simply put on the agenda (exactly as we do with the grievances of the fellows in the General Council). . . .

Greetings.

Yours,

K. M.

---

3. In his speech at the Brussels Congress on September 11, 1868, Hess attacked the Proudhonist theory of "free credit" and "barter bank," citing Marx's anti-Proudhon book, *The Poverty of Philosophy.*

4. At the General Council session of November 3, 1868, a letter from the committee was used to show that Vésinier had no proof against Tolain and that Vésinier should therefore be expelled as a slanderer.

From letter to Engels (in Manchester)
LONDON, SEPTEMBER 19, 1868

Dear Fred:

   . . . Next Tuesday [September 22], at the first session of the General Council, it will be stormy. Dupont is also very furious at Eccarius, because he had taken practically no part in the Congress. I will try to protect Eccarius against any "positive" steps, but this time I cannot come out for him as partisanly as I did last year against Fox, Carter, etc.[1] . . .

   Greetings.

Yours,

K. M.

   The report of *L'Opinion Nationale* on the Brussels Congress says, among other things: "I must mention here the General Report of the Association, edited by the Council in London. *Mention* is actually the only word I can use, because I am not sufficiently versed in law to sort and prune the incriminable phrases under French law which may be contained in the report." He then mentions the passages relating to "*le gouvernement français.*" "The criticism here is occasionally sharp, and often ironic. I repeat, I can pass no judgment on it; but I must admit that the public has been less timid than your correspondent; it has received all the passages which I refrain from citing with delirious applause."

   Twelve reporters from France were there.

   Emancipation and *Journal de Bruxelles* attacked the Congress in much the same way they treated us twenty years ago.

   One Russian journalist was there. He said he would send the General Council the Russian newspapers dealing with the Congress.

---

   1. On October 8, 1867, Peter Fox, James Carter, and Robert Shaw brought before the General Council accusations against Eccarius for his distorted reports of the Lausanne Congress in the London *Times*. See Marx's letter to Engels, October 4, 1867.

From letter to Engels (in Manchester)
LONDON, SEPTEMBER 26, 1868

Dear Fred:

. . . For the German working class, the most necessary thing is to stop agitating under the order of high authority. Such a bureaucratically schooled race must go through a complete course of "self-help." On the other hand, they have the advantage of beginning the movement under much more developed contemporary conditions than the English, and, as Germans, they have heads for generalization on their shoulders. Eccarius is full of praise for the parliamentary decorum— particularly as compared with the French at Brussels—that prevailed in the Nuremberg congress . . .

Greetings.

Yours,
K. M.

From letter to Engels (in Manchester)
LONDON, OCTOBER 10, 1868

Dear Fred:

. . . Enclosed a letter from Schweitzer,[1] together with a copy of the *Social-Demokrat,* which he sent me with it. . . .

In regard to Schweitzer's letter, it is clear that he does not feel himself quite at ease. His threat of "open war" is silly, even though the phrase "ostensibly" is directed only against Liebknecht & Co. His assertion that the cat did it is by no means correct. His alleged identification with the International Working Men's Association is in some contradiction to his hints in the *Social-Demokrat* after the Nuremberg affair that his association had "not" joined the International. Above all, however, it appears from his whole letter that Schweitzer has not yet been able to rid himself of the *idée fixe* of having "his own workers' movement." On the other hand, of all current German labor leaders,

---

1. In a letter of October 8, 1868, Schweitzer complained to Marx, as "secretary of the International," against the activities of the German socialists August Bebel and Wilhelm Liebknecht, claiming that his own General German Workers' Association had affiliated with the International "as far as the law allows."

he is absolutely the most intelligent and the most energetic, while
Liebknecht, in point of fact, has been forced by Schweitzer to remember that a workers' movement independent of the petty-bourgeois
democratic movement does exist.

My plan is, not to apply diplomacy, but bluntly to give Schweitzer
my opinion of his doings and to make it clear to him that he must
choose between "sect" and "class." If he is willing to come to a
rational understanding with the "Nuremberg majority,"[2] I, as "secretary for Germany," am prepared to be helpful in reasonable-seeming
terms. If he should not want this, I can promise to maintain the
necessary objective impartiality vis-à-vis his agitation. What I cannot
promise, however, is not to attack publicly the Lassallean superstition,
whenever I should deem it necessary to do so in my private capacity.

It is a fine and authentically Lassallean conception of Schweitzer's
that "two organizations can only do harm," and that, because his
preceded the other, it is, if not legally, nevertheless morally obligatory to a certain extent that the latter "merge" in him.

Mr. Odger is running [for Parliament], as you know, for Chelsea,
but I do not believe with any expectation of success. Throughout all
of the past year Odger has shown us the cold shoulder, ever since, at
my proposal, "the presidency of the International," and thereby also
"President" Odger, was abolished once and for all. Now he is thankful for his reelection by the Brussels Congress and wishes us to support
his campaign through a letter to his electioneering committee. We
have acceded to his request only because it is a step that is useful to
the International and recommends itself in the eyes of the London
workmen. . . .

Greetings.

Yours,

K. M.

From letter to Ludwig Kugelmann (*in Hanover*)
LONDON, OCTOBER 12, 1868

My Dear Friend:
. . . I am having much "bother" just now in Germany in connection with the quarrels of the leaders, as you can see from the enclosed
letters, which you will please return. On the one side Schweitzer, who

2. At the Nuremberg congress a majority voted to affiliate with the International.

has nominated me pope in *partibus infidelium*,[1] so that I can proclaim him workers' emperor in Germany. On the other side Liebknecht, who forgets that Schweitzer, in point of fact, forced him to remember that there is a proletarian movement apart from the petty-bourgeois democratic movement.

I hope you and our family are well. I hope I have not fallen into disfavor with your dear wife. Apropos: The International Women's Association, *duce* [leader] Frau Gögg (read "Geck"), sent an epistle to the Brussels Congress[2] inquiring whether ladies may join. The answer, of course, was a courteous affirmative. Therefore, should you persist in your silence, I shall send your wife a mandate as Correspondent of the General Council. . . .

Yours,

K. M.

Draft of letter to Johann Baptist von Schweitzer (in Berlin)
LONDON, OCTOBER 13, 1868

Dear Sir:

If you did not receive an answer to your letter of September 15, the fault was a misunderstanding on my part. I had read your letter to mean that you were planning to "present" to me your views for my information. I waited for it. Then came your congress,[1] and—being much overworked—I considered it no longer urgent. Before your letter of October 8 arrived, I, in my capacity as the International's secretary for Germany, had *repeatedly* called for peace. They answered me (and included citations from *Social-Demokrat* to prove it) that you yourself had provoked the *conflict*. I declared that my role must necessarily confine itself to being "nonpartisan" in this duel.

I believe that in return for the great confidence in me which your letters express, I can do no better than to report to you openly, without any diplomatic circumlocutions, my view of the situation. I assume that you, like me, are concerned only with the matter itself.

I completely recognize the intelligence and energy with which you work in the labor movement. I have never concealed this opinion from any of my old friends. Whenever I had to speak in public—in the

---

1. In the land of the infidels; that is, an official without an office.
2. September 6–13, 1868.

---

1. The General German Labor Association Congress, in Berlin, September 26–29, 1868.

General Council of the International Working Men's Association and in the local German communist society[2]—I always treated you as a man of our party and *never dropped a single word* about the *points on which we differ.*

Nevertheless, there are such points.

D'abord, in regard to the Lassalle Association,[3] it was established in a period of reaction. After a fifteen-year slumber, Lassalle reawakened the workers' movement in Germany—and this remains his immortal service. But he committed great mistakes. He permitted himself to be dominated too much by the immediate circumstances of the time. He made a small starting point—his opposition to a dwarf like Schulze-Delitzsch—into the central point of his agitation: state help versus self-help. Thereby he merely took up again the slogan which Buchez, the leader of Catholic socialism, had propounded in 1843 and subsequently against the real workers' movement in France. Much too intelligent to regard this slogan as anything more than a temporary *pis-aller* [makeshift], Lassalle could justify it only on the ground of its (alleged) immediate practicability. For this purpose, he had to maintain that it could be carried out in the *near* future. Hence *the* "state" became transformed into the Prussian state. Thus he was forced into concessions to the Prussian monarchy, the Prussian reaction (feudal party), and even the clericals. With Buchez's state aid for associations he combined the Chartist cry for universal suffrage. He overlooked the fact that conditions in Germany and England were different. He overlooked the lessons of the Second Empire with regard to French universal suffrage. Moreover, from the outset—like every man who maintains that he has in his pocket a panacea for the sufferings of mankind—he gave his agitation a religious and sectarian character. In fact, every sect is religious. Furthermore, precisely because he was the founder of a sect, he denied all natural connection with the earlier movement in Germany, as well as abroad. He fell into the same error as Proudhon, and instead of looking among the actual elements of the class movement for the real basis of his agitation, he tried to ascribe its course to these elements according to a certain dogmatic recipe.

Most of what I am saying here *post festum* [after the event] I predicted to Lassalle in 1862, when he came to London and invited me to place myself with him at the head of the new movement.

You yourself have experienced in your person the contrast between the movement of a sect and the movement of a class. The sect seeks

---

2. The German Education Society for Workers, organized in London in 1840; after the founding of the International in 1864, the Society, including such members as J. Georg Eccarius, Friedrich Lessner, Georg Lochner, and Carl Pfänder, joined it.

3. The General German Labor Association, founded in 1863.

its *raison d'être* and its *point d'honneur* [point of honor]—not in what it has in *common* with the class movement, but in the *particular shibboleth* which distinguishes one from the other. Hence, when in Hamburg[4] you proposed the congress for the formation of trade unions, you were able to defeat the sectarian opposition only by threatening to resign from the office of president. Furthermore, you were obliged to play a double role and announce that in one case you were acting as head of the sect and in the other as the organ of the class movement.

The dissolution of the General German Workers' Association gave you the occasion to accomplish a great step forward and to declare— to prove, *s'il fallait* [if necessary]—that a new stage of development had now been reached, and that the sectarian movement was ripe for entering into the class movement and putting an end to all "independence." As for the real substance of the sect, it would, as with all previous working-class sects, be carried in the general movement as an enriching element. Instead of this, you have actually demanded that the class movement subordinate itself to the movement of a particular sect. Those who are not your friends have concluded from this that you want to preserve your "own workers' movement" at all costs.

In regard to the Berlin congress, the time was at first not urgent, as the coalition law had not yet been voted. You should have come to an agreement with the leaders *outside* the Lassallean circle, and, together with them, worked out a plan for convening the congress. Instead, you now have left open to you only the alternative of joining *them* or of making a common front *against* them. The congress itself appeared only as an extension of the Hamburg congress.

In regard to the draft of the statutes,[5] I consider it faulty in principle, and I believe I have as much experience in the field of trade unionism as any other contemporary. Without going into further details here, I only remark that a *centralized* organization, while appropriate for secret societies and sectarian movements, is contrary to the essence of trade unionism. If it were possible—and I state *tout bonnement* [flatly] that it is impossible—it would not be desirable, at least in Germany. There, where the worker is bureaucratically regulated from childhood on and believes in the supreme authority of the government, it is necessary *to teach him to act independently*.

Your plan is otherwise impractical also. In the "Union" you have three independent powers of various origins: (1) the committee, chosen by the unions; (2) the president (here an entirely superfluous person. In the Statutes of the International Working Men's Association

---

4. The General German Workers' Association Congress, August 22–26, 1868.
5. Drafted by the congress in Berlin, September 26–29, 1868.

a president also figures. But in reality he has no other function than to preside over the session of the General Council. At my motion, the office, which I proposed in 1866, was abolished in 1867 and replaced by a chairman, selected at each weekly session of the General Council. The London Trades Council likewise has only a chairman. Its only permanent official is a secretary, because he has a continuing function), elected by universal suffrage; (3) the congress, selected by the localities. Hence collision everywhere, and this is expected to promote "rapid action"! Lassalle made a great mistake when he borrowed the phrase *"président élu du suffrage universel"* from the French Constitution of 1852. And in a trade-union movement at that! The latter revolves chiefly around money questions, and you will soon discover that here all dictatorship soon ends.

Still, no matter what the shortcomings of the organization are, they can perhaps be more or less extirpated by rational practice. I am prepared, as Secretary of the International, to serve as mediator between you and the Nuremberg majority,[6] which has directly joined the International—on rational grounds, it goes without saying. I have written the same thing to Leipzig.[7] I do not ignore the difficulties of your position and I never forget that every one of us depends more on his circumstances than on his own will.

I promise you, under all circumstances, my impartiality, which is my duty. On the other hand, I can promise nothing which someday I, as a *private author*—as soon as I consider that the interests of the workers' movement dictate it—may want to explore in open criticism of Lassallean superstition, as I once did in the case of Proudhon.[8]

Assuring you of my best personal wishes,

Faithfully yours,

K. M.

From letter to Engels (in Manchester)
LONDON, OCTOBER 24, 1868

Dear Fred:

. . . Last Tuesday [October 20] the twelve ragamuffins of the so-called French Branch held a public meeting in London under the

---

6. The Union of German Labor Associations met in Nuremberg September 5–7, 1868.
7. To Liebknecht.
8. In *The Poverty of Philosophy* (1847).

chairmanship of Pyat, with a reading of one of his melodramatic revolutionary pufferies. In addition, large wall posters as follows: *République Française, La Branche Française de L'Association Internationale*, etc. etc. Then *Félix Pyat* in huge letters. Among the points of discussion, *in French*, No. 3 was: *Vote d'adhésion au manifeste* [Vote to adhere to the manifesto] (the one that Pyat read and which he himself manufactured as a manifesto of the Commune of Paris, which exists only on the moon) *et protestation contre l'indifférence en matière politique professée à Bruxelles au dernier Congrès de l'Association Internationale* [and protest against the indifference to political matters professed at Brussels in the last Congress of the International Working Men's Association].

Below this, in English (and also distributed as a handbill) was: *Democrats of all Nations* are invited, etc., "for the purpose of DECIDING whether the Workingmen's International Association is to be a *Political Association*."

Last Tuesday I was empowered, in case the London dailies treated or mentioned this as our manifesto, immediately to disavow the fellows publicly. Fortunately no notice was taken of them.

This evening, however, there will be a subcommittee meeting, where witnesses will be heard in connection with the fact that one of these dozen characters was formerly a *marchand d'hommes* [slave dealer] and brothel keeper, another a gambler, a third a spy in the pay of the masters in the local tailors' strike, etc., etc.[1] On the basis of the "moral paragraph" of the Statutes, these gentlemen will probably be ejected. Naturally, they are doubly angry that policies which relate to laddies such as they will leave them out of the game. . . .

Yours,
K. M.

Letter to Sigfrid Meyer and August Vogt (in New York)
LONDON, OCTOBER 28, 1868

Dear Meyer and Vogt:

From the enclosed mandate to Meyer (I have added one for you) you will see that your wish was fulfilled on October 13. The *Bee-Hive*'s issue of October 13 published Meyer's nomination. The General Council has resolved that German correspondents correspond with

1. Between April and October, 1867, 3,000 London tailors vainly struck to establish a uniform wage scale for the trade in all of England.

me, Pelletier (for the French) with Dupont, and Eccarius with Jessup. I personally proposed the latter, as I have no time for more correspondence. You can hand over this letter to Jessup and at the same time show him your mandates.

In regard to Eccarius, there is a misunderstanding. I have never quarreled with him; on the contrary, to date I have supported him against the attacks of the English, etc. But he—his predominant, often narrow-minded egoism is perhaps due to his circumstances—has committed unpleasant stupidities from time to time. Ordinarily I take no notice of them. In exceptional cases, my patience gives out. I then give him a piece of my mind, and all is right again until next time. The poor devil is now very sick, and he always uses such moments to say his *pater peccavi* [father, I have sinned]. What, according to Vogt's letter, Liebknecht refers to is completely unknown to me. I at least have never written a word to any man against Eccarius, except in my letter to Meyer[1] at a moment when our other delegates to the Brussels Congress denounced Eccarius in their letters and I became hot under the collar. But it is very possible that without my knowledge Eccarius wrote to Liebknecht something that may have given the latter reasons for his assertions to Vogt. This would be strange, as at that time I got into a big row with the English because of Eccarius, whose side I took.

In regard to Sorge, no other action is needed. My letter to Jessup will explain the temporary character of the mandates.

Cards for members have been exhausted, and we must print new ones. Liebknecht makes too much of South German patriotism; nor should he publish in *Staat und Gesellschaft* such stupidities, which are in opposition to our own views.

Salute. In great haste.

Yours,

MARX

Apropos. Do you know Dietzgen? He has now returned from Petersburg to the Rhineland, in order to establish himself as a small tanner. He is one of the most gifted workers I know, I mean in regard to letters. I do not know him personally.

A translation of my book [*Capital*] now appears in Russian in St. Petersburg. Or did I write you about this already?

[Enclosure]   256 High Holborn, W.C.

On October 13, 1868, Citizen A. Vogt was appointed, by the General Council of the International Working Men's Association, Cor-

---

1. See Marx's letter to Sigfrid Meyer, September 14, 1868.

responding Secretary of the International Working Men's Association (German Section in America) for the year 1868–69.

By Order of the General Council,

Karl Marx,
Secretary for Germany

Letter to Hermann Jung (in London)
LONDON, NOVEMBER 14, 1868

Dear Jung:

Before you went to Brussels I gave you the *secret circular* (the one by Stepney) of the *États-Unis de l'Europe*,[1] which speaks of the necessity of making common cause with the International Working Men's Association. Since Gustav Vogt—that is, that paper—is now making himself uppity toward us, please return the thing to me. I will use it in Liebknecht's paper[2] against G. Vogt.

How come that in the last two issues of *Bee-Hive* there has not been a word about the resolutions of the Geneva and Brussels congresses?

Greetings to you and family.

Yours,
K. M.

From letter to Engels (in Manchester)
LONDON, NOVEMBER 23, 1868

Dear Fred:

. . . As for Ernest Jones, I find him exceedingly cool. *I* am to represent him as his electioneering agent (for Greenwich)! I told him I did not see a ghost of a chance for him:

1. If Baxter Langley were the local candidate, neither Mill nor Beales could stand without his permission.

2. The General Council of the International does not mix in electioneering. But in any case we could under no circumstances come out

---

1. The Peace and Freedom League's weekly publication, of which Gustav Vogt was editor.
2. *Demokratisches Wochenblatt.*

against B. Langley, since—and this is a fact—B. Langley and his Sunday League[1] have concluded a friendship agreement with us since the Brussels Congress. (Our meetings, in fact, take place in their hall.[2])

3. He (Jones) is presently unpopular in London (and this is true). The articles in *Reynolds's*, "Traitors in the Camp," did him harm. . . .

Yours,

K. M.

Letter to Engels (in Manchester)
LONDON, DECEMBER 5, 1868

Dear Fred:

Enclosed [letters from]: (1) Von Schweitzer, (2) Mineworkers from Lugau, (3) The Russian Serno-Solovyevich (author of the pamphlet against Gögg).

So Schweitzer is determined to become the tailor king of Germany! Good luck to him. On one point he is right—Wilhelm [Liebknecht]'s incompetence! His demand that the Nurembergers—under penalty for treason—enroll under his leadership is very cool indeed.

That Wilhelm becomes more stupid every day. What a lousy sheet![1] From the letter from Lugau, it appears that he has hitherto done *nothing* in matters connected with the International. At the same time he is playing fine tricks on us. In his "genial" way he lets it be known that the International Working Men's Association costs *nothing*, hence anybody can join *without a fee*. Becker complains from Switzerland about this absurdity.

Yours,

K. M.

---

1. The National Sunday League was organized, in the face of church opposition, to keep cultural institutions (museums, concert halls, etc.) open on Sunday, so that working people could attend.

2. From June, 1868, to February, 1872, the General Council of the International met in the hall of the Sunday League: 256 High Holborn, London. W.C.

---

1. *Demokratisches Wochenblatt.*

From letter to Ludwig Kugelmann (in Hanover)
LONDON, DECEMBER 5, 1868

Dear Kugelmann:

. . . For some time now I have promised you a few words about the French Branch. Half or two-thirds of these ragamuffins consist of *maquereaus* [pimps] and similar rabble, but all—since our people have withdrawn from them—are heroes of the revolutionary phrase, which, from a safe distance, of course, kills kings and emperors, and especially Louis Napoleon. In their eyes we are, naturally, reactionaries, and they have drawn up against us a formal act of accusation, which was actually laid before the Brussels Congress in its secret sessions. The spite of these blacklegs was increased by the fact that Felix Pyat, an unlucky French melodramatist of the fourth rank—used in the Revolution of 1848 only as a *toastmaster* (this is what the English call the paid men who make toasts at public dinners and who see to it that the other toasts are in sequence)—who is possessed of a true monomania "to shout in a whisper" and to play the dangerous conspirator, has gotten control over them. Through this gang Pyat wanted to transform the International Working Men's Association into his own tail. Specifically, the aim was to compromise us. Hence at a public meeting, which the French Branch announced and trumpeted through wall posters as a meeting of the International Association, Louis Napoleon, alias Badinguet, was *formally condemned* to death, the execution naturally being left to the unknown Paris Brutuses.[1] Since the English press took no notice of this farce, we too passed it off in silence. But one of the gang—a certain Vésinier, a dealer in blackmail literature—published the whole muck in a Belgian paper, *La Cigale,* which claims to be an organ of the International, a "comical" kind of paper such as surely exists nowhere else in Europe. Certainly there is nothing more comical in it than its seriousness. From *Cigale* the stuff found its way into *Pays, Journal de l'Empire.* This was a natural treasure trove of swill for Paul de Cassagnac. Thereupon we—that is, the General Council—declared in six lines officially in *Cigale* that F. Pyat was in *no way* connected with the International, of which he was not even a member. *Hinc illae irae!* [Hence that fury!] The battle of the frogs and mice ended with the French rancorously seceding from us, pursuing business on its own, under Pyat's aegis. Their London *succursale* [branch] is the so-called German Agitation Association, founded by a dozen and

---

1. See Marx's letter to Engels, July 7, 1868.

a half people, and with an old Palatinate refugee, the half-crazy watchmaker Weber, as chief. Now you know all that is to be reported about this bombastic and important event. Only one thing more. We had the satisfaction of seeing Blanqui, through one of his friends, also in the *Cigale*, ridicule Pyat to death, leaving him to be, as the only alternatives, either a monomaniac or a police agent!

Yesterday I received a letter from Schweitzer[2] in which he indicates that he is again going to *cachot* [jail] and that an outbreak of civil war—that is, war between him and W. Liebknecht—is unavoidable. I must say that on one point Schweitzer is right, namely Liebknecht's incompetence. His paper is really lamentable. How a man whom I have drummed at orally for fifteen years (he has always been too lazy to read) can print such stuff as, for example, "Society and State," wherein the "societal" (also a nice category!) is treated as secondary and the "political" as essential, would be inconceivable if Liebknecht were not a South German, and if, as it would seem, he had not always confused me with his old chief, the "noble" *Gustav Struve*. . . .

Lafargue and his wife have been in Paris for the past two months. But they refuse to recognize there the medical degrees he acquired in London and demand that he pass five new "Paris" examinations!

In consequence of a settlement, my "economic" (not political-economic) circumstances will take on satisfactory form beginning with next year.

With best regards for our dear wife and Fränzchen.

Yours,

K. M.

Is your wife also active in the big German women's emancipation campaign? I think German women should begin by driving their men to self-emancipation.

From letter to Engels (in Manchester)
LONDON, DECEMBER 9, 1868

Dear Fred:
. . . I forgot to enclose the letter from the Russian [Serno-Solovyevich]. Here it is. Also one from Sigfrid Meyer.[1] (The Drury of whom

---

2. Dated December 2, 1868.

---

1. On October 28, 1868, Meyer wrote Marx that he and August Vogt were preparing to organize a Section of the International in New York.

he speaks is a lazy lad who was previously in London and wanted to force his way into the Central Council. He impressed S. Meyer with his public appearance in New York. Meyer wrote us that we ought to name Drury our agent. I replied that Drury had already let himself be "recommended" to us for this by Cremer, Huleck, etc. We did *not* want him). . . .

Greetings.

Yours,

K. M.

Letter to Engels (in Manchester)
LONDON, DECEMBER 15, 1868 (PAST MIDNIGHT)

Dear Fred:

I beg you to study the enclosed document[1] carefully—despite its *fadaise* [tastelessness]—to write your marginal notes in French, and to return the thing itself *next Saturday at the latest*.

Herr Bakunin—who is behind this whole story—is condescending enough to want to put the whole movement under Russian leadership.

This shit has existed for two months now. Only this evening did Becker report it by letter to the General Council. This time Schaute [Borkheim] is right. The Alliance, as Becker writes, is to restore the "idealism" that is lacking in our Association. *L'idéalisme Russe!*

This evening there was great anger in our General Council, especially among the French, over this document. I have known about this shit for a long time. I considered it stillborn but wanted to let it die in peace, out of respect for old Becker.

But the matter has become more serious than I thought. Hence considerations for old Becker are no longer admissible. This evening the Council has resolved *publicly* to repudiate this interloping society —in Paris, New York, Germany, and Switzerland. I am charged with drafting the repudiation decree (for next Tuesday [December 22]). I am sorry about the whole thing, because of old Becker. *Mais* [but] our Association cannot commit suicide for his sake.

Yours,

K. M.

---

1. "Marginal Remarks on the Program and Rules of Bakunin's International Alliance of Socialist Democracy." See page 157.

Michael Bakunin, letter written in French to Marx (in London)
GENEVA, DECEMBER 22, 1868

My Old Friend!

Serno reported to me the part of your letter relating to me. You asked him whether I am still your friend.[1] Yes, more than ever, dear Marx, because I now understand more than ever how very right you are when you follow the grand route of economic revolution and invite us to march along, and when you denigrate those among us who lose themselves in the side paths of partly national and partly exclusively economic undertakings. I am now doing what you have been doing for more than twenty years. Since my solemn and public leave-taking of the Bern Congress,[2] I know no other society, no other milieu, than the world of workers. From now on, my fatherland is the International, of which you are one of the principal founders. You see thus, dear friend, that I am your disciple—and I am proud to be. This is all that is necessary to explain to you my position and my personal feelings.

Let us go on to other questions.

You say in your letter to Serno that at Bern we put the question wrongly in that we spoke of equalizing classes and individuals. This observation is perfectly correct in regard to the expressions and the formulations we used. But this formulation has been, so to speak, forced upon us by the stupidity and the infinite inexperience of our bourgeois public. They have been stupid enough to yield us the terrain of equality without a struggle, so to speak—and our triumph consisted precisely in the fact that we have been able to substantiate that they rejected all conditions of a real and serious equality. It is this that has made them so furious, and still does. For the rest, I sincerely admit that it would have been better if we had expressed ourselves differently; if, for example, we had said: The radical suppression of the economic causes of the existence of various classes and the economic, social, and political equalization of the environment and the conditions of existence and development for all individuals, without regard to sex, nation, or race.[3]

Under separate cover I am sending you all the speeches I delivered

---

1. See Marx to Engels, January 13, 1869.
2. The Peace and Freedom League.
3. In its reply of March 9, 1869, the General Council of the International stated: "The great aim of the International Working Men's Association is, not the equalization of classes, which is a logical contradiction and hence impossible to carry out, but rather the abolition of classes. . . ."

at Bern, with one exception. M. Herzen has asked me for permission to reprint it in his last Mohican, that is, the last issue of his journal, which has gone under for lack of readers.[4] I had no reason to reject his request. But I beg you to believe me that there is absolutely no solidarity between him and me. Specifically, since 1863 all political and now also private relations between us have been broken off. He has begged me to change to his sense the speech I gave in Bern on Russia, as a reply to a speech by my friend Mroczkowski, which you will find in *Kolokol*. Like all my Russian Social-Democratic friends, whose program, which I edited, I am sending to you, I have maintained that the first condition of a real, that is, economic, social, and political emancipation of the Russian and non-Russian peoples within the Russian Empire, is the radical destruction of that Empire: this was too much for Herzen and we have had a falling out.

I am also sending you the program of the Alliance, which we founded together with Becker and many Italian, Polish, and French friends. We would have much to talk about on this subject. Next time I will send you a copy of a long letter—practically a brochure—which I wrote to friend César De Paepe on it.

Now a few more words about what is taking place here.

In Basel there is a considerable strike, which perhaps will have as a consequence that the International will acquire 5,000 new members. Geneva is acting splendidly. We have had a big popular meeting which set up a permanent central committee to make contact with Basel. I belong to it, Becker also. Among the workers I have found really splendid people.

Give my regards to Engels, if he has not died a second time—you know they have already buried him once—and please give him a copy of my speeches; also to Messrs. Eccarius and Jung.

Devotedly yours,

M. BAKUNIN

Please remember me to Madame Marx.

Letter to Hermann Jung (in London)
LONDON, DECEMBER 28, 1868

Dear Jung:

Hardly had you gone away when I received a letter from Bakunin in which he specifically assured me of his friendship.

4. *Kolokol*, a revolutionary journal published in Geneva by Alexander Herzen —in Russian from July, 1857 to 1865, and in French, under the title *La Clôche*, from 1868 to 1869.

From his letter I see that he has again written at length to De Paepe, to lure him into the *Alliance Internationale*. It is necessary, in order to obviate later mischief or accusations of lack of timely information, that you transmit a copy of our decision on the Alliance to De Paepe as soon as possible.[1] You must, of course, tell him at the same time that in the present situation in Switzerland, and in order to avoid any semblance of a split, we did *not want* to make the decision *public*, but confined ourselves to communicating it confidentially only to the respective central councils in the various countries.

Do not forget to invite Applegarth in time for the Saturday session [January 2, 1869]. It would also be good to do the same with Odger.

Yours,

K. M.

From letter to Engels (in Manchester)
LONDON, JANUARY 1, 1869

Dear Fred:

. . . In the enclosed *Vorbote* you will see about the scandal in Basel.[1] Those damned fellows—I mean our spokesmen there—have a special talent for making the International Working Men's Association responsible for every local quarrel between master and men. At the same time they neglect *every measure* that would prepare for conflict, for example, the founding of trade unions. Hence they cry the louder. The cantonal government interferes. Hence the smallest incident becomes important to them. Then comes the appeal to the International Working Men's Association in general and to the London General Council in particular to pay the cost of the Swiss conflict on the shortest notice. Then old Becker writes that we should not, after all, compromise ourselves, as we did in the Geneva affair, etc. . . .

Addio.

Yours,

K. M.

---

1. See "The International . . . and Bakunin's International Alliance of Socialist Democracy," page 162.

---

1. Marx discussed the Basel strike in his "Report of the General Council to the Fourth Annual Congress . . .," page 37.

From letter to Engels (in Manchester)
LONDON, JANUARY 13, 1869

Dear Fred:

. . . A brief report now on "International events."

(a) *International Alliance of Socialist Democracy*: A unanimous decision of the General Council, December 22, 1868, providing: (1) All the articles of the rules of the Alliance, etc., relating to the International Working Men's Association are declared null and void; (2) the Alliance, etc., is not admitted as a branch of the International Working Men's Association. The motivation of the decision (edited by me) is couched in entirely juridical form, showing the contradiction of the rules of the intended Alliance with our own Statutes, etc. A final consideration, wherein old Becker in particular must see his folly, is that the Brussels Congress had already prejudged the question regarding the League of Freedom. It wanted to join the International, but the Congress declared: As the League claims to have the same principles and to pursue the same ends as the International, it has no *"raison d'être,"* adding in conclusion that "several members of the initiatory group in Geneva" had voted to that effect at the Brussels Congress.

In the meantime we received letters from Brussels, Rouen, Lyon, etc., declaring absolute support of the General Council's decision. Not a single voice was raised for *le groupe initiateur de Genève* [the initiatory Geneva group]. That that group had not acted with entire honesty is already clear from the fact that it informed us of its founding and carryings-on only *after* it had sought to win over the Brusselers, etc. I consider the matter finished, although we have not yet received an answer to our "decision" from Geneva. In any case, the attempt has miscarried.

(b) *Ad vocem* [in regard to] Bakunin:

To understand the ensuing letter,[1] you must know the following: *D'abord*, it crossed our "message" about the Alliance. Bakunin therefore still gives himself the pleasant delusion that he will be quietly let alone. Furthermore, the Russian Serno was, in his previous correspondence with Borkheim, definitely *against* Bakunin. In *my* reply to Serno I expressed the wish to employ this youth to report on Bakunin. Since, however, I do not trust any Russian, I did it in this form: "How is my old friend (*I don't know whether he still is*) Bakunin, etc., etc.?"

---

1. Bakunin's letter to Marx, December 22, 1868.

The Russian Serno has nothing more urgent to do than report this letter to Bakunin, and Bakunin uses this for a sentimental entrée!

(c) *Ad vocem* old Becker:

This one has become very obstinate. *D'abord*, he sends us a letter, dated Geneva, December 21, of four pages on the Basel story, but without a single *fait précis* [precise fact]. But we are to act *immediately*. At the same time he writes to Lessner that we (the General Council) have already "compromised" ourselves in the Basel affair, and that this should not happen again. Or, he says literally (in the letter to Lessner), "does the General Council exist, like God, only in the faith of the stupid?" In Geneva, he says, they speak of us only with shrugs, etc.

Old Becker got a reply to this from Jung telling him that his four-page epistle contained *nothing*. How could he believe that money could be had in London in such a vacuum?

In his letter of December 21 Becker indicated a subsequent elaborate report. Instead of that, we received the *Vorbote*. You have seen yourself that the *Vorbote* actually reports only the now "concluded" lockout of the ribbon weavers, but in no way makes clear how the widened conflict has developed. In brief, to this very moment we do not know anything more than what is in the *Vorbote*. Not only can the trade unions not take a step on this, but it is also impossible to make anything public on the situation in the name of the General Council. After all, we cannot expose ourselves to the Basel usurers' charge that we cry out to the world without any factual knowledge.[2]

Summa Summarum: Eight days ago yesterday, the General Council resolved to reprimand Becker as well as Perret (the French correspondent for Geneva) for not having sent us the necessary material on the Geneva affair before now. . . .

Yours,

K. MORO

---

2. Minutes of the General Council, January 5, 1869: "Jung then stated that a great many ribbon weavers at Basel were locked out, but his information was so scanty that he could not make out a case."

From letter to Engels (in Manchester)
LONDON, FEBRUARY 24, 1869

Dear Fred:

Best thanks for the report.[1] It is transparently clear. I changed nothing, except to cross out the last sentence (or rather, a few words in it). I read it yesterday in the General Council. Adopted. Will be sent first to the *Times* (or rather, taken there by Eccarius). If the *Times* does not take it, then the *Daily News*. Then the English clipping will be sent to *Zukunft*, to *Social-Demokrat*, and to Wilhelm [Liebknecht]. The Lugauers [miners], poor devils, will have great satisfaction at being featured in the English press.

Enclosed the Resolutions,[2] etc., six pieces. This is the situation: By the decision of the Brussels Congress we were obligated to print its resolutions. On the pretext that the Geneva resolutions were part of the platform, we also printed a part of those proposed by the London Central Council and adopted by the Geneva Congress, and left out those proposed by the French in Geneva, *as well* as the adopted amendments, etc. idiotic stuff. That part was also written by me. On the other hand, I took no part in the drafting of the Resolutions of 1868. The only word by me is the first "considering"—"on the effects of machinery." . . .

Greetings.

Yours,
K. M.

From letter to Engels (in Manchester)
LONDON, MARCH 5, 1869

Dear Fred:

The enclosed little document[1] arrived *yesterday* (although dated February 27). You must send it back as soon as you have read it, as

1. On the coal miners in Saxony.
2. Of the Brussels Congress, September 6–13, 1868.

1. Notification from the Geneva section of the Bakunin "Alliance" of its desire to affiliate with the International.

I have to lay it before the Council on Tuesday next. The gentlemen
of the "Alliance" have taken a long time to achieve this opus.

As a matter of fact, we would rather they had kept their "innu-
merable legions" in France, Spain, and Italy for themselves.

Bakunin thinks if we approve his "radical program" he can make
a big noise about this and compromise us *tant soit peu* [just a little
bit]. If we declare ourselves against it we shall be decried as counter-
revolutionaries. Moreover, if we admit them, he will see to it that he
is supported by some riffraff at the congress in Basel. I think the
answer should be on the following lines:

According to Paragraph I of the Statutes, every workers' association "aiming at the same end, viz., the protection, advancement, and
complete emancipation of the working classes" shall be admitted.

As the stage of development reached by different sections of workers in the same country and by the working class in different countries
necessarily varies very much, the actual movement necessarily expresses
itself in very various theoretical forms.

The community of action which the International Working Men's
Association called into being, the exchange of ideas by means of the
different organs of the sections in all countries, and, finally, the direct
discussions at the general congresses, will by degrees create for the
general workers' movement its common theoretical program also.

With regard to the program of the "Alliance," therefore, it is not
necessary for the General Council to submit it to a critical examination. The Council has not to examine whether it is an adequate, scientific expression of the working-class movement. It has only to ask if
the *general tendency* of the program is in opposition to the general
tendency of the International Working Men's Association—the complete emancipation of the working classes.

This reproach could apply to only one phrase in the program, par.
2: "above all things it desires the political, economic and social equalization of the classes." "The equalization of the classes," literally interpreted, is nothing but another expression for the "harmony of capital
and labor" preached by the bourgeois socialists. Not the logically
impossible "equalization of classes" but the historically necessary
"abolition of classes" constitutes the final aim of the International
Working Men's Association. But from the context in which this phrase
occurs in the program it would appear that it is only a slip of the
pen. The less, therefore, does the General Council doubt that this
phrase, which might lead to serious misunderstanding, will be removed
from the program.

This being assumed, it is in accordance with the principle of the
International Working Men's Association to leave to each section the

responsibility for its own program. There is therefore nothing to prevent the transformation of the sections of the Alliance into sections of the Working Men's Association.

As soon as this has taken place, an enumeration of the newly joined sections according to country, locality, and number must be sent to the General Council in accordance with the regulations.

This last point—the census of their legions—will especially tickle the gentlemen. Tell me everything you want altered in this draft of the reply when you return the letter. . . .

Greetings.

Yours,

K. M.

From letter to Engels (in Manchester)
LONDON, MARCH 14, 1869

Dear Fred:

. . . The reply to the Genevans has gone off.[1] In the French text I kept the tone icy cool and *passablement ironique* [passably ironic]. Fortunately, the English, who of course know only my English translation, did not notice this.

In addition to the official letter reported to me, the gentlemen [in Geneva] also sent a four-page *private letter* to Eccarius, according to which only the efforts of Becker, Bakunin, and the writer, Perret, prevented a *direct break*. Their "revolutionary" program is supposed to have a greater effect in Italy, Spain, etc., in a few weeks than that of the International in years. If we reject their "revolutionary program," we bring about a separation between the countries of "revolutionary" workers' movements (these are, according to the count: France, where they have two whole correspondents, Switzerland [!], Italy—where the workers, with the exception of those belonging to us, are a mere tail to Mazzini—and Spain, where there are more priests than workers) and the countries of *slower* development of the working class (viz., England, Germany, United States, and Belgium). Hence separation between the volcanic and Plutonic workers' movement on the one side, and the aqueous on the other.

That the Swiss represent the revolutionary type is really amusing.

---

1. See "Letter of the General Council to the International Alliance of Socialist Democracy," page 164.

How dumb old Becker must have become, really to believe that Bakunin had invented a new program!

Yours,

K. M.

From letter to Engels (in Manchester)
LONDON, MAY 1, 1869

Dear Fred:

The enclosed letter to our Belgian secretary [Bernard] will be made clear to you by the enclosed *Cigale,* the organ of the French Branch, from which one analogue was formed in Brussels and another (*Comité de l'avenir* [Committee of the Future]) in Geneva—altogether a few dozen men under Pyat's leadership.

From letter to Engels (in Manchester)
LONDON, MAY 8, 1869

Dear Fred:

. . . After the addresses, as you will see from the enclosed papers, poured in from every corner, it was finally necessary for the Central Council really to speak out on this important matter. I was named editor of the Address.[1] If I had declined, the thing would have fallen into the hands of Eccarius, who is as right for such demonstrative documents as a fist in the eye. Hence I accepted. With my present liver ailment, this was already painful enough to do in English—as such things require a certain rhetorical style—but then there was the additional pain of doing it afterwards in French! But necessity knows no law, and I did it in French. At first I wanted to send it to the Belgians in the English original, but our Belgian secretary, Bernard (Frenchman by birth), said (last Tuesday) before the assembled *patres conscripti* [members of the General Council] that if one left the translation to the Belgians, who know only half English and no French, one might as well leave the whole matter alone. So I had to give way. You will get the thing to enjoy in both languages. But I left to Eccarius, who,

---

1. See "The Belgian Massacres," page 97.

moreover, has a financial interest in it, the translation into German, with which I am not concerned.

Indeed, writing in French, with or without the liver, is very easy. . . .

Yours,

Mohr

From letter to Engels (*in Manchester*)
LONDON, MAY 14, 1869

Dear Fred:

. . . Swinish press, the local one! Not only did they, to a man, suppress every word of our Belgian missive (after all of them, last week, had published some deliberately stupid lines, composed in Cherval's terms, probably by the "police member" of the Brussels separate committee)—they also, to a man, suppressed the Address to the American Labor Union[1] (written by me and adopted last Tuesday[2]), although it was *against* war between the United States and England. But there were things in it which these scoundrels don't like.
Greetings.

Yours,

K. M.

From letter to Engels (*in Manchester*)
LONDON, JULY 3, 1869

Dear Fred:

. . . Enclosed a content-heavy letter from Wilhelm.[1] From it you will see that he has suddenly appointed himself my *curator* and prescribes to me each and every thing that I "MUST" do.

I *must* come to their Congress,[2] *must* show myself to the German

---

1. See "Defense of America Against England," page 102.
2. May 11.

---

1. On June 29, 1869, Liebknecht wrote a long letter to Marx about Social-Democratic policies and problems and about his break with Schweitzer's General German Workers' Association.
2. The Social-Democratic congress at Eisenach, August 7-9, 1869.

workers, *must* immediately send the International [membership] cards (after they did not reply to questions asked about them twice in three months), *must* reprocreate the *Communist Manifesto, must* come to Leipzig.

Is it not highly naïve that in the same letter in which he complains of not being able to return the £2 (which I had transmitted to him through Eccarius) he offers me *travel expenses to Germany! Toujours le même!* [Always the same!]

He seems to be morally indignant at you. I have already answered that he has interpreted your letter falsely. It is completely incomprehensible to the man that political opinions and business ability are not absolute polar opposites, as he assumes in his administration of the newspaper, and as others have to assume also, if they are not to become suspect.

Our Wilhelm is an optimist and a liar. Thus strong exaggeration again in the account of his victory over Schweitzer. Still, there is something in the affair. Schweitzer would not have made the retreat from the Hatzfeldt church[3] if he had not been shaken up by his own organization. On the other hand, he hastened the general dissolution by the stupid staging of his last *coup d'état*.[4] I hope that as a result of this affair the German labor movement will at last grow out of its stage of Lassallean infantile disease, and that the residue of the same will die out in mere sectarian isolation.

In regard to Wilhelm's "absolute commandments," I answered him to this effect:

I feel no positive need to show myself to the German workers, and will *not* come to their congress. If they really want to affiliate with the International, and if they have established a decent party organization—and the Nuremberg Congress showed how little mere promises, tendencies, etc., are to be trusted—then there will be opportunity for that by-and-by. Moreover, it must be clearly understood that for us the new organization must be as little a *Volkspartei*[5] as a Lassallean church. If we came over now, we would, after all, have to speak out against the *Volkspartei*, which Wilhelm and Bebel would not like! And if they—*mirabile dictu*—agreed to this themselves, we would still have to throw our weight directly into the scales against Schweitzer & Co.,

---

3. The General German Workers' Association, founded by Lassalle and supported after his death by his intimate friend, the Countess von Hatzfeldt.

4. In the June 18, 1869, issue of the *Social-Demokrat*, Johann Baptist von Schweitzer, president of the General German Workers' Association, and Fritz Mende, president of the Lassallean German Workers' Association, published a proclamation that the two groups had united and demanded that the members approve the union within three days. This virtual ultimatum was considered a *coup d'état*.

5. The *Deutsche Volkspartei*—German People's party—was a middle-class anti-Prussian party.

instead of the transformation appearing to be a free act by the workers themselves.

As for fixing up the *Manifesto*, we will think it over after we have seen the decisions of your congress, etc.

He can keep his £2 and not worry about my travel expenses.

I praised his proceeding against Becker.[6]

So much for that. . . .

Best compliments to all.

EL MORO

From letter to Engels (in Manchester)
LONDON, JULY 17, 1869

Dear Fred:

. . . The worthy Wilhelm [Liebknecht]—always amiably disposing of things foreign to him—naturally sends Fritzsche to me, to borrow £300 from the local trade unions! And *he* guarantees their repayment! And needlessly puts me in the embarrassing position of having to refuse Fritzsche!

Moreover, he does not even seem to read the letters one writes him. I sent him 900 [membership] cards and told him that one penny per card constitutes the annual contribution. Of these 900, I put 500 at his disposal gratis, so that the fellows could at least be able to be represented at the Congress.[1] And now he asks me whether one has to pay fixed annual contributions!

That Schweitzer is forced to let Mende begin a quarrel with the International in the *Social-Demokrat* shows strikingly under what hard conditions he has returned to the lap of Hatzfeldt. For he knows best how dangerous this operation is for him!

For the rest, it was not necessary for that old ass Becker to meddle officially in this dissolution of the Lassallean church;[2] he should have maintained an appropriate reserve, instead. The old beast does much harm with his urge for action . . .

Best regards for all.

Yours,

K. M.

---

6. See Marx's letter to Engels, July 27, 1869.

1. The Congress in Basel, September 6–11, 1869.
2. An article in the *Social-Demokrat*, July 14, 1869, presumably by Fritz Mende, accused Johann Philipp Becker and the International of meddling in the affairs of the General German Workers' Association.

From letter to Engels (in Manchester)
LONDON, JULY 22, 1869

Dear Fred:

The effrontery of Wilhelm [Liebknecht] in issuing bulls of ex-communication in the name of the General Council of the International is really colossal. I wrote him that I personally mean to stay out of that scandal (the old sow Hatzfeldt would like nothing better than to drag me into it), the more so as I have just now decided against the Lassalle clique and against the *Volkspartei*. I added that Wilhelm can announce (this against Schweitzer) that only representatives of *real* members (according to the decisions of the Brussels Congress) can be admitted in Basel. This he did in a paragraph of the *penultimate* issue.[1]

Now, after he vainly solicited me to take official steps against Schweitzer, he has the effrontery to force me into that scandal! Upon receipt of the last issue of the *Wochenblatt* I immediately wrote him a rude letter in which I reminded him how often he had already compromised me and told him directly that I will *disavow* him *publicly* as soon as he commits another such insolence. (Insolence which is in addition a direct *lie*, in that, in the matter of Schweitzer, etc., the General Council had never had any discussion and, even less, made any decisions.)

Now it depends on how Schweitzer, who is *severely provoked*, will react. I will "shake off" Herr Wilhelm if he involves me in beastliness a third time. The fellow does not even have the excuse that he is with us through thick and thin. He commits his stupidities on his own initiative, betrays us when he thinks it proper, and identifies with us when he does not know how to save himself otherwise. . . .

Greetings.

Yours,
MOHR

---

1. Of the *Demokratisches Wochenblatt*, July 10, 1869.

Letter to Engels (in Manchester)
LONDON, JULY 24, 1869

Dear Fred:

I can write you only a few lines today. The thing is full of pus, hence very painful, but will soon be done with. The arsenic treatment[1] must begin again.

This morning I received the enclosed scrap from Liebknecht.[2] What is more amazing, the stupid impudence or the impudent stupidity? Thus this philistine allows *official lies*, such as nonexistent decisions by the General Council, to come from his own mouth, but deems them highly objectionable in the mouth of Schweitzer. And why did he reconcile himself with the monster Schweitzer in Lausanne? And his theory of action! It consists of this, that Herr Wilhelm has the right to use my name and that of the General Council "arbitrarily," whenever it seems to him to be appropriate. Added to that, the courage of this philistine! He pretends to be against Lassalle, and therefore takes the side of the "genuine" as against the "nongenuine" Lassalleans! His own Bracke reproaches Schweitzer for having declared Lassalle's theory of state credit merely a means of agitation and for not believing in the panacea. He has involved me in "wars"! I wrote him it was in "scandal."

Greetings.

Yours,
K. M.

---

1. For carbuncles.
2. On July 22, 1869, Liebknecht wrote Marx explaining his quarrel with Schweitzer, the latter having claimed Marx's friendship: "You would not, after all, want to appear in the eyes of German workers as a patron of this scamp. That I acted *arbitrarily* I admit—when one is at war, one always acts arbitrarily, or not at all. Schweitzer's eventual rejection by the Congress was necessary of itself. The Statutes of the International Working Men's Association exclude 'dishonest' persons—and if Schweitzer had been admitted despite this, admission of the German workers . . . would have been made impossible. . . ."

Letter to Engels (in Manchester)
LONDON, JULY 27, 1869

Dear Fred:

Among the newspapers I am sending you, look particularly at pp. 105, 106 of the *Vorbote*, which I have underlined.

You will find that old Becker cannot leave pompousness alone.[1] Through his system of linguistic grouping, he throws overboard all our Statutes and the spirit of our Statutes, and transforms our natural system into an artificial piece of work made up of *arbitrary linguistic connections* rather than *actual political and national connections*. Arch-reactionaries, an economy worth of Pan-Slavs! And all this because we allowed him provisionally, before the International in Germany grew stronger, to remain the center of its former correspondents.

I immediately attacked his attempt to pose as the German center at the Eisenach Congress.[2]

Bebel sent me 25 Taler for the Belgians [miners] from his Workers' Education Association. Today I acknowledged its receipt and used the opportunity to write about Becker's fantasy plans.

I called his attention to Article 6 of the Statutes,[3] recognizing only national Central Committees, directly connected with the General Council, and, where this is impossible because of police regulations, obligating the local groups in every country to correspond with the General Council direct. I explained to him the folly of Becker's pretensions, and finally told him that if the Eisenach Congress—*quoad* [in regard to] the International—adopted Becker's proposal, we would immediately dismiss him publicly as violating the Statutes.

---

1. In *Vorbote*, July, 1869, Johann Philipp Becker, then under Bakuninist influence, denied the necessity of national proletarian parties.

2. The congress of the German Social-Democratic Workers' party at Eisenach, August 7-9, 1869.

3. Article 6 of the Rules and Regulations of the International, adopted at the Geneva Congress, September 5, 1866, reads: "The General Council shall form an international agency between the different national and local groups of the Association, so that the workingmen in one country shall be constantly informed of the movements of their class in every country; that an inquiry into the social state of the different countries of Europe shall be made simultaneously, and under a common direction; that the questions of general interest mooted in one society shall be ventilated by all; and that when immediate practical steps should be needed—as, for instance, in case of international quarrels—the action of the associated societies shall be simultaneous and uniform. Whenever it seems opportune, the General Council shall take the initiative on proposals to be laid before the different national or local societies. To facilitate communications, the General Council shall publish periodic reports."

For the rest, Bebel and Liebknecht had written me spontaneously beforehand that they had written Becker they did *not* recognize him but corresponded directly with London.

Becker himself is not dangerous. But his secretary, Remy, as they report to us from Switzerland, has been imposed on him by Bakunin, whose tool he is. This Russian obviously wants to become the dictator of the European workers' movement. He had better look out. Otherwise he will be excommunicated.

Yours,

K. M.

From letter to Engels (in Manchester)
LONDON, JULY 29, 1869

Dear Fred:

. . . The *Bee-Hive* is now under the control of Samuel Morley, and since then everything antibourgeois in the reports of our sessions is being stricken out. This happened to the whole development of the subject of Roman and German testamentary and untestamentary law which I presented at the last session of the General Council.[1] . . .

Greetings.

Yours,

K. M.

From letter to Engels (in Manchester)
LONDON, AUGUST 4, 1869

Dear Fred:

. . . Yesterday there was a tragicomic session of the General Council. Dunning letters for cards, rent, pay in arrears for the secretary, etc. In brief, international bankruptcy, so that we do not know yet whether we will be able to send a single deputy. On the other hand, a letter from Geneva, French side, wherein the General Council is politely requested to issue a circular in the three languages, demanding (and that immediately) that all branches collect money for the

1. See "The Right of Inheritance," page 107.

purchase of a building in Geneva (for meetings), which would cost only
£45,000 and would become the property of the International. Isn't this
a modest request from these lads who have not yet paid their one-
penny contribution?

Becker, the chief of the German-language [groups], sent 280 pence
for his "myriads."

The long and the short of the story is: The local committees (including the Central Committee) are spending too much money, and are
taxing their people too much for their national and local needs, to
have any money left for the General Council. There is always money
to print idiotic addresses to the Spaniards, etc., and similar follies. We
will be obliged to declare to the next Congress, in writing or orally,
that we can no longer conduct the General Council in this fashion, but
that before it gives us a successor, it should be so kind as to pay our
debts, which would have been even larger if our secretaries had not personally borne the cost of the correspondence.

If I could see anywhere any individuals who would not get us into
asininities, I would see the Central Council removed from here with
the greatest pleasure. The thing becomes *ennuyant* [boring].

Greetings.

EL MORO

From letter to Engels (in Manchester)
LONDON, AUGUST 18, 1869

Dear Fred:

. . . Received the £10.[1] But cannot send the receipt before Saturday, the day of the session of the subcommittee. The money [to pay
rent] comes extremely opportunely, before we are locked out.

Yesterday Dupont reported that the French (Parisian) trade unions
(bronze workers) paid back the £45, that is, they sent it back to be
repaid. Part of the money was borrowed through our mediation a
year ago, and part of it was a gift from the local unions. (Prior to that,
at our request £20 was sent from Paris to Rouen.) I arranged for
députés [deputies] to be sent to the unions here, to appeal to their
consciences for the repayment of the money. Altogether, the Paris
unions have behaved very decently.

---

1. Engels to Marx, August 16, 1869: "Enclosed a banknote of £10, of which
£5 is from Moore and £5 from me, as contributions to the International."

This is a blow to old Becker, and especially to the "language-group treasury." . . .

Yesterday there came an affiliation of a group (Italian) from Trieste. Ditto from Barcelona; I am enclosing a copy of the organ[2] of this new group.

In Posen—as Zabicki informed us—the Polish workers (carpenters, etc.) ended a strike victoriously with the help of their Berlin colleagues. This struggle against Monsieur le Capital—even in the subordinate form of a strike—will do away with national prejudices in different fashion from the peace declamations of the bourgeois gentlemen . . .

EL MORO

The sudden death of Sylvis (forty-one), president of the American Labor Union, is greatly to be regretted; it happened just *before* the meeting of the Labor-Union Congress, for whose objectives he agitated across the length and breadth of the United States for almost a whole year. Part of his work is thus lost.

From letter to Engels (in Manchester)
HANOVER,[1] SEPTEMBER 25, 1869

Dear Fred:

 . . . On this tour through Belgium, my stay in Aachen, and my voyage up the Rhine, I have become convinced that the priests, especially in the Catholic districts, must be energetically attacked. I shall work along these lines through the International. The dogs (for example, Bishop Ketteler in Mainz, the priests at the Düsseldorf Congress, etc.) are flirting, where they find it suitable, with the labor question.[2] Indeed, it was for them we worked in 1848; only they have enjoyed the fruits of victory during the period of reaction. . . .

 Greetings.

Yours,
K. M.

2. *La Federación.*

1. Marx visited Dr. Ludwig Kugelmann in Hanover from September 18 to October 7, 1869; he had arrived there after traveling through Belgium and the Rhineland for about a week.
2. At the Twentieth General Convention of the Catholic Societies of Germany, meeting in Düsseldorf, September 6, 1869, it was decided to appeal to Christians of all classes to show concern for the working classes, as a counter to socialist propaganda among them.

From letter to Engels (in Manchester)
LONDON, OCTOBER 30, 1869

Dear Fred:

. . . That Serno should have committed suicide is natural. But that Bakunin, with whom he had bad relations up to the end, should have seized his papers is a revolting discovery.[1] Apropos. The secretary of our French Committee in Geneva has had Bakunin up to his ears and complains that his "tyranny" has disorganized everything. In *Égalité* Bakunin announces that the German and English workers have no need for individualism and that they therefore accept our *communisme autoritaire*. In contrast, Bakunin represents *le collectivisme anarchique*. The anarchy is indeed in his head, wherein there is room for only one clear idea, that Bakunin must play first fiddle. . . .

A consequence of the Basel Congress to be considered is the founding of the Land and Labour League (instigated directly by the General Council), through which the workers' party withdraws entirely from the bourgeoisie, with nationalization of land as a starting point. Eccarius is named the active secretary (next to Boon as the honorary one), and is paid for it.

I was instructed by the General Council to write a few words to the English working class on the Irish prisoners' demonstration last Sunday. With my present occupations, I am by no means inclined to it, but it must be done.[2] The demonstration has been quite falsely described in the London papers. But it was splendid. . . .

Yours,
K. M.

---

1. Serno-Solovyevich committed suicide on August 16, 1869, and *L'Égalité* of October 1, 1869, announced that his literary remains were going to Bakunin.
2. See Marx's letter to Engels, November 18, 1869.

Letter to Engels (in Manchester)
LONDON, NOVEMBER 18, 1869

Dear Fred:

I am sending you today by book post a packet containing (1) a volume of Irish pamphlets[1] (especially Ensor, of some value), (2) the *Social-Demokrat* and *Volksstaat*, and (3) three copies of the *Report on the Basel Congress*,[2] one for you, one for Moore, and one for Schorlemmer. I don't know whether I had already sent you this. If I did, then give the copies to other people.

I will carry out your commissions.[3]

The *Bee-Hive* has entirely suppressed the report (by Eccarius) on the last session [of the General Council], on the pretext that it was received too late. The real reason was

(1) that he [Potter] did not want to announce that the General Council would open up a discussion of the Irish Question at its next session;

(2) that the report contained references to the Land and Labour League displeasing to him (i.e., Mr. Potter). Mr. Potter, be it stressed, has been *blackballed* with éclat as candidate for the Committee of that League.

Last Tuesday[4] I opened the discussion of Point No. 1, the position of the British Ministry regarding the Irish Amnesty Question. Gave a speech of about three quarters of an hour, much cheered, and then proposed on Point No. 4 the following resolutions. . . .[5]

Harris (an O'Brien man) seconded. The president (Lucraft), however, pointed to the clock (we are supposed to stay only until eleven);

---

1. Marx to Engels, November 6, 1869: "One of these days I will send you a volume, which I picked up accidentally, containing all kinds of pamphlets on Ireland. The one by Ensor (whom I also cited in *Capital* [Vol. I, Ch. 24]) has all sorts of piquant stuff. Ensor was a political economist of English origin (his father still lived in England at the time of Ensor's birth), a Protestant, and withal one of the most resolute Repealers [of the Anglo-Irish Union] before 1830. As he was himself indifferent to religious matters, he could wittily defend Catholicism against the Protestants. . . ."

2. A brochure printed in London in 1869.

3. Engels to Marx, November 17, 1869: "Prendergast [John Patrick], *Cromwellian Settlement of Ireland* [London, 1865] is *out of print*. I would be much obliged if you would immediately order it for me from an antiquarian. Butt's [Isaac] *The Irish People and the Irish Land* [Dublin, 1867]: none in London. Other Irish pamphlets, for example, those of Lords Rosse and Lifford: cannot find."

4. November 16.

5. See "On the Irish Amnesty Question," page 115.

hence it was adjourned until next Tuesday. But Lucraft, Weston, Hales, etc., in fact the entire Council, declared their provisional approval in an informal way.

Another O'Brienite—Milner—stated that the language of the resolutions was too weak (that is, not declamatory enough); moreover, he demanded that what I said in explanation should be included in the Resolution. (A nice story, this!)

So, since further discussion is next Tuesday, now is the time for you to tell me, to write me, what you would like to see changed in or added to the resolutions. In the latter case, if you want to have an additional paragraph on the amnesties in all of Europe, in Italy, for example, write it out in the form of a resolution!

An incident at the last Council's sitting. Mr. Holyoake—every man his own Cromwell—shows up, and then, after disappearing, has himself proposed for admission by Weston. Temporarily resolved, that he should first get a card as member of the International Working Men's Association, otherwise he could not be proposed. His aim was simply to make himself important—and to be able to figure as a delegate to the next General Congress! The discussion over his admission will be stormy, since he has many friends among us and could also play some practical jokes on us as an offended intrigant. What is your opinion on the tactics to follow?[6]

Enclosed a scrap from Liebknecht, who also complains bitterly in a letter to Borkheim that we support him neither spiritually nor materially. Return the two enclosed letters from Wilhelm [Liebknecht] which are addressed to Borkheim.

In Dundee, establishment of a Branch of the International, ditto a new branch in Boston, New England.

Carbuncles not yet vanquished.

Greetings.

Yours,

K. M.

Apropos L. Blanc. When Reclus was here, he also visited L. Blanc and told me afterwards: The little one is shitting in his pants out of fear at the very thought of having to return to France. He feels himself devilishly well off here as a danger-exempt *"petit grand homme"* [little great man]—he, as he told Reclus directly, having absolutely lost all confidence in the French.

---

6. Engels to Marx, November 19, 1869: "With Holyoake, the matter is awkward. The fellow is purely a go-between between the radical bourgeois and the workers . . . To the best of my knowledge, Mr. Holyoake has never done the slightest thing for the working class *as such. A priori*, everything speaks against his admission, but if rejecting him would cause splits in the Council, while his admission would perhaps cause but few practical changes in the make-up of the General Council, *eh bien* [well, then]!"

From letter to Engels (in Manchester)
LONDON, NOVEMBER 26, 1869

Dear Fred:

. . . Last Tuesday's [November 23] session was very fiery, heated, and vehement. Mr. Muddlehead,[1] or the devil knows what the fellow's name is—a Chartist, or an old friend of Harney's—had providently brought Odger and Applegarth along. On the other hand, Weston and Lucraft were absent because they were attending an Irish ball. *Reynolds's* had published my resolution in its Saturday issue[2] and also an abstract of my speech (as well as Eccarius, who is no stenographer, could do it); *Reynolds's* printed it right on the front page of the paper, after its leading article. This seems to have scared those flirting with Gladstone. Hence the appearance of Odger and a long rambling speech by Mottershead, who got rapped over the head for it by Milner (himself an Irishman). Applegarth sat next to me and therefore did not dare speak *against* it; on the contrary, he spoke *for* it, evidently with an uneasy conscience. Odger said that if the resolutions were forced to a vote, he would vote for them. But unanimity was surely better and could be attained by means of a few minor amendments, etc. I thereupon declared—because he was just the one I wanted to sail into—that *he* should submit his amendments at the next session! At the last session, although many of our most reliable members were absent, we would thus have carried the resolution against *one single* vote. Tuesday [November 30][3] we shall be there in full force.

Greetings.

Yours,

K. M.

---

1. Marx's pun on the name of Thomas Mottershead, his colleague in the General Council.
2. Of November 20.
3. Minutes of the General Council, November 30: "Par. 1 of the resolution on the British Government in the Irish Amnesty affair was then read . . . Citizen Marx had consented to withdraw the word 'deliberately.' The Par. was unanimously adopted with that omission. The Par. 2 Citizen Odger thought to be altered so as not to throw the whole blame on Gladstone . . . Citizen Milner stated . . . Gladstone could not be treated differently to any other government . . . Citizen Marx said if Odger's suggestions were followed the Council would put themselves on an English party standpoint. They could not do that. The Council must show the Irish that they understood the question and the Continent that they showed no favor to the British Government . . . The Par. was carried unanimously."

From letter to Ludwig Kugelmann (in Hanover)
LONDON, NOVEMBER 29, 1869

Dear Kugelmann:

... I have come more and more to the conviction—and it is only a matter of bringing this conviction home to the English working class—that it can never do anything decisive here in England until it most definitely separates its policy with regard to Ireland from the policy of the ruling classes, until it not only makes common cause with the Irish, but even takes the initiative in dissolving the Union established in 1801 and replacing it with a free federal relationship. And, indeed, this must be done, not as a matter of sympathy with Ireland, but as a demand made in the interests of the English proletariat. If not, the English people will remain in the leading strings of the ruling classes, because *it* must join with them in a common front against Ireland. Every one of its movements in England itself is crippled by the quarrel with the Irish, who even in England form a very significant section of the working class. The first condition of emancipation here—the overthrow of the English landed oligarchy—remains impossible, because its position here cannot be stormed so long as it maintains its strongly entrenched outpost in Ireland. There, however, once the matter is in the hands of the Irish people themselves, once they are made their own legislators and rulers, once they become autonomous, the abolition of the landed aristocracy (for the most part the same persons as the English landlords) will be infinitely easier than here, because in Ireland it is not only a simple economic question, but at the same time a *national* question, since the landlords there, unlike those in England, are not the traditional dignitaries and representatives, but the mortally hated oppressors of the nation. And not only does England's internal social development remain crippled by the present relation with Ireland, but its foreign policy also, particularly with regard to Russia and the United States.

But since the English working class undoubtedly throws the decisive weight into the scales of social emancipation generally, it is necessary to apply the lever here. In fact, the English republic under Cromwell was wrecked over—Ireland. *Non bis in idem!* [Not twice the same thing!] The Irish have played an exquisite joke on the English Government by electing the "convict felon" O'Donovan Rossa to Parliament. The government papers are already threatening a renewed suspension of the Habeas Corpus Act, and a renewed system of terror! In fact, England never has and—so long as the present relationship lasts—never *can* rule Ireland otherwise than by the most revolting reign of terror and the most reprehensible corruption. . . .

Yours,

K. M.

Letter to Engels (in Manchester)
LONDON, DECEMBER 4, 1869

Dear Fred:

The resolutions carried unanimously, despite Odger's constant verbal amendments. I yielded to him on only one point, to omit the word "deliberate" before "insults" in Par. 1. I did that on the pretext that everything a Prime Minister did publicly must be presumed *eo ipso* [of itself] *to be deliberate.* The real reason was that I knew that once this concession in the first paragraph was made, all further resistance would be in vain. I am sending you two copies of the *National Reformer,* containing the report on the first two sessions, but not the last one. This report is poor, too, and much in it is false (through misunderstanding), but it is better than Eccarius' reports in *Reynolds's.* It is by Harris, whose currency panacea you will also find in the last issue of the *National Reformer.*

With the exception of Mottershead, who acts as John Bull, and Odger, who always acts the diplomat, the English delegates have behaved splendidly. The general debate on the relation of the English working class to the Irish Question will take place on Tuesday.

One has to battle not only with prejudices here, but also with the stupidity and miserableness of the Irish spokesmen in Dublin. The *Irishman*[1] (Pigott) knew about the proceedings and resolutions not only from *Reynolds's,* which it admires and extracts. They (the Resolutions) had already been sent to it direct by an Irishman on November 17. Until today, *deliberately not a syllable.* The jackass had acted similarly during our debate and petition for the three Manchester men.[2] The "Irish" Question is to be treated by him [Pigott] as something separate, to the exclusion of the outside world, and specifically it is to be kept quiet that English workers sympathize with the Irish! What an ox of the bovine race! To act like this in the face of the International, which has organs in all of Europe and the United States! This week he has officially received the resolutions, signed by the

---

1. A pro-Fenian weekly in Belfast, later published in Dublin.
2. See "On the Fenian Prisoners in Manchester," page 87.

PERSONAL LETTERS

foreign secretaries. The thing was also sent to the *People*. *Nous verrons*. [We will see.] Mottershead supports the *Irishman* and will certainly use this opportunity to poke fun at "high-souled" Irishmen.

Nevertheless, I will play a trick on Pigott. Today I will write to Eccarius that he should send the resolutions with the signatures, etc., to Isaac Butt, as president of the Irish Workingmen's Association. Butt is not Pigott.

To explain to you the enclosed letter from Applegarth, the following:

At the end of the last session, at which he behaved very well, he took me aside and told me the following: An eminent member of the House of Commons[3] wrote him that he was commissioned by an eminent member of the House of Lords (Lord Leachfield!) to ask him whether he had voted for the abolition of all private property at Basel.[4] Applegarth's reply would be decisive for his relationship with his parliamentary patrons. He (Applegarth) wants to reply definitively, but I should write him briefly the "reasons," and on the next day at that. I was very busy, and in addition still suffering in the underarm [from a carbuncle] and from a cold, aggravated by the atrocious fog after the Tuesday evening session. Hence I wrote to Applegarth on Wednesday [December 1] that I had been delayed but was ready, after he had received the answer, to support him. With English obstinacy, he did not agree, and wrote the enclosed letter. Thus, willy-nilly, I was compelled to send him yesterday eight closely written pages, which he will have to chew for a long time, on landed property and the necessity for its abolition. The man is very important, because he is the officially recognized representative of the English trade unions in both houses of Parliament.

Enclosed, a letter from Bracke.[5] I have nothing against Bonhorst, but I told Kugelmann only that I thought he had a Catiline-kind of existence. Kugelmann, with his usual tact, reported this to Bracke with amplifications.

Tussy[6] thanks Dido[7] for his letter and sends greetings to everybody.

Greetings.

Yours,

MOHR

---

3. Probably Anthony John Mundella.
4. The Congress of the International in Basel.
5. On November 11, 1869, Wilhelm Bracke informed Marx of the arrest of Leonhard von Bonhorst, the secretary of the Brunswick Committee of the Social-Democratic Workers' party.
6. Eleanor Marx.
7. Engels' dog.

From letter to Engels (in Manchester)
LONDON, DECEMBER 10, 1869

Dear Fred:

. . . *Ad vocem* [in regard to]: *Irish Question.* I did not attend the Central Council session last Tuesday [December 7]. My family would not permit me—although I had undertaken to open the debates—to go out in this fog and in my present state of health.

In regard to the *National Reformer*, not only is the nonsense ascribed to me, but also what is *correctly* reported is *falsely* reported. But I did not want to protest. *D'abord*, I would thereby insult the reporter (Harris). And second, so long as I did not interfere at all, all these reports have nothing official about them. If I correct anything, I admit thereby that the rest is correct. And everything, as it is reported, is false. Besides, I have reasons for not turning these reports into legal evidence against me, which would happen the moment I corrected the details.

The way I will bring up the matter next Tuesday is this: that apart from all "international" and "humane" justice-for-Ireland phrases— which are self-evident in the Council of the International—it is in *the direct and absolute interest of the English working class* TO GET RID *of their present connection with Ireland.* And this is my fullest conviction, and for reasons which in part I *cannot* communicate to the English workers themselves. I have long believed that it would be possible to overthrow the Irish regime through English working-class ascendancy. I have always expressed this view in the *New-York Tribune.*[1] A deeper study has convinced me of the opposite. The English working class will *never achieve anything* until it has got rid of Ireland. The lever must be applied in Ireland. This is why the Irish Question is so important for the social movement in general.[2] . . .

Yours,

K. M.

---

1. See "Forced Emigration—Kossuth and Mazzini—The Refugee Question . . ." in the *New-York Daily Tribune*, March 22, 1853.
2. See The Question of the General Council's Resolution on the Irish Amnesty, part 5 of the Circular in "Confidential Communication," page 166.

From letter to Engels (in Manchester)
LONDON, DECEMBER 17, 1869

Dear Fred:

. . . From the enclosed copy of *L'Égalité,* which I must have back, you will see how insolent Signor Bakunin is becoming. This lad now has at his disposal four organs of the *Internationale (L'Égalité, Progrès* in Locle, *Federación,* and *Eguaglianza* in Naples). He is trying to gain a foothold in Germany through an alliance with Schweitzer, and in Paris through flattery of the journal *Le Travail.* He believes the moment has come to begin an open conflict with us. He poses as the true guardian of proletarianism. Still, he will wonder. Next week (fortunately, the Central Council is adjourned until the Tuesday after New Year's Day [January 4, 1870], so we in the subcommittee can act freely without the genial interference of the English) we are sending a missive to the Romansh Federal Committee in Geneva with threats, and since these gentlemen (of whom, moreover, a significant, perhaps the major, part is *against* Bakunin) know that, in accordance with decisions of the last Congress, we can *suspend* them if necessary, they will think twice about it.

The main point about which our missive will revolve is: The only representation of the *branches romandes en Suisse* [Romansh Branches in Switzerland] vis-à-vis us is the Federal Committee there. The latter has submitted to us its demands and reprimands *privately* through its secretary, Perret. They have absolutely no right to turn over their functions to the *Égalité* (nonexistent *for us*) and expect the Central Council to enter into a public explanation and polemic with this *remplaçant* [substitute]. Whether or not the replies of the General Council are to be published in the organs of the branches of the International depends entirely on the decision of the General Council, which alone is *directly* responsible to the Congress. On this occasion, the blows will fall on the intriguers, who are usurping an authority that does not belong to them and who are trying to subject the International to their private rule.

In regard to the outcry of the Cossacks[1] about the *Bulletin,* the matter is so:

At the Brussels Congress, it was decided that we were to publish bulletins on strikes, etc. "in the several languages," "*as often as its*" (*the General Council's*) "*means permit.*" But on condition that we, on

---

1. Bakunin and his followers.

our part, receive reports, documents, etc., from the federal committees at least every three months. Since we neither received the reports nor had the "means" to print them, this decision naturally remained a dead letter. In reality, it became superfluous because of the establishment of many international newspapers (*Bee-Hive* as register of English strikes, etc.), which made mutual exchanges.

At the Basel Congress the question was warmed up again. The Congress treated the Brussels decisions on the bulletin as nonexistent. Otherwise it would have simply ordered the Central Council to carry them out (which, again, without providing the means, would have been a *lettre morte* [dead letter]). What is involved is a bulletin in another sense (not, as before, a résumé of strikes, etc., but rather general reflections on the movement). On this, however, the Congress did not come to a vote. Hence at the moment there exists *no* decision on this question. But to tell the public, through published replies to *L'Égalité*, that the former Brussels decisions remained *impossible of execution* because (1) the members did not pay their pence, and (2) the federal committee did not carry out their functions—that would have been some politics!

In regard to Schweitzer, Herr Bakunin, who understands German, knows that Schweitzer and his gang do not belong to the International. He knows that Schweitzer has *publicly rejected* Liebknecht's offer to have the General Council serve as arbitrator.[2] His formulation of the question is thus the greater *canaillerie* [blackguardism], since his friend Ph. Becker, president of the German-language groups, sits in the Geneva *Federal Council* in order to provide them with the necessary information there. His [Bakunin's] aim was to find a handle in Schweitzer. *Mais il verra!* [But he will see!]

I have written to De Paepe at length about the affair (to be submitted to the Brussels Central Committee).

As soon as a Russian creeps in, there is the devil to pay. . . .

Greetings.

Yours,

K. M.

---

2. In the February 20, 1869, issue of the *Demokratisches Wochenblatt* Liebknecht asked that the General Council mediate between his Social Democrats and the General German Workers' Association, of which Johann Baptist von Schweitzer was president. Schweitzer rejected the offer in the *Social-Demokrat* of February 24, 1869.

Letter written in French to César De Paepe (in Brussels)
LONDON, JANUARY 24, 1870

Dear Citizen De Paepe:

I am writing you with some difficulty, as my left arm is bandaged. A glandular abscess began to develop near the hollow of my shoulder at the end of last month. I neglected the thing and am now punished for this sin. A few days after I wrote my letter to the Brussels Committee [January 8], the pain became unendurable and I fell into the hands of the doctors. I had to suffer two operations. I am improving now but am still under treatment and must remain in my room.

I am writing you today because I want to ask you a personal favor. You probably know that a portion of the English bourgeoisie has founded a kind of Land League,[1] which is in opposition to the workers' Land and Labour League.[2] Its official aim is to transform the English landed property into parceled property and to create a peasant class for the greater welfare of the nation. Its real aim is to attack the landed aristocracy. They want to put the land into free circulation, so as to take it from the hands of the landlords and transfer it to the capitalists. For this purpose they have published a series of popular essays under the title *Cobden Treatises*, in which small ownership is extolled in rosy colors. Its great parade horse is Belgium (primarily the Flemings). In that country the peasants are made out to be living under paradisiacal conditions. The Land League made contact with M. Laveleye, who supplies them with material for their declamations. Since I am now dealing with landed property in the second volume of *Capital*, I consider it suitable to enter into a few details about Belgian landed property and agriculture. Would you be so kind as to send me the titles of a few important books which I could consult?

My illness has, of course, prevented me from attending the sessions of the General Council in the last few weeks. But the subcommittee (of the executive committee), to which I belong, visited me last night. Among other things, they reported the contents of a letter from M. Hins to Stepney. As Stepney assumed that I would be in condition to attend the session of the General Council (on January 25), he had re-

---

1. The Land Tenure Reform Association, founded by John Stuart Mill in July, 1869.
2. The Land and Labour League was founded by the General Council of the International in October, 1869.

ported to me the contents of that letter. I knew about it only from hearsay.[3]

In the first place, they probably believe in Brussels that the Geneva catastrophe, the change in the editorship of *L'Égalité*,[4] was called forth by the decisions of the General Council. This is an error. Jung was so busy with his work as watchmaker that he could not find the time to copy the decisions and send them to Geneva *before January 16*. In the meantime he received two letters from H. Perret, the secretary of the Romansh Committee. The first letter, dated January 4, is an official one. It is a report of the Romansh Committee to the General Council saying that a few of the editors of *L'Égalité* agreed to start a public campaign against the General Council *and* the Swiss Committee, with which they were not in agreement, but that they acted *against* the latter's will.

The second letter, dated later, but which also arrived *before* Jung sent off the decisions of the General Council, is a confidential communication addressed by Perret to Jung.[5] I am giving you literal excerpts, so that you may be informed. I need not add that this is a private letter, that the excerpts should not be reported to the Belgian Council, and the name of the author should remain secret.

". . . Bakunin has left Geneva. So much the better. These fellows continue to create division among us. They were the head of the Alliance. These democrats are authoritarian, they tolerate no contradiction, such are men like Bakunin, Perron, and Robin; all three headed *L'Égalité*. Bakunin with his personal attacks has cost us two or three hundred subscribers in Geneva. Robin is even more authoritarian than he; he presumes to change everything among us; he will not succeed in this, for we will not let ourselves come under the tutelage of these gentlemen, who consider themselves indispensable. They tried to exert pressure on the Federal Committee, but did not succeed; we will not let them drag us into adventures or permit a split among our sections. But do believe that the Alliance is dangerous for us, particularly now. Its plan in Geneva—I have long surmised it—was to bring Alliance men into all the societies and thus put the Federation under its domination. If you only knew what means they employed: *slandering* in the sections the men who refused to yield to them; they have done everything to thwart my candidacy in Basel; the same is true of Gosselin . . . You see, their maneuver was to send to Basel only mem-

---

3. Eugène Hins' letter to Cowell Stepney, written January 21, 1870, was transmitted to Marx on January 27, 1870.

4. See "Circular to the Swiss Romansh Council," in "Confidential Communication," page 166.

5. Both of Perret's letters to Jung were dated January 4, 1870.

bers of the Alliance—Heng, Brosset, Bakunin. In this they did not altogether succeed. In addition, he [Bakunin] procured mandates from
Lyon and Naples; all these methods dispense with every morality.
They left here to prepare their intrigue in Basel . . . At the Congress[6]
there was one fact which I sensed but had no sure proof of. Martinaud, delegate of the Neuchâtel section, had a mandate signed by
Guillaume's brother, a lying, false mandate; *now we have the proof in
our hands.* The Neuchâtel section was not yet definitely constituted
then, and the provisional committee wrote us that it knew neither
Guillaume nor Martinaud. Such is the morality of the apostles of the
Alliance, for Guillaume and a few men from Locle are among their
friends. Furthermore, the publication of *Progrès* and *L'Égalité* has cost
us subscribers, while our own paper, which we have to support,
was founded by all of us in common.

"Latest news: the adventurers of the Alliance have just withdrawn
from *L'Égalité:* Perron, Robin, and a few other more or less competent
persons. A small *coup d'état* against Bakunin and à la Robin. They
wanted *to force the Federal Committee to dismiss* a member of the
editorial board who had shown himself to be refractory and who had
criticized the attacks on the various committees and on the General
Council. We do not wish to exert pressure in favor of these people; we
will still have to fight a secret battle with them; but it seems that the
Alliance is losing many members, and if it declines, so much the better."

So much for the extracts from Perret's missive.

If M. Hins has not yet communicated my letter (and the decisions
of the General Council) to the Belgian Council, he would *do well to
leave out entirely the paragraph dealing with Bakunin.* I have no copy
but I know that I wrote it when I was irritable because of pain. Hence
I do not doubt that M. Hins is critical of the form of this paragraph.
However, in regard to the contents, where facts are concerned, they
depend neither on my bad mode of expression nor on the good opinion
M. Hins has of Bakunin. The fact is that the Alliance, called into life
by Bakunin and now only *nominally* dissolved, is a danger for the
International Association, an element of disorganization.

In the paragraph regarding Bakunin, I am told, M. Hins disap-
proved of the phrase *"le bonhomme Richard"* ["simple Richard"].
This is a *slip of the pen* which I deplore the more since Richard is one
of the most active members of the Association. I used the word only
because I wanted to say that in the correspondence mentioned he
accepted too many *bonhomie* [credulous] opinions, whose contents he
never examined. For the rest, when I wrote those words Richard had

---

6. The Congress of the International in Basel, September 6–11, 1869.

shown another proof of his thoughtlessness. He sent the Council a letter which contained an already formulated judgment to the effect that certain persons belonging to a so-called recreant section in Lyon were *vile* and should be considered *traitors* to be *excluded* from the Association. We were asked to copy this judgment, put our seal and signatures on it, and return it posthaste. And this without any proof, without any documents, without giving the condemned the right to defend themselves!

I have been told, furthermore, that M. Hins reproaches the English-language "Report on the Basel Congress"[7] with suppressing everything relating to the question of inheritance. This is obviously a misunderstanding. On pages 26–29 one will find the Report of the General Council as well as the report of the Basel committee and a rendering of the discussion on this question. For the rest, the English report on the work of the Congress was written by Eccarius. The Council appointed a committee to examine it. Although I was a member of this committee, I declined to participate in its work, because I was not at the Congress and hence was not competent to judge the accuracy of the report. My whole contribution was confined to a few purely stylistic corrections.

If, finally, the decisions taken by the General Council do not have the good fortune to please M. Hins, they did clearly satisfy the Romansh Council, as, two weeks before it accepted them, it resolved to emancipate itself from the dictatorship of the Alliance.

Yours,

K. M.

From letter to Engels (in Manchester)
LONDON, FEBRUARY 10, 1870

Dear Fred:

. . . You will recall that *L'Égalité*, under Bakunin's inspiration, attacked the General Council, made public all sorts of interpellations, and threatened more. Thereupon, a Circular—which I composed— was sent to the *Comité Romand* in Geneva and all other French-language committees in correspondence with us.[1] Result: The whole

7. *Report of the Fourth Annual Congress of the International Working Men's Association, held at Basel, in Switzerland* (London, 1869).

1. See "Circular to the Swiss Romansh Council," in "Confidential Communication," page 166.

Bakunin gang has resigned from *L'Égalité*. Bakunin himself has given up his residence in Tessin and will continue his intrigues in Switzerland, Spain, Italy, and France. Even the armistice between us is at an end, since he knows that on the occasion of the latest Geneva events I vigorously attacked and denounced him. The beast actually imagines that we are "too bourgeois," and therefore incapable of grasping or respecting his lofty conceptions of the "right of inheritance," "equality," and the replacement of the existing political systems by the "International." His "Alliance of Socialist Democracy" has been suspended in name but in fact it continues. From the enclosed copy of a letter (which you must return to me) from H. Perret, secretary of the *Conseil Romand*, to Jung, you will see that the catastrophe in Geneva actually took place before our Circular was received there. Nevertheless, this strengthens the new *status rerum* [state of things]. The Belgian *"Conseil"* has officially declared itself entirely in favor of our position against *L'Égalité*, but the secretary of the Belgian Council, Hins (brother-in-law of De Paepe, but who has fallen out with him), sent a letter to Stepney in which he takes Bakunin's side and accuses me of supporting the reactionary party among the Geneva workers, etc., etc. . . .

K. M.

From letter to Engels (in Manchester)
LONDON, FEBRUARY 19, 1870

Dear Fred:
   . . . Tonight—although going out last night did not agree with me—I must again go into the City. I have been summoned by the subcommittee. And the matter is in fact important, since the Lyonnais expelled Richard from their Association and the General Council has to make a decision about it. Richard, until now leader in Lyon, is a very young fellow, very active. Apart from his infeudation to Bakunin and his being a know-it-all in connection with it, I don't know that there is anything to reproach him with. It seems that our last Circular caused a great sensation in Switzerland, and there, as well as in France, a hunt after Bakuninists has begun. But there is a *modus in rebus* [a way of doing things] and I will see to it that no injustice occurs. . . .
   Greetings.

Yours,
K. M.

From letter to Engels (*in Manchester*)
LONDON, MARCH 5, 1870

Dear Fred:

. . . In the meantime, all sorts of things have been happening in Fenian affairs. A letter I wrote to the *Internationale* in Brussels, in which I also attacked the French republicans for their narrow-minded nationalist tendency, was printed and the editors announce that they will publish their reflections on it this week.[1] You must know that in the Central Council's Circular to the Genevans—which has also been communicated to the Brussels men and to the main centers of the International in France—I developed at length the meaning of the Irish Question for the movement of the working class in general (through its reaction on England).

Shortly thereafter Jennychen flew into a passion over a lousy article in the *Daily News*, the private gazette of the Gladstone Ministry, wherein this dog of a journal turns to its "liberal" brothers in France and warns them not to confuse the cases of Rochefort and O'Donovan Rossa. The *Marseillaise* really fell into the trap, agreed with the *Daily News*, and, furthermore, published a miserable article by the chatterbox Talandier, wherein this ex-Procurator of the Republic, now teacher in the French Military School at Woolwich (also ex-tutor in the home of Herzen, of whom he wrote a glowing obituary), attacked the Irish because of their Catholicism and accused them of having caused the defeat of Odger—because of his participation in the Garibaldi Committee.[2] In addition, he adds that they cling to Mitchel despite the latter's support of the slaveholders, as if Odger had not supported Gladstone despite the latter's party support of the slaveholders,[3] which was much more important. Hence Jennychen—*ira facit poetam* [anger makes the poet]—in addition to a private letter, wrote an article to the *Marseillaise*, which was *published*.[4] More-

1. Marx's letter on the Fenians was published in *L'Internationale*, February 27, 1870. The editors stated that they would comment on the mistreatment of the Fenians in their March 6 issue.

2. Talandier's article, *"L'Irlande et le Catholicisme,"* was published in *La Marseillaise*, February 18, 1870; his obituary of Alexander Herzen appeared in the Brussels *Internationale*, February 6, 1870.

3. In a speech at Newcastle, October 7, 1862, Chancellor of the Exchequer Gladstone hailed Jefferson Davis; the speech was published in the London *Times*, October 9, 1862.

4. Writing under the pseudonym "J. Williams," Jenny Marx published a series of eight articles on the Irish in *La Marseillaise* (February 27; March 9, 19, 21, 29; April 12, 17, 24, 1870). Marx was coauthor of the March 19 article.

over, she received a letter, a copy of which I am enclosing, from the
rédacteur de la rédaction [editor of the edition.] Today another letter
goes off to the *Marseillaise*, containing, in connection with Gladstone's
reply (this week) to the interpellation regarding the treatment of the
[Irish] prisoners, excerpts from a letter by O'Donovan Rossa (see
Irishman, February 5, 1870). Here Gladstone is presented to the
French, from Rossa's letter (insofar as G. is in fact responsible for the
treatment of prisoners, also under the Tories), not only as a monster,
but at the same time also—as the author of *Prayers, The Propagation
of the Gospel, The Functions of Laymen in the Church* and *Ecce
Homo*—as a ridiculous hypocrite.

In these two papers—the *Internationale* and the *Marseillaise*—we
shall now pull the masks off the Englishmen before the Continent. If
you should find anything, one day or the other, that is appropriate
for one of these papers, you must participate in our good work. . . .
Greetings.

Yours,

K. M.

From letter to Engels (in Manchester)
LONDON, MARCH 19, 1870

Dear Fred:

Enclosed a copy of *La Marseillaise*, which must be returned together with the previous copies. I have not seen them yet myself. The
article was written by Jennychen, together with me,[1] because she
did not have sufficient time at her disposal. This is also the reason why
she did not answer your letter and why she lets me thank Mrs. Lizzy
[Burns] provisionally for the shamrock.

From the enclosed letter from Pigott to Jenny, you can see that
Mrs. O'Donovan, to whom Jenny sent a private letter and a copy of
La Marseillaise, took her for a gentleman, although she had signed
herself Jenny Marx. At Jenny's suggestion, I wrote to Pigott today
and took the occasion to explain briefly my views of the Irish Question.

Your hint about Bruce's forgery has been used already in the
article which Jenny sent to the *Marseillaise* yesterday. We have the
report of Knox and Pollock (but have not looked it over yet) and
ditto "Things not generally known." You would oblige me if you

---

1. See "The Imprisoned O'Donovan Rossa and the English Press," page 128.

would send me *immediately:* (1) Lassalle's piece against Schulze-Delitzsch, and (2) the book of the crazy Frisian, "Clement."

The sensation which Jennychen's second article (containing the condensed translation of O'Donovan's letter) created in Paris and London kept the repugnant and importunate (but very fluent with mouth and pen) Talandier from sleeping. In *Marseillaise* he had denounced the Irish as Catholic idiots. Now, full-mouthed as ever, he takes their side in a review of what the *Times*, the *Daily Telegraph*, and the *Daily News* had said about O'Donovan's letter. Since Jennychen's article was not signed (by accident), he clearly flattered himself with the notion that he would be considered its secret author. This has been frustrated for him in Jennychen's third article. For the rest, the fellow is a teacher of French at the military school of Sandhurst.

Last Tuesday [March 15], for the first time, I once more attended a session of the General Council.[2] Felix Holt, the rascal, was with me. He was very much amused because, for a change, something interesting was taking place. As is known, the Paris *prolétaires* "*positivistes*" [positivist proletarians] had already sent a deputy [Mollin] to the Basel Congress. That Congress had argued whether or not he should be admitted, as he belonged to a philosophic, rather than a workers', organization (although he and associates "personally" belong to the working class). In the end he was admitted as a delegate of the personal members of the International. Those lads have now constituted themselves into a branch of the International in Paris—an act over which the London and Paris Comteists have made a great fuss. They considered this a thin entering wedge. The General Council, upon receiving the notice of affiliation from the "*prolétaires positivistes*," reminded them politely that it could approve only after seeing their program. So they sent a program—real orthodox Comteist—which was debated last Tuesday. The meeting was presided over by Mottershead, a very intelligent (although anti-Irish) old Chartist and a personal enemy and connoisseur of Comteism. After a long debate, the conclusion: Since they are workers, they can be admitted as a simple branch. But not as a "*positivist* branch," because the principles of Comteism are in direct contradiction to our Statutes. Moreover, it is their affair how they make their private philosophic views compatible with our Statutes.

Tomorrow, about the scraps of writing from Solingen.

Greetings.

Yours,

Moro

---

2. Because of illness, Marx had not attended any sessions since January 11.

Letter to Wilhelm Bracke (in Brunswick)
LONDON, MARCH 24, 1870

Dear Friend:

Yesterday I sent 3,000 membership cards at Bonhorst's address.

I have some not uninteresting occurrences inside the International to report to you. They will reach you in a roundabout way.[1] According to the Statutes, all national committees that are connected with the General Council have to send in reports on the state of the movement every three months. While I call your attention to this, I beg you to keep in mind that such reports are *not* designed for the public and hence they should be written factually, without embellishment.

From Borkheim and from Bonhorst's last letter, I know that the financial state of the "Eisenachers" is bad. For your consolation, I report that the finances of the General Council are below zero, a constantly growing *negative* quantity.

Letter written in French to Philippe Coenen (in Antwerp)
LONDON, MARCH 24, 1870

Citizen:

Yesterday I received the *Proefblad* [proofs] of *Het Volk*, published in Amsterdam, and a letter from the publisher, Philipp von Roesgen von Floss,[1] in which, among other things, he requested an International membership card. I know neither Herr Ph. von Roesgen von Floss nor the state of our relations in Rotterdam. I presume that you are better informed, and so I beg you to give me an answer to

---

1. Marx to Ludwig Kugelmann, March 28, 1870: ". . . I am sending you the enclosed, for the Brunswick Committee, Bracke and associates. It would be best if, after reading it, you would deliver it personally, with the reminder that this report is confidential, and not designed for the public."

---

1. Marx to Engels, March 24, 1870: "The letter from the publishers of *Het Volk*—herein enclosed—was addressed to me without address, merely stating on the envelope: 'to Herr Karl Marx, *Algemeen Correspondent voor Nederland der International Arbeiders Vereeniging, London.*' This position of '*Algemeen Correspondent voor Nederland*' ['General Correspondent for the Netherlands'] has hitherto been entirely unknown to me. Before going any further with 'Herr Philipp von Roesgen von Floss,' I thought it safer to write first to our Flemish branch in Antwerp, asking for information about his lengthy name."

the following two questions: (1) What is the situation of the International in Rotterdam? (2) Can the General Council enter into contact with Herr Phil. von Roesgen von Floss?

With fraternal greetings,

KARL MARX

From letter to Engels (in Manchester)
LONDON, MARCH 24, 1870

Dear Fred:

. . . I enclose a letter from the Russian colony in Geneva. We have admitted them and I have accepted their commission to be their representative in the General Council and have also sent them a short reply (official, with a private letter as well) and given them permission to publish it in their paper. A funny position for me to be functioning as the representative of young Russia! A man never knows what he may come to or what strange fellowship he may have to submit to. In the official reply I praise Flerovsky and emphasize the fact that the chief task of the Russian section is to work for Poland (i.e., to free Europe from Russia as a neighbor). I thought it safer to say nothing about Bakunin, either in the public or in the confidential letter. But what I will never forgive these fellows is that they turn me into a *"vénérable."* They obviously think I am between eighty and a hundred years old. . . .

Yours,

MOHR

From letter to Sigfrid Meyer and August Vogt (in New York)
LONDON, APRIL 9, 1870

Dear Meyer and Dear Vogt:

. . . Among the materials sent, you will find some pieces you know about—the resolutions of the General Council of November 30 on the *Irish amnesty*,[1] which originated with me, as well as an Irish pamphlet on the treatment of Fenian convicts.

---

1. Throughout this letter words and phrases which Marx wrote in English are in italics.

I had intended to introduce additional resolutions on the necessary transformation of the present Union (that is, Ireland's enslavement) into *a free and equal federation with Great Britain.* For the time being, further progress in this matter, *as far as public resolutions go,* has been suspended because of my enforced absence from the General Council. No other member of it has sufficient knowledge of Irish affairs or adequate prestige with its *English* members to be able to replace me here.

Meanwhile time has not been spent idly, and I ask you to pay particular attention to the following:

After occupying myself with the Irish question for years, I have come to the conclusion that the decisive blow against the English ruling classes (and it will be decisive for the workers' movement *all over the world*) *cannot* be delivered *in England* but *only in Ireland.*

On January 1, 1870, the General Council issued a confidential circular drawn up by me in French (for reaction about England only the French, not the German, papers are important) on the relation of the Irish national struggle to the emancipation of the working class, and therefore on the attitude which the International Association should adopt in regard to the Irish question.

I shall give you here only quite briefly the decisive points. Ireland is the bulwark of the *English landed aristocracy.* The exploitation of that country is not only a main source of the aristocracy's material wealth; it is its greatest *moral* strength. It represents, in fact, the *domination of England over Ireland.* Ireland is therefore the great means by which the English aristocracy maintains *its domination in England* itself.

If, on the other hand, the English army and police were to withdraw from Ireland tomorrow, you would at once have an agrarian revolution there. But the overthrow of the English aristocracy in Ireland involves and has as a necessary consequence its overthrow in England. Thereby the prerequisite for the proletarian revolution in England would be fulfilled. Since the *land question* in Ireland has hitherto been the *exclusive form* of the social question, being a question of existence itself, *a matter of life and death* for the immense majority of the Irish people, and at the same time inseparably a *national* question—the destruction of the English landed aristocracy in Ireland is an infinitely easier operation than in England itself. Quite apart from the Irish being more passionate and revolutionary in character than the English.

As for the English bourgeoisie, it has in the first place a common interest with the English aristocracy in turning Ireland into mere pasture land which provides the English market with meat and wool at the cheapest possible prices. It has the same interest in reducing, by eviction and forced emigration, the Irish population to such a small number that *English capital* (leasehold capital) can function there with "security." It has the same interest in *clearing the estate of Ireland* as it had in the clearing of the agricultural districts of England and Scotland. The £6,000 to £10,000 absentee and other Irish revenues, which at present flow annually to London, must also be taken into account.

But the English bourgeoisie has even more important interests in Ireland's present-day economy. Owing to the constantly increasing concentration of farm leasing, Ireland constantly supplies its own surplus [labor] to the English labor market, and thereby forces down wages and lowers the material and moral position of the English working class.

And most important of all! Every industrial and commercial center in England now possesses a working class that is *split* into two *hostile* camps, English proletarians and Irish proletarians. The ordinary English worker hates the Irish worker as a competitor who lowers his *standard of life*. In relation to the Irish worker, he feels himself a member of the *ruling nation* and so makes himself a tool of the aristocrats and capitalists of his country *against Ireland*, thereby strengthening their domination *over himself*. He cherishes religious, social, and national prejudices against the Irish worker. His attitude toward him is much the same as that of the *poor whites* to the *niggers* in the former slave states of the United States. The Irishman *pays him back with interest in his own money*. He sees in the English worker at once the accomplice and the stupid tool of the *English domination in Ireland*.

This antagonism is artificially kept alive and intensified by the press, the pulpit, the comic papers, in short, by all the means at the disposal of the ruling classes. *This antagonism is the secret of the impotence of the English working class*, despite its organization. It is the secret by which the capitalist class maintains its power. And that class is fully aware of it.

The evil does not stop here. It continues across the ocean. The antagonism between English and Irish is the hidden basis of the conflict between the United States and England. It makes any serious and sincere cooperation between the working classes of the two countries impossible. It enables the governments of both countries, whenever they think fit, to break the edge of the social conflict by their mutual *bullying* and, *in case of need*, by war between the two countries.

England, the metropolis of capital, the power which has hitherto ruled the world market, is for the present the most important country for the workers' revolution, and moreover the *only* country in which the material conditions for this revolution have developed to a certain degree of maturity. To hasten the social revolution in England is, therefore, the most important object of the International Working Men's Association. The only means of hastening it is to make Ireland independent. Hence it is the task of the International everywhere to put the conflict between England and Ireland in the foreground, and everywhere to side openly with Ireland. It is the special task of the Central Council in London to awaken a consciousness in the English workers that *for them* the *national emancipation of Ireland* is no *question of abstract justice or humanitarian sentiment* but *the first condition for their own social emancipation.*

These are, approximately, the main points of the circular, which thereby, at the same time, gave the *raisons d'être* of the resolutions of the Central Council on the Irish amnesty. Shortly thereafter, I sent a strong anonymous article on the treatment of the Fenians by the English, etc., against Gladstone, etc., to the *Internationale*[1] (organ of our Belgian Central Committee in Brussels). In that article I at the same time accused the French republicans (the *Marseillaise* had printed some stupid stuff on Ireland, written by the miserable Talandier) of saving all their anger for the Empire out of national egoism.

This had an effect. My daughter wrote, under the name of J. Williams (in her private letter to the editors she called herself Jenny Williams), a series of articles in the *Marseillaise*,[2] publicizing, among other things, O'Donovan Rossa's letter.[3] Hence the immense noise. Gladstone, after many years of cynical refusal, finally was *thereby* forced to authorize a *Parliamentary inquiry* into the treatment of the Fenian prisoners. Jenny is now the regular correspondent on Irish affairs for the *Marseillaise*. (*This is, of course, a secret between us.*) Furious anger on the part of the English Government and press that the Irish Question is now the *ordre du jour* [order of the day] in France and that they, the *canaille*, will now be watched over and exposed by the whole Continent via Paris.

Another fly was hit with the same swatter. All this has forced the Irish leaders, press men, etc., in Dublin to enter into contact with us, something that the General Council has not succeeded in achieving until now!

In America you have a wide field in which to do this kind of work. *A coalition between the German and Irish workers* (naturally also the English and Americans, who may wish to join) is the greatest

---

1. Published February 27, 1870.
2. *La Marseillaise*, March 1, 9, 19, 21, 29; April 12, 17, 24, 1870.
3. March 9.

work you can now undertake. This must be done in the name of the International. The social significance of the Irish Question must be made clear.

Next time, some special reports on English labor conditions.
Salut et fraternité!

KARL MARX

From letter to Engels (in Manchester)
LONDON, APRIL 14, 1870

Dear Fred:

... I am enclosing two issues of a Vienna workers' paper[1] and one of *L'Égalité*, and beg you to return all three after reading them. ...

From *L'Égalité* you will see that at the Congress of the *Suisses Romands* in La Chaux-de-Fonds, it came to an open war between the Bakuninists, led by Guillaume (the animal calls itself Professor, is editor of *Progrès*, Bakunin's personal gazette at Locle), and the *Conseil Romand* (Geneva).[2] The report is very confused. On Tuesday evening [April 12] Jung submitted [to the General Council] an official report on the Geneva Council, written by the Russian Outine, who functioned as secretary of the Romansh Congress. The anti-Bakuninists, representing 2,000 men, were outflanked and therefore forced to *secessio* [secession] by the Bakuninists, representing 600 men, who, however, had assured themselves of a larger number of delegates *fas et nefas* [in a legal and illegal way], that is, through false mandates. It came to vehement explanations of Bakunin's doings, which Outine, among other things, exposed. Now the Romansh Council, supported by the decision of the last (Basel) Congress, has requested that the Central Council decide. We replied: All the facts, together with the protocols of the sessions, must be sent over. We authorized Jung to write ditto to Guillaume, so that he could submit his *plaidoyer* [pleadings] ditto.

Recently we also had to settle a quarrel in Lyon.[3] Finally, in

---

1. *Volkswille.*
2. The Congress of the Romansh Federation took place at La Chaux-de-Fonds, April 4–6, 1870.
3. A quarrel in the Lyon Section of the International between left-wing republicans and Bakuninists, led by Albert Richard. The General Council decided, on March 8, 1870, in favor of the latter as corresponding secretary of the International.

Basel one clique (under State Procurator Bruhin) complained to us about another (more proletarian). But we referred the latter case, it being entirely a local one, to J. Ph. Becker as mediator. . . .

Greetings.

Yours,

K. M.

Letter written in English to Paul and Laura Lafargue (in Paris)
LONDON, APRIL 18, 1870

Dear Paul-Laurent:[1]

I send enclosed the credentials for M. H. Verlet. Let him give to the new section he is about to establish no sectarian "name," either communistic or other. *Il faut éviter les "etiquettes" sectaires dans l'Association Internationale.* [One should avoid sectarian "labels" in the International Association.] The general aspirations and tendencies of the working class emanate from the real conditions in which it finds itself placed. They are therefore common to the whole class although the movement reflects itself in their heads in the most diversified forms, more or less fantastical, more or less adequate. Those to interpret best the hidden sense of the class struggle going on before our eyes—the communists—are the last to commit the blunder of affecting or fostering sectarianism.

Mr. Verlet would do well to put himself in communication with our friend Jules Johannard, 126 Rue d'Aboukir.

One thing which ought to be done as quickly as possible, and which might be done by Paul-Laurent, is to publish in the *Libre Pensée* a true and literal translation of the International Statutes. The French current translation, emanating from our first Paris Committee, Tolain et Co, is full of *intentional* mistakes. They suppressed everything which they did not like. If a true translation was made, it would be well to send it me *before* its publication.

In Germany people would much wonder at Verlet's appreciation of Büchner. In our country he is only considered, and justly so, as a *vulgarisateur.* You know how much I admire le "Roman de Conspiration."[2] I was, therefore, truly delighted to see it so well appreciated by Paul-Laurent.

---

1. Paul-Laurent was Paul Lafargue's literary pseudonym, made from his first name and that of his wife, Marx's daughter Laura. Marx used the pseudonym in writing to both of them.
2. The title of an article by Lafargue in *La Libre Pensée*, April 16, 1870.

I am now forced to say a few words which Paul-Laurent will a little fret at, but I cannot help doing so.

Your father wrote me a letter to Hanover which I have not yet answered, because I did not know what to say.

I feel quite sure that Paul has discarded all notion of finishing, or occupying himself with, his medical studies. When at Paris I wrote to his father in a different sense, and I was warranted in doing so by Paul's own promises. Thus I am placed in quite a false position toward M. Lafargue *aîné*. I cannot remain in that fix. I see no other prospect of getting out of it but by writing to him that I have as little influence with his beloved son as himself. If you see any other way of escape for me, any other means of clearing my position, please communicate it to me.

In my opinion, which however I neither pretend nor hope to see accepted and acted upon, Paul-Laurent *cum filio* ought to pay a visit to their parents at Bordeaux and try to coax them by the many means personal intercourse permits of.

Yours truly

From letter to Engels (in Manchester)
LONDON, APRIL 19, 1870

In all haste
Dear Fred:
I am sending you two parliamentaries on Ireland and the last issue of *L'Égalité*, ditto *La Solidarité*. From the enclosed letter by Perret,[1] ex-secretary of the Federal Committee in Geneva—which I must have back *by Friday* [April 22]—you will see how the Muscovite animal acts. He also, of course, has been forced—as did happen—to appeal to the Central Council, through his Secretary General, Robert. I am enclosing this letter too.[2] What do you think we should do with the fellow? . . .

Greetings.

Yours,
K. M.

---

1. Perret's letter to Hermann Jung, April 15, 1870, reporting on the split in the congress at La Chaux-de-Fonds.

2. Engels to Marx, April 21, 1870: "It is clear that the Alliance [Bakunin's], even if it were tolerated by the General Council, has no place in a local organization like the Romansh Swiss . . . Either the former should stay out of it, or it should give up its international character . . . If Bakunin succeeded in winning over the majority of the Romansh Swiss workers to his side, what could the General Council do? The only tenable point would then be that of absolute abstention from all politics, but even this handle is not certain."

Letter written in English to Paul and Laura Lafargue (in Paris)
LONDON, APRIL 19, 1870

Dear Paul-Laurent:

I shall have proposed [you] by Dupont on Tuesday next. Meanwhile I call your attention to the presence in your committee of Robin, Bakunin's agent who, at Geneva, did all in his power to *discredit the General Council* (he attacked it publicly in the *Égalité*) and to prepare *la dictature de Bakunin sur l'Association Internationale.* He has been expressly sent to Paris to act in the same sense.

Hence this fellow must be closely watched without becoming aware of having a surveillant at his side.

In order to *vous mettre au courant* I must give you a succinct review of Bakunin's critique.

Bakunin does not belong to the International but for about 1½ years. *C'est un nouveau venu.* At the Lausanne Congress (September 1868) of the *Ligue de la Paix et de la Liberté* (he was one of the executive committee of this international middle-class association founded in opposition to the proletarian International) he played one of the mountebank parts he delights in. He proposed a series of propositions, stupid in themselves, but affecting an air of swaggering radicalism calculated to frighten *les crétins* bourgeois. In that way, being outvoted by the majority, he made his noisy exit from the Ligue and had this great event triumphantly announced in the European press. He understands *la réclame* almost as well as Victor Hugo, *qui, comme Heine dit, n'est pas simplement égoiste, mais Hugoiste* [as Heine said, is not simply an egoist but a Hugoist].

Then he entered our Association—its Geneva *branche Romande.* His first step was a conspiracy. He founded *l'Alliance de la Démocratie Socialiste.* The program of that society was nothing else but the series of resolutions proposed by Bakunin on the Lausanne Peace Ligue Congress. The organization was that of a sect with its head center at Geneva, constituting itself as an International Association which was to have General Congresses of its own, which was to form an independent international body, and, *at the same time,* to be an integral member of our *Internationale.* In one word, our Association was by this interloping secret society by-and-by to be converted into an instrument *du Russe Bakunin.* The pretext was that this new society was founded for the special purpose "*à faire la propaganda théorique.*" Very funny indeed, considering that Bakunin and his acolytes know nothing of theory. But Bakunin's program was "*the* theory." It consisted, in fact, of three points.

1. That the first requirement of the social revolution was *the abolition of inheritance, vieillerie St-Simoniste, dont le charlatan et l'ignoramus Bakunin se faisait l'éditeur responsable.* It is evident: if you had the power to make the social revolution in one day; *par décret plébiscitaire,* you would abolish at once landed property and capital, and would therefore have no occasion at all to occupy yourselves with *le droit d'héritage.* On the other hand, if you have not the power (and it is of course foolish to suppose such a power), the proclamation of the *abolition of inheritance* would be not a serious act, but a foolish menace, rallying the whole peasantry and the whole small middle class around the reaction. Suppose f. i. that the Yankees had not had the power to abolish slavery by the sword. What an imbecility it would have been to proclaim the *abolition of inheritance in slaves!* The whole thing rests on a superannuated idealism, which considers the actual jurisprudence as the basis of our economical state, instead of seeing that our economical state is the basis and source of our jurisprudence! As to Bakunin, all he wanted was to improvise a program of his own making. *Voilà tout. C'était un programme d'occasion.*

2. "*L'égalité des différentes classes.*" To suppose on the one hand the continued existence of *classes,* and on the other hand the *égalité* of the members belonging to them, this blunder shows you at once the shameless ignorance and superficiality of that fellow who made it his "special mission" to enlighten us in "theory."

3. The working class must not occupy itself with *politics.* They must only organize themselves by trade unions. One fine day, by means of the *Internationale* they will supplant the place of all existing states. You see what a caricature he has made of my doctrines! As the transformation of the existing states into "Associations" is our last end, we must allow the governments, these great trade unions of the ruling classes, to do as they like, because to occupy ourselves with them is to acknowledge them. Why! In the same way the old socialists said: You must not occupy yourselves with the wages question, because you want to abolish wage labor, and to struggle with the capitalist about the rate of wages is to acknowledge the wages system! The ass has not even seen that every class movement, *as* a class movement, is necessarily and was always a *political* movement.

This then is the whole theoretical baggage of Mahomet-Bakunin, a Mahomet without a Koran.

His conspiracy he went secretly on with. He had some affiliates in Spain and Italy, a few dupes at Paris and Geneva. Good old Becker was foolish enough to allow himself to be put forward somewhat in a leading character by Bakunin. He regrets his blunder at present.

The General Council was only informed and called upon to sanction the statutes of the "Alliance" after Bakunin considered that concern as *fait accompli.* However he was mistaken. In an elaborated document the General Council declared the "Alliance" to be an instrument of disorganization, and rejected every connection with it. (I shall send you the document.)

A few months later, the *Comité Directeur* of the "Alliance" addressed a letter to the General Council to this effect: The great men were willing to dissolve their organization and merge it into the *Internationale,* but on the other hand, we were to declare categorically, *Oui ou Non!,* whether we sanctioned their principles! If not, there would be a public secession on their part, and we would be responsible for such a misfortune!

We answered that the General Council was not the Pope, that we allowed every section to have its own theoretical views of the real movement, always supposed that nothing directly opposite to our Statutes was put forward. We hinted in a delicate way that we considered their "theory" to be a sham. We insisted that "*l'égalité des classes*" be changed for "*l'abolition des classes,*" what they have never complied with. (You will also get this second document.) Thus the Alliance was nominally dissolved. In fact, it continued to form an *imperium in imperio.* Its branches had no connection at all with the General Council, but that of conspiring against it. It acted under Bakunin's dictatorship. He prepared everything to *frapper un grand coup au Congrès de Bâle* [bring off a great coup at the Basel Congress]. On the one side, he made the Geneva Committee propose *la question d'héritage.* We accepted the challenge. On the other side, he conspired everywhere to discredit us and to have the seat of the General Council transferred from London to Geneva. At that Congress, *ce saltimbanque figurait comme "délégué de Naples et de Lyon"* [this buffoon figured as a "delegate from Naples and Lyon"] (at that latter place, Albert Richard, otherwise a very active and well-meaning youngster, is his acolyte). Where the fellow got the money for all his secret machinations, travels, missions of agents, etc., remains to this moment a secret. Poor like a church mouse, he has never in his life earned a farthing by his own work.

At the Congress he was baffled. After the Congress he commenced to attack us publicly by his private *Moniteur, Le Progrès* (de Locle), edited by his valet James Guillaume, a Swiss schoolmaster, and by the *Égalité* (de Genève). We allowed this to go on for some time, and then sent a missive to the Federal Council of Geneva. (This document—copy of it—is in the hands of Varlin.) But before our circular arrived, the Federal Council of Geneva, never friendly to Bakunin and the Alliance, had broken loose from him. Robin et Co. were expulsed from the editorship of the *Égalité*. The Federal Council of the Swiss Romand Section made his pronunciamento against the intrigues of the Alliance and its Muscovite dictator.

Meanwhile Bakunin had left Geneva to reside at Tessin. His circumstances were changed. Herzen died suddenly. Bakunin, who had attacked him fiercely during the latter times (probably because Herzen's purse shut against him), all at once became the fiery apologist of Herzen in the French, etc., press. Why? Because Herzen (although a millionaire) received annually for his *Clôche*[1] and *"propagande Russe"* a rather large sum from the *"Panslavistes démocrates"* in Russia. Although a fierce enemy *de l'"héritage,"* Bakunin wanted to inherit Herzen's position and salary. He succeeded by his panegyrics of the dead man. He had the *Clôche*, the subvention, etc., transferred to himself. On the other hand there had grown up at Geneva a colony of Russian émigrés, enemies of Bakunin, because they knew the mere personal ambition of this very mediocre man (although an accomplished intriguer) and because they knew that in his "Russian" writings he propagates doctrines quite contrary to the principles of the *Internationale*.

The late Swiss Romand Congress at La Chaux-de-Fonds (5 April this year) was seized upon by Bakunin and his wantons to bring about an open split. The Congress was split into two Congresses, on the one hand a Congress of Bakunites proclaming abstention from all politics, representing about 600 men; on the other hand the Congress of the Federal Comité of Geneva, representing 2,000 men. Outine (*c'est un des jeunes Russes*) *dénonça publiquement les intrigues de Bakunin.* His (B.'s) men have constituted themselves as a "Federal Central Council" *pour la Suisse Romande* and have founded their own organ, *La Solidarité*, edited by Bakunin's *valet de chambre*, James Guillaume. The "principle" of that paper is "Bakunin." Both parties have appealed to the General Council. Thus this damned Muscovite has succeeded to call forth a great public scandal within our ranks, to make his personality a watchword, to infect our Working Men's Association with the poison of sectarianism, and to paralyze our action by secret intrigue.

He hopes to be strongly represented at our next Congress. To direct to himself the attention of Paris, he has opened a correspondence

---

1. *Kolokol (Clôche)*, a journal published in Geneva, first in Russian and then (1868–69) in French.

with the *Marseillaise*. But we have spoken with Flourens, who will put a stop to this.

You are now sufficiently informed to counteract Bakunin's movements within our Paris branches.

My thanks to Laurent for her letter. Another time try to find an envelope for your missives which is not easily opened. Apropos. Look whether you possess still the article of the *Queen's Messenger* on Lord Clanricarde. We want it here and can get it from nowhere else.

Yours,

OLD NICK

From letter to Engels (in Manchester)
LONDON, APRIL 28, 1870

Dear Fred:

. . . Last Tuesday [April 26] the General Council unanimously adopted my proposal (supported by Mottershead): to sever our connection with the *Bee-Hive* and to publish that resolution. Mr. Applegarth sat opposite me with a diminished head when I explained the reasons. He and Odger are on the editorial committee of the *Bee-Hive*. I denounced the paper as having been sold out to the bourgeoisie (S. Morley, etc.), also mentioned especially its behavior in connection with our resolutions and debates, etc.[1] Pursuant to the decision of the Council, I am to bring in the *formulated* decision next Tuesday.

Greetings.   *Yours,*

MOHR

From letter to Engels (in Manchester)
LONDON, MAY 7, 1870

Dear Fred:

All kinds of interesting things have happened this week. But at the moment the English post is too inquisitive, and I do not feel called upon to supply it with news indirectly. Hence orally later.

The *Marseillaise* did not arrive today. Possibly it has been con-

---

1. See "The *Bee-Hive*," April 26, 1870, page 177.

fiscated. Last Wednesday [May 4] we informed it telegraphically that it would receive the decision of the General Council next Thursday in the original French and that it should not translate it from the English. This telegram, of course, came immediately to the attention of the Paris police, and Pietri probably did not want our announcement the day before the plebiscite.

The insipid Reuter-Havass telegrams have at last given us the long-hoped-for opportunity to declare to the Paris journals that the so-called London French Branch does *not* belong to the International.

Yesterday and the day before, the *Standard* published two swinish articles against the International, dictated directly from the French Embassy, as was also the article in the London French paper, *L'International.*

All London papers have received instructions from Bruce—and of course they obey them like born dogs—not to mention a word in their columns about the steps the English police quietly took last week in regard to Flourens and the International General Council (they make a hodgepodge of both).

Ten thousand copies of the above-mentioned issues of the *Standard* have been sent to France. This is also a way of payment, or did the Society of December 10[1] suddenly learn English?

Last Tuesday [May 3] the rumor suddenly spread in London that we would be arrested in our meeting hall. Hence news-hungry press reporters showed up, for a change.

In England, in a moment of panic the fellows immediately forgot their own laws and let themselves be carried away—in part by the press, which lies partly out of ignorance and partly deliberately.

Even granting the police that everything Grandperret, Reuter, and the *Journal Officiel* report is gospel truth, the English Government could do *nothing*, except at most to make itself ridiculous.

D'abord, there can be no question of trying to extradite Flourens—which, according to *Gaulois*, has been requested. There exists only one extradition treaty between France and the United Kingdom, that of 1843. In 1865 the French Government declared it would give notice of withdrawal after six months, because in practice it was not enforcible under English laws of evidence. Hence a few formalities connected with evidence were changed in 1866, without in any way altering the content of the treaty. In that treaty the crimes calling for extradition are clearly specified—among others, murder (parricide, infanticide, and poisoning) and attempted murder, *notabene*, would-be murder in the sense *qu'il y avait un commencement d'exécu-*

---

1. Marx discussed the Society of December 10, an organization that backed Louis Bonaparte, in *The Eighteenth Brumaire of Louis Bonaparte* (1852).

tion [that there was a beginning of carrying it out], "the direct consequence of which would probably be the death of the individual whose life was attacked."

According to *that* treaty, therefore, Beaury, for example, if he took refuge in England, could *not* be extradited, and even less so Flourens.

The only question is whether a foreigner *here* could be condemned by an English tribunal for *complicity in a conspiracy to commit the crime of murder abroad.*

Up to 1828, nobody—neither Englishman nor foreigner—could be prosecuted here for a murder committed outside the United Kingdom. English duelists took advantage of this. According to Sec. 7 of 9 George IV, it is provided "that if any of H. M.'s Subjects should be charged with murder or with any accessory to murder committed on land out of the United Kingdom he should be *triable* for such offenses in the United Kingdom."

This law was in fact passed for English duelists and therefore applies only to "Her Majesty's Subjects."

In 1858, at the trial of Dr. Bernard, he therefore pleaded "that the Court had no jurisdiction." The servile court reserved this point, without making a decision about it, and then ordered that a plea of not guilty should be recorded. His acquittal prevented any further decision on this legal point.

Soon after the Orsini plot in 1858, Palmerston brought in a *conspiracy bill* in the House of Commons, "with the object of making conspiracy to commit murder either within the United Kingdom or within the territory of any Foreign State a *felony*." This bill was justified on the ground that:

1. "Conspiracy was only a *misdemeanor* and that according to English law, a conspiracy to murder was no less and no more than a conspiracy to blacken a man's character."

2. And it was very thoroughly demonstrated by the Attorney General—Sir R. Bethell—"that the 9 George IV Sec. 7 applied only to *natural-born British subjects*, and that *foreigners resident in this United Kingdom could conspire to commit murder abroad with impunity*."

The conspiracy bill, as is known, fell through, and with it fell Lord Palmerston for the time being.

The whole uproar of the English and French press is therefore pure imbecility. At worst, Flourens could be prosecuted for misdemeanor, to finally get a definitive judicial decision on 9 George IV Sec. 7, sure to be negative, and then the government would be forced to submit a conspiracy bill. Gladstone will try like the devil to succeed where Palmerston failed.

If this plot for the assassination of Badinguet[2] is not a mere police invention, then it is the biggest absurdity humanly possible. Fortunately, the Empire itself can no longer be saved by the stupidity of its enemies.

Bakunin's agent Robin, now in Paris and a member of the Paris Federation (of the International), immediately proposed in the latter that the new *Conseil Romand* be recognized as the legitimate one, and that it be announced in the *Marseillaise* that only the followers of the latter were the real members of the International. But we had forewarned our people in Paris. Robin was therefore splendidly defeated with his proposal. It was decided that the *Fédération Parisienne* had no authority whatever for interference, that the matter belongs to the General Council in London. The thing, however, is characteristic of the *modus operandi* of Gospodin Bakunin.

The Paris plot puts a fearsome end to the already well-developed plan to hold the Congress in Paris and to take that opportunity to move the General Council there. . . .

EL MORO
(The beard becomes whiter every day)

From letter to Engels (in Manchester)
LONDON, MAY 18, 1870

Dear Fred:
. . . Our French members are demonstrating *ad oculos* [before the eyes] of the French Government the difference between secret political organizations and genuine workers' unions. Hardly had it imprisoned the members of the Paris, Lyon, Rouen, Marseilles, etc., committees[1] (some of them fled to Switzerland and Belgium) when *double that many* committees announced themselves in the newspapers with the most audacious and the most defiant declarations of being their successors (supplying, in addition, their *private addresses*). The French Government finally did what we had so long hoped for—transformed the political question: Empire or Republic, into a question *de vie ou de mort* [of life or death] for the working class.

---

2. One of Marx's nicknames for Napoleon III.

1. At the end of April, 1870, while Napoleon III's government prepared for a May 8 plebiscite asking for approval of its policies, hundreds of socialists were arrested throughout France; they were accused of being members of the International, as well as of conspiring against the Emperor.

Altogether, the plebiscite gives the Empire its final blow! Because so many yeas were cast for the Empire, *avec la phrase constitutionelle* [with the constitutional phrase],[2] Boustrapa[3] now believed that he could restore the Empire *sans phrase, c'est à dire le régime du Décembre* [without a slogan, that is to say, the December regime]. In Paris—according to all private information—the *Société du 10 Décembre* has been fully restored and is in renewed action.

Greetings.

Yours,

K. M.

The removal of the Congress to Mainz—voted on unanimously yesterday[4]—will make Bakunin dance!

From letter to Engels (in Manchester)
LONDON, JULY 28, 1870

Dear Fred:

. . . The *Times* had given us every expectation, via Eccarius, that it would print our (the International's) Address.[1] It did not do so, probably because of a blow at Russia. Therefore (Monday last [July 25]) I immediately sent it to *Pall Mall* and also wrote the editor, following a conversation with its war correspondent (Thieblin, now in Luxembourg) about military correspondence, asking for a reply. No reply. Nor was the Address printed. Today, when I sent your article to the editor of *Pall Mall*, I wrote him a brief letter, *speaking only of the military correspondence*, asking him simply whether it is yes or no.

Last Tuesday the General Council voted to print 1,000 copies of the Address. I expect the proof sheets today.

The singing of the *"Marseillaise"* in France is a parody, like the whole Second Empire. But at least the dog [Napoleon III] feels that *"Partant pour la Syrie"*[2] would not do. In Prussia, on the other hand, such humor is not necessary. "Jesus Is My Shepherd," sung by

---

2. The plebiscite resulted in 7,358,000 yeas, 1,571,000 nays, and about 1,900,000 abstentions.
3. Napoleon III.
4. The Mainz Congress did not take place; see Marx's letter to Johann Philipp Becker, August 2, 1870.

---

1. See "First Address . . . on the Franco-Prussian War," page 49.
2. "On to Syria," an early-nineteenth-century French song, sung on official occasions during Napoleon III's Second Empire.

William I, with Bismarck on his right and Stieber on his left, is the German *"Marseillaise"*! As in 1812. The German philistine seems to be downright enchanted that he can now give his inborn servility free vent. Who would have considered it possible that twenty-two years after 1848 a national war would have *such* a theoretical expression in Germany!

Fortunately, the whole demonstration emanates from the middle class. The working class, with the exception of Schweitzer's direct followers, takes no part in it. Fortunately, the war of classes in both countries, France and Germany, is so far developed that no war abroad can seriously turn back the wheel of history. . . .

Greetings.

Yours,

K. M.

From letter to Johann Philipp Becker (in Geneva)
LONDON, AUGUST 2, 1870

Dear Becker:

My long silence is due entirely to lack of time. I hope we know each other sufficiently to be convinced that our mutual friendship is unbreakable.

I sent the manifesto of the General Council on the war[1] first of all to *L'Égalité*, because I knew that it was too late for publication in *Der Vorbote*. Today I expect proofs, so I can send them to you. . . .

In regard to the Congress, under present circumstances it obviously cannot take place in Mainz. The Belgians have proposed Amsterdam. We are convinced that the Congress must be postponed until conditions are more favorable.

First, we stand on quite weak ground in Amsterdam, and it is important to hold the Congress in countries where the International has already struck strong roots.

Second, the Germans cannot send anybody—or at most only *one* person—because of the lack of money caused by the present war. The French cannot leave their country without passes, that is, permission of the authorities. Our French sections have been exploded, the most experienced members being in flight or captured. *Under these circumstances* there could easily be a repetition of the farce that was played in

---

1. See "First Address . . . on the Franco-Prussian War," page 49.

Switzerland.[2] Certain intrigants could put together a *majorité factice* [artificial majority] in Amsterdam. For such maneuvers they always find the necessary money. Where? *C'est leur secret* [It's their secret].

On the other hand, under Par. 3, the General Council cannot postpone the date of the Congress. Nevertheless, under the present *extraordinary* circumstances, it would take upon itself the responsibility for such a step if it got the necessary support from the various sections. Hence we would appreciate receiving an *official* proposal of this nature from the German Swiss group and from the Geneva Romansh group.

Bakunin has, as you know, a fanatical instrument in the Belgian Council, Hins, the scatterbrain. To the circular letter which the General Council sent to *L'Égalité* early in January[3]—since the Belgian secretariat was finished—I added a denunciation and characterization of Bakunin under my own name. Thereupon Hins wrote the General Council an extremely rude letter against me personally (he spoke of my *"manière indigne d'attaquer Bakunin"* ["infamous manner of attacking Bakunin"]). It is to his influence that one may well ascribe the fact that yesterday we received from the Belgian General Council an official letter full of complaints, stating, among other things: "The Belgian General Council has resolved to instruct its delegates to the next Congress to demand an accounting from you about your resolution regarding the Romansh Federal Council." It said that we had no right at all to meddle in this local Swiss affair! Strangely enough, the Brussels men themselves, as well as the Paris *Fédération*, had *directly* asked us to intervene! Short memory!

In any case, we shall have to explain our decision at greater length in another circular letter. We would therefore be much obliged to you if you would send us details about the intrigues of the Alliance, the congress of La Chaux-de-Fonds, and the Swiss brawl in general.

I received the letter from the Russian friends in Geneva. Convey my thanks to them.

It would in fact be best if you wrote a brochure on Bakunin, but it has to be done *soon*. In this case, you do not have to send me any further documents on Bakunin's machinations.

You ask me what Bakunin did in 1848. During his stay in Paris in 1843–48 he played the resolute socialist. After the Revolution he went to Breslau, where he joined the bourgeois democrats and worked among them for the election of Arnold Ruge (to the Frankfurt parlia-

2. The Congress of the International's Romansh Federation, which met in La Chaux-de-Fonds, April 4–6, 1870, where a split occurred between the Bakuninists and the followers of the General Council over the question of political action.

3. See "Confidential Communication," page 166.

ment), who was then a firm enemy of socialists and communists. Later —in 1848—he organized the Pan-Slavic congress in Prague.[4] Pan-Slavists themselves reproached him for having played a perfidious role there. But I do not believe that. If (from the point of view of his Pan-Slavic friends) he made mistakes there, they were, in my opinion, "involuntary." In the beginning of 1849 Bakunin made public his Address (pamphlet)[5]—sentimental Pan-Slavism! The only laudable thing that can be reported about his activities during the Revolution is his participation in the Dresden insurrection of 1849.[6]

Of importance for an understanding of his character is the role he played immediately upon his return from Siberia. On that there is sufficient material in *Kolokol,* and also Borkheim's "Russian Letters" in *Die Zukunft,*[7] which you must certainly have. . . .

Yours,

KARL MARX

From letter to Engels (in Manchester)
LONDON, AUGUST 3, 1870

Dear Fred:

. . . The Belgian members have proposed that the Congress be held in Amsterdam on September 5. This is the plan of Herr Bakunin. The Congress would consist *mainly of his tools.* Against this, I proposed: Appeal to all the sections whether they did not think that, under present circumstances, where the French and German delegates would be excluded from the Congress, power should be given to the General Council:

1. To postpone the Congress;

2. To enable the Council to convoke Congress at the moment it shall consider opportune.[1] This happened.

The matter is the more urgent, since, from the open attack on us in the last issue of *Solidarité*[2] (on the pretext of our decision in the

---

4. June 2, 1848.

5. Bakunin, *Appeal to the Slavs. From a Russian Patriot* (Koethen, 1848).

6. The Dresden insurrection took place May 3–8, 1849.

7. Sigismund Borkheim, "Russian Letters. VIII–X. Mikhail Bakunin," a series which appeared in the Berlin paper *Die Zukunft* July–November, 1869.

---

1. The whole sentence beginning with "Appeal" was written in English.

2. *La Solidarité,* July 23, 1870, challenged the General Council's right to make decisions in matters regarding the Swiss Romansh Committee.

Swiss affair), we can see that Bakunin has already carefully prepared his measures for the Amsterdam Congress. Without the German element in Switzerland, he would have defeated us in the Basel Congress. . . .

Greetings.

Yours,

K. M.

Letter to Friedrich Adolph Sorge (in Hoboken)
LONDON, SEPTEMBER 1, 1870

Dear Mr. Sorge:

My continued silence in regard to your various letters was due to two circumstances; at first "overwork," later very serious illness. At the beginning of August the doctors sent me to the seashore.[1] There, however, a violent sciatica bent me double for weeks. I have been back in London only since yesterday, in no way fully recovered yet.

First of all, my best thanks for what you have sent me, especially the Labor Statistics,[2] which are very valuable to me.

Now I will answer briefly the questions in your various letters.

Hume was authorized to carry on propaganda among the Yankees, but has exceeded his authority. I will submit the matter to the General Council next Tuesday, with an exhibition of his "cards."

In regard to the "secretaryship" for the United States, the matter stands thus: I am secretary for the German branches there, Dupont for the French, and lastly Eccarius for the Yankees and the English-speaking section. In our public declarations, therefore, Eccarius figures as "Secretary for the United States." Otherwise we should have to employ useless prolixity. For example, I would have to sign as "Secretary of the Russian Branch" in Geneva, etc. Moreover, Eccarius himself has plainly explained the state of affairs in a New York paper—in connection with Cluseret.

Next week I shall send you a new pack of membership cards.

The miserable behavior of Paris during the war—its appalling defeats which still allow it to be ruled by the mamelukes of Louis Bonaparte and the Spanish adventuress Eugénie—shows how much the French need a tragic lesson in order to regain their manhood.

---

1. From August 9 to 31, 1870, Marx and his family stayed at Ramsgate.
2. "Report of the Bureau of Statistics of Labor . . . from August 2 to March 1, 1870" (Boston, 1870).

What the Prussian jackasses do not see is that the present war is leading just as inevitably to a war between Germany and Russia as the war of 1866 led to a war between Prussia and France. This is the *best result* that I expect from it for Germany. "Prussianism" as such has never existed, and can never exist, except in alliance with and subjection to Russia. And such a war No. 2 will act as the midwife of the inevitable social revolution in Russia.

I regret that some incomprehensible misunderstanding on the part of my friend Vogt has led to a wrong opinion about Schily. Schily is not only one of my oldest and most intimate personal friends; he is one of the ablest, most courageous, and most reliable members of the party.

I am very glad that Meyer is going to Cincinnati as delegate.[3]

Your most devoted

KARL MARX

I should like to have a look at the Kellogg money nonsense[4] (a mere variation of Bray, Gray, Bronterre O'Brien, etc., in England, and of Proudhon in France) in the original. The thing cannot be obtained here.

Letter written in English to Edward Spencer Beesly (in London)
LONDON, SEPTEMBER 12, 1870

My Dear Sir:

Last Wednesday A. Serraillier, a member of the General Council of the International Working Men's Association, went to Paris as the plenipotentiary of the Council. He thought it his duty to remain there, not only for taking part in the defense, but to bring his influence to bear upon our Paris Federal Council, and he is, in point of fact, a man of superior intellectual quality. His wife was today informed of his resolution. Unfortunately, she is not only *sans sou* [penniless], she and her child, but the creditors of Serraillier having claims to the amount of about £12, threaten to sell her furniture and throw her on the street. Under these circumstances I and my friends have resolved to come to the rescue, and it is for this that I take the liberty to call, by this letter, also on you and your friends.

---

3. The Congress of the American National Labor Union took place in Cincinnati from August 7 to 10, 1870.

4. Marx read and annotated Edward Kellogg's *A New Monetary System* after receiving a copy from Sorge in February, 1871.

You will find that the Address I laid before the General Council Friday last, and which is in course of printing, coincides on many points almost literally with your pamphlet.[1]

My opinion is that Paris will be forced to capitulate, and from the private letters I receive from Paris it appears that some influential members of the Provisional Government are prepared for such a turn of events.

Serraillier writes me today that the haste with which the Prussians march upon Paris is the only thing in the world able to prevent a new Insurrection of June! Paris fallen, France will be far from lost if the provinces do their duty.

The Federal Council of Paris bombards me with telegrams, all to this effect: *Recognition of the French Republic by England.* In point of fact, it is *most important* for France. It is the only thing you can at present do for her. The King of Prussia treats officially Bonaparte as the ruling Sovereign of France. He wants to restore him. The French Republic will not exist officially before its recognition by the British Government. But no time is to be lost. Will you allow your Queen and your oligarchs, under the dictation of Bismarck, to abuse the immense influence of England?

Yours faithfully,

KARL MARX

Letter to Ludwig Kugelmann (in Hanover)
SEPTEMBER 14, 1870

Dear Wenzel:[1]

Enclosed the Address.[2]

My time is so wholly taken up with "International works"[3] that I never go to bed before three in the morning. Therefore my obstinate silence is to be excused.

Best regards for Madame la Comtesse and Fränzchen.[4]

Yours,

K. M.

---

1. E. S. Beesly, *A Word for France: Addressed to the Workmen of London* (1870).

---

1. Wenzel, or Wenceslaus, was Marx's nickname for Kugelmann.
2. See "The Second Address . . . on the Franco-Prussian War," page 54.
3. The two words in quotation marks were written in English.
4. Kugelmann's wife and daughter.

From letter written in English to Edward Spencer Beesley (in London)
LONDON, SEPTEMBER 16, 1870

My Dear Sir:
    . . . From the Continent, where people were and are used, even at Moscow and St. Petersburg, even in the French papers under the Bonapartist rule, even now at Berlin, to see the manifestoes of the International treated seriously and reproduced in full by some journal or other, we have been once and again taunted for our negligence in not using the "free" London press. They have, of course, no idea whatsoever, and will not believe in the utter corruption of that vile concern, long since branded by William Cobbett as "mercenary, infamous, and illiterate."
    Now I believe you would do the greatest possible service to the International, and I should take good care to have your article reproduced in *our* journals in Spain, Italy, Switzerland, Belgium, Holland, Denmark, Hungary, Germany, France, and the United States—if you in the *Fortnightly Review* would publish something on the International, the manifestoes of the General Council on the war and the treatment we have to undergo at the hands of that paragon press, that "free" English press! Those fellows are in fact more enslaved to the Prussian police than the Berlin papers. . . .

Your devoted
KARL MARX

Letter to Frau Wilhelm (Natalie) Liebknecht (in Leipzig)
LONDON, JANUARY 13, 1871

My Dear Frau Liebknecht:
    The General Council of the International has begun a collection for the families of German patriots persecuted by the Prussian Government[1]—patriots in the true sense of the word. The first £5 which I am sending you is for you yourself and Frau Bebel.
    The London liar-correspondent of the professorial Biedermann indisputably belongs to the police personnel of the local Prussian

---

1. On December 17, 1870, Wilhelm Liebknecht, August Bebel, and Adolf Hepner were arrested for their, and the Social-Democratic party's, opposition to the Franco-Prussian War; they were released on March 28, 1871.

Embassy, which was active in much the same way during the Communist trial in Cologne in 1852. We will investigate the subject in order to expose the game of this clique in the local press and thereby also throw light on this most recent phase of the Christian-Prussian-Germanic morality.

In the issue of the *Volksstaat* which arrived today I find a notice showing that Mr. Nechayev is once again being taken with ill-deserved seriousness. Everything this Nechayev had published in the European press about his deeds and sufferings in Russia was *shameless lies*. I have the proof in hand. One should never, therefore, mention the name of this individual.

My wife and daughters send you, your children, and Liebknecht their most cordial regards.

With best wishes for the New Year.

Faithfully yours,

KARL MARX

From letter to Sigfrid Meyer (in New York)
LONDON, JANUARY 21, 1871

Dear Meyer:
The establishment of the so-called Central Committee in New York was by no means to my taste. I delayed its recognition by the General Council as long as possible, but was disarmed as soon as it appeared from a letter of Mr. Charnier's that our French secretary, Dupont—a very excellent fellow, but too impetuous and often led to false steps by his urge for action—was the initiator of this matter. *Alors, il n'y avait plus rien à faire.* [Well, there was nothing more to do.] He received a reprimand from the General Council, *mais le jeu était fait* [but the play had been made]! Engels (who now lives here in London) and I remind you and Vogt that according to our Statutes the General Council can veto only where there are open violations of the Statutes and principles of the International, but that for the rest, it is our invariable policy to accept the sections and leave them to govern themselves. The only exception, owing to the exceptional circumstances at the time of the Empire, was France. Our friends must therefore act according to circumstances. We here in London work together with the English, a portion of whom are in no way appealing to us and who, we know very well, only want to exploit the International as a milch cow for their petty personal ambitions. Nevertheless, we make *bonne mine à mauvais jeu* [the best of a bad bargain].

If we were to withdraw indignantly from these people, we would only give them power, which our presence now paralyzes. And you must do the same. . . .

Yours,

Karl Marx

Letter to Friedrich Adolph Sorge (in Hoboken)
LONDON, JANUARY 21, 1871

Dear Mr. Sorge:

All the reports of the American German sections are to be sent to me. Eccarius is correspondent only for the Yankees. As secretary of the General Council, he has nothing to do with foreign correspondence.

I had completely forgotten the history of the "contribution" of the German section. Hence upon receiving your letter[1] I immediately wrote Eccarius, whose enclosed reply may also serve as the receipt.

Regarding the formation of the Central Council (we would have preferred to call it it Central Committee, in order to avoid confusions), I have already written about it.

I have not yet received Kellogg. It was probably in the yellow envelope which I received at the post office. It was opened and stamped: "No contents." The envelope was probably not strong enough.

Several weeks ago I sent you a *large packet* containing General Council publications of various dates, but have not yet received an acknowledgment. The things belonged to me personally, because the General Council's stock (like that of most of its publications) is quite exhausted.

From letter to Frau Wilhelm (Natalie) Liebknecht (in Leipzig)
LONDON, MARCH 2, 1871

My Dear Frau Liebknecht:

The alas too meager contribution which I sent you for the families of those in prison did not come at all from the General Council of the

---

1. On December 29, 1870, Sorge wrote Marx that the German section had not received a receipt for its contribution.

International, which really has no funds for such purposes. The General Council was chosen by the contributors simply as "guarantor." For the rest, no receipt is necessary. . . .

Amicably yours,

K. M.

Letter written in English and French to Paul Lafargue (in Bordeaux)
LONDON, MARCH 23, 1871

General Council of the International
Working Men's Association
256 High Holborn, London, W.C.
London, 23 March, 1871

Dear Paul,

I enclose Serraillier's declaration in the *Courrier de l'Europe*, 18 March, 1871 (this French paper is published at London), in regard to the impudent mystification of the *Paris-Journal* of March 14, of which you are probably aware.

The following is published in the *Times* of 22 March, 1871, under the title "The International Association:" "M. Karl Marx asks us to contradict the statement contained in a letter published by us on the sixteenth of March, from our Paris correspondent, that 'Karl Marx has written a letter to one of his principal *affiliés* in Paris, stating that he is not satisfied with the attitudes which the members of that society have taken up in that city, that they violate the Statutes of the Association in dabbling in politics, that they disorganize labor instead of organizing it, etc.' M. Karl Marx says this statement has evidently been taken from the *Paris-Journal* of the fourteenth of March, where also the publication in full of the pretended letter is promised, and that the *Paris-Journal* of the nineteenth of March contains a letter dated London, February 18, 1871, purporting to be signed by him, *which letter M. Marx declares is from beginning to end an impudent forgery."* I come now to the second trick of that dirty Parisian reactionary press. When we were informed of the pretended exclusion of the German "Internationals" by the *Paris* "Internationals" we wrote to the "*frères et amis*" at Paris, who replied that this story was nothing but an invention of the Paris press scum. Meanwhile, the false news spread like wildfire through the London press, which indulged in long leaders upon that pleasant event proving at the same time the decomposition of the International and the incorrigible perversion of the Paris workmen.

In today's *Times* (23 March, 1871) the following declaration of the General Council is published:

"The Anti-German League of Paris"

To the Editor of the *Times*
Sir,

A statement has gone the round of the English press that the Paris members of the International Working Men's Association had insofar joined the so-called Anti-German League as to declare all Germans to be henceforth excluded from our association.

This statement is the very reverse of fact. Neither the Federal Council of our Association in Paris, nor any of the Paris sections represented by that council, have ever passed any such resolution. The so-called Anti-German League, as far as it exists at all, is the exclusive work of the upper and middle classes; it was started by the Jockey Club, and kept up by the adhesions of the Academy, of the Stock Exchange, of some bankers and manufacturers etc. The working classes have nothing whatever to do with it.

The object of these calumnies is evident. A short time before the outbreak of the late war the International was made the general scapegoat for all untoward events. This is now repeated over again. While the Swiss and Prussian press accuse it of having created the late outrage upon Germans in Zurich, French papers, such as the *Courrier de Lyon, le Courrier de la Gironde, la Liberté,* etc., tell of certain secret meetings of Internationals having been held at Geneva and Bern, the Prussian Ambassador in the chair, in which meetings a plan was concocted to hand over Lyon to the united Prussians and Internationals for the sake of common plunder.

By order of the General Council
of the International Working Men's Association
Lond. March 22. J. G. Eccarius, General Secretary

I have today still so many letters to write that I must shut up. Tell Laura that I was greatly delighted with her.

Yours,

K. MARX

Your letter to Jenny has just arrived. It is not my juvenile ardor, as you believe. These are *manifestoes,* published by the Federal Council of Paris during the war and communicated to us *officially,* leading the General Council to believe in a stupidity such as the exclusion of the German Internationals by the Paris International. Today I sent to the *Volksstaat* in Leipzig (Liebknecht's journal) and to the *Zukunft* in Berlin (fruit of Dr. Jacoby) a declaration on the fantasies of the *Paris-Journal* and the so-called exclusion of the German Internationals by the Parisians, which has caused such a stir in the "good press" of Germany. I ended that declaration with these words: "It is in the nature of things that the big dignitaries and the dominant classes of the old society, who would not know how to perpetuate their power and exploit the productive masses except by antagonisms and *national* wars, should treat the International Working Men's Association as the common enemy."

Serraillier's Note, in French, in the *Courrier de l'Europe:*[1]

Monsieur: Under this title (The Main Chief of the International), *Paris-Journal* does not hesitate to affirm that "I have just received a letter from Citizen Karl Marx, in which he insinuates that he '*lives in Berlin.*'" According to this journal, Citizen Karl Marx, who is "the main chief of the International," shares with Blanqui, Flourens, and Company the honor of having been condemned to death at least once. Let us add, furthermore, that the Citizen includes in his life the honor of having been expelled successively from Prussia in 1843, from France in 1844, and from Belgium in 1848, at the demand of the Prussian Government. Returned to Prussia at the outbreak of events, he was again expelled, in May, 1849, and after having sought refuge in France he was expelled a second time, in September, 1849, at the demand of the same Prussian Government in the fine old days of the [French] presidency.

It would be strange to see Citizen Karl Marx, who has lived in London ever since that period, addressing from Berlin a letter to the "big Parisian priest" Serraillier in Paris, while the latter, who has lived in London ever since his return there on February 22, was in contact there with his "friend and German—worse than German, Prussian!—brother," on whom the General Council has not yet bestowed the all-powerful title of "Main Chief," which would at least have avoided his having to beg "the Parisian members not to lose sight of the unique objective of their society by indulging in too much politics." This journal's origin and its campaign during the siege of Paris sufficiently indicate the source of these maneuvers which properly crown the "predated" articles, written in the coziness of his own hearth and signed "a *franc-tireur,*" but who was nobody other than a messenger of the Seventh Light Infantry, occasionally invited to the table of General Schmitz, before *Siècle* informed the public that the resolutions of the Council of War for National Defense were known to the Prussians as soon as they were taken by the Bonapartist General Staff.

Chase away this Bismarck, and he returns at a gallop.

Accept, M. l'Éditeur, the thanks of one of the big Parisian priests of the International.

A. SERRAILLIER

---

1. Dated March 16, published March 18, 1871.

Letter to Wilhelm Liebknecht (in Leipzig)
LONDON, *ca.* APRIL 10, 1871

Dear Wilhelm:

In all haste, two notes which you can arrange for use in the *Volksstaat*.

1. In the now officially published *Papiers et Correspondance de la Famille Impériale*, under the letter "V" (the money recipients are listed alphabetically)—*verbo tenus* [literally]: "*Vogt, il lui est remis en août, 1859, 40,000 frs.*"

2. While the Bismarck Government makes any correspondence with me (*vide* the Brunswick trial and the earlier Communist trial in Cologne) more or less a criminal offense, in Germany it tries to put me (and through me, the International in Paris, which is the *purpose* of the whole maneuver) under suspicion of being an agent of Herr Bismarck. This is done through the organs of the old-Bonapartist police, which is still—and particularly so under the Thiers regime—tied in an international bond to the Stieber police.

So I was compelled to deny diverse lies in the *Paris-Journal*, in the *Gaulois*, in the *Times*, etc., because this idiocy was reported to the English papers by telegram. The most recent lie was spread by the *Soir* (the journal of About, the well-known Plon-Plonist[1]), recently suppressed by the Commune, and from there to all the French reactionary provincial papers. Thus, for example, I received from Laura (by the way, Lafargue is at this moment the delegate from Bordeaux in Paris) the following excerpt from the journal *La Provence* (yesterday I received the same excerpt from a Belgian parsons' paper):

"Paris, April 2. A revelation arriving from Germany has caused a great sensation here. It is now authentically substantiated that Karl Marx, one of the most influential chiefs of the International, was *private secretary to Count Bismarck* in the year 1857 and has never ceased to remain in contact with his former *patron*."

That Stieber is really becoming "frightful."

Greetings.

Yours,

K. M.

---

1. Plon-Plon was one of Marx's nicknames for Napoleon III.

Letter to Friedrich Adolph Sorge (in Hoboken)
LONDON, *ca.* APRIL 20, 1871

Dear Mr. Sorge:
My best thanks for Kellogg,[1] which this time did arrive, and ditto for the other consignments.

In the future, the Committee[2] will receive its answers more expeditiously, but in the last few weeks the European continental business, together with the local agitation among the English,[3] has absorbed much time, the more so as the non-English secretaries are in Paris.

Faithfully yours,
K. M.

Draft in French of letter to Leo Frankel (in Paris)
LONDON, *ca.* APRIL 26, 1871

Dear Citizen:
The General Council has instructed me to reject sharply, in its name, the base calumnies that Citizen F. Pyat has spread about Serraillier. The vileness of the man is fed by a single source: *his hatred of the International*. Through the *so-called* French Section in Paris, which was expelled by the General Council and into which police spies, Imperial guards, and scoundrels had crept, Pyat had tried to pose before the world as the secret leader of our Association, to which he did not belong at all, and to make us responsible for his grotesque manifestations in London and his compromising indiscretions in Paris, for which Citizen Tridon gave him his proper comeuppance during his stay in Brussels.[1] Hence the General Council found itself obliged to publicly disavow this cheap intrigant. Thus his rage against Dupont and Serraillier. When Serraillier threatened to sue the miserable handyman Pyat in the so-called French Section

1. See Marx's letter to Sorge, January 21, 1871.
2. The Central Committee of the International in New York City.
3. Workers' meetings in London, Manchester, and other cities were organized by the General Council in defense of the Paris Commune.

1. On July 19, 1868, Edmé-Marie-Gustave Tridon published a letter in the Brussels *Cigale* attacking Félix Pyat.

and hale him before an English court in order to stop the calumnies that Pyat is now repeating in Paris, the former were disavowed by the *French Section itself*, and Pyat was branded as a slanderer. Since Serraillier's political life offered no chances for calumnies, they went after his private life. If Pyat's private life had been as pure as Serraillier's, he would not have found it necessary to ignore certain bloody aspersions against him here in London.

The General Council will soon make public an Address on the Commune.[2] The publication of this manifesto has been delayed, in the daily expectation of precise information from the Paris Section. In vain! Not a word! The Council could no longer delay, as the English workers awaited its explanation with growing anxiety.

Nevertheless, they did not lose time. Through correspondence with various secretaries in the continental sections and in the United States, workers everywhere received explanations of the true character of this exalted revolution in Paris.

We received the letter from the Citizen.[3] He has been in contact in my house with the person you know who was sent to me. Paris is wrong not to have sent the necessary particulars for facilitating the operations. You must now have 3-percent bonds that are freely quoted and can be traded daily on the Exchange. The Citizen will give you all other necessary explanations. He can be entrusted with securities, which are entirely safe with him.

Letter to Ludwig Kugelmann (in Hanover)
LONDON, JUNE 18, 1871

Dear Kugelmann:

You must excuse my silence; even now I have time only for a few lines.

You know that throughout the whole period of the recent Paris Revolution I was constantly denounced by the Versailles papers (Stieber collaborating) and, by repercussion, in the local journals as the *"grand chef de l'Internationale."*

Now about the Address,[1] which you should have received by now. It makes a devilish noise, and I have the honor of being at this

2. *The Civil War in France*, which Marx wrote in April and May, 1871.
3. Probably N. Eilau.

1. *The Civil War in France.*

moment the best calumniated and most menaced man in London. That really does one good after a tedious twenty-year idyll in the swamp. The government paper—the *Observer*—threatens me with court action. *Qu'ils osent! Je me moque de ces canailles-là!* [Let them dare! I scoff at that riffraff!] I am enclosing a clipping from the *Eastern Post*, which contains our answer to Jules Favre's Circular.[2] Our reply appeared originally in the *Times* of June 13. That honorable sheet received a heavy reprimand from Mr. Bob Lowe (Chancellor of the Exchequer and member of the Supervision Committee of the *Times*) for this indiscretion.

My best thanks for Reuter[3] and my best compliments to Madame la Comtesse *et ma chère* Fränzchen.

Yours,
K. M.

Letter to Ludwig Kugelmann (in Hanover)
LONDON, JULY 27, 1871

Dear Kugelmann:

Be so good as to send the enclosed note to Liebknecht immediately.

I find your silence highly surprising. I cannot assume that the various printed matter I sent you did not reach you.

On the other hand, it would be very silly if you—following the ancient eye for an eye, tooth for a tooth—wanted to chastise me this way for not writing. Consider, *mon cher*, that in recent months if the day had forty-eight hours, I still would not get through my daily work.

The work for the International is immense, added to which London is overrun with refugees we have to care for. In addition, I am overrun with other people. Newspaper fellows and other types, wanting to see the "monster" with their own eyes.

Hitherto it was believed that the Christian myth-building under the Roman Empire was possible only because printing was not yet invented. On the contrary. The daily press and the *Telegraph*, which

2. Favre, the French Foreign Minister, sent a circular letter to French diplomats abroad urging that European governments take common steps against the International. On June 12 Marx and Engels wrote a reply in the name of the General Council of the International and sent it to various English newspapers, including the London *Times*.
3. As a birthday gift, Kugelmann sent Marx a book by the German critic and humorist Fritz Reuter.

instantly spread their inventions throughout the whole earth, fabricate more myths (and the bourgeois cattle believe and spread them) in one day than could previously be done in one century.

My daughters have been in the Pyrenees for months. Jennychen, who was still suffering from the aftereffects of pleurisy, is recovering visibly, she writes me.

Best thanks for the German clippings.

I hope that you, as well as your dear wife and Fränzchen—to whom I send warm greetings—are well.

Apropos. You were probably surprised that in my last letter to *Pall Mall* I hinted at duels. The matter was quite simply this. If I had not given the editor this pretext for making a few cheap jokes, he would have suppressed the whole thing. In this way, however, he fell into the trap and fulfilled my main objective—he printed verbatim the accusations against Jules Favre & Co. from the Address.[1]

Greetings.

Yours,

K. M.

Draft in French of letter to Nicolai Issakovich Outine (in Geneva)
LONDON, JULY 27, 1871

Dear Citizen:

Last Tuesday the General Council resolved that (in view of the extraordinary circumstances) this year there should be no Congress, but that, as in the year 1865, an *internal Conference* should take place in London. The different sections will be asked to send delegates here. The Conference will not occupy itself with theoretical questions but exclusively with *questions of organization.* The question of conflicts among the different sections within each country will also be added. The conference will *open in London on September 17* (the third Sunday in September). Jung will report these resolutions to Becker and Perret.

At last Tuesday's session of the General Council, Guillaume asked two questions: (1) He had sent copies of two letters; one, from Eccarius, dated July 28, 1869, recognized the Alliance as a section of the International; the other, dated August 25, 1869, is from Jung. This is a receipt of the Alliance's contribution (for the year 1868–69). Now Guillaume asks if these letters are authentic.

We replied that there was *no doubt about it.*

---

1. *The Civil War in France.*

(2) "Did the General Council adopt a resolution which excludes the Alliance from the International?"

We replied that *no such resolution* corresponding to the facts as stated *was adopted.*

So far, only facts were to be determined; but when Robin, in the interest of his employers, attempted to present the facts in such a way as to settle the Swiss dispute in advance, the Council rejected it energetically!

Next, it was established that in a letter from Eccarius the *conditions* for the admission of the Alliance were precisely stated, that they were accepted by the Alliance, and that now it is merely a question of determining whether the Alliance had fulfilled those conditions—a question the Conference must decide.

In regard to the contributions for 1868–69, it was established that this payment of the Alliance was made in order to buy its participation in the Basel Congress of 1869, and that the Alliance thereafter ceased to pay.

In regard to the second question, it was established that while the General Council adopted no resolution excluding the Alliance, this in no way proved that the Alliance, by its behavior, had not excluded itself.

The Council, therefore, resolved that, although the answers to Guillaume's questions were given in accordance with the facts, this matter should be presented to the conference, which should make the decision.

L'Égalité arrives here quite irregularly.

I would be obliged if you would send me an acknowledgment of this letter.

Greetings and fraternity.

K. M.

P. S. In the Council's manifesto I do not sign myself as secretary for Russia, in order not to compromise my friends in Russia.

From draft in French of letter to Adolphe Hubert (in London)
LONDON, AUGUST 10, 1871

Dear Citizen:
. . . The public prosecutor of Versailles has drawn up a grotesque indictment against the International.[1] Perhaps it would be useful to

1. The indictment of a group of French Communards.

communicate the following facts to M. Bigot in the interests of the defense:

1. Enclosed herein (marked No. 1) are the two Addresses of the General Council on the Franco-Prussian War. In its first Address, dated July 23, 1870, the General Council declared that the war was not the handiwork of the people of France but of the Empire, and that at bottom Bismarck was as culpable as Bonaparte. At the same time the Council appealed to the German workers not to let the Prussian Government change the war of defense into a war of conquest.

2. The second Address, of September 9, 1870 (five days after the proclamation of the Republic), is a very emphatic denunciation of the Prussian Government's plans of conquest. It is an appeal to the German and English workers *to take the part of the French Republic.*

As a matter of fact, the workers in Germany belonging to the International Association opposed Bismarck's policy so vigorously that he had the principal German representatives of the International illegally arrested and cast into Prussian fortresses on the trumped-up charge of "conspiring" with the enemy.

In London, on appeal of the Council, the English workers held large meetings to force their government to recognize the French Republic and to oppose with all its strength the dismemberment of France.

3. And now, is the French Government ignorant of the support which the International gave France during the war? Quite the opposite. M. Jules Favre's consul in Vienna, M. Lefaivre, even committed the indiscretion of publishing, in the name of the French Government, a letter of thanks to Messrs. Liebknecht and Bebel, the two representatives of the International in the German Reichstag. In that letter, he said among other things (I shall retranslate it from a German rendition of Lefaivre's letter): "You, gentlemen, and *your party*" (that is to say, the International) "are the only ones to maintain the ancient German tradition, that is, the humanitarian spirit, etc."

Well, this letter figures in the criminal proceedings for high treason which Bismarck forced the Saxon Government to institute against Liebknecht and Bebel and which are still going on at this moment. It served Bismarck as a pretext for having Bebel arrested after the adjournment of the German Reichstag.

At the very time when the reptile press denounced me to Thiers as an agent of Bismarck, Bismarck imprisoned my friends for being guilty of high treason against Germany and gave orders to arrest me should I visit Germany.

4. Some time before the armistice,[2] the worthy Jules Favre—as

2. Of January 28, 1871.

the General Council declared in a letter to the *Times* on June 12, a reprint of which is herewith enclosed (No. 2)—asked us through his private secretary, Dr. Reitlinger, to arrange public demonstrations in London in favor of the "Government of Defense." Reitlinger added, as the General Council said in its letter to the *Times*, that one should not speak of the "Republic" but only of "France." The General Council refused to give any assistance to demonstrations *of this sort*. But all this goes to show that the French Government itself considered the International an ally of the French Republic against the Prussian conqueror—and in fact it was the only ally France had during the war.

With fraternal greetings,

K. M.

Letter to Friedrich Bolte (*in New York*)
BRIGHTON, AUGUST 25, 1871

Dear Mr. Bolte:

I have been here for about two weeks, sent by my doctor, as my health has been very upset from overwork. Nevertheless, I will return to London probably next week.

Next week you will receive an appeal from the General Council for the refugee Communards. The main body of them is in London (now more than eighty or ninety). Hitherto the General Council has kept them from starvation, but in the past two weeks our financial means have so melted away, while the number of newcomers has been growing daily, that they now find themselves in a very deplorable position. I hope New York will do everything possible. In Germany, all the means of the party are still absorbed by the victims of the police persecutions there, and likewise in Austria, Spain, and Italy. In Switzerland they not only have to support a part, even though a small one, of the refugees, but also, as a result of the St. Gall lockout, the International itself. In Belgium, finally, where a small number of the refugees is also to be found, they must also support those Belgians who are en route to London.

As a result of these circumstances, all financial means for the mass of refugees in London have been raised exclusively in England.

In the General Council there are the following members of the Commune: Serraillier, Vaillant, Theisz, Longuet, and Frankel; and the following agents of the Commune: Delahaye, Rochat, Bastelica, and Chalain.

I sent a statement to the *New York Herald* in which I repudiated all responsibility for the tasteless and entirely false report its correspondent gave of his interview with me.[1] I don't know if it was printed.

Give my regards to Sorge. Next week I will answer his letter.

Yours,

KARL MARX

Letter to Friedrich Adolph Sorge (in Hoboken)
LONDON, SEPTEMBER 12, 1871

Dear Mr. Sorge:

Be so good as to transmit the enclosed letter from our Irish secretary McDonnel to J. Devoy.

I have had no time to write you in greater detail. At this moment we are so busy that for three months I have been (and still am) forced to interrupt very urgent theoretical work.

In regard to the Statutes, I only say that the *English* edition is the only authentic one. The Conference[1] will arrange for authentic editions in English, French, and German, which is necessary because various Congress decisions about the Statutes must be incorporated in them.

The Central Committee in New York must not forget:

1. That the General Council had contacts of long standing in America before the Committee was founded;

2. In regard to the Address,[2] it is being sold in London, hence everybody has the right to send it at his own cost to friends in America.

3. Paragraph 7 of the Statutes says specifically: "No independent local society shall be precluded from corresponding directly with the General Council," and the branch in Washington, for example, states that it does not want to enter into contact with New York.

Fraternal greetings,

KARL MARX

---

1. Interview of August 3, 1871; see page 326.

1. The London Conference of the International, September 17–23, 1871.
2. *The Civil War in France.*

Letter to Mrs. Jenny Marx (*in Ramsgate*)
LONDON, SEPTEMBER 23, 1871

Dear Jenny:

Today the Conference[1] is finally coming to an end. It was hard work. Morning and evening sessions, committee sessions in between, hearing of witnesses, reports to be drawn up, and so forth. But more was achieved than in all previous conferences together, because there was no public—before whom to play rhetorical comedies. Germany was not represented, and from Switzerland only Perret and Outine.

Last week the revolutionary party in Rome gave a banquet for Ricciotti Garibaldi, whose report in the Roman journal *La Capitale* was sent to me. A speaker (*il signore Luciani*) proposed a toast, which was received with great enthusiasm, to the working class and "*a Carlo Marx che*" (*qui*) "*ne*" (*en*) "*é fatto*" (*à fait*) "*l'instancabile instrumento*" (*l'instrument infatigable*) [to Karl Marx, who has made it into an indefatigable instrument]. A bitter pill this, for Mazzini!

The news of my death resulted in a meeting in New York of the "Cosmopolitan Society," whose resolution, as printed in the *World*, I am sending you.[2]

Tussy also received from friends in St. Petersburg an anxious letter about me.[3]

It went badly here for Robin and Bastelica, Bakunin's friends and coconspirators. The exposés of Robin's activities in Geneva and Paris were indeed strange. Jennychen's article[4] went off to America today.

Your
KARL

1. The Conference of the International, important in view of the Commune debacle in France, began in London on September 17.
2. The Resolution of the "Cosmopolitan Society," a radical club, referred to Marx as "one of the most devoted, most fearless, and most selfless defenders of all oppressed classes and peoples."
3. On September 12, 1871, N. F. Danielson wrote to Eleanor Marx, inquiring about the truth of the story in the Russian press that Marx was gravely ill.
4. For this article, on the arrest of her sister and herself by the French at the Spanish frontier in August, 1871, see page 297.

Letter to Gustav Kwasniewski (in Berlin)[1]
RAMSGATE, SEPTEMBER 29, 1871

The Conference of the delegates of the International Working Men's Association, which took place in London last week, decided that in the future the General Council will not issue any membership cards. Instead, the General Council will send out stamps (like postal stamps), which every member is to paste on his Statutes or on his membership card, wherever such are issued, as in Switzerland, for example. Hence I will send you a certain number of such stamps as soon as they come out.

In regard to the Statutes, a new edition will be prepared here (in London) in the English, French, and German languages (the latter must be printed in Germany). Pursuant to the decisions of the Conference, every member must possess a copy of the Statutes. For supplements and alterations have been made in them as a result of the various conference decisions since 1866.

At the Conference Germany was represented neither by delegates nor by reports, nor has it made any financial contributions since September, 1869. This hitherto purely Platonic relationship to the International of the German Workers' party, which expects only services without equivalent returns, cannot go on. It compromises the German working class. I therefore summon the Berlin Section to enter into direct correspondence with me and I will send the same demand to all other sections, so long as the leadership of the Social-Democratic party continues to do nothing about the organization of the International in Germany. The laws may prevent the regular organization, but cannot prevent the existing organization of the Social-Democratic Workers' party, from actually doing what has been done in other countries, namely, enrolling individual members, paying contributions, sending reports, etc.

As a member of the control committee of the Social-Democratic Workers' party, perhaps it will be possible for you to take steps in this direction.

Amicably yours,
KARL MARX

---

1. A copy of this letter was found in the Berlin police archives and was published in *Die Gesellschaft*, No. 3, March, 1933.

Letter to Friedrich Adolph Sorge (in Hoboken)
LONDON, NOVEMBER 6, 1871

Dear Friend:

Today I am sending to New York 100 copies (50 French and 50 English) of the Resolutions of the Conference.[1] The resolutions not designed to be made public will be sent subsequently.

The new *revised* edition of the Statutes and Regulations will appear tomorrow in England, and you will receive 1,000 copies for distribution in America (1 penny per copy). The thing ought not to be translated into French and German in New York, as we are issuing *official* editions in both languages. Write us how many copies in both languages you want.

I have relinquished to Eccarius the correspondence with the German Section and with New York (he was nominated for it at my suggestion), as my time does not allow me to carry out these functions properly.

Section No. 12 (New York) has proposed to the General Council to constitute itself as leader in America. The resolutions against these claims, in favor of the present Committee, Eccarius will already have sent to Section No. 12.

In regard to the Washington Branch (which sent the General Council a list of its members), the New York Committee has gone too far. It has no right to demand anything more than the number of members and the names, etc., from the corresponding secretary.

More in the next letter (*this week*).

Yours,
K. M.

Letter to Ferdinand Jozewicz (in Berlin)[1]
LONDON, NOVEMBER 6, 1871

Dear Friend:

I am enclosing a copy of the French translation of the Resolutions

---

1. See "Resolutions of the [London] Conference of . . . September, 1871," page 61.

1. Jozewicz was the corresponding secretary of the International in Berlin. This letter, found in the Berlin police archives and first published in *Die Gesell-*

of the Conference. They appeared likewise in English, and a German translation of the same is being sent tomorrow to the *Volksstaat*.

The English edition of the Statutes and Regulations of the International will be issued tomorrow. We will probably issue a German edition in Leipzig and a French one in Geneva. Pursuant to the latest resolutions of the Conference, every member must possess a copy. I will send you the stamps as soon as they are issued.

In regard to Berlin, my opinion is that no "general" public meetings are to be held until more propaganda has been made there. But meanwhile one should exploit certain occasions of general importance and public interest, in meetings as well as in printed manifestoes.

The next proper occasion would be the infamous trial of the members of the former committee of the Social-Democratic party in Brunswick, since the International constitutes the central point of the indictment. There it would be a good idea to wait until the official opening of the court proceedings, which would attract Germany's attention to Brunswick.

Similarly, the drafts of laws about the International which the government plans to submit to the German Reichstag would offer a favorable opportunity. I hope the German workers will stand up against them as energetically as the Spanish did against similar governmental meddling.

I made a mistake in my last letter.[2] In 1870 Bebel did send me *one* detailed report, at the moment when we were postponing the Mainz Congress (shortly before the outbreak of the war).

It is not my duty as corresponding secretary for Germany, but I would appreciate it if I could be in constant correspondence with you, Kwasniewski, and other friends in Berlin.

Greetings and fraternity.

KARL MARX

---

schaft, No. 3, March, 1933, had an attached note from Police Chief Wurmb to the Prussian Minister of Interior, Count zu Eulenburg, November 13, 1871: "I have the honor of respectfully enclosing to Your Excellency a copy of a private letter from the communist chief Karl Marx to one of the local partisans. The genuineness of the letter, the original of which I have seen, is beyond doubt and the content affords a view into the apparatus of the 'International,' whose general secretary for Germany and Russia is Karl Marx."

2. Marx to Kwasniewski, September 29, 1871.

Letter to Friedrich Adolph Sorge (in Hoboken)
LONDON, NOVEMBER 9, 1871

Dear Friend:
The day before yesterday I sent you 100 copies of the Conference resolutions, 50 English and 50 French.

This week, 1,000 copies of the revised and official Statutes and Regulations, in English, will be sent you. Try to dispose of them.

The General Council has had great expenses in carrying out the various tasks which the Conference commissioned it to do.

We will print an official French edition of the revised Statutes, etc., in Geneva and an official German one in Leipzig. Write us approximately how many copies of both could be used in the United States.

A section of the International has been constituted here among the French refugees, "Section française de 1871" (approximately twenty-four members), which immediately tangled with the General Council because we demanded changes in their statutes. It will undoubtedly come to a split. These people collaborate with a portion of the French refugees in Switzerland who, for their part, are intriguing with the "*Alliance de la Démocratie Socialiste*" (Bakunin), which we have dissolved. The objects of their attack are not the governments and ruling classes of Europe that are allied against us, but the General Council in London, and especially my humble self. This is my thanks for having lost practically five months working for the refugees and acting as the savior of their honor with my *Address on the Civil War* [in France].

Even at the Conference, where the delegates from Spain, Belgium, Switzerland, and Holland expressed fears that the General Council was in danger of losing its international character by too great an admixture of French refugees, I defended them. But in the eyes of these "Internationalists" it is already a sin that "German" influence (because of German science) predominates in the General Council.

Regarding the New York Central Committee, the following:

1. Pursuant to the Conference resolutions, see II, 1, it must in future change its name to Federal Council or Federal Committee of the United States.

2. As soon as a more significant number of branches have been founded in the different states, the most practical thing—following the example of Belgium, Switzerland, Spain—would be to convene a conference of the various sections to select a Federal Council or Committee in New York.

3. In the various states—as soon as they have a sufficient number of branches—Federal Committees can be constituted for which the New York Committee would serve as the central point.

4. The definitive special statutes, those of the New York Federal Committee as well as subsequent committees, must first be sanctioned by the General Council before publication.

In Italy we are making rapid progress. A great triumph over the Mazzini party. In Spain the progress is significant too. In Copenhagen a new section has been formed, already containing 1,500 members and publishing a newspaper, *Socialisten*.

I have been informed that the Brunswick court has indicted the former committee members [of the Social-Democratic Workers' party], Bracke and comrades—an infamous act.

We all regret that you wish to resign from the Committee. Still, I hope that your decision is not final. I personally often think of doing the same, as the business of the International absorbs too much of my time and interrupts my theoretical work.

Apropos. I would like to have twelve copies of *Woodhull & Claflin's Weekly* of October 21, 1871, which has my daughter's story.[1] We saw a copy only by accident.

Fraternal greetings.

KARL MARX

Letter to Carl Speyer (in New York)
LONDON, NOVEMBER 10, 1871

Dear Speyer:

Lessner has reported on your letter. Overwork and subsequent sickness prevented my answering you sooner. There are many mistakes in your letter.

1. According to the Statutes, the main duty of the General Council in Yankeeland is to keep an eye on the Yankees.

2. But *the General Council has absolutely nothing to do* with private correspondence to West, etc. Some individual members of the General Council, namely G. Harris and other sectarians of the school of O'Brien, the currency quack doctor, are in contact with West & Co. Whatever they write to the United States has no official character. If you could bring proof that Harris, etc., pretend to correspond with

---

1. See page 297.

America in the NAME of *the General Council*, this mischief would be promptly eliminated.

3. As for other correspondence of members of the General Council, we cannot forbid this.

First: In regard to Eccarius' correspondence with Jessup, I see nothing against it. I am not aware that Jessup, one of our oldest correspondents in the United States, has acted against the New York Committee.

Second: My correspondence with Sigfrid Meyer. Meyer and Vogt have been proxies of the General Council; I do not know them personally, but I have considered Meyer and Vogt active members of the workers' party for a long time. I long ago advised both of them to join the Central Committee of the organization founded in New York.

I have received no letters from Vogt for years, but if he should carry on intrigues, he would certainly find no supporter in me; I am only interested in your movement, not in private individuals.

In regard to Sorge, I know him personally as little as I do Meyer and Vogt. But it is my conviction that the General Council is most indebted to him for his effectiveness—an opinion which I have frequently expressed in the General Council.

4. You must try to win over the trade unions at all costs.

This letter is addressed to you personally. You must not communicate it to anybody except Sorge.

Write me soon.

Fraternal greetings.

Devotedly yours,

KARL MARX

Letter to Wilhelm Liebknecht (in Leipzig)
LONDON, NOVEMBER 17, 1871

Dear Liebknecht:

1. On the subject of the Statutes, etc., my next letter.

2. Your remarks about my advice to Berlin[1] rest entirely on a misunderstanding. I expressed myself against demonstrations for which there was no occasion, but did, on the contrary, indicate "occasions,"

---

1. Liebknecht to Marx, November 11, 1871: "Furthermore, you do the party a *very poor service* when you advise the Berliners to hold no 'meetings.' You thereby confirm them in their abominable quietism, which we have to thank for the fact that the Swiss have the upper hand in Berlin."

including imminent ones, for which demonstrations would have a reason and a prospect of success.[2]

3. First you and Bebel do not come to the Conference, take no steps for other delegates to come, and then you publish Boruttau's correspondence in which he, perhaps an unconscious tool of the Geneva conspiracy against the General Council, reproaches the latter with not having invited any delegates from Germany. This has already been used in Geneva by the Bakuninists and the wretched tail end of the emigration allied with them, as an indication that Marx himself has lost influence in Germany!

4. You can safely assume that I am more intimately informed about the intrigues inside the International than you are. Therefore, when I write you that none of Boruttau's letters which *in any way* relate to the International (including the announced *Manifesto*, which the same Boruttau has sent you) is to be printed in *Volksstaat*, you simply have to decide whether you want to act *against* or *with* us. In the latter case, my hints based on precise knowledge of conditions, are to be obeyed implicitly.

5. As we are very dissatisfied with the manner in which the business of the International has hitherto been carried out, I have the duty, pursuant to the order of the General Council, to establish contact with the main cities of Germany, which I have already begun to do.

6. We are so overwhelmed here with the work of the International that Engels and I have not found the time to write the preface for the *Communist Manifesto*. In any case, we will not write it in order to open up a polemic with Herr Boruttau in the *Volksstaat*.

Yours,

K. M.

Letter written in French to Adolphe Hubert (in London)
LONDON, NOVEMBER 22, 1871

Dear Citizen:

My illness keeps me house-bound, so that I am prevented from doing what I want to, namely, to come out for the good element in *Qui Vive!*[1] Nevertheless, I have spoken with many of my French friends without knowing whether they have started anything.

---

2. See Marx's letter to Ferdinand Jozewicz, November 6, 1871.

---

1. A French-language publication in London.

In regard to the conditions for joining the International, it suffices to recognize our principles. I am sending you thirty membership cards which you can dispense to the extent that you win new members. The latter have to pay only one penny annually, but they can pledge more if they wish. You only need to fill in the names of the new members.

I am also sending you thirty copies of the Statutes. Every member must have a copy, which costs one penny.

Pursuant to the resolution of the last Conference, glued stamps, worth a penny each, are now being printed; the members are to paste them in the Statutes.

Whoever has already paid for the card is not obligated to pay again for the stamps.

The pamphlet on *The Civil War in France* is sold at Truelove, 256 High Holborn.

With fraternal greetings,

KARL MARX

Letter to Friedrich Bolte (in New York)
LONDON, NOVEMBER 23, 1871

Friend Bolte:

Yesterday I received your letter, together with the report from Sorge.[1]

1. As regards the position of the General Council vis-à-vis the New York Federal Council, I hope the letter I have meantime written Sorge (and another to Speyer, which I authorized him to report to Sorge *privately*) will have eliminated the highly erroneous views of the German sections.

In the United States, as in any other other country where the International was to be established, the General Council originally empowered a few individuals and appointed them its official correspondents. However, from the moment the New York Committee achieved some consistency, these correspondents were dropped one by one, because one could not do it all at once.

For a long time the *official* correspondence with the formerly authorized agents was confined to one between Eccarius and Jessup,

---

1. Bolte's letter to Marx, November 7, 1871, included a report by Sorge on the work of the New York Central Committee of the International during October.

and from your last letter I see that you have nothing to complain of in regard to it.

But aside from Eccarius, nobody had the right to carry on any official correspondence with the United States except Dupont and me, the latter as the (then) correspondent for the French Sections, and insofar as he carried on a correspondence it was confined to the latter.

Except for you and Sorge, I have absolutely not carried on any official correspondence. My correspondence with S. Meyer is private; he never made it public in the slightest, and in its very nature it could *in no way* hinder or hurt the New York Committee.

On the other hand, there is no doubt that G. Harris and perhaps also Boon—two English members of the General Council—carry on a private correspondence with members of the International in New York, etc. Both belong to the sect of the late Bronterre O'Brien, are full of foolishness and crotchets, such as currency quackery, phony women's emancipation, etc. They are thus by nature allies of Section 12 in New York[2] and its soul relatives.

The General Council has no right to forbid its members private correspondence. If, however, it could be *proved* to us that such correspondence either pretends to be official or that—whether for publication or for mischief-making against the New York Committee—it counteracts the effectiveness of the General Council, the necessary measures to avoid the nuisance would be taken.

These O'Brienites, despite their follies, often constitute a necessary counterweight against the trade unionists in the General Council. They are more revolutionary, in the land question more decisive, less national, and not susceptible to bourgeois bribery in one form or another. Otherwise we would have ousted them long ago.

2. I was greatly astonished to hear that German Section No. 1 suspected the General Council of partiality in favor of bourgeois philanthropists, sectarians, and amateur groups.

The situation is precisely in reverse.

The International was founded in order to replace the socialist or semisocialist sects with a real organization of the working class for struggle. The original Rules and the Inaugural Address show this at a glance. On the other hand, the International could not have maintained itself if the course of history had not already smashed sectarianism. The development of the socialist sectarianism and that of the real working-class movement always stand in inverse ratio to each other.

---

2. Section 12, under the leadership of the suffragettes Victoria Woodhull and Tennessee Claflin, pursued its own objectives, which helped to split the International in New York into two councils. In March, 1872, the General Council in London expelled Section 12.

Sects are justified (historically) so long as the working classes are not yet ripe for an independent historical movement. As soon as they attain this maturity, all sects become essentially reactionary. Nevertheless, what history shows everywhere was repeated in the history of the International. The obsolete tries to reestablish itself and maintain its position within the newly acquired form.

And the history of the International has been a *continual struggle of the General Council* against the sects and amateur experiments which sought to assert themselves within the International against the real movement of the working class. This struggle was conducted at the Congresses, but even more in the private negotiations between the General Council and the individual sections.

In Paris, since the Proudhonists (Mutualists) were cofounders of the Association, they naturally held the reins there for the first few years. Later, of course, collectivist, positivist, etc., groups were formed there in opposition to them.

In Germany—the Lassalle clique. I myself corresponded with the notorious Schweitzer for two years and proved to him irrefutably that Lassalle's organization was a mere sectarian organization and, as such, hostile to the organization of the *real* workers' movement striven for by the International. He had his "reasons" for not understanding.

At the end of 1868 the Russian Bakunin joined the International with the aim of forming inside it a *second International* under the name of "*Alliance de la Démocratie Socialiste*" with himself as chief. He—a man devoid of all theoretical knowledge—claimed to represent in that separate body the scientific propaganda of the International, and wanted to make such propaganda the special function of that second International within the International.

His program was a hash from the right and the left, superficially scraped together—equality of classes (!), abolition of the right of inheritance as the *starting point* of the social movement (St. Simonian imbecility), atheism as a dogma dictated to the members, etc., and as the main doctrine (Proudhonist), abstention from the political movement

This infantile primer found favor (and still has a certain hold) in Italy and Spain, where the real conditions for the workers' movement are as yet little developed, and among a few vain, ambitious, and empty doctrinaires in Romansh Switzerland and in Belgium.

To Mr. Bakunin, doctrine (the mess he has brewed from Proudhon, St. Simon and others) was and is a secondary matter—merely a means to his personal self-assertion. Although a nonentity as a theorist, he is in his element as an intriguer.

For years the General Council had to fight this conspiracy (supported up to a certain point by the French Proudhonists, especially in Southern France). At last, by means of Conference Resolutions 1, 2, and 3, IX, XVI, and XVII,[3] it delivered its long-prepared blow.

It goes without saying that the General Council does not support in America what it combats in Europe. Resolutions 1, 2, 3, and IX now give the New York Committee the legal weapons with which to put an end to all sectarianism and amateur groups, and, if necessary, to expel them.

3. The New York Committee would do well to express its agreement with the Resolutions of the Conference in an *official communication to the General Council.*

Bakunin (moreover, personally threatened by Resolution XIV, and publications in *L'Égalité* about the Nechayev trial, which will expose his infamous Russian activities) is doing everything possible to organize protests against the Conference with the remnants of his followers.

For this purpose he has made contact with the ragged portion of the French émigrés (a numerically small element, however) in Geneva and London. Their announced watchword is that Pan-Germanism (i.e., Bismarckism) dominates the General Council. This, of course, is a reference to the unforgivable fact that I am a German by birth and exercise a decisive intellectual influence on the General Council. (*Notabene:* The German element in the Council is numerically two-thirds weaker than the English and ditto weaker than the French. The offense, therefore, is that the English and French elements are, in matters of *theory*, dominated by the German element, and that they find this domination, that is, German science, very useful and even indispensable).

In Geneva, under the patronage of the bourgeoisie and Madame André Léo (who at the Lausanne Congress was so brazen as to denounce Ferré to his Versailles executioners[4]), they started a newspaper, *La Révolution Sociale,* which uses almost literally the same polemical expressions against us as the *Journal de Genève,* the most reactionary paper in Europe.

In London they established a French Section, a sample of whose work you will see in Number 42 of *Qui Vive!,* which I am enclosing. (Ditto the number which contains a letter by our French secretary, Serraillier[5]). This section, consisting of twenty people (among them

---

3. See "Resolutions of the [London] Conference . . .," page 61.
4. At the Peace League Congress in 1871 Madame Léo accused Charles Théophile Ferré, who was then in prison awaiting execution, of having advocated sanguinary action by the Commune.
5. *Qui Vive!,* November 16, 1871.

many *mouchards* [police informers]), has not been recognized by the General Council, but another, much more numerous, has.[6]

In reality, despite the intrigues of this gang of scamps, we make great propaganda in France—and in Russia, where they know how to judge Bakunin and where they are now printing my book, *Capital,* in Russian.

The secretary of the above-mentioned French Section (not recognized by us, now in complete dissolution) was the same Durand whom we expelled from the Association as a *mouchard.*

The Bakuninist abstentionists from politics, Blanc and Albert Richard of Lyons, are now *paid Bonapartist agents.* The proof is in our hands. The Correspondent Bousquet (of the same clique in Geneva) in Béziers (southern France) has been denounced to us by that section as a policeman.

4. In regard to the Resolutions of the Conference, it is to be observed that the whole collection was in my hands, and that at the *very first* I sent it to New York (Sorge), as being the farthermost point.

If previous reports on the Conference—half true and half false—reached the press, it was the fault of the Conference delegate [Eccarius] against whom the General Council has started an inquiry.

5. In regard to the Washington Section, it had first applied to the General Council, in order to establish contact with it as an independent section. The matter is now finished, hence it is unnecessary to revert to it.

In regard to the sections in general, the following observations are to be made:

a. According to Article 7 of the Statutes, sections which want to be independent can apply directly to the General Council for admission ("no independent local society shall be precluded from corresponding directly with the General Council"). II, Articles 4 and 5 of the Regulations: "Every new branch or society" (this applies also to "independent local societies") "intending to join the International is immediately bound to announce its adherence to the General Council" (II, Article 4) and "The General Council has the right to admit or to refuse the affiliation of any new Branch, etc." (II, Article 5).

b. According to Article 5 of the Regulations, the General Council, nevertheless, has to consult the federal councils or committees prior to admission, etc., and

c. according to the Resolution of the Conference—see V. Article 3, of the Regulations—no section will be accepted from the beginning,

---

6. Another French Section in London affiliated with the International on November 18, 1871.

if it gives itself sectarian names, etc., or, V, Article 2, if it does not constitute itself simply as a Section of the International Working Men's Association.

Please communicate this letter to the German sections you represent, and use the contents for action, but not for publication.

Salut et fraternité,

KARL MARX

Capital has not yet come out in English or French. A French edition was in progress, but has been interrupted by events.

At my request, Eccarius has been appointed secretary for *all* sections of the United States (except the French, for which Le Moussu is secretary). Despite this, I shall answer with pleasure any questions you or Sorge ask me in private. Engels sent the article on the International in the *Irish Republic*[7] to Italy for publication.

In the future, the *Eastern Post*, which carries the reports of the General Council sessions, will be sent to New York regularly.

Notabene on Political Movement.

The political movement of the working class has, naturally, as its final objective the conquest of political power for itself, and this, of course, necessitates a previous organization of working class development up to a certain point, being itself an outgrowth of its economic struggles.

But on the other hand, every movement in which the working class as a *class* confronts the ruling classes and tries to vanquish them by pressure from without, is a political movement. For example, an attempt in a particular factory or in a particular trade to force shorter working hours on individual capitalists through strikes, etc., is a purely economic movement; on the other hand, a movement to compel the enactment of an eight-hour law, etc., is a political movement. And in this way, out of the workers' separate economic movements there grows everywhere a *political* movement, that is, a movement of the *class*, aiming to effect its interests in a general form—in a form which possesses universal socially coercive force. Although these movements presuppose a certain degree of previous organization, in turn they are equally a means for the further development of this organization.

Where the working class is not yet sufficiently far advanced in its organization to undertake a decisive campaign against the collective power, that is, the political power, of the ruling classes, it must in any case be trained for this by constant agitation against (and a hostile

---

7. The *Irish Republic* was a weekly for Irish immigrants, published in New York from 1871 to 1898.

attitude to) the policies of the ruling classes. Otherwise it remains a plaything in their hands, as the September [1870] Revolution in France has shown and as is also proved to a certain degree by the game that Messrs. Gladstone & Co. still succeed in playing in England to this very hour.

Letter to César de Paepe (in Brussels)
LONDON, NOVEMBER 24, 1871

My Dear Friend:

I would have written you sooner if my time had belonged to me. During the last four weeks I kept to the house; I had abscesses, operations, etc., *secundum legem artis* [according to all the rules of the art]. In addition, owing to the affairs of the International on the one hand and the refugees on the other, I did not even get to the point of working on the Russian translation of *Capital*. As the friends in St. Petersburg kept urging me more and more, I was obliged to leave the chapter as it was and make only a few small changes. I have already told you in London that I have often asked myself whether the time has come for me to withdraw from the General Council. The more the Association develops, the more time is lost, and finally I do have to complete *Capital* once and for all. Furthermore, my withdrawal would save the International from the *Pan-Germanism* which, according to Roullier, Malon, Bakunin, Robin, & Co., I threaten it with.

I have discussed your affairs with a doctor here. He told me the following:

1. If you want to settle in London as an *English doctor*, it is not enough to pass the examinations here. You would be obliged to spend at least two years of study in a London hospital (or university). Belgian courses are accepted in some branches of the sciences, but not in all.

2. On the other hand, you can establish yourself here as a doctor with your Belgian diploma, without taking new examinations or English courses. There are French and German doctors who practice here. To be sure, in certain areas, although they are not numerous ones (for example, forensic medicine), you could not function, but these are insignificant.

3. Finally, you could—as many foreigners have—combine both methods, start practicing immediately and at the same time take the

necessary measures to transform yourself later into an English doctor, and in the end, become the physician of Her Most Gracious Majesty.

Thus you see, my dear friend, many roads lead to Rome. Drop me a few lines on this subject.

The attitude of the Belgian Federal Council vis-à-vis the General Council seems to me suspicious. Mr. Hins and his wife—I speak to you quite frankly—are Bakuninists, and Mr. Steens has probably concluded that his oratorical cleverness has not been sufficiently admired. In Geneva, it was even said, as Outine has told me (he, of course, did not believe it himself), that they placed themselves on the side of the Alliancers and joined with André Léo, Malon, Razoua, etc.

This matter, slight in itself, could lead to bad consequences. England, the United States, Germany, Denmark, Holland, Austria, the majority of the French groups, the Italians of the North, Sicilians and Romans, the overwhelming majority of the Swiss Romande, all of German Switzerland, and the Russians in Russia (whom one has to distinguish from some Russians abroad who are tied to Bakunin) go along with the General Council.

On the other side, the Jura Federation in Switzerland (that is, the men of the Alliance who hide behind this name), Naples, perhaps Spain, a part of Belgium, and some groups of French refugees (who, for the rest, judging by some letters from France, seem to have no serious influence there) all constitute the opposition camp. Such a split, not too dangerous in itself, could become awkward at a certain point, as we must march against the common enemy with closed ranks. Our opponents do not in any way deceive themselves about their weakness, but they count on receiving great moral support by joining the Belgian Federal Council.

People inquire daily here about the *Anti-Proudhon*.[1] I could make a certain propaganda among the best minds of the French emigration if I had a few copies of my book against Proudhon, which you were so kind as to promise me.

With fraternal greetings,
KARL MARX

---

1. Marx's book *The Poverty of Philosophy.*

Letter written in English[1] and French to Paul and Laura Lafargue
(in San Sebastián)
LONDON, NOVEMBER 24, 1871

My Dear Laura and Toole:[2]
What with the International business, what with the visits of the
Communards, *I have not found the time to write. How my time is
encroached upon you may judge from one case. At Petersburg they
have been translating* CAPITAL *into Russian, but they had reserved the
first chapter because I had asked them to do so, since I intended to
rewrite it in a more popular manner. Since the events of Paris I was
continually prevented from fulfilling my promise and was at last
compelled to limit myself to a few alterations, in order not to stop the
progress of the publication altogether.*

As to the calumnies against Toole, *it is all moonshine,* a canard of
the French Branch No. 2. Serraillier, the secretary for France, *wrote
immediately to Bordeaux. The six sections there existing have answered
by a vote of absolute confidence in the illustrious Toole.*

*As to the scandals that have taken place at London and Geneva, I
must begin from the beginning.*

*Amongst other French refugees, we had admitted to the General
Council Theisz, Chalain, and Bastelica. The latter was hardly admitted
when he proposed Avrial and Camélinat, but est modus in rebus* [there
is method in things], *and we found that there were now enough
Proudhoniens in our ranks. On different pretexts the election of these
two worthies was therefore delayed until the Conference, and dropped
after the Conference, the latter having passed a resolution inviting us
not to admit too many refugees. Hence* the great anger of Citizens
Avrial and Camélinat.

*On the Congress itself the resolution on the political action of the
working class was violently opposed by the Bakuninists—Robin, the
Spaniard Lorenzo, and the Corsican Bastelica. The latter, an empty-
headed and very pretentious fellow, got the worse of it and was rather
roughly handled. His main quality—that is to say his amour propre—
got him into steam.* There was still another incident.

On the affair of the "Alliance of Socialist Democracy" *and the
dispute in the Swiss Romansh, the Conference appointed* a committee
(of which I was a member) and which met in my house. Outine on

---

1. The sentences and phrases written in English are in italics.
2. Lafargue's nickname.

the one side, Bastelica and Robin on the other, were summoned as witnesses. Robin behaved in the most shabby and cowardly manner. After having had his say (at the beginning of the session) he declared that he had to leave, and rose to go out. Outine told him that he ought to stay, that the interrogation should be a serious one, and that he did not like to speak of him in his absence. Robin, in a series of admirable tactical movements, approached the door. Outine apostrophized him violently, saying that he must accuse him of being the mainspring of the Alliance's intrigues. *Meanwhile, to secure a safe retreat,* the great Robin partly opened the door and, before going out, hurled these truly Parthian words at Outine: In that case, I despise you. On September 19, using Delahaye as intermediary, he communicated the following epistle to the Conference:

> Summoned as witness by the committee to look into the Swiss dispute, I went there in the hope of contributing to an appeasement.
> Being directly attacked, I declare formally that I do not accept the role of an accused and I abstain from attending the sessions of the Conference when the Swiss question is being discussed.
> 19 September, '71. P. ROBIN

Several Conference members, like De Paepe, demanded the immediate expulsion of this worthy Kerame (?) of the General Council, but, upon my advice, it was resolved that he be asked to retract his letter and, in case of refusal, to leave the matter in the hands of the General Council. Robin stubbornly stuck to his letter and the upshot was his expulsion by the Council.

Meanwhile, he had addressed to myself the following billet doux of September 28:

> Citizen Marx, I have had great personal obligations to you that did not weigh on me as long as I believed that nothing could alter the respectful friendship that I felt for you. Today, unable to subordinate my gratitude to my conscience, in my regret of having to break with you, I believe that I owe you this declaration.
> I am convinced that in yielding to personal hatreds, you have carried or supported unjust accusations against members of the International, objects of these hatreds, whose sole crime has been in not sharing them.
>
> P. ROBIN

I did not think it worth my while to answer to R. R. R. Robin sheep (Rabelais already knew it under this name and introduced it especially among the sheep of Panurge). Now I return to our other business.

After the Conference, Avrial and Camélinat pushed to establish a

French Branch ("French Section of London of 1871"). Theisz, Bastelica (who had already decided to return to Switzerland and wanted to create support for Bakunin in London before his departure), and Chalain (a worthless humbug) collaborated on that. They published their particular statutes in the journal *Qui Vive!*, about which I shall speak later. These statutes were contrary to those of the General Council. Among other things, these gentlemen (there were twenty of them, among them some stool pigeons; their secretary was the illustrious Durand, whom the General Council had publicly castigated as a stool pigeon and expelled from the International) had arrogated to themselves *the* right of naming the delegates to the General Council with imperative mandates, deciding at the same time that no one belonging to their section could accept an appointment as a member of the General Council unless he was sent as delegate by the section itself.

Even before any confirmation of their statutes by the General Council, they had the impudence to send to it as their delegates Chautard (a cretin who was the laughingstock of Paris during the Commune) and Camélinat. They were politely invited to withdraw and to await the confirmation of their statutes by the General Council. I was charged with the task of making the critical analysis. This first missive of the Council to the new section was still written in a conciliatory manner. We asked only that the articles contrary to the letter and the spirit of the Statutes and General Rules be eliminated.

They were furious. Avrial (with the collaboration of Theisz and Camélinat) made a reply which cost them two weeks of work *and to which the last literary finish was given* by Vermersch (Père Duchesne).

This individual had sneaked himself in among them because they, together with a few typographers (refugees), had founded the journal *Qui Vive!*, under the provisional editorship of Le Verdet (Schopenhauerian philosopher). Vermersch flattered them and incited them against the General Council in order to secure the journal for himself, and *he succeeded in this*.

They sent Bastelica to Switzerland and received from there the password: The General Council was under the yoke of Pan-Germanism (that was me), authoritarian, etc. The first duty of every citizen was to work for the overthrow of this usurping Council, etc. All this emanated from Bakunin (acting through the Russian, N. Zhukovsky, secretary of the Alliance in Geneva, Guillaume, etc.), whose clique (which, for that matter, has only a very few members in Switzerland) allied itself with Madame André Léo, Malon, Razoua, and a small group of other French refugees, discontented with playing a secondary role or *no part whatever*.

In passing: all the imbeciles who had been members, or who had falsely pretended to have been members, of the Federal Council of Paris, such as, for example, Roullier, this brawler, glutton, drunkard, flattered themselves that they would be admitted—as if by right—to membership in the General Council.

Theisz (who had been appointed *treasurer*, not secretary for France, of the General Council) and Bastelica handed in their resignations as members of the Council, using as pretext the article of their statutes which forbids them to accept appointment by the Council. I finally replied to the letter, which was embellished by Father Vermersch, whose spirit is more Flemish than French. My reply was so crushing and at the same time so ironic that they resolved not to continue their correspondence with the Council. Hence they were not recognized as a section of the International.

Father Vermersch became editor-in-chief of *Qui Vive!* In issue No. 32 he published the letter by Chautard, Chouteau (who had already been denounced by Rigault in *Patrie En Danger* as a stool pigeon), Landeck, who gave his word to M. Piétri (see the last court trial of the International in Paris) that he would withdraw from the International and from politics—*and similar riffraff*—in which they denounce the Conference and say that the German workers (who had demonstrated against the annexation of French provinces and, later, in *favor of* the Paris Commune, and many of whom are still exposed to persecutions by Bismarck) had done their duty, and offered this as proof of flagrant "Pan-Germanism"!

This was a bit too strong for the simple fellows Theisz, Camélinat, and Avrial. They refused to sign. As members of *Qui Vive!*'s administrative council, they also got into other squabbles with Vermersch because of an immoral romance which he published in the literary section. Vermersch, who no longer had any need for these gentlemen, then attacked them in *Qui Vive!*, without naming them. He also quarreled with other refugees because of his nauseating articles, and I believe that yesterday he was slapped in the face by Sicard. Now they want to remove him from the editorship at all costs. We shall see! It is believed that he is being paid by Versailles to compromise the Communards. To finish the thing: in London, the conspiracy miscarried. The French Branch No. 2 is in complete dissolution (it goes without saying that Le Lubez, Bradlaugh, Besson, etc., pushed it there). Another French section, much more numerous and in accord with the General Council, has been established.

To replace those who have resigned, we have appointed Antoine Arnaud, F. Cournet, and G. Ranvier as members of the Council.

At Geneva, the "Alliance," and André Léo, Malon, etc., is publishing a small journal, *La Révolution Sociale* (edited by a certain

Claris), in which they openly attack the General Council and the Conference. Pan-Germanism (German heads and Bismarckians), authoritarian, etc., etc. The "Jurassic Federation" (again the same clique under a different name) held a very small congress at Sonvilliers (Bernese Jura), which resolved to invite all the sections of the International to join the Jurassic Federation in urgently calling together a special congress which would examine the conduct of the General Council and would annul the resolutions of the Conference as contrary to the principle of autonomy which those resolutions "openly violate." It protests particularly against Resolutions II, 2, 3, IX (*political action of the working class*), XVI, and XVII. It dares not speak of Resolution XIV, which is particularly disagreeable to Bakunin, because it exposes before all of Europe the turpitudes he committed in Russia.

The attitude of the Federal Council of Madrid (worked over by Bakunin and Bastelica) is very suspect. Since the departure of Lorenzo, Engels has received no answer to his numerous letters. They [the Spaniards] are imbued with the doctrine of abstention from politics. Engels wrote them today that if their silence continues, measures will be taken. In any case, *Toole must act.* I will send him English and French copies of the new edition of the Statutes and Rules, revised and enlarged.

Our adversaries are unlucky. As I have said before, the first secretary of the dissident section in London was G. Durand, whom we exposed as a Versailles agent. The Bakuninists Blanc and Albert Richard (of Lyon) have sold themselves to Bonaparte. They were here to enlist members under his banner—since Bonaparte is worth more than Thiers!

Finally, the correspondent of the refugees hostile to Geneva at Béziers—practically their sole French correspondent—has been denounced to us by the Béziers Section as a policeman (he is secretary of the central police commission).

I hope soon to receive good news of the health of my well-beloved Schnaps[3] and of the whole family.

OLD NICK

Postscript added by Engels:

Apropos Theisz. He has lost all influence in Paris because of the praises the Versailles newspapers have bestowed on him and on Father Beslay.

Bastelica *heads Bakunin's valets.*

I should also add that the attacks on us by the *Révolution Sociale*

---

3. Marx's nickname for his grandson, Charles-Étienne Lafargue.

of Geneva are couched in virtually the same terms as those of the *Journal de Genève* (the most reactionary newspaper in Europe) and the *Times*, which I am sending you. The newspaper which the *Times* mentions is the *Journal de Genève*.

My dear Toole, I thank you for your letter, of which I have made good use in the Council. This very day, my ultimatum to the Federal Council of Madrid goes off by *registered mail*, telling them that if their silence continues, *debuemos proceder como nos la dictarà el interés de la Internationale* [we will have to proceed as the interests of the International dictate]. If they do not reply, or do so in an inconvenient manner, we will then send you full powers for all of Spain.

Meanwhile, you have, as do all other members, the right, according to our Statutes, to establish new sections. It is important that, in case of a split, we always have a foothold in Spain, even if the whole actual organization were to desert with arms and baggage to the Bakuninist camp; and it is only on you that we can count for this. Therefore, do all you can to renew communications everywhere with men who would be useful to us in such a case. The Bakuninists want absolutely to transform the International into an *abstentionist society*, but they will not succeed. The *Federación* of Barcelona and the *Emancipación* of Madrid come here too irregularly for me to know whether or not the intrigue has already begun to be unveiled in those journals. But they have always preached abstentionism, which probably seems to them to be more important than economic questions. This is what they have come to with their abstention from politics: They themselves make politics the most important point! Give my best to Laura and kiss little Schnaps for me. Ever yours,

F. E.

Letter written in English to Friedrich Adolph Sorge (in Hoboken)
LONDON, NOVEMBER 29, 1871

My Dear Sorge:

I hope you have at last received in New York the Resolutions of the Conference[1] and the various letters I sent you. Along with this letter I am sending you the three last *Eastern Post* reports on the sessions of the General Council, which, of course, contain only what is appropriate for publication.

---

1. The Conference of the International in London, September 17–23, 1871.

In regard to financial matters, I have only to remark:

1. The New York Committee has to pay only tuppence per piece for the pamphlets, *The Civil War in France*, it has received. It will pay one penny per piece for the Statutes and Regulations, *à fur et à mesure* [in proportion] as they are sold. But you should write us how many French and German editions of the Statutes, etc., you need. Aside from what you require at the moment, you would do well to have some stock in reserve.

2. In regard to the money sent to us for the refugees, the General Council wants a positive written declaration that it alone is responsible for the distribution of the funds among the French refugees, and that the so-called "Society of French Refugees in London" has no right of control over the Council.

This is necessary because, although the mass of the above-named society are honest people, the committee at its head consists of ruffianly fellows, so that a large part—and the most meritorious portion of the refugees at that—does not want to have anything to do with the "Society," but prefers to be supported directly by the General Council. Hence we give a weekly sum to the society for distribution and distribute another sum directly.

It is the above-mentioned ruffians who have spread the most atrocious calumnies against the General Council, without whose aid (and many of its members have not only sacrificed their time but also paid out of their own pockets) the French refugees would have *crevé de faim* [perished of hunger].

Now I come to the question of McDonnel.

Before admitting him, the Council instituted a most searching inquiry as to his integrity, since he, like all other Irish politicians, has been harshly traduced by his own countrymen.

After the most incontroversible evidence about his private character, the Council chose him because the *mass of Irish workers in England* have more confidence in him than in *any other person*. He is entirely above religious prejudices, and as to his general views, it is absurd to charge him with "bourgeois" tendencies. He is a proletarian in his way of life and his ideas.

If accusations are to be brought against him, let it be done in specific terms, and not by vague insinuations. In my opinion, Irishmen, having been imprisoned for such a long time, are not competent judges. The best proof of this: their relations with the *Irishman*, whose editor, Pigott, is a mere speculator, and whose business manager, Murphy, is a ruffian. Despite the exertions of the General Council on behalf of the Irish cause, that paper has always intrigued against us. McDonnel was constantly attacked in it by an Irishman (O'Donnell), a man connected with Campbell (an official of the London police), a habitual drunkard, who for a glass of gin will tell the first constable he meets all the secrets he may happen to know.

After the appointment of McDonnel, Murphy attacked and slandered the International (not only McDonnel) in the *Irishman*, and at the same time secretly asked us to appoint him (Murphy) secretary for Ireland.

In regard to O'Donovan Rossa, I am surprised that you still quote him as an authority after all you have written me about him. If ever there was a man obligated to the International and the French Communards, it was he, and you have seen what thanks we have received at his hands.[2]

Let the Irish members of the New York Committee not forget that, to be useful to them, we need above all to have *influence on the Irish in England*, and for this purpose, so far as we have been able to ascertain, there is no better man than McDonnel.

Yours fraternally,

KARL MARX

Train has never received credentials from the General Council.

Letter to Ferdinand Jozewicz (in Berlin)
LONDON, FEBRUARY 24, 1872

Citizen Secretary:

I can reply only in a few words. As a result of the conspiracy of the "international police" with certain *faux frères* [traitors] inside the International, the General Council has so overwhelmed me with work that I have to stop my own theoretical writings. Now to the point:

1. By a decision of the General Council, based on the four-month delay in printing the stamps (in consequence of unforeseen obstructions in London), the term for the unused stamps has been postponed from March 1 to July 1. (Please inform Liebknecht of this, as I have no time to write him now.)

2. As for double payment for the stamps, all you have to do is simply state in your report of July 1 that such-and-such a sum of the money sent in comes from that source.

---

2. After Rossa and other Fenians were imprisoned, the General Council exposed their mistreatment in jail. See "The British Government and the Imprisoned Fenians," page 124. Rossa and the Fenians were pardoned on condition that they emigrate.

3. As for the "corresponding secretary," the General Council leaves it to the Berlin Section to arrange things as it sees fit.

4. The Berlin Section falls into the category of countries where "legal obstructions" stand in the way of the regular organizations, and the sections of those countries have absolute freedom to constitute themselves in accordance with the law of the land, without thereby losing *any right* appertaining to any other section.

5. The next Conference will take place in September, 1872. The General Council has not yet decided on the place of meeting. The Social-Democratic party would do well to inform us immediately when it intends to hold its own congress.

6. The periodic reports of the General Council are supplemented by its weekly reports in the *Eastern Post*, the first of which is being sent you today.

7. The *Volksstaat* belongs to the organs [of the International] in question.

8. The General Council thanks the Berlin Section for appointing a statistical committee.

9. It asks, through me, what the relation is between the Hamburgers (that is, the committee of the Social-Democratic party) and the General Council. We have hitherto not received a word from there.

10. The General Council requests the Berlin Section to give its approval to the resolutions of the last Conference of the delegates of the International (in London).

With fraternal greetings,

K. M.

Letter to Friedrich Adolph Sorge (in Hoboken)
LONDON, MARCH 8, 1872

Dear Sorge:

Only today did Liebknecht send us the German Statutes, and they cannot be sent out before Monday [March 11]. They seem to imagine there that the General Council can handle anything on the spur of the moment, whereas on the contrary, without private contributions from its members or personal friends, *absolutely nothing* can be done. I notice in your letters, as well as those of Speyer and Bolte, and the correspondence from other countries, the same thing. Each country believes that our whole time can be devoted to it. If we were to complain about every detail, we could mention, for example, that your reports to us appear simultaneously in the *Volksstaat*.

As I have finally been instructed by the General Council to prepare a report (we were obliged to postpone the matter from session to session, owing to the confusion of the International in Europe) on the split in America, I went carefully through all the correspondence from New York as well as what has been published in the press, and found that we were in no way informed in time about the elements that led to the break. One part of the resolutions which I submitted has already been adopted, the other part will be taken up next Tuesday, and the final decision will be expedited to New York.

You will receive 1,000 copies of the German Statutes. Hales will send you 500 English ones. I am sending 200 of the French, which are now completely disposed of.

Eccarius says that the things should be sent to Gregory (his private correspondent), because you wrote him that you have resigned your position and did not mention any new correspondent.

The complaint about [no longer having] an exclusive "French" correspondent, on the ground that the Germans had their own correspondent, is entirely unjust, because the secretary for the United States—Eccarius—could correspond in German and English, but not in French. Furthermore, the complaint was impolitic because it seemed to confirm the opinion of the French members of the Council that Section I aimed at establishing a dictatorship over the other sections. The complaint arrived at the same time as the one of the counter-committee, to the effect that, contrary to the Statutes, Section I was strongly represented in the old committee.

The costs of the Statutes for the countercommittee were greater because the admission fees had to be paid (at least so they say).

I hope your committee will be satisfied with the decision of the Council.

Our side will publish in Geneva a brochure against the dissenters[1] as big as that on the Civil War. In the meantime they have tried to blunt the points of the polemic, in that they pulled in their horns in their last circular.

In all haste.

Yours,
K. MARX

---

1. See "Fictitious Splits in the International," page 190.

Letter written in English to Friedrich Adolph Sorge (in Hoboken)[1]
LONDON, MARCH 15, 1872

Dear Citizen:

I enclose the Resolutions of the General Council (in English and French). The other council will receive them from Le Moussu.

Eccarius, at the end of the sitting of 12 March told me privately that he would not send the resolutions to New York and that, at next sitting, he would hand [in] his resignation as Secretary for the United States. As this affair cannot be settled by the General Council before Tuesday next [March 19], the Resolutions sent by me and Le Moussu are not signed by a secretary, the which considering the form chosen, was not necessary. They will be printed in next week's *Eastern Post*. During the discussion Eccarius spoke in a spirit most hostile to your Council. He was moreover offended because, in order to save time, I had not entrusted the resolutions to the subcommittee of which he forms a part, but laid them at once before the General Council. As the latter fully approved this proceeding, after my statement of the reasons which had induced me to act as I have done, Eccarius ought to have dropped his personal spleen.

For the *private* information of your Council I add that Mr. and Madame Huleck—he is an imbecile and she is *"une intrigante de bas état"* [a low-grade intrigante]—had for a moment slipped into the General Council at a time when most of us were absent, but that, soon after, that worthy couple was forced to withdraw consequent upon their intrigues with the *soi-disant Branche Française* [so-called French Branch], the which was excluded from the *International* and denounced by us in the *Marseillaise* and *Réveil* on the eve of the plebiscite as *"une section policière"* [police section]. Moreover, the two persons, after their arrival at New York, cooperated in the foundation of a society hostile to the International and were in constant connection with *les beaux restes de la Comité française* [the remnants of the French Committee] at London. The same facts have been communicated by Le Moussu to the other council.

Section 10 (French) has written a letter to the General Council on the American split.

Yours fraternally,
KARL MARX

---

1. The original of this letter is in the New York Public Library, Manuscript Division (Sorge Papers).

Letter written in French to Paul Lafargue (in Madrid)
LONDON, MARCH 21, 1872

My Dear Toole:

I am enclosing an excerpt from our circular against the dissidents in connection with the functions of the General Council.

All the General Council can do in a given case, in regard to the applications of the general Statutes and the decisions of the Congress, is to consider them as decisions of a court of arbitration. But carrying them out depends entirely on the International in each country. From the moment the Council ceases to function as the instrument of the general interests of the International, it becomes absolutely meaningless and impotent. For the General Council is itself one of the active forces of the International, and in order to preserve its unity it is necessary to prevent hostile elements from seizing it. The moral influence that the present Council (notwithstanding all its shortcomings) has managed to maintain in the face of the common enemy has hurt the egotism of some people, who never saw in the International anything besides an instrument of personal vanity.

Above all, one should not forget that our Association is the *fighting organization* of the proletariat and in no way a society founded to advance dilettantish doctrinaires. To destroy our organization at this moment would mean to lay down one's arms. The bourgeoisie as well as the governments could not wish for anything better. Read the report of the country bumpkin Sacaze on Dufaure's project.[1] What does he most admire and fear in the Association? "Its organization."

We have made excellent progress since the London Conference.

New federations have been established in Denmark, New Zealand, and Portugal; there is a great extension in the United States, France (where Malon & Co., according to their admission, do not have a single section), in Germany, in Hungary, in England (since the establishment of the Federal Council). Only recently, Irish sections have been founded. In Italy, individual groups belong to separate sections; those in Milan and Turin, to us; the leadership of the others is in the hands of lawyers, journalists, and other doctrinaire bourgeois. (Apropos: Bakunin harbors a personal animosity for me, because he has lost all influence in Russia, where the revolutionary youth is with me.)

The decisions of the London Conference have already been

---

1. Jules Dufaure drafted the law, passed by the French Assembly on March 14, 1872, providing for the imprisonment of members of the International.

recognized in France, America, England, Ireland, Denmark, Holland, Germany, Austria, Hungary, and Switzerland (with the exception of the Jurassians), as well as by the real labor sections in Italy and finally by the Russians and Poles. Because of this, those who do not recognize the decisions will change nothing, but will be forced to separate from the vast majority of the International.

I am so overwhelmed with work that I do not even find time to write to my sweet Cacadou[2] and the dear Schnappy (from whom I would be happy to hear). In reality, the International takes so much of my time that if I were not convinced that my presence in the General Council at this moment is still necessary, I would have withdrawn long ago.

The English Government has thwarted our proposed celebration on March 18;[3] I am enclosing the resolutions which were adopted at a meeting of English workers and French refugees.

Lachâtre is an abominable charlatan. He steals one's time with absurdities (for example, his reply to my letter that obliged me to make changes).

Roy (6 Rue Condillac, Bordeaux) is a splendid translator. He has already sent me the manuscript of the first chapter (I sent to him in Paris the manuscript of the second German edition).

Entirely yours,

OLD NICK

Letter to Johann Georg Eccarius (in London)
LONDON, MAY 3, 1872

Dear Eccarius:

You[1] seem to have gone crazy, but since I still think this is a passing aberration, you will excuse me for not addressing you as either sir or mister or master, and for writing you in German instead of English.[2]

If you have not also lost your knowledge of the German language along with your memory—and this can be ascertained by the minutes of the General Council—you will recall that all the rows I have ever

---

2. Marx's nickname for his daughter Laura Lafargue.
3. The first anniversary of the Paris Commune.

1. Marx used the familiar *Du* throughout this letter.
2. On May 2, 1872, at the time the International was breaking up, Eccarius, long-time secretary of the General Council, wrote Marx a curt note in which he addressed him as "sir."

had with Englishmen, from the founding of the International until now, have been due simply to my always taking your part:[3] first, in the case of the *Commonwealth* against Odger, Cremer, Howell, etc., then against Fox, with whom I had been on the most friendly terms, and finally against Hales during the period of your general-secretary-ship.

If collisions occurred subsequently, the question is *who* caused them. I have attacked you only twice.

First, over the premature publication of the decisions of the Congress of the International [September 23–27, 1871], which you well know was a violation of your duty.

Second, over the affair in America [where the International split in March, 1872], in which you caused great mischief. (I overlook the fact that you have hung around my neck the abuses in the American papers supported by Karl Heinzen & Co. I am as indifferent to those insults as I was to the public and private praises that used to come from that direction.)

But you seem to imagine that when you make blunders you should receive compliments instead of being told the truth, as one would to anybody else. . . .

Finally, let me give you a bit of good advice. Do not believe that your old personal and party friends are any the less devoted to you when they believe it is their duty to oppose your *freaks*. By the same token, do not imagine that the small clique of Englishmen, which is using you for certain purposes, consists of your friends. I could, if I wished, prove to you the contrary.

And with this, I salute you. Since the day after tomorrow is my birthday, I do not wish to enter it with the disagreeable conviction that I have lost one of my oldest friends and staunchest comrades.

Salut fraternel,

KARL MARX

Letter to Friedrich Adolph Sorge (in Hoboken)
LONDON, MAY 23, 1872

Dear Sorge:

A few words in a hurry.

I am over-busy.

Apart from the business of the International—which is in flames

---

3. See Marx to Engels, September 19, 1868.

everywhere—I am kept busy daily correcting the German proof sheets of the second edition of *Capital* (it will be issued in separate parts) and the *épreuves* [proofs] of the Paris French translation, which I often have to redo entirely in order to make it clear to Frenchmen; in addition, the *épreuves* of the *Address on the Civil War* [*in France*], which we are issuing in Brussels in French. You will be receiving constant deliveries from me in German and French.

A splendid Russian translation came out in Petersburg. The Russian socialist paper, *Die Neue Zeit* (that is, in German translation; the paper is written in Russian), has recently published a very laudatory leading article of five columns on the book, which, however, is only an introduction to a whole series of articles on it. Whereupon it received threats of suppression from the police. . . .

Next time I will explain to you the reasons why the General Council is sticking to its resolutions for the time being, without making any further aggressive moves. There will be no more correspondence with the fellows. But Le Moussu has been instructed to ask you for the letters of Eccarius (who has probably already given an order to print his letter there) and Hales.[1]

(*Between us*. Eccarius has been demoralized for some time and is now a real bum—yes, *canaille*.)

Your amicably devoted

KARL MARX

Letter to Friedrich Adolph Sorge (in Hoboken)[1]

LONDON, MAY 27, 1872

Dear Friend Sorge:

I am swamped with proofs, French (of which I have to rewrite an extraordinary amount, as it has been translated too literally[2]) and German,[3] which have to be sent off soon. Hence I can write you only a few lines.

---

1. After the General Council excluded the members of the American Section 12, and thereby splintered the International in March, 1872, John Hales, the Council's secretary, and Johann Georg Eccarius, corresponding secretary for the United States, protested the action. Hales's letter was published in *Socialiste*, May 18, 1872.

1. The original of the letter is in the New York Public Library, Manuscript Division (Sorge Papers).
2. The French translation of *Capital*, by Joseph Roy.
3. The second German edition of *Capital*, which appeared in separate parts between June, 1872, and May, 1873, and as a book in 1873, with the publication date given on the title page as 1872.

I am sending you in German and French the declaration of the General Council on the farce of the *"Conseil fédéraliste universel,* [Federalist Universal Council], *etc."* Ditto *notre circulaire privée sur les Jurassiens* [our private circular on the Jurassians]. (As soon as we get the bulk of the copies, you will receive more.) Eccarius handed in his resignation before his case was investigated. Provisionally, Le Moussu is now [the secretary] for *toute l'Amérique* (we now also have contact with South America). Send everything to me, as I see Le Moussu daily, and not to Hales, who out of self-important fussiness constantly commits stupidities. An investigation of him is also pending, in connection with the American affair, as was the case with Eccarius.

Eccarius has become a fool and a scamp. I will write you further about it in the course of the week.

I will insist on the 1,000 copies tomorrow at the General Council.

Yours,

K. MARX

Letter written in French to César De Paepe (in Brussels)
LONDON, MAY 28, 1872

My Dear Friend:

Enclosed a statement by the General Council against Vésinier & Co. for the Brussels *Internationale.* It was also sent to *Liberté,* (1) because it must get public notice, and (2) because M. Steens has *suppressed* the Reply of the General Council to the English Parliament, which had been sent him.

I have read the report on the Belgian Congress[1] in the *Internationale.* How is it there were no Flemings among the delegates? Furthermore, judging by the information received from their countrymen by the French here, the International in Belgium does not seem to have had much success in Belgium since the events of the Commune.

For my part, I would be prepared to accept Hins's plan[2] (with changes affecting details), not because I consider it good but because it is always better to make certain experiments than to cradle oneself in illusions.

It is very characteristic of the tactics of the Alliance: In Spain, where it controls a powerful organization even though it has lost the

---

1. The Congress of the Belgian Federation met May 19-20, 1872, and inconclusively debated the abolition of the General Council (in London).

2. Eugène Hins, a Belgian Bakuninist, proposed the abolition of the London General Council.

support of the Spanish Federal Council, it has, in the Council of Barcelona, attacked every organizational element, the Federal Council as well as the General Council, etc. In Belgium, where one must reckon with "prejudices," the proposal has been made to abolish the General Council and to transfer its functions—yes, even to enlarge them—to the Federal Councils (which are opposed in Barcelona).

I await the next Congress with impatience. This will be the end of my slavery. Then I will become a free man; I will no longer accept any administrative functions, whether in the General Council or in the British Federal Council.

Yours,

KARL MARX

Letter to Friedrich Adolph Sorge (in Hoboken)
LONDON, MAY 29, 1872

Dear Friend:

En toute hâte [In all haste].

At yesterday's meeting of the General Council, which nearly all the members of the Commune attended,[1] Hales read the letter from Praitsching.

Whereupon I reported, partly from your letter and partly from the [New York] *World* which you sent me, the adventures of the countercouncil and pointed out how these events confirmed the necessity of the resolutions proposed at my suggestion.[2] Eccarius was thunderstruck.

Whereupon there occurred a useful incident, which I immediately exploited.

---

1. Arnaud, Delahaye, Frankel, Dupont, Le Moussu, Martin, Margueritte, Ranvier, Serraillier, Vaillant.

2. Minutes of the General Council, May 28, 1872: "Citizen Marx said he had received news from New York: a so-called convention had been held at the Apollo Music Hall, ostensibly to nominate Mrs. Woodhull to the presidency and Douglass, a colored man, for vice-president. The proceedings had become the laughingstock of America. Owing to the action taken, Section 6 had withdrawn Grosse and appointed a new delegate. Millot of the French Section No. 2 had rushed into print and repudiated the Woodhull nomination. Though the name of the International was used, it was a fact that only three sections were represented: Sections 9, 12, and 35, one of which [Section 12], it was well known, was only organized for political purposes. In three weeks the humbug would break up and it was a good job the Council took the initiative.

"In concluding he proposed that a thousand copies of the Rules be at once sent."

Eccarius received a letter from St. Louis, in which a German section there inquired to which of the two Federal Councils it should belong. I said, naturally to the Council that goes along with us, the old one. Hales and Eccarius (although deadly enemies) spoke against it. I replied, and the decision was adopted by the very well-attended session with only three votes against it (Hales, Eccarius, and Delahaye, whom the other Communards don't think much of).

Le Moussu will report this officially to you tomorrow, and you will then do well (it goes without saying, of course, not at London's orders) to make it public that the General Council, in connection with this German Section, decided that your Council is the only one which is *en règle* [legitimate], and therefore the recognized one.

Tout à vous,

Karl Marx

From letter to Friedrich Adolph Sorge (in Hoboken)
LONDON, JUNE 21, 1872

Dear Friend:

Your consignments of June 7 (along with enclosed letter), received yesterday.

In the meantime, you will have received my second letter, as well as that of Le Moussu, which definitely establishes the General Council's position in regard to the United States.

The next Congress will be held (the official announcement will be sent to New York next week) on the first Monday in September, 1872, in The Hague (Holland). *That Congress will be a matter of life or death for the International. You and at least one other, if not two, must come.* As for the sections that send no direct delegates, they can send mandates (delegates' mandates).

The Germans: mandates for me, F. Engels, Lochner, Carl Pfänder, Lessner.

The French: for G. Ranvier, Auguste Serraillier, Le Moussu, Édouard Vaillant, F. Cournet, Antoine Arnaud.

The Irish: for McDonnel, who does very well, or, if you prefer, one of the above-mentioned Germans or Frenchmen.

Every section, of course, no matter what its number [of members], if it does not number over 500, is entitled to one delegate.

By now you will already know of the beautiful Belgian project for the revision of the Statutes. It originates with an *ambitieux impuissant* [ambitious impotent], Hins, who, together with his Russian wife, is under Bakunin's orders. One of its lovely features is the *abolition of the General Council*. The whole project has been properly publicized in *La Emancipación* (Madrid), organ of the Spanish Federal Council. That same paper had very much approved our American resolutions.

From the enclosed copy of *L'Égalité* you will see that the Romansh Congress had also rapped Hins on the knuckles.

I am mailing you four copies of the General Council's circular, *Fictitious Splits in the International*.[1] Engels has sent 200 copies by parcel post. . . .

We have issued a French translation of the "Address on the Civil War,"[2] at 2½ pence per copy. Please let me know if it is in demand in the United States.

As for the Nicholson affair,[3] it is best not to mention it in the General Council for the time being.

Greetings.

Yours,

K. M.

Letter to Ludwig Kugelmann (in Hanover)
LONDON, JULY 23, 1872

Dear Kugelmann:

If nothing happens in between, I shall be at The Hague[1] on September 2 and will be very glad to see you there. I had already sent you the "*Scissions*,"[2] etc., but it seems to have been confiscated. I am, therefore, enclosing a copy in this letter. You must excuse me for not writing more today. I have sent *épreuves* [proofs][3] to Paris and am generally overwhelmed with business.

Yours,

K. M.

---

1. See page 190.
2. *The Civil War in France.*
3. On June 7, 1872, Sorge had informed Marx that Nicholson, the treasurer of the provisional Federal Council in New York, had absconded with the Council's money and records and had not been heard from in several weeks.

1. The Hague Congress, September 2–7, 1872.
2. See "Fictitious Splits in the International," page 190.
3. Of Joseph Roy's French translation of *Capital*.

Letter to Ludwig Kugelmann (in Hanover)
LONDON, JULY 29, 1872

Dear Kugelmann:

At the Congress of the International (The Hague, opening September 2), it will be a matter of life or death for the International, and before I step out, I want at least to protect you from the disrupting elements. Hence Germany must send as many representatives as possible. Since you will come, do write to Hepner that I beg him to provide you with a mandate as a delegate.

Yours,

K. M.

Letter to Hermann Jung (in London)
LONDON, LATE JULY, 1872

Dear Jung:

Voilà Article 8[1] in the French and English texts:

Against the collective power of the propertied classes the working class cannot act, as a class, except by *constituting itself into a political party, distinct from, and opposed to, all old parties formed by the propertied classes.*

This conversion of the working class into a political party is indispensable in order to insure the triumph of the social revolution and its ultimate end—the *abolition of classes.*

The combination of forces which the working class has already effected by its economical struggles ought at the same time to serve as a lever for its struggles against the political power of landlords and capitalists.

The lords of the land and the lords of capital will always use their political privileges for the defense and perpetuation of their economic monopolies and for enslaving labor. To conquer political power has therefore become the great duty of the working class.

Salute.

KARL MARX

---

1. In September, 1872, the Hague Congress incorporated this Article as Article 7 of its General Statutes. (The English text is given here; the French text is omitted.)

Letter to Friedrich Adolph Sorge (in Hoboken)
LONDON, AUGUST 4, 1872

Dear Sorge:

My long silence is not to be excused at all; *cependant il y a des circonstances attenuantes* [however, there are extenuating circumstances]. That damned liver illness has made such headway that I have been absolutely unable to continue the revision of the French translation[1] (which in reality amounts to practically a complete rewriting), and I am very reluctantly submitting to the doctors' orders to go to Karlsbad. . . .

The few Frenchmen (I mean of those who stuck with us at the Hague Conference) have since turned out to be scoundrels, particularly M. Le Moussu, who has cheated me and others out of considerable sums of money and then through infamous calumnies tried to whitewash himself as a beautiful soul.

In England the International is as good as dead for the present; the Federal Council in London exists as such only nominally, even though some members are active individually. The great event here is the reawakening of the agricultural laborers. The failure of their initial efforts does no harm; *au contraire* [on the contrary]. As to the urban workers, it is to be regretted that the whole gang of leaders did not get into Parliament. That is the surest way to get rid of the rascals.

In France, workers' syndicates are being organized in the various big cities and are in correspondence with each other. They restrict themselves to *purely professional* matters, nor can they do anything else. Otherwise they would be suppressed without further ado. Thus they retain some form of organization, a point of union for the time when freer movements will again be possible.

By their impotence in practice, Spain, Italy, Belgium demonstrate their supersocialism.

In Austria, our people are working under the most difficult conditions; they are compelled to move with the greatest caution. Nevertheless, they have made great progress; specifically, they have prevailed upon the Slavic workers in Prague and elsewhere to act together with the German workers.[2] During the final period of the General Council in London, I had vainly tried to achieve such an understanding.

---

1. Of Vol. I of *Capital*, by Joseph Roy.
2. On April 5–6, 1874, the Social-Democratic Labor party was founded, as an organization for the whole Austro-Hungarian Empire.

In Germany, Bismarck is working for us.

General European conditions are such that more and more they drive toward a *general European war.* We shall have to go through it before any decisive activity of the European working class can be thought of.

My wife and children send you their best regards.

Yours,

KARL MARX

The publication of B. Becker's brochures on the Lassalle movement, despite all kinds of errors in them, are very useful for putting an end to sectarianism.

You will have noticed that from time to time there appear in the *Volksstaat* half-baked philistine fantasies. The stuff comes from schoolmasters, Ph.D.s, students. Engels has told Liebknecht off about it, something that seems necessary to do from time to time.

In judging French conditions, particularly those in Paris, one should not forget that the official military and political authorities, working hand in glove with the gang of epauletted Bonapartist scoundrels [*Lumpenhunde*] which the great Republican Thiers made into military courts for slaughtering the Communards, is still active. They constitute a sort of secret tribunal of terror, their *mouchards* are everywhere and, in particular, make the Parisian workers' districts unsafe.

Letter written in English to Nicolai Frantzevich Danielson (in St. Petersburg)*

LONDON, AUGUST 15, 1872

Dear Sir:

. . . I am writing in all haste today about a special, highly urgent matter. Bakunin has worked in secret for years to undermine the International, and has now been driven by us into a corner, so that he must now throw off his mask and publicly disavow the blockheads he leads. It is he who had managed the Nechayev affair. It is this Bakunin who was once entrusted with the translation of my book [*Capital*]. He took the money for it in advance, but instead of delivering the work, he wrote or had somebody write to Lyubavin (I believe that is the name), who had arranged the matter with him on behalf of the publisher, a thoroughly infamous and compromising letter. It would be of the highest value to me if this letter were

* Translated from a German translation.

promptly forwarded to me. As it concerns a purely business matter and the name would not be used, I hope you can provide the letter for me.[1] But there is no time to lose. If it is to be sent, it should be done immediately, since I am leaving at the end of this month for the Hague Congress.

Very devotedly yours,

A. WILLIAMS[2]

Letter to Ludwig Kugelmann (in Hanover)
LONDON, AUGUST 26, 1872

Dear Kugelmann:

In The Hague[1] the delegates should wear blue rosettes, so that those who meet them at the station can recognize them.

In case they miss each other:

Private address: Bruno Liebers, 148, Jacob Catstraat.

Public hall of the Congress: Concordia, Lombardstraat.

In all haste.

Yours,

K. M.

From letter to Nicolai Frantzevich Danielson (in St. Petersburg)
LONDON, DECEMBER 12, 1872

Dear Friend:

From the enclosed you will see the results of the Hague Congress. I had read Lyubavin's letter, under the seal of silence and without giving his name, to the Committee of Inquiry on the Alliance.[1] But the secret was not kept, first, because on the committee there was the Belgian lawyer Splingard, who was in reality only an agent of the Alliancers; second, because Zhukovsky, Guillaume, & Co. had already revealed the whole thing left and right *in their own way*, with apologetic turns of phrase—as a preventive. Thus it came about that the

---

1. For the fate of the letter to Lyubavin, see Marx to Danielson, December 12, 1872.

2. Marx's cover name, as a protection against the Russian police.

---

1. The Hague Congress met September 2–7, 1872.

---

1. Bakunin's Alliance of Socialist Democracy.

committee in its report to the Congress was obliged to inform it of the facts about Bakunin contained in Lyubavin's letter (of course I did not give the letter writer's name, but Bakunin's friends in Geneva already knew it). Now the question is whether the committee on the publication of the Congress' protocols (of which I am a member) can make public use of the letter or not? It depends on Lyubavin. Still, I must remark that the facts themselves—since the meeting of the Congress—have already made the rounds of the European press without our doing. For me the whole course of affairs has been the more distasteful in that I had counted on the strictest discretion and had solemnly demanded it.

As a consequence of Bakunin's and Guillaume's expulsion, the Alliance, which controlled the International in Spain and Italy, started a war of calumny against us everywhere, and, in alliance with all the rotten elements, seeks to bring about a split into two camps. Nevertheless, it is sure to be defeated in the end, and it only helps us to *cleanse* the International of the unclean and weak-brained elements that had penetrated it here and there.

The murderous attack by Bakunin's friends on Outine in Geneva is a fact. At this moment Outine himself is in a very perilous state of health. The rascally deed has already been reported in many papers of the International Association (among others, in the *Emancipación* of Madrid)and will figure in detail in the *Compte Rendu* [Report] of the Hague Congress. This gang of rascals had already made two similar attempts on their opponents in Spain. They will soon be pilloried before the whole world. . . .

Faithfully yours,

A. WILLIAMS

Letter to Friedrich Adolph Sorge (in Hoboken)
LONDON, DECEMBER 21, 1872

Dear Sorge:

Now a few words in a hurry.

The alleged majority of the British Federal Council (consisting to a very great extent of sham sections founded on behalf of that scamp Hales by a couple of individual delegates) has seceded from the minority (which alone represented the large English sections in London, Manchester, Birkenhead, etc.). The fellows have secretly fabricated a circular to the Federation (on the tenth of this month) (it will be sent to you), wherein they invited the sections to a

Congress in London to make common cause with the Jurassians, with whom Hales has been in constant contact since the Hague [Congress].

Our people—who now constitute the only legal Federal Council—immediately sent out printed postal cards to the various sections to make no decisions until they received the countermanifesto, on which they met for consultation (setting up the main points) in my house yesterday. You will receive it immediately. It will be printed early next week. It will also include the formal resolution to recognize the Hague Congress and the General Council.

At the same time, Engels, at the demand of the Manchester sections, prepared a reply to the scamps' circular (among them also the old idiot Jung, who cannot get over the removal of the General Council from London and has been Hales's fool for some time now), which they will receive at their session today and which will be printed promptly.

It is my opinion that for the time being you should remain as passive as possible, and leave the struggle to the local sections. In the meantime, of course, it is very good to have such circulars as those directed at Spain, which I found in the *Emancipación*.

Apropos. The organ, the *International Herald,* and its owner Riley (member of the Federal Council) have made themselves independent, on my advice. We will probably make a contract that *we* will issue our own weekly international supplement. Today I am sending you a copy, in which Engels and I are opening a polemic with Hales and Company.[1]

In regard to Poland, your letter cannot be sent there. The old General Council could admit Poland to membership *only* on condition (necessary, given the situation of the country) that it deal *only* with Wróblewski, who reports what he considers necessary or proper.

In this case, you have no choice. You must give Wróblewski the same absolute power as we did, or give up all claim to Poland.

Because of the French translation,[2] which gives me more work to do than if I had done it without a translator, I am so overworked that I could not write you for a long time, as I wished to do.

Cuno has promised to deliver the details of the session of the Hague [Congress] Investigation Committee. Tell him that if he does not do it

1. Marx and Engels, letter to the editor of the *International Herald,* December 21, 1872: "We have hitherto considered it superfluous to answer the calumnies and lies which the 'autonomous' Mr. John Hales is spreading about us. But when such calumnies are spread in connection with the name of the British Federal Council and its alleged authority, it is done with the intention of doing damage to the International in general, and we are obliged to break our silence. . . ."
2. Of *Capital,* by Joseph Roy.

immediately we cannot wait for him any longer, and that his own personal honor is involved in the matter.

Best regards from the whole family.

Yours,

KARL MARX

From letter written in English to Nicolai Frantzevich Danielson
(in St. Petersburg)
LONDON, JANUARY 18, 1873

Dear Friend:

. . . As to Lyubavin,[1] I should prefer suppressing that whole part of the inquiry from publication rather than expose him to the least danger. On the other hand, boldness is perhaps the best policy. According to something which Bakunin has published in Switzerland, not in his name, but in that of some of his Slavonian friends, they intend giving their own account of the transaction as soon as circumstances permit them to do so. The indiscretion of their accomplices at The Hague was intentional and, I suppose, was meant as a sort of intimidation.

On the other hand, I cannot judge of the possible consequences of the publication, and therefore should wish our friend to communicate [to] me through you his decision, after quietly *reconsidering* the case. . . .

Devotedly yours,

A. WILLIAMS

Letter to Johann Philipp Becker (in Geneva)
LONDON, FEBRUARY 11, 1873

Dear Becker:

The second part of the French translation[1] has just been published. If it is not intercepted, you will have received it before this letter reaches you.

---

1. On the use, or misuse, of Lyubavin's letter about Bakunin, see Marx to Danielson, August 15 and December 12, 1872.

1. Of *Capital,* by Joseph Roy.

The German parts, like the others, have obviously been intercepted. In a few weeks the whole first volume will come out, and I will send it to you through a bookseller, and I hope you will be so good as to acknowledge it.

For Kostecki I can do absolutely nothing. (1) I am myself under great pressure, having run into significant debts for *Messieurs les réfugiés français* [the French refugees], who properly abuse me for it. (2) Mr. Kostecki was in no way sent by me. On the contrary. He could not remain in London, told me he was going to Galicia, and wanted support from the International. I told him the treasury was empty, but added that perhaps something could be done for him once he got to Geneva. (3) All this took place long before the Hague Congress. Kostecki took leave of me, but long afterwards I found he was still in the streets of London and heard no more from him. Since then everything has changed. Our relations with Galicia, where many Poles went at that time, are lively and proper, likewise with other parts of Poland. Hence no emissary is necessary. For the rest, Wróblewski does not think much of Kostecki, who in general is little esteemed by our Polish people.

One of these days I will write you about the internal conditions of the International.[2]

Yours,

K. M.

From letter to Friedrich Bolte (in New York)
LONDON, FEBRUARY 12, 1873

Dear Friend:

. . . In recent weeks the secessionists in England—-Mottershead, Huber, Roach, Alonzo, Jung, Eccarius, & Co.—in a so-called Congress of the English Federation have repeated the farce of the London Universalist Federal Council. The gentlemen represented only themselves; two of them, Jung and Pape, had already been removed by the sections in Middlesbrough and Nottingham; hence they did not even nominally represent anything. The various "hole-and-corner sections" those fellows have put together hardly add up to fifty in all. The congress—with the exception of a small notice which Eccarius, as a serf of the *Times*, had smuggled into that paper—went unnoticed, but will be exploited on the Continent by the secessionists. Jung's speech

2. See Marx to Becker, April 7, 1873.

at the congress surpassed everything in absurdity and infamy. It is an old wives' web of lies, twistings and idiocy. This vain lad seems to suffer from softening of the brain. There is no help for it; one has to get used to it; the movement wears the fellows out, and as soon as they feel they are outside it they sink into vileness and try to persuade themselves it is this or that one's fault that they have become scamps.

In my opinion the General Council in New York committed a great mistake when it suspended the Jura Federation. Those fellows had already *withdrawn* from the International when they declared that the Congress and its Statutes did not exist for them. They formed the center of the conspiracy for the creation of a Counter-International. As a result of their congress at Saint-Imier,[1] similar congresses have taken place at Córdoba,[2] Brussels,[3] and London, and finally the Alliancers of Italy will hold one too.[4]

Every person and every group has the right to withdraw from the International, and as soon as that happens the General Council has simply to substantiate that withdrawal officially, but in no way to *suspend.* When groups (sections or federations) challenge the authority of the General Council, or violate the Statutes or Regulations on this or that point, *suspension* is considered. On the other hand, the Statutes do not contain any article on groups that reject the whole organization, and this for the simple reason that it is self-evident from the Statutes themselves that such groups no longer belong to the International.

It is in no way a formal question.

The secessionists have resolved in their various congresses to organize a combined secessionist congress for the creation of their *new* organization, independent of the International. Such a congress is to take place in the spring or summer.[5]

But the gentlemen wanted to keep a door open in case of failure. This is seen in a ponderous circular of the Spanish Alliancers. Should

---

1. A congress of the Jura Federation at Saint-Imier, Bern Canton, Switzerland, on September 15, 1872, protesting the exclusion of Bakunin and his followers from the International.

2. At the congress in Córdoba, December 25–30, 1872, only Bakuninists were represented.

3. At the Belgian Federation's congress in Brussels, December 25–26, 1872, the majority of the delegates were Bakuninists.

4. The second congress of the Italian anarchist organizations took place at Bologna, March 15–17, 1873.

5. The Congress of the Jura Federation, held in Geneva September 1–6, 1873, refused, under the influence of the anarchists and Bakuninists, to recognize the decisions of the Hague Congress of 1872.

their congress fail, they are prepared to visit the Geneva Congress,[6] an intention which the Italian Alliancer Gambuzzi . . . was naïve enough to confide to me when he was in London.

If, therefore, the New York General Council does not change its proceeding, what will be the result?

Following that of the Jura, it will suspend the secessionist federations in Spain, Italy, Belgium, and England; the result: The whole gang of scamps will show up again in Geneva and there paralyze all serious work, as happened in The Hague, and again compromise the general Congress for the benefit of the bourgeoisie. The great result of the Hague Congress was to drive out the rotten elements and *to exclude itself*, that is, to withdraw. The action of the [New York] General Council threatens to negate this result.

In *open opposition* to the International, these people do no harm, and are useful, but as hostile elements *inside* the organization they ruin the movement in all countries where they set foot.

The trouble that these people and their emissaries cause us in Europe can hardly be imagined in New York.

To strengthen the International in those countries where the main struggle is being fought needs above all the energetic measures of the General Council.

Since the mistake in regard to the Jura Federation has already been committed, it would perhaps be best to ignore the others for the time being (except when our own federations demand the contrary) and await the general secessionist congress, and declare to all its [the General Council's] constituencies that they have withdrawn—excluded themselves—from the International, and that henceforth they are to be regarded as alien and even hostile societies. In the local London congress, Eccarius himself has naïvely declared that one *must play politics with the bourgeois*. His soul has long thirsted for such a sellout.

The news of the great misfortune that has befallen Sorge[7] has grieved us all deeply. My warmest regards to him.

Salut fraternel,

KARL MARX

---

6. A Congress of the International, held in Geneva September 8–13, 1873, no longer had an international character; virtually all delegates were Swiss.

7. The death of Sorge's daughter in February, 1873.

From letter to Johann Philipp Becker (in Geneva)
LONDON, APRIL 7, 1873

Dear Becker:

If I don't write you in detail, you must ascribe it to over-busyness. . . .

The General Council will surely decide on Geneva for the next Congress.[1] You people must now begin to plan for a numerous representation. This is the more indispensable as the Alliance gang of scamps expects to come there en masse. They cannot, of course, be admitted. We must at least have the advantage over the Hague Congress in that the gang is removed from our midst. But for this it is necessary to find among you a strong-fisted local representation.

With best regards from the whole family.

Yours,
KARL MARX

Letter to Friedrich Adolph Sorge (in Hoboken)
LONDON, SEPTEMBER 27, 1873

Dear Sorge:

My wife has written you a number of times about the state of my health; I have been in great danger of apoplexy and still suffer from pains in the head, so that I am forced to restrict my working time. This is the only reason for my prolonged silence. Insofar as I can recall, I have written to New York only once, to Bolte,[1] since it appeared to me from your letter that an intervention on my part would be useful for calming and clarification.

The fiasco of the Geneva Congress[2] was unavoidable. From the moment it became known that no delegates would come from America, the thing was already on the skids. They had sought to present you in Europe as pure figments. If you don't appear and we do, this

---

1. Held in Geneva September 8–13, 1873, but attended primarily by Swiss delegates.

1. See Marx to Friedrich Bolte, February 12, 1873.
2. The Sixth Congress of the International, which met in Geneva September 8–13, 1873.

therefore becomes for our opponents a confirmation of their anxiously spread rumors. Moreover, it would prove to them that your American Federation was only a paper one.

Furthermore: the English delegation did not raise money for a single delegate; the Portuguese, Spaniards, and Italians informed us that under the circumstances they could send no direct delegates; from Germany, Austria, and Hungary news was equally bad; participation by the French was out of the question.

It was certain, therefore, that in these circumstances the great majority of the Congress must consist of Swiss, and particularly local Genevans. From Geneva itself we had no news. Outine was no longer there; old Becker maintained a stubborn silence, and M. Perret wrote us once or twice—in order to mislead us.

Finally, at the last minute, there came a letter from the Geneva Romansh Committee to the English Federal Council, wherein the Genevans expressed hesitation about accepting even English mandates, wrote propitiatingly, and enclosed a pamphlet (signed Perret, Duval, etc.) aimed directly at the Hague Congress and the old General Council in London. In this the fellows in many respects went further than the Jurassians; for example, they demanded the exclusion of the so-called *brain workers*. (The queerest thing about this is that this wretched piece of work was written by that miserable military adventurer Cluseret—in Geneva he calls himself the founder of the "International" in America. The gentleman wanted the General Council to be in Geneva, so he could exercise a secret dictatorship from there.)

That letter, including the enclosure, came just in time to keep Serraillier from going to Geneva (as was also the case with the English Federal Council) to protest against the doings of the chums there and to tell them in advance that their congress would be treated merely as a local Geneva affair. It was very good that nobody went, so his presence could not create doubt about this character of the congress.

Despite all that, the Genevans did not manage to take hold of the General Council, but as you already know, they have frustrated all the work of the first Geneva Congress and even carried through many decisions contrary to those passed by the latter.

As I view European conditions, it is quite useful to let the formal organization of the International recede into the background for the time being, but if possible not relinquish control of the central point in New York, so that no idiots like Perret or adventurers like Cluseret can seize the leadership and discredit the whole business. Events and the inevitable development and complication of things will of themselves see to it that the International shall rise again in improved form. For the present, it suffices not to let the connection with the most capable [people] in the various countries slip altogether out of our hands, and for the rest, not give a hang for the Geneva local decisions and simply ignore them. The only good decision adopted there, to postpone the Congress for two years, facilitates this mode of action. Furthermore, it upsets the calculations of the continental governments that the specter of the International will fail to be of service to them during the impending reactionary crusade; besides, everywhere the bourgeoisie considers the specter laid, luckily for them, for good.

Apropos. It is absolutely necessary that the account book of the moneys for the refugees of the Commune be returned to us. We need it urgently for our own defense against calumniating insinuations. This has absolutely nothing to do with general functions of the General Council, and in my opinion should never have left our hands.

I hope the American panic will not assume too great dimensions and will have no great effect on England and, thereby, on Europe. Such partial crises always precede periodic general ones. If they are too violent, they only discount the general crisis and break off its spearhead.

With heartiest regards from my wife,

Yours,

KARL MARX

I would appreciate receiving clippings from the Yankee papers about the crisis.

What is the address of our mutual friend [Hermann Meyer], the testamentary executor of Weydemeyer?

Next week, Engels will send you another 25 copies of the *Alliance*.[3]

Frederick Engels, draft in English of letter to Philip Van Patten
(in New York)
LONDON, APRIL 18, 1883

Esteemed Comrades:

My statement in reply to your inquiry of the 2nd April[1] as to Karl Marx's position with regard to the anarchists in general and Johann Most in particular shall be short and clear.

---

3. A brochure by Marx and Engels entitled *A Plot against the International Working Men's Association*. See note page 251.

---

1. On April 2, 1883, Van Patten, secretary of the Central Labor Union in New York, wrote to Engels that at a meeting in honor of Marx the anarchist

Marx and I, ever since 1845, have held the view that one of the final results of the future proletarian revolution will be the gradual dissolution and ultimate disappearance of that political organization called the state; an organization the main object of which has ever been to secure, by armed force, the economical subjection of the working majority to the wealthy minority. With the disappearance of a wealthy minority the necessity for an armed repressive state force disappears also. At the same time we have always held that in order to arrive at this and the other, far more important ends of the social revolution of the future, the proletarian class will first have to possess itself of the organized political force of the state and with this aid stamp out the resistance of the capitalist class and reorganize society. This is stated already in the *Communist Manifesto* of 1847 [*sic*], end of Chapter II.

The anarchists reverse the matter. They say that the proletarian revolution has to *begin* by abolishing the political organization of the state. But after the victory of the proletariat, the only organization the victorious working class finds ready-made for use is that of the state. It may require adaptation to the new functions. But to destroy that at such a moment would be to destroy the only organism by means of which the victorious working class can exert its newly conquered power, keep down its capitalist enemies, and carry out that economic revolution of society without which the whole victory must end in a defeat and in a massacre of the working class like that after the Paris Commune.

Does it require my express assertion that Marx opposed these anarchist absurdities from the very first day that they were started in their present form by Bakunin? The whole internal history of the International Working Men's Association is there to prove it. The anarchists tried to obtain the lead of the International, by the foulest means, ever since 1867, and the chief obstacle in their way was Marx. The result of the five years' struggle was the expulsion, at the Hague Congress, September, 1872, of the anarchists from the International, and the man who did most to procure that expulsion was Marx. Our old friend F. A. Sorge of Hoboken, who was present as a delegate, can give you further particulars if you desire.

Now as to Johann Most. If any man asserts that Most, since he turned anarchist, has had any relations with, or support from Marx,

Johann Most and his friends claimed to have had a close relationship with and the approval of Marx. Van Patten added: "We have a very high opinion of the capacities and the activity of Karl Marx, but we cannot believe that he was in sympathy with the anarchistic and disorganized methods of Most, and I should like to hear your opinion as to the attitude of Karl Marx on the question of anarchism versus socialism."

he is either a dupe or a deliberate liar. After the first No. of the London *Freiheit*[2] had been published, Most did not call upon Marx and myself more than once, at most twice. Nor did we call on him or even meet him accidentally anywhere or at any time since his new-fangled anarchism had burst forth in that paper. Indeed, we at last ceased to take it in as there was absolutely "nothing in it." We had for his anarchism and anarchist tactics the same contempt as for those people from whom he had learnt it.

While still in Germany, Most published a "popular" extract of *Das Kapital.* Marx was requested to revise it for a second edition. I assisted Marx in that work. We found it impossible to eradicate more than the very worst mistakes, unless we rewrote the whole thing from beginning to end, and Marx consented to his corrections being inserted on the express condition only that his name was never in any way to be connected with even this revised form of Johann Most's production.

You are perfectly at liberty to publish this letter in the *Voice of the People,* if you like to do so.

Yours fraternally,

F. E.

2. An anarchist German-language weekly founded by Johann Most in 1879.

Bibliography

GUIDES

Egbert, Donald Drew, and Persons, Stow
  Socialism and American Life (Princeton, N.J., 1952), II, 51–55
Répertoire International des Sources pour l'Étude des Mouvements Sociaux au XIXe et XXe Siècles (Paris, 1958), I, 83 pp.
Rubel, Maximilien
  Bibliographie des Oeuvres de Karl Marx (Paris, 1956)
  Supplement (Paris, 1960)
Stammhammer, Josef
  Bibliographie des Socialismus und Communismus (Jena, 1893, 1909), I, 286; III, 422–23
The Tamiment Institute Library Bulletin
  "The First International, 1864–1878," No. 27, September–October, 1960

DOCUMENTS

Founding of the First International: A Documentary Record (New York, 1937)
The General Council of the First International, 1864–1872 (Moscow, Foreign Languages Publishing House, 1964), 5 vols.
Gerth, Hans, ed. and tr.
  The First International. Minutes of the Hague Congress (Madison, Wisc., 1958)
Guillaume, James
  L'Internationale: Documents et Souvenirs (1864–1878) (Paris, 1907–1910), Vols. II–IV
Postgate, R. W.
  "Papers of the First International," in *Tamiment Institute Library Bulletin*, No. 27 (1960), 3–7

BOOKS AND ARTICLES

"Amsterdam Meetings of the First International in 1872," in *Bulletin of the International Institute of Social History*, VI (1951), 1-15

Bach, M.
   "Beiträge zu einer Geschichte der Internationale," in *Die Neue Zeit*, February, 1920, 549-58

Beer, M.
   A History of British Socialism (London, 1920), II, 200-25

Bernstein, Samuel
   The First International in America (New York, 1962)

Bourgin, George
   "La Lutte du Gouvernement Français contre la Première Internationale," in *International Review of Social History*, IV (1939), 39-137

Brupbacher, Fritz
   Marx und Bakunin: Ein Beitrag zur Geschichte der Internationalen Arbeiterassociation (Munich, 1913)

Cole, G. D. H.
   A History of Socialist Thought (London, 1957), II, 88-133, 174-212

Collins, Henry, and Abramsky, Chimen
   Karl Marx and the British Labour Movement: Years of the First International (London, 1965)

Eichhoff, Wilhelm
   Die Internationale Arbeiterassociation (Berlin, 1868)

Guillaume, James
   Karl Marx Pangermaniste et l'Association Internationale des Travailleurs de 1864 à 1870 (Paris, 1915)

Harrison, Royden
   "E. S. Beesly and Karl Marx," in *International Review of Social History*, IV (1959), 22-58

Hillquit, Morris
   History of Socialism in the United States (New York, 1903)

Jaeckh, Gustav
   Die Internationale (Leipzig, 1904)

Jellinek, Frank
   The Paris Commune of 1871 (London, 1937)

Karl Marx and Frederick Engels on the Paris Commune (Moscow, 1971)

Lehning, A. Muller
   "The International Association (1855-1859). A Contribution to the Preliminary History of the First International," in *International Review of Social History*, III (1938), 185-286

Lissagaray, Prosper Oliver
   History of the Commune of 1871, tr. from the French by Eleanor Marx-Aveling (London, 1886)

Lorenzo, Anselmo
"Reminiscences of the First International," in his *El Proletariado Militante* (Barcelona, 1923), Vol. I
Lorwin, Lewis
Labor and Internationalism (New York, 1929)
Maximoff, G. P., ed.
The Political Philosophy of Bakunin: Scientific Anarchism (New York, 1964)
Nettlau, Max
Bakunin e l'Internazionale in Italia del 1864 al 1872 (Geneva, 1928)
Postgate, R. W.
The Workers' International (London, 1920)
Puech, Jules L.
Le Proudhonisme dans l'Association Internationale des Travailleurs (Paris, 1907)
Rothstein, Th.
From Chartism to Labourism (New York, 1929)
Schluter, Hermann
Die Internationale in Amerika (Chicago, 1918)
Lincoln, Labor and Slavery (New York, 1913)
Stekloff, G. H.
History of the International (London and New York, 1928)
Testut, Oscar
L'Internationale (Paris, 1871)
Le Livre Bleu de l'Internationale (Paris, 1871)
Villetard, Edmond
Histoire de l'Internationale (Paris, 1872)
Ward, C. Osborne
The International; the New Idea. Universal Co-Operation and Theories of Future Government (New York, n.d.)
Zacher, Dr.
The Red International (London, 1885)

Biographical Index

About, Edmond (1828–1885), French Bonapartist journalist, 525

Adams, Charles Francis (1807–1886), American Minister to London, 1861–1868, lv, 16n, 17n, 19, 378n

Aldovrandi, P., Italian worker in London, member of International Working Men's Association,* 17

Alexander I (1777–1825), Czar of Russia, 1801–1825, 84

Alexander II (1818–1881), Czar of Russia, 1855–1881, 57–58, 84–86, 151 & n

Allen, George R., American house painter, member of the New Democracy in New York City, 235, 236, 245

Alonzo, English labor leader, 576

Amadeus, Duke of Savoy, 261

André, P. Fox (see Fox, Peter)

Anne (1665–1713), Queen of England and of Great Britain, 1707–1713, 89, 432

Applegarth, Robert (1833–1925), English trade unionist, IWA member, xxiin, 4n, 48, 53, 60, 68, 101, 104, 121n, 274, 353, 462, 481, 484, 508

Arnaud, Antoine (1831–1885), French Blanquist, Communard, émigré in London, IWA member, 553, 566, 567

Assi (or Assy), Adolphe Alphonse (1841–1886), French mechanic, Proudhonist, Communard, IWA member in Paris, deported in New Caledonia after the Commune's defeat, 281, 286, 296, 330 & n

Auer, Ignaz (1846–1907), German saddlemaker, member of Socialist Labor party, member of Reichstag, 360

Avrial, Augustin (1840–1904), French mechanic,

* Hereafter referred to as IWA.

Proudhonist, Communard, émigré in London, IWA member, 204, 550, 551–552

Badinguet (see Napoleon III)

Bagnagatti, G., secretary of the Mazzini-led Italian Association of Mutual Progress, IWA member in London, 17–18

Baillie-Cochrane (see Cochrane-Baillie)

Baines, Sir Edward (1800–1890), English economist, Liberal member of Parliament, 391 & n

Bakunin, Mme., wife of Michael Bakunin, 160

Bakunin, Michael Alexandrovich (1814–1876), Russian revolutionist, anarchist leader, member of IWA, from which he was excluded at The Hague Congress (1872) after conflict with Marx and the IWA General Council, xxii, xxiii, xxiv, xxx–xxxii, xxxv–xl, xliii–xliv, xlviii–l, lvii, lix, 155–176, 180–181, 189n, 190–214, 216n, 219, 222, 227–228, 248, 251–266, 269–270, 310, 312–313, 317, 329n, 343–344, 347, 365, 386, 427, 459, 460, 462–464 & n, 465–468 & n, 474n, 475, 478 & n, 486–487 & n, 489–492, 497, 501 & n, 503 & n, 504–507, 511–512, 514–516 & n, 534, 538, 541, 544–546, 548–550, 552, 554–555, 561, 565, 568, 571–573, 575n, 582

Banks, Theodore H., house painter, IWA member in U. S., 235, 236

Bara, Jules (1835–1900), Belgian statesman, Minister of Justice, 1865–1870, 1878–1884, 34, 435

Barry, Maltman (1842–1909), English journalist, IWA member, xlixn, 240

Bastelica, André (1845–1884), Franco-Spanish typesetter, Bakuninist member of IWA in France, 143, 196, 197, 201, 205, 532, 534, 550–554

589

Subject Index

[605]

Propaganda, xxii, 19, 35, 42, 62, 65, 143, 167,
  176, 191, 195, 209, 214, 219, 264, 265,
  305, 345, 374, 378, 389, 396, 415, 437,
  477, 504, 507, 516, 537, 544, 546, 549
Property, xxxviii, 17, 55, 74, 94, 108, 110, 114,
  117, 121, 229, 260–262, 281, 335, 337n,
  339
  abolition of, xxxvii, lvii, 339, 484, 505
  classes of, 7
  collective, 158
  communal, lvii, 85, 105, 355
  enjoyment of, xliv
  landed, xxxii, 89, 171, 173
    abolition of, 339, 505
  political economy of, 10
  private, xxxvii, xliv, liii, 108, 110, 111–112
    121–123, 179n, 332, 333, 338
    abolition of, xxxvii, lvii, 339, 484, 505
  public, xliv, 338
  rights of, 121
  social, 137
Property tax, 8
  (See also Taxes)
Protestantism, 89, 125, 435, 479
  (See also Religion)
Proudhonist, xiv, xxi, xxiii, xxx, xliv, lvi, lvii,
  lviii, 114, 143n, 269, 403, 418, 422, 425,
  427, 428, 441, 444, 445, 544, 545, 550
Provence, La, xlvii, 525
Prussia, Prussian, xvi, xxviii, xli, xlii, xliii, xlv,
  lviii, 34, 42, 46, 51, 52, 54–58, 69, 72–74,
  76, 82, 85, 86, 108, 114, 116, 139, 148,
  149, 151, 196, 197, 218, 271, 275, 279, 280,
  284, 290–292, 305, 360, 366, 382, 400,
  438, 450, 512, 517, 518, 524–531, 532
  (See also Franco-Prussian War)
Public Opinion, xlviin, 294–295

Queen's Messenger, 508 ,
Qui Vive!, 203, 204, 541, 545, 552, 553

Racism, 155, 193
Radical, 203
Radical causes, xxii
Radical journalism, xxxv
Radical papers, xx, xlviii
Radical revolution, xxxi
Radicalism, radical, xii, xiv, xvi, xx, xxv, xxvi,
  xxix, xxxii, xxxv, xxxvi, xl, xliii, xliv, liv,
  131, 155, 168, 172, 213, 235, 317, 341,
  342, 365, 504, 534n
Radicals, American, xlix
Railroads, public ownership of, lvii
Rappel, Le, 270
Realpolitik, 382
Rebellion, xxxv
  (See also Revolution)
Reform, reformist, xvii, xxi, xliv, 220, 225, 229,
  231, 233–235, 244, 245, 396, 412–413,
  423
  (See also Communism; Democracy; Liberal-
  ism)

Reform, 390
Reform League, The, xxi, 142n, 274, 383, 384,
  388, 391, 402, 405, 408, 410, 411, 420
Reformation, Protestant, 89
Reichstag, 147, 360, 531, 537
Religion, xlviii, 31, 74, 85, 107, 125, 148, 173,
  197, 217, 220, 231, 235, 260, 281, 301,
  305, 337, 346, 347, 358, 399, 450, 499,
  556
  (See also Catholicism; Priests)
Reminiscences (by Theodor Cuno), 343–345
Rents, 108, 110, 123, 139, 431
  (See also Landlords; Property; Tenant)
Report on the Basel Congress, 479, 491
"Report . . . of the International . . . to the
  Fourth Congress in Basel" (by Marx), lvii
Republic of France (see French Republic)
Republic of Paris (see French Republic)
Republicanism, republican, xxxv, xliii, xliv, 102,
  116, 124, 149, 159, 220, 243, 254, 329,
  387, 398, 401
  French radical, xiv, 493, 500
Resistance Society of the English Foundrymen,
  the, 214
Resolutions on the Anniversary of the Paris
  Commune, 69–70
Resolutions of the London Conference, 61–68
Restoration, English, 89
Réveil, Le (Paris), xxiii, 50, 200, 270, 560
Révolution, La, 161
Revolution, xxx, xxxi, xxxii, xxxiii, xxxiv,
  xxxv, xli, xliii, xliv, xlvii, 83, 108, 109,
  115, 143, 144, 148, 155, 198n, 257, 260,
  261, 263, 320, 333, 337, 357, 428
  agrarian, 498
  (See also Agriculture)
  American, 17, 90, 103
  economic, xxxi, xxxii, 171, 460, 582
  economic determinism of, xxxi
  in economic relationships, xxxii
  European, xxxvi, 16
  February (1848), 86, 342
  French (1789), xliii, 56, 57, 90, 108, 358
  French (1830), xliii, 82
  1848–1849, xii, xv, xviii, xxviii, xxx, xxxv,
    xlii, xliii, 9, 32, 59, 77, 83, 100, 178,
    342, 357, 438, 457, 513, 514
  international, xxxv
  Polish (1830), 373
  proletarian, xiv, xxx, xxxii, xxxiv, 172, 498,
    582
  social, xxxi, xxxiii, 65, 69, 86, 108, 109, 111,
    149, 167, 172–174, 227, 418, 435, 500,
    505, 517, 582
  triumph of, lviii, 65, 150, 209n
  violent, xxi
  workers', xxxvii, 500
  world, xxxii
Révolution Sociale, La, 199, 217, 220, 222,
  270, 545, 553, 554
Revolutionary, revolutionaries, xvi, xvii, xxi,
  xxii, xxxi, xxxii, xxxiii, xxxvi, xxxviii,